THE MORMON MISSIONARY

Who *Is* That Knocking at My Door?

ROBERT L. LIVELY JR.

THE MORMON MISSIONARY
WHO IS THAT KNOCKING AT MY DOOR?

Cover illustration by JD&J Book Cover Design
Interior design by 52 Novels

Robert Lively is Dean Emeritus, University of Maine at Farmington.
He holds the Doctor of Philosophy degree from
the University of Oxford, Oxford, England.

For my family, for my students,
and for the many missionaries who shared their stories with me.

Missionary work is the lifeblood of the Church.

SPENCER W. KIMBALL (1895-1985), PRESIDENT OF THE CHURCH OF JESUS CHRIST OF LATTER-DAY SAINTS, 1973-1985

CONTENTS

PROLOGUE

"Do we have *to invite them?"*

Missionaries in the Religion Classroom

My students were not pleased when I suggested we invite Mormon missionaries to speak to our religion class at the University of Maine at Farmington, a public liberal arts college of 2,000 students located in west-central Maine. This surprised me, because they generally enjoyed visits from representatives of faiths we were studying—from Adventists to Zen Buddhists—but for some reason they balked at the idea of Mormon missionaries.

Most in the class of thirty acknowledged that people had knocked on their door, wanting to talk about religion (although they frequently confused Mormons with Jehovah's Witnesses), but few had invited them in. They found them a mild irritant. One student said he didn't like people trying to force their religion down his throat; an older woman admitted she had chased them off her porch "a time or two"; while a third said she went into the basement and did her laundry when she saw two well-dressed young men coming down the road.

The students chuckled; but then some became self-reflective. One student said she always turned them away but felt bad doing so because they seemed so nice, while an older student admitted their appearance made him realize he wasn't as patient as he thought he was, for he would close the door before they could finish saying hello.

"So," said a young man sitting in the front row and wearing a Boston Red Sox baseball cap, "if we don't invite them into our homes, why should we invite them into our classroom? Do we *have* to invite them?"

Exercising my professorial prerogative, I said, "Yes!"

I extended an invitation to two young women and two young men who were serving their missions in our area, which is a rural region characterized by small towns, pristine lakes, and forests of pine, birch, and maple. I asked them to say something about themselves, to talk about the history and beliefs of their church, and to describe what it is like to be a missionary.

They were nicely dressed. The young women wore conservative blouses, calf-length skirts, and practical shoes. The young men wore dark suits, white shirts, and plain ties. Since there was an autumn chill in the air, they all wore black trench coats. Each wore a black nametag with white lettering. They referred to each other as "Sister" and "Elder," and they smiled a lot. The women were somewhat older—twenty-one and twenty-two—while the young men were nineteen and twenty. Two were from Utah, one was from Idaho, and one was from California. They came from families of four to eight children. All had been raised in the Mormon Church, and one could trace his family roots back to the beginnings of the Church in the nineteenth century.

They talked of their families, pets, and interests, of their plans to go back to college after their missions, and of their plans to get married and to raise families: interests and goals that mirrored those of many of my students. And no, they said, they were not going to return home and enter into polygamous marriages. It was "Fundamentalists" who practiced plural marriages, they said, not Mormons, who had banned the practice in 1890.

"We get asked that all the time," said the senior elder, "even though it hasn't been practiced for over one hundred years."

The students smiled with the missionaries.

We were told that young, single men are expected to go on missions and that they serve two years. Young, single women don't have the same obligation and are counseled by Church authorities to accept a viable offer of marriage over serving a mission. Lacking such an offer, sisters are free to serve a mission, should they wish. They serve eighteen months.

Three of the missionaries' fathers had gone on missions, none of their mothers had, and all had siblings who had served or who were currently. One had a sister in Belize, and one had brothers in Japan and in Kentucky.

"So there are three from your family who are currently on a mission?" a student asked.

"Yes," replied the sister, "plus I have a cousin in Brazil, and the ones who went foreign had to learn a new language."

The students began to exchange glances with one another.

Our guests explained that while many refer to them as Mormons, their official name is The Church of Jesus Christ of Latter-day Saints. As their name indicates, they believe themselves to be Christians who are living in the "Latter Days" or the End Times spoken of in Revelation. They spoke of Joseph Smith (1805-1844), the nineteenth-century American prophet and the founder of their Church, of his miraculous visions and revelations, and of his discovery and translation of a set of golden plates, which were published as the Book of Mormon, a scripture they said complements the Bible. With the publication of the Book of Mormon and the founding of the Latter-day Saint Church in 1830, it was believed the truth of the original Christian church had been restored, an event they referred to as the "Restoration."

The missionaries described the early persecution of the Saints and their westward migration from New York to Ohio, then to Illinois. They told of Smith's martyrdom in Illinois and of the trek across the Plains led by Brigham Young to the Great Salt Lake Valley, where the Latter-day Saint Church is headquartered today. They also spoke of the rapid worldwide growth of the Church.

They explained the purpose of their activities is to take the "restored gospel of Jesus Christ" to others, and they cited Mt 28:19-20 as their mandate, in which Jesus told his disciples to take his message throughout the world. It was not an easy task in Northern New England (a region identified as the least religious in the United States), they said, and they spent much of their time knocking on doors trying to find people who were interested in hearing their message. Most responded to their knocking with, "Thanks, I'm all set," or, "No, I'm not interested." A few slammed doors in their faces.[1]

The sisters and elders described their disciplined lifestyle. They have no choice where they are sent for their mission, they may not travel outside of their mission area without permission, and they may not return home, even for family emergencies. They always must be with a companion, except when in the bathroom. They are assigned many different companions during their mission, and they have no say in who their companions will be. They are moved to a new location every three or four months. They must follow a rigorous daily schedule, which has them rising at 6:30 A.M. and in bed by 10:30 P.M. They are not allowed to work, date, watch television, listen to the radio, play popular music, surf the internet, play video games, engage in social networking, have a personal cell phone, have a personal computer, or go to a movie theater. They can call home only on Mother's Day and on Christmas, and they have to follow the "Word of Wisdom," requirements that apply to all Latter-day Saints, which preclude the use of tobacco, alcohol, coffee, tea, and illegal drugs.

In addition, they pay a monthly fee of $400 while serving.

I watched my students exchange glances with one another as they heard about the regimented lives the missionaries volunteer to live and even have to pay for.

The elders and sisters concluded by discussing the personal benefits missionaries gain by serving: they travel to parts of the world they have never seen before; many learn a new language; and all learn skills that will benefit them personally and professionally, including public speaking skills, interpersonal communication skills, dealing with adversity and rejection, and time and money management. And, most importantly, they added, the experience strengthens their faith and their commitment to the Latter-day Saint Church.

The presentation was followed by animated discussion. Students were respectful, but direct. Their interest had become obvious. Evangelical Protestants questioned the need for a new prophet and a new scripture, saying Jesus and the Bible are all that are needed for salvation. Many students questioned why they needed to live such austere lives, and they wondered how missionaries dealt with rejection and with people being rude to them.

The missionaries, as they are taught, didn't argue; they merely shared their beliefs and experiences. The senior elder and sister took the lead in discussing the thornier theological issues, saying Joseph Smith, through divine inspiration, was instrumental in bringing about the "restoration of the truth" that had been lost since the early days of the Christian church, and while other faiths may have part of the truth, the "fullness of the gospel" is to be found in the Book of Mormon. The younger sister explained their austere lifestyle allowed them to focus on their primary goal, of sharing their message with others, while the younger elder said they were just normal people who were passionate about what they were doing. They agreed it is difficult to live with rejection and with people calling them names and slamming doors in their faces. They try not to let it bother them; people are rejecting their message, not them personally—but rejection is still hard to live with on a daily basis, they admitted.

Some students said they would not want to be separated from their families for so long, while another, after doing a quick calculation, announced that at $400 a month, the women were paying $7,200 toward their mission, while the men were paying $9,600. The missionaries agreed it was difficult both personally and financially, but, as one sister observed, "My mission involves sacrifice, but if something isn't worth a sacrifice, then it has no worth."

While appreciative and fascinated, the general tenor of the class was one of skepticism; although one older student ended the class by saying she had always been impressed by the Mormon Tabernacle Choir, and as a result she had an ongoing interest in the Latter-day Saint Church. She said if they can produce something that is that good, then perhaps there is something about their message she should consider; she hadn't completely rejected them.

I took the missionaries to lunch after the class to thank them for their participation. The younger elder, who had just arrived in the mission field a week earlier, and who had had a deer-in-the-headlights look during the class, said he found the experience "scary." He had been raised in Utah, had attended Brigham Young University for a year, and had never been in a classroom where Mormons were in the minority. He said no one told him his mission would begin by talking to thirty college students, most his own age, none Latter-day Saint, who would ask him difficult questions. The senior sister comforted him, saying he would get used to it, that she too was scared when she began her mission, but it got easier each time she faced these kinds of challenges.

I asked if they would be willing to come to other religion classes. The senior sister and elder enthusiastically embraced the offer. The junior two weren't quite so sure, but they eventually said yes.

My students continued the conversation during the next class period, speaking more bluntly without the missionaries present. Evangelicals felt Latter-day Saints should not be considered Christians, in spite of the fact that "Jesus Christ" appears in their name. They considered it blasphemous to suggest there is need for a new prophet and a new scripture. The term "cult" was used more than once. Those with an academic interest in religion found the idea of progressive revelation, which suggests that the potential exists for new prophets and new scriptures, to be an interesting concept. They just weren't sure Joseph Smith and the Book of Mormon had a part in the process.

But it was the missionaries' rigorous and disciplined lifestyle that intrigued students the most, and while many said they neither would, nor could, do what Mormon missionaries do, they did appreciate what the Latter-day Saint Church and the missionaries gained from it: the Church gained converts and a more committed membership, and missionaries came away with a stronger faith and with knowledge and skills that would serve them for a lifetime.

At the end of the class period, when I asked if I should invite Mormon missionaries back in subsequent semesters, students responded with an enthusiastic, "Yes!"

Their curiosity had been piqued.

The Need for This Book

I continued inviting Latter-day Saint missionaries to my religion classes and students began asking a question that would be repeated semester after semester: had a non-Mormon ever written a book that told the story of the missionaries—that explained their reasons for serving, their training, their experiences in the field, and what they and the Latter-day Saint Church gained from it? I replied I wasn't aware of such a book. I said there are numerous how-to-have-a-successful-mission books written by returned missionaries and there are books that include accounts of missionary labors, but I wasn't aware of a comprehensive overview of the missionary program written by an outsider.[2]

After the question was raised enough times, it finally dawned on me that I, a non-Mormon, should write such a book.

It is surprising this book hasn't been written before. Missions have played a central role throughout the history of the Latter-day Saint Church, and the experience can have a profound spiritual and personal impact on the individuals involved. The Church's mission statistics are staggering. In 2007, it announced that it had sent out its one-millionth missionary since the founding of the Church in the nineteenth century, and during 2014, over 88,000 were serving worldwide.

The LDS mission experience is also a unique example of a religious rite of passage: unique because of its length, especially for young men.

Perhaps missionaries are taken for granted. For Latter-day Saints, the missionary experience is such an integral part of their culture that they may not fully appreciate how unusual it is. A sister from Ogden, Utah, serving in Northern New England, said as she was growing up she "watched a steady stream of missionaries come and go," but she didn't think much about it. Going on a mission is something a young man does in the Latter-day Saint Church, and devout members only raise an eyebrow when an eligible candidate does not go.

This book is written primarily with non-Mormons in mind. While many say they have encountered Mormon missionaries in some way, and while most tell missionaries they are not interested in hearing their message, an increasing number are genuinely curious about the Latter-day Saint Church. Their interest has been piqued by the Church's rapid growth over the past five decades (from fewer than three million members in 1970, to over fifteen million members in 2015), by the Church's popular short ads on television, and by the attention given the Church when it served as the backdrop for the 2002 Winter Olympics in Salt Lake City, an event witnessed worldwide by millions of viewers.

More recently, there have been high-profile events such as the 2008 and 2012 presidential bids of Mitt Romney, in which opponents sought to turn his Latter-day Saint identity into a political liability. Further interest in the Church was generated when fellow Mormon Jon Huntsman Jr. joined the 2012 presidential race for a short period of time.

Attention was also drawn to the Church with the opening of the popular Broadway play *The Book of Mormon*, which follows the haps and mishaps of two mismatched missionaries from Utah serving in Uganda. It opened in the spring of 2011 to rave reviews. It went on to win nine Tony awards that year, including Best Musical. It is not an LDS Church production, but rather the work of the creators of the popular TV-MA rated animated series *South Park*. The play, while it contains positive messages, makes ample use of profanity, spoofs, and parodies, which offend many Church members.

Concurrent with the 2012 presidential race and *The Book of Mormon* on Broadway, the Church launched its "I am a Mormon" series on www.mormon.org, which includes profiles of everyday people—such as homemakers, blue-collar workers, artists, professionals—who, as they say in their vignettes, are also Mormons. The most dramatic ad appeared in Times Square in New York City, where a large neon sign touting www.mormon.org and the "I am a Mormon" series greeted viewers in the Square, including those going to *The Book of Mormon*, just a few blocks away at the Eugene O'Neill Theatre. In 2014 the Church released the feature film *Meet the Mormons*, which looks at the lives of six faithful members from around the world. It portrays them as normal people, with struggles and successes like the rest of us, and it has enjoyed box office success.

Those seeking information about the Church are also encouraged to visit the Church's website: www.lds.org.

These efforts, together with the always popular Mormon Tabernacle Choir and the ubiquitous presence of the Church's highly committed missionary workforce, have contributed to what the media in 2011 labeled as the "Mormon Moment," a time of intense public interest in the history, beliefs, and practices of the Latter-day Saint Church.[3]

While non-Mormons may have a growing interest in the Latter-day Saint Church and may have questions they would like answered about Mormon missionaries (*Who are these people at my door? Why are they here? Who pays for it? What do they and their church gain from it?*), they may not be comfortable asking questions of the missionaries themselves. They fear missionaries will want to talk more about their religion than their life stories.

This book seeks to answer those questions.

This book will also be of interest to members of the Latter-day Saint Church. Missionaries are held in very high regard in the Church, and Church members seem to have an insatiable appetite for stories about missionaries and the missionary experience. Their status in the Church was attested to me by an elder serving in 2012, who said missionaries are treated like "rock stars" in Utah; people will blow their horns and wave when they see missionaries on the street.

Equally as important, Church members are especially interested in how they are perceived by outsiders. Boyd J. Peterson of Utah Valley University says that Latter-day Saints have "a divided sense of self," which is a sense minorities often experience in wider society. They live with a contradictory public image: they are revered for their work ethic, their clean living, and their family centeredness, but they are also perceived as being outside the mainstream of American religious life, as being clannish, and as relegating women to an inferior position in the Latter-day Saint Church. They have a strong sense of themselves, of being "a peculiar people," but their divided sense of self also causes them to look closely at how others view them. They are constantly looking at themselves through the eyes of others.[4]

The Interviews

This work is based on my interviews with over 275 past, present, and future missionaries: young men, young women, and older, senior missionaries. These interviews began in the 1970s and extended into 2015. Interviewees included individuals who served in every decade since the 1930s, in the United States and in forty-seven countries around the world. Interviews were conducted in various parts of the United States, and in Mongolia, Russia, Germany, and England.

When approaching prospective interviewees, I made a point of explaining that I wasn't a member of the Latter-day Saint Church, but that, as a religion professor and college dean, I was interested in telling *their* stories; of sharing with non-Mormons what it is like to be a Mormon missionary.

No one refused an interview. Every one wanted to tell their missionary story, and they seemed pleased someone would ask them about it. They freely shared their challenges and low points, as well as their fondest memories and high points. Some became emotional, even those who had served decades earlier; their voices quivered, and their eyes filled with tears. This was true even for some who had left the Church. To witness the depth and significance of the missionary experience for these interviewees was one of the most memorable aspects of this study. I am deeply indebted to them for sharing their stories. Their names have been omitted to protect their privacy.

Church officials were also very supportive of my project. Once convinced of the worthiness of my work (helped by much-appreciated endorsements from my friends within the Church), they willingly helped. I had the opportunity to interview Church officials in Salt Lake City and elsewhere, including "General Authorities" such as Gordon B. Hinckley (1910-2008), president from 1995 to 2008, mission presidents, stake presidents (a "stake" is an administrative unit that includes multiple congregations), and Church leaders at the local level. I also had the rare opportunity of visiting Missionary Training Centers (MTCs) in Utah and in England and the Senior Missionary Training Center in Utah (these sites are generally off-limits, even to Church members), where I conducted interviews with missionaries in training and with MTC presidents and their staff.

The organizational structure of the Latter-day Saint Church is very hierarchical, and members normally don't enjoy direct access to General Authorities, nor do they enjoy open access to the MTCs. But my being an outsider and pursuing a significant project gave me access. As a jealous, young elder quipped: "You can get in edgewise with all the higher-ups, and we can't."

The help of these officials, offices, and friends is greatly appreciated, for they have contributed to a much deeper understanding of the missionary program.

Some Church members find it odd that I would undertake this study and devote so many years to it, yet remain dispassionate about the missionaries' message. Their experience has been that people either accept their message or reject it. Few remain in-between.

Some Church members questioned my motives, or my ability, to carry out the project. Such was the reaction of a senior missionary I met at London's Gatwick Airport, who was on his way home to the United States after an eighteen-month senior mission in Scotland. I was at the airport with the president of the England Missionary Training Center and we were meeting a group of new Italian missionaries who were coming to the MTC for training. The president introduced me to the senior missionary and told him I was writing a book on Mormon missionaries. The president also mentioned I was not a member of the Latter-day Saint Church. The returning missionary, a man in his sixties, good-naturedly, but pointedly, asked me: "Why are you, a non-member, writing a book on this topic? What do you know about the Church? Have you ever been a missionary? How can you 'tell *my* story'? How do I know that you aren't going to turn your book into yet another anti-Mormon work?"

I explained I had been interested in the Church for decades; I had written about the Church in nineteenth century England in my Oxford University doctoral dissertation; I had interviewed hundreds of missionaries, including General Authorities; I had been allowed into various MTCs; I tried to be evenhanded in my writing; and I even had met and twice interviewed the president of the Church, Gordon B. Hinckley. And no, I had never served as a missionary.

He looked me up and down and then said: "Most people who look at us in depth either end up joining the Church or rejecting us. It's an either-or thing. I have never met anyone who just kind of dribbles on and on, without making a definite decision one way or the other. I don't know about you, Lively!"

Most Church members aren't as blunt as my senior acquaintance, but he did raise legitimate concerns. The question of who can speak for a religious group is an ongoing conversation. Whose perspective is more valid: an insider's or an outsider's? Which approach is more valid: the confessional or the objective? Proponents of the insider, confessional approach question how an outsider can understand a religious community's faith, motivation, and inner workings, while proponents of the outsider, objective approach suggest they bring a perspective that allows them to more fully appreciate the unique features of the group. I fall into the latter category, and while I am sure I may not fully grasp some of the subtleties of the faith's beliefs and practices, I don't think members always appreciate and understand the distinctiveness of their missionary program. I expect both approaches are useful and necessary.

I also can appreciate my friend's concern that this could be yet another tool for anti-Mormon propaganda. The Latter-day Saint Church has been persecuted perhaps more than any other religious group in American history. An immense amount of anti-Mormon literature has been generated; it began not long after the Church was founded in 1830, and it continues today. I leave it to the reader (and my senior missionary acquaintance) to decide if I have been successful in providing an authentic picture of these missionaries, the missionary program, and the Latter-day Saint Church.

There are also members who have said they appreciate the fact that I undertook the study. A returned missionary who served in South Africa in the mid-1980s, said: "I am surprised you have delved so deeply into our faith without either joining it or becoming antagonistic towards it. In my own experience, this rarely occurs. I must also say that I very much appreciate your efforts to accurately and objectively understand and portray our faith as a professor and writer."

I explained that is what professors of religion try to do.

The Age Change

A significant event in October 2012 is having a profound effect on the Latter-day Saint missionary program: the ages when missionaries may serve were lowered. Young men can now serve at eighteen instead of nineteen, and young women no longer have to wait until they are twenty-one: they can serve at nineteen. This is described as optional; a person may still serve at an older age, should she or he desire. But the effect of the changes was immediate. There was a significant influx of younger men and women seeking to serve, such that the missionary ranks swelled from 55,410 in January of 2012, to over 88,000 in 2014, with the greatest proportion being young women. (Around 64 percent of serving missionaries are young men, 28 percent are young women, and 8 percent are senior missionaries.)

This has had the effect of causing overcrowding at the MTC in Provo, Utah; stays at the MTC have been shortened to accommodate the numbers. The number of "missions" or geographical areas around the world to which missionaries are assigned increased from 347 to 406, and the number of missionaries assigned to a particular mission has increased from 150 to over 200—contributing to the already stressful responsibilities of the mission president.[5]

The reasons for the age changes appear to be manifold. The leaders of the Church say it is a reflection of their belief that we are living in the End Times and that Christ's return will be hastened if more missionaries are called. (They refer to it as "hastening the work.") I suggest there are also practical reasons. The number of eligible nineteen-year-old young men in the United States is declining, and lowering the age to eighteen increases the chances they will serve right out of high school. To have to wait a year increased the chances that they would lose interest in serving if working or attending college. Plus, the change decreases the chances of moral lapses during the gap year, which would affect their eligibility to serve.

When young women had to wait until they were twenty-one, their chances of serving a mission decreased considerably—they were near completing their education, they were working, or they were married. Church leaders encourage "marriage over mission" for young Latter-day Saint women, but young Latter-day Saints, to a certain extent like their counterparts in the wider US society, are delaying marriage. Church leaders recognize this fact, and I would suggest they decided to let sisters serve at an earlier age since they weren't marrying; the Church could put their numbers, talents, and desire to serve a mission to good use. And when the sisters return home, they might be in a better position and frame of mind to marry.

It remains to be seen what the long-term effects of this change will be, but the remark of an eighteen-year-old elder in 2015, who entered the mission field right out of high school, is telling: "Being able to serve at eighteen makes everything so much easier and more convenient. If I would have had to wait until I was nineteen, I doubt that I would have served. I would have been moving on with other parts of my life by then."

Nearly all of the interviews in this book were conducted prior to the change in requirement age; thus they reflect the earlier practice of elders being at least nineteen and sisters at least twenty-one. This is frequently reflected in the text. While some of the new practices and dynamics will lead to significant changes, it seems that many missionary experiences remain consistent over time, regardless of their ages when they begin their missions.

Overview of the Book

The introduction looks at the religious impulse behind missionary efforts, while chapters one through seven follow the chronological experiences of Latter-day Saint missionaries. Chapters 1 and 2 look at the expectations, pressures, and early preparations for a mission.

Chapter 3 focuses on the Provo Missionary Training Center and on the knowledge, skills, and attitudes the Church seeks to instill in its new missionaries. Chapters 4 and 5 follow the missionaries into the mission field, with a consideration of the structure and organization of the mission, the role of the mission president, and companion relationships. Chapter 6 considers how missionaries find people to teach, while Chapter 7 looks at what they teach, the process of baptism, and the efforts made to integrate new converts into the Church. Chapters 8, 9, 10, and 11 concentrate on the unique experiences of particular sub-groups of missionaries: those on international missions; sister missionaries; and senior missionaries. Chapters 12 and 13 then consider the often awkward experience of returning home, the reasons some interviewees chose to leave the Latter-day Saint Church, as well as the future of missionary work.

This work fills a significant gap in the study of one of the most dynamic religious groups today. In an age when large mainline churches are losing members or, at best, holding their own, the story of the Latter-day Saint Church and its missionaries is a testament to the strength that can be found in committed volunteers, as well as the value that can come from individualized contact with people in their own homes.

I am seeking neither to aid nor to hinder the missionaries' efforts, nor am I seeking to determine whether their message is "true." I leave that up to the reader. What I *am* interested in is looking at a practice that I think Mormons and non-Mormons alike take for granted, but which is really quite unique. If the reader comes away with a greater understanding of the missionaries and the missionary program, as well as a greater appreciation for their importance to the Latter-day Saint Church, then this work will have served its purpose.

ACKNOWLEDGEMENTS

A work of this scope requires the help of a myriad of people—from the technical, to help with the content, to those who provided general support and encouragement. My thanks go out to: Elizabeth Cooke; Karl and Jeanine Franson; Bonnie Frost; Jennifer Johnson; Joyce King; Angie LeClair; Sandy Lord; Lynn Payne; the faculty, staff and administration of the University of Maine at Farmington; my agent, Jim McCarthy, my digital manager, Sharon Pelletier, and my copyeditor, Trinity McFadden; for translations, Linda Britt and Odessa Deffenbaugh; colleagues in the Mormon Social Science Association; the Farmington, Maine, Ward of The Church of Jesus Christ of Latter-day Saints; and especially my students, my family, and all the missionaries who shared their stories with me. This work could not have been completed without your help. I am eternally grateful.

THE MORMON MISSIONARY

INTRODUCTION

The Missionary Impulse

"Of course."

THE RESPONSE OF A VANCOUVER, BRITISH COLUMBIA, RESIDENT IN 2008, WHEN ASKED IF SHE HAD EVER BEEN APPROACHED BY MORMON MISSIONARIES. A RESIDENT OF ALBANY, NEW YORK, GAVE AN IDENTICAL RESPONSE TWENTY-FIVE YEARS EARLIER.

Missionizing Faiths

Many have answered a knock at the door to find two young men standing there. Polite, well-dressed, and wearing black nametags with white lettering, they introduce themselves as "Elder Smith" and "Elder Jones" of The Church of Jesus Christ of Latter-day Saints. They are Mormon missionaries, and they want to share their faith with you.

It is an awkward moment. They always seem to show up at inconvenient times, American culture does not welcome strangers at the door, and their appearance raises a fundamental question: should they be so aggressive in trying to convert us to their faith? Don't they understand that if we want to know about their church, we will ask them? As a result, most are turned away, and not always in a friendly manner.

Their approach to missions reflects a philosophy of recruitment shared only by a few religions, most notably Christianity and Islam. Many faiths are focused on particular peoples or places, and adherents would find it strange to suggest they should seek members among other peoples or in distant lands. Orthodox Jews, for example, will not appear at your door, nor will followers of Shinto, an indigenous Japanese religion which combines religion and patriotism and is only practiced by the people of Japan.

In contrast, Christianity and Islam share an aggressive approach to evangelism, where each looks to a founder who said his message had universal relevance and should be carried to all humankind. Christianity is the largest of the world's religions, with over two billion members, while Islam is the next largest, with over one and a half billion adherents.

Jesus told his disciples: "Go ye therefore, and teach all nations, baptizing them in the name of the Father, and of the Son, and of the Holy Ghost: Teaching them to observe all things whatsoever I have commanded you: and, lo, I am with you alway (*sic*), even unto the end of the world" (Mt 28:19-20).[6] Popularly referred to as the "Great Commission," Jesus's exhortation, along with the example of the apostle Paul, who is one of the greatest Christian missionaries of all time and whose missionary efforts are chronicled in the book of Acts, have served as the impetus for subsequent Christian missionary activity. Jesus warned his disciples that missionary work would not be easy, for they would be ignored, harassed, and persecuted. This should not be a deterrent, he said, for those who persevered would find favor in the sight of God (Mt 10:16-22).

Christian missionaries have faced challenges and setbacks over the centuries; some have suffered greatly, and some have lost their lives in service to the faith. But it is due to their efforts, aided by advances in transportation and communication, that Christianity enjoys its worldwide presence today.

Of particular interest to this study is the rise of a new approach to missions that occurred in the nineteenth century, which transformed the mission landscape: the rise of volunteer, lay missionaries.

Christian Mission in the Nineteenth Century

In the nineteenth century, Christian mission and expansion occurred on a scale and at a speed never previously attained. Evangelical religion swept across Protestant Europe, England, and America during the century, and part of its impact was seen in the development of a new approach to missions: the propagation of the spread of Christianity was increasingly seen to be the responsibility of *all* Christians, not just that of a professional clergy. Lay involvement became a powerful factor in the worldwide spread of Christianity, and the chief vehicles by which this was carried out were numerous voluntary benevolent and missionary societies.

In the United States, the first half of the nineteenth century was a period of intense missionary activity for practically all Protestant denominations. Benevolent and missionary associations, fueled by the Second Great Awakening (a period of intense religious and social excitement characterized by enthusiastic revivalist preaching), were especially active in New England, central and western New York, western Pennsylvania, and the Great Lakes region. The key individuals were traveling missionaries who were frequently sent on missions of a year or more at a time, taking with them Bibles, tracts, and pamphlets, and preaching at churches wherever they could.[7]

The Second Great Awakening had a considerable impact on Upstate New York. The term "burned-over district" was coined to describe the religious character of western New York during the first half of the nineteenth century. It was a region and a time in which enthusiastic religion and millenarian expectations flourished—when the faithful looked forward to Christ's return and the beginning of a thousand year reign on earth—and the fires of evangelistic revivalism swept across the area repeatedly during the period.

The birth of The Church of Jesus Christ of Latter-day Saints occurred in this time and place, and subsequent Latter-day Saint missionary activity reflects the new understanding of who is responsible to spread the gospel: all are responsible, for all are considered missionaries.

The Church of Jesus Christ of Latter-day Saints

The Church of Jesus Christ of Latter-day Saints has its origins in the revelations of Vermont native Joseph Smith Jr. (1805-1844). It is said that in 1820 the fourteen-year- old Joseph, confused by the excitement of the Second Great Awaking and by the existence of so many competing religious denominations, prayed to God asking which church was right and which he should join. Smith reported that God the Father and God the Son appeared to him in a vision and told him to not join any of them; all were wrong, for all had strayed from the teachings of Jesus. Instead, Joseph would be called as a prophet of God through whom the fullness of the gospel of Jesus Christ was to be restored to the earth. This vision, often referred to as the "First Vision," was the first of many revelations Joseph Smith was said to receive.

Other revelations followed from 1823 to 1827, and it was these that Smith said ultimately led to his discovery and translation of a set of golden plates, which were subsequently published as the Book of Mormon. The Book of Mormon is said to be an account of the earliest inhabitants of the American continent, their Hebraic origin (it is said they were a remnant of the Lost Tribes of Israel), and the "fullness of the everlasting Gospel," which Christ preached to these inhabitants in America after his death, but before his ascension into heaven (3 Nephi 11-26). It is said to complement the Bible and that it represents another testament of Jesus Christ. Smith received additional revelations that were subsequently published as *Doctrine and Covenants* and *Pearl of Great Price*. It is also reported that the New Testament figure John the Baptist, acting under the direction of the apostles Peter, James, and John, appeared to Smith, baptizing and ordaining him.[8]

With the calling of Joseph as a prophet and the establishment of the Church in Fayette, New York, on April 6, 1830, it was believed that a new and final dispensation had begun, which would bring humankind back into fellowship with God. It was Joseph's duty to restore the Church of the Latter Days with its priesthood and ritual to the simplicity and purity of the Apostolic Church. Accordingly, the ancient Melchizedek and Aaronic priesthoods were restored, and the offices of the Church were patterned after the first-century Church, including twelve apostles, elders, priests, teachers, deacons, and a patriarch. Church members were told their activities were apostolic, for two months after the Church was established, Joseph spoke of their being "engaged in the very same order of things as observed by the holy Apostles of old."[9]

Thus miraculous experiences, a living prophet who received revelations from God, a new scripture, and the Church's structure and activities served as the basis for its claim that it wasn't just another fragment of Protestantism but that it was the divine restoration of the Ancient Church in the Last Days that would meet Christ at his Second Advent.

The Latter-day Saint Church was established as a lay organization (meaning it has no paid, professional clergy) where all are considered member missionaries and where the philosophy and goals of the Great Commission are embraced. They believe they have a message with universal relevance, and they feel a responsibility to share the message with the world. *Doctrine and Covenants* echoes this responsibility: "And this gospel shall be preached unto every nation, and kindred, and tongue, and people" (*D&C* 133:37).

The early Saints also found a role model for their missionary activity in the Book of Mormon. There are missionary passages in the books of Alma and Mosiah in which Ammon, the most famous missionary depicted in the Book of Mormon, is credited with baptizing thousands of idolatrous unbelievers, or "Lamanites." Ammon is often held up as the missionary model for Latter-day Saints, and he was a favorite figure of Ezra Taft Benson, president of the Church from 1985 to 1994. President Benson particularly enjoyed citing Alma 26:3-4, which reviews the accomplishments of Ammon. Said Ammon: "...for our brethren, the Lamanites, were in darkness, yea, even in the darkest abyss, but behold, how many of them are brought to behold the marvelous light of God! And this is the blessing which hath been bestowed upon us, that we have been made instruments in the hands of God to bring about this great work. Behold, thousands of them do rejoice, and have been brought into the fold of God."

Latter-day Saint missionaries were sent out soon after the Church's founding in 1830, and they were expected to travel "without purse or scrip," a practice referred to in the New Testament where Jesus sent his disciples out as missionaries without money or food. "Scrip" was a bag used by travelers to carry food and other items, and the idea was that they would be housed and fed along the way by sympathetic listeners (Mark 6:8). Mormon missionaries could be gone from their homes and families for periods of a year or more, frequently leaving them in dire circumstances. They carried with them the Book of Mormon, Church periodicals, and handbills announcing meetings. They spoke of the prophet Joseph Smith, his First Vision and subsequent revelations, the golden plates, Smith's divinely inspired translation of the Book of Mormon, and his duty to restore the Church to the purity of the Apostolic Church. They approached relatives and friends and went where they felt led by the Spirit. They went eastward in the United States and into Canada, and in 1837 they went on their first overseas mission to England, where the LDS Church enjoyed some success until the mid-nineteenth century.

A unique feature of the missionaries' message was that new members were encouraged to move to the new Mormon community being built, first, in Kirtland, Ohio, then in Nauvoo, Illinois, and, finally, in the Great Salt Lake Valley. This migration became characteristic of the Latter-day Saints, and it soon became associated with the idea of "The Gathering," the building of the millennial kingdom of God ("Zion") on earth—the building of the utopian society in America for the redemption of humankind, which will greet Christ at his Second Advent. The American continent is believed to hold a primacy of place in the Divine Plan. The Book of Mormon refers to it as "a land of promise, a land which is choice above all other lands" (2 Nephi 1:5). It is the land of favor that Christ visited after his resurrection but before his ascension, to establish the true Church, and it is the land where the faithful will gather to meet the Lord at his Second Advent.

The idea of "The Gathering" is one of Mormonism's oldest doctrines, and it quickly became one of the most important.

Harassment and persecution dogged the Saints from the earliest days. The idea that Smith was a new prophet of God and that the Book of Mormon was scripture that complemented the Bible did not sit well with the religious establishment. The Saints also came into conflict with their neighbors when they sought to build their communitarian society, resulting in their being forced to move westward from New York to Ohio, and then to Illinois, where Joseph Smith was martyred in 1844. Choosing to remove themselves from their detractors, the majority of Saints, under the direction of Brigham Young, made their famous trek across the Plains to the Great Salt Lake Valley where the LDS Church remains headquartered today and where the greatest concentration of Latter-day Saints is found.

The Saints also ran afoul of public sentiment and the federal government due to their practice of polygamy, and it delayed Utah's entry into statehood until after the Church officially abandoned the practice in 1890.

It is not unusual for new religious groups to alter members' marriage patterns. Two nineteenth-century American contemporaries of the Latter-day Saints did just that: the Shakers practiced celibacy, and the Oneida Community practiced matched-marriages, or eugenics. But polygamy is what caught the public's eye, and it generated a massive amount of anti-Mormon literature and sentiment, both in the United States and in Europe.

Today the Latter-day Saint Church excommunicates those who engage in the practice, but the activity has permanently branded the group. This perception is fed in part by the fact that there are "Fundamentalists" in the Mountain West and elsewhere who are polygamist. The Church of Jesus Christ of Latter-day Saints disassociates itself from these groups, but missionaries today are still asked if they plan to live in a polygamous marriage when they return home from their mission.

From these experiences evolved a unique lifestyle, a sense of mission and community, which, when coupled with persecution and forced migrations, were instrumental in forming the Mormon self-image of being "a peculiar people."

During the conflict with the federal government over the polygamy issue, Church authorities decided to shift their attention to international efforts, reflecting their disaffection with their federal protagonists and with the United States in general. Missionaries were dispatched to countries around the world, where they enjoyed mixed success, with the United Kingdom and Western Europe being the most fruitful. Converts were encouraged to "gather to Zion" in order to help build the Kingdom of God in the Mountain West, and tens of thousands of converts immigrated to America in the nineteenth century in pursuit of that goal. This practice weakened the local branches of the Church, both in the United States and overseas, and it was stopped in the first decade of the twentieth century. Converts were discouraged from immigrating to America thereafter, and they were told to stay in their communities and countries and to build the worldwide Church. As a result, the Latter-day Saint Church took on an international identity in the twentieth century.

The missionary system became more formalized once the Saints were in the Mountain West. Missions to a specific place for a set period of time became standard; men waited for "the call" to a mission field, and the ceremony of "the farewell" developed, where friends and relatives gathered and gave money and presents to the departing missionary. Not all men looked forward to the call, fearing the hardship it would pose for their families.

Married men went on missions well into the middle of the twentieth century, when young, single males replaced them, which remains the practice today.

The twentieth century also saw greater attention given to the organization of the missionary system, to improving proselytizing techniques, and to making materials and practices more uniform. A series of lessons that missionaries present to interested people (or "investigators") were developed in the 1950s, and they have been periodically refined since. Memorization of a preset script was emphasized until the 1990s, when greater attention was placed on addressing the needs and concerns of the investigator. A call for missionaries to provide nonproselytizing community service for up to four hours a week was also introduced in the latter part of the twentieth century.

The role and limits of the individual missionary also became more sharply defined, such that today's missionary is typically a young, single male who will receive training at a Missionary Training Center prior to leaving for his assigned mission. He will serve for two years in a defined location, and his behavior will be closely monitored.

In 1974 the newly sustained president of the Church, Spencer W. Kimball, called for increased attention to international missionary efforts and for members to "lengthen our stride" so that they might meet Jesus's challenge to teach all nations. Every young man was exhorted to prepare for a mission, and each country was asked to provide its own missionaries. Improved language training accompanied the Church's worldwide expansion. As a result of President Kimball's challenge in 1974 and of subsequent presidents' calls for missionary service, there has been a dramatic increase in the number of missionaries serving: from 9,811 called in 1974, to over 88,000 serving in 2014. Church membership has also shown an impressive increase—from 3,409,987 in 1974, to over 15,000,000 in 2015.[10]

However, care needs to be taken when considering LDS membership statistics. Except in very specific circumstances (when they request that their names be removed from membership rolls, or they are excommunicated), names of members remain on the membership rolls whether they still attend a Latter-day Saint church, have joined another church, or no longer consider themselves Mormon.

The Church's rationale for leaving names on the membership rolls is that special efforts are made to reactivate inactive members. Reactivating "inactives" is a particular consideration and goal of the current president, Thomas S. Monson.

What is the appeal of the Latter-day Saint Church? The appeal appears to be multi-faceted: the Church's conservative stance on political and social issues, its emphasis on the family, and its advocacy of basic values such as hard work, discipline, and thrift, resonate in today's society. Many are also attracted to the Church's claim that its head, the president, is a prophet who continues to receive divine revelations. The process by which members are brought into the Church is also significant. People respond to the Church because they are *asked* to do so. Few faiths are that bold. There is also something to be said for a faith that requires engagement of its members. Latter-day Saints are given a "calling" in the Church, a responsibility they are expected to carry out. Such engagement can have the effect of strengthening the commitment level of its members.

Four significant events occurred at the turn of the twenty-first century that impacts the current missionary program. For the first time in the Latter-day Saint Church's history, more of its members are found *outside* of the United States than inside it; English is no longer the predominate language in the Church; in 2007, the Mormon Church sent out its one-millionth missionary, a remarkable achievement for a faith that has only been in existence since 1830; and there was a significant increase in the number of young men and women applying for missionary service when the age requirement for young missionaries was lowered in 2012.

The Latter-day Saint Church can rightly claim to have one of the most extensive and successful missionary programs in the world.[11]

The LDS Church continues to struggle with its public image, because the image persists that Latter-day Saints are outside of the religious mainstream and that their beliefs are, at best, unusual, and, at worst, heretical—which makes the work of their missionaries that much more difficult. Their claims that a fourteen-year-old boy received revelations from God and that he translated a new scripture from golden plates lead many to assert that the Latter-day Saint Church is not Christian at all, but a "cult" centered on Joseph Smith. Critics say there is no need for further prophets and the Bible says there is no need for further revelations. They cite Revelation 22:18 as proof: "For I testify unto every man that heareth the words of the prophecy of this book, If any man shall add unto these things, God shall add unto him the plagues that are written in this book." The Latter-day Saint Church counters by noting that the Bible in its current form did not exist until centuries after the writing of Revelation and that the passage cited applied only to that particular book, not to the Bible as we know it today.

The Latter-day Saint Church stresses its Christian connections by including "Jesus Christ" in its official title, and in 1995 it further emphasized this identification by changing the font in its title from "The Church of Jesus Christ of Latter-day Saints," to "The Church of JESUS CHRIST of Latter-day Saints." The title is prominently displayed on Church buildings, Church publications, and missionaries' nametags, where the name JESUS CHRIST visually jumps out at the viewer.

But not all are convinced. Various surveys show that many Americans believe Latter-day Saints hold beliefs and values at variance from their own and that they do not have a favorable impression of Mormons.[12] Gary C. Lawrence, public opinion pollster, LDS Church member, and author of *How Americans View Mormonism: Seven Steps to Improve Our Image,* found that Americans generally have a negative perception of Mormonism. In a 2008 poll of 1,000 randomly chosen adults, Lawrence found: only 12 percent knew (unaided) the Church's claim to be a restoration of the first century Church; 67 percent are uncertain whether Mormons believe the Bible; 77 percent are uncertain whether Mormons are Christian; and 75 percent are uncertain whether Latter-day Saints practiced polygamy. Forty-nine percent had an unfavorable impression of Mormons, whereas 37 percent had a favorable impression. Thirty-seven percent said they didn't know a Mormon, and 55 percent said they hadn't met one.[13]

Lawrence is not alone in his findings. The Latter-day Saint Apostle L. Tom Perry, speaking at Women's Conference at Brigham Young University on May 1, 2009, said there are significant misperceptions surrounding the Latter-day Saint Church. He said the Church has employed professional firms to help it define and project its image to the world and to better understand how the organization should approach its missionary efforts. He reported that when pollsters asked respondents to provide one-word impressions of the LDS Church, they said "polygamy," "family," "cult," "different," and "dedicated." Perry sadly observed that three negative impressions out of five is not a good batting average for the Church.[14]

Other surveys and focus groups have yielded even more negative images among non-Mormons, with respondents using adjectives such as "secretive," "cultish," "sexist," "controlling," "pushy," and "anti-gay."[15]

Mitt Romney's presidential bids in 2008 and 2012 serve as examples of how one's Latter-day Saint faith can be a lightning rod for anti-Mormon sentiment and concern. In a famous October 2011 episode, Robert Jeffress, a Baptist pastor of a Dallas megachurch, introduced Romney's Republican opponent Rick Perry, and then described Mormonism as a "cult," adding that he thought Mormons are not Christian. This created an uproar in the presidential campaign, but Jeffress refused to back down. Jeffress eventually warmed to Romney and even said he would vote for him, but he also said he would "hold his nose" while doing so.[16]

A 2011 Quinnipiac University poll found similar discomfort for a Mormon president. Thirty-six percent of respondents said they were somewhat, or entirely, uncomfortable with the idea of a Mormon president.[17]

These negative perceptions can make it difficult for Latter-day Saint Church members to engage non-Mormons in discussions about the LDS Church, and it is particularly true for those who are expected to initiate the conversations: Mormon missionaries.

The Mormon Missionary

We traditionally think of the Mormon missionary as a young male, and this is predominately the case. Approximately 56,000 unmarried, young men are serving worldwide in 2015 (up from 43,000 in 2012), along with around 24,500 women (up from around 8,000 in 2012) and 7,000 older, retired members, who serve as senior missionaries (up from 4,000 in 2012).[18]

The youthful missionaries traveling two-by-two on their bicycles, walking along the street, and going door to door, are performing signature activities of Latter-day Saint missionaries; but since most are ignored or turned away, non-Mormons know little about them. Most are not aware of the preparation missionaries undergo prior to their missions, nor do they appreciate what missionaries experience in the mission field. The Latter-day Saint Church prepares its missionaries from an early age to accept, and even welcome, serving a mission in early adulthood. Informal training begins in the home and church, while formal training takes place at a Missionary Training Center just before beginning the mission. Once in the mission field, missionaries follow a rigorous daily regimen; they experience emotional and spiritual highs and lows; and they struggle with rejection and exhaustion. But they also gain converts for the Church, come away with new knowledge and skills, and many develop a deeper spirituality.

The missionaries' common appearance leads many to assume they are a homogeneous group, but in reality they have varying personalities, backgrounds, and differing mission experiences. This is becoming increasingly so as the number of converts increases and as more non-American missionaries serve.

The mission has symbolic significance. The three stages of the missionaries' experience—separation (at a Missionary Training Center), isolation with hardship (the mission itself), and reintegration into the community—are features common to a rite of passage, an experience designed to move an individual from one status to another in a community. The Mormon missionary experience is such a rite, and few religions, if any, have developed as elaborate or lengthy a process to prepare their youth (primarily the males) for adulthood.

Perhaps what is most surprising is that the missionary system works at all. Late adolescent males traditionally are not associated with fervent religious convictions, nor are they known for their commitment to religious organizations. Thus to entrust the expansion of a faith to that group is unusual. They also are essentially untrained, in spite of their informal and formal preparation. With their brief formal training period at a Missionary Training Center, they stand in stark contrast to other denominations' clergy, who generally have years of training and experience prior to entering the mission field.

The Latter-day Saint missionary program appears to be working, though, and the benefits are not limited to, or even dependent upon, Church growth alone. While the Latter-day Saint Church obviously benefits from the work of missionaries and their steady influx of new converts, the personal growth of missionaries must be of equal value to the Church in the long run. The missionary experience is a formative personal and religious experience requiring diligence, commitment, and sacrifice, carried out within the supportive structure of a complex religious organization. Granted, there are variations in the quality of the missionary experience, and there have been changes in the missionary experience across time due to changes in the system itself, but most missionaries seem to enjoy a variety of benefits from their experience: strengthening of their faith and testimony; greater commitment to the LDS Church; independence from family; self-sufficiency; personal discipline; self-motivation; management of time and finances; practice with interpersonal relations; development of communication and teaching skills; experience dealing with adversity; growth of concern for others; experience traveling; exposure to different (often foreign) cultures and values; and (for many) the acquisition of a foreign language. These traits are developed within a tight-knit organization and support system that also provides counsel and guidance from a mission president and his wife.

The Latter-day Saint Church also benefits from the knowledge and skills missionaries gain in the field. As a lay organization, it is dependent upon its members to provide leadership, instruction, and service. The mission experience is excellent preparation for these roles and responsibilities.

One's mission doesn't stop at the end of eighteen months or two years, for all members, regardless of whether they went on a mission, are expected to be "member missionaries," a concept enunciated by the head of the Church, President David O. McKay in the 1950s (president from 1951 to 1970). Therefore, it is not surprising that members, in general, and many returned missionaries, in particular, continue throughout their lives to invite their friends, neighbors, and colleagues to investigate their faith.

These benefits—personal growth, Church growth, and lifelong commitment to the Latter-day Saint Church—are perhaps the most pervasive rewards of the missionary program for the individual and for the Church.

Granted, not all have a positive mission experience—some leave the Church because of negative experiences in the mission field, and some later leave the Church for various reasons—but many still point to the positive aspects of their mission. They are glad they served.

Of particular interest to me, and I think to non-Mormons in general, is the increasing number of young women who are choosing to serve a mission. Historically, the role and status of single women serving as missionaries has not been the same as of the men; women's service is entirely voluntary. Single, female missionaries began serving in the latter part of the nineteenth century, and their participation extended throughout the twentieth century, (albeit in much smaller numbers than men's). But their participation was seen as being unusual, since the Church teaches that the primary role of women is to marry and have children. Up until the last quarter of the twentieth century, most women were content with that role and did not even consider serving a mission. If a woman did go on a mission, it was often seen as a last resort; it meant she wasn't able to find a mate.

This negative stereotype of sister missionaries has changed dramatically since the 1980s, such that today serving a mission is considered a worthy endeavor for young women—that their desire to witness to their faith, to gain significant life skills, and to deepen their spiritual lives is to be applauded. "Marriage over mission" is still the counsel of Church leaders for young women, and while this can lead to internal conflicts for women—"Should I marry, or should I go on a mission? Should I follow the counsel of the Brethren, or do I follow my dream of serving a mission?"—today many young Latter-day Saint women are postponing marriage so that they too can have the mission experience.

The sisters' missionary stories provide an insightful perspective on this trend and will be of special interest to non-Mormons, who often perceive Latter-day Saint women as having second-class status in the Latter-day Saint Church. The women's missionary stories provide non-members with a window through which to observe the evolving experience of women in the LDS Church.

PART I

Preparation

CHAPTER 1

Called to Serve: Expectations

"I always assumed I would go on a mission.
I never even questioned it."
A FREQUENT REMARK OF MALE INTERVIEWEES

"It would have been more difficult for me
***not** to go on a mission, than to go."*
A RETURNED MISSIONARY WHO SERVED IN
MEXICO IN THE MID-1960S

When the phone rang at 6:00 A.M. at his home in a small, Utah town, Mark knew it was either very good news, or very bad news. He was relieved when he heard the local postmaster say, "It's here!"

"It's here!" shouted Mark to his family, who were coming out of their bedrooms, looking sleepy and worried.

"It's here!" they repeated excitedly to one another.

Mark was tempted to call his grandparents in Arizona and his sister at college to give them the good news, but he decided to wait until he had it in hand.

He was at the post office when it opened, and the postmaster handed him a large white envelope, the envelope that would tell him where he would serve his mission for the next two years. He nervously had checked the mailbox for the past two weeks, wondering when it would arrive. Now that he had it in hand, he became even more nervous, wondering where he would go, what language he would speak, and if he would like it.

He hurried home and, surrounded by his parents and younger sisters and brothers, with his grandparents and sister on the speakerphone, he opened the envelope. He began reading:

> "Dear Elder Johnson,
>
> You are hereby called to serve as a missionary of The Church of Jesus Christ of Latter-day Saints. You are assigned to labor in the New Hampshire/Manchester Mission."

His younger sister interrupted him: "Are you going to England? To Manchester, England?"

"No," said her mother, "he is going to New Hampshire."

"Where's that?" asked a younger brother.

They quickly found a map and discovered that it was in New England, on the other side of the country.

"Oh," said the siblings.

His father, who had served his mission in Brazil, detected a bit of disappointment on Mark's face, for Mark shared that he too wanted to "go foreign"—to learn a new language and to go to a foreign country. Mark's grandfather, who also knew of Mark's desire to go foreign and who had served his mission in Boston, assured him that it indeed would feel like a "foreign" mission, given the way they talk there and given the differences in cultures between Utah and Northern New England.

Mark's sister Jenny, who was a senior in college and who served her mission in South Carolina, echoed her grandfather's assessment when she said, "Believe me, Mark, *anywhere* outside of Utah is foreign!"

They all laughed.

Mark began to feel better about his call, believing he was going where he was needed. But he had lingering doubts: Would he get along with his companions? Had he studied the Book of Mormon and the Bible enough? Would he return home being able to say his mission had been a success?

The expectation is clear in the Latter-day Saint Church: young men should serve a mission. Church leaders, official publications, and family expectations contribute to a culture that extols the obligations and benefits of serving. This is especially true since the 1970's, when a renewed emphasis was placed on missionary work.

From a young age, Latter-day Saint boys are counseled to prepare for missionary service, to live righteous lives, to acquire knowledge and skills that will serve them in the mission field, and to develop a "testimony," an inward assurance that the Latter-day Saint message is true. Young people are advised to start a mission fund, because they and their family share responsibility to pay for the mission. Their worthiness is monitored yearly by Church leaders and more frequently by parents. They go through a rigorous personal interview as part of the mission application process: a process that since the early 2000s has seen increased expectations with regard to personal worthiness. They then wait with great anticipation for the call, including the assignment to a specific field of labor and the date to enter. When the large envelope arrives, opening it becomes one of the most memorable moments of the missionary experience. There is then a flurry of activity as they prepare for the next phase of the process, entering a Missionary Training Center, which we will discuss in Chapter 3.

While young women are not obligated to serve a mission, thousands today choose to do so. Their mission experiences parallel those of young men in many ways. However, the fact that sisters have a choice doesn't make their decision to serve any easier; if anything, it makes it more difficult. The elders know what is expected of them. In a sense the sisters do, too—get married and start a family—but, for many, their hearts are set on serving a mission, and they have to decide whether to postpone marriage or not.

Early Preparation

The success of the missionary program rests in large part on the close cooperation between the Latter-day Saint Church and families, for each play a vital role in preparing and sustaining missionaries. The Church makes clear its expectations and provides institutional support, while the family reinforces these expectations and provides nurturing, counsel, and financial support.

The Church

Expectations and benefits. Addressing young men in the Church in 1981, particularly those twelve to eighteen years old, President Spencer W. Kimball wrote: "It is your responsibility to attend to this missionary work, and we hope you will not excuse yourself from this responsibility. Every worthy young man should fill a mission. The Lord expects it of him."[19] Missionary service is a frequent topic at General Church Conferences, held twice yearly in Salt Lake City and broadcast to LDS meeting houses around the world. Parents are to reinforce this theme at home, and those who served missions are encouraged to discuss their missionary experiences with their children, with the hope that it creates a home environment that prepares their boys, in particular, to serve.

The current president of the Church, Thomas S. Monson, has stressed the obligation that young men have to serve: "I repeat what prophets have long taught that every worthy, able young man should prepare to serve a mission. Missionary service is a priesthood duty—an obligation the Lord expects of us who have been given so very much. Young men, I admonish you to prepare to serve as a missionary."[20]

Planting the seed. Youth are introduced to the idea of serving a mission at a very early age. One of the songs primary children (those three to twelve years old) sing is "I Hope They Call Me on a Mission."

I hope they call me on a mission
When I have grown a foot or two.
I hope by then I will be ready
To teach and preach and work as missionaries do.

I hope that I can share the gospel
With those who want to know the truth.
I want to be a missionary
And serve and help the Lord while I am in my youth.

Numerous interviewees cited this song as planting the seed that they should consider serving a mission. An elder who served in Portugal in the early 1990s said when he was little and sang the song, "it created a feeling" in him that he would become a missionary someday, and he never let anything get in the way of his goal. An elder from Utah who served in England recalled the impact that it had when, at the age of six, he was asked to sing the song for his grandfather. From that point on, he "had a good feeling" whenever he sang the song, and he renewed his commitment to serve a mission. And when asked in 2008 of his earliest memories of considering going on a mission, a Brazilian elder at the MTC in Provo, Utah, immediately responded, "When I sang, 'I Hope They Call Me on a Mission' in Primary!"

Moral purity. The Latter-day Saint Church sets high moral standards for its members. They are counseled to remain chaste, not lie, cheat, or steal, not use profanity, avoid degrading media influences (especially pornography), avoid tattoos and body piercings, dress modestly, honor the Sabbath, fast once a month, pay tithing (10 percent of their gross income) to the Church, and observe the Word of Wisdom. Those who transgress are advised to confess to the head of their local congregation or "unit" and repent.[21]

It appears many Latter-day Saint youth meet the high moral standards of the Church. *The Princeton Review*, which provides yearly rankings of colleges to aid high school students in their selection, consistently ranks Brigham Young University (BYU), the Latter-day Saint Church-sponsored university in Provo, Utah, as the most "stone cold sober school" in the country, listing BYU students as number one in avoiding beer and hard liquor. The school is also ranked number one in student religiosity.

Education. LDS youth attend an educational program ("Seminary") for students in grades nine through twelve, where they study the "Standard Works" or scriptures of the Church: the Old Testament; the New Testament; the Book of Mormon; and *Doctrine and Covenants*. The students meet for an hour each weekday (many meet at 6:00 A.M.) and devote a year each to the study of the four works. Anticipating that many Seminary students will serve a mission, the Church correlates the Seminary curriculum with what is useful in the mission field. While students don't come away from Seminary with an in-depth knowledge of their scriptures, they become familiar with important passages, and they learn the principles of the Latter-day Saint faith that they are expected to teach as missionaries.

Many Seminary teachers are returned missionaries, and they draw on their mission experiences to enliven their scripture lessons. A sister from Utah who served in the early 2000s told how her Seminary teacher illustrated many of his points with stories from his mission, even though he had served ten years earlier. "It became part of his life," she observed. She still remembers his stories today.

Returned missionaries also are invited to visit Seminary classes to speak about their missionary experiences. Such visits are found to be especially helpful for those who will be the first in their family to serve a mission; they may find the prospect of going somewhere they have never been, and meeting people they have never known, frightening. The returned missionaries show it can be done.

Many interviewees in the mission field confessed they wished they had worked harder and listened more closely in Seminary. When asked what advice they had for prospective missionaries, to a person they said, "Pay attention in Seminary!"

Spiritual preparation. Spiritual preparation for the missionary-to-be includes daily reading of the Book of Mormon and of the Bible, daily prayer, monthly fasting, moral worthiness, and obedience and dedication. They are advised to become familiar with the missionary manual *Preach My Gospel* and to study the doctrines of the Church. They are also advised to read *For the Strength of Youth: Fulfilling Our Duty to God*, which outlines the Church's moral standards and expectations, including advice on dating, avoiding pornography, and maintaining sexual purity before marriage.[22]

Finances. Prospective missionaries are encouraged to set up a mission fund and to contribute to it regularly, since they and their families are responsible to pay missionary expenses ($400 per month in 2015). Non-Mormons find this requirement of missionary service especially surprising: not only are Latter-day Saints expected to volunteer to serve, they also are expected to pay for it.

The teenage years. Increased attention is given to the obligation to serve a mission as boys enter their teenage years. Sunday school lessons for young men ages thirteen to seventeen make constant references to missionary labor. They stress that missionary service is both a privilege and a responsibility and that all are expected to serve (except those with severe health problems). The common excuses for not going—school, employment, having a girlfriend, cost—are given short shrift. They are advised to maintain their health, watch their weight, work on social skills, develop good work and study habits, study a second language, develop household skills such as cooking, cleaning, and sewing, and practice personal cleanliness and good grooming.

Bishop's annual interview. The head of the local congregation, the bishop, holds annual interviews with teenagers to discuss their lives, their worthiness and faithfulness, and their plans for the future. Young men are specifically asked about their mission plans, whether they have a mission fund and if they contribute to it. Young women may also be asked about their mission plans, but since they do not share young men's obligation to serve, it may not be stressed.

More recently, Church authorities have encouraged bishops to take a more proactive role in the lives of their youth and to help them establish timetables for their lives, including steps to take to prepare for a mission, a vocation, and marriage. They are encouraged to start these discussions in the preteen years, since, while it is hoped such conversations occur in the family, it doesn't always happen there; some young men reach the age of missionary service and suddenly realize they have not made adequate preparation for their mission.

An elder who served in the mid-1990s recalled that missions were never discussed much in his home as he was growing up, and when his older brother left for his mission, it took the family by surprise. The interviewee said serving a mission seemed a long way off at that time for him, for he was in his early teens when his brother left, but it came upon him more quickly than he expected. Suddenly he was nineteen, and he thought, "Oh, shoot, now what am I going to do?"

The need for advanced planning and preparation has been especially important since 2002, when the bar to qualify for missionary service was raised.

Raising the bar. While Latter-day Saint youths project the image of moral wholesomeness, not all live up to it. Since the first decade of the twenty-first century, there has been a renewed emphasis in the Latter-day Saint Church on ensuring the candidates' lives are in order, that they are not "repent-and-go" missionaries.

There had been concern for some years among Church authorities that some missionaries had not dealt with moral issues in their lives or that they lacked motivation to serve a mission. The individuals responsible for missionaries in the field, mission presidents, reported an increase in missionaries sent home because they did not fully repent before entering the field or because they didn't want to be there in the first place. Bishops and stake presidents, responsible for vetting prospective missionaries, may have been overly anxious to get wayward youth into the mission field as a way of straightening them out, not unlike the military. Thus candidates who were found to be less than morally worthy were given a short period of probation and then recommended for a mission, but when they got to the mission field it was discovered they hadn't repented much and couldn't do the work, so they were sent home.

There had also been talk about addressing the notion, prevalent particularly in Utah, that a teenager could have a pretty free life and do what he wanted (sex, alcohol, drugs, tobacco), repent, and then go on a mission. This became such a concern that Church authorities decided to act: they placed renewed emphasis on the potential missionary's moral character; they raised the bar.

At General Conference in Salt Lake City in October 2002, Apostle M. Russell Ballard said what the Church needs is "the greatest generation of missionaries in the history of the Church."

"We need worthy, qualified, spiritually energized missionaries. This isn't a time for spiritual weaklings. We cannot send you on a mission to be reactivated, reformed, or to receive a testimony. We just don't have time for that. The bar that is the standard for missionary service is being raised."

He went on to say that some young men have the idea they can behave pretty much as they wish up to six months before they are eligible to serve, repent, and then go on a mission. That will no longer be the case, he said; while they can repent of their sins, it doesn't necessarily mean they will be qualified to serve.

"The day of the repent-and-go missionary is over," he emphasized.[23]

President Hinckley acknowledged that stricter standards may appear unreasonable and harsh to many parents, but he expressed optimism that, by raising expectations, it will lead to greater self-discipline, especially among young men. The Church wants to get back to the original purpose for the missionary program, he said, to preach the gospel to the unconverted, and not to use it as a way to reform wayward Mormon youth. If they want to serve, he said, they should first get their lives in order.[24]

Interviewees who were in their formative teen years at this time said it had an impact on their behavior; they knew they would be held to a higher standard and had to be careful. When asked what advice he gives prospective missionaries in their teens, an interviewee who had served in Vermont said, "Just don't do dumb things." Another spoke of the importance of choosing one's friends wisely, of sharing common values and goals, with the most important goal being serving a mission. "Whenever my teenage friends and I did things," he said, "this was taken into consideration. We weren't going to do something stupid that would keep us from going on a mission."

Missionaries-to-be are counseled not to waste time playing video games, surfing the Internet, or engaging in social media, as they do not contribute to the knowledge and skills missionaries need, particularly interpersonal and communication skills. Weaning young missionaries and missionaries-to-be from technology, computers, cell phones, texting, video games, and social networking sites is becoming a concern for the Church. There are reports of young men choosing not to serve a mission because they don't want to give up playing video games. They cannot give them up.[25]

The sense among current missionaries is that raising the bar has had a positive impact in the field. They report missionaries are now more worthy, and, while not suggesting previous generations of missionaries were not hardworking, they say missionaries are taking to heart the literal meaning of being "set apart," of living to a higher standard than that found in the world. As a result they feel they are able to "hit the ground running," in the words of an elder serving in Pennsylvania, and they feel they reach a higher level of success while on their mission.

But interviewees also say they know missionaries in the field who shouldn't be there, who have said "the right things" to their bishop and stake president so that they can go on a mission and thus not disappoint their families and girlfriends.

Statistics indicate the Latter-day Saint Church carried out its intention to be more selective of its missionaries. There was a 15 percent decline in those called between 2002 and the end of 2010 (from 36,196 to 30,563).[26]

Church demographics also may have contributed to the decline, because the Church now has a smaller pool of eligible young men from which to draw. The Latter-day Saint Church is not alone in witnessing this drop. Schools, colleges, and universities also are impacted by the decline of the teenage cohort in the United States, resulting in fewer being in school.

But as we have seen, lowering the age requirements has helped the numbers rebound, and in a dramatic way.

The Family

Many non-Mormons are familiar with the Latter-day Saint Church's emphasis on the family, a frequent subject of the Church's popular ads on television. I asked an interviewee from California who identified himself as coming from "a typical Mormon family" what that meant. He said that while Mormon families tend to be larger, they still are similar to non-Mormon families in many ways: children are involved in school, sports, and music; parents support these activities by asking about homework, providing rides, and attending events; and families experience stresses and strains common to all families, including separation and divorce. (Some interviewees spoke of being children of divorce or of coming from dysfunctional homes.)

What he felt set his family apart from those of his non-Mormon friends was that his was a "gospel-centered home." As a family they regularly read from the scriptures, engaged in personal and family prayer, and attended church together. The teenagers attended Seminary, young men were expected to go on a mission, and all showed respect for Church leaders. The family observed "family home evening," a night (Mondays) set aside by the Church when no Church meetings are scheduled and when families are encouraged to engage in wholesome family activities like playing games, reading scriptures, and praying.

One of the family's greatest contributions to the missionary program is that it provides a powerful intergenerational support system for missionaries. Serving a mission is part of Mormon culture, it becomes a family tradition, and it provides structure to the family experience. This became apparent during my interviews, for a striking number of interviewees said that one, and in many cases more than one, of the following also served a mission in their family: fathers, brothers, uncles, male cousins, and grandfathers (and, to a lesser extent, sisters and mothers). Many who served in the late 1900s and 2000s were children of parents who were part of the wave of missionaries who responded to the call for more to serve in the 1970s; thus they represented a second generation of missionaries resulting from that call. Almost all said they were committed to seeing their own children be part of the next generation of missionaries.

An interviewee who served in Germany in the 1960s and who came from a long line of missionaries extending back to the early pioneer days of the Church said a "legacy of missionary service" is strongly felt in his family. Another interviewee who described himself as coming from "traditional Mormon stock" said that as he turned nineteen he thought, "Okay, it's my turn now."

Status. Latter-day Saint families achieve status in the Mormon community when their children serve missions. An interviewee who had served in Latin America in the late 1990s spoke of how proud his father was that all six of his sons served missions. The father had not been allowed to go because his father thought it was more important that his son pursue his education. The interviewee said his father felt bad about it, but he could now say that all his sons went on missions.

"There is status associated with that," said the returned missionary.

A sister missionary spoke of the pressure this creates for young LDS males. She knew a woman who had six sons, five of whom went on missions, but the sixth balked at the idea. The young man eventually went because he knew that had he not, his mother would not be able to say for the rest of her life, "All six of my sons went on a mission."

But it was not to be. He returned home early; a mission was not for him.

Spiritual benefits and blessings. There is a belief among Latter-day Saints that families receive spiritual benefits while supporting missionaries. When I asked what that meant, a returned sister missionary from Idaho who served in the mid-1990s explained that while there isn't a doctrinal basis for it, it is something that is understood among Mormons. She drew a parallel with the blessings received from tithing (Latter-day Saints tithe 10 percent of their gross income to the Church): while one has less money because of tithing, what remains seems to go farther. In a similar vein, while supporting a missionary can be financially and emotionally challenging, she said there could be a greater outpouring of the Spirit on those who remain at home, resulting in increased family harmony and unity.

An elder who served in Bolivia in the mid-1970s provided an example of this. His brother was on a mission at the same time, and their serving together created a serious financial burden for their family, because their father was an auto mechanic with a limited income. But he said his father's business increased dramatically while he and his brother were away, the family was able to support both missionaries, and it was considered a blessing.

A Canadian from a very poor family of nine children, all of whom worked on the family farm, told a similar story. The tradition of missionary service extended back at least as far as his great-grandfather, but as a twelve-year old boy in the 1940s he still was shocked when his father came home from church, called the family together, and said the bishop asked if the family would support sending the oldest son on a mission.

"What did you say?" asked his mother.

"Well," responded his father, "I told him that we didn't have the money, but if the Lord needed him to go, then the Lord would open the way and we would do what was needed to support him. I told him we would unite as a family and the Lord would work things out."

The interviewee reported it seemed impossible that his brother could go, since he was a significant contributor to the family income. Plus, the $100 per month it would cost to support him would be a huge financial burden for the family. He said he could remember thinking as his father talked, "That was a dumb thing to say! Why did you say that? How are we going to have any more income when such an important person in our family is gone? Plus, a mission is adding a financial burden on top of it!"

"I didn't say anything," he continued during our interview, "but of course it showed how shallow my faith was."

The son was called to France for thirty months. (Missionaries at that time did not receive language training prior to departure. Their mission was extended six months, and they spent the first months learning the language in the field.) The interviewee said he vividly remembers "observing thirty consecutive miracles." The family never had enough money in advance; month by month they didn't seem to have enough, and toward the end of each month his parents started praying a lot longer and a lot harder that it would be there. And it was.

The family was actually better off financially when the brother returned home and the same thing happened as six more children served. The interviewee also recalled that as a teenager he once expressed disappointment to his father that the farm had not done as well that year as he had hoped. His dad responded: "Well then, I guess it is time to send another son on a mission, for we will be blessed for it."

However, as we will see, not all are able to consider the financial burden of funding a mission a blessing.

Family members and returning missionaries as role models. Many interviewees said role models played an important part in their decision to serve a mission, with the most powerful being family members and other missionaries returning from the field. A missionary from Utah whose father served in London in the late 1970s said his father always shared missionary stories and how things he learned on his mission helped him address challenges and problems he currently faced. He found his father's stories entertaining, and he was sure part of his father's motivation was to teach him lessons. And he listened. A missionary from the state of Washington said his father talked all the time about his mission to Canada, what he learned, and how important it was in his life. The interviewee said he grew up with that and as a result he always planned on a mission. A sister missionary whose mother served in the Central States Mission in the 1970s, said her mother told her about being a missionary her whole life, and that is why it felt normal for her to serve as a sister missionary.

Some parents spoke of the challenges they faced on their mission. An elder from Utah, whose older sister was serving at the same time, said their father spoke frequently about his mission to Germany as they were growing up; he told exciting stories, but he also shared his struggles. A sister from Salt Lake City said her father encouraged his children to go on missions, and he shared the hard experiences of his mission as well as the good experiences. He told them the reality: it wasn't just a time to play and take it easy. She was glad he did. Her companion added that her father also talked about his mission and how hard it had been, and she initially thought it was not something she wanted to do. But he talked about his experiences with a big grin on his face, as if it were the best thing that ever happened to him.

She thought, "You are crazy, Dad!"

An unusual story was told by an elder who served in the late 1990s, who is a direct descendent of a first cousin of Joseph Smith, five generations removed. He said as he was considering serving a mission, he thought back to his ancestors and the sacrifices they endured. He asked himself what his ancestors would do in his situation. He started to weigh his options as he was driving to a family reunion. He reflected back on his family roots, and that made up his mind for him; he needed to do what they did before—he needed to serve a mission.

Some missionaries said family home evening provided the context when their fathers or mothers talked about their mission experiences. Old missionary pictures, slides, and films were viewed, and missionary stories were told. Some parents read from their missionary journals and from letters they sent home to their parents.

This is not to suggest that all parents who are returned missionaries talk about their missions with their children. Some discuss it only when asked, and some don't mention it at all. And some, those who served frustrating missions where they saw few or no baptisms, who returned home with a sense of failure, said they are ambivalent about encouraging their children to serve. They don't share missionary stories, and they don't want their children to go through similar negative experiences. Thus they do not push their children to serve, and in some cases the children don't go.

Siblings are also powerful role models. A sister said her older sister serving a mission set an example for her, and she thought if her sister could do it, so could she. An elder from California serving in the early 2000s told how frightened he was as he was growing up by the idea of serving a mission, but how his older brother's example as a missionary helped him get over his fears and motivated him to want to serve.

He then explained, with amusement, the whole story. When he was around fourteen years old, he had a mental image of his parents dragging him out the door, kicking and screaming, when he turned nineteen, and sticking him on a plane for his mission. He decided he would hide from them on that day so he wouldn't have to go. But then his older brother went on his mission, and as he read his brother's letters and heard his missionary experiences, he got over his fears and decided that he too wanted to serve.

Observing older siblings as they return from the mission field, seeing how much they have changed, also has a significant impact on younger siblings. An elder serving in Northern New England in the mid-2000s said his older brothers set the example for him as he was growing up, and as they returned from their missions he saw how much they had matured and learned, and he decided at an early age that he, too, wanted to have the same growth and to help other people.

Missionary homecomings are popular events in the Latter-day Saint Church and it is common for the newly returned missionary to speak at a Sunday sacrament service soon after returning home. Such events can have a powerful effect on the youth of the Church. A returned missionary who served in Hungary in the early 1990s said watching missionaries return home "in glory" had a profound impact on him when he was young. He would sit there and think, "I want to be like that guy when I grow up." He said Mormon culture encourages it, and the homecoming was an inspiration and encouragement for him to go.

Missionaries serving in the area as role models. Numerous interviewees said as they were growing up, missionaries serving in their area had a powerful influence on their decision to serve a mission. Missionaries speak at Seminary classes and talk with young men and women at church, and it is common for missionaries to be invited to homes for a meal and to interact with the children. A father whose family has missionaries to dinner once a month observed that in some ways he feels his children admire missionaries more than they admire him, and, since missionaries are typically young, enthusiastic, athletic, and fun-loving, being with them motivates younger members to want to be one. By interacting with them regularly, the children get to see what is like to be a missionary, and eventually they will decide that this is what they want to be. Seven of his children served missions. One who served in Japan said he admired missionaries who came for a meal because they always seemed so much smarter and more mature than he.

Young people occasionally have a chance to serve a mini-mission or to go on "splits," where teenage women and men serve with full-time missionaries (of the same sex) for short periods of time as youth missionaries. They may help in planning the day's activities, accompany the sisters or elders while tracting ("tracting" is when missionaries of any religious stripe go door-to-door, frequently leaving pamphlets or "tracts"), teach part of the lessons, invite investigators to get baptized, and speak at district meetings. The experience can have the effect of strengthening their testimonies and motivating them to serve a mission. They are thus better informed and prepared when they do serve. It also has the effect of getting parents involved in the missionary endeavor, with the result that they are more supportive of their child going on a mission.

Boy Scouts of America

The Latter-day Saint Church has a close affiliation with the Boy Scouts of America, and it serves as the largest single sponsor of scouting units. Many of the local branches sponsor their own Boy Scout troop. While LDS scouts engage in activities common to any scout troop, the Church uses the scout movement as a platform to encourage young LDS boys to prepare for and to go on a mission. At the 2010 National Scout Jamboree held in Virginia, Latter-day Saint scouts were challenged by their leaders to commit to serving a mission, to prepare for it, to engage in missionary work at the Jamboree by passing out copies of the Book of Mormon to non-Mormon scouts, and to share their testimonies with them.[27]

"I Never Questioned It"

The majority of male interviewees reported they never questioned if they would go on a mission; it is such a part of Mormon culture that it is something they just do. It is "the expected norm," as a physician who served in the mid-1970s described it: it is something he always assumed he would do. Serving a mission is a given, like attending college is a given, commented another physician who served in the Northwest states in the late 1980s. "Serving a mission was always a part of me as I was growing up," observed an elder who served in Switzerland. "I never had thoughts of not going; it was never an option as far as I was concerned."

While an outsider might think missionaries only serve because of family pressure, and while some did admit to feeling pressure to serve, some said they saw it differently, that they saw it as fulfilling an expectation. A returned missionary who served in Scandinavia, whose family roots extended back to the earliest days of the Church and whose father served a mission, said that there was always the expectation (never the pressure, but clearly the expectation) that serving a mission was what he should do. A young man who was applying to go on his mission in 2002 said for a young Mormon man there is the expectation that he will go on a mission. He said it is more of a given, rather than a pressure to go; it is something that is going to happen. An elder who served in the Midwestern United States, whose father and mother went on missions, said he knew from an early age that he would go on a mission: "That was the thing you did. There was no question about it. You just did it."

The logic was perhaps most clearly described by a missionary who served in Germany in the late 1990s. He said once he decided the Latter-day Saint Church was true, serving a mission then followed. That is one of the things young Mormon men do, he said: if they believe the Church is true, then going on a mission follows. He knew by the seventh grade that the Church was true; therefore he went on a mission.

This is not to suggest that none feel pressure from family to serve, even if indirectly. A missionary who served in California said "there can be considerable social pressure to serve a mission," but he thought his parents perceived themselves as not pressuring their children to go on a mission (he was the third in his family to serve). At the same time there was subtle social pressure when they said, "When you go on your mission at nineteen...." and, "After your mission you will be doing...." During our interview he recalled a recent conversation with an LDS friend who introduced his small son as "our little missionary."

Some parents are more direct in communicating that they want their children to serve a mission. An elder serving in the Mid-Atlantic states said his parents clearly told him they wanted him to serve a mission, while another said from an early age he felt "pushed" to serve by his parents. Yet another elder recalled being at a friend's house and the parents telling his friend, "You *will* serve a mission!"

And there are stories of parents bribing their sons with promises of a new car if they serve.

And there are plenty of stories of a girlfriend saying she won't marry her boyfriend unless he serves a mission.

I expect some missionaries do get a new car on their return, but very few marry their old girlfriend. In the vast majority of cases, she has married someone else before he returns.

A returned missionary who served in Japan said he felt he didn't have a choice whether to serve, but he isn't unhappy about it, even though he has since left the LDS Church. He found his mission exciting, and it gave him status and rewards in the Church. He described it as part of the "male trajectory" in Latter-day Saint culture: a young man finishes high school, serves a mission, gets married, starts a family, gets an education, gets a job, and moves on with his life.

CHAPTER 2

Hesitations, the Call, and Rituals

"It would have broken their hearts."

THE RESPONSE OF AN AMERICAN ELDER IN MONGOLIA, WHEN ASKED HOW HIS PARENTS WOULD HAVE FELT HAD HE NOT SERVED A MISSION.

Hesitations

The right decision? While there is the expectation that young men serve a mission, and while some do not question it, others say they need to come to the decision on their own, to make sure it is the right choice for them. They question the timing of the mission in their lives and their weak (or lack of) faith. They ask themselves: "Do I want to spend two years of my life serving a mission?", "Will I be acting on the faith of my parents?", and "How can I serve, because I have so many doubts of my own?" The sense of urgency to address these questions grows stronger the closer they approach the age when they will be expected to serve. One young elder who was forced to go to church by his parents when he was growing up, recalled that when he was sixteen he realized what would be expected of him in a few years' time and thought, "Oh, crap, I have to go on a mission!" But by the time he came of age, he had warmed to the idea, and he went on to serve.

Some questioned if it was a good idea to put their education on hold: the world is a very competitive place, and they would be two years behind when they returned. "Will I be able to compete when I return?" asked an elder. Others spoke of giving up good jobs. An elder from Idaho said he had such a good job prior to his mission that he questioned whether Satan had a hand in it—if the job was there to tempt him to not go.

Watching others struggle with the question of whether to serve caused some to question their own futures. Some reported watching older brothers delay entering the mission field. An elder from the Northwest who served in the mid-2000s said he always planned on serving at the age of nineteen, but as he watched an older brother struggle with the decision (who didn't go until he was twenty-one), he began to wonder if serving a mission was the right choice for him; perhaps he should go to school instead. As he succinctly put it: "It came down to: do I want to do this, or do I not want to do it?" After an intense period of study and prayer, just before his nineteenth birthday, he said he found out for himself that serving a mission was what he wanted to do for the next two years of his life.

Some from small towns, with limited travel experience, question if they can cope with being in another part of the world for such a long period of time. Others wonder what they will do if they don't like their mission assignment. An elder from California said he worried because missionaries are told where they will serve, and if they decide they don't want to be there, they can't just decide to go somewhere else; they have to go home.

It can be very traumatic for parents who are faithful Church members but whose son chooses not to go on a mission, either because of a lack of interest or commitment or because he cannot meet the moral standards. A father of a teenage son who had strayed from the Church wrote an anonymous piece in a Church publication, in which he shared how difficult it was for him and his wife. They were "devastated" when, after years of faithful church attendance and family counseling, their son began hanging out with the wrong crowd, didn't live up to the moral standards of the Church, and dropped out of high school. The expectation that young Mormon men should serve a mission, and that it appeared their son wouldn't, made it even more difficult for these parents. "As our son turned nineteen, it became increasingly difficult for us to hear departing missionaries speak in Church. We questioned ourselves over and over again, wondering where we had gone wrong." This went on for some years, but the father was able to report that, through patience and prayer, his son eventually got his life in order, and at the age of twenty-five (the upper age limit for serving) he served a mission.[28]

Whose faith is it? For some, it is not so much indecision as it is coming to the realization that they haven't nurtured their own faith, or as one elder put it, that he was "living off of the faith of his parents." In a similar vein, some who grew up in communities where Latter-day Saints are in the majority say they never had occasion to doubt their faith, and they took the claims of the Church for granted. An elder from Utah said he never really questioned his faith or had reason to. A sister from "Happy Valley" (Utah County, south of Salt Lake City, also known as Utah Valley, and approximately 88 percent Latter-day Saint) questioned how much the culture shapes the beliefs of those who live there. She said as she was growing up, everyone around her believed the Latter-day Saint Church was the only true religion: "It was just common knowledge. Oh, yes, Joseph Smith, prophet of God." She felt some elders left on their missions on blind faith. She said they had "no clue what is up or down as far as the religion is concerned," how much they really believed it, and how much was their culture and their being brought up in it.

For those living off the faith of their parents and for those living off the faith of their community, the realization often comes that going on a mission will bring them into frequent contact with those who will challenge their faith, reject their claims, and tell them they are deluded. As a result, many interviewees spoke of going through an intense period of prayer, study (especially of the Book of Mormon), and soul-searching prior to their mission, because they realized their faith and their knowledge of the Church were weak, and if they were going to serve as missionaries they needed to be convinced of the truthfulness of their message.

For some, coming to the realization that their faith was weak became a dramatic turning point in their lives. An elder reported that while he had always had the desire to serve a mission, he knew he lacked a solid foundation for his faith. So he read and studied the Book of Mormon from cover to cover, and he came away with a newfound faith in the teachings of the Church. He said as he was reading the Book of Mormon, he felt compelled to open it to Alma 26. He said he knew nothing about it at the time, and what he found was the story of the missionary Ammon, who was going through things similar to what the young man was experiencing—doubt, people were laughing at him, telling him he wasn't going to convert anyone—but he trusted the Lord, he felt the Spirit was strong, and he got on his knees and thanked his Heavenly Father. He said it was a turning point in his life.

Another elder said he had his own conversion at the age of eighteen. He said he knew the Church was true, and he lived according to that belief, but he felt there comes a time when a person is really converted. He said he experienced it, and it "really fired him up" about his mission.

Some came to the realization that they had been taking their faith and the Church for granted. On seeing the effect of the Latter-day Saint message on a friend who was a recent convert, an elder from New Mexico observed that it really opened his eyes. He said he realized he did have a lot to be grateful for, and he wanted to be able to help others so they could have similar blessings. He decided he did want to go on a mission, and not just because it would make his parents and grandparents happy.

An elder who served in 2000 said there are missionaries who serve for the wrong reason—pressure from parents and girlfriends being the most common. But for him, and for most of the missionaries he knew, the young men did it because they wanted to, not because they were pressured into it. He said he decided around the age of seventeen to go on a mission, and it was not for his parents or for his bishop, but for him and for the people he was going to serve.

A crisis of faith. At a more profound level, some say they first have to address their own lack of faith before they can commit to a mission. A sister from California shared that she "had fallen away inside" in her late teens and that she had to regain her faith before deciding to serve a mission. A returned missionary who served in Western Europe in the 1960s said prior to his mission he came into contact with anti-Mormon professors who picked on Mormon students. It adversely affected him, and he stopped attending church for three months. While he had always planned on a mission, at that point he realized he would be exposed to similar negative attitudes while on a mission, and he needed to have a solid foundation for his faith. He read through and studied the Book of Mormon and became convinced it was true. He then served a mission.

His crisis of faith after experiencing anti-Mormon sentiment is not unique; many missionaries reported similar struggles of faith after being subjected to constant rejection and negative comments in the mission field.

A more dramatic story was told by a man who grew up in Utah and who served his mission in France in the mid-1970s. He walked away from the Church after high school, choosing to go to college on the East Coast so he could leave behind his Mormon culture and identity. But during his first year at college he decided he needed to ensure he made the right decision. He decided to read the Book of Mormon, to which Latter-day Saints believe are attached great sorts of promises if a person reads the book and engages God in questions about its veracity and importance. He assumed he wouldn't get an answer, or he would decide Mormonism was false, concocted by Joseph Smith. He said he had "the first and most extraordinary religious experience of his life" reading it: not so much because of the teachings he received (because they were part of the teaching he picked up in primary school), but because of an immediate religious experience with the Divine. He said one has to have these kinds of experiences to know what he was talking about, and from this he decided he had to take it more seriously.

He became active in the ward where he went to school, and the community immediately embraced him (even though his long hair reached his waist, which generally is perceived quite negatively in the Latter-day Saint Church). He was given positions of importance that belied his age and recent conversion. At that point he realized the Latter-day Saint community and its teachings meant more to him than he had imagined; it could transform people's lives. He felt he had a serious obligation to go on a mission, which he then did.

While he has since left the Latter-day Saint Church, to this day he said he does not doubt his encounter with the Divine.

Delaying the decision. Some may take extra time to sort out issues with their faith before serving a mission, but they can't wait too long. While young men technically can go on their mission through the age of twenty-five, there appears to be a much smaller window of time in which the decision must be made before social expectations and pressure come to bear.

A returned missionary from Utah shared how he grew up with the expectation that he would go on a mission at the age of nineteen, but he was going through a period of religious doubt when he reached that age, so he chose not to apply. His family and friends soon began asking why he wasn't going on his mission. By waiting to go later (he left for his mission at twenty-one), he said it became "a cause for concern" for his family and neighbors. An elder from California who served in the mid-2000s said he remained in college until he was twenty before going on his mission, but at the expense of having people tell him he should go on a mission when he turned nineteen. He said he didn't see anything wrong with going to college first. In fact, he was glad he did. A couple who served a Senior Mission in the early 1980s, whose son waited until he was twenty-three to go on his mission, said by that point they "had given up hope" that he would ever serve.

To delay is thus perceived as a red flag. An elder said that young men in his hometown in Utah feel considerable pressure to go by the appointed age and that if a person hasn't gone on his mission by that year, people will say, "Whoa! What is wrong with that guy?"

But there are those who express respect for young men who choose to wait so they can sort out issues in their lives and so they can be sure the decision to serve is their own and not somebody else's. A sister from California said she knew Latter-day Saint young men in high school who were not ready to serve a mission because their behavior precluded them from being good ambassadors for the Church. But when they became of age they began to get serious, they changed their habits, and while they had to wait an extra year before serving, and while the delay was embarrassing to them and their families, the young men were better missionaries for it. But some certainly felt pressure to serve during the process. Girlfriends said they wouldn't marry the young men unless they served a mission, while some parents wanted them to serve because their friends' sons were serving. She said they took the extra time to make the necessary changes in their lives and decided, on their own, that they wanted to serve, and she respected them for it.

Losing interest. A bishop reported that enthusiasm for serving a mission tends to wane with age. There is great enthusiasm for missionary work at the primary level (ages three through twelve), but as young men reach their teen years and competing interests arise, the idea of serving a mission becomes secondary for some. Reasons given for not serving include school, employment, lack of money, and marriage. Many girlfriends have derailed potential missionary careers, saying the young men should marry instead. In order to preclude this eventuality, Sunday School lessons for teenagers emphasize the responsibilities of youth to help, not hinder, future missionaries' preparation. Young men are advised not to form serious relationships, and young women are advised to let their young men go.

Many religious groups have trouble retaining males in their mid-to-late teen years, and while Latter-day Saints may be able to retain a higher percentage of this population than most, a large percentage of young LDS men are lost between the ages of fifteen and nineteen. One wonders whether some are put off by the prospect of serving a mission, and if their leaving is a way to avoid the demand the Church will place on them. One interviewee residing in Boston described the missionary obligation as the "razor's edge" that forced him to decide on which side of the line he stood: would he stay in the Church and serve a mission, or would he leave?

He chose to leave just prior to his nineteenth birthday.

Social Pressure to Serve a Mission

There can be considerable social pressure placed on a young man to serve a mission. A returned missionary who was raised in Utah and who served his mission in the southern United States in the mid-1980s, but who struggled prior to his mission with doubts that he wanted to serve, said that in the end he had to. He said the social pressure to do it was "overwhelming." He felt he had no choice. He served a mission, but he left the Church soon after.

The pressure to serve a mission is perhaps most strongly felt at Church-sponsored Brigham Young University (BYU) in Provo, Utah, a campus with 34,000 students.

It is said social pressure to serve a mission is pervasive on campus. Multiple interviewees shared the following scenario: a young man arrives on campus with little interest or inclination to serve a mission; he asks a young woman out on a date; her first question on the date is, "Where did you go on your mission?" He responds, "Oh, I didn't go on a mission." "Well," she asks, "when *will* you go?" Interviewees reported that if they said they weren't going on a mission, they weren't going to get another date.

All went on to become missionaries.

A BYU professor observed that going on a mission is an integral part of BYU culture. He indicated that one is a "normal" male sophomore at BYU if he has been on a mission, but if he is a sophomore, junior, or senior and has not gone on a mission, then, in the professor's words: "He is not 'normal' and no one even has to say it. That is just what is 'normal.' And that is part of the capital he acquires by going on a mission—he becomes 'normal' on campus."

A returned missionary, who spent his first year at BYU and then served a mission in Japan, noted that all his BYU friends served a mission. Had he not gone, he would have been the "oddball" of the group.

Both of the observations above, the professor's and the student's, date prior to the age change, when young men had to wait until they were nineteen before they could serve. Thus they typically had completed one year of college before serving. In talking with two nineteen-year-old sisters serving in 2015, who had both attended BYU as chemical engineering majors in their first year, they said that while technically it is optional for young men to begin serving their mission at eighteen, they perceived a "stigma" on campus associated with young men who waited until they were nineteen to serve.

Young men who choose not to serve a mission, but who remain active in the Church, can find themselves in an awkward position. The Apostle Quentin L. Cook, speaking at the semiannual 181st General Conference of the Church in April 2011, told how a group of young men in Tonga resisted the strong encouragement of Church leaders to serve a mission at the traditional age. When they were in their late twenties and early thirties and thus too old to serve, they felt like "second-class" citizens in the Church. It wasn't clear whether they felt that way of their own accord, or whether they were made to feel that way by other members. Perhaps it was a combination of the two.[29]

Girlfriends and Boyfriends

The LDS Church advises its youth not to date before the age of sixteen and not to enter into serious relationships prior to a mission. When they do date, they are told they should dress modestly, should go in groups or double date, and should not engage in passionate kissing, sexual touching, or sexual activity. Young women are counseled to help young men prepare for missionary work, and those who are dating prospective missionaries are advised not to hold them back, but to let them go. Some interviewees, both sisters and elders, said they actively avoided dating as they approached the time of their mission; they didn't want a budding relationship to interfere with their mission plans. Missionaries in the field said they wrote to younger brothers and sisters offering the same advice—don't date, and don't get married; go on a mission first.

Many interviewees reported knowing missionaries whose girlfriends told them they wouldn't marry them unless they served a mission, but the interviewees then quickly pointed out the irony of the demand: only a miniscule number of relationships last the entire mission. The others send or receive "Dear John" or "Dear Jane" letters before returning home.

Parental and Family Opposition

Parents and family members aren't always supportive of a mission, especially if they are nonmembers or are inactive. Missionaries are told they are brainwashed, wasting their time and money, and that the family won't support them while in the mission field. Interviewees reported knowing missionaries whose parents disowned them when they joined the LDS Church and went on to serve a mission. A returned missionary from Utah recounted how his older brother, who didn't serve a mission, considered his serving a mission "a horrendous waste of time," and when the missionary-to-be told of his plan to serve, his brother threw a chair at him.

A mother, very active in her mainline Protestant church, related how her family and she were shocked when their twenty-year-old son, who was also active in their Protestant church as he was growing up, told them the "explosive news" that he was joining the Latter-day Saint Church. "Perhaps I erred in not explaining our faith as well as I might have," she said. Further shocks awaited the family when the son informed them he was going on a mission in two and a half weeks. The family was "speechless." "Stunned" members of the family's church hugged the father and mother and expressed their sympathy. Said the mother, "When we tell our Protestant and Catholic friends about his mission, they say, 'Incredible. We're so sorry!'"

The mother and brother attended the son's missionary farewell ceremony, but the father refused to go.[30]

There were interviewees who chose to serve in the face of parental opposition. A returned missionary who served in New England in the late 1950s reported how his father, an inactive member, was not supportive when the young man said he wanted to go on a mission. The father told him it was a waste of time and money and that he would disown him as a son if he went. Describing himself as stubborn like his father, the prospective missionary told his father that he loved him, but that he was going anyway. The father came to the young man's missionary farewell, the first time he had been in the Church in twenty years, and even spoke a few sentences at the service.

Some said even their Latter-day Saint Church-attending parents didn't like the idea of them serving a mission. Mothers in particular resisted the idea of the Church mandating such limited contact between the missionary and the family. They didn't like that the missionary wasn't allowed to visit home while on the mission and could only call on Christmas and Mother's Day. Some parents supported the idea of a mission but felt interrupting college was not a good idea, and they counseled their children to finish college first. Some missionaries did complete their education first, but some chose to put their education on hold and serve. Those who did said their parents eventually supported their decision.

Parents may not be supportive if they feel the Church has mishandled or mistreated their child. A parent who had sent older children on successful missions reported how a younger child had medical issues that were only discovered in the mission field, and, as a result, the missionary was sent home early. To be sent home early can be perceived quite negatively in the Latter-day Saint Church, and the parent felt the local leadership and membership didn't handle this instance well; they accused the young man of being lazy or of having done something woefully wrong. The parent said the criticism and gossip were very painful, and it was only after the missionary's medical condition was correctly diagnosed that people became more understanding. While not bitter and while remaining active in the Church, the parent commented: "I was glad I didn't have any more children. I had nothing more to give spiritually, emotionally, or financially. There was nothing left."

The Athlete as Missionary

Young Latter-day Saint men and women who interrupt successful athletic careers to serve a mission have caught the attention of the national media. After Brigham Young University won the NCAA Division I-A national football title in 1984, *Sports Illustrated* ran a feature article on BYU football players who could have played on the winning team but instead chose to serve a mission.[31] The commitment to their church and their mission was greater than their commitment to the team.

Historically, the sense among avid Mormon fans and some coaches has been that exceptional Mormon athletes should remain on the team and help it achieve national rankings, which to them is seen as a mission in its own right—it's bringing national and international attention to the Church—just as the Mormon Tabernacle Choir brings positive attention to the Church. To do otherwise is considered athletic suicide: athletes return home from a mission out of touch and out of shape.

Today, LDS athletes who interrupt their athletic careers are fairly common, many coaches accept it, and it is a popular subject with the media. But returning missionaries still find it a struggle to regain their strength, weight, and positions on the team.

Why They Serve at the Age They Do

Elders at eighteen or nineteen. Non-Mormons frequently ask why elders begin their missions at such a young age. They find it odd that the Church entrusts its missionary efforts primarily to late adolescent males who have limited life experience and theological training. When I asked an elder who was nearing the end of his mission why they are sent at that age, he quickly answered, "To keep us out of trouble!" He said it is an age when many young men experiment with alcohol, drugs, sex, and tobacco, which the Mormon Church doesn't permit. He said the Church gets them at the point when they may drift away and may never find their way back. He said it is also a time just before many of life's major decisions are made: what college to attend, whom to marry, what occupation to pursue.

"Plus," added his energetic companion, "we are in better shape than older people, and we can go out and do the work for twelve or thirteen hours a day."

An elder who served in Brazil in the early 2000s explained the timing of the mission in terms of taming a young man's pride. It is an age when males try to prove themselves, he said, and by calling them at that age it is a way for them to forget themselves, to overcome their pride, and to realize the importance of serving others. Seeing the humble circumstances of the Brazilian people and realizing the importance of serving others helped him to be a less prideful person, he felt.

A returned missionary and one-time college president said as an educator he finds the missionary program to be an excellent way to develop leaders. He said it essentially has two purposes: to proclaim the gospel and to develop leaders. It is an expensive way to develop leaders, he said, but it works; it puts people in difficult, crucible-kinds of experiences in which they are forced to confront themselves, their faith, and life, resulting in growth and maturity. Not all missionaries have a good experience, he added, and not all returned missionaries remain active in the Church, but those that do "become committed to the Lord, to the gospel, and to the Latter-day Saint Church, and they become great leaders." From an educational standpoint, he felt it is a "marvelous education in life" for a young man.

A biology professor who served in the 1960s agreed, saying young men don't have much experience, they have limited knowledge of the scriptures, and they haven't taken courses in preaching, beyond being told not to argue and not to try to prove that the Church is true. He said the biggest benefit is that young men get a spiritual grounding that will stay with them for the rest of their lives. He believes it is a "real builder of spiritual men."

An Assistant to the President in the mission office in Germany described the process in more colorful terms. He said he felt there are better ways of proclaiming the gospel than of sending "hormonal" eighteen and nineteen year old boys out, but without sending them out as boys and having them return as men who are ready to lead, he didn't think the Mormon Church would survive. He said without a paid ministry, they require boys of the Church to grow up and become men who can lead.

President Hinckley commented on the importance of the mission's timing in a young man's life: "What a wonderful program to take a young man at the most impressionable time of his life and, at a time when he is most prone to think of himself, send him out in the world to lose himself in the service of others. That's a tremendous thing in its own right, this great [missionary] program."[32]

But it is reported that President Hinckley also marveled at the young age of the missionaries: "At times it seemed almost incredible to him that the progress of the Church rested largely in the hands of young missionaries—hence the countless hours he spent teaching, interviewing, encouraging, and blessing them."[33]

The youthful age of elders is of ongoing amazement in the Church, too, and it once prompted a Church member with a comedic bent to observe that the Latter-day Saint Church must be true—otherwise, young missionaries would have destroyed it long ago.

Sisters at nineteen or older. Non-Mormons also ask why, until 2012, young women had to wait until they were twenty-one years of age before they could go on a mission. There were practical reasons for this. By being two years older than elders, it created an elder sister/younger brother dynamic; it was hoped this would have the effect of limiting the potential for romantic relationships to form. It seemed to work, for many sisters reported some of the younger, immature elders reminded them of their irritating younger brothers.

At a more fundamental level, the Latter-day Saint Church prefers young women to marry and have children, and by requiring them to wait until they were twenty-one it increased the likelihood that marriage would come first. This is not to suggest that Church authorities don't appreciate the value of a mission for young women. Sister interviewees serving since the 1990s and 2000s said if they expressed interest in a mission to their bishop, he first asked if they had marriage opportunities; if they didn't, then most bishops strongly encouraged them to go on a mission.

In general, however, the Church takes a conservative stance. Given its emphasis on marriage and families, the Church advises young women that if they have a choice between a viable marriage offer and serving a mission, they should choose marriage, for it is considered the "higher calling." [34]This was brought home to me in 2008 when I asked a Church member in her late twenties if she had served a mission. She simply said, "No, I got married and had babies instead."

But as we will see in Chapter 10, an increasing number of Latter-day Saint women (like women in the wider American society) are postponing marriage in order to pursue other interests first, be it further education, employment, or, in the case of LDS women, serving a mission. Lowering the age when they can serve to nineteen has made serving a mission a much more viable option for them, which has stimulated a marked increase in the number of sisters serving.

Traditionally, when elders left on their mission at the age of nineteen, many had completed one year of college. Now many will go straight from high school into their mission. When sisters had to wait until they were twenty-one, they frequently had completed two, three, or even four years of college prior to their mission. Now they can leave after one year of college. Some (elders and sisters) choose to work after high school instead of going to college, in order to contribute to their mission fund.

It remains to be seen what effects lowering the age requirements will have. As a college dean, I have worked with many students right out of high school, particularly males, and while it is a significant developmental period in their lives, they don't always make the best choices. It will be of interest to see, given their younger age, what particular challenges, if any, they pose for the leadership in the field, particularly the mission presidents.

The Application Process

Bishop and stake president interviews. Prospective missionaries may apply to go on a mission three months prior to when they are eligible to serve. The bishop and the stake president interview candidates before they apply. Both ask candid and searching questions, since they are seeking to assess the stability and general worthiness of the candidates. They want to know if the candidates can handle the pressure of serving a mission and if they can reach the new moral standard; if they can "reach the bar" that was set higher in 2002.

Prospective missionaries are questioned about their belief in Christ and their knowledge of Church doctrine, and they are asked to share their testimony. Special talents are discussed (for example, the ability to speak Spanish is a desirable talent), as well as restrictions or limitations such as physical issues and the inability to learn a second language. Those with physical limitations will probably be assigned to their home country. Emphasis is placed on exploring any unresolved problems of a physical, dental, or emotional nature and ensuring they are addressed before the candidates are recommended for a mission. Issues of a moral nature are also discussed, such as swearing, stealing, cheating on exams in school, problems with following the Word of Wisdom, masturbation, molestation of others, and sexual activity. It is felt that shortcomings in these areas reveal a level of self-absorption that indicates the mind is not focused on other people. Successful missionaries need to focus on others, they are told, not themselves. Recent practices of masturbation can put them on probation and delay their entry into the mission field. In the case of serious transgressions, such as having engaged in a sexual relationship, the local leadership will recommend the application not go forward until there is contrition, confession, and cessation of the activity in question. The probationary period may last six months to a year. Counseling may be recommended for those who can't overcome the behavior.

A college professor who served his mission in the western United States and who has served as a bishop and stake president says the interviews can be a healthy but painful process. It causes the prospective missionaries "to clear the slate." Lives are assessed, problems sorted out, and wrongdoings are confessed. They are asked if there are any misdeeds in their lives that ought to be cleared up at that time. "It is good," he reported, "for when they go out on their mission they are not flawless, but they are clean with God."

A physician who served his mission in Southeast Asia said the main goal of his stake president interview with missionary candidates is to ascertain that their lives are clean and in good order, and that they will be able to teach effectively soon after arriving in the field. Not all live up to that expectation, he said. He said that as he looks at missionaries who have failed, "who have returned without honor," he finds it's usually because there is something in their lives they haven't resolved. He said prospective missionaries normally will have addressed these issues before the interview, but there are instances where they still need to address specific issues, and their missionary application will be delayed until they are dealt with.

Some candidates will not be entirely truthful during the interview process. An elder from Idaho shared that he wasn't completely honest about his background with his bishop. The bishop knew the prospective missionary wasn't being entirely honest because the ward was small and the bishop was aware of what went on in the lives of youth, but he chose not to say anything, to see what the young man would do. The elder said it "ate at his conscience" until he finally went back and confessed. His bishop then helped him overcome the issue so he could serve his mission. "He knew what he was doing," the young man observed.

In cases where shortcomings go unacknowledged and un-confessed, there is a good chance they will come back to haunt the missionary at the Missionary Training Center, or in the mission field, because intensive environments such as these have the effect of bringing lingering issues to the surface. A bishop said he always makes it clear to prospective missionaries that they need to clear up issues in their lives before going on their mission, because, once in the field, any unresolved issues will rise to the surface, they won't be able to ignore them, and they will experience considerable feelings of guilt until they go through the repentance process.

Some potential candidates don't even apply. They may not want to confess to their behavior, to change it, or to be an embarrassment to their family and to themselves. Most are moral worthiness issues. An elder serving in 2008 said he had friends who knew they couldn't "reach the bar"; some had relationships with young women, and some knew they weren't prepared. They knew it was a serious matter to serve, and they weren't ready for it. "They didn't even try," he said.

Completing the paperwork. Once candidates have committed to serve a mission, have reached the required age, and have been deemed worthy by their bishop and stake president, they complete an extensive, electronic application that includes personal and family information, doctor's and dentist's reports, educational background, school grades, and ability to do schoolwork. They are asked if they speak any languages with native or near-native ability and what language or languages they have studied at school, and for how long, and what grades they earned. They are asked how interested they are in learning and using another language on their mission and how successful they think they will be in learning it.

The application form, recommendations from the bishop and stake president, medical and dental records, and a photograph of the candidate are then electronically forwarded to the Missionary Department in Salt Lake City.

Some can't wait to send in their application. "Once I decided to go, I wanted to go really bad," reported an excited sister. "I was anxious to go. I was twenty and one-half years old when I decided to go and I had to wait until three months before my twenty-first birthday. I sent my papers in on that day!"

While this quote shows the enthusiasm of the prospective missionary, it illustrates a point that will be addressed later: for some, sisters particularly, serving a mission can be a last-minute decision, which creates issues of its own.

The Missionary Department

The Missionary Department at Church headquarters in Salt Lake City manages the missionary program, and, in collaboration with the Twelve Apostles of the Church, is responsible for choosing ("calling"), assigning, and training missionaries. The department is also responsible for the fifteen Missionary Training Centers around the world, their staffing, and the training that takes place in them. It provides teaching materials used in the field. It manages the logistics of the missions throughout the world, including calling and training the individuals responsible for the day-to-day oversight of the various missions: the mission presidents.

Responsibility for missionary callings is shared by the Twelve Apostles. An apostle sits in front of two computer monitors and "prayerfully reviews" each missionary application. On one screen is a picture of the missionary candidate, their recommendations, academic background, medical history, and interest expressed in learning a new language. The apostle consults the second monitor, which shows where vacancies and needs exist in the various missions around the world. He then receives a "spiritual impression" of where the missionary should serve, sometimes in less than a minute. Depending on the number of applications received that week, the process can involve the efforts of multiple apostles spending hours in front of their computers.[35]

There are instances in which applications will be denied. Missionary department physicians review the medical reports and, if necessary, follow up with the local physician, dentist, and stake president to see if they feel the individual can handle the demands of the mission. There are physical expectations. Missionaries must be able to walk six miles a day or to bike twelve. They are required to have a body mass index not higher then thirty-seven, which borders between obesity and morbid obesity.[36] Young men and young women with serious mental, emotional, or physical limitations are excused from full-time missionary service and are told they shouldn't feel guilty about it, for there are other ways for them to serve.

Those whose hearts are set on serving a mission are not always happy with the prospect of alternative service. A sister with health issues, who completed her application accurately and honestly, said her stake president warned that she included information that could preclude her from serving a mission. She said it almost broke her heart when he told her that. She "so badly" wanted to serve. She felt she needed to serve. She waited a very long time for a response from Salt Lake City, a wait she described as "agonizing," and the longer she waited, the greater her fear was that she would receive a rejection letter. There were nights when she cried herself to sleep, praying and begging them to let her go. One night she finally prayed that she couldn't take the agony any longer; she asked to know one way or the other, so that she didn't have to worry about it anymore. She reported she had a dream that night that she received her mission call, but it was a very strange call, for all it said, in capital letters, was MANCHESTER. She shared the dream with her parents and some friends, and they thought it was an answer to her prayers and that she was going to England.

Her missionary call arrived a few days later, informing her that she would be serving in the New Hampshire/Manchester Mission.

The Missionary Call

The time between submitting their paperwork and receiving their call is nerve-racking for prospective missionaries. It generally takes two to four weeks to hear from Salt Lake City. Many talk of daily visits to the mailbox, of being on edge, and of wondering if something is wrong if they don't hear within the normal time. An impatient sister who hadn't heard by four weeks said she was afraid she was going to receive a letter from the Church saying, "Thanks, but we think you should get married instead." She received her call not long thereafter.

It is the question of the unknown that keeps them on edge. A sister who served in Guatemala in the mid-1990s said she experienced a "mysterious feeling" as she waited for her call, knowing she could be sent anywhere in the world. A sister who served in Italy in the late 1980s described the wait as a "big, blank, vague cloud" in front of her, where she had no idea where she would be sent and the kinds of experiences she would have.

Some receive a quick response from Salt Lake City. An elder applied for his mission during the spring semester of his first year at college, and his call arrived within a matter of days, informing him he was to enter the Missionary Training Center the day following the end of the semester. He said, "I guess the Lord didn't want to waste any time with me."

The large white envelope. The missionary call and supporting documents are sent in a large, white envelope, and its arrival is one of the highpoints of the missionary experience. It is not uncommon in smaller towns in Utah for the postmaster to make an early morning call to the prospective missionary, informing her or him of the envelope's arrival. Parents and family members call candidates at school or work to tell them it has arrived, and in a few cases sympathetic employers (returned missionaries themselves) gave interviewees permission to go home early to open it.

Missionaries react in a variety of ways when faced with the envelope. It is a Mormon tradition to open the call in the presence of family, and many will wait hours to give them a chance to gather. A sister who worked a late evening shift returned home at 2:00 A.M., woke her family, and they opened it together. One talked of being away at college and of opening it over the phone with his father. Some want it to be a private moment and take it to a favorite spot to open it alone. Some have trouble opening it at all. One elder talked of sitting and staring at the envelope for many minutes before opening it. He said that as he looked at it, he thought of how its contents determined the next two years of his life, where he would be going, and what language he would be speaking. He described it as a "very emotional, spiritual moment."

The most pressing question missionaries want answered is, "Where will I serve?" The world is divided into geographical areas or "missions"; as of 2015 there are 406. A mission president oversees each, and missionaries are assigned to a particular mission. While the application asks about their foreign language skills, they have no control over where they will be assigned. This is by design. The Church does not want missionaries to have a say, otherwise some may choose comfortable or exotic places. (While the Latter-day Saint Church may not be a fan of the Broadway hit, *The Book of Mormon*, parts of it are authentic. One missionary had his heart set on serving in Orlando, Florida, because of the recreational attractions there. He was shocked to end up in Uganda.) Instead, the Church wants missionaries to display the attitude of an elder who served in Argentina, who said, "I will go anywhere," or the attitude of a sister from New England who served in the Salt Lake City/Provo area who said: "I don't really care where I go. I know the Lord calls us where we are needed. I know it is where I am supposed to be."

Not all interviewees were so open to being called just anywhere, and this affected how they chose to open their envelope. Some, fearing they would not be called to a desired location, chose to open it alone, in case they needed time to work through the disappointment. "What if I didn't like it?" said a sister who chose to open her call alone. "What if I opened it and thought, 'Yuck, _____ (location)!'" She didn't want people to see the reaction on her face; by being alone, she could adjust to it in case it was some place she didn't want to go. Another sister had a similar concern and opened her envelope alone. Holding it in her hand she knelt and prayed, "Heavenly Father, I know this is not where I want to go, so please help me like it." She said initially she was disappointed with her assignment, but she soon grew to love it.

A returned missionary who served in the early 1990s told a touching story. He came from a family in which his parents and six brothers and sisters had served missions. His mother, brothers, and sisters had all gone to other countries, and everyone predicted he would also go somewhere exotic. Fearing he would be called stateside, to a very non-exotic place, he chose to open the envelope alone so that he didn't have to worry about what others saw when he opened it. He said a prayer, opened it, and as soon as he saw where he was going it felt right and he was happy. He rushed home and told his family he was going to Switzerland. He reported they were very excited, especially his mother, who had served in that very same mission thirty years earlier.

The Letter

The Church of Jesus Christ of Latter-day Saints
Office of the First Presidency
47 East South Temple Street
Salt Lake City, Utah 84150

(Date)

Dear (Elder) (Sister) _______,

You are hereby called to serve as a missionary for The Church of Jesus Christ of Latter-day Saints. You are assigned to labor in the (location) Mission. It is anticipated that you will serve for a period of 24 months [18 months if a sister].

You should report to the Missionary Training Center at (location) on (date). You will prepare to preach the gospel in the (name of language) language. Your mission president will modify your specific assignment according to the needs of the mission.

You have been recommended as one worthy to represent the Lord as a minister of the restored gospel. You will be an official representative of the Church. As such, you will be expected to maintain the highest standards of conduct and appearance by keeping the commandments, living mission rules, and following the counsel of your mission president.

You will also be expected to devote all of your time and attention to serving the Lord, leaving behind all other personal affairs. As you do these things the Lord will bless you and you will become an effective advocate and messenger of the truth. We place in you our confidence and pray that the Lord will help you meet your responsibilities in fulfilling this sacred assignment.

The Lord will reward you for the goodness of your life. Greater blessings and more happiness than you have yet experienced await you as you humbly and prayerfully serve the Lord in this labor of love among His children.

You will be set apart as a missionary by your stake president. Please send your written acceptance promptly, endorsed by your bishop.

Sincerely,
(signed)
President

After reading the call, recipients and family members run to the map to see where they are going, and then connect with girlfriends, boyfriends, family, and friends.

Going stateside, or going foreign? In the parlance of missionaries from the United States, one is either "going stateside," or "going foreign." A sister reported that most American missionaries think they will go foreign, and to a certain extent this is true. More than three-fourths of missionaries at the MTC in Provo were learning a new language when I visited there in 2008. While some were to serve stateside (primarily Spanish-speaking), most were going foreign. Many interviewees said they hoped they would serve an international mission, because they found the idea of learning a new language, living in a new country, and being exposed to a new culture appealing. A sister who served in the late 1980s reported that she was thrilled to be called to Italy. She said that a mission is a mission wherever missionaries go, and they don't go to travel to exotic places; but she found it "a plus" to be able to learn another language, experience another culture, and get to know people from another country while on her mission.

Since some interviewees thought they would go foreign, but didn't, they reported initial disappointment, but most seemed to adjust quickly. An elder from the Southwestern United States who wanted to go foreign, but who was assigned to Northern New England, said it was "a shock and disappointment" for the first thirty seconds, but then he decided that was where he was supposed to be. An elder who served in the mid-2000s, who said his family had a legacy of going foreign (his father and three older brothers had), said he was "shocked and had mixed emotions" when called to the Northeastern United States. Another elder serving in the mid-2000s had a stronger reaction. He said he wanted to go to South America, speak Spanish or Portuguese, live on a dirt floor, sleep in a hammock, and experience what it is really like to live in another country. He thus was quite disappointed when he opened his call and saw he was assigned to the United States. He said most of his family was there as he opened his call, and his dad commented later that he saw disappointment on his son's face. "But sometimes God has a different purpose for us," observed the missionary, philosophically. "It took a couple of days to adjust, but I am happy with my assignment now."

Some Americans experience a double disappointment of not going foreign and of not liking where they are sent in the United States. An elder from the East Coast was called to a mission in Utah. He said at first he was disappointed, since Utah is the center of Mormonism, and he thought, "Forget it, I don't want to go." It took him almost two weeks to send in his acceptance letter, but eventually he decided if that was where he needed to be, then he would go. He quipped, "As I was soon to find out, there was plenty of missionary work to be done in Utah!"

Some said they were just as happy with their stateside assignment; they didn't want to go foreign. A hardworking convert assigned to the Pittsburgh area in the mid-2000s said he received condolences from his foreign-going friends because he was going stateside, but he said he preferred his assignment because it allowed him to reach his greatest potential as a missionary quicker. He didn't have to spend the first six months of his mission becoming comfortable with a new language and adjusting to a new culture. Others expressed relief at not having to learn a new language, that it was not one of their strengths. A sister serving in the United States confided that, given a preference, she would like "indoor plumbing, a bed and a pillow, and being warm in the winter and cool in the summer." She added, "I was willing to go wherever Heavenly Father wanted me, but the thought of going foreign really scared me."

Others expressed a similar fear. A sister said her parents were convinced she would go foreign, but when they heard she was going stateside, they both let out a huge sigh of relief, and for the next few days they found themselves sighing and saying, "Our daughter is going stateside!" The sister said she too thought she would go foreign, and it was a relief not to. She said she would have gladly done so and put up with "giant spiders," or, like her brother on his mission, "get bit by bed bugs every night." She would deal with it. But when she found she didn't have to do any of those things, but could still do what the Lord wanted her to do without copping out, she was happy. She would have hot water. She said her whole family found they were walking around breathing giant sighs of relief, and they hadn't even known that they were stressed about it. Afterwards they all joked about how stressed they were about her going foreign.

There is a perception among some missionaries that there is more status associated with serving in a foreign country. A returned missionary from Utah said he and his two best friends applied for their missions at the same time. One friend was called to South America, he to Japan, and the other to South Dakota. The interviewee said to this day, many decades later, the friend sent to South Dakota still complains about his assignment. The interviewee said that for a kid from Utah to go foreign is desirable and exciting; it is the call of the exotic. He said the call to South Dakota is not quite so exotic.

A General Authority who lived in Utah and was called to Colorado in the 1940s said his friends who were going foreign laughed at him when he received his assignment, just one state away. But he put a positive interpretation on his call when he said that maturing comes when missionaries accept wherever they are sent as best for them. Plus, being so close, he has been able to stay in touch over the years with people he baptized.

There are those who are perfectly happy regardless of where they are called. An elder from Utah who served in the early 2000s said where people go is never where they expect. He said he never thought he would be in Maine, but he felt the thing to remember was that his call came from God through a prophet. He also said God knows him better than he knows himself, and He knows what is best for him.

People also find humor in their assignment. An elder from California told his father he wanted to serve in Chile. "Well," responded his father, "perhaps you will serve in some place chilly." He was called to Northern New England. An elder serving in 2010 said his assignment showed that God has a sense of humor. He wanted to go foreign, and while he was called to Northern New England, he said he still traveled the world because he had served in Bethlehem, Egypt, and Jericho—in Vermont—and Canaan, China, Mexico, Norway, and Poland—in Maine.

Other stateside missionaries discovered it is possible to "go foreign" even in one's own country. A sister from Utah who hoped to go foreign so she could be exposed to a different culture, observed that once she arrived in New England, the culture was very different from what she was used to in the West, and she felt she was indeed having a different cultural experience. A sister from Idaho who served in Maine in the late 1990s observed: "I did go foreign. Maine is as foreign to me as you can get, without the language barrier. Well, even that, too." An elder from Utah serving in Maine in 2010 said at his very first door, on his very first day of knocking on doors, an old Mainer told him, "Get out of my doh-wah yahd, ayuh."

He thought the man was speaking a foreign language.

Perhaps the distinction between "going stateside" and "going foreign" is a relative concept for young people who haven't traveled much. As the young woman quipped in our story at the beginning of Chapter 1, which is an actual quote from a missionary from Utah who served in the Northeast in the late 1990s, "*Anywhere* outside of Utah is foreign!"

What to bring, and what not to bring. In addition to the call letter, the large envelope includes a pre-departure to-do list, medical and travel information, and a checklist of what to bring. Missionaries are given detailed instructions on the clothing to purchase, based on the region of the world in which they will be serving. Young men are to bring two dark, conservative suits, white shirts, conservative ties, a dark, conservative raincoat, and conservative shoes. They are not to bring sports coats or baggy, pegged, or light-colored slacks. Young women are to bring modest dresses, skirts, blouses, sweaters, conservative shoes, and a dark, conservative raincoat. They may not wear slacks or pantsuits. Until 2011, dresses and skirts had to reach between mid-calf and ankle, and quiet colors were the rule; but in that year the sisters' dress code was updated: skirts may now be shorter (but still below the knee), and sisters are permitted to wear more colorful clothing. Jewelry in moderation is permitted, and nylons are no longer required.[37]

Sisters report they feel much better wearing more modern and fashionable clothing and it contributes to their self-perception and self-confidence. Plus, they say, they don't appear so dowdy when talking with potential converts. A non-Mormon friend, when she saw the earlier outfits sisters were required to wear, said she wouldn't be interested in joining such a church, because she assumed she would be required to wear similar clothing.

A sister reported that friends who had served missions told her not to buy dresses, because she would get sick of them. Rather, she should buy skirts and blouses that she could mix and match. She took their advice and only bought one dress, which she soon tired of and didn't wear very often. A sister reported that one of her companions bought really nice things for her mission—nice suits, nice dresses, nice shoes—but they stayed in the closet because they weren't good for tracting in the mud and snow, for running from dogs, and for kids spitting on them.

Once sisters arrived in the mission field many said they hated what they had bought. Some of it was impractical, and some they quickly grew bored with. Sometimes companions would tell sisters they were bored with looking at them wearing the same clothes. A lot of trading of clothes between companions and other sisters is the norm. Later they will recognize yet another sister wearing their dress (which was traded with a companion) at a zone conference. "Clothes go all over the place," remarked a sister, "and it is fun to get someone else's. We call them a designer HMD; a designer Hand-Me-Down."

With the change in the sisters' dress code in 2011, allowing them to wear more colorful and fashionable clothing, perhaps they won't get so bored with their wardrobe so quickly.

While conservative ties are the expectation, elders worldwide on occasion will intentionally choose the ugliest tie they can find.

The Church's strict guidelines requiring elders to wear dark, conservative clothing make them seem out of place in some parts of the world. A young woman from Central Europe reported that nobody wears dark suits where she comes from. And the black trench coats? She said the elders look like they are gangsters. They scared her, and she wouldn't open the door to them. While the Church recognizes their clothing will set missionaries apart, sometimes negatively, it prefers to follow the adage, "You never have a second chance to make a first impression." The Church doesn't want its missionaries wearing jeans, T-shirts, or short skirts, because it knows a person's encounter with them may be that person's only contact with the Latter-day Saint Church, and it wants the lasting impression to be a positive one.

The missionary and their family are responsible for purchasing a bicycle and helmet if needed in the mission field.

Missionaries are also told what they may *not* bring: books not Church-approved, smart phones, computers, video games, DVD players, video recording devices, radios or clock radios, musical instruments, playing cards, games, sports equipment, or weapons. Nor may they engage in social networking. It is felt all of the above are both a temptation and a distraction.

Preparations and Last-Minute Activities

Some interviewees said they were ready to leave the day their call arrived, but there is an approximate three-month period between the time the candidates' applications are sent to Salt Lake City and when they enter the Missionary Training Center. Interviewees did a variety of things during the interim. Some continued working and earning money for their mission; some finished their semester at college; some went on vacations with their families; others fulfilled individual goals such as visiting all of the Church temples in their region. Most got serious about their studies and spent more time reading the Bible and the Book of Mormon. A conscientious sister from the Northwest said it is a time of intense preparation for missionaries, when they prepare themselves mentally, spiritually, and physically, when they have more of a desire to read and study the scriptures. Another sister spoke of getting up an hour earlier each day to study the scriptures. Parents, siblings, and friends talked about their mission experiences and gave advice. Some found the three months to be exciting, nerve-racking, and scary. More than a few admitted to having second thoughts. "Is this really what I want to do?" they asked themselves. Some felt Satan was raising doubts and concerns, and they found it a stressful time.

Some found themselves in embarrassing, but in retrospect, humorous situations. A sister from Idaho had to buy cigarettes and beer for the seventy-eight year old non-Mormon she cared for. When she took the items to the checkout counter, store employees, many of whom were Latter-day Saints, looked at her and said, "Yeah, and you are planning on going on a mission, right?"

Stores that market goods for and about missionaries are popular in Latter-day Saint circles, where one can purchase how-to-have-a-successful-mission books, inspirational and reference works, stationary, journals and supplies, gifts and care packages. Countdown calendars in the shape of the Salt Lake Temple spires are popular with families, girlfriends, and boyfriends. Comprised of eighteen or twenty-four months of boxes representing each day the missionary is gone, a sticker is placed on each passing day until the missionary returns home (see DeseretBook.com).

Missionaries also receive a letter from their new mission president prior to their departure to the MTC, which welcomes them to the mission and says something about the area where they will be serving. An elder who served in the mid-2000s received a letter from his mission president, who said he had observed that missionaries who are the happiest and most successful on their mission are those who are obedient, humble, and focus on serving others. The mission president said if the young missionary did that, he would witness miracles and find joy and satisfaction like he had never experienced before. The new elder was also given an assignment to read passages in the Book of Mormon. The elder said the themes of obedience, humility, and service was repeated in the orientation session held once he arrived in the mission field. Many missions have a web site, and new missionaries consult their mission's site to gain local information and to connect with missionaries who served there in the past.

The period before leaving for the mission can be a time for serious family conversations and decisions. A missionary who served in England in the 1960s said his mother suffered from a heart condition that was going to require open-heart surgery while he was on his mission. Before leaving, his father talked about the possibility of her passing while he was gone and whether he should request to come home at that time. The interviewee was pleased to report he received a phone call from his mission president saying that a telegram had arrived, which said the operation was a success and his mother would be fine. Aging parents of an older couple about to leave for England on a senior mission told the couple that if they died while the couple was gone, not to come for the funeral, not to interrupt their mission. They too were pleased to report that deaths didn't occur while they were on their mission.

Departure Rituals

Young missionaries participate in three important rituals prior to leaving for their mission: a missionary farewell; a visit to a temple; and a setting-apart ceremony. These are rituals that signal they are moving from one status to another in the Latter-day Saint Church. This is a significant rite of passage—moving from being merely members of the Church to becoming its ambassadors and missionaries.

The farewell. Missionary farewells are popular events in the Church, and they represent an important transitional ritual for missionaries, their families, and their congregations. Relatives, friends, Church members, and non-Church members will travel miles (even hundreds of miles) to attend the ceremony. An appreciative sister who served in the early 1990s described her farewell as a special day. She said she felt fear, excitement, and anxiety—all wrapped into one. But she knew she had made the right choice to serve a mission. She said it was a good feeling to have family, relatives from out-of-state, and ward members attend.

Traditionally held during Sunday morning "sacrament" service the Sunday before their departure, farewells prior to 2004 had evolved into fairly elaborate events where budding missionaries, their parents, sisters, brothers, other relatives, and Church officials spoke, musical selections were performed, and the tone ranged from light-hearted to serious. Some played tapes from siblings already in the mission field. Tears were common. "Everyone was crying," reported a sister who served in the mid-1990s. "It was neat though, for they said really nice things about me."

An elder who served in the mid-1980s recalled that his farewell felt like a graduation; it was a very big event at which a number of people spoke. After the service, family and friends gathered at his home for a picnic and celebration.

A sister from Utah had fond memories of her farewell. She had a huge family and a lot of people were there: parents, brothers, sisters, all of her aunts and uncles, and her cousins. She said it was good to be surrounded by people she loved.

By the early 2000s it was felt that farewells and homecomings (another popular ritual in the Church, discussed in Chapter 12) were taking up too much time in the sacrament service. It was found (especially in Utah and in other areas of large LDS populations) that so many missionaries were leaving for or returning from their missions that practically every Sunday saw either a farewell or a homecoming, with the result that the goal of the sacrament service (of teaching the principles of the gospel) was not being met. Thus in 2004 the First Presidency curtailed the events to a fifteen-minute talk given by the missionary on an assigned theological topic.

A bishop from the Northeast who does not see nearly as many farewells and homecomings a year as seen in Utah said he has to walk a fine line with regard to following the counsel of the Church leadership, while at the same time meeting the needs of the missionary, the family, and the congregation. He said the rituals do take up sacrament meeting time and farewell talks tend to be pretty much the same—family and friends say nice things about the departing missionary, the missionary thanks the parents and the Sunday School teachers, some elders feel a need to apologize for causing trouble as they were growing up, etcetera—but he feels it is also important to personalize the event for the individual and families involved. He added that a more personal approach may inspire younger members of the congregation to serve. He assigns a topic the missionary will be teaching in the mission field and asks that it be placed in the context of some personal remarks. He feels it is a reasonable compromise: he has some control over the topic, the event is personalized to a certain extent, and gospel principles are taught.

Some congregations choose to hold the more traditional, longer farewell outside the sacrament service at a different time.

While something is gained by shortening the missionary farewell, I wonder what is lost, because beyond the symbolic, transitional importance of the event, the longer missionary farewells had emotional and psychological significance as well. They gave speakers a chance to express their pride, feelings, and concerns regarding a person they would not see for the next eighteen or twenty-four months. A mother who spoke at the farewell of a third child observed:

> "They say the more often you do something the easier it gets, but this isn't the case when children go on missions. It almost gets harder the more you do it. But it is the best thing

> for them to do. Thus it is hard and easy at the same time for me to get up here and say goodbye to them."

A mother tried to remain stoic while speaking at her son's farewell in 2002, but her true emotions were revealed when these words caught in her throat: "Mothers are to be left."

Missionary safety is always a concern for parents. The mother of a son who was leaving for a remote country thousands of miles away, a mother who had already seen five children leave on missions, made these moving and emotion-filled comments at his farewell in the late 1990s:

> "We are safe when we are doing right, thus we should not worry. Although some missionaries get hurt, become ill, and even lose their lives, there is safety in serving the Lord. There are forces beyond the veil that protect us when we are doing the Lord's work. I know he will be safe while he is on his mission."

It would appear these mothers would not be afforded the same opportunity to speak at their children's sacrament service farewells today.

Some missionaries reported how their longer, pre-2004 farewell was a time when family wounds began to heal. Some came from families marked by divorce or separation, or where there had been a breakdown in relationships between parents or siblings, and including them in the farewell program had a healing effect. A sister serving in the late 1990s said her mission was a means whereby some of her family got back together. She said her farewell was a point where she could begin to relax; her family had overcome the divorce, a lot of things. She reported there were a lot of "happy-sad" tears. Another missionary talked of how a parent had stopped attending missionary farewells because they were too upsetting. An older sibling had planned on a mission, but his girlfriend talked him out of it. That relationship ended soon thereafter, and he never went. This distressed the parent so much that she couldn't sit through others' farewells. The interviewee was the first to go from the family, and thus it was especially important to the parent. The parent spoke at the farewell and started attending farewells again.

One missionary told the unusual story of growing up in a family that did not attend religious services, but when he converted to the LDS faith as a teenager, his father revealed that he had been raised as a

Latter-day Saint but had fallen away. The father attended the farewell, his first time back in years, and he started attending church again.

The farewell can also be the occasion for humorous events. A sister said her grandfather fell asleep and snored throughout the service, while another recalled that her grandfather said the longest prayer she had ever heard in her life. She said he was getting "kind of old," kept forgetting what he was saying, and kept repeating himself. They started laughing. A third said that during the service her mother kept saying what a good child she was, but it wasn't true. After the service, she said to her mother, "Mom, you lied! Why did you lie? I was not a good child growing up!"

Some missionaries receive cash gifts at their farewells. The practice varies depending on the economic well-being of the ward members, as well as the region of the country. It seems to be more common in the West than in the East.

While I wonder whether the shortened service takes away some of the ritualistic and psychological significance of the farewell ceremony, some missionaries (especially elders) report they are just as happy to give a fifteen minute talk and not have to plan an entire event.

The farewell of an elder from California who served in the mid-2000s reflects the new shape of the ritual. He reported that he spoke on a topic assigned by his bishop, he thanked his parents, he shared his testimony, and he ended on time.

Temple visit. Temples are sacred buildings in the Latter-day Saint Church in which various rituals or "ordinances" are performed, including washings, anointings, the endowment, celestial marriages, the sealing of families, and baptisms for the dead. Participation in these rituals is considered fundamental to one's salvation. A detailed discussion of their nature and role, along with a description of temples, is included in Chapter 11. For the purposes of this chapter, the ordinance that involves new missionaries will be outlined.

New missionaries visit a temple prior to leaving for the Missionary Training Center so that they may receive their "endowment," an event that marks a change in their status in the religious community. They participate in a ceremonial washing and anointing, engage in a course of instruction on the Creation, the Fall, and the Plan of Salvation, and make sacred covenants to uphold the teachings, commandments, and obligations of the faith. It is at this ceremony that they receive their sacred undergarments, which they wear throughout their lives. It is believed their endowment will protect, inspire, and uplift them spiritually. A number of interviewees spoke of this experience as a high point of their spiritual lives.

Being set apart by the stake president. Missionaries meet with their stake president, who sets them apart for their mission just prior to their departure for the Missionary Training Center. Parents frequently witness the ceremony. It includes words of encouragement and admonition from the stake president and the laying on of hands, in which he blesses the individual and commits her or him to full-time missionary service.

The Challenge of Paying for a Mission

With the missionary-to-be poised to enter missionary service, another obligation begins—that of paying for the mission. It cost missionaries $400 per month in 2015, regardless of where they were assigned in the world. This totaled $9,600 for elders and $7,200 for sisters, and those figures don't include personal care expenses or clothing, which can cost upwards of an additional $1,000. Serving a mission thus makes significant financial demands on the missionary and the family, and they are counseled to start saving early on. Advice on financial planning for missionaries and their parents, along with success stories, periodically appear in Church publications.

The Latter-day Saint Church encourages prospective missionaries to assume responsibility for saving money toward their mission, for it is found that the more missionaries contribute, the more committed and effective they are. Many prospective missionaries have a mission fund, but few are able to save the entire amount. They receive help from parents, family, friends, ward members (who contribute to a ward missionary fund), anonymous donors, and, for those who need extra help, a general missionary fund in Salt Lake City. No qualified missionary is turned away because of a lack of funds.

Occasionally there are stories of tragedies that provide inspiration and motivation for prospective missionaries to do more. At the semiannual General Conference held in October 1993, Elder Gordon B. Hinckley told the story of a young man who had been killed in an accident two days prior to the arrival of his mission call. His mother wrote a letter explaining her son's accident, and she enclosed a check representing his mission savings. She asked that it be donated to the International Missionary Fund. She told how her son had saved all of the money himself; that from his earliest years he had set aside 50 percent of all he earned for his mission fund, plus another 10 percent for his tithing. "This money was dedicated to the Lord's work, so we are sure he wants it to be used for this purpose," wrote the mother.

The check was for nearly $9,000.[38]

The bishop collects the money monthly and deposits it in the general fund in Salt Lake City. Missionaries then receive back a monthly amount that covers their living expenses. Those who live in areas with a lower cost of living are given a smaller amount than those living in an area with higher living expenses. Missionaries serving in Maine in 2015 receive $150 per month for living expenses, while those serving in expensive urban areas would receive many times that amount.

Prior to 1990, missionaries paid the actual cost of their mission. This led to disparities in what they paid, since the cost of living varies around the world. The unfairness of the approach became apparent to Church authorities as the Church expanded worldwide, since some missionaries were able to support their missions on as little as $100 per month, while others were paying considerably more. The equalization of cost (the Equalized Missionary Support Fund program) took effect in 1990.

Up until 2012, senior missionaries paid all the costs of their mission, which adversely affected their ability to serve. As we will see in Chapter 11, the Church placed limits in 2012 on what seniors are expected to pay, hoping it will attract more seniors.

Parents are advised not to send extra money to their missionaries in the field, because tensions and hard feelings can arise if one companion has more pocket money than another.

It was striking during my interviews that in a fair number of cases the interviewee was not the only child in the family serving a mission at that time; that another one, even two, siblings were also in the mission field. I eventually realized this is to be expected. Given that Latter-day Saints tend to have large families and that children are spaced closely together, there is a steady progression of children reaching the age to serve.

The costs are significant. A mother who witnessed seven of her children serve missions over a sixteen-year period, children who also attended college before and after their missions, said it had been "the most financially stressful time in the family's life," for they normally had three on a mission or in college at the same time, with about equal payments for each ($350 per month each at the time of the interview).

Said she: "That is a lot of money to say goodbye to automatically every month, but it is well worth it, for you can't put a dollar amount on the experience." The family also continued to tithe 10 percent of their gross income to the Church during the entire period, as is the practice in the Latter-day Saint Church. The mother recalled that her parents faced similar challenges, because she turned twenty-one when her younger brother turned nineteen, and they left on their missions at the same time.

A sister from Utah said there were three from her family on missions at the same time; she, an older sister, and a younger brother. Serving a mission was her parents' first priority, followed by going to college. She said her dad was "ecstatic" when she decided to go, that it was his biggest dream for her. When she expressed concern about the expense of having three on a mission at the same time, she thought he would have sold the house, if necessary, for all of them to go.

While some siblings don't serve concurrently, many serve in close succession. An elder who served in Germany reported that his parents dropped him off at the door of the Missionary Training Center in Provo, drove to Salt Lake City airport, and flew to Rome to pick up his brother, who was finishing his mission. The interviewee's first day of his mission was his brother's last. Thus there was no break in the family's four-year obligation to provide a monthly contribution in support of a child on a mission.

The timing of missions also impacts family relations. The interviewee observed that except for forty minutes in the Salt Lake City airport when he flew to Germany, he and his brother did not see each other for four years.

Those who decide late to serve a mission (this tends to be truer of young women than of young men) typically have to scurry to find funding, and some sisters said they initially experienced resistance from their parents to the idea of serving. While their parents didn't explicitly state it, the sisters felt the last-minute, unexpected financial obligation for the family was the reason why their parents balked. But, their parents eventually became supportive.

Support may also come from unexpected sources. A sister missionary told how she had not considered serving a mission because she couldn't afford it, but when a family friend passed away, it was discovered he had set aside enough money in his will for her to serve. She was then able to go.

Even those supporting just one missionary at a time spoke of the challenges they faced. A mother who supported three sons who served their missions in quick succession said it was very hard financially for the family. It "got her down." She thought the promise was that the Lord would help, but it didn't seem like it was there. But in the end she said the Lord must have been watching, because they didn't lose their home. Another family who also supported three sons who served in quick succession found they couldn't recover financially, and they had to sell their house and move into a smaller condominium.

"You Can Do It"

Early preparation for a mission is a complicated psychological process, reported a lifelong Church member who served his mission in California and who is the father of seven returned missionaries. While acknowledging that cynics might say it is brainwashing, he says the Church's early emphasis on missions and missionary work makes sense if one accepts the premise that it is the duty of all young men to go on a mission. Given that, the Church will want to prepare its youth as best it can to help them fulfill their obligation. It can be an intimidating prospect, he conceded, especially for those who have led sheltered childhoods, who have not been away from home, or who have not worked hard as a youth. A mission would scare someone like that, he observed. He went on to say that the Church works especially hard to convince its youth that they can do it, that people just like them have had successful missions. They are also assured the Mormon Church stands behind them to help and guide them. From the cradle on, the message is, "You can do it."

Most budding missionaries are not so optimistic at this point in their missionary careers. Almost to a person, interviewees reported they felt unprepared when they received their call. They wished they had studied harder, been more diligent in reading the scriptures, and saved more money. Their instincts told them they were not ready to go into the mission field, that they lacked the knowledge and skills necessary to have a successful mission. And they were right. That is why their first stop is a Missionary Training Center; that will be considered in Chapter 3.

CHAPTER 3

Missionary Training Center, Provo, Utah

"The Missionary Training Center prepares missionaries to fulfill their role of sharing with others the restored gospel of Jesus Christ."
INTERVIEW WITH THE MISSIONARY TRAINING CENTER PRESIDENT, PROVO, APRIL 6, 1994

"Being at the MTC is like trying to drink from a fire hose."
AN ELDER WHO ATTENDED THE PROVO MTC IN 2001.

Elder Jones thought he wanted to go foreign, but now he was having second thoughts. He had been studying Mongolian for five weeks at the Provo Missionary Training Center (MTC), and there were days when his fellow students and he were reduced to tears, the language was so hard. The teacher was a BYU student and returned missionary who had served his mission in the country. He was patient and understanding, because he too had found the language difficult. He tried to motivate the young missionaries by saying that if he could do it, so could they. A native Mongolian speaker living in the area was invited to talk with the missionaries in his native tongue, but MTC officials knew that once the young missionaries arrived in Ulaanbaatar, they would think they were in the wrong country; people would talk so fast that they would not understand what was being said.

It didn't help that the missionaries' lives were so highly regimented—study, eat, sleep; study, eat, sleep—with practically no contact with the outside world. Homesickness was a problem for Elder Jones, while his companion sorely missed his girlfriend. Tension arose between the two because of their personal struggles and because they always had to be together. Two older sisters in their district tried to keep the peace between them.

However, after twelve weeks at the MTC and realizing how far he had come in learning the language, Elder Jones pointed to what he felt was Divine help in what he had accomplished. He felt a nervous knot in his stomach as he boarded the bus for the Salt Lake City airport. He had never been outside of the Mountain West before, and, while he had learned the rudiments of the language, Elder Jones was fearful of having to approach people and talk about the Latter-day Saint faith in a language he was still learning. He also wondered if he would get along with the many different companions with whom he would be paired over the next two years.

These and many other concerns swirled through his head as the plane took off and he took one last look at the Great Salt Lake Valley and one last look at home.

As noted in Chapter 1, informal preparation of missionaries begins in the home and in the Church. Formal training occurs at fifteen MTCs located around the world, where young missionaries gain knowledge, skills, and spiritual preparation that will aid them in the mission field. The twentieth century saw an increasing rationalization of the missionary program with training, dress, and expected behavior becoming uniform worldwide. Thus the curriculum and standards at the MTCs in São Paulo, Brazil; Preston, England; and Accra, Ghana, are the same as those at the MTC in Provo, Utah—the subject of this chapter.

MTCs are akin to monastic communities. Missionaries are allowed only limited access to the outside world, their behavior is closely monitored, and they follow a rigorous daily schedule, which includes personal study, classroom work, and devotional meetings. Some have significant religious experiences while at the MTC, and most struggle in some way. Issues include homesickness, missing a significant other, being with a companion at all times, and exhaustion. A few return home early because they choose to, or because they are told to. The rest complete their training and move on (albeit with some trepidation) to the mission field (which is discussed in Chapter 4.)

Missionary Training Center, Provo, Utah

The oldest and largest MTC is located on the edge of the BYU campus in Provo, Utah. Built in 1976, expanded in 1994, and in the midst of a ten-year remodeling plan that began in 2007, the MTC is comprised of over nineteen buildings on approximately ten acres of land. It includes residence halls, cafeterias, classrooms, a medical center, a counseling center, a bookstore, a gymnasium, laundry facilities, a barber/beauty shop, administrative offices, a maintenance shop, and auditoriums. It is an enclosed, self-contained facility; no one need go beyond its fence—nor is anyone allowed to, except to go to the Provo Temple across the street or to participate in off-campus MTC-sponsored events.

It houses the Referral Center, the department that handles incoming and outgoing calls and e-mails in support of the Church's media offers for free materials and information. It also includes the Training Resource Center, where missionaries develop their teaching skills with volunteers from the community.

Attendance ranged from 1,800 to 2,500 when I visited there in 2008. By the end of the current renovation campaign (around 2017), the facility will be able to house up to four thousand missionaries.

Provo trains the majority of missionaries. In 2010, 31,755 missionaries were trained at MTCs around the world, with Provo educating 20,750 of them.[39] Prior to the age change in 2012, missionaries spent three to twelve weeks at the Provo MTC, depending on whether they were learning a new language. With the significant influx of missionaries after the age change (the number of missionaries at the Provo MTC went from under three thousand in 2011 and 2012, to nearly eight thousand the next year[40]), missionaries who are not learning a new language stay only twelve days at the MTC. This certainly has implications for their training and for their preparedness once they are in the mission field.

It is reported that 50 percent of all missionaries worldwide serve in their homelands, but that percentage is lower for American missionaries serving in the United States.[41]

Responsibility for the young missionaries rests with the MTC president. Always male and always married, many presidents have interrupted professional careers to serve this three-year calling. The president's wife assumes special responsibility for sister missionaries. The full-time employees at the facility are mostly in training, development, and administration, while the part-time instructors are largely returned missionaries and students at BYU. The MTC also depends on over a thousand volunteers a week to help with training.

The MTC is normally off-limits to outsiders, including family, friends, and Church members. It is felt such interruptions detract from the MTC experience. But I was given the rare and much appreciated opportunity in 1994, and again in 2008, to spend a day at the Provo MTC with missionaries, teachers, and staff. I was also accorded a visit to the MTC in England and to the Senior MTC in Provo. These are discussed in Chapters 8 and 11. The visits provided a richer understanding of the inner workings of the MTCs.

Wednesdays: New Missionary Orientation

Preparing to go to the MTC can be an emotional and trying time. Many talked of losing their appetites the week before entering and of not being able to sleep. Hundreds of new missionaries enter the Provo facility each week, while hundreds more depart from there for the mission field.

Wednesday is intake day for new missionaries, and a large orange dot is placed on their lapels as they walk into the MTC—a beacon identifying them as newcomers or "greenies." Referred to as a "dork dot" by missionaries, some throw them away after the orientation, but many place them in their journals or on the back of their nametags, where it remains for the duration of their mission.

I was permitted to attend a new missionary orientation in 1994. Hundreds of us—new missionaries, family, and friends—were in the auditorium, a windowless room with a stage and a podium. It was a somber, yet moving, event. The MTC president's wife made welcome remarks. She said she appreciated how difficult the day was for families ("You want them to go, but you don't want them to leave"), that missionaries would find the MTC challenging but that it was a safe environment where they would be in good, caring hands. We then viewed the stirring missionary video *Called to Serve*. Then the president spoke, reminding missionaries that it was a privilege for them to serve, that they should expect to work hard, and that he understood their anxieties. He quoted 2 Timothy 1:7 for comfort: "For God hath not given us the spirit of fear; but of power, and love, and of a sound mind." He reviewed their missionary call letter paragraph by paragraph, provided general words of encouragement, and bore his testimony. He concluded by saying elders should always wear their suit coats, parents should not return to the MTC to visit, and goodbyes should be said quickly.

There was a spectrum of emotions at the moment of separation, when missionaries went out one door and everyone else out another—when missionaries and their families knew they would not see each other again for eighteen or twenty-four months.

Some remained stoic. A dry-eyed father gave his son a brief hug and merely said, "Do the work."

At the opposite end of the emotional spectrum was an entire family crying. The young woman leaving for her mission said her grandmother was "such a big baby" and that when they brought her to the MTC for such an event, she got them all crying.

One of the most moving images was that of a tall, thin, Central European sister, standing alone, crying. Her tears surprised her, since her family was thousands of miles away. "There I was standing by myself, crying," she said, "but I didn't have anyone to cry for."

Most of us were teary-eyed that Wednesday—even my host, an administrator who had been at the MTC for thirteen years and who had seen thousands of missionaries, including his four daughters, pass through the door.

The moment of separation can be a time of rare expressions of affection and emotion. A sister recalled how much she appreciated it when her mother hugged her and told her she loved her; it was only the second time her mother had said that to her.

For many, it is the first time they see their fathers cry. A sister recalled how her father, whom she described as not one to share his feelings very much, "sobbed uncontrollably" at the moment of separation and would not let go of his daughter. She expected her mother and sisters to cry, but it hit her dad the hardest, and it was especially hard for him to say goodbye.

It was only later that she learned that her father feared he had a life-threatening illness. The reason for his tears became clear: it could have been the last time he saw her. She was relieved to report that it was eventually determined that he was not terminally ill.

While many missionaries confess to being anxious and nervous on that day, some remain more composed than their parents. An elder from Utah reported that he handled the separation better than his family, especially his mother. She was more worried than he was. He saw it as a new adventure, a new learning experience, while she was thinking, "I am losing my son for two years." What worried him was what missionary life would be like and who his companions would be.

A sister reported that her family kept giving her hugs and wouldn't let her go. Finally, she gave them one last hug and walked away. "I just wanted to get on my way," she said, "I wanted to go through that door."

Parents exited through a door at the back of the auditorium, while missionaries left through one at the front, and it was at the point of going through the door that many realized they had become missionaries, that they were entering a new phase in their lives. An elder recalled walking through the door and thinking that he was now a missionary, the responsibility was on his shoulders, and that it was up to him to do his best. Another reported that as he went through the door he knew it was the start of something new. He was taking "a leap of blind faith"; he didn't know how it was going to end, but he hoped it would work out. A sister said she was "in a daze" as she said goodbye to her family, but once through the door, she knew she had entered a whole new world.

The moment of separation, when missionaries left through one door and everyone else left through another, was rich in ritualistic symbolism. The missionaries were engaging in a rite of passage, of moving from one status to another in the religious community, and their transition was clearly demarcated as they disappeared behind the door. They were moving from the separation phase of the rite, to the isolation phase, with hardship.

A significant change that impacted the ritualistic power of entry into the Provo MTC was introduced to the orientation program in 2009. The MTC wanted to phase out family involvement in the orientation session, because over one thousand people were going in and out of the MTC each week. (Multiple orientation sessions have been held on Wednesdays.) During the swine flu (H1N1) scare of 2009, MTC officials said goodbyes should be said at the curb outside, so as to decrease the possibility of spreading flu in the MTC. The new practice, which took effect June 3, 2009, remained in place after the swine flu scare passed and remains in effect today.

What used to be a powerful symbol of the separation and isolation phases of the missionary experience, when missionaries and families exited through separate doors, has now become a routine saying of goodbyes at the MTC curb. Indeed, only one car per missionary is permitted inside the MTC gate, and families are encouraged to say their goodbyes before arriving in Provo. This is in stark contrast to the way it used to be, as it wasn't uncommon for family, relatives, friends, girlfriends, and boyfriends to join them. One elder talked of a motorcade of five cars, filled with family and friends, who followed him to Provo and who participated in the orientation.

While appreciating the need to control the crowds, I fear something has been lost.

Behind the Door: A Whole New World

In 1994 I was permitted to join the missionaries when they walked through the door. We were led to another part of the MTC where medical and personnel records were checked, the length of elders' hair was inspected (I was told my hair was too long), and nametags were distributed. When the elder in front of me was handed his nametag, he turned and said it was one of the best days of his life. A sister added that she too was excited, that this is where she wanted to be.

Some weren't so sure. They spoke of an immediate sense of loneliness. A sister said her heart sank as she stood in line; she felt "very much alone," even though surrounded by people. Another sister simply said, "I don't know anyone. All I know is prayer."

Missionaries were given their dormitory assignments; they would room under spartan conditions with three others, one of whom would be their new companion, or "comp." After finding their rooms, meeting their companion, and unpacking, they had personal interviews with an MTC administrator, ate dinner, and attended an evening orientation on missionary conduct. It had been a long day.

Reflecting on her first day, a sister said she knew the MTC experience would be challenging but exciting. She was surrounded by other young people—elders dressed in dark suits, white shirts, and muted ties, and (since it was pre-2011) sisters with skirts at mid-calf and blouses with long sleeves—doing the same thing as she, who, "for the most part," wanted to be there. It was like no other place she had ever been. She said it was incredible.

Some experienced insecurity on that first day. A sister said she felt like a kindergartener in a brand new school; she didn't know anything, and she didn't like the feeling. Another sister said after she and her companion put on their nametags, it struck them that they were missionaries. They were in shock. Together they said, "Wait a minute! What are we doing?"

Another questioned whether she was prepared to serve. The MTC president had said to get out a notebook and pen at the orientation session and to write down an important point. She said she didn't have a notebook, or a pen, and she thought: "Am I really prepared to be a missionary?"

Some questioned whether they had made the right decision. An elder described his first day as "the longest day of my life" and as a "reality check." He wondered if he wanted two years of it. Another elder lay in bed staring at the ceiling that first night, realizing he was now a missionary, and that in two month's time he would be in Europe. "What in the world did I just get myself into?" he asked himself. "This better be true and worthwhile, for I am giving up two years of my life." Had he decided it was not true, he said he would have returned home.

An MTC administrator said it is recognized that there are some who have theological doubts when they enter the MTC and that part of the function of the MTC is to have the new missionaries go through the same process they will ask others to go through—to have them ask themselves the questions they will ask of investigators: Is this message really from God? Is the Book of Mormon divine scripture? Was Joseph Smith a prophet of God? They assume missionaries already believe these things when they arrive, but, if not, they help them identify the issues and help them work through their doubts.

Other challenges present themselves at the MTC: homesickness; missing a significant other; exhaustion; restlessness from being cooped up all day; and, because of the daily pattern of study-eat-sleep, gaining weight.

But one of the most difficult, yet most memorable, experiences is learning to live every hour of every day with a companion.

Companionships. Companionships are a distinctive feature of the Latter-day Saint missionary experience. Drawing on Jesus's example of sending disciples out two-by-two, LDS missionaries are paired for two reasons: mutual support and protection. There is the practical advantage of two heads being better than one, of missionaries combining their respective knowledge and skills to make them more effective in the field. Companionships also protect missionaries from detractors who might try to mislead them or harm them, of which there are some in the field. And it protects them from themselves. Being with another missionary makes it less likely that they will be tempted to stray from the strict rules and regulations imposed on them.

Missionaries are never to be alone, except in the bathroom, and they stay with their companion at all times, except in very specific instances. At the MTC these include choir practice, physical education activities, and short-term illnesses. Companions must sleep in the same room, eat all meals together, and attend all classes and meetings together.

Companionships are comprised of senior and junior members. In the field the senior companion is the one who has served the longest, while at the MTC they are assigned. The senior companion is to set a good example, conduct daily and weekly planning meetings with the junior companion, and give weekly reports on the status of the companionships to those in authority. Problem areas such as disobedience are reported. The junior companion is to live up to the high standards expected of missionaries, provide support and counsel to the senior companion, and share goals and progress with the senior companion in daily planning sessions.[42]

The MTC companion is the first of many that missionaries will have during their mission. Living with someone, whom they have no say in selecting and whom they might not chose as a friend, twenty-four hours a day, seven days a week (their "shadow," as they call them), is for many the biggest challenge they face during their mission.

When asked if there were any low points during his time at the MTC, an elder who served in the Northwest responded that the hardest part was being with a companion. He said the fact that one is never alone is a common struggle. "It is weird, it is very strange," he said.

It is not without reason that the elder quoted above at the orientation said he was more worried about whom his companion would be than about saying goodbye to his parents. In a similar vein, a sister said she was happy to move on from the orientation meeting to find her companion, "to see if she was normal."

Rules and regulations. There is a sense of formality at the MTC. Missionary nametags announce the wearer as "Elder (last name)" or "Sister (last name)," and that is how they are addressed. First names are never used. Elders must wear their missionary attire (they call it "the uniform"), while sisters must wear dresses, or skirts with blouses or sweaters. Physical contact between the sexes is limited to handshakes. These requirements contribute to a sense of distance between missionaries, which is intentional: they are there to train as missionaries, not to develop relationships.

Missionaries live under a number of restrictions at the MTC. They cannot watch television, listen to the radio, or listen to popular music. They are not allowed to have computers or cell phones, and only emergency phone calls may be made or received. Friends and family may not visit. They may not chew gum, sunbathe, or arrange for outside food delivery. They are not allowed to leave the MTC campus except to visit the Provo Temple across the street or to attend MTC-arranged events. They may not leave the MTC to attend births, baptisms, marriages, funerals, or other family or friend events.

They are not to call girlfriends or boyfriends, nor are these people allowed to visit. Missing a significant other is a common issue. A sister who was preparing to serve in Latin America observed that much of the MTC experience is a time of learning to let go. She saw many elders who lived for their girlfriends' letters, and some would sneak off to call them. Some elders made it difficult for themselves: one had a companion who had a picture of his girlfriend laser-printed on his pillowcase, while another had her picture "everywhere." Another interviewee described how his companion's girlfriend mysteriously appeared in the MTC parking lot one day and how he and other missionaries had to stop them from talking.

He said he learned two important lessons that day: "I learned very clearly why there is the two-by-two rule, and the episode also convinced me of the power of a girlfriend."

Infamous "Dear John" and "Dear Jane" letters announcing the break-up of relationships start to arrive. An elder who was in the MTC in 2011 said when the two thousand missionaries were asked how many had already been "Dear Johned," he estimated that two hundred hands went up.

Missing significant family events is hard for many. An elder who was at the MTC for both Thanksgiving and Christmas said he cried on Thanksgiving, but had adjusted by Christmas. He was kept busy on Christmas putting together first aid kits for humanitarian projects.

Many regret not being allowed to attend weddings and funerals. A sister from Provo had to miss her sister's wedding, held just ten minutes away.

The Latter-day Saint Church places these restrictions on missionaries because it feels contact with the outside world interferes with the basic purpose of the MTC: preparing young men and women to become effective ambassadors and missionaries of the Latter-day Saint Church. Reflecting on the various rules and regulations, an elder said they helped him learn to be a "conformist in the right ways," that they set the tone for the rest of his mission and that his work would have been compromised had he been allowed to engage in "worldly pursuits" while in the mission field.

More colorfully, a sister said the enforced isolation strips away unimportant, distracting, and negative influences. "The MTC is like a giant vacuum cleaner," she said. "Its role is to suck the world out of you." While it is a bit of an overstatement, since missionaries have already avoided or renounced many worldly behaviors in order to gain entry into the MTC, it does attest to the isolation they experience and to the narrowly defined behavior that is deemed acceptable in the MTC.

Not all have agreed with the restrictions. They said they feel stripped of their identity. They referred to the MTC as a "spiritual boot camp," and some admit to intentionally breaking rules in order to reassert their individuality, including leaving the grounds to get pizza or to play a round of golf (according to interviewees who served in the 1980s).

Such infractions are rare. When asked if she had ever been tempted to break the rules at the MTC, a sister responded: "Never. You are so exhausted, you don't even try to do things you shouldn't."

Some are not patient with those who complain about the rigors of the MTC. A sister observed that if people don't like it, it is their own fault. She said there are so many good things about it, the complainers have to convince themselves not to like it. Another said it boils down to attitude: missionaries knew what they were getting into before they signed their mission papers; they knew they would be cooped up all day long and live under numerous rules. Thus it is not unexpected. She didn't know what some people thought they would be doing; it was not going to be a big party. "It all depends on one's attitude, on what one makes of it."

Sisters and Elders. Proper relations between sisters and elders are stressed. Dormitories of the opposite sex are off-limits, and physical contact between the sexes is restricted to handshakes. At the New Sisters' Orientation conducted by the MTC president's wife, she said in order for sisters to uphold their callings they needed to maintain a "reverent relationship" with elders. They were not to give them "high fives," slap them on the back, or sew for them. If asked to do the latter, sisters were instructed to tell the elders to do it themselves.

Elders and sisters are continually reminded they have to be careful what they do; they have to remain at arm's length. This was brought home to a sister who saw her brother outside the Provo Temple. When she went to hug him, he said not to, because people would assume he was her boyfriend.

Restrictions on physical contact can lead to awkward situations. A sister fell and sprained her ankle at the MTC, and when an elder offered to help her up and assist her to see the nurse, she yelled: "Don't touch me! You are not allowed to touch me! Get away!"

A sister succinctly summed up the feelings of many sisters and elders: "You are just weird about people of the opposite sex when at the MTC, and when on a mission."

Most sisters and elders seem to get along well, although their relationships can be strained at times. It is not unusual for sisters to initially perceive some elders as being immature. Since new elders are typically younger than sisters, their antics can seem childish. A sister recalled that she had just finished her junior year at college, had been dating older men, and had friends who were married. Now she found herself with nineteen-year-old young men, some of who had just graduated from high school. Describing them as "scared, little boys," she found them irritating and immature: they were homesick, they cried about their high school girlfriends, and, "they had trouble adjusting to the fact that there are rules in life."

When asked if they initially got along with elders, two sisters responded in unison: "They are nineteen-year-old guys. What can you say? What *can* you say!

One sister confessed that she got fed up with immature elders, whom she described as "horrible and awful." She got into verbal battles with them, which she said was not very Christ-like.

For some elders, sisters can be seen as bossy, superior, and trying to act like their mothers. Some are fond of referring to sisters not as "sisters," but as "blisters," because "regardless of where they are, they hurt."

These perceptions and attitudes (both the sisters' and the elders') generally soften with time. In many cases it even grows into mutual respect, and the place where this change occurs is in their districts.

Districts. Missionaries in the MTC generally are divided into groups of ten or twelve (sometimes more, sometimes less) called "districts." Some include two or four sisters, but since there are a disproportionate number of elders to sisters, some may have no sisters. District members attend all classes together, eat together, and in some cases serve in the same mission after leaving the MTC. They represent what in higher education is called a "learning community," which research has shown is a high-impact learning environment that leads to improved learning, a greater sense of community, and increased retention.

A number of districts together form a "zone," and they report to a branch president, which is an MTC staff position. The branch president selects an elder from each district to serve as a district leader, and a zone leader is selected to assist the district leaders. The district leader's role is to set a good example and to encourage district members to live obedient lives in the classroom and in the residence hall. If problems arise, such as improper conduct, district leaders are to address it with the individual involved. Each missionary submits a weekly report to the district leader and the district leader submits those reports, along with a weekly district report, to the zone leader and to the branch president. The progress of each missionary is shared with the branch president, and issues such as homesickness, disobedience, and lack of motivation is discussed. In districts that have sisters, a coordinating sister fulfills a similar role with the sisters.

Similar positions of responsibility are found in the mission field, and they provide valuable opportunities for missionaries to develop leadership skills.

Serving as a district leader isn't an easy task. When I asked an elder if he experienced any low points at the MTC, he said they came while fulfilling his responsibilities as a district leader. There were elders in his district who weren't very mature and were doing things they shouldn't: writing letters to their girlfriends every day, instead of once a week as instructed, and staying up late talking, when they should be in bed. He said he experienced some "struggles" with them. Finally, he stood in front of the group and said he didn't ask to be their district leader, but since he was called to do it, he was going to do the best job he knew how. They were there to become the best missionaries they could be, and they needed to focus. They talked as a group, and things improved after that.

Another district leader spoke of two missionaries who had personal problems and had difficulty adjusting. It was a challenging experience, but they "pulled together" as a group and got through it.

Working through issues can lead to a greater sense of cohesion in districts. A sister whose district included six elders and two sisters reported one of the elders was weak in his faith when he arrived, so they fasted and prayed for him. His testimony grew, and the district grew closer together as a result.

"We became like a family," she reported. "We did nice things for each other, and we looked out for each other."

Most find their district to be a source of support during the MTC experience, but getting to that point can sometimes be a challenge. Some jell quickly; others take time. It depends on the personalities and backgrounds of those involved.

A sister shared how there was "pride, shyness, insecurity, and guilt" in her district, and so the missionaries initially didn't get along well. The first two weeks were hard, while they looked at themselves and worked through their issues. Things eventually changed, including her. She came to the MTC as a "straight arrow," with narrowly defined goals and a clear idea of how she was going to achieve them. But with time she loosened up and decided she could be obedient and do what she was supposed to do, but still have a good time—and others could do the same.

Some confessed to feeling inferior around their peers, which led to insecurity. An elder gave a candid, but wrenching, description of his self-perception while at the MTC: everyone seemed so spiritual and knowledgeable, except him; he felt inadequate compared to everyone else. That was the hard part for him, he said: "Seeing all of the great missionaries, and I was not one of them." He prayed "a lot" about it. He said it helped when he shared his feelings with sisters.

Many sisters reported that elders sought them out to talk about their personal concerns. Unique bonds can form in districts, in spite of the formal atmosphere of the MTC. A sister observed that she and the elders in her district were good friends "on a spiritual level." A special trust and relationship grew between them, because, "It wasn't physical like in the outside world." An elder agreed. Most of the conversations they had in his district were on a very personal—almost intimate—level, about family, about personal problems, about things they only told their best friends. It was an everyday occurrence, and he found it "wonderful."

Sisters can have a profound impact on districts. They can have a calming, spiritual effect, bringing a level of seriousness that is sometimes lacking in all-male districts. A returned sister missionary who teaches Spanish at the MTC said sisters, being older and more mature, usually are more committed and know exactly why they are there. No one has told them to go on a mission, and they have made up their minds to serve. She finds they are more serious and more focused on what they are doing, and they set a positive tone for the district. It is sometimes "rough" when she has districts of only elders, because there can be friction between them. She has never struggled with a sister, but she has with some elders. Another instructor said she had two elders who she thought were going to start fighting, but the group "pulled them back together with a song."

Another Spanish instructor said he enjoys having sisters in a district because they create a different atmosphere; they are more likely to share their feelings and be more open to spiritual experiences. A sister agreed. She had heard something is lacking in districts with no sisters, as sisters are more emotional and are more willing to talk about their feelings. "Sisters are touched by the Spirit a little bit more easily than the elders," she said. "Feelings are good. Feelings are what the gospel is all about." The sister Spanish instructor observed, "I guess sisters don't have the walls that men sometimes have."

When asked what effect sisters have on districts, elders said they probably watch their manners more and are less competitive, and sisters keep them from becoming too comfortable, because, as one elder explained, "Sisters keep you remembering who you are and what you are doing." An elder confessed to something most elders know, but may not admit: "Sisters are more mature, and they are typically smarter and more spiritual than we are. In general, I think they are our superiors. There is no doubt about that."

This is not to suggest that sisters don't bring issues to the district, including doubt. One sister asked herself why she was going on a mission, while another confessed she wondered if she really wanted to do it. Some questioned their ability. One asked if she was able to do it, while another confessed to sitting in class and thinking she couldn't knock on someone's door and ask if they wanted to learn about the Latter-day Saint Church.

While sisters are older and typically more mature than elders, there is an important dimension that influences the dynamic in the male/female relationship. Since only males "hold the priesthood," elders hold spiritual authority over sisters. The perceived incongruity between some elders' behavior and their authority is a problem for some sisters. A sister commented: "The elders were nineteen-year-old brats. It was hard for two whole weeks. It was really hard. I just wanted to smack them. 'I know you are my leader, but' Whack!"

An independent-minded sister said her returned-missionary father tried to warn her about the elders' higher status, that he was worried how she would react to a nineteen-year old male having authority over her. He asked if she understood what that meant. She said that she did and that she could deal with it.

"No, I don't think you can!" he responded.

"And he was right," she confessed. "I am not good at reporting to nineteen-year-old pipsqueaks, not at all. They think they know so much, but you just want to slap them and say, "Oh, grow up!"

But by the end of the third week the elders had become much more mature; she and her companion had become attached to them and did not want to leave them. She said it was one of her favorite experiences at the MTC, to see how much the elders changed. Other sisters observed a similar transformation. They conceded that elders can act reverently when they need to, and they admitted watching elders develop leadership qualities was a highpoint for them at the MTC.

As we will see, the tensions between sisters and elders, as well as the growing respect between them, carry into the mission field.

The daily schedule. Missionaries are subject to a rigorous and disciplined routine at the MTC. They follow a demanding daily schedule, spending their days in study, classes, and devotional meetings.

6:00 A.M.	Arise and Prepare
6:45 A.M.	Book of Mormon Personal Study
7:30 A.M.	Companionship Study
8:00 A.M.	Breakfast
8:45 A.M.	Class (all morning)
11:30 A.M.	Exercise in Gymnasium
1:00 P.M.	Lunch
1:45 P.M.	Class (all afternoon)
6:00 P.M.	Dinner
7:00 P.M.	Class (or large meetings)
9:30 P.M.	Companionship Prayer
10:30 P.M.	Lights Out

Attendance at all classes, meetings, and physical education activities is mandatory, and missionaries make a serious effort to conform to the schedule. A sister recalled that at the orientation session the MTC president promised the new missionaries that if they were strictly obedient to the daily schedule, they would be blessed, everything would come easily to them, and they would have a better MTC experience. She said as a result she and her peers were constantly striving to live that schedule; they never got up after 6:00 A.M., and they never had lights on after 10:30 P.M.

When I commented to a stake president and returned missionary that it seemed like a pretty rigid routine, he agreed. He said there is no doubt that it is fairly regimented and that there are many rules. "But how else do you do it?" he asked. "It is instruction on how missionaries will live for the next eighteen or twenty-four months. They get up and go to bed when they are supposed to, not when they want to. If they follow the rules, they will succeed, but if they don't, they will run into trouble." Some do run into trouble because they don't always understand why they are missionaries. His advice: "If you can hang in there and do what is asked, you will be okay."

Many said they found the daily schedule exhausting. A sister recalled how excited she was to be at the MTC; on the first day she was ready to "learn everything"—but by the third day she was so tired she had trouble staying awake. Reflecting on her first week at the MTC, a sister said by the second night it felt like she had been there a week, and by the next night it felt like it had been a month. They sat through classes and got up and ate. They sat through more classes, and they got up and ate. They sat through more classes, until 9:30 P.M. Then they went to bed, got up, and did it all over again. "It was draining. It was exhausting." But she also alluded to what missionaries call "the mystery of time" at the MTC: while the days drag on, the weeks fly by.

Some grow weary of the routine. An elder who was at the MTC for two months said the experience was good for the first two and a half weeks, but after that he and his peers began to "feel like cattle. Herded to eat, herded to class, herded to sleep." He didn't really care for the regimented lifestyle, but he knew it was preparation for what he would face in the mission field. A fellow elder added that the MTC is meant to be rigorous, because it is where they begin their mission.

Missionaries are given a break on Preparation Day, or "P-Day," which is when they do laundry, write (mandatory) letters or e-mails home, and perform "celestial service," a euphemism for helping clean the MTC facility. It is also a time when the pent-up energy of cooped-up young men can lead to intense basketball games. A very competitive elder recalled that things sometimes got out of control during such games and that sprained ankles were common. He confessed they sometimes got in trouble taking things "a bit too far." When watching such a game with my MTC host, I asked him what mission presidents worry about most. His quick reply, "P-Day!"

In the Classroom

Emphasis in the classroom is placed on developing the knowledge and skills missionaries need in the field, on gaining a firm understanding of Latter-day Saint beliefs and practices, and on how best to share this information with "investigators"—those who show interest in learning more about the Church. Particular emphasis is placed on gaining scriptural and doctrinal knowledge, along with developing interpersonal, communication, and teaching skills.

Missionaries attend classes as a district, so classes are relatively small. Missionary instruction has taken a decided shift in recent decades, reflecting a trend taking place in American higher education in general. Greater attention is now focused on the learner rather than on the teacher, on whether the student actually understands what is being taught, rather than on how deftly the material is presented. This has had a direct impact on missionary training, which historically had emphasized memorization; entire lessons were memorized and presented to investigators in a lockstep manner.

Church authorities began to question this approach in the early 1990s, feeling that it led to wooden or mechanical presentations. Emphasis now is placed on missionaries learning general concepts and principles and how best to present the information. Their task is to determine the questions and needs of investigators and to tailor their message accordingly. Special emphasis is placed on attentive listening, effective planning, and creating individualized lesson plans.

This new approach was developed by a team of five staff members and was reviewed by General Authorities in the early 2000s; it resulted in the creation of a new guide to missionary service, which was introduced in 2004: *Preach My Gospel: A Guide to Missionary Service.* It is said to have reinvigorated missionary preparation, and the Church stresses its usefulness among the general Church population for personal study and prayer and for fulfilling their role as member missionaries.

Preach My Gospel.[43] *Preach My Gospel* takes its title from *Doctrine and Covenants* 50:13-14: "Wherefore, I the Lord ask you this question—unto what were ye ordained? To preach my gospel by the Spirit, even the Comforter which was sent forth to teach the truth." The guide contains the expectations and requirements that shape missionaries' lives in the field, practical suggestions on how to find and teach investigators, and a review of Church beliefs and practices missionaries are to share. Chapter headings include:

1. What Is My Purpose as a Missionary?
2. How Do I Study Effectively and Prepare to Teach?
3. What Do I Study and Teach?
4. How Do I Recognize and Understand the Spirit?
5. What Is the Role of the Book of Mormon?
6. How Do I Develop Christlike Attributes?
7. How Can I Better Learn My Mission Language?
8. How Do I Use Time Wisely?
9. How Do I Find People To Teach?
10. How Can I Improve My Teaching Skills?
11. How Do I Help People Make and Keep Commitments?
12. How Do I Prepare People for Baptism and Confirmation?
13. How Do I Work with Stake and Ward Leaders?

Missionaries read, study, and discuss the various chapters in the classroom. Special attention is given to Chapter 3, "What Do I Study and Teach?", for it contains five lessons that outline the core beliefs and practices of the Latter-day Saint Church. This is the material missionaries present to investigators in the field. The lessons include:

1. The Message of the Restoration of the Gospel of Jesus Christ
2. The Plan of Salvation
3. The Gospel of Jesus Christ
4. The Commandments
5. Laws and Ordinances

The lessons address Latter-day Saint teachings regarding the nature of God, Christ's role in the salvation of humankind, the need for the prophet Joseph Smith, the role of the Book of Mormon, the importance of genealogical study, the place of the family in God's plan, the importance of chastity, and the fact that we are living in the Latter Days, or End Times. Since the lessons are at the heart of what missionaries teach, a detailed discussion of their contents is found in Chapter 7, where consideration is given to what missionaries say once they are invited into a home.

Missionaries are subject to periodic assessment in the classroom, including pre-and post-tests on their knowledge of scripture, Church doctrine, and the contents of *Preach My Gospel.*

I was allowed to sit in on various classes. The instructors I observed showed understanding and compassion for their students. Since most instructors were returned missionaries, they knew and appreciated what young missionaries were experiencing, and they attempted to create a supportive, collaborative environment where missionaries looked to both the teacher and their peers for help and support.

A returned missionary teaching Japanese said what he noticed when he entered the classroom, first as a missionary, and then as a teacher, was the camaraderie that existed between students and teachers; each wanted the other to succeed. When I asked another language instructor what gave her the greatest satisfaction in the classroom, she said it was watching her students grow and develop, to see them "get the vision," to see them progress in their skills, in their love of the work, and in their desire to do what is right. Another instructor described the classroom experience in spiritual terms. He felt "there was a powerful feeling of the Spirit in the classroom and if missionaries humbled themselves and worked hard, God would work miracles in them and through them; that in a short period of time they would be different people, both academically and spiritually."

Some interviewees spoke of this Divine inspiration in the classroom. An elder who attended the MTC in 1987 said he felt a motivation he had never experienced in his life. Suddenly he was memorizing massive amounts of scripture, and he thought to himself, "Where is this coming from? What is driving this?" He described his three-week stay at the MTC as "a very spiritual experience."

An elder who served in France in the early 1970s, in an era when discussions were memorized, said he felt Divine assistance in the classroom. He wasn't always sure he understood what he memorized in French, but he *did* memorize it. For him, there was "a very spiritual side" to being able to learn the basics of a language and to speak it in just two month's time. He said he couldn't have done it on his own.

While instructors don't serve as counselors, their day-to-day contact with missionaries in the classroom and in one-on-one sessions can lead to relationships of trust where missionaries feel comfortable sharing personal concerns with their teachers. Some elders, reported an instructor, shared they didn't know why they were there (especially those who came from a family with a tradition of serving missions), and they didn't want to be there. Others, both elders and sisters, struggled with homesickness, missing significant others, and worrying about difficult issues at home. When appropriate, referrals are made to MTC administrators, who may refer them to the Counseling Center.

The students generally praise their teachers and appreciate the MTC's supportive learning environment. They like teachers who tell good missionary stories, stories that inspire them to go out and work hard. One elder said he especially liked his teachers' obedience stories, of instances where they remained faithful to the mission rules, even when it didn't seem important at the time, but which had important ramifications for their effectiveness as missionaries.

(As we will see in Chapter 5, "In the Mission Field," obedience stories, whether based on fact or found in myth, circulate among missionaries and play an important role in shaping their behavior in the field.)

As in any classroom, there is a range of abilities among students, from those who excel to those who struggle. A sister who didn't attend church very often while growing up, and who didn't attend Seminary in high school, found that she lagged behind her peers in her knowledge of scripture and Church doctrine. She struggled in the classroom, until one day she finally broke down and cried. "I loved the MTC," she said, "but it was so hard. I just didn't know as much as the others."

Her experience—both the struggles and the tears, especially for those learning a new language—is not unusual.

Language training. There is a prophecy in *Doctrine and Covenants* 90:11: "Every man shall hear the fullness of the gospel in his own tongue, and in his own language, through those who are ordained unto this power." The LDS Church has labored to fulfill this prophecy since its earliest days. When I visited the Provo MTC in 1994, language instruction was provided in forty-four languages. When I returned in May 2008, the number had risen to fifty-two—from Albanian to Vietnamese. Of the 1,800 to 2,400 missionaries at the MTC at any one time that year, three out of four were learning a new language, with 41 percent learning Spanish, the most common language studied. Fifty-five languages were being taught in 2014.[44]

Instructors include returned missionaries fluent in the language, or native speakers living in the area.

Those learning a new language typically remain at the MTC for eight to twelve weeks, depending upon their fluency in the language when they arrive. They spend long hours each day in the classroom. A missionary who studied Spanish in 2006 said they spent the first week studying *Preach My Gospel* in English, and thereafter everything was said in Spanish, including (at least in theory) conversations at dinner and in the residence hall. It took him a while to see progress.

A student studying French said he and his fellow students lived with a dictionary in their hands, and at first they didn't talk much outside of the classroom.

Some experience pleasant surprises. An elder studying German discovered he had a long attention span and found he didn't have a problem sitting in class eight to twelve hours a day. Others who felt they weren't good at learning a language were surprised they could do it, attributing it to increased motivation and Divine inspiration.

An elder who put a very successful college football career on hold in order to serve a mission in South Africa in the mid-1980s studied Afrikaans at the MTC and found that it took a month of concentrated work before he began to see progress; but two weeks prior to his departure, he had memorized all of the discussions. He said it was very painful in the sense of creating a mental discipline he had never had before, but he could see the reward of it. He said it was probably his favorite time of his mission, because of the radical change in his life. It really "broke him"; he had been focusing on football, but suddenly his beliefs were the most important thing in his life. It brought about such a change. He described it as "cathartic" during our interview.

Many struggle with learning a foreign language. They talk of frustration with the language, with their ability to learn it, and with the long hours. An elder studying Hungarian said there were days when he was reduced to tears because the language was so difficult. His low point at the MTC wasn't homesickness, but frustration with the language and his performance. He didn't think he would ever learn it. And he wasn't alone. Others have felt the same way. They "wracked their brains," they sat in the classroom "all day long and into the evening. Study, study, study," but eventually they did learn it.

A Japanese instructor said some missionaries get discouraged because the language is so difficult. He felt not all would have had the ambition to learn Japanese had they not been called on a mission, but they all wanted to do well. They found the experience very demanding, but in the end most found it rewarding.

The sense of camaraderie seems especially strong in language classes. An elder who spent twelve weeks learning Mongolian said the key to success in learning a language is to work in groups, that the support of the group is vital.

Language training is provided in modern facilities at the MTC, and I visited a classroom that utilized computer-assisted learning. A student studying Japanese demonstrated a computer program that allowed him to choose between a number of options relating to Japan, including a discussion of Japanese customs and a presentation of the lessons in Japanese. His screen showed the inside of a Japanese home and missionaries arriving, removing their shoes, and talking with the occupants in Japanese. The elder was able to stop the program and speak into a microphone, and the computer played back his speech as well as theirs, so he could see how close his pronunciation was to that of native speakers.

There was a direct impact on language instruction at the MTC when the missionary program adopted *Preach My Gospel*, with its emphasis on understanding concepts and principles rather than on memorization, so missionaries could tailor their presentations to the needs of investigators, instead of repeating preset discussions. Under the earlier approach of memorizing lessons, it was clear what vocabulary and grammar needed to be taught. Under the new approach, instruction focuses on teaching the words, phrases, and grammar appropriate to each of the five lessons, with each topic, concept, and principle being addressed with appropriate phrases. The result is that how to communicate the principle is given higher importance, while accuracy in grammar is given lower importance. This approach gives missionaries the ability to communicate more freely and with greater flexibility. Language training has continued to evolve since 2004, but language professors at BYU say they have noticed that returned missionaries are not as strong in grammar as they used to be.

Most leave the MTC with only a rudimentary knowledge of the language, and it is not uncommon for missionaries to think they have been sent to the wrong country when they first arrive and hear native speakers talk. It may take months for them to become comfortable with the language. An American elder I spoke to in St. Petersburg, Russia, said it took him eight months before he could carry on a normal conversation.

The usual practice, however, is to give fledgling missionaries a baptism by fire once they arrive in the country. The young elder who struggled to learn Hungarian said his mission president had him and the other new missionaries participating in a street meeting the day after they arrived in Budapest. When I asked how that went, he responded: "It was scary. We were suffering from jet lag, none of us knew what we were doing, but we were enthusiastic about it!"

Training Resource Center

Missionaries develop their teaching skills through role-playing in the classroom with their peers and through practice sessions at the Training Resource Center (TRC), a division of the MTC with rooms furnished as living rooms, where missionaries present lessons to volunteer investigators from the community. Volunteers are given a scenario to follow, challenges to present to the missionaries, and suggestions on how to respond to the missionaries' responses. Missionaries are given the same scenario and it is their task to determine the needs of the investigator and how to address them. Comments and questions investigators might raise include: "I don't believe in Joseph Smith. My minster says he is a fraud." "I already have the Bible. Why do I need to believe in the Book of Mormon?" "I have already been baptized. I am already saved. Why do I need to be baptized again?" Twenty-minute teaching sessions are videotaped, played back, and evaluated with a teacher. Strong points are discussed, along with recommendations for improvement. Missionaries then teach for another twenty minutes, the tape is reviewed, and they complete a self-assessment. Particular attention is given to their knowledge of *Preach My Gospel*, their communication and teaching skills, and, for those learning a new language, their language skills.

A teacher supervisor said sisters initially do better at this than most elders. Sisters seem more comfortable with the exercise, they show better social skills, and they have better listening skills. Sisters tend to know when to nod, pause, and repeat, whereas some elders tend to be more mechanical: they will ask a question, wait for an answer, and then move on to the next question. The elders don't do anything wrong per se, reported the supervisor, but teachers help them communicate to the investigator that they are interested in what is being said by smiling, nodding, and making it seem more natural. But they do learn, he said.

Experience in the mission field has shown that investigator interest in hearing additional lessons after the first lesson declines with each succeeding lesson, and missionary training reflects this fact. Lesson one, "The Message of the Restoration of the Gospel of Jesus Christ," receives the most attention at the MTC, while lessons two, three, and four receive somewhat less. Lesson five is mastered in the field.

The MTC depends on over one thousand volunteers a week to serve as investigators. They may be BYU students, returned missionaries, Church members from the community, or, as in my case, non-members. An LDS friend and I served as investigators during a visit to the MTC in May 2008. Our scenario had us relaxing in a park and being approached by two young men. The elders in our session had been called to Taiwan and were in the early stages of learning Mandarin Chinese. Since this was their first visit to the TRC, and since neither my friend nor I spoke Mandarin, the exchange was conducted in English. The elders engaged us in friendly conversation, quickly moving to questions about our feelings about family, the Divine, and the afterlife. They also discussed Joseph Smith's First Vision and the Book of Mormon. We responded with appropriate questions and comments, but I eventually chose to digress, asking about American life, American culture, and the 2008 presidential campaign. The digression was intentional, because it is something missionaries going foreign frequently experience, and it causes them to wonder: is this investigator interested in our message, or is he more interested in learning about the United States and in practicing his English?

The missionaries returned to the TRC a few weeks later, and they attempted to conduct the conversation in Mandarin with "investigators" who were either returned missionaries fluent in the language or native speakers. They were also exposed to the fact that investigators in Taiwan will be coming from a cultural and religious background very different from their own.

The Referral Center

Many non-Mormons are familiar with the Church's media advertisements and with the offer of free materials if a toll-free number is called. The calls come into the Referral Center at the Provo MTC and are answered by missionaries going stateside (those going foreign are busy learning their new languages). Seated at computers with headsets and prompt sheets, missionaries handle requests for the Book of Mormon, DVDs, and the King James Bible. They ask callers if they would like the item mailed to them or if Church "representatives" may deliver it to their home. If the item is to be delivered personally, missionaries in the area are notified of the request and are asked to deliver it as soon as possible. The young missionaries at the Referral Center may also share their testimony with the callers during the conversation. They are advised to keep their calls short, ideally no more than five minutes, and a supervisor may monitor their conversations.

Many enter into this activity with trepidation, as it represents their first real missionary encounter with non-members. Describing the Referral Center and missionaries' initial feelings about serving there, a shy sister said calls are coming into the MTC and are being answered by brand-new missionaries, "who don't know what they are doing, and who are scared to death."

One of the reasons for their fear is that stories abound of being yelled at, of being sworn at, and of having the phone hung up on them. A sister admitted she was petrified her first day and she sat for the longest time, praying for strength and courage. Another sister said she had similar fears, and for good reason: one of her first callers was a woman who yelled at her and who said the sister was inspired by the Devil.

Follow-up calls are made at three, six, and twelve-month intervals to those who requested items. The missionary's computer screen shows the requester's name, the item requested, and a dialogue to follow. Recipients are asked if the item was received, what was their reaction to it, and if they have questions or concerns. Additional information or items are offered, and they are asked if representatives may visit them at home.

Missionaries prefer to handle incoming calls, since callers typically have an interest in receiving the materials (although some call just to yell at them). They tend not to enjoy making follow-up calls at three, six, and twelve-month intervals, because they often don't get a positive reception. "Why do you keep calling me?" asked one person, and another said, "Oh, you Mormons!" and hung up. An elder said people felt he was "hounding" them and that a man yelled at him, "You just called three months ago, and I don't want anything more!"

Many young callers, when making their first callback, admit they hope the person isn't home.

A bashful sister described the difficulties she experienced on her first day of making outbound calls: of being new to the job, of trying to follow a script, and of dealing with a recalcitrant person. She was making a third follow-up call to a man who had been sent a Bible a year earlier. She offered him a Book of Mormon, and as she was explaining that it was another testament of Jesus Christ written by ancient prophets who lived on the American continent, the man interrupted her and said: "You are wrong! There never were ancient prophets on the American continent!"

Taken aback by his outburst, and not knowing what to say, she continued following the script. She talked about Joseph Smith, the First Vision, and how the current head of the LDS Church is a prophet.

The man interrupted her again and yelled, "There are no prophets today! God wouldn't do that. And Joseph Smith didn't see God the Father and Jesus Christ!"

Even more bewildered, the young caller pressed on with the script, offering to send representatives so the man could talk with them about his concerns.

He didn't want them to come, he said, because they had visited before, but they didn't want to talk about things he wanted to talk about.

He then hung up on her.

Shaking, the sister thought, "That guy was so rude. I am about to cry!"

But with time, missionaries become comfortable with the task, gain confidence in their abilities, and appreciate the fact that they are finally engaged in real missionary work. An elder was pleasantly surprised to discover that talking with people was easier than he thought—to tell them things he had known all his life—whereas initially he thought he would have "no clue," that he wouldn't know what to say.

Many gain a sense of satisfaction from their efforts: questions are answered, materials are shared, and home visits are arranged. A compassionate sister reported a woman started crying while talking with her, and she was able to have the missionaries visit her. An elder appreciated how it prepared him for the mission field. He got to talk to people, he had conversations with them that most teenagers don't have, and, in his words, he was "able to practice how to avoid putting my foot in my mouth."

Missionaries also learn valuable lessons through the experience. They learn the power of the Church's media efforts and how it helps shape the public's perception of the Mormon Church. They also come to appreciate the value of following through on promises made to non-members; they feel a special commitment to act on referrals once they themselves are in the mission field.

They also learn to appreciate the importance of first impressions. A sister recalled calling a woman who had ordered a Book of Mormon, and her husband answered the phone. He started talking about being in the trenches with "some young Mormon boys" during World War II and what a good example they had set: they were always the first to do their work, and they didn't drink or smoke. "They were great people and great workers," he said. The sister said she thought about what a positive impression the Mormon soldiers made on the man, that he was talking about them sixty years later. She came away with the realization that non-members watch them, and they remember what Church members do and say.

Questioners can now post their queries online at www.mormon.org. There is a chat button, "Chat With Us," which allows visitors to post questions at the site. Missionaries at the MTC respond to them, just as they do to telephone calls.

While some find working at the Referral Center a challenge—dealing with disinterested, rude, and sometimes hostile people—the experience helps prepare them for what they will encounter in the field. But it is just a foretaste. While reviewing their calls at the end of a day, missionaries asked their supervisor how their experiences compared to what they will find in the field. He told them their work has the positive effect of helping them learn how to present their message and how to deal with rejection, but he also warned, "If you think this is hard, you haven't tasted anything yet."

"Feeling the Spirit"

Many say the most important dimension of the MTC experience is the spiritual, and it is nurtured through the study of scripture, personal and companion prayer, and group devotional meetings. The most commonly used phrase to describe it, "feeling the Spirit," is said to denote a feeling, a perception, and an attitude.

While walking on the MTC grounds one evening with her companion, a sister remarked on how strong the feeling of the Spirit was inside the boundaries of the MTC. She was "in a wholly different world, in the Spirit world," because the Spirit felt so strong there. She said, "It felt like there was glass all around us and we couldn't go out; it was so peaceful and generous." But once they walked out to the fence, they felt a different Spirit.

Some speak of an immediate sense of the Spirit at the MTC. A perceptive sister remembered feeling the Spirit as soon as she walked into the MTC, and her first impression was, "This is serious business here." Her companion agreed. She said the feeling of the Spirit is strong at the MTC. "The Spirit is running through here. You can't get away from it. They really catch you on fire." They said it was a spiritual high for them, all the time.

Many say they have significant spiritual experiences during the large group "firesides" held on Sunday evenings, when a General Authority speaks, and during Tuesday evening devotionals, when MTC administrators or other Church officials share a spiritual message. All missionaries are required to attend these events. An elder recalled how important they were to his spiritual development. He said firesides were the "pinnacle" of his spiritual experience at the MTC.

The large group meetings also have a powerful impact on the perceptions of new missionaries, because it is there, surrounded by thousands of fellow missionaries, that they see the size and scope of the missionary endeavor they are engaged in. An especially stirring moment is when they sing the popular missionary song, "Called to Serve":

1. Called to serve Him, heav'nly King of glory
Chosen e'er to witness for his name,
Far and wide we tell the Father's story
Far and wide his love proclaim.

Chorus
Onward, ever onward, as we glory in his name;
Onward, ever onward, as we glory in his name;
Forward, pressing forward, as a triumph song we sing.
God our strength will be; press forward ever,
Called to serve our King.

2. Called to know the richness of his blessing—
Sons and daughters, children of a King—
Glad of heart, his holy name confessing
Praises unto him we bring.

Text: Grace Gordon
Music: Adam Geibel, 1855-1933[45]

"It's incredible to hear missionaries sing 'Called to Serve' for the first time," recalled an excited sister. "It is very spiritual. We would really belt it out!" Another said: "After hearing that, I just knew the Church is true. Oh, it has to be something good. I never realized it before." "When singing 'Called to Serve,' your heart just swells," said a third. "You think, 'We *are* going to flood the earth. We *are* all united!'"

Other popular songs at the MTC are: "Put Your Shoulder to the Wheel," and, "I'll Go Where You Want Me to Go." Missionaries studying a foreign language are expected to sing in their adopted language.

The MTC serves as a motivator, or as one elder described it, "a cheering camp," where they get missionaries fired up about going on their mission. Another elder reported it created "a great feeling," while a third said it gave him a "spiritual boost," and he had never "felt so alive" before in his life.

Many say visits to the Provo Temple across the street are spiritual high points for them. A sister who struggled at the MTC said she found refuge in the Provo Temple, because it was the only place where she felt completely at peace; she "found the feeling of the Spirit in the temple to be incredible."

Some speak of being born again spiritually while at the MTC. An elder who served in the late 1980s spoke of this experience. It wasn't that he didn't have faith and a testimony when he entered the MTC; he did. But his time there had a "profound and drastic effect" on him; he considered it a spiritual conversion. He felt a motivation to study and learn that he had never experienced before. He said it was not that he was a bad kid, but that in the first week he went from being a good kid to being a really driven person. His teachers commented on the change they saw in him. He wrote to younger brothers and friends, telling them everyone should have the MTC experience, where they come and focus on the gospel. He wrote similar letters to his parents, and they wondered, "Who is this kid?" The whole thing was a high point for him and he had a profound change: "I came to realize how powerful salvation is, the atonement of Jesus Christ, how important the restoration of the gospel is, the prophets the priesthood; they all fit." Even though he always had felt they were true, by the time he left the MTC, he had a completely different viewpoint of the Latter-day Saint Church.

For some it is a time when they gain a deeper understanding of the Church's teaching regarding Joseph Smith and his role in the restoration of the gospel. An elder described how he always had believed Smith was a prophet of God, but he had never gotten on his knees and prayed for confirmation. After attending a group meeting in which he saw a film on Joseph Smith's First Vision and they were asked to write down their feelings about him, he went back to his room and, "letting go of my pride," he got down on his knees and felt he received assurances from the Spirit that Joseph Smith was indeed a true prophet of God.

High Points and Low Points

Given the intense and restrictive nature of the MTC experience, it is not surprising that missionaries react to it in varying ways. Some love it, describing it as the most spiritual place on earth; some hate it, saying it is a spiritual prison; but most are somewhere in-between, liking some aspects, but disliking others. All struggle in some way, and most agree a positive attitude helps.

In addition to devotional talks by General Authorities, singing "Called to Serve," and feeling the presence of the Spirit, missionaries said the high points included companionships (some became friends), companionship prayer at the end of the day, and feeling a sense of closeness in their districts. Many enjoyed exercising in the gym, and receiving mail was always a high point. An elder commented that he never realized how much he appreciated a letter until he was at the MTC.

Challenges included always needing to be with a companion, physical exhaustion, and living under a regimented routine. Some spoke of the loss of individuality, and more than a few used the term "boot camp" when referring to the MTC. Not receiving mail was the low point for some. An elder sadly recounted that he didn't receive much mail in the MTC, and he would go to the mailboxes and watch others read their letters.

Given the nature of companionships (always needing to be together) when one companion struggles, the other suffers. A sister said she was a "basket case" at the MTC because she was homesick, and it put "a real toll" on her companion. They would have a good laugh about it later, but she could tell her companion was pretty frustrated. She knew she would be if the roles were reversed.

While concerns are expressed about certain aspects of the food, many complain of gaining weight—as much as twenty-five pounds in some cases. An elder explained that the pattern of study, eat, sleep leads to people putting on the pounds.

Others feel a sense of isolation. An elder said the whole world seemed so far away that he felt isolated from everything. Another elder half humorously, half pathetically gave voice to this sense of isolation when he and a group of sisters and elders were reminiscing about what they would be doing were they not at the MTC. He said, "Can we go out by the fence and watch people drive by, people who have lives?"

Most missionaries successfully cope with the stresses and strains of the MTC. They credit help from teachers and peers: "When you are low, there is always someone who is up and who will build you up." They say the good days outweigh the bad, and they remind themselves why they are there. A sister said when things got hard, she told herself that she was engaged in the greatest work she could do, and while it was a sacrifice, it was the least she could do; what she was doing was important. Another sister agreed. She felt the MTC was where she needed to be, so she just "hung in there" when it was hard. She got through it and moved on. An elder who served in France agreed perseverance pays, but recalling his time at the MTC—how concentrated, intense, and difficult it was—he said he needed to do it, but he wouldn't want to do it again.

Leaving the MTC Early

While missionaries point to the many stresses and strains that dispirit them at the MTC, none is worse than when one of their own quits or is sent home early.

Great emphasis in the Church is placed on serving an honorable mission. While the vast majority of missionaries successfully complete their stay at the MTC and go on to serve worthy missions, there are those who have to return home early. For some, it is to address medical issues. They have to give attention to preexisting conditions, they require surgery, or they even have to begin treatment after a diagnosis of cancer. If the problem can be cured, the missionary is permitted to return to the MTC.

Some are sent home for psychological reasons, including schizophrenia and obsessive-compulsive behavior. In cases where counseling and medication can correct the condition, they may be allowed to return.

In some cases, missionaries have not confessed to or repented of transgressions committed prior to arriving at the MTC. Such confession and repentance should normally occur before or during the pre-mission interviews with the bishop and stake president. Missionaries are sent home, and in some instances are allowed to return to the MTC after a probationary period. Whether they are allowed to return, and how long their probationary period lasts, depends on the severity of the infraction.

Self-examination is stressed at the MTC, and missionaries are implored to identify and root out any lingering issues. An elder who attended the MTC in 2007 said they were repeatedly told the bar had been raised; they should search themselves, and if they had not repented of all their sins, they should go home and deal with them.

He said he began to feel paranoid. "What have I done?" he asked himself. "I don't think I have done anything!"

Another elder found the MTC to be a very stressful place, with a strong emphasis on whether missionaries are worthy to be there. He arrived thinking he was qualified and a good person, but he began to wonder if he was. He ended up "feeling very unworthy, very inadequate."

Another elder put a more positive interpretation on the process. He said the MTC helped him sort out things in his life. He described it as "a cleansing process."

An elder serving in the mission field said he could appreciate the importance of cleaning up one's past before arriving in the field, since it is much harder to do it from there. That is the MTC's rationale for stressing that missionaries sort things out before leaving the MTC; issues are much more difficult to address in the field. Also, mission presidents don't want, or need, the extra headaches.

Some choose to leave the MTC of their own accord. They find the rules and regulations too constricting, their freedom of thought and action too circumscribed, and they decide to leave—sometimes in a dramatic fashion. A missionary recalled hearing of an elder who jumped the fence, ran to a convenience store, and after lighting a cigarette, called a friend and said, "Come and get me, I am not doing this." His parents were informed, and there was an angry reception when the young man returned home. He was not allowed to return to the MTC, and his clothes were shipped home.

Whether this actually happened is unknown, and while there is probably some embellishment if it is true, it is typical of disobedience stories that circulate among missionaries: they tend to be dramatic and to have significant consequences.

There are also those who are sent home for what are considered less-than-honorable reasons: disobedience at the MTC, or serious moral transgressions. To return home under these conditions is one of the worst fates that can befall missionaries and their families, as it creates disappointment, tension, and embarrassment at home and in the Church—especially if there were elaborate farewells and donations of money.

The last category, which accounts for most of the early departures, are those who should not be, and who do not want to be, at the MTC. Some are desperately homesick. Others are terrified at the thought of going to another part of the country, or to a foreign country. Some are preoccupied with a girlfriend or boyfriend, or are under intense pressure to return home and marry. Others do not have the support of their families. They are told they are wasting their time and the family's money and they should return home.

Some never wanted to be a missionary in the first place. A great deal of pressure can be placed on young men to serve a mission. There may be a family tradition of parents, brothers, sisters, uncles, aunts, cousins, and grandparents serving missions, and it is assumed they will do the same. But not all want to, and as the time grows closer for them to leave the MTC and go into the mission field, they finally share their true feelings with their families and MTC officials, and they return home early.

This may lead the way for others to do the same. An elder said when someone from the dorm floor left early because he didn't want to be there, it opened the door for others who had similar feelings but had stayed on because of social pressure. Once the precedent of leaving early was set, others felt more comfortable doing the same.

Professional help is available for those who struggle. Administrators meet with the individual and discuss the issues. When appropriate, they refer the missionary to the medical center, which is staffed with physicians and nurses, or to the counseling center, which is staffed with full-time counselors.

Sometimes administrators can solve the problem on their own. A very thin sister was losing weight because she would not or could not eat the food served in the MTC cafeteria. She was ready to return home, but her branch president and his wife began bringing home-cooked meals to her. She started eating again, gained weight, and went on to serve a mission.

Missionaries frequently rally around peers who are having difficulties. Interviewees spoke of praying for them, fasting for them, and crying for them when they left early. Early departures can have a devastating effect on the district. A sister said an elder announced that he was going home to "clear up some things," and they wept and felt very bad for him; it was hard to know that he had done something so wrong that it was holding him back. An elder said it is difficult to see someone go home early and it takes time for a district to get over it.

Some praise their peers who chose to return home. A supportive elder said he has a lot of respect for those who go home because they want to take care of some things from their past. They are being honest; if they try to ignore it, "it eats at them." In a similar vein, an elder recalled a neighbor who attended the MTC under considerable family pressure but who returned home after only three days. He said the young man was thinking of applying again, but this time he wanted to do it for himself, and not for others.

It can be especially difficult for those who come home early. While there is a difference between *choosing* to return home for personal reasons and being *sent* home early for dishonorable reasons, members of the home congregation may still frown on it and have judgmental attitudes. They wonder, "What happened, and why couldn't you do it?"

Missionaries return home early from the MTC for a variety of reasons, and, as we will see, they return home early from the mission field for very similar reasons.

Blowing Off Steam and Leaving Their Mark

While missionaries are held to higher moral standards and live more regimented lives than their peers in secular colleges and universities, their behavior is still similar in some ways: pranks are played; they see how far they can bend the rules; and they try to leave their mark. Elders penny each other into their rooms, alarm clocks are set at odd hours and hidden in rooms, and various roughhouse games are played in the hallways. After a particularly raucous game of stickball in the hall, an elder said the resident assistant yelled at them, reminding them they were servants of God. The elder confessed they went out of their way to irritate him, that they were "nineteen-year-old guys blowing off steam."

A returned missionary who served in Germany summed it up well: "If you have a bunch of eighteen and nineteen-year old guys together, you are asking for trouble."

Some push the envelope. Gaudy ties and old suits are passed down, and elders wear them. While I was having lunch with the MTC president, an elder walked by wearing such a tie, and the president commented, with a certain note of disapproval, "Nice tie, elder."

Sisters find the elders' behavior strange, and they fail to see the humor in many of their antics. A sister recalled that a number of elders went into a bathroom stall, sang a song, and recorded it. She said sisters would never do anything like that—although she reported that she and some sisters went "tracting" in their dorm one night. "Now, that *is* funny," she said. ("Tracting" is when missionaries go door to door seeking to share their faith with people. It frequently involves leaving pamphlets, or "tracts.")

Sisters and elders also like to leave their mark. Messages are written on the bottom of mattresses, and notes are left in sockets, vents, and in the tubing of furniture. In one of the most unique cases, missionaries left messages, poems, and drawings on the reverse side of drop-down ceiling tiles in the old Language Training Center on the BYU campus. They were discovered during the demolition of the building in 1977.[46]

Experiences and Perceptions of Earlier Generations of Missionaries

Prior to the construction of the Provo MTC in 1976, training took place at a Church Mission Home that was established in Salt Lake City in 1925 and at the Language Training Mission later established on the BYU campus. While the goals of training earlier generations of missionaries parallel those of today—learning the fundamentals of the faith, getting along with your companion, motivating the missionary—the manner in which it is now done is very different. Today's training is highly structured, in contrast to previous generations that depended to a great extent on on-the-job training.

An interviewee who entered the mission field in 1947 provided my earliest detailed description of missionary training. He recalled spending about a week in Salt Lake City in an old house that served as the Mission Home. The young missionaries were taught the basic teachings of the Church, how to seek and be directed by the Spirit, and how to get along with their companion. They were provided literature to distribute, and they were given advice on how to approach people. The training was rudimentary, he said; there was little of the "how-to-stuff," the expectation being that they would learn much of what they needed to know once they were in the mission field. Those going foreign were given no language training. Their mission was extended by six months to thirty months (twenty-four months for sisters), and they were expected to learn the language in the field. He felt the purpose of the time in Salt Lake City was to boost morale and to get missionaries excited about serving: "To get you in the mood, pawing the ground, to get you to go and do the Lord's work."

A steady stream of Apostles and General Authorities came to speak to them, who shared "wonderful old Mormon war stories" and whose names showed they were direct descendants of the founders of the Mormon Church. He said it was a terribly charismatic experience, to have the feeling as a nineteen-year-old kid that he was being addressed by an Apostle of the Lord, and chances are he was a direct descendent of a pioneer Mormon leader of some kind and who might have a last name like Young, Smith, Richards, or Kimball. These apostles told stories of their Pioneer roots.

Some things have not changed since the 1940s; this missionary from 1947 said his mission home president addressed an issue that is still addressed today: "Will my girlfriend wait for me while I am gone on my mission?" The interviewee recalled how he and around thirty other young elders followed the mission president to the Salt Lake Temple to participate in their endowment ceremony. Stopping outside the Temple, the president pointed to the statue on the top of the spire and asked, "What do you see?"

"The angel Moroni," answered the elders.

"Look at him for a minute," said the president. "If he winks at you, it means your girlfriend will wait for you. If he doesn't, then she won't be there when you return."

The interviewee reported there was a lot of good-natured talking about it at the time, but it was also an "emotionally excruciating thought": that the promises that had been made at the final good-byes just a few days earlier were for naught and their girlfriends would not wait.

He reported the mission president was right.

An interviewee who served in the late 1950s spoke of receiving similar training and advice at the Mission Home, along with practical suggestions on how to take care of himself and how to iron his shirts. He had taken a mission preparation class at BYU and had memorized ninety-three scriptural passages. He described himself as "a fired up missionary" when he went out.

A sister who served in the mid-1960s recalled spending a week at the Salt Lake Mission Home. The majority of the sessions were on the principles of the gospel, on what it meant to be a missionary, and on developing a testimony. The mission president's wife held sessions on how to do their laundry, on grooming, on diet, and how to take care of their feet. They went to the office of a General Authority to be set apart as missionaries. She recalled the experience as being inspiring. She found it a thrilling experience to be with a group of young people who were all dressed up and who were excited about doing the same thing as she.

Others trained in the 1960s recalled memorizing the first lesson by the end of the week, being given advice on how to live with a companion and how to resolve conflicts, and how to iron shirts and pack clothes so they didn't wrinkle.

Very Practical Information

Missionaries receive practical information relating especially to issues of health and safety. Those serving in areas with poor sanitation conditions face a variety of potential ailments, with diarrhea being the most common medical problem faced in foreign missions. Other ailments include ingrown toenails, upper respiratory infections, skin rashes, and injuries. When I visited the Provo MTC in 2008, missionaries were given the handout "Ten Basic Commandments of Good Health," with the goal of helping to preclude such ailments. The commandments included:

- drinking pure water;
- eating food that is prepared sanitarily;
- eating a balanced diet;
- keeping their hands and bodies clean;
- keeping living quarters clean;
- protecting themselves from animals and insects that carry disease;
- staying away from dogs, cats, monkeys, or other animals;
- getting adequate rest;
- learning to manage stress;
- exercising regularly (at least twenty minutes a day);
- preventing accidents;
- getting proper medical care when needed.

As will be seen in later chapters on international missions, it isn't always easy to follow these guidelines.

Missionaries are also counseled to show great reserve around children; due to the increased threat of litigation, they should not put themselves in situations where there is even the appearance of inappropriate behavior. They are never to be alone with children, and they are not to have physical contact with children including tickling, changing diapers, holding them, or allowing them to sit on their lap. They should never babysit children. Two sisters said there are sessions on the policy at the MTC where missionaries are given scenarios and coached on how to act. They said it is okay if an investigator asks if they can hold her baby while she runs after her two year old, but generally they should not pick up or hold children.[47]

Departure for the Mission Field

After days, weeks, or months of preparation, the time for departure to the mission field finally arrives. Missionaries typically are excited, nervous, and somewhat insecure. They give voice to their concerns: "What will it be like where I am going?" "Who will be my trainer?" "Have I learned everything I need to know?"

To the last question, they generally feel the answer is, "No." An insecure sister said as she was getting ready to leave, she felt like she didn't know anything. She was excited, but she felt "clueless." The thought of what she was getting into "scared her to death."

A fearful sister who grew up in Salt Lake City and who was used to being surrounded by Latter-day Saints, said as she was leaving the MTC to go to Northern New England, she suddenly realized that she was going to an area where there were few Latter-day Saints and where there would be few who would be interested in what she had to say. The thought "freaked her out."

An elder also spoke of his anxiety. He had never been so nervous in his entire life as when he was leaving the MTC; he even became sick on the bus on the way to the airport. Other than that, he felt the MTC was a great transition to missionary life.

Some find it hard to leave the MTC. While relationships with their companions and in their districts can be rocky at times, they speak of how sad it is to leave their fellow missionaries; it is difficult to say goodbye to people they have only known for a few weeks but with whom they have shared intimate, deep feelings. "You become a lot closer than you normally would," observed a sister. Another sister said it was almost harder to leave her companion and district than it was to leave her family.

Having minimal contact with the opposite sex can feel awkward at the moment of separation. A sister said it seemed strange not to hug the elders but instead to shake their hands when they left for the mission field.

There is a touching ritual that is held in the sisters' dorm on the evening before a group is to leave. All gather in the stairwell and sing, "God Be with You Till We Meet Again." Those who have learned a new language sing the first stanza in their new tongue, and all sing the final stanza in English. A sister reported they all cried when they sang.

Elders aren't quite so emotional. One reported that on their final evening, elders in his district passed a saltshaker around to remind them that they are the salt of the earth. They also held a soft drink toast and told each other to work hard, good luck, and goodbye. "We felt like we were going off to battle," he recalled.

Continuing with the military imagery, an elder whose heart was not in serving a mission said he felt like a draftee as he left the MTC, "going to do my time."

Missionaries are given detailed pre-departure instructions and advice. They are to have their hair cut five days before leaving; they are to be in bed by 10:30 P.M. on the eve of their departure; they should not engage in horseplay or practical jokes; and they should leave their rooms clean. At the airport, they should be alert, watch their carry-on bags, and keep their wallets, purses, and passports in a safe place. Those who share a common destination are organized into districts and a district leader is chosen who has the general responsibility for the group during the trip. An elder chosen for this role interpreted it to mean he had earned the respect of MTC administrators; he thought they selected him because of his sterling character and leadership abilities. It was only later that he learned they choose the elder whose last name begins the closest to the beginning of the alphabet. His last name began with "C."

Missionaries are shuttled in buses to the Salt Lake City airport, where they board planes for destinations around the world. Until the early 2000s, family and friends saw them one more time if they traveled to the airport and said goodbye as the missionaries departed. Church authorities called a halt to the practice because it caused too much confusion and congestion, especially after the increased security after 9/11. It was also found that saying goodbye a second time undermined the separation and transition that began at the MTC. Final goodbyes are now said when missionaries are dropped off at the MTC.

Boarding the plane and liftoff are defining moments for many. A sister who lived within walking distance from the MTC struggled throughout her entire time at the MTC, questioning whether she should stay or whether she should go. She found the MTC very stressful; she felt unworthy and inadequate, and she missed her family and boyfriend who were so close yet so far away. A relative who knew of her struggles told her not to put on her running shoes, because if she did she would run home and never return to the MTC. But as soon as she boarded the plane, all of her anxieties "just melted away." It represented her first clear separation from home, and she was finally beginning a journey that would take her thousands of miles away. This had a "liberating effect," and she was finally able to relax.

Another sister recounted her humorous, but real, thoughts and feelings as she sat on the plane. She thought, "What am I doing?" and realized that if she started yelling and screaming, they would allow her to get off. But the plane started down the runway, and as she felt the wheels lift off, her stomach sank, and she thought, "Eighteen months."

"Then I was fine," she reported, "For I knew there was no turning back."

Describing the same moment, a laconic elder related: "As we took off, I looked out at the Great Salt Lake Valley, and then down at my nametag, and I thought, 'This is it.'"

Most missionaries look back on their time at the MTC as helpful and as setting the tone for their mission, but they also say preparation for much of what they faced on a day-to-day basis in the mission field came only with on-the-job training. We will now follow them into the mission field, join them as they gain this training, and watch them adjust to missionary life. It is not always an easy task.

PART II

The Mission Field

CHAPTER 4

To the Mission Field: Mission Presidents, Trainers, and "Greenies"

"I felt like a rubber band, stretched and stretched, even over-stretched, and then I was let go into the mission field."

AN ENGLISH ELDER, REFLECTING ON WHAT IT FELT LIKE WHEN HE LEFT THE PROVO MTC FOR HIS MISSION

"It is awesome to know that somebody makes sure we are okay."

AN EIGHTEEN-YEAR-OLD AMERICAN ELDER, TALKING ABOUT HIS MISSION PRESIDENT, AND THE MISSION PRESIDENT'S WIFE

Missionaries aren't thrust into a formless experience in the mission field. They are integrated into a complex but caring organization designed to help them fulfill their evangelistic responsibilities. They are assigned to a particular geographical area, or "mission." A mission president (a position that represents one of the most challenging callings in the Latter-day Saint Church) oversees their activities. The mission president is assisted by his wife, who plays a complementary and equally important role, and by two trusted elders, who hold the title of Assistant to the President. The missionary's first companion in the field is known as his or her "trainer," and it is that person's responsibility to help the new missionary assimilate into the mission culture and to fulfill mission expectations. Being new to the mission, "greenies" hold the lowest status in the mission, and they periodically are reminded of that. But they also bring new energy and enthusiasm that longer-serving missionaries find they occasionally need.

CHAPTER 4

To the Mission Field

The realization they have become missionaries occurs at different times and in different ways for new sisters and elders. For some it comes when they are handed their black nametag at the MTC, as was the case for the Italian sister I observed at the MTC in England, who exclaimed: "Now I am missionary!" (*sic*). For many it is when they are en route to the mission field and they see people reacting to them in airports and train stations: people stare at young men in dark suits, white shirts, and ties, and at young men and young women wearing nametags. A self-conscious elder who served in the early 2000s observed, "A lot of people gawk at you when you are a missionary."

In some cases, the role of missionary is thrust upon them. A young elder en route from the Mission Home in Salt Lake City to Mexico in the mid-1960s sat next to a woman who recognized him as a missionary. She shared that she had recently reactivated her affiliation with the LDS Church after years of inactivity, but her daughters remained indifferent, and she felt guilty about it.

She asked, "What should I do?"

He told her he felt God would give her time to work it out, although ultimately it would be her daughters' responsibility.

The interviewee said it was when he gave this counsel that he realized he had assumed a new role; he had moved from being a young boy to being a missionary.

Some see their trip to the mission field as the beginning of their missionary responsibilities. Elders en route to Mongolia gave out "pass-along" cards to fellow travelers; these cards list the Latter-day Saint Church website and a telephone number to call to obtain a free Bible, Book of Mormon, or Church DVD. During a layover in Chicago, a gutsy sister approached strangers, introduced herself as a new missionary for her church, said she was a little nervous, and would they mind if she "practiced" on them. Some were nice and listened to her, while others "steered clear of her."

Some felt they should begin their missionary activity en route, but confessed they came up short. Two sisters said they tried to talk to people next to them on the plane, but it didn't work; they said they didn't know what they were doing. They wished they had been given a Book of Mormon at the MTC, with the challenge to give it away before reaching their destination; then they would have had a goal in mind. Some seatmates didn't appreciate the missionaries' evangelistic efforts. An elder sat next to a woman on the plane to Chicago, and he and his companion tried to talk with her. She soon put on headphones, which stopped the conversation. They later noticed the headphones weren't plugged in.

Some realize in retrospect that they are so new at being missionaries that they are not savvy enough to take advantage of opportunities presented to them. In 2006 a timid elder sat next to a woman for three hours, and neither said a word until their plane was taxiing to the terminal gate. The woman then asked him where he was going and what he was doing. That is when it struck him—he had been like "his usual self," and not like a missionary. He had had three hours alone with her, and she had nowhere to go; she couldn't close the door on him or walk away.

"I blew it," he said.

For some, their journey anticipates the challenges they will face in the mission field. A sister en route to Europe in 1989 recalled that she sat next to a man she described as a "determined atheist," who tried to convince her there was no God. She felt secure in her beliefs, but he was "a very smooth talker." She tried to explain her beliefs, but he kept asking questions. She began to doubt that she knew enough to be a missionary, and she hoped she would learn a lot more very quickly. "What in the world do I think I am doing?" she asked herself.

And some are left in ambiguity, because they will have one-time chance encounters with people and will have no idea what long-term effect their message may have. A sister traveling from Salt Lake City to Chicago said her plane sat on the tarmac for forty-five minutes; she was very tired, and she closed her eyes and said a quiet prayer that the plane would soon take off. The man sitting next to her said, "I know what you are doing, sister."

Startled, she quickly opened her eyes and said, "You do?"

"You are praying, aren't you?" he asked.

She felt self-conscious but told him he was right. He then shared his story. He was a member of the Latter-day Saint Church, but had not attended since he was a child. He had had a hard life, he was going through a difficult divorce, and he was involved in a painful custody battle to get his child back. They talked about him getting his life back on track. The sister told him that it says in both the Bible and in the Book of Mormon that if he sought first the Kingdom of God, then everything else would fall into place. She felt if he started attending church again, he would get his life in order, and things would probably work out.

"We had a really good conversation," she said, "but I never saw him again. I have no idea if it had any effect."

The journey to the mission field is also the missionaries' first venture back into the world, and some speak of the discomfort they feel of returning to their old environment. A conscientious elder said he tried to avoid glancing at the movie during his flight, while another said he experienced cigarette smoke, loud music, and profanity at a connecting airport. It struck him that he had left the sheltered cocoon of the MTC.

"Oh, no," he thought as he walked through the airport. "I'm in hell!"

For some, the realization they've become missionaries comes during those first few days in the mission field. A sister serving in Vermont discovered she had a teaching appointment on her first night, and she thought, "I can't do that." It occurred to her that she was now a missionary and that she was expected to teach. She tried to review in her mind all that she had been taught at the MTC, but, she said with some relief, the person cancelled. An elder new to Maine reported it took him a couple of days in the field to realize that he was a missionary, but it finally hit him when, as he was trudging thorough ice and snow and knocking on doors, he looked down and saw that he was wearing his "church shoes." That's when he knew.

Non-Mormons are sometimes incredulous when they encounter young missionaries fresh from the MTC. A non-Mormon friend was on a Salt Lake City to Chicago flight with a number of new missionaries. She said they seemed so young and naïve; the young man sitting next to her didn't look any older than sixteen, and he looked frightened. She talked with him, but as a mother she kept thinking, "I would never let my children do such a thing."

The Mission Field

The Latter-day Saint Church is aware of the emotions and anxieties new missionaries experience, and it provides a structured yet caring organization into which they are integrated. Each is assigned to a particular geographical area or "mission," of which there are 406 worldwide in 2015. There are approximately two hundred or more missionaries now assigned to a mission (it had been around 150 prior to the age change requirement), and its physical size depends on the population base of the area. Urban missions can be relatively small when compared to the vast expanses of missions in more rural areas, which can cover thousands of square miles. A mission is divided into units called zones (the number of zones vary widely, depending on the size of the mission), and zones are divided into smaller units called districts, with typically four to eight missionaries per district. Missionaries showing leadership skills are chosen to serve as zone leaders and district leaders. Each mission has a central office staffed with administrative personnel, and it serves as the home base for the person responsible for the mission: the mission president.

The Mission President and the Mission President's Wife

The person charged with day-to-day oversight of the mission is the mission president, and it has to be one of the most difficult responsibilities in the Latter-day Saint Church. Always male and always married, he is responsible for two hundred or more missionaries, who may be spread over a large area, some who have emotional problems and some who don't want to be there. The role calls for a complex set of knowledge and skills: teacher, preacher, leader, diplomat, administrator, supervisor, motivator, counselor, disciplinarian, adjudicator, and father figure. It is a three-year, full-time calling, which requires that he and his family put their personal, professional, and financial lives on hold. They reside in the mission, generally at a centrally located mission home. They are provided a house, a car, and a living allowance, but they don't receive a salary. Some still have children living at home, and they must balance mission and family responsibilities.

Given the range of knowledge and skills required and the necessity to suspend nearly all aspects of one's life for three years, mission presidents tend to exhibit similar personal, religious, professional, and socioeconomic profiles: all are married men; almost all are middle-aged; almost all have served missions; they have held Church callings of increasing responsibility; many have impressive professional resumes (corporate presidents, chief executive officers, chief financial officers, successful business people, physicians, dentists, health care administrators, educators, attorneys, etc.); they are able to put their personal and professional lives on hold for three years; and they are financially able to serve. While the majority of mission presidents are from the United States, a growing number of men from around the world are being call to these positions.

Mission presidents' wives play an important, complementary role. There is a standing joke among General Authorities that when choosing a new mission president, they should look for the hardest-working, most spiritual, most dedicated person they can find, and then call her husband to the mission presidency. (A General Authority confirmed that wives *are* an important consideration when selecting men for Church offices.) They too have held a variety of responsibilities in the Church, but as of 2015, and typical of their generation (being middle-aged like their husbands), few served as sister missionaries in their early twenties. That profile should change with time, given the greater number of sisters now serving missions.

A mission president's wife assumes particular responsibility for sister missionaries and meets with them individually and as a group. She may speak at sisters' zone conferences on topics such as companionships, relationships, and grooming. She typically handles medical issues. If missionaries are sick and need to see a doctor, they must first get permission from her. She may need to balance family and mission responsibilities. If she still has children at home, her activities outside of the home with her husband may be more limited. She prepares meals for new missionaries arriving at the mission home en route to their first assignments, and she provides meals for those having their final interviews with the mission president as they leave for home.

An elder who lived in the mission home while his father served as a mission president described his mother as, "a saint. She was amazing, and she could cook for an army." A sister missionary observed that the mission president's wife has to be a strong woman; she is as important to the mission as the mission president himself. A missionary who served in the 1980s said on occasion there were rumors of "Sister Mission Presidents"—that the mission president's wife actually ran the operation. The president would say no, and she would say yes. An elder summed up the more common feeling of missionaries regarding the mission president's wife: "She is like a mom."

But mission president's wives may enter the role with trepidation. One, the wife of a newly called mission president with three teenagers and an eighteen-month-old baby at home, confessed the call "scared her to death."

Mission presidents don't apply for the position. Rather, as in all positions in the Latter-day Saint Church, they are "called" to the role by those in authority above them. The convention is that members neither seek nor refuse a calling, whether it is to serve as a Sunday School teacher, a mission president, or an Apostle. To be called seems especially appropriate in the case of mission presidents, since probably few would volunteer, given the personal, professional, and financial challenges of the positions, not to mention the emotional, psychological, and physical demands that accompany it.

I asked a returned missionary who served as an assistant to the mission president if he ever wanted to be one. He said he has a list of Church callings he does *not* want, and serving as a mission president is near the top of the list. He feels being in charge of two hundred young missionaries is "a disaster waiting to happen," and that much of a mission president's time is spent putting out fires before they get too big.

The Apostle Ronald A. Rasband spoke of the challenges of being a mission president. He served as a mission president in the New York City area, and he said the calling "brought him to his knees" more than any other assignment he had previously held. He said regardless of one's occupation, there was nothing that prepared one, "or even closely" prepared one, for the role. "I was caught in situations that I had no experience in, things I didn't know how to deal with," he said. As a result he said he learned the power of prayer and "the power of being spiritually dependent on a higher source."[48]

Of all the interviewees in this study, only one said he aspired to the position; he loved missionary work and looked forward to serving in the role some day. He added he is probably the only person in the Latter-day Saint Church with such a goal, given the demands of the position. He said most people dread the call from Church headquarters: "It's the Prophet on the phone."

Such calls are necessary, though, in a church in which there is no paid clergy and lay members hold all positions. The fact that the call to serve as a mission president is ever accepted is an amazing testament to members' commitment to the Latter-day Saint Church and to its missionaries. It also speaks to the regard members hold for what are believed to be Divinely-inspired decisions by the General Authorities who call them, and to the social pressure that accompanies accepting such a calling.

While new mission presidents and their wives know they will face many challenges, they say they also look forward to the opportunity to expand the reaches of the Church and to serve in a role in which they can have a significant impact on the personal and spiritual development of the young men and women in their care.

Calls to new mission presidents are typically made in early spring. Formal training takes place at the Provo MTC, and they enter the mission field in July. Announcements and pictures of new mission presidents and their wives are a common feature of *Deseret News Church*

News. A brief biography and summary of Church service is included for both, and notice is made of their assignment, along with the number of children in the family (an important piece of information in any LDS biography). Roughly one-third of new mission presidents are called each year.

Informal training begins at home. Newly called mission presidents are assigned a tutor from the MTC who helps them work through *Preach My Gospel*, as well as any language training that may be necessary. A DVD on understanding *Preach My Gospel* is provided. Initial discussions are held over the telephone. The tutor also role-plays various scenarios that relate to how the president can help missionaries in various situations. He is encouraged to practice the proselytizing principles found in *Preach My Gospel* and to attend zone conferences held in his area to observe how mission presidents already in the field handle these meetings.

Formal training for new mission presidents and their wives takes place during a Seminar for New Mission Presidents held at the Provo MTC. It is a four-day event where the training is as much inspirational as it is practical.[49] The intellectual, emotional, and social processes by which missionaries and prospective converts are motivated are considered, along with the quasi-parental role that mission presidents and their wives play in the lives of young missionaries. Many will receive additional training from their Area Presidency once in the field. (Area Presidencies are General Authorities who are assigned to supervise specific regions around the world.) Many Area Presidencies set policies based on local conditions and on their own preferred strategies for Church growth. A one-time mission president reported that the reason for the focus on spiritual matters in mission president training is that in the LDS Church there is the belief that the Spirit is the surest guide. He said that it is for this reason that, at all levels of leadership in the Church, they try to resist the temptation to prescribe strategies and methods, although he acknowledges that the temptation to do so is powerful.

One hundred twenty-nine couples from twenty countries attended the Seminar for New Mission Presidents in 2014. During the event, Thomas S. Monson, President of the Church and a one-time mission president, gave attendees some practical advice: greet newly arriving missionaries and get to know them through a personal interview; choose the best missionaries to serve as trainers for new missionaries; carefully monitor what missionaries do on their Preparation Day and counsel them to avoid activities on that day that could lead them astray;

encourage missionaries to follow what he calls "The Monson Rule"—send an e-mail home weekly; and work closely with Church leaders and members in the area where they serve, because it is they who hold the greatest potential for introducing missionaries to interested people in the community.[50] (The last piece of advice is in contrast to the approach of some interviewees who served during the mid-twentieth century, who said they had little or no contact with local Church leaders or members. The newer approach is far more effective.)

Addressing the wives at the 2010 seminar, the Apostle Boyd K. Packer gave voice to General Authorities' appreciation for what they bring to the task: "You have the tender heart and you [have] the insight, a spiritual insight superior to that of your husband. We do not like to admit it, but it is true."[51]

The role and training of current mission presidents is in stark contrast to that of decades past. An interviewee who served in the late 1940s said mission presidents in those days had much more autonomy than they do now. His father was a mission president in the Far East in the early 1950s, and he had limited experience in the Latter-day Saint Church prior to then. He had been a missionary to Japan as a young man, and he had served as a bishop in his local congregation, but that was about it. When he was formally set apart in Salt Lake City by President George Albert Smith (President from 1945 to 1951), he asked President Smith if he had any special instructions, handbooks, or materials for him. President Smith said he did not, that he should just follow the Spirit and everything would be fine. The interviewee went on to say that his father had an enormous amount of autonomy, but he feels this is not true of mission presidents today. Today they arrive on a specific day, and they leave on a specific day, "and they kind of almost leave soup cooking on the stove as they leave and the next family moves in." They have limits on what they can and cannot do, and they bear a heavy responsibility in keeping track of their missionaries.

While husband and wife bring an impressive array of knowledge and skills to their new roles, not many have formal counseling training, and it is a skill they will need to develop fairly quickly as they deal with two hundred young men and women. An elder who lived in the mission home as a teenager while his father served as a mission president said the phone rang constantly and his father was gone a lot, taking care of young missionaries spread over the countryside, some of whom did dumb things. It was really difficult, he reported, since his parents also had responsibility for three children at home.

Where and when mission presidents are posted influences the level of stress and difficulty they experience. The early days of opening a mission can be particularly challenging. A mission president who served in South Africa in the mid-1950s described it as the most intense experience he ever had in any Church assignment. His mission area was immense, covering thousands of square miles. He interviewed every missionary every six weeks and those who were struggling, weekly. He flew to a different area each weekend, where he held zone conferences. He also had responsibility for helping local congregations get organized. It was an extremely demanding and exhausting assignment. He said he never had a breather as a mission president, and the pressure was always on him.

An elder who served in England in the early 1990s said he found his mission president to be an incredible man; he had to be, because he was constantly on the go and it was physically draining for him. Some missionaries confessed to contributing to the stress of mission presidents, of bending the rules and, as one described it, "of horsing around." An elder who served in the mid-1990s quipped that he probably caused the mission president to grow a few gray hairs now and then. The elder who served in England said he and his mission president arrived in the mission field around the same time, and at that point the mission president's hair was black. When the missionary returned home two years later, the president's hair was entirely gray.

While mission presidents experience the heavy demands of the position, they also speak of the rewards. The president who served in South Africa said he found the experience extremely rewarding, being so close to the missionaries; while the elder who lived in the mission home as a teenager said he wouldn't trade the experience for anything, and he was sure his father felt the same way.

As one would expect when dealing with 406 individuals, mission presidents exhibit a wide range of personalities and approaches. Some are strict. A sister missionary who served on the East Coast in the early 1990s recalled her mission president's rules: elders had to stand when sisters entered the room; elders and sisters could not inform people they were transferring to a new location until the night before they were leaving; and they couldn't call new missionaries "greenies" (a common practice among missionaries). A senior sister missionary who served in Canada in the early 1990s (a woman in her sixties) said her mission president, a retired military officer, made missionaries stand for inspection: fingernails, shoes, elders' hair, their weekly planners. Elders didn't seem to mind, she recalled, but her senior companion (also a woman in her sixties) refused to do it. She thought it was "too much," and she sat and watched. (Senior missionaries are sometimes able to express their opinions more forcefully, and more successfully, than younger missionaries.)

Not all mission presidents inherit a situation in which their predecessor has been strict, in which missionaries are conforming to the rules and are hardworking. A sister who served in California in the late 1990s said when her mission president arrived he found there were some missionaries who were "really relaxed" and some who were disobedient. He "tightened things up quite a bit," and he implemented strict rules for the mission. She found it good, but hard. In a similar vein, an elder who served in Switzerland in the early 1990s said when his mission president arrived, he found things pretty lax, and some missionaries lacked respect for the mission presidency. The new president "whipped things into shape." In fact, the elder was amazed at the turnaround brought about by the new president: missionaries became obedient, and they respected him.

There is a saying among missionaries: "New president, new rules."

Those who serve under successive mission presidents are able to observe the extent to which they can differ and how their personality sets the tone for the mission. An elder who served in the mid-twentieth century spoke of having two contrasting presidents. The first came from the judicial system and seemed to assume that missionaries were generally up to no good, and it led to a sense of distrust in the mission. A mission president followed him who had a background in scouting and who had a more positive attitude toward the young missionaries. "The feeling and attitude in the mission was the difference between night and day," said the interviewee. He felt the former president was always watching over his shoulder, whereas the latter valued him and trusted him to do what was right.

When I asked what effect the mission president has on the mission, a sister from Idaho said he makes all the difference in the world. How he acts has a direct effect on how missionaries act and on the trust they put in him. If he isn't very strict, the missionaries react similarly. She was happy with her mission president. He was strict and made them follow the rules, but at the same time he was very caring and took time out for them. He called her five times in three days when a relative of hers was diagnosed with a life-threatening illness. He wanted to see how she was doing emotionally and to see if there was anything he could do to help.

Many interviewees spoke affectionately of their mission presidents. An elder who served in the Northeast said a special relationship developed between his mission president and the missionaries; a bond of trust was built between them, and there was a spiritual affinity if the missionary was sincere and worked hard. An elder who served in Japan spoke of forming a strong affiliation with his president; he and his wife were "warm and genuine," and they really cared. An elder who served in England said he couldn't have asked for a better president: he was totally selfless and would do anything for the missionaries.

Not all gave such positive descriptions. An elder who served in the mid-1980s described his mission president as "an MBA, draconian, produce-results type of guy," whose primary interest during the personal interviews was numbers: numbers of contacts made, lessons taught, and baptisms performed. The missionary described him as a "bean counter." Another interviewee who was a returned missionary said if she had children, she would not encourage them to go on a mission, because she would worry about who they would have as a mission president. She had worked professionally with men who were called as mission presidents, and she was not always impressed. "It's such Russian roulette on who the mission president will be. There are some control freaks out there. They called people to be mission presidents that I had worked with for years and I thought, 'Thank God I don't have a kid old enough to go to that mission.' There are good ones, but you don't have any say in it."

It is recognized that not all missionaries will get along with their mission president and that there may be conflicts between them. A stake president said he gave his home telephone number to departing missionaries and told them to call him if they felt they were facing issues they couldn't discuss with their president. Occasionally he received such calls. Missionaries would say they felt their mission president didn't understand them or didn't appreciate the issues they were facing.

It may be difficult to follow a popular mission president, or one who experiences tragic circumstances. A sister whose mission president died in an accident in Central America said she and her fellow missionaries initially didn't want to accept the new president, especially when he did things differently from the president who died.

Mission presidents and their wives serve as important role models for missionaries. A returned missionary who taught at the MTC in England said the whole mission watches them: their character, their behavior, and the quality of their marriage. The couple's relationship, as perceived by missionaries, can have a powerful influence on sisters and elders. The president of the MTC in England told me that many young elders told him that when they returned home they hoped to marry someone like his wife.

Serving as a role model sometimes puts the mission president in an awkward position. A one-time mission president said he quickly discovered that his stronger missionaries looked to him in "an exalted manner," almost to the point of thinking he made no mistakes.

When I asked a General Authority what makes a good mission president, he said he exhibits five qualities. First, he leads the mission. He is not intimidated by the missionaries, but rather is part of their world and helps provide focus and direction for them. Second, he is thoughtful. The good mission president gives positive feedback when the missionary does good work, and he tells the missionary's parents. Third, he has to have vision and be a motivator. The mission president continually works to keep his missionaries focused and working. When he served as a mission president, he told his missionaries how well they did on their mission was an indicator of how well they would do in their lives. This motivated them to work even harder. Fourth, missionaries must feel the mission president trusts them, but he realizes a few missionaries will make some serious mistakes. The good mission president trusts his missionaries, but he also has sleepless nights. Fifth, the mission president must work at getting along with local units of the LDS Church. He is an uninvited, three-year guest in the area, and local congregations have no say in his selection. He should not arrive with the attitude that he has the answers to their problems.

Not all mission presidents have a good experience. According to the same General Authority, some do come into the mission acting like they have all the answers, and they alienate themselves from local congregations. Some work so hard and experience such stress that they never quite get over it, while others feel the Church "owes" them something—perhaps a position with greater status—for working so hard and for so long. And some suffer financially and never fully recover from it.

A mission president has many responsibilities: he supervises, motivates, and adjudicates the whole mission; he insures discipline, interviews missionaries on a regular basis, and keeps peace among them; he speaks at zone conferences and provides training; and he decides which areas will be opened and which will be closed. He can't do all these things by himself, and he is assisted in the central office by paid administrative staff, senior missionaries (if available), missionaries who have particular skills that can be put to good use in the office, and, occasionally, by missionaries whose misbehavior has brought them into the office for closer scrutiny. There are two others the mission president depends upon and who can have a significant impact on the success of the mission: his trusted assistants to the president.

Assistants to the President. Two mature missionaries who hold the position of Assistant to the President, or "A.P.," join the mission president in the mission office. Being an A.P. represents the highest level of leadership a missionary can achieve. Only elders serve in this role, except in sister-only missions such as at Temple Square, Salt Lake City. A.P.s typically excel in proselytizing, have strong communication and interpersonal skills, are hard workers, follow the mission rules, and are trustworthy. When I asked why he was chosen for the position, an elder who served as an A.P. in Peru said he had asked himself the same question many times before. He said he is not super-intelligent, and he didn't baptize as many converts as some of his fellow missionaries, but he is humble, hardworking, and trustworthy. He is also obedient, conscientious, and he never let his mission president down. "He knew that he could trust me," he said. The mission president said he chose the young man as his assistant because when he was a district and zone leader, those serving under him were the most excited and engaged missionaries in the mission. They praised his ability to relate to them, and they appreciated his desire to help them become better missionaries. This caught the attention of the mission president.

A.P.s are based at the central mission office and their duties include serving in the office, working in the field, and assisting the mission president. They perform administrative functions such as collecting and compiling weekly mission progress reports and sharing the information with the mission president. These reports include the number of hours missionaries worked, first lessons taught, other lessons taught, and baptisms. They travel throughout the mission and serve as mediators between the mission president and the missionaries. They deal with issues that don't rise to the level of the mission president. They may speak on behalf of the mission, they may make decisions for the mission president, and they communicate the needs and concerns of the missionaries to the mission president. Together they decide what follow-up action is necessary in order to address particular needs, problems, or concerns. These may be addressed at zone conferences or district meetings, which assistants help organize.

A.P.s travel with the mission president, and on occasion have to look into serious problems such as missionaries who are disobedient or are ill. An A.P. who served in California said they occasionally had to serve as "snoopervisors," appearing at missionaries' doors early in the morning to see if they were awake. They didn't have to do it very often, but they did have cases of missionaries who were known to be flagrant late-sleepers, and they periodically checked in on them.

Some say A.P.s almost run the mission, although the mission president ultimately decides how much responsibility and authority he wants to give them. An A.P. who served in the Northwest said when their new mission president arrived, he and his fellow assistant felt it was their responsibility to introduce him to every missionary in the mission. They set up a schedule where he went to every corner of the mission, speaking thirty times in twenty days. The mission president was worn out after this initial burst of activity. "We ran him ragged," said the A.P. The mission president's wife wondered if this was how it was going to be for the next three years. It was then that the mission president realized that *he* was going to run the mission, not the A.P.s.

A.P.s consider it an honor to be in the mission office, and many say that their greatest enjoyment and most rewarding experiences come from working so closely with the mission president. They gain valuable knowledge and skills. They develop their speaking, training, and motivational skills, and they develop their leadership styles.

But they also point to what they consider to be downsides to the position. It involves far more administrative work than they have ever done before (which is off-putting to some), and while success for them in the field is based on their individual efforts and accomplishments, as A.P.s they have to base their success on the activities of others. An A.P. who served in Japan said at times he felt almost overwhelmed with having to deal with other peoples' problems, including their lack of motivation, poor teaching skills, and weak testimony. There were days when he wished his only tasks were to teach investigators and to deal with his own issues.

Some A.P.s tire of the administrative duties and ask to go back to teaching. This is understandable, because for many it is their teaching abilities that helped get them the A.P. position in the first place. And many miss teaching. An elder who served in Hungary said it was an honor to serve in the office, but it was also difficult, because he thrived on teaching. He was excited to go back into the mission field and teach again.

Missionaries whose mission includes administrative responsibilities thus have a different kind of missionary experience than those who don't.

An A.P. who served in Europe in the late 1990s said some missionaries have a false perception of what A.P.s do; they are seen as not doing much, as having an easy job, because it is so different from what they do in the field. His trainer badmouthed A.P.s not long after he arrived. He called them "apes" and said they never work. (Scratching under one's arms like an ape is common behind the backs of A.P.s.) Thus when the interviewee became an A.P., he found it very different from what he had expected. He found the position very demanding, staying up sometimes until 2:30 A.M., planning training sessions and zone meetings and trying to meet the needs of individual missionaries. Other A.P.s concurred. One who served in Japan said he spent every day, even Preparation Day, thinking about what needed to be done; he never had the chance to relax.

In spite of the kidding and misperceptions, there is prestige serving as an A.P., and some vie for the position because of the status and influence that it carries. Some interviewees said they heard of girlfriends who told their missionary boyfriend they would only marry him *if* he became an A.P.

An A.P. who served in Portugal said missionaries who exhibit the desired qualities but have to be coaxed into the position better serve mission presidents. Becoming an A.P. is not a goal, it just happens. The A.P. who served in Peru said there were missionaries who wanted to take his place when he left. Their actions and motives were clear, but the mission president said it would never happen. "That is not the way it works," said the president. "Rather, it works as it did in your case. When I called you to the position, you responded, 'I wasn't expecting it at all.'"

Arrival at the Mission Home

New missionaries arriving in the mission field are typically met at the airport or train station by the mission president, his wife, and/or the A.P.s. They are taken to the mission home for a one or two day stay, where the mission president interviews them and they receive an orientation to the mission. It is their first home-cooked meal in weeks, if not months. At the end of the orientation they are introduced to their trainer, who takes them to their first assignment in the mission field.

Many missionaries spoke of their initial impressions of those greeting them at the airport or train station: serious, awe-inspiring, and somewhat frightening. A sister serving in 2000 recounted her impressions as she entered the airport terminal. There stood the mission president, who was very tall, flanked by his A.P.s with their arms crossed, all looking very formal in their dark suits, white shirts, and conservative ties.

She said it looked like the F.B.I. was there to arrest them and to take them away.

A shy elder confessed to being intimidated by his mission president when he first met him. The president was very distinguished looking and had been very successful in business prior to serving as a mission president. The elder said he felt like "a deer in the headlights" as he shook his hand, and as the president looked at him the young missionary said it felt like he could see into his soul. He didn't know what to do, but he said he would have done whatever the president told him to do: where to stand, what to do, just tell him. An elder who served in Oregon said his mission president struck him with awe; he was a man of accomplishment and leadership in the Church and in the world. He was tall, charismatic, and warm, and his wife was energetic and "free-flowing." They knew General Authorities, and they told stories about them. They seemed larger than life, he felt.

While missionaries may be given warm welcomes by the mission president and his wife, they typically are very nervous when they arrive at the mission home and sit down for their first meal. Many have never eaten at a mission president's home before. A sister serving in 2000 said the mission president and his wife made her feel very much at home but she was very, very nervous at the first meal. She thought she must have looked "as white as a ghost" that first evening, and looking back at pictures, she knew she was. An elder reported the president's wife was "really big" on etiquette, and it made him nervous. She told them not to chew with their mouths open. In an interview with the mission president and his wife, she confirmed that she often talks about etiquette, because she is surprised how much help missionaries (especially elders) need in the area of table manners.

Interview with the mission president. The mission president meets with new missionaries for a personal interview during the orientation period and then every four to six weeks thereafter. He wants to get to know them as people and as budding missionaries during the first interview. Personal information and interests are shared. He may ask them how they perceive their roles as missionaries, and he will ask them to share their testimony of Jesus Christ, of Joseph Smith, of the Restoration, and of the Book of Mormon. They will return to these themes in future meetings.

Obedience is a common theme during the first interview. A missionary mentioned in Chapter 2, who served in Northern New England in the mid-2000s and who received a letter from his mission president prior to his departure, said his mission president returned to the themes that were stated in his letter—obedience, humility, and serving others. The mission president said those who practice these traits are the happiest and most successful. An elder who served in Japan said during his initial interview with his mission president, the president stressed the importance of obedience and the importance of seeking understanding through prayer and study, rather than through logic.

Missionaries may also discuss their personal goals during the first interview. An elder who served in the American Southwest and who converted to the faith in Western Europe a year earlier, said during his initial interview he told the mission president that he wanted to be the best missionary he could be, that he was determined to work hard, and that he was committed to being obedient "one hundred percent." He told his mission president he felt it was a privilege to come to the United States, "a country of freedom, and a promised land as it says in the Book of Mormon," and he wanted the president to let him know if he ever was "slacking off," because he was not only representing his Church, but also his financial supporters in Europe.

The commitment and dedication that can be typical of recent converts is especially apparent with this young man.

Missionaries occasionally get off on the wrong foot at the initial interview with their mission president. A new missionary who attended an Ivy League college for a year prior to going on his mission, said his mission president, an attorney, noted the newcomer's educational background with a certain amount of perceived sarcasm when he said, "An Ivy Leaguer, huh?" To which the new missionary responded, "A lawyer, huh?"

Their relationship deteriorated thereafter.

The interviewee is no longer a member of the LDS Church; he chose to leave it.

Orientation. Missionaries are introduced to the mission during orientation: its characteristics, unique features, and the current state of missionary efforts. Practical information is shared, including how to access their monthly allotment of money and the rules and regulations regarding driving a car.

Missionaries are given a monthly allowance of a predetermined amount, based on the cost of living where they are serving. Mission presidents realize that many missionaries have never used a budget before, and they advise their new missionaries to budget their money wisely, to be frugal, and to keep track of all money spent. Otherwise they will find themselves, in the words of a handout given at the orientation session, "with too much month at the end of the money." They should never lend or borrow money, and they must pay all bills before transferring to another location. Missionaries are expected to pay fast offerings on each Fast Sunday. (Latter-day Saints observe the Law of the Fast, which typically is the first Sunday of each month, when members go without food or drink for two consecutive meals. The money that would have been spent on meals is donated to the Church for the care of the poor and needy.) Missionaries don't pay the 10 percent tithe expected of Church members on their monthly allotment.

While it is common to see missionaries walking along the street or riding bicycles, cars are available for those who serve large areas, or who are required to do a considerable amount of traveling, such as A.P.s. Mission cars are to be used only for Church-related business, and missionaries are not permitted to drive beyond their assigned area without permission from the mission president. Drivers are typically restricted to a certain number of miles per month. Missionaries may not drive vehicles owned by Church members or non-members, nor may they allow others to drive or ride in Church-owned vehicles. They are allowed to ride in members' and non-members' cars. New missionaries watch a car safety training film during orientation that includes a discussion of the use of seat belts and turn signals, how to take care of the car, and how to back up—including the requirement that the companion who is not driving get out of the car, stand to the rear, and help direct as the driver goes in reverse. Mission officials say the practice cuts down on accidents, while non-Church bystanders watch in disbelief and with some amusement, especially in situations in which there are no other cars or traffic around. They are told to go the speed limit, and they are sometimes subject to road rage and rude gestures because of this. If they get two tickets, they lose the right to drive.

Near the end of orientation new missionaries are told where they will be serving and who their trainer will be. A sister who served in the mid-1990s said her mission president called new missionaries to the front of the room and pointed to red dots on the mission map to show them where they were going. He then called their trainers forward, and they were formally introduced.

Trying to guess who one's trainer will be from the mix of trainers who show up at orientation is an exercise most new missionaries engage in. Sisters appear to have stronger feelings about this than elders, for many sisters said that when looking at the sisters who came to collect them, they had a strong preference just by looking at them. "You have a lot of strong feelings about your trainer and companions," said a forthright sister, "and you ask yourself, 'Am I going to like this person?'"

The Trainer

Trainers are seasoned missionaries who take new missionaries to their first assignment and serve as companions and mentors for the first three or four months. Care is taken in choosing them. According to the Missionary Training Manual given to trainers in Northern New England in the mid-2000s, they are chosen for the role because they are obedient, can be trusted to follow mission rules, are effective missionaries, have good communication skills, and have a love for their fellow missionaries and for the people in the area. They are told their greatest responsibility is to serve as an example for their new trainee and that they must follow the daily schedule with exactness.

Trainers play an important role because they can set the tone for the newcomer's entire mission. If trainers are hardworking and set high standards, new missionaries will likely behave in a similar way. If trainers are tired or unmotivated, or if the chemistry between trainers and trainees isn't good, it can have a negative impact on how new missionaries behave. As a sister candidly observed: "It is scary. Your trainer can make or break your mission."

During the first week together, the trainer and new missionary review the mission rules that are spelled out in the *Missionary Handbook* (known as the "Little White Book"), read sections of *Preach My Gospel* together (with particular attention given to what it says about companionships), and agree on a plan that has the new missionary reading the Book of Mormon in its entirety. They work on developing the trainee's proselytizing skills, including how to approach potential investigators, how to prepare lesson outlines, and how to present the material in an effective manner. The new missionary is taught how to use the Area Book, which keeps track of individuals missionaries have spoken to, and how to keep their Daily Planner. They begin to plan daily activities together, and the trainer checks in periodically on the trainee's study habits. The trainee is introduced early to district and zone leaders, to local members, and to those who hold positions of authority in the local Church.

Weekly trainer and trainee reports are sent to the mission president during the training period. At a more mundane level, they discuss the schedule for cooking meals, washing dishes, and cleaning the apartment they share.

Appropriately, missionaries refer to their first area as their "birthplace," and some refer to their trainers as their "mom" or "dad."

When I asked what makes a good trainer, a perceptive sister serving in 2000 used her own trainer as an example. She felt her trainer had a perfect balance between asking the new missionary what she wanted to do, even though she had only been out for a week, and the trainer sharing what she learned during her year in the mission field. Her trainer made her feel as though what she said mattered; she let her learn things on her own, and they worked as a team.

The sister gave an example of her trainer allowing her to discover something on her own: there are regional differences in how people behave and missionaries have to be aware of them and adjust to them. In this case it was what appeared to be a rather simple question: "What door do I knock on when I go to someone's home?" The new sister was from Utah, and she said it would be very unlikely that she would go to someone's back door, which is considered a private entrance. Thus it made her very uncomfortable for the first few weeks after her arrival in Northern New England when her trainer went to the back door (typically a side, "mudroom" entrance, common in older New England homes and farmhouses). She told her trainer of her discomfort and her reason why. Instead of telling the new missionary that that is what people do, the trainer suggested she go to the front door and knock. The sister did, but no one came to the door. She knocked again, but still no answer. Eventually she realized the occupants couldn't come to the door because it was blocked with furniture. Later, in the winter, she observed that people who use their mudroom entrance don't even shovel the snow away from their front doors. Thus it is never used. It only took two front doors to realize that she should go to the mudroom entrance in older homes. In a number of different situations the trainer let her find out things for herself, which she felt was the best way for her to learn.

The sister observed that some trainers don't approach their role in the same way; they are overbearing, pushy, and bossy, which she feels defeats their purpose, because trainees may or may not follow them.

New missionaries whose trainers are quite strict generally come to appreciate them, but sometimes only after the fact. Initially they find such strictness difficult, but in retrospect they come to a greater appreciation of their trainer because they learn strict obedience. Trainers set the tone; if they are "slackers" (a term used by interviewees), new missionaries may become slackers, too. A sister said she appreciated her trainer in hindsight. They worked hard, and she learned what it meant to be a good missionary. She got more gentle companions after that, who taught her they could have fun, too.

An American elder who served as a trainer in southern England had a companion new to the mission field who wasn't a very strong worker, but with whom he thought he got along well. After the young missionary was transferred, their landlady said he had "hated the trainer's guts" and that he thought the American trainer was working him too hard. The missionaries would come for lunch, and when the trainer was out of the room, the young elder would complain to the landlady: "Do you know what he made me do today?" However, months later, after they each had been given new companions, the young missionary told his trainer he was glad he had worked him so hard, because it was a good way for him to begin his mission.

From the trainer's perspective, an elder who served as a trainer in Brazil said he felt that what makes a good trainer is being sensitive to the needs of new missionaries, of not being too hard on them, and of letting them take the initiative when appropriate. He needed to let his new trainee do things on his own, to let him "spread his wings."

Many first-time trainers said they entered into their new roles nervously. A sister who was called as a trainer soon after she was trained was astonished with the call and she said she felt like she had been "thrown to the wolves." It initially put her in a very awkward position, because her trainer had done everything—scheduled meetings, took the lead in teaching, dealt with problems—and she didn't even know how to get to the mission home to pick up her trainee. Things eventually worked out, but not without some discomfort. Her trainee assumed she knew what she was doing, and the new trainer tried to "fake it" for a while, but the trainee soon figured out what she was doing. They had a good laugh about it. The trainer said she must have done okay, because they let her continue training other new missionaries.

Learning to make judgment calls is a challenge for new trainers. A trainer told of teaching a couple that was having marital difficulties. The missionaries felt as though they were in the middle of the conflict, and it was hard to know the best course of action. She advised the couple to seek marital counseling.

When I asked what it is like to work with missionaries who don't want to be there, trainers said it is difficult, because there are days when it is hard enough to motivate themselves, let alone someone else. One trainer described having an unmotivated trainee as having a lot of extra weight to carry around.

While trainers may struggle with some of their new trainees, some say they grow from the experience. An elder who served in the late 1950s said his first trainee was very skeptical, and he kept asking why they were there and why they were doing what they were doing. The trainer said he found the skepticism healthy, for he had experienced it himself, and it forced him to come to have answers to some basic questions: the validity of the scriptures, the place of Christ in the plan of salvation, the Restoration, and Joseph Smith's role as a prophet. He worked with his new companion on his skepticism, and they were able to move beyond it to a more profound level. The trainer was able to show there are spiritual realities, because he had experienced them himself.

Some trainers don't devote their full attention to their role, especially when they are close to returning home. They are exhausted, their mind is elsewhere, and this can have a negative effect on their new trainee. An elder who served in Paris in the early 1970s spoke of how frustrated he felt at the beginning of his mission. He had arrived "fired up" and ready to find investigators, but his trainer was finishing in a few weeks. He was preoccupied with home and what he would be doing there. His mission had, in effect, already ended for him. A sister spoke of a similar experience. She too was "fired up" when she arrived in the mission field, but she felt very frustrated in her first city, because her trainer was preparing to go home and get married, and so they spent their first couple of days shopping for the wedding. She had arrived "ready to push every minute, to study hard, to work hard, and to keep my mind on missionary work, and then this." She was "terribly deflated." She said it was a challenge to pull together as a team, because they were different people at different stages of their mission. It wasn't until both new missionaries received other trainers that their missions really began.

A conscientious trainer who served in England and who had seen this dynamic in other companionships vowed that he wouldn't let it happen to him. When he was informed he would be training a new missionary one month before his return home, he chose not to tell the new missionary this fact until about a week before his departure. He found it difficult not to think and talk about home, since he would be home just in time for Christmas. So he pressed on, worked hard, and finally told the new missionary he was going home. The trainee was given a new trainer, and things worked out okay.

Missionary Housing

The mission president approves all missionary housing. Typically it is a rental unit in the area where missionaries are serving, and successive missionaries who rotate through the area use it. It must have its own entrance and bathroom, and they aren't to live where single people of the opposite sex live, or where the spouse is frequently absent. Generally only two missionaries live in a unit. They are told not to roughhouse in the apartment and that they are responsible for any damages. While current generations of missionaries tend to stay in rented apartments, earlier generations spoke of staying in rented rooms of members and non-members and in motel rooms.

An elder who served in England in the mid-1960s said many missionaries roomed with families and ate meals with them. They normally weren't member families, because they didn't want to overburden the families financially, since member families may have felt an obligation not to charge missionaries very much. Plus, by living and interacting with non-members, they could share their gospel message with them. Missionaries occasionally lived in flats, but that was relatively rare. Conversely, a sister serving in Lyon, France, in the mid-1960s, said she lived in a room in an apartment owned by Church members, as did an elder in Johannesburg, South Africa, in the mid-1980s.

An elder who served in Portugal in the early 1990s said missionaries frequently rented rooms from non-members. They had the use of the bathroom, and the landlady did their laundry and cleaned their room. Missionaries sometimes found the owners hard to get along with—they had the attitude, "Don't touch my things, but it's okay for me to touch your things." It upset many of them. Missionaries were responsible for finding their own rooms. They would live with other missionaries until they found a place. He said things really became cramped in those situations. Today the Church finds housing for missionaries.

Discussions of housing arrangements sometimes prompted unusual or fond memories from interviewees. An elder who served in California in the 1960s once had to live in the library of an older Latter-day Saint chapel. He and his companion cooked in the kitchen and had cots in the library. They found it a little eerie living there at night. An elder who served a building and proselytizing mission as a carpenter in Austria in the early 1990s had fond memories of his landlady. While she was Roman Catholic and had no interest in their message, she knew the missionaries struggled financially, and she returned some of their rent money to them. An elder who served in Paris in the early 1970s had an eighty-year-old landlady who had rented an apartment to missionaries for years. She delivered the mail each morning around 8:00 A.M., but she entered without knocking. The elder recalled she just walked right in, whether they were dressed or not. They knew they had to get dressed by then, because they knew she would come barging in.

Keeping the apartments clean may be a challenge. Cockroaches and other bugs and insects may be a perennial problem. Hand-me-down clothing and shoes left in closets from previous missionaries contribute to the clutter. Donated furniture isn't always in the best shape. When sisters replace elders in an area and they move into what had been an elders' apartment, it will sometimes show an elder's touch. A sister described moving into such an apartment, where there were stacks of soda cans around the apartment and the toilet seat was repaired with tape.

The apartment and its cleanliness are subject to inspection by the mission president, his wife, the zone leader, or the A.P.s. Some mission presidents hold periodic meetings with the missionaries in the apartment and will inspect it for cleanliness at that time. Inspection visits are typically prearranged, and missionaries will clean the apartment in anticipation of the visit. Junior companions and greenies are frequently taxed with the cleaning duties. An elder serving in Kentucky said the mission president and his wife made twice-yearly apartment inspections tours to make sure missionaries were keeping their apartments clean—at least on those two days. The visitors knew it was a temporary condition, and they would say something to that effect. An incredulous sister reported their inspector wore white gloves and wiped them over surfaces. They were told they could do a better job keeping the place clean. Missionaries refer to overzealous inspectors who show up unannounced as "snoopervisors."

Accidents do occur. Two careless elders admitted burning a hole in a porch rug as they were burning worn-out shirts to celebrate the one-year anniversary of their mission, while two rambunctious elders broke a window and some dishes while throwing a football in the apartment. Upon reflection, the elders said that's when they decided to take their mothers' advice and not throw footballs inside. It took the accident to realize their mothers were right.

As one might expect, young men aren't always the neatest housekeepers. An elder who served in Spain told of reporting a break-in in the elders' apartment to the police. After walking through the apartment the police officer observed, "The intruders really trashed the place, didn't they." To which the embarrassed elder replied, "Well, uh, no. It always looks like this."

Another elder reported a break-in in Indiana. As they returned to their apartment, the elders found the police and building superintendent in the apartment. Someone had broken in, and the elders were asked to look around to see what was missing. The elder immediately went to see if his scriptures and missionary journal were still there, which they were. Then he noticed that his bike and camera were gone. The police and super thought it was unusual that he valued his scriptures and journal more than his bike and camera, and they commented on it.

An elder who served in the Southwest said they were housed in a rough area known for crime and someone had been shot in front of his apartment building three days before he arrived. He felt scared. There were three hospitals in the neighborhood, and the sound of ambulance sirens kept him awake at night. He had frequent requests for blessings at the hospitals for Church members and for some non-members, too.

Daily Schedule

The Latter-day Saint Church recommends a daily schedule for missionaries, which is followed worldwide, with allowances made for certain local customs and practices such as siesta times, when practically all activity stops. The schedule is found in *Preach My Gospel*:

6:30 A.M.	Arise, pray, exercise (30 minutes), and prepare for the day.
7:30 A.M.	Breakfast
8:00 A.M.	Personal study: The Book of Mormon, other scriptures, doctrines of the missionary lessons, other chapters from *Preach My Gospel*, the *Missionary Handbook*, and the *Missionary Health Guide*.
9:00 A.M.	Companion study: share what has been learned during personal study, prepare to teach, practice teaching, study chapters from *Preach My Gospel*, confirm plans for the day.
10:00 A.M.	Begin proselytizing. Missionaries learning a language study that language for an additional thirty to sixty minutes, including planning learning activities to use during the day. Missionaries may take an hour for lunch and additional study, and an hour for dinner at times during the day that fit best with their proselytizing. Normally dinner should be finished no later than 6:00 P.M.
9:00 P.M.	Return to living quarters (unless teaching a lesson; then return by 9:30 P.M.) and plan the next day's activities (30 minutes). Write in your journal, prepare for bed, pray.
10:30 P.M.	Retire to bed.

Missionaries are to attend church services, district and stake meetings, and to view the semi-annual general conferences held in Salt Lake City if available. They are encouraged to invite non-members to attend services.

Initial Impressions and Adjustments

The first weeks in the field are a time of adjustment for missionaries: to their new life, their new role, and their new companion. They may experience a range of emotions including doubt, fear, and homesickness. They may be dealing with leftover emotional baggage. It may take time for them to adjust to being a missionary, and they may be aided or hindered in the process by how others perceive them; they receive positive reinforcement in the Latter-day Saint Church, where they are revered, whereas they may feel negative emotions from non-Mormons in the community. Learning to adjust to the many rules and regulations is a challenge for some, while learning to live with their trainer is one of the biggest and most important adjustments they will make, for that person holds the keys to their early success.

Some missionaries had vivid memories of their drive from the mission home to their new assignment with their trainer. One said she found it scary and that eighteen months sounded like forever, while another was so nervous she became sick to her stomach and her trainer had to stop the car. Another said she was impressed and somewhat amazed at the ease with which her trainer interacted with people and was able to bring the conversation around to the LDS message. They stopped at a gas station, and as the trainer was pumping gas she engaged the person at the next pump in a conversation about spiritual things. "I will never be able to do that," thought the new missionary. But she said eventually she could, and did, in many different and equally unusual contexts.

Missionaries' first impressions in the field may be that of unease. An elder serving in the early 2000s spoke of his discomfort when his trainer and he first arrived at their apartment. As he unpacked, he thought to himself that he didn't know anybody, he didn't know what he was doing, and he didn't know anything about the person he would be living with all the time. He decided it was "the weirdest" thing he had ever done in his life.

Recalling her feelings of inadequacy and panic when she arrived in the mission field, a sister said she was scared and in shock; she couldn't believe what she was doing, and she was wondering what she had gotten herself into. She felt inadequate and wished she had studied harder. Her sense of panic was heightened when she compared herself to her fellow missionaries, who seemed relaxed, excited, and prepared. She felt there was something wrong with her, that there was something she "didn't get." But then she settled down. She said: "I knew I had strong faith and if I did what was right, was obedient, and tried my hardest, Heavenly Father would help me. That was the one thing I always relied on—that God would help me if I did my part."

A few confided that once they arrived in the mission field and saw the realities of missionary life, they wanted to go back to the sheltered and predictable world of the MTC.

More than a few, elders as well as sisters, confessed to crying themselves to sleep that first night.

Homesickness can be a significant problem, and it can have an immediate onset. A sister said her departure from Salt Lake City was very painful. Her whole family came to the airport, she was the last to get on the plane, and she immediately felt homesick. She sat with her companion, who talked at length about her boyfriend, who wondered if they would get married when she returned.

The homesick sister just sat there and cried.

An elder serving in 2001 said he struggled with homesickness for the first few weeks. He often thought of home, of what he would be doing if he were there. Prayer and letters from home helped, as did coming to the realization that it was his choice to serve a mission, that no one forced him into it. He found there were days when he thought he couldn't face another, but the longer he held on and served, the easier it became.

An elder who served in California echoed the importance of receiving letters while in the mission field. He hadn't really been homesick, because he had been away from home before, but during the first month he wrote twenty-four letters to family and friends and received nothing in return. He eventually started receiving replies, but he felt "abandoned" that first month.

A sister from Nebraska and in the mission field a month when she talked to me said homesickness was an issue for her the first few weeks: she dreamt of home, her family, her work. She would wake up and it would dawn on her that she was on a mission, and she didn't want to be there. She moped; she wasn't talking to her trainer. She considered calling the mission president and telling him she was going home, but she didn't. Resolution came a few weeks later when she and her companion were returning from a teaching appointment. Quite unexpectedly, "a total sense of contentment" fell over her; she came to the realization that serving a mission was what she was supposed to do. While she thought of home thereafter, she was not as homesick as those first weeks. "I'm getting there," she reported during our interview.

Her advice for new missionaries suffering from homesickness: don't look back, because missionaries make it too hard on themselves if they continue to keep one foot at home and one foot in the mission field. "Just go for it," she said.

Some who experience ongoing homesickness call home, in spite of mission rules against it.

All missionaries, not just new ones, struggle when there are problems or issues back home, and this leads to frustration, because mission rules don't allow them to return home. They are so far away, and there is nothing they can do about it.

Being away from home during family holidays is hard on new missionaries. An elder who served in South America said his first Christmas in the field was one of the hardest days of his life, that he went into his bedroom and cried; it was one of the few times during his mission that he entertained thoughts of going home. He said the experience was common among new missionaries spending their first Christmas away from home and family. He got over it in a few days, and by the second Christmas it didn't even bother him.

Finances can be a problem if one companion has access to outside funds but the other doesn't. Parents are encouraged not to send their sons or daughters extra money, since it can create tension between companions. An interviewee told of having a companion who came from a wealthy family, who regularly ate steak for supper, while he struggled to afford more modest meals, even meals of rice and tomato soup.

It also takes time for missionaries to adjust to being misidentified. In stores, people will assume they are store employees since they are wearing nametags, but then there is the awkward moment when they say they don't know the location of an item and the person stares at them strangely. Missionaries say they eventually get used to these reactions.

Some say their appearance causes them to become the butt of jokes and derision. A self-conscious sister, a month into her mission, told of standing in line with her companion in a fast food restaurant, when four teenage girls in front of them started giggling and laughing at them. She asked her companion why they were doing it, and her companion looked her in the eye and said, "We are religious freaks, and don't you know?" It then struck her how much of a "people pleaser" she was, that she wanted people to like her and think she was normal. Thus she had a hard time at the beginning of her mission when she realized that people thought she was "a religious weirdo, one of those crazy Mormons, probably the seventh wife of someone."

A sister in 2001 said it helped her adjust to the idea of being a missionary when people in the Latter-day Saint Church began to respond to her in that role. She remembered as she was growing up that Church members felt adulation for missionaries and that they were beginning to react to her in a similar manner. People (especially youth) wanted to talk with her and be her friend. She said after being in the field a month, with everyone treating her like that, she thought maybe she was a real missionary after all.

Church members can certainly help in the adjustment process. A sister described her mother as a "missionary mom," someone who invited missionaries for frequent meals, took them places, and had them over at Christmas, Easter, and on their birthdays. She also went proselytizing with sisters. An elder who served in the early 1960s in New

York observed that members of the Church make a mission "survivable," while a sister praised the members where she was serving: "They give you rides, feed you, refer people to you, and are really nice." Such a close relationship with members is not always the case. An elder serving in Colorado in the early 1950s said missionaries had little contact with local members. In his words: "We just went in and worked the area."

Food/Eating

Food can be a memorable part of a missionary's experience. Some have never cooked before, and being on a mission forces them to plan, purchase, and prepare meals. It's common for members to invite missionaries for a meal in areas where the LDS Church is well-established and members can afford it, but such invitations may be rare in poorer areas or where there are few members. Missionaries generally appreciate such invitations, since it means they will probably have at least one good meal that day. In some cases they are fed too well and gain weight. Those in foreign lands frequently are faced with food they haven't tried, and in some cases can't identify, and so they tend to lose weight.

Missionaries are counseled to eat safe, balanced, and nutritious meals. An elder who served in California said his mission president and wife would look in the refrigerator during their periodic apartment inspections to make sure the missionaries were eating well. In preparation for their visit, the elders would stock the refrigerator with foods from various food groups. The visitors knew what they were doing and made comments to that effect: they were glad the elders would be eating well—at least for the next few days.

In areas where members can afford it and where there are sufficient numbers of them, missionaries may be invited to dinner many evenings a week. There may be sign-up sheets on the Church bulletin board where members can commit to feeding the missionaries on a particular date. Referred to as dinner appointments (or "D.A.s" by missionaries), it saves missionaries money, draws them into the community, and, for families with children at home, the missionaries' presence can serve as a motivator for children to serve a mission.

To help insure they don't commit social faux pas, missionaries may be coached by the mission president's wife on proper table manners. An interviewee had a trainer who passed down an ugly, polyester tie that he wore to dinner appointments. They called it "the bib." In case he spilled food on it, he could wash it afterwards.

Missionaries are held to strict expectations while eating in homes. They are reminded that they need to keep in mind that they are missionaries and that people (especially children) are watching them. They may not watch television, they should not be alone with younger members of the opposite sex, and they should not flirt. When talking with members at dinner, they should try to get members to give them names of friends or neighbors who might be interested in talking with the missionaries. (Ideally the member will go with them to the friend's house.) They should stay no longer than an hour; they are to share a spiritual message with the family, say a prayer, and then leave to continue working. Some say they find it difficult to eat, talk, plan, and motivate all in one hour, especially when members want to continue talking.

There have been instances when the practice has been abused, such as staying longer and socializing, watching television, or not returning to their tracting a soon as they are done eating. As a result, mission presidents have suspended the privilege throughout the mission until offending missionaries have committed to mending their ways. Once they understood it was a privilege not to be abused, they were permitted to engage in the practice again.

Eating out can create problems for missionaries who have a number of dinner appointments a week. Since Church members generally hold them in high esteem and want to serve their biggest and best meal of the week, missionaries assigned to the United States tend to gain weight. Elders spoke of ripping their pants because of weight gain. One said he gained fifty pounds on his mission. Two sisters said they felt bad not finishing their meals and refusing seconds, but they found that members were used to feeding elders, "who eat a ton," and they would pile food on their plates. The sisters couldn't finish eating it, and they gained weight.

Another challenge can be that they are served food they either don't like or it doesn't agree with them. Some told of feeding some of their dinner to the family dog under the table when the hostess went into the kitchen to get more food, of putting food in baggies in their backpacks, and of heaping food they didn't like on their companion's plate when the hostess was away from the table. An elder was served a thick, red steak at a member's home one evening, and he thought, "I can't eat this, but I can't decline it and be rude." So he cut it up and fed it to the cat sitting under the table. He continued talking, and the cat ate it. During the meal his companion, who hated peas, piled them on his plate when the hostess left the room.

Those from different parts of the country may be confronted with foods they have never eaten before. Lobsters present a challenge to missionaries new to Maine; they see them live before dinner and then struggle to figure out how to eat them after they are cooked. An elder told of spraying his hostess with shells while trying to crack a lobster claw. A sister from Utah had never eaten shrimp or scallops. She swallowed the shrimp whole, and she kept chewing the scallops, but she couldn't swallow them. When she started making strange faces, the twelve-year old daughter of the hostess asked her what was wrong and why she kept chewing. "Sometimes you just have to choke stuff down," added an elder. An elder from the East Coast serving in California spoke of similar issues while eating cow's tongue, cow intestine, and pig's feet.

Sisters and elders are always playing tricks and pranks on each other. In one instance elders left a frog in the sisters' bathtub, while in return the sisters baked the elders brownies laced with a laxative. An example I observed of the good-natured kidding that goes on is when I noticed a monthly dinner sign-up calendar on a bulletin board at a LDS meetinghouse, where members could sign up to have the missionaries to dinner. One of the calendars was for sisters and one was for elders. The sisters put a calendar twice the normal size on the bulletin board with "Sisters" written across the top, while next to it was a calendar they had shrunk so small that it couldn't even be written on, with the word "Elders" written on it.

Periodic Meetings with the Mission President

Missionaries meet individually with the mission president on a regular basis, typically every four to six weeks. It can take place at zone conferences, or he may come to the missionaries' apartment. Topics for discussion may include: the missionary's testimony; his or her self-understanding of what it means to be a missionary; insights gained from recent personal and companionship study; the review of a lesson plan developed for a current investigator; challenges and successes in finding and teaching investigators; discussion of the Book of Mormon and how to communicate its importance to investigators; if the missionary is learning a language, periodically interviewing her or him in the language; review Area Books and Daily Planners; discussion of companion relationships; and any physical or emotional issues.

The mission president may also do a visual inspection of the missionaries. He might tell elders to shave their sideburns, to get a haircut, or that they need to wear more conservative ties.

The personal interview is also a time when missionaries may share personal problems. Money is sometimes an issue. Some are not adept at managing their money, and in some cases their monthly allotment is more money than they have ever managed before. A mission president told of a young missionary who met with him on the tenth of the month, who said he had run out of money for the month. When pressed, the missionary admitted he bought a boombox with his monthly check. He had always wanted one but could never afford it. The mission president took the missionary and the boombox back to the store where it was purchased, explained the situation, and the missionary was given back his money.

The mission president also uses the interviews to identify missionaries who show potential to become effective leaders in the mission, including those who can serve as trainers, senior companions, district leaders, zone leaders, and A.P.s.

Depending on the size of the mission and where missionaries are assigned, they may only see the mission president at monthly zone conferences and during individual interviews.

Many interviewees developed very positive impressions of their mission president based on their personal interviews with him. An appreciative elder said his mission president always asked how he was doing and how he could help, and he gave good advice. An elder who served in Germany said his mission president had a way of working with missionaries, even troubled ones, and he had a good relationship with all of them. If companions were slacking off, he challenged them and said they should make a difference, and they would; he had a way of making them look at and face their issues. A thankful sister said she didn't leave the interview without feeling the mission president's love and spirit. Even talking to him on the phone made her feel "ten times happier." She felt the Spirit was really strong in his life.

"Greenies"

Missionaries are informally labeled as "greenies" while in their first area but lose the designation once they are transferred to a new area, typically after three or four months. (The term is not universal. New missionaries in Germany were introduced to me as "goldens" in 2000. Some mission presidents ask that the term "greenie" not be used.)

Newly arrived missionaries are a common target for good-natured greenie jokes played on them by fellow missionaries and by Church members. Serving green meals is popular: green milk and green pancakes for breakfast; green mashed potatoes, green beans, and green milk at dinner, served on green plates with green napkins. A new elder serving in England, when he commented on the green milk, was told all English milk is green because the grass is so green there. Another elder thought it must be St. Patrick's Day. A convert from a Middle Eastern country serving in the Southwest said on his first evening in the field he and his companion had dinner with Church members, and everything on the table was green. He initially didn't understand the symbolism, and when he asked why everything was green, they just laughed. But he figured it out later when he realized that he was the one who was "green."

A bewildered elder who served in the Northeast in the early 1960s said on his first day in the mission field as he, his companion, and two other elders knelt to pray, his companion said that since they pray so often, and it could be so time-consuming, they always prayed "by the numbers." Confused, the greenie kept his head bowed and didn't say a thing. After a pause, an elder said, "Number seven." There was another pause, and a second elder said, "Number three." "Number twelve," said the third elder. They then said "Amen" and stood up. The greenie didn't know what to do or say. They all then laughed and welcomed him to the mission.

Companions sometimes lure new missionaries into uncomfortable situations. A new elder and his trainer were to teach his first lesson to a supposed investigator, and he was made very uncomfortable because the investigator agreed with everything the trainer said but disagreed with everything the greenie said. He began to question his faith and his ability to teach. He eventually was told the "investigator" was actually a Church member.

Another common initiation rite is that under the guise of going to the home of a non-member who has expressed interest in hearing more about the Latter-day Saint Church, missionaries are confronted by an angry spouse or family member who doesn't want them there and who demands they leave. After a period of awkwardness, it is revealed that they are Church members. In one instance, the "irate" husband appeared with a baseball bat. The new missionary recalled: "I was never so close to wetting my pants during my whole mission as on that day." (Such experiences aren't always a joke. An interviewee told of literally being thrown out of a house by an irate, non-member father.)

His trainer told a new elder on his first day that they would be following up with a woman who had been given a Book of Mormon. She appeared at her door looking very angry, and the greenie assumed she would give it back and they would not return. He was prepared to say, "Have a nice day," and leave, when the woman grabbed his companion by the tie, dragged him into the house, and closed and locked the door. The greenie panicked, looked in the window, and pounded on the door. His companion yelled for help. The greenie ran to the car, and as he was leaving his companion came out of the house and said, "Oh, by the way, this is where we are having dinner this evening." The woman was a Church member.

Strange visitors will appear at the missionaries' apartment and eat from the fridge or ask to spend the night. They are Church members.

Mission presidents ask that such jokes not be played, or that initiations into the mission field be avoided. But missionaries do it anyway.

New missionaries also suffer from the lower status that being a greenie brings to the companionship. An elder said that as a greenie his trainer made him get up and shower first so that the trainer could sleep later. He also had to clean the toilet, and he had to clean the cockroaches out of the sink each morning. As the greenie, he had to do all of the things the trainer didn't want to do.

While new missionaries hold the lowest status in the mission, and while they suffer through good-natured practical jokes, it is recognized that they bring something positive to the mission field. A returned missionary who teaches at the MTC said missionaries just coming from the MTC are "spiritual giants" compared to those already in the field, who may be tired and discouraged. New missionaries are involved and ready to go, he said. An A.P. who served in Portugal said new missionaries arrived full of fire when he met them at the airport; the MTC "had cranked them up," they were full of "greenie fire," and they were ready to serve. They want to find people, baptize them, and build the Church. He said those who were willing to work were a great asset to the mission, and to him. Their energy motivated him and it strengthened his faith.

But "greenies," regardless of what they bring to the mission, will always be the butt of jokes. An A.P. reported that when he delivered new missionaries from the airport to the mission home, he would point to an airplane flying high overhead and ask, "Elders, how far away is that plane?" "Thirty-five thousand feet?" they would ask. "No," the A.P. would respond. "Two years."

Mission presidents, Assistants to the President, and trainers play important roles in the acculturation of new missionaries. They set a tone that can have a long-lasting effect on the missionaries' perceptions and experiences. Other forces are also at work that shapes their lives in the field, including myriad rules and learning to live with and adjust to many different companions over the length of their mission.

These serve as mirrors that force missionaries to look at themselves—their beliefs, attitudes, and self-perceptions—and they aren't always happy with what they see. We will now turn to these aspects of the missionary experience in Chapter 5.

CHAPTER 5

In the Mission Field: Rules, Relations, and Reflections

"People think we are just a bunch of robots in suits and ties. We are human, just like everybody else."

AN ELDER WHO SERVED IN NORTHERN NEW ENGLAND IN THE EARLY 2000'S

As at the MTC, missionaries in the field are held to strict standards of behavior and a rigorous daily schedule, and they are assigned a companion with whom they are always to be together. They can expect to be transferred to another area within their mission every three or four months, and they will be assigned a new companion every two to four months. While missionaries are responsible to the mission president and meet with him periodically, they may not see him very often; some missions are large, and missionaries may be based hundreds of miles from the mission office. Day-to-day responsibility for their activities thus rests entirely with the missionary. Most respond well to this freedom and responsibility, although some take advantage of the lack of daily oversight and bend the rules.

Missionaries face significant challenges. Living successfully with a companion twenty-four hours a day, seven days a week is frequently cited as the biggest hurdle. A small percentage goes home early for medical or emotional reasons, and some are sent home for flagrant infractions of mission rules. Except for serious illness, injury, or death, the worst fate that can befall a missionary is to be sent home early for moral infractions.

Missionaries also speak of gaining new knowledge and skills, of strengthening their testimonies, and of gaining self-confidence; they find it encouraging that the Latter-day Saint Church puts faith in them, their character, and their ability to serve on the front lines of its evangelistic endeavors, in spite of their youth. But this growth frequently takes time, and it only comes after they have struggled with their role, their companion, and themselves.

This chapter looks at the structure of the missionary program and how it shapes the lives of missionaries in the field. Chapter 6 will consider their day-to-day activities as they seek to find interested non-members; significant (and even greater) challenges accompany these efforts.

Living by the Rules

Missionaries get a foretaste of what life will be like in the mission field while still at the MTC; it is a life of discipline and structure, except for one very important difference—while discipline is imposed at the MTC, once in the field the motivation to follow the rules has to come from within. Since most missionaries live at a distance from the mission office and their time is unsupervised, self-discipline plays a key role in whether they remain faithful to the rules and they accomplish anything.

While adjusting to the rules may be a challenge and take time, it seems the vast majority of missionaries try to remain faithful. Indeed, they say the more they conform to the rules and assume responsibility for their actions, the better they feel about themselves and the more effective their work becomes. The reverse is also true. As a truthful missionary commented, if they don't keep the rules, if they don't study, if they don't care about people, it feels like "a weight on their shoulders." They feel responsible, for they believe that someday they will be judged before God about how they used their time, which creates "a huge amount of pressure" on them.

On a positive note, the missionary added, it is pressure that helps them grow spiritually.

Missionaries live under a number of rules and regulations. They are not allowed to date, watch television, listen to the radio, or see movies. They may only watch videos or DVDs approved by the Church. They may only listen to religious or classical music. The Church must authorize all reading material, including books and magazines. They are not to participate in musical groups, clubs, or athletic teams.

They are to avoid activities that hold the potential for personal injury. They are not allowed to swim, play football, ski, ride motorcycles or horses, ride in private boats or airplanes, climb mountains, or handle guns. They must avoid alcohol, tobacco, coffee, tea, and illegal drugs.

Missionaries are not allowed to have personal computers. They must use computers in public places such as libraries, and companions must sit side-by-side so each can see what is on the other's screen. They aren't allowed to play computer or electronic games or to engage in social networking. They are to write to their families on their day off (Preparation Day), but they must use the filtered Internet service provided by the Church, MyLDSMail.net. They are not allowed to use members' computers. They are reminded their primary purpose is to perform their missionary duties, not to stay in touch with family and friends back home.

They are not allowed to have personal cell phones, and they are severely restricted in who they may call on the mission-provided cell phone. They are not to phone friends or relatives, nor are they to communicate with people in their area except on Church-related matters. They are only allowed to receive calls from home or to make calls home—on Mother's Day, Christmas, and (in some missions) on Father's Day. Otherwise, the mission president must authorize all calls to or from home.

Missionaries are not allowed to leave their assigned area without permission from the mission president, and they are not allowed to return home for visits—even for emergencies. Family members, friends, and acquaintances are not allowed to visit missionaries in the field. Such visits are considered disruptive and can cause missionaries to lose sight of their primary responsibilities. Emergencies are to be reported to the mission president.

They are never to be separated from their companion, except in very specific circumstances: when in the bathroom; during a personal interview with the mission president; or during a companion exchange when they are paired with another missionary. They should always be within sight and hearing of each other, even when in a home or building. Companions are to sleep in the same bedroom (though not in the same bed). They are to go to bed and to get up together; they can't get up early or stay up late to be by themselves. It is for good reason that missionaries refer to their companion as their "shadow." It is also for good reason that a senior sister missionary said, "Thank goodness for the bathroom!"

Companions are told they have a responsibly to watch out for the physical and spiritual well-being of one another. If a companion appears to be straying from the mission rules and expectations, he or she should be given constructive criticism or guidance. If the behavior isn't corrected, the companion is to discuss it with the mission president. If a companion doesn't report serious violations of mission rules to the mission president, he or she may be subject to disciplinary action, along with the offending missionary. The Latter-day Saint Church has been quite aggressive in counseling members to avoid pornography. It is a frequent topic in Church publications. Missionaries are counseled to avoid it at all costs and to watch out for their companions in this area.

If a companion disappears, which is rare, but does happen, the mission president is to be notified immediately.

Missionaries are reminded that they are ambassadors of the Latter-day Saint Church and that their appearance and conduct can have a direct impact on their effectiveness as missionaries: if they take their appearance and work lightly, others will regard them lightly; if they take their appearance and work seriously, then others will regard them seriously. Thus they are to look, dress, and act in ways that reinforce their message, not detract from it. Elders are to keep their hair trimmed, above the collar and ears, they may not wear mustaches and beards, and they are to shave their sideburns below the middle of the ear. They should shave each day. They may not wear earrings, necklaces, or bracelets (save MedicAlert bracelets). Tattoos and nose rings are not allowed. They are to dress conservatively: dark business suits, white shirts, conservative ties.

The term "modest" is often used to describe sisters' appearance. Their hairstyle should be conservative and easy to maintain, and their makeup and jewelry be understated. Their clothing shouldn't be too tight or too loose, or transparent in any way, and it should not draw attention to any part of the body. The sisters' dress code was updated in 2011—away from drab colors and skirts that had to reach the mid-calf—to skirts below the knees and more colorful blouses, sweaters, and outfits. They may wear suits, skirt-and-blouse combinations, skirt-and-jacket combinations, dresses, or jumpers. They may not wear T-shirts, sweatshirts, or pants suits. Their clothes and shoes are to be kept neat and clean, and they are counseled to bathe frequently and use deodorant.

Missionaries should avoid slang and inappropriate language. Companions and fellow missionaries are never addressed by their first name, nickname, or surname alone. They should be addressed as

"Elder (Last Name)," or "Sister (Last Name)," even when companions are alone together. Church and missionary leaders should be addressed by their titles. Members and investigators are addressed as "Brother" and "Sister."[52]

Do missionaries live up to these standards? Yes and no. A sister received a call from the administrative assistant at the mission office informing her that her grandfather had died of a heart attack. She was tempted to call her parents and grandmother right away, but she waited until the mission president called back and gave her permission to do so. She was glad she waited, because she felt she had a better conversation since she had been given permission. "It's the obedience thing," she said.

Missionaries may not be able to live up to the standards, even if they try. Staying neatly dressed and well-groomed in a tropical climate is a case in point. A sister serving in Central America said when she and her companion left their house in the morning they looked like missionaries, but after a day of walking along muddy roads in the heat and the rain, they started to look "shabby," and it was hard to keep a good attitude because of it.

Some admit they don't keep every rule, every day. They say there are so many, and there are some that are so contrary to their personality, that they don't come naturally to them. They may try, but as one sister confessed, "I just can't do it." A returned missionary who admitted he was pretty lax about the rules (he especially liked to sleep late), said there was always a "feeling-out period" with a new companion, a time when he tried to gain a sense of just how strict or relaxed the new companion would be. Those who were more impressionable became more lax like him.

Missionaries admit that sometimes they don't act like they should, or like people expect them to. They are the first to acknowledge they aren't perfect, but Church members tend to think they are, or that they should be. Thus they find it a big responsibility for a young adult. Two outgoing and rather boisterous sisters said sisters are supposed to show "quiet dignity"—peacefulness, not laughing out loud, not cracking jokes, looking immaculate—which they found difficult. "Neither one of us has an ounce of quiet dignity," they said with a laugh.

And they were right.

Missionaries are sometimes surprised by how closely their behavior is watched, both by non-members and members. A bishop received a call from a non-member who reported two elders going to a movie the night before and they got in trouble for it. Two sisters were surprised and very upset when a Church member said they were observed gambling; a non-member saw them playing a game of bingo at a county fair, and he reported it to the member. The member told the sisters he felt they were setting a bad example. They pleaded ignorance. They said they had never played bingo before in their lives, and, yes, they each had put down a quarter with the hopes of winning a T-shirt they liked (which they didn't win), but it didn't occur to them that they were "gambling."

The sisters went through a great deal of turmoil, fearing they would be sent home for setting a bad example (they were not). One of the sisters observed, "Everybody's eyes are on us." Her companion agreed, saying people were constantly watching them.

When I asked if they would like to see some of the rules relaxed, such as being allowed to sleep in separate rooms and to go out by themselves, missionaries almost uniformly said, no, that the rules were for their own good. There would not be a problem if *they* slept alone and were allowed to go out, they said, but they suspected there were those who would abuse the rules if given that much freedom. They said the longer they were on their mission, the more they realized the rules were there for a reason; they had been established over the years based on the experiences of earlier missionaries. Thus they felt it was important that they conform to the rules.

"A good missionary is obedient," said one. "In obedience there is freedom," echoed an A.P.

There is also a sense of personal and spiritual responsibility. When commenting on the importance of obeying the rules and keeping the schedule, a sister said it was up to her whether her mission was going to be successful, and she found it "scary."

For most missionaries, having a companion helps them conform to the rules. An elder observed that he found the rules difficult, but having a companion always at his side ensured his strict obedience.

Non-Mormons comment on what they consider to be the isolated and sheltered lives of missionaries; they seem disengaged from the world, and non-Mormons question if that is a good thing. They ask if missionaries aren't shirking their civic responsibilities. Missionaries agree that they live in a bubble; they don't listen to the news, watch television, or read newspapers. But some say they prefer it that way. They agree they have to be good citizens and to be informed when they are "in the world," but, while on their mission, they have to stay focused on their work.

Non-Mormons seem especially interested in the rules missionaries live by. A sister said they may not be interested in their message, but people do ask about what missionaries can and cannot do. She had been asked if she could eat potato chips, why she had to be in by 9:30 P.M.—and was once asked if she wanted to go out for a drink later that evening. (This last question led to a discussion of the Word of Wisdom.) When she asked to use the bathroom of an investigator, the woman asked if she was allowed to go to the bathroom.

Companionships

As we saw in Chapter 3, missionaries are always teamed with a companion. It draws on Jesus's example of sending disciples out two-by-two (Luke 10:1), and it has a dual purpose: persuasion and protection. It is believed companions can strengthen each other's message; if two people attest to the truthfulness of a message, it will have a greater impact on the listener. Companions also provide mutual support and protection. Being paired with someone who shares their values and goals, they learn from and support each other during difficult times, such as dangerous situations, false accusations, and when others may try to tempt or harm them. It also protects them from themselves—from the temptation to ignore or bend the rules.

The trainer is the first of many companions missionaries have in the field. The time with the trainer generally lasts around three of four months, at which point the young missionary is assigned a new companion. Thereafter, missionaries can expect to have a new companion every two to four months.

Companionships are comprised of a senior companion and a junior companion, with the senior companion having served longer and having the final say on what they will do.

Those who move into the senior position are sometimes surprised at the amount of responsibility it entails. A rather relaxed elder who had just moved into a senior companion position, said he loved being a junior companion because he didn't have many responsibilities. As a senior companion he had to make calls, take the lead with investigators, and arrange baptisms. Initially he didn't like the extra work, but he grew accustomed to it and it helped him to "grow a bit."

An elder who served in Brazil said he was shocked when he was made a senior companion after only seven months in the field, when it became his responsibility to make decisions about things he hadn't thought about before; planning each day's schedule, working with leaders of the local church, arranging appointments, and planning baptisms. It was a shock, he said, because as a junior companion, "you walk 'behind' the senior companion in your mind." It helped him "grow a lot," he added, including making him more tolerant.

Another elder spoke of the challenges of being a senior companion, especially when a junior companion chose to remain disengaged. The junior companion would sit around, and when the senior companion would ask him what he wanted to do, the junior companion would say, "Oh, I don't know, you decide. You're the senior comp." He would make a decision, and the junior companion would complain about it. The senior companion found it stressful. He had to bring his junior companion along because he had to have him as a companion, but he found it drained his energy to tell the junior companion constantly, "Okay, let's go."

An elder who converted to the faith just a year before he went on his mission said he was surprised to discover, when he became a senior companion, that missionaries showed various levels of commitment; not all were dedicated and hardworking as he was and as he thought they would be. He began with the impression that all missionaries were going to be perfect and if asked to do something, they would do it. Nagging and being impatient with companions who didn't want to be there didn't work, and telling them what to do *certainly* didn't work.

In order to motivate his companions to get up, he stopped nagging them and instead he set an example as a positive role model. Some reacted positively and they developed a desire to follow his lead. He said he gained valuable leadership skills from the experience, but learning to be a motivator and a leader were some of the hardest aspects of his mission.

Others spoke of stresses and strains created by companions who had different work ethics. A sister who served in France said she didn't recall any missionaries who didn't want to be there, but she did recall (diplomatically) "some who were certainly more relaxed about exerting themselves than others." She found it frustrating. An elder who served in Brazil said he had some companions who weren't as hardworking, and it made things "kind of tough." A sister who served on the East Coast of the United States spoke of being assigned a companion who had been the companion of the least obedient sister in the mission. The new companion admitted they left the house at noon, "hung around," and watched television in members' homes. The senior companion informed her they were going to work hard, and they did. When they would go into members' homes where the television was turned on, she would ask them to turn it off. The mission president told her parents, "She is the boldest missionary we have."

Some I spoke with chafed at having to be junior companions. Two elders who served in Mexico reflected on their feelings about the junior/senior relationship. They hated being dependent on their senior companion, which was the case in the early days of the mission, since their companions' language faculties were better than theirs. They hated being subordinate to their companions' wishes, because their companions bossed them around. They felt like "little kids, when we weren't little kids." They had arrived at the MTC from military basic training and they were tired of being bossed around. But it also varied depending on who the senior companion was: some they found to be good and admirable, while others, the bossy ones, they didn't respect. The relationship also depended on what phase of the mission they were in. The authority relationship changed over time, because as they became more competent in the language and the work, they were more able to assert themselves and their preferences.

Living with someone all the time is frequently cited as one of the most difficult aspects of the missionary experience. Companions' personal habits and idiosyncrasies take on a magnified importance, which can lead to tensions in the relationship. Unless the tensions are addressed, they can escalate into eruptions, which can have a negative impact on the missionaries' work. Even those who get along well have to continually monitor their relationship. As an elder observed, it's like being married, except they don't get to pick their companion, and they can't walk away for a while.

Some companions are harder to get along with than others, depending on their personalities, their attitudes, and their habits. Interviewees spoke of companions who were arrogant, bullheaded, and selfish. An elder said a low point for him was living with a companion who was not living according to the rules. He tried to work with and help him, but "it was a struggle." Another spoke of being frustrated with a companion who didn't clean up after himself.

A sister said effectively communicating with her companion was a learning experience. Initially she wasn't very good at it. With a new companion every two to four months, she went through a similar process with each of them; she had to learn how to adjust to living with a new person, each with a different background, personality, and perspective on life. It always took time to get to know them, their habits and idiosyncrasies, and what bothered them. Initially she would let things bother her, but she wouldn't say anything. She would get upset, and her anger would build up, until finally she would explode. With time and each succeeding companion, she got better at knowing how and when to discuss issues so that she didn't hurt their feelings. She learned how to peacefully tell her companions, "You left your dirty dishes in the sink, and could you please wash them and put them away." It was a skill she was glad she was learning on her mission, so she could better communicate with her husband and children later in life. She felt the key was being patient with one another.

An elder who had "a complainer" for a companion spoke of its negative effect on him. He read from his journal: "I was really disgusted today. All that my companion could do was complain and I think everyone doesn't like a complainer. I let it get under my skin, so to speak, and I couldn't even talk to people. I realized I am going to have to fight to keep my enthusiasm and to build my testimony."

Sometimes things will build up until there is an eruption. A sister said she had a companion who left her hair in the shower, and she would have to go in later to clean it out with toilet paper. It made her so angry that she would be upset with her companion for the next hour. It eventually ended in a shouting match. An elder had a fistfight with a companion over groceries; the companion kept eating his food. After the fight, they agreed they wouldn't tell anyone.

While these reactions are rather extreme, they are instances where a number of irritations festered over time until they eventually got out of control. A sister summarized the dynamics with companionships simply and distinctly: "Some people you get along with, and some you don't."

Even companions who are easier to get along with wear on each other over time. An elder said there were times when little things bugged him, and his companion would do them over and over again, and over a three month period it became irritating. A sister said she never fought with any of her companions, but small habits had a way of magnifying themselves. She gave the example of wanting to work hard and get a lot done each day, but she had a companion who always "walked at a snail's pace," which she found to be a challenge. An elder had an opposite experience with a companion's irritating walking habits: the companion intentionally walked one step ahead of him, always.

Missionaries also face challenges when their companions are ill or when they are mentally or physically challenged. If a companion is ill, the companion cannot stay alone in the apartment. Both companions have to remain together indoors, unless a Church member of the same sex can be found to stay with the sick companion while another Church member of the same sex can be found to go proselytizing with the companion who is well. This may not be an issue for short-term illnesses, but some interviewees had companions who were ill for several weeks or who had ongoing medical issues that required frequent trips to the doctor. The healthy companion frequently became frustrated, impatient, and wanted to get out and "do the work." Some companions suffered from mental illness, which also kept them both indoors.

Missionaries who the mission president perceives as being especially supportive of people with physical or mental illnesses may be assigned successive companions with these conditions, or they may keep the same companion for a longer period of time than normal. A distressed sister who was assigned a succession of companions with health issues expressed her frustration and concern to the mission president: she wasn't able to do the work because of this, so couldn't she be assigned to someone else? The president said he understood her frustration, but he felt she was the most sensitive and most supportive among the sisters. He was sorry for the strain it put on her, but it was best for the troubled missionaries.

"I need you to help me," he said, "for you are a strong missionary. You are the only one who can do it."

The interviewee frequently cried herself to sleep because it was so hard, and because she wanted to do the work. She said she needed to talk to "a mom" at times, and she would call the mission president's wife. The president would come on the phone and build her up, telling her she was a good missionary and that he would try to work it out. This went on for three months and she cried each time she met with the president. He would apologize, but he told her she was the only one who could do it.

An elder who served in Switzerland said he had been assigned a number of missionaries who were struggling, including an elder whose girlfriend wanted him to come home and get married, and an elder whose non-member parents kept writing and telling him to come home because he was wasting his time and their money. He found it a challenge, but the mission president felt he would be a good influence on the struggling missionaries. Another elder said he was assigned companions who were struggling, but for the opposite reason: they didn't want to be there, but their family and girlfriend had pressured them to serve.

While missionaries face challenges when their companion has physical, mental, or motivational issues, they do learn from the experience. A sister with a companion who had a lot of emotional problems confessed it was hard to have patience and to treat her with respect. She did so outwardly, she said, but her battles were inward, "in my mind and in my heart," and she learned patience from it. An elder had a companion who had a physical issue and initially it bothered him, but from the experience he learned to be kinder and more patient. A sister whose companion was sick a lot said there were days when it was very hard, but it was those times when she grew the most, because she was forced to address her reactions.

The Latter-day Saint Church recognizes that it is difficult for missionaries to live around the clock with people they don't know and may not choose as roommates or friends, and it counsels them to communicate with one another; if there are issues, they should discuss them and work through them. They are told to focus on the positive aspects of their companions and to not criticize them behind her or his back.

While they should confront concerns as they arise, the Church also says there should be a formal time each week when issues are addressed. They are to hold a "Companionship Inventory," which is typically held on Friday morning. They are counseled to discuss all aspects of their missionary experience at this session: their work, their goals, their relationship, strengths, challenges, and ways to improve. Companions are to share their perceptions of their companion's strengths and to ask for suggestions of how they can improve themselves. They are to discuss specific concerns that keep them from working as a team or from being obedient. They are to work through conflicts and to set goals for how to improve their work and their relationship. Honesty, combined with sensitivity, is encouraged.[53]

Two mature elders described companionship inventory sessions they had held with companions. Taken together, they had had twenty different companions. The process involved putting issues on the table and discussing them, with the goal that companions learned to communicate and relate. They said the extent to which the goal was achieved varied depending on the companion. In some cases, issues remained unaddressed, and they tried to ignore them. In some cases, there was silence. In some instances, one of the elders wanted to discuss the issues, but his companion did not. The interviewee said he would ask what he could do to improve their companionship, and the companion would say, "Oh, nothing." But there were also situations that were addressed and corrected. They pointed to small things, such as not putting the cap back on the toothpaste or one always pouring a larger glass of orange juice, which had festered into bigger frustrations and eruptions. These they were able to address and remedy.

The process can be painful, they said, because they are asking their companion to tell them what they need to do to improve, and, conversely, they are telling their companion the same thing. Concerns may relate to their teaching and how they interact with others. In one instance an interviewee said he had to point out to a companion that he wasn't a very good listener, while a companion pointed out to him that he interrupted investigators when they spoke.

On a positive note, an adaptable sister said since it is a two-way street, she had to be willing to change, too, so she learned a lot about herself in the process. Another sister said she made a point of trying to learn at least one new thing from each companion.

Companion inventories aren't only negative; they are also to let companions know what they do well, be it being a good cook, a good teacher, or a good listener. Reflecting on their multiple companionships, two elders agreed it was a good experience to learn to live with another person and that the companionship inventory was a good thing. "It gets things out so that at the end you can shake hands and say, 'Let's go do the work.'"

While all have issues with their companions at some point, most seem to work through them. But some don't; they may experience the spiraling effect of poor communication, frustration from daily rejection, and boredom—such small irritations can erupt into major confrontations. In cases where companionships break down, it requires reassignment to new areas and new companions. A stubborn elder said he had a companion he couldn't get along with, and vice versa. Each had irritating personal habits, each did things the other didn't like, and "they were at each other's throats" for the two months they were together. They eventually informed the mission president, and he transferred them to different areas and different companions.

Missionaries recognize that unresolved strains in their relationship can have an adverse effect on their missionary effectiveness. A sister who served in Japan said nothing makes the process fail more quickly than tension between companions.

Another sister said if she and her companion had an argument and went into an investigator's home before it was resolved, the investigator could sense it. "They know," she said. A third sister said given the sensitive nature of what they were teaching, companions need to be in harmony. She said people could sense if companions don't get along. "They won't listen to you," she said. "You are an odd couple, trying to be nice."

Interviewees also spoke of the many positive aspects of companionships. An accommodating elder said living with a companion was his first experience of trying to love someone he didn't necessarily like, so he started to learn to care for people. An elder in Mongolia said getting along with a companion is the hardest part of the missionary experience, but because of it he felt he would be a better Church member. Many said learning to live with a companion was excellent preparation for marriage.

An eternally optimistic elder agreed there are challenges in living with anyone all the time; if missionaries look for the negatives they will find them, but if they focus on the positives, they will find them, too. He learned something of value from every companion. His advice: look for the positives, and you will find them.

Interviewees discussed other positive dimensions of their companionships. A thankful sister who served in Spain described her companion as being the only constant she had in a very fluid situation, while a sister serving in Northern New England said she appreciated having a companion because it was good to be with someone who knew what she was doing and who shared similar values and ideas.

A perceptive elder said that on occasion, companions may need to sort through their differences before they can arrive at their commonly shared beliefs and values. To an outsider, missionaries may look the same and act the same. "When you look at us with our white shirts, ties, and suits, we look like a bunch of robots," he said; but what struck him about his companions was how different each had been. Some were more outgoing, while some were more introverted. They included: "the 'athlete type'; the 'math type'; the 'whatever-I-don't-care type'; and the 'it's-my-way-or-nobody's-way type.'" They all had different interests, he added, but the thing that bound them together was that they shared the same goal as far as the mission was concerned. Other than that, companions could be as different as night and day.

Interviewees also understood some things wouldn't change and that they had to remain philosophical about their situations. An elder said he learned to adjust; there were times when little things his companion did irritated him, but he knew he just had to live with him for a while. It was not going to be forever, although things started to wear on him (like the companion who didn't clean up after himself). Another elder said he had a companion who was very different from him (the companion was very athletic, and he wasn't), and they didn't see eye-to-eye on much of anything. If he had a problem with his companion, he would bring it up at the weekly inventory. If things improved, then he was fine, but, if not, he would bring it up again at the next inventory. If things still didn't improve, he just lived with it. They agreed to disagree, and he was fine with that. "Some things you just have to let go," he observed. "It is a sign of maturity."

Missionaries who described themselves as "a private person" chafed at the loss of personal space that came with having to live all of the time with a companion. They tended not to want to display their emotions in front of others, and it bothered them that they didn't have a choice. A sister said she had a pretty high tolerance for things that annoyed her, but what she didn't have a high tolerance for was when she couldn't be by herself. If she was having a hard time, she didn't want other people to know it. She was a very private person as far as emotions went, and if she hid emotions from her companion, her companion knew something was wrong. The companion wanted to know what the problem was, and she didn't want to tell her, but she had to be with her. She described it as being "really tough."

She already knew what she would do once she returned home: "I am going to sit, *by myself*, in a room, *by myself*, and do whatever I want, *by myself*!"

Elder/Sister Relations

The tensions, as well as the growing respect, seen between sisters and elders at the MTC carry into the mission field. Younger elders can seem immature to sisters, verbal battles may occur, and they may have different views of the world. A sister recounted that when some elders played what sisters thought was an immature joke on them, they said: "We are on a mission, and you aren't supposed to act this way!"

But over time both come to appreciate the other. Part of the issue is that there is a huge maturation difference between a male in his late teens and an older female (especially when sisters had to wait to serve until they were twenty-one). A sister said she observed considerable growth take place during the elders' missions, especially in their people skills and leadership skills. Her companion added, "You basically watch them grow up." Another sister said the relationship with elders depended on how the elders acted. She could tell they were younger, especially when there were several of them together. But she said they usually became close friends, even best friends. "Then they don't seem young and they have the Spirit with them and they are good, really good. It's good to have elders."

A sister who served in California said she had mixed relations with elders, depending on how mature the elders were. Some she thought were fantastic; they took their callings seriously and tried to do their best. They were there when she needed help. Some she thought really needed to do some growing up; they seemed so young, and they didn't know how to behave. Some were slackers. For the most part, she had a good experience with elders—as long as they were following the rules and not doing "stupid stuff."

It remains to be seen what effect having even younger eighteen-year-old elders in the mission field has on elder/sister relations. The same can be said for younger, nineteen-year-old sisters.

Service

Since the early 1990s, missionaries have been expected to provide up to four hours of community service each week in activities that may or may not be related to the Latter-day Saint Church or Latter-day Saint Church members. All community service normally takes place during the day on weekdays; the mission president must approve them, and companions are to stay together during the service activity. They should not put themselves in danger or in compromising situations. In order to preclude the potential for legal action, they are not to serve where they will have direct contact with children, as in day-care centers or schools. (This is a twenty-first century change. Interviewees who served in previous decades spoke of serving in schools and orphanages and of coaching young athletic teams.) While they may not proselytize during service activities, conversations with non-members may lead to discussions about the LDS Church. The immediate supervisor of the activity determines whether the missionary nametag may be worn during the service activity and whether missionaries may talk about their religious duties.

Interviewees spoke of volunteering in hospitals, soup kitchens, secondhand clothing stores, and nursing homes and of teaching English classes, mowing grass for elderly members and non-members, and assisting in disaster and emergency relief work. Missionaries are frequently enlisted to aid in disaster relief, including the delivery of supplies and cleaning up debris after hurricanes, tornadoes, earthquakes, floods, and fires. They wear distinctive yellow T-shirts and vests with a logo showing two hands and the words "Mormon Helping Hands." Almost all say they enjoy the community service aspect of their mission. They see it as yet another dimension of their role as missionaries; it gives them something different to do, and in most cases they see tangible results from their efforts, such as shoveling snow or helping clean up after a flood. This is in contrast to their proselytizing efforts, where they don't always see obvious results. There is also a public relations aspect to their engagement in the community: it contributes to a positive image of missionaries and of the Latter-day Saint Church. They are "those nice young Mormon missionaries who have come to help."

A service-minded elder who served in Japan said he and his fellow missionaries went on health drives, and they did service projects for those with special needs. If there was a natural disaster, the mission president immediately told them to go and offer help. He said he and his fellow missionaries were pleased to help, because they perceived themselves as servants, and this was an example of it. They would sometimes go for weeks without having to buy fruit, because people were so appreciative of their efforts and would give them fruit baskets in thanks.

An elder who served in England said he thought serving people and helping them in whatever way he could is what the gospel of Jesus Christ is all about. He said people didn't realize it, but missionaries were there to serve them. He cited a passage from the Book of Mormon that he said played a key role in his mission: "And behold, I tell you these things that ye may learn wisdom; that you may learn that when ye are in the service of your fellow beings ye are only in the service of your God"(Mosiah 2:17).

An elder who served in California said he and his companion took an aggressive approach to service. When they opened a new area, they started by going door to door, telling people that they were missionaries and that they wanted to help them, for free, whether it was mowing their lawn, weeding their garden, or washing their car. He said it was amazing to see people's looks; many would respond, "Are you serious?" People would say they didn't have any money to pay them, and the missionaries would say they couldn't accept money or donations (maybe a sandwich for lunch, but no money). It "threw them for a loop," he reported, and they ended up helping a lot of people. After pruning an older lady's trees and helping with her garden, she said: "Boys, nobody could be prouder of you than I am. Not even your moms. I am so proud of you." It made them feel good to do things like that, said the elder; she needed help, and they were able to provide it. And they didn't make her listening to their message a condition of their helping; in fact, he said, they didn't teach her any of the lessons, and that was fine. It was purely service, and it was a way to help out in the community. It was a way for people to get to know them, and it worked.

Preparation Day, or "P-Day"

Each week (frequently on Mondays) missionaries are given a day off from normal proselytizing activities: Preparation Day, or "P-Day." On this day they attend to personal matters such as laundry, haircuts, writing home (they are told to write home once a week on Preparation Day, but to limit other letter writing or emailing), grocery shopping, and cleaning their apartment. It is a time to get some exercise and pursue cultural interests. It is also a day that makes mission presidents very nervous, since injuries and wayward behavior occasionally occur on these days.

Their day begins with their usual personal devotions, and they are then free to pursue their P-Day activities. While it is a different routine, missionaries are advised to plan P-Day just as carefully as they plan a regular day. As with any other day, companions are required to stay together. They return to their normal proselytizing schedule at 6:00 P.M. that evening.

They are encouraged to exercise on P-Day but are not to do anything that might injure them. They are allowed to play basketball, though they do experience their share of injuries. I encountered two American missionaries in St. Petersburg, Russia, and one of them was on crutches. As we passed on the sidewalk, I said, "Basketball?" He looked surprised and then said, "Yes." An A.P. who is an avid basketball player and who confessed to being very competitive and aggressive on the court, sustained injuries in two successive games; the first required thirteen stitches to his forehead, and the second required six stitches under his eye. His mission president looked at him and said if he got one more stitch there would be no more basketball in the mission—and if that happened, he would not be very popular with the other missionaries. The A.P. became a little less aggressive on the court after that.

Even when missionaries do things as instructed on P-Day, things don't always turn out as hoped. An elder who served in England spoke of playing basketball on P-Day, of obeying all the mission rules, including playing half-court instead of full-court, and, as they did before they started any physical activity, they began with a prayer and asked that no one get hurt. Unfortunately, he fractured his fibula, and, as he lay on the floor, he found it ironic that he was the one who had offered the prayer.

Missionaries are encouraged to engage in cultural activities on P-Day and to visit museums, art galleries, historical sites, zoos, special exhibits, and cultural centers. They generally enjoy these outings. In an unfortunate and bizarre incident, a lion mauled an elder serving in Guatemala when he went too close to the lion's cage at a zoo. His arm and a leg were seriously injured.[54]

They are advised to wear clothing appropriate for their P-Day activities, to remain neat and clean looking, and to not pass up opportunities to proselytize, even if it is their day off.

P-Day has psychological and emotional benefits. An elder who served in Canada in the late 1990s said missionaries need to have a day "when they can ease the tension"; they are under so much pressure that little things can "set them off." He said they need to recoup from the emotional distress of continual rejection.

Mission presidents worry about P-Days. Not only do accidents occur and missionaries are injured, but some use the time to engage in forbidden activities. For those who bend the rules and are caught, consequences follow, and there is a wealth of stories, some true and some apocryphal, that shows the consequences if missionaries do things they shouldn't.

Apocryphal and True Missionary Stories: Designed to Keep Missionaries in Line

There is a rich tradition of missionary stories in the Latter-day Saint Church, which recount the adventures and misadventures of missionaries. While some are probably apocryphal, they still convey clear meanings and serve clear purposes—warning them that if they disobey, they will be caught and punished.

A popular story has missionaries wanting to go to a major league baseball game on their Preparation Day. To do so means leaving their mission area, something they are not allowed doing without the consent of the mission president (which they know he won't give). Since the president's office is one hundred miles away, the missionaries believe they can get away with it, so they leave their mission boundaries and attend the game. During the game a foul ball comes in their direction, and one of the missionaries makes a spectacular one-handed catch to the thunderous applause of the crowd. His catch is replayed numerous times on the giant screen. As luck would have it, a Church member from the elder's area is watching the game on television. He sees the spectacular catch, knows the elder is breaking mission rules, and calls the mission president to report the misbehavior. The mission president and A.P.s are waiting at the apartment when the missionaries return, and they receive a severe reprimand.

Another popular story has missionaries wanting to go on a two-week vacation. They feel they have earned the break, given the stresses of their work. They want to go to the ocean, which is outside their mission area. They know the mission president won't approve the trip, so they devise a plan to make him think they are faithfully working during the time they are away. Missionaries are required to submit weekly activity reports, and their plan is to make up two reports: one for their first week away, and the second for the second week. They carefully date the reports (one a week ahead and the other two weeks ahead), place them in stamped envelopes, and instruct their landlady to send the first report at the end of the first week, and the second report at the end of the second. Unfortunately, she sends both reports at the same time, thus alerting the mission president that something is awry. The mission president awaits them when they return, with their bags packed. They are sent home.

An elder who served in Japan in the 1990s said the story is told in just about every mission. The missionaries went to South Korea in the version he heard, and he and his fellow missionaries believed it had actually happened.

While the above stories may be apocryphal, the following one *is* true. Two elders in upstate New York were meeting with an investigator who wanted to go to New York City, which was outside the mission boundaries. The missionaries left a message on their answering machine covering themselves. They spent the weekend in the city and thought they had gotten away with it. But the investigator sent pictures of them in front of the Statue of Liberty to the mission president, not knowing they were not allowed to be there. The elders were chastised.

The message is always clear in these stories, whether they actually occurred or not: obey the mission rules, because if you don't, you will get caught and will be in serious trouble.

Continuing Education

Missionary continuing education is an important feature of their time in the field, and it is achieved through personal study, companion study, district meetings, and zone conferences. The goal is to increase their knowledge and skills and to strengthen their testimony. During personal study, missionaries increase their knowledge of Church beliefs and practices through studying *Preach My Gospel*, reading the "standard works" of the Latter-day Saint Church (the Book of Mormon, the Holy Bible, *Doctrine and Covenants*, and *Pearl of Great Price*), and through studying the approved "mission library" (*Jesus the Christ*, *Our Heritage*, *Our Search for Happiness*, and *True to the Faith*).[55] Particular attention is given to the study and understanding of the Book of Mormon, followed by the New Testament and, to a lesser extent, the Old Testament. Emphasis is placed on the Book of Mormon, since it is new to investigators and central to the missionaries' message. Investigators are generally more familiar with the New and Old Testaments.

Companion study focuses on building a positive relationship between companions, sharing insights gained from one's personal study, devising lesson plans for current investigators, and planning the day's activities. District meetings occur weekly and are attended by missionaries in the district (generally four to eight missionaries, both elders and sisters). The district leader plans the meetings with the help of the district members and the A.P.s, and the goal is to provide mutual support through mini training sessions, updates on work with investigators, success and challenges in the district, and insights gained from personal and companion study.

A number of districts together form a "zone," and the mission president calls zone conferences approximately every three months. The mission president and the A.P.s organize them. Topics can include: motivational talks by the mission president and A.P.s.; short presentations by missionaries on scriptural and doctrinal topics; and small group work in which missionaries discuss theological subjects, teaching techniques, and proselytizing strategies. They may study particular topics in *Preach My Gospel*, including how to teach, what to teach, and how they can become better missionaries. It may include guest speakers, including recent converts reflecting on their conversion experience and the missionaries' role in it.

Individual mission presidents approach the continuing education of missionaries in a variety of ways. They are concerned that missionaries gain knowledge of the scriptures, Church beliefs, and the lessons so that they can communicate effectively with investigators. Special attention is given to new missionaries and how their trainers can help them. One mission president I spoke with put together a study guide that was spread over the first two months after arrival. Referred to as "certification," it included practice presenting the lessons to a member or non-member, memorizing forty-two scriptures from the lessons, and a list of "objection" questions missionaries get asked, such as: "Why is there a need for the Book of Mormon? Isn't the Bible enough?" "I don't believe in modern day prophets, including Joseph Smith. Why do we need him?" "I have already been baptized. Why do I need to do it again?"

Both trainers and new missionaries find this type of guidance helpful. A new missionary commented: "I am glad for certification. After the clear guidelines of the MTC, it is good to have some direction and structure, to have help setting goals."

Transfers

Missionaries can expect to be moved to another location within the mission boundaries every two to four months, at which time they are assigned a new companion. They have no say in the matter. The mission president, with help from his A.P.s, decides when the missionaries will be transferred and where they will be assigned. Missionaries typically don't have much advance notice. Some mission presidents don't want missionaries to inform their local congregations and investigators that they are moving until the last moment; they want to avoid going-away parties and tearful farewells, as well as people forming too-close relationships with missionaries.

Emergency transfers, or "E.T.s," take place when necessary, typically when there are issues between companions or between missionaries and members or non-members. An A.P. described the process: typically they received a call from a companion who said they needed to transfer Elder Smith, or Sister Jones, because a local person was showing a romantic interest in him or her, or vice versa. Occasionally the missionaries themselves made the call, which the A.P. appreciated.

They always respected the missionary who made the call, and they followed through on the request before it became a problem. An attractive sister who served in Central America received a number of emergency transfers, because local men followed her around and said they loved her, they wanted to marry her, and they wanted her to teach them. Some of her transfers took place in the middle of the night.

Being responsible for transfers gives A.P.s a new and different perspective on how things operate in the mission and in the Latter-day Saint Church. An A.P. who served in Germany said he and his fellow A.P. were in charge of assigning transfers and choosing senior companions. They worked at large wallboards with cards for every missionary, which included a picture, areas previously served, and a list of previous companions. They moved them around based on their understanding of the needs of the mission, the missionaries' previous assignments and their personalities.

The A.P. said in the process of doing this it occurred to him that when he was a missionary in the field and notice of a transfer came, his first thought was that God wanted him somewhere else. He had never really thought about the mechanics of how it worked. But suddenly *he* was deciding where missionaries were to be assigned, and he asked himself—how did he know where God wanted them to go? He and his fellow A.P. prayed before, during, and after the process, but it was a revelation to him that there was "no pillar of light" telling them what to do, that there was "no mysterious hand" moving the cards around. "The way God works is through us," he said, "and that is true at any level of the Mormon Church. We all have the same tools to work with. We are given revelation, but we have to work for it."

Girlfriends and Boyfriends

Missionaries are prohibited from dating or entering into relationships in the mission field. They are also advised not to enter into relationships prior to the mission, because it has been found that girlfriends or boyfriends waiting at home are a distraction to those serving in the field. Some begin their mission trying to maintain a long-distance relationship (for elders it is frequently their high school sweetheart) with expectations of marriage after returning home. But the vast majority of these relationships fizzle out, some as late as one or two months before the end of the mission; the missionary can return home only to find his significant other married to someone else. Both sisters and elders spoke of this experience during their interviews.

Very few relationships last the entire two years and end in marriage. Only three interviewees had this experience (two were a couple before they each went on a mission). In the process of breaking up missionaries often receive or send the infamous "Dear John" or "Dear Jane" letter.

A sister serving in Northern New England in the early 2000s described a typical scenario for receiving a "Dear John" or "Dear Jane" letter. She and her boyfriend wrote faithfully each week for a year, repeating their undying love for each other. But then his letters stopped for a month. His next letter indicated he had met someone new whom he was dating seriously, and he wanted to call off the relationship with the missionary. A month later he announced they were engaged, and a week later she received a wedding announcement.

She said she didn't anticipate it happening, and she was surprised how quickly things changed; he had only known the new girlfriend for two or three months. Looking back on the experience, she knew it was the right thing to do, but it wasn't easy at the time. Each destroyed the other's letters and pictures.

Most interviewees who entered the mission field with a significant other back home and who received "the letter" spoke of a similar quick pattern of events. They also spoke of how difficult it was emotionally. One described the experience as the lowest point of his mission, while another had a friend "who never really recovered from it." Another had a friend who had even set a date for the wedding. He was "Dear Johned," and it "destroyed him emotionally." He returned home a month later, though he had a full year left to serve on his mission. An elder who served in the early 1960s said he really liked his girlfriend and had plans of marrying her upon his return, but he told her if she found someone who loved her more than he did before he returned, she should marry him.

He reported, with dismay, "And she did!"

Most who received such letters while serving their mission—while acknowledging that it could be painful—eventually said that it was probably for the best, because it allowed them to stop thinking about home and to focus their full attention on their mission. Among interviewees who didn't have a girlfriend or boyfriend back home, the general consensus was that long-distance romances were not a good idea for a variety of reasons, the most important being that it was a distraction from the work at hand. An elder said when his companion received a letter from his girlfriend telling him how much she loved him and how she couldn't wait until he returned home, the elder wouldn't be able to work for two days, because he would be thinking of her.

Many also felt that it is unfair to both parties to try to keep the relationship going from a distance. An elder spoke of a friend who wrote his girlfriend throughout his mission, and she him, but after he returned home and they had one date, they called it off; they both had changed so much that they realized they had little in common. "What a waste," observed the elder. "He didn't give his mission his undivided attention, and she sat home alone for two years."

Sometimes it is the missionary in the field who calls off the relationship. An elder said his girlfriend said she wanted to be "part of his mission" and they should talk every week. Missionaries are not allowed to make such calls, and it was too much of a distraction for him. He "Dear Janed" her.

Couples frequently engage in ritualistic counting while on a mission, counting the days until they are together again. An interviewee had a boyfriend on a mission who gave her a jar of M&Ms, one for each day he was gone. She was to eat one each day, and he would return the day the jar was empty. But she eventually "Dear Johned" him and ate the remaining candy all at once.

Traditions

Missionaries engage in traditions that contribute to a sense of community in the mission. Some are unique to particular missions or areas, while some are practiced worldwide. They can include serving others on Christmas day and giving them presents (Christmas is typically a difficult day for missionaries), leaving messages and autographs on apartment message boards and furniture when transferring, swapping clothing with fellow missionaries, and ritualistically destroying worn-out clothing (typically at six-month intervals).

An elder who served in Paris said he and his companion weren't invited to members' homes on Christmas, so they started their own tradition of baking yogurt cakes and taking them to people in the area. An elder and companion serving in Singapore baked cinnamon buns and distributed them on Christmas to members and non-members alike. They approached a man on the street and said, "We have a gift for you." The man responded, "No one has a gift for me." The elders gave him some buns, and he went away, crying. An elder who served the Spanish-speaking population in California said he and his companion pooled their money at Christmas and bought presents for each of seven members of a Church member's family who was struggling financially and who otherwise would not have a Christmas for the children. Other Church members donated gifts and a turkey, which the missionaries delivered. The elder said it was one of the best Christmases the family had ever had, and him, too.

Traditions are also carried on in missionary apartments. When missionaries have stayed in the same place for years, there may be collections of ties, clothes, and a quote wall. They will frequently sign their bed or bureau when vacating an apartment, leaving their name, the months they served in the area, and where they were from. An elder who saw it practiced both in California and Kentucky said the furniture looked like the autograph page of a school yearbook. He could see evidence of missionaries who had served eight to ten years earlier.

There is a tradition of sharing clothing among missionaries. An elder described it as a "barter economy." They get tired of their clothes, and sisters trade dresses and blouses. They then check to see who is wearing their swapped clothing at district meetings and zone conferences. Elders' ties are the only thing of variety they can control, and tie swapping is common. One described how they each threw three ties into a pile and then took three others back. Trading ugly ties is also popular. One sister had the reputation of cutting off elders' ties with scissors if she didn't like them.

Many missionaries engage in rituals of destroying worn-out articles of clothing at six-month intervals, with each interval representing a particular milestone in the mission. For elders, six months equals a "bump" (they have gotten over the initial adjustment to the mission); twelve months equals a 'hump" (they are halfway through and headed down the other side); eighteen months equals a "slump" (they are getting tired and perhaps thinking about home, but they still have six months to go); and twenty-four months equals a "dump" (they are sent home). At six months elders may burn a tie, at twelve months a white shirt, at eighteen months a pair of shoes, and at twenty-four months, when they return home, they may destroy a suit. At six months, sisters may burn a pair of nylons, at twelve months a pair of shoes, and at eighteen months they may cut a dress into pieces, write a message on each piece, and pass them among sisters.

None of these clothes are worth saving and taking home because they are worn out.

These traditions are practiced worldwide. Occasionally these rituals go awry; an elder spoke of burning a hole in a balcony rug while burning his white shirt.

An elder described how he took delight in destroying his mission suit because he had ripped his pants on multiple occasions—in a bike accident, in a car accident, and when he had gained weight. An elder who served in Paris in the early 1970s said the evening before they returned home they took their threadbare suits and holding the two legs, ripped them apart at the crotch. Pictures are frequently taken to commemorate these events.

The mission president and his wife may participate in similar (but less dramatic) rituals. Collages, wall hangings, or quilts may be made from pieces of sisters' dresses and elders' ties, with their signatures on the backs of the pieces.

Unusual Experiences

Missionaries occasionally have unusual experiences for which their Church background and the MTC haven't prepared them. A Uruguayan sister serving in North Carolina told how she and her companion were asked by a Spanish-speaking Church member to be present at the birth of her baby. They remained with her during the nine hours she was in labor, translated for her, coached her during the delivery, and watched the baby being born. A sister who served in France told how she and her companion had to dress the body of a Church member for burial. "That was a pretty grim experience for someone our age," recalled the sister. When two sisters passed a house in the winter of 2015 in Maine, a man who had been on his roof shoveling snow experienced a heart attack. His wife screamed for help, and one of the sisters climbed onto the roof and administered CPR until paramedics arrived. Thereafter the wife referred to the sisters as "her angels."

A returned missionary told how he helped convert two atheists at once—one of whom was his companion. They began teaching a self-confessed atheist who had been in the military and who had seen things in his life that would have convinced anybody there is no God. The man would ask the interviewee's companion how their message manifested itself in his life. The companion struggled to answer his questions, and it soon became obvious to both the investigator and the interviewee that the young man didn't have a testimony. Finally the young man confessed to his companion, "To be honest with you, I don't have a testimony." The interviewee continued: "Right then, I took it as a challenge to help this missionary to feel the Spirit, to recognize the Spirit, and to gain a testimony." They continued teaching the man, and eventually both the man and the companion "became converted to the truthfulness of the gospel."

I said to the interviewee: "You didn't expect that when you left the MTC, did you?" "Not at all," he responded.

Missionary Health

At the spring 2010 meeting of the Collegium Aesculapium Foundation, Inc., an organization of LDS health professionals, Elder Richard G. Hinckley, Executive Director of the Church's Missionary Department, spoke of the Department's efforts to ensure the good health of missionaries. He reported that attention was initially focused on missionary health in developing countries and that a study conducted in Chile in 1987 showed that on any one day about 30 percent of missionaries were sick in bed and unable to fulfill their duties.

The Missionary Department Health Services was created to develop policies and procedures for maintaining missionary health and safety. Health Services grew over the years to include medical doctors, nurses, dentists, and mental health providers. There were about ninety healthcare professionals serving full-time missions in 2010: forty doctors who served as Area Medical Advisors, around the same number of nurses, and ten psychiatrists and mental health therapists. There were an additional 125 healthcare professionals serving in a volunteer capacity in Church Headquarters in Salt Lake City, where they screened missionary applications, served on various committees, and provided telephone consultation for missionaries in the field. Another fifty physicians served as consultants from their homes.

These services are now available worldwide and it is estimated that on any given day less than 2 percent of missionaries are sick. Elder Hinckley reported that in 2009 the Missionary Department had around 52,000 missionaries in the field (including 3,500 senior missionaries), and 68,850 missionary contacts were made for health reasons with the Area Medical Advisors. Eighty to 90 percent of the issues were addressed without the need for referrals to other health care providers.

Some missionaries struggle with mental health issues. Over four thousand missionaries with mental health issues were served in 2009, representing 8 percent of the missionary force. They received on average four telephone counseling sessions, and 89 percent remained in the field.

Elder Hinckley ended his presentation with an appeal to health professionals to consider serving a full-time mission in support of the physical and mental health of Church missionaries. Missionaries have to be in good health, he reminded them; otherwise their poor health can have a negative impact on their companion, on other missionaries, and on the mission president.[56]

Health missionaries may be single registered nurses between the ages of nineteen and twenty-five, single seniors, or senior couples in which one is a registered nurse or a physician.

An interviewee physician said in his professional role as a doctor he had worked with missionaries over the previous decade who had serious problems with depression and emotional issues, and he felt they represented a new breed of troubled missionaries. (This trend is not unique to Latter-day Saint missionaries. A similar trend of increased mental health issues is observed among U.S. college students.)

This helps account for the response of a sister when asked what her mission president did. She said a large part of his job was counseling discouraged missionaries.

Going Home Early

Some do not complete their mission for reasons similar to why some do not complete their stay at the MTC; they either choose to return home, or they are sent home. Those who choose to return home early do so because of homesickness or of pressure from girlfriends, boyfriends, or family, or because they discover serving a mission isn't for them. An elder who served in the mid-1980s said some missionaries come into the mission field because of social or family pressures, but they don't believe in what they are saying, so they can't survive, especially when things get difficult. So missionaries do a lot of self-introspection, and, for some, they decide a mission isn't for them, and they choose to return home early.

A trainer had a greenie companion who went home early because of homesickness. The young missionary, who had never been away from home before, would "wake up and look like he was going to die; he would look so sad, and then he would start to cry." The trainer kept him very busy, trying to get his mind off it, and the homesick missionary even went to the mission home for a while, but he finally returned home and got married, though he remained active in the Church.

A sister described how an elder went home after only a week in the field. He became terribly homesick, and he packed up and left without even discussing it with the mission president. It was hard on the other missionaries in his district, and she predicted his home congregation would look upon it negatively. His departure was a low point for her, but it strengthened her resolve to stay until the end, because she "didn't want to be perceived as a quitter."

Interviewees spoke of companions who went home early because of girlfriends, and some returned home early because of family issues. Some struggled with the decision. An elder said he wanted to return home because so many things were going wrong in his life: his parents were getting a divorce, he had been involved in two accidents on his mission, and he wondered, "Why is this happening to me? I am serving a mission, aren't I?" He was "sorely tempted" to go home, thinking the events were an indication that he shouldn't serve a mission. But while it was the lowest point of his life, he decided to stick it out. Help from his companion, regular calls from his mission president, and "a lot of prayers" helped him through the crisis.

Other interviewees admitted they too thought about leaving early. An elder who served in the early 1990s considered returning home, but decided against it, because he knew he would eventually regret it.

A missionary's physical condition can change in the field. Some become ill or develop disabilities and face being sent home early. Many resist the idea, wanting to complete a task they are committed to doing. They may seek to be reassigned to accommodate their condition. This can include being reassigned to their home country after serving foreign, or being reassigned to a role that doesn't require as much physical activity, such as working in the mission office, a temple, or in a Church history center.

Or they may be sent home. A sister suffering from painful arthritis faced this possibility and was disappointed, but she tried to remain philosophical: she loved missionary work, but realized she may be reassigned, or even return home, where she would finish her college education. Wherever she went, she felt her Heavenly Father needed her there for a particular reason.

Some don't think returning home for a health reason is a worthy option for them. A sister who had minor surgery halfway through her mission in France said she was given the option of returning home early because of it. She refused, considering it a "disgraceful choice."

The Latter-day Saint-published magazine *Ensign* reported in 2007 that 3 percent of missionaries return home early because of physical or mental health issues.[57]

To return home early, especially under what are (or are perceived to be) less-than-honorable conditions can be traumatic for the missionary, the family, and the congregation.

Some are sent home early to deal with serious sins or transgressions they should have addressed through their bishop and stake president prior to their mission, but didn't. They may be sent home and placed on probation, a period of time during which appropriate steps of repentance are taken, after which the missionary is allowed to return to the field.

Some are sent home for acts of disobedience and are not given the option of returning to complete their mission. Some don't get along with their mission president, are rebellious, or question authority. A bishop told of knowing missionaries who decided to take a break and spend a weekend in a city outside their mission boundaries. Their vacation was discovered by the mission president, and while the event in and of itself may not have been grounds for being sent home, they had committed other acts of disobedience, which, when taken together, served as the basis for several of them being sent home early, though some were near the end of their mission.

While we generally assume it is elders who get in trouble, in this case it was sisters.

Sometimes missionaries are purposely led astray. A colleague told of observing a college student attempting to see how far she could entice an elder to stray from his mission rules. When the A.P.s became aware of the situation, the elder was immediately sent to a new area under an emergency transfer. In another instance, an interviewee told of two young women who tried to entice him and his companion. Reading from his journal, he recounted: "A common thing happened today. Two girls walked around the car about four times, just tempting us. They made it quite obvious. I am sure glad I didn't indulge in a few moments of unholy pleasure, which would have left me incapacitated to a greater degree. Satan sure puts things in pretty packages. I am glad I only have eight months left. It gives me courage to stick it out."

Not all missionaries are so strong, and some allow themselves to get into compromising situations that prove disastrous for their missionary careers. They are under strict guidelines to avoid all situations that could possibly end with them committing serious moral infractions. Young Church members of the opposite sex are not to communicate with missionaries in their area, flirt with them, or lead them on. Missionaries are not to be alone with the opposite sex or to communicate with them. But a few missionaries let their passions get the best of them, get involved with someone, and are sent home.

Those who find themselves in compromising positions with either sex are subject to a disciplinary council, or Church court, conducted by the mission president and the A.P.s. While I don't know how common such events are, many interviewees who were A.P.s said they had served at least once in this role. An A.P. who served in the Northwest said there were three such situations in the six months he served as an A.P., all because elders got involved with local girls; one elder was sent home having served twenty-two months.

A.P.s said it is "a heavy burden" sitting in judgment of a fellow missionary and making decisions that involve sending her or him home in disgrace. An A.P. told of having to arrange the return home of an elder who was in a compromising situation and who was excommunicated while in the mission field. The excommunicated elder came to the A.P. and asked if he was making his travel arrangements. The A.P. said he was. Crying, the devastated young man said he could send him anywhere in the world, but don't send him home. He could face anyone, even General Authorities, but he couldn't face his parents. The A.P. said he had no choice. The missionary was sent home.

While excommunication and being sent home in disgrace seems especially harsh to non-Mormons, the Church says when serious moral transgressions occur it breaks the bonds between the individual and her or his ordination; in order to serve as a missionary they have to remain worthy of their calling. This includes keeping the commandments, following the missionary standards of conduct, and honoring Christ's name by their actions.[58]

Some will complete their mission, but under a personal cloud. A General Authority serving in an Area Presidency in Europe told of an elder who masturbated as a teenager, didn't tell his bishop or stake president, and didn't stop while in the field, and, while he served a decent mission, he struggled until he finally went to his mission president, near the end of his mission, and said he had a moral problem. He wasn't sent home dishonorably, but the General Authority said he felt the missionary never blossomed as he should, because he was carrying such guilt. When the young man returned home he went to the stake president, confessed, and wept. The General Authority said few missionaries go through the experience of serving that long without confessing. He said a missionary couldn't serve effectively and honorably with that sort of skeleton in his closet.

When dealing with issues of disobedience or moral transgressions, mission presidents have to determine their own balance of keeping missionaries in the field, where they can have a direct impact on them, or when their behavior is such that it is affecting the mission negatively and they should be sent home. "Raising the bar" raised the stakes. An A.P. who served prior to the raising of the bar said his mission president told him he would let a missionary "walk all over his chest" before sending him home. The president said he felt a personal obligation to put his pride aside, and it didn't matter if a missionary opposed him or was rebellious because as long as the missionary was in the field the potential existed that the mission president could have a positive influence on the individual. Once home, that influence was gone.

But mission presidents also have to weigh how much they are willing to tolerate before the missionary's actions have a negative influence on other missionaries, on the local congregation, and on the image of the Latter-day Saint Church in the community. The A.P. said many mission presidents looked at it as his mission president did, but with the raising of the bar their options became much more limited.

Certainly not all mission presidents are as lenient as the above-mentioned one. Another interviewee spoke of a disobedient elder who the mission president tried to work with, but as soon as the president was replaced by a sterner mission president, the A.P.s were dispatched to the missionary's apartment, packed his bags, and sent him home the very next day.

"New president, new rules," he said.

How early-returning missionaries are received back home (or how they perceive they are received) varies with the family, the congregation, and the individual. In general, there are negative perceptions and judgmental attitudes, especially if no reasons or details are given for the return. When I asked what it is like to be sent home early and how Church members may react to it, a bishop said, "You don't want to be in that position." How members should act, and how they *do* act, are two different things, he said. Some will assume the worst, especially if there is secrecy around the return. This leads to awkward moments and people not knowing what to say to the returnee. The bishop said he hopes people will be sympathetic and supportive, but it is not always the case.

A sister who served in Europe in the 1960s, at a time when elders served thirty months and sisters served twenty-four, returned home after serving twenty months. She had a crisis of conscience and of faith.

The initial response of Church members was that she should be mortified and ashamed—and she was. She walked into the church on the first Sunday, and one of the members said, "What are you doing here? You are not supposed to be here. Go back!" She felt her mission had been a failure.

Instead of leaving the Church, the failure of the mission kept her "struggling desperately" with the Church for a long time thereafter. She followed the rules, trying to prove that she was a faithful Church member. She remained active in the Church, she married in the temple, and she became a stake relief president. In hindsight, she felt she probably lasted ten yours longer than she would have had she not served a mission. She was trying to make amends for her sense of failure in the eyes of the LDS Church and her family. She is no longer a member.

In some instances, missionaries probably perceive congregations as being more negative than they actually are, and they are harder on themselves than they need to be. An elder observed that when people return home early "it crushes them." Some re-engage with the congregations right away, some stay out of sight for a while, and some leave the Church altogether. A sister who had friends return home early said they left the Church because they felt a sense of failure; they felt they couldn't handle it, and the feeling stayed with them for a very long time. "I would feel the same way," added her companion. "Had I gone home early, I would never had been able to look a sister missionary in the eye, thinking, 'Oh, I couldn't do it.'"

Perhaps it is a little easier to return early if others from the same ward have done so before them. An interviewee said she has observed that coming home early is something that feeds upon itself; when a missionary returns home early, it makes it easier for the next person to do it.

It is still awkward to return home early, especially in light of the celebrations that marked the departure. Prior to the recent, more formalized farewells, missionaries would have gone through rather elaborate missionary farewells with talks, accolades, and gifts (frequently money) from family and Church members. An announcement regarding their departure to the mission field, along with a picture, may have appeared in the local newspaper. To return home early and have to face the congregation and the community is not something missionaries want to do.

Missionaries returning home early can have a devastating effect on their families. When an elder chose to return home because of emotional issues after a few months in the mission field, his mother kept asking, "Where have I gone wrong and what will members of the Church think?" Her biggest fear was that people would think he came home for dishonorable reasons. It was a painful trial for the family. A parent whose child returned home early because of an undiagnosed medical problem said the family was "treated poorly" because Church members assumed he had done something wrong. "I could have become bitter," said the parent, "but didn't." Her son still goes to church, but she knows missionaries who left the Latter-day Saint Church because of similar receptions.

An elder who served in Europe said he feels congregations can do better—the Mormon Church can do better—in accepting back missionaries who can't handle missionary life and who return home early. He wasn't thinking so much of those who transgress, but of those who just can't handle missionary life. He gave the example of a missionary he knew who was a good person, who wasn't very strong emotionally, and who "just couldn't do it." He was not received well back home. The interviewee said that just because people are called to do something and they couldn't do it, it shouldn't be held against them. I asked him if he came back early under similar circumstances, and while people would shake his hand and smile, would he be wondering what they were really thinking?

His response: "Yes."

An elder had two older brothers who returned home early from their missions, and he felt a responsibility to take their place and make up for them. One brother got homesick and came home twice before finally finishing his mission. The other's girlfriend kept asking him to come back home, which he finally did. Their bishop didn't speak to the returned young man for a while, and he now lowers his eyes when missions and missionaries are mentioned. The interviewee said he has seen quite a few early-returning missionaries drift away from the Latter-day Saint Church.

An elder who served in California said being sent home early from a mission is like coming back early from the Army with a dishonorable discharge. It's not something that is honorable, so being sent home early is regarded by Church members as meaning that something serious happened.

A sister who served in the mid-1960s said she grew up with the expression, "I would rather have you return home from your mission in a casket, than return home in disgrace."

The expression is still heard in the Church today.

Missionary Safety, Illness, Injury, and Death

The Latter-day Saint Church is naturally concerned for the safety and well-being of its missionaries, and accidents are a constant worry of mission presidents. With nearly eighty thousand missionaries serving worldwide, where sanitation practices and the access to healthcare vary widely and where missionaries ride bicycles, drive cars, and travel on foot in unfamiliar environments surrounded by unpredictable drivers, they face the potential for illness, injury, or even death. They are advised to be careful what they eat and drink, to avoid animals, to avoid using faulty appliances and heaters, to ride their bicycles prudently, to drive safely, and to be aware of their surroundings. But missionaries are robbed at gunpoint, and their cars are stolen. They become ill, are bit by dogs, are injured, die in accidents, and die of carbon monoxide poisoning because of faulty heating appliances. Some are even murdered. Some, especially those serving in third world countries, contract serious illnesses that require they return home early, and from which some never fully recover.

The mission president is to be informed of illnesses and accidents, and traditionally it is the mission president's wife who handles such situations.

Missionaries on bicycles are a familiar sight. They are required to wear helmets, and accidents are fairly common. An elder who served in California said bike injuries are part of missionary life, and missionaries learn to grin and bear it. Cars run into them, they run into cars, and car doors are opened in front of them. Clothes are ripped, injuries occur, and some have died as a result of their injuries.

Interviewees spoke of using mopeds (motorized scooters or bicycles) in France in the 1960s and early 1970s, and while they were found to be a great means of transportation, there were so many accidents (and even deaths) that they were banned from use. They were replaced with ten-speed bicycles.

Car accidents can be serious. An elder serving in Northern New England was knocked unconscious and the Jaws of Life was needed to extricate him after the car he was driving was broadsided and knocked on its side by a driver who ran a red light. Mission presidents and missionaries have died in automobile accidents, and missionaries have been struck and killed while walking along roads or standing on sidewalks. While driving a car in France during his mission, twenty-one-year-old

Mitt Romney was struck head-on by a Mercedes that crossed the centerline. Tragically, the mission president's wife, who was a passenger, died of her injuries. Romney was seriously injured and was pried out of the car. The police officer on the scene thought he was dead and wrote, "Il est mort," ("He died") in his passport.[59]

A sister interviewee who served in Belize in the mid-1990s recounted the tragic story of how her mission president died in a plane crash. It was devastating to her and to the mission. She had just met with him. She said it felt like her father had died.

Accidental deaths occur. Two sisters in the Argentina Bahia Blanca Mission died in their sleep in their Comodoro Rivadavia apartment in 1989 as a result of a faulty natural gas heater. Two elders died of carbon monoxide poisoning in their apartment in the Romania Bucharest Mission in 2010. An elder died while trying to save a drowning thirteen-year-old boy in Gualeguaychú, Argentina, in 2003. Both were electrocuted when a power line came in contact with the water.[60] An elder died after being struck by a stray bullet that hit him while he was riding in a van in 2011.

Missionaries are sometimes murdered. Terrorists killed two missionaries in the Bolivia La Paz Mission in 1989. An interviewee serving in the mission at the time of the murders said the missionaries were serving in a poorer area, and the reason for the murders was unclear. Elder Ballard, an Apostle, came and helped allay nervousness. Sister missionaries were immediately reassigned to other missions, and missionaries whose missions were ending in the next four months were sent home early. Those remaining were initially told to remain indoors, and then they were given a curfew to be in by dark. Bolivian missionaries replaced some of the Americans as they left. The interviewee reported that non-member Bolivians stopped him on the street in the wealthier section where he served and told him to keep up the work, to not let the tragedy stop his efforts.

A Latter-day Saint interviewee, a mother of eight children, seven of whom served missions, said after the death of the missionaries in Bolivia, a non-member stopped her on the street and said she took the Bolivian incident as a sign from God that one shouldn't be sending children on missions. The Latter-day Saint mother, who served a mission herself, responded that it was surely a case of bad things happening to good people, but it didn't negate the reasons for going on a mission. She said missionaries serve out of gratitude for their blessings because they know the gospel is true and because Jesus asked that his word be spread. Sacrifice is painful, she continued, but we don't give enough to adequately thank God for the blessings we receive. Someone who doesn't understand what they really do feel and experience as members of the LDS Church may not understand this rationale, she continued, but they believe the answer to every problem is found in the gospel of Jesus Christ. "Not everyone will accept it," she said, "but everyone deserves an opportunity to hear it."[61]

Looking in the Mirror

Missionaries are to maintain a journal and write in it daily. Some just state the facts, while others write introspectively. An elder fresh from the MTC said he spent the time en route to his mission assignment writing in his journal, taking stock of his two months at the MTC. He wrote bullets of what he had learned, and he was surprised to see how much he had grown. He felt he had become a different person; he had learned most about himself through experiences living with a companion. "I recognized my weaknesses and I wrote them all down," he said. It showed him who he was, things he didn't know about himself, things he wanted to change while on his mission.

President Kimball's and succeeding presidents' directive that all young LDS men should serve a mission places a heavy obligation on them, and some confess to spending the first few months of their mission dealing with the fact that they experienced considerable pressure to serve; that they came because they were trying to please someone else. Most eventually realize they would regret not serving, and they come to the conclusion that they are there because they want to be and that it is their choice. "I still chose to go on a mission and I am going to make the most of it," said an elder who initially struggled. "That is the biggest key for me; taking responsibility for my actions, taking responsibility for who I am and that I am a representative of the Lord, and just go for it."

In spite of their perceived wholesomeness, missionaries don't come into the mission as pure vessels; and they don't come out as perfect people. They may carry guilt, doubt, and issues from the past. They have emotional baggage they haven't gotten rid of, and it surfaces while working long, stressful hours. This, together with the fact that their faith is challenged on a day-to-day basis, creates doubt, and they have to decide what they really believe. Was Joseph Smith a prophet of God? Is the Book of Mormon divine scripture? Is the Latter-day Saint Church true? They can't hide anything as a missionary; all of their issues are magnified because the mission is "a pressure cooker experience," as many missionaries described it.

A sister shared that she had the misconception that once she became a missionary, everything would be perfect. But, she quickly found out, "Being out here I am still the same me and I still have the same weaknesses." Another sister observed that since being on her mission and facing her weaknesses, "I have learned that I am so human that it's not even funny."

They talked of being impatient with themselves, with their companions, and with investigators. They confessed to being judgmental of their companions and others, of lacking social skills and study skills, and of lacking knowledge of beliefs and practices of other faiths. Some reported their weaknesses became more apparent when living with a difficult companion than when living with someone they got along with. Some struggled because they compared themselves to missionaries who they felt were better than they were.

Missionaries must address these questions and issues in order to become grounded in the faith and to strengthen their testimony. This must take place before they can become truly effective.

A truthful sister said the early days of her mission were like living through a process of personal and spiritual purification, and it wasn't easy. It seemed like a low point at the beginning, but it became a high point, because she became a better person as a result. Her companion echoed her experience; weaknesses came to the surface, but she also found new strengths and abilities; she found she could do things without her parents being there. It was only after they began to deal with their issues that their confidence began to grow and that they began to feel more comfortable with themselves and with their roles as missionaries.

While reflecting on this difficult process of self-examination and change, a sister said she carried a picture of Jesus in the Garden of Gethsemane and under it a quote: "I never said it would be easy, I only said it would be worth it."

A returned missionary read from his missionary journals during our interview. While some of his writing was factual, most was introspective. He described his relationships with companions, Church leaders, and investigators, and his feelings (both positive and negative) about them. Some were easier to get along with than others, he noted. The journal writing process was an inner dialogue for him, and he felt it was an important endeavor because before he could understand others he had to first understand himself.

We will return to this early period of trials and stress, this "dark night of the soul," when we consider international missions: when missionaries not only have to learn to adjust, but have to do so in the context of learning a new language and living in a new culture.

Missionaries live rigorous, disciplined lives, which in and of themselves would present a challenge to many; but that is only the beginning, because the reason they are on a mission—to find investigators, share their message, and baptize new members into the Latter-day Saint Church—presents even greater challenges. They face rejection and hardship, their faith and dedication are tested, and at times they struggle to understand what they are doing and why they are doing it. Remaining optimistic and motivated under such circumstances is an ongoing challenge. But they say one positive experience, just one baptism, wipes away a score of negative experiences. In Chapter 6 we will follow them in these day-to-day activities and consider how they find investigators, which is not always easy. In Chapter 7 we will consider what they teach, how they baptize, and how they weather the struggles along the way.

PART III

Find, Teach, Baptize, Confirm

CHAPTER 6

Find

"We all remember our first door."

ALDIN PORTER, GENERAL AUTHORITY RESPONSIBLE FOR THE MISSIONARY PROGRAM, SALT LAKE CITY, APRIL 4, 1994

"Mercenaries."

THE RESPONSE OF A TWELVE-YEAR-OLD BOY WHEN ASKED BY HIS MOTHER WHO WAS AT THE DOOR. IT WAS TWO MORMON MISSIONARIES.

Most missionaries leave the MTC excited, nervous, and optimistic. They are happy to be finally going into the mission field. They don't quite know what to expect, but they are confident they will be successful. They have "greenie fire." Their goal is to locate potential converts, teach them the doctrines and practices of the Latter-day Saint Church, and baptize them into the faith.

This chapter looks at their efforts to find those who are interested in hearing their message: "investigators." Many missionaries have the impression—gained, they say, from Church videos and other Church sources—that finding such people is relatively easy. Whether this is true or not depends in large measure on where and when they are assigned. Interest in the LDS Church is strong in Latin America and the Philippines, especially when missionaries first arrive in an area. They struggle in other parts of the world, particularly in New England and Western Europe, and they wonder if they have been given too rosy a picture.

The Latter-day Saint Church employs a number of strategies to approach and recruit new members. It extols its members to reach out to their non-member relatives, friends, and neighbors and to introduce them to missionaries. Non-Mormons who visit historic Mormon sites and visitors' centers are encouraged to fill out cards that indicate an interest in meeting with missionaries. The Church also has a history of a sophisticated use of media, particularly short ads on television, to generate interest in the Church. Even greater use is now made of the Internet to advance its purposes.

Missionaries set weekly goals and maintain records of their activities. They pray constantly. They speak frequently of "the Spirit" and of the powerful impact it has on their lives as they seek listeners for their message.

All face rejection, some encounter rude behavior, and a few experience assault. Apathy is the most common response to their appeals. They encounter anti-Mormon sentiment, and it challenges their faith in the Restoration, in the Book of Mormon, and in Joseph Smith as a prophet. They are forced to come face-to-face with their own beliefs, and they prayerfully struggle with the question, "What *do* I believe, and is all of this worth it?" As a result, many become frustrated and struggle to find the inner resolve to carry on, day after day, in the face of such experiences. Most learn to not take rejection personally.

Chapter 6 looks at the missionaries' attempts to find investigators, and their trials and successes along the way. Chapter 7 then considers what they teach once they are invited into a home and the baptismal and confirmation process for those who choose to join the Latter-day Saint Church. These include challenges as well.

Referrals

The missionaries' task is to share with the investigator a series of lessons that outline the basic beliefs and practices of the Latter-day Saint Church, with the goal that the individual will be baptized into the faith. The first step in this process, finding those who are willing to listen, isn't always an easy task.

The Church has identified a range of approaches and techniques for finding investigators, from the most effective to the least effective. Experience and research have shown that referrals are the single most effective source for finding investigators and potential converts: referrals from members, recent converts, investigators, television ads, and the Internet—instances where personal contact has already been made, or where personal interest has been expressed. In 2003 the Church estimated that 59 percent of converts were referred by Church members and that 20 to 30 percent of investigators referred to missionaries by members go on to become baptized.[62]

Referrals certainly make the job of missionaries easier. An appreciative elder who served in Maine in the mid-2000s observed that missionary work is hard without the support of members and that some wards are more "missionary minded" than others. Wards that give missionaries referrals produce the most results, because it means a personal connection has been made, and it frees up missionaries' time to teach; they don't have to go out and knock on doors to find people.

While the importance of members finding investigators is clear, the Church has identified what it considers a disturbing trend: member participation in referring investigations has declined over the years. The percentage of investigators referred to missionaries by members declined from 42 percent in 1987 to 20 percent in 1997.[63] This trend continued into the 2000s. At the Seminar for New Mission Presidents held in 2002, the Apostle Joseph B. Wirthlin observed: "We see an ironic trend in the Church. At the very time when we are confirming the importance of members in the conversion process, evidence from studies suggest that members are playing a proportionally smaller role in finding people to teach."[64]

There appear to be a number of reasons why members have become less engaged in the proselytizing process. Some say they have little time to devote to the effort because of work and family responsibilities. Some are reluctant to share their faith with their neighbors, friends, and colleagues, since active evangelization is not looked upon favorably in American society. And, paradoxically, members are not always comfortable referring friends to the missionaries serving in their area. President Gordon B. Hinckley made a significant comment about this dynamic when speaking at a Church leadership conference broadcast worldwide on January 11, 2003: "Where the members have confidence in the missionaries, they will work to find investigators for them to teach."[65]

This alludes to an important issue: the relationship between missionaries and the local branch or ward is not always positive. On occasion there are missionaries who are lazy or irresponsible, and Church members don't want them meeting with friends or neighbors. Some interviewees spoke of witnessing this when, in their words, missionaries "messed up the ward" because they didn't obey the rules or because they didn't show respect for their calling. It made it difficult for other missionaries, because if there is one "bad apple," then all are assumed to be that way. Succeeding missionaries who are more disciplined and diligent find it very difficult to overcome these lingering perceptions and attitudes, and they have to work very hard to regain the trust of the local congregation.

Speaking about this issue, the Mormon science fiction author Orson Scott Card said he is very careful when he refers missionaries to his non-LDS friends, because they are his friends and he wants to keep it that way, whether or not they join the Latter-day Saint Church. He avoids missionaries whom he perceives as being interested mainly in numbers or who appear to be in competition with their fellow missionaries to teach the greatest number of lessons and perform the greatest number of baptisms. He waits until these missionaries are transferred and are replaced with missionaries whom he feels are serving for the right reason, before he introduces them to friends.

Thus it's not necessarily the case that Church members are lazy or not interested in missionary efforts, it's just that they have to have faith in the motivation and ability of those serving in their area.[66]

The first decade of the twenty-first century saw the Latter-day Saint Church making a concerted effort to re-engage members in the missionary process. Renewed emphasis was placed on the responsibility of all Church members to be missionaries. Hearkening back to the call of President David O. McKay in the 1950s, who said that all Latter-day Saints are to be "member missionaries," Church leaders sought to rekindle a sense of commitment and enthusiasm for the recruitment process among Church members. Speaking at the above-mentioned leadership conference in 2003, President Hinckley told Church leaders that missionary work is the responsibility of everyone in the Church, not just missionaries, and should become part of the culture of the Latter-day Saint Church. Members should make a concerted effort to reach out to friends and neighbors, with particular emphasis placed on recruiting families.

Missionaries are told they have a role in helping members become member-missionaries. They are encouraged to work with members to help them think about who might be interested in hearing about the Church, they are to share success stories to motivate members to get involved, and they are reminded that missionary work is a good topic of conversation when members invite them for a meal. A sister who served in Washington, D.C., said their mission president told them that when talking with members at dinner they were to ask them to give them names of friends and neighbors who might be interested, and, ideally, that the member would accompany them to the friend's house, or invite the friend to theirs.

The Internet has opened up unlimited possibilities for the Church to spread its message. Non-members can learn more about the Church, obtain free materials, and find the location of local congregations at the Church's official website, www.lds.org. The Church also encourages members to post their personal and spiritual stories on www.mormon.org. Thousands of Latter-day Saints from all walks of life have shared how their faith affects their lives. The site has as many as one million unique visitors per month.[67] Both sites offer visitors the opportunity to request that missionaries visit them in their homes.

Pass-along Cards

The Church provides other convenient ways to help members engage non-members in discussions about the LDS faith. Members are encouraged to use "pass-along cards," small cards that offer the holder a free Church DVD or Book of Mormon if they call a toll-free number. They are also referred to the official Church websites.

Media Ads

Media ads generate self-referrals from non-members. Many Americans are familiar with the short television ads sponsored by the LDS Church. They typically portray scenes centered on the family or on one's spiritual journey, and they offer viewers the chance to call a toll-free number to obtain a free Bible, Book of Mormon, or to request a visit by missionaries (referred to as "representatives" in the ads). The calls come into the Provo MTC and are screened by missionaries-in-training. They determine what the individual is requesting, and they try to answer questions the caller may have. Callers are given the option of having the requested material mailed to them or having it delivered to them by missionaries.

Some balk at the idea of a personal visit. A sister who worked at the MTC call center in the 1990s said the number of calls received increased when TV ads clearly stated that no one would visit the caller if material was requested.

Media campaigns are expensive to air and only 1 to 2 percent of investigators found through media ads are baptized. They do have an effect, though, for the Church reports that around 60 percent of adults who convert to the Church are positively influenced by the ads before their baptism.[68]

Missionaries report that non-members frequently comment on the TV ads. While they may not be interested in converting to the faith, they do like the ads.

Historic Sites and Visitors' Centers

Missionaries also receive referrals from Church-maintained sites that document significant individuals and events in the Church's history and from visitors' centers that are affiliated with Church temples and historic sites. There are over fifty historic Church sites, including the birthplace of Joseph Smith in Sharon, Vermont, the location of Smith's First Vision in Palmyra, New York, and Temple Square at Church Headquarters in Salt Lake City, Utah, the administrative and spiritual center of the Latter-day Saint Church. Millions of members and non-members visit these sites each year. Salt Lake City receives more visitors than any other location in Utah: between three and five million visitors come to Temple Square each year, Americans and non-Americans alike. The Church caters to its international visitors. Temple Square tours are available in an amazing number of languages (over forty), from Albanian to Urdu.[69]

In an effort to capitalize on visitors' interest, non-members are encouraged to fill out a card requesting more information or to have missionaries visit them at home. They are also asked to list names of others who may be interested in knowing more about the Church. This information is conveyed to local missionaries who follow up on the request.

Member-visitors to historic sites are asked to provide names of non-members who might be interested in hearing from missionaries. In 2001, members provided 150,000 such names, and it is reported that nearly 50 percent of those identified agreed to have missionaries visit them. This strategy is increasingly being seen as a fruitful approach to finding investigators.[70]

Over twenty-five temples have a visitors' center associated with them, where non-members can gain information about the Church and its beliefs and where they can request a visit from missionaries.

Historic sites and visitors' centers are overseen by a site director and his wife, who are frequently assisted by senior missionary couples, sisters, and (to a lesser extent) elders and they assume much of the day-to-day responsibility for tours and informational lectures. A visit to a site or center may be the non-member's first contact with the LDS Church or the first time they are able to have their questions answered by a member. This places increased responsibility on missionaries to be knowledgeable and articulate about the history and doctrines of the Church and the significance of the site, and to have good communication and inter-personal skills.

Inactive Members

Thomas S. Monson, President of The Church of Jesus Christ of Latter-day Saints (from 2008 to the present), places particular importance on missionaries reaching out to inactive members and reengaging them in the life of the LDS Church. Conversations are held, issues and concerns are addressed, and attempts are made to rekindle the feelings the person experienced at baptism. Some have fallen back into old habits of smoking, drinking alcohol, or drinking coffee. Some have personal issues with other Church members. Two sisters serving in 2012 reported that they are to spend 50 percent of their time working with "inactives," and 50 percent of their time seeking converts.

The Church's practice of not removing names from membership rolls, except in cases of self-request or excommunication, is based on the hope and expectation that inactives will become re-engaged in the congregation.

Missionaries are also expected to work with part-member families, former investigators, non-members who attend baptism services of relatives and friends, and new residents in the community.

But once they run out of referrals and have exhausted the other means of finding investigators, they must resort to what is referred to as "cold contacting."

Cold Contacting

"Cold contacting" includes knocking on doors (or "knocking doors," as missionaries call it), street contacting, and generally talking with everyone they meet. These approaches are among the least effective in finding investigators, but many missionaries have to engage in them at some point during their mission. Most don't enjoy it, because it can be tedious work. For many, however, cold contacting provides vivid memories—high points and low points, awkward or dangerous situations, as well as humorous experiences.

"Knocking Doors"

The common stereotype of Mormon missionaries is of two, polite, well-dressed young men going door to door, talking with people about their faith. This aggressive style of evangelism, in which only a few religious groups engage (mostly Latter-day Saints and Jehovah's Witnesses), is referred to as "tracting," since it frequently involves distributing religious literature known as tracts. Some Latter-day Saint missionaries do it almost exclusively throughout their mission, whereas others do it only rarely. Some don't do it at all: door-to-door proselytizing is illegal in some countries, and missionaries must find other ways to spread their message.

Irritating, but legal. Many non-Mormons, particularly in North America and Western Europe, are uncomfortable when approached in this manner. They don't respond well to strangers knocking at their door, seeking to convert them to another faith. Many find it irritating.

When asked how she responds to Mormons or Jehovah's Witnesses knocking at her door, an older woman living in Woodstock, England, told me: "I put a flea in their ear and send them packing. We all have our own religion, and they shouldn't come 'round and try to convert us to theirs."

I asked an English friend what it meant to "put a flea in their ear." He explained that it is a sharpish retort, halfway between a polite brush-off and being told to "shove off."

Such an attitude is not restricted to the English. An American interviewee observed: "Most people have the philosophy, 'If I want to know about your religion, I will ask you.' They find it invasive if people try to proselytize."

As a result, most Latter-day Saint missionaries are turned away.

While many Americans find door-to-door evangelism bothersome, it is legal. The town of Stratton, Ohio, passed an ordinance that said people wishing to go door to door had to obtain a permit from the town before being allowed to go onto people's private property to distribute literature, poll their opinion, or advocate for a particular cause. Jehovah's Witnesses said it was an infringement on their First Amendment rights of the free exercise of religion, freedom of speech, and freedom of the press, and they sought an injunction against the ordinance. The case went all the way to the Supreme Court, who, in 2002, sided with the Witnesses, saying the ordinance violated the First Amendment.[71]

Door approaches. Missionaries typically approach knocking on doors in a methodical manner, beginning on one side of the street and progressing from door to door, seeking to find people at home. They use a variety of "door approaches," or opening lines, when people answer the door. Their hope is to immediately engage the person's attention so that the person will want to continue the conversation. An elder in the Northeastern United States used this approach: "My name is Elder

Smith, and this is my companion Elder Jones. We are in the neighborhood today sharing a message about Jesus Christ and how His gospel has been restored to the earth. We would like to share this message with you."

Elders serving in 2003 reported this approach: "We are representatives of The Church of Jesus Christ of Latter-day Saints. We are here to share a message about our Heavenly Father that comes from the Book of Mormon. Have you heard of the Book of Mormon?"

An American elder serving in Tokyo, Japan, used this approach: "We have recently transferred to this area as missionaries of The Church of Jesus Christ of Latter-day Saints, and we have a short message we would like to share with you. We would like to speak with you for a few minutes and ask you how you feel about a few questions we have for you. Would that be okay?"

If people say yes to the approach, missionaries will talk with them, get to know something about them, give their testimony, and talk about Joseph Smith, the First Vision, and the Book of Mormon. They may pursue further pleasantries and then ask if they can come back to talk further with them. If they say no, the missionaries will say it was nice to meet them and to have a nice day, and leave. They keep smiling throughout.

For those who agree to further conversations, a meeting time will be set, and they will then work through a series of five lessons (or as many as the person wants to hear). We will discuss the contents of these lessons in Chapter 7.

Missionaries keep detailed records of their experiences at doors, especially those who express interest. They also record personal information such as children's names and the family's plans for the future. These records are passed on to missionaries who serve after them.

A sister said most people want to know immediately who is at their door, so she and her companion told them. She didn't start by mentioning the Book of Mormon, because she found that if people had preconceived notions they would slam the door in her face. Rather, she began by talking about Jesus Christ and God, and she explained that there is a plan and a reason for humans being on earth. We can find out about that plan, she told them, because it has been revealed through modern-day prophets. She then introduced the Book of Mormon, explaining it is a scripture that complements the Bible. She and her companion would talk casually with the person, about their respective families, about something they saw in the house, such as family pictures or trophies, in the hope of establishing a relationship that would encourage the person to want to listen to their message. It was also a way of showing the person that they were not, in the sister's words, "religious freaks," but that they wanted to share a message that was very important to them.

People weren't always interested in what she had to say or to accept a Book of Mormon, but they generally had pleasant conversations, and many said they respected the missionaries for what they were doing. She knew not all would seek baptism or even be interested in her message, but if she could get them to understand a little bit more about the LDS Church, then she felt she was doing a good job.

Missionaries develop the skill to carry on such extended conversations with time and experience.

Non-members may be confused by the missionaries' names when they introduce themselves. People may not realize that "Elder" and "Sister" are titles in the Latter-day Saint Church. Thus when elders say, "Hello, I am Elder White and this is Elder Black," the person may respond, "How interesting that you both have the same first name, and that it is so unusual." When sisters say, "Hello, I am Sister Jones and this is Sister Brown," they are sometimes asked, "Are you Roman Catholic nuns?"

Reactions of the Public

The public reacts to the missionaries' knock in a variety of ways. A few chase them away, some slam the door in their faces, and some pretend not to be at home. Some invite them in but try to convert them to *their* faith, while some have little interest in their message but invite them in to give them respite from the heat or cold. Some invite them in to hear what they have to say, and some find their message compelling and join the Latter-day Saint Church.

Most, however, are indifferent and turn them away.

Assault. While assaults are rare, they do happen. An irate father physically threw an elder serving in England out of a home. A son who was interested in their message had invited the elders into the home, but the father was not happy with their presence. Instead of getting upset with his son, he became upset with the missionaries and gave them quite a shove out the door. Others told of having knives and guns pulled on them, of threats to sic dogs on them, and of being chased off porches with people swinging sticks at them. A hesitant sister confessed to having a fear of knocking on doors. Her brother told her stories of his mission in Kentucky, when a man shot at him and his companion as the man chased them off of his property. She feared that when she knocked on a door, someone would start shooting at her.

Verbal abuse. Some missionaries experience verbal abuse while tracting. A woman whose nephew was baptized a Latter-day Saint against her wishes shouted at sisters at her door, telling them they were witches and that she was going to pray for them. Another sister described what she called "a very frightening experience" while knocking on a door in a high-rise apartment in Paris. A person answered the door and started screaming at the sisters. The sister said she "had never felt so evil a spirit," and the person continued to yell and scream as the sister and her companion ran down the stairs. She thought the person was a woman, but she wasn't sure.

Another sister said she and her companion knocked at the door of what should have been a condemned house, but people were living there. They introduced themselves to a man who said his eleven-year-old daughter might be interested in what they had to say. They went in and found the young girl reading her Bible. They started teaching her about the Latter-day Saint faith, when suddenly "a totally huge, loud woman" came bustling in and confronted the sisters:

"What are you doing in my house?" she shouted. "You shouldn't be in my house! I want you to leave!"

As they were departing, one of the sisters said, "Have a nice day," to which the woman responded, "Have a bad day."

The sister, trembling, thought, "Just don't kill me!"

A woman threatened two elders in 2000: "If I ever see you pimple-faced boys on my porch again, I will have a string of lawyers waiting to prosecute you!"

Harassment. Being on bicycles or in cars doesn't protect missionaries from harassment. An elder who served in California, who rode a bike during his mission, said people yelled at him and his companion, spit on them, and threw things at them. He initially wanted to go back and confront the attackers, but he quickly decided that Christ went through a lot more than he did, so he wiped it off, shook it off, and went on to the next door. He and his companion talked about it later, and he considered making a journal entry about it to get it out of his system, but both tried to not let it bother them. He said they had to guard against feeling persecuted.

They were assigned to rougher areas, where there was gang-related activity and bikes were stolen, missionaries were held up at gunpoint, and they were robbed. Their white shirts, "which seemed to glow in the dark," marked them as easy targets. But at times they were referred to as "Jesus People," and gang-members afforded them a certain amount of protection.

They did find that there were advantages to riding on bicycles, as it was easier to interact with people on the street. Young people came up to them and talked to them.

Missionaries driving cars may also face issues. An elder who drove a car said kids enjoyed squashing bugs and caterpillars on the windshield.

Going to Hell. Missionaries are frequently told they are false priests, the Antichrist, and deceived, brainwashed, and going to Hell. "If I had a nickel for every time someone told me I was going to Hell," said an irritated elder, "I would be a millionaire."

Don't talk to missionaries. Various non-Mormons told missionaries that their priest or minister told them not to talk to missionaries, because Mormonism is a cult and Mormons aren't Christians. While tracting in a rural area, two sisters knocked at a door, and, when a woman answered, one of the sisters began, "Hi, we are representatives from The Church of Jesus Christ of Latter-day Saints and", at which point the woman interrupted and said, "I would never be a Mormon, because you don't believe in Jesus Christ and you aren't a Christian Church."

As the woman was closing the door, the sister said, "We are representatives of the Church and we would be happy to talk with you about what we really believe."

"I am not interested," responded the woman. "Anyway, I know what you believe. My minister told me." She then closed the door.

This frustrated the sisters. They felt people were closed-minded about new things, and they found peoples' ignorance about the Church frustrating, especially that they didn't think they were Christian and that they took someone else's word for what they believed.

At another door, a woman told the same sisters that she didn't need to talk with them because she had watched a video and she knew what they believed. The sisters said it was obvious from her comments that she was misinformed, and while they didn't want to argue with her, they struggled between trying to explain their beliefs and just walking away.

Pastoral criticism. Missionaries can be subject to pastoral criticism firsthand. Most missionaries who grew up in the Latter-day Saint faith have limited contact with other religions, and some use their time on the mission to gain knowledge about other religious groups. They do it out of curiosity and to gain a better understanding of their common beliefs, which can serve as a basis for conversations with non-members. Missionaries are told to respect other faiths because this attitude can contribute toward a positive public perception of them and the Latter-day Saint Church.

Missionaries attend other services with these goals in mind, but at times it backfires on them because they become the target of anti-Mormon sentiment during the service. At least half-a-dozen interviewees said that when they attended services at conservative Protestant churches, the minister—either by coincidence or because they were there—chose to preach against the Latter-day Saint Church. At one service parishioners were told Mormonism is a cult and not to let missionaries into their homes. At another service the pastor said the Book of Mormon is wrong and that Joseph Smith was a false prophet. A third pastor warned his congregation that if they read the Book of Mormon, "the great evil Mormon spirit" would enter their body and they would become possessed.

At another service, missionaries were told they were going to Hell, they belonged to a cult ruled over by Satan, and, as a missionary described it, "then one of them got in our faces and started speaking in tongues at us. It was an eerie experience. There are definitely people around here who don't want us around. And it is hard. They weren't nice to us at all."

A female pastor invited two elders to the front of the church to join her in prayer. Thinking it was an ecumenical gesture, they joined her, but as the elders bowed their heads, she placed her hands on their heads and prayed that they be healed of their misguided beliefs.

Myths about missionaries. Numerous myths persist among non-Mormons regarding LDS missionaries and why they shouldn't be allowed into homes. One man recalled that as a young boy his mother told him to run upstairs and hide under his bed when missionaries knocked, because if they saw him they would kidnap him and take him to Salt Lake City, where they would brainwash him and put him to work for the Mormon Church. "They will steal you right out of the house," she told him.

Another myth is that missionaries should never be allowed to open the Book of Mormon in a home, because if they do, demons will be set free and infest the place.

Perhaps the most common myth is that missionaries have horns and tails—that they are in league with the Devil. When a woman asked an elder if he had horns, he offered his head to her, inviting her to feel for herself.

Where are you from? Sometimes people will make rude comments about missionaries' real or perceived country of origin. An elder serving in Pennsylvania was asked where he was from. When the elder told the man he was from Canada, the man said he should go back to his own country. An elder from Africa was given the same advice while serving in the American Southwest. An elder serving in the Northeast who had a Hispanic-sounding name was told by a man to go back to Mexico. The elder was from Oregon.

Surprising reactions. Non-Mormons are sometimes surprised at their reactions to missionaries at their door. A colleague from a Southern university said he doesn't respond well to people arriving at his door unannounced and uninvited. He "tends to be a bit rude with them, spending only a millisecond with them," before saying he is not interested. But then he feels bad, because he realizes he is not as accepting, patient, and polite as he thought he was.

A sister serving in the Northeast said a man was very rude when she and her companion knocked on his door. He "blew up at them." A few days later, they approached a man sitting on a park bench and started talking with him. He said he had been feeling bad because he had yelled at two missionaries a few days before, and, yes, he would like to hear what they had to say. They taught him the first lesson. When he realized it was they he had yelled at, he apologized for his behavior. He said he was having a bad day.

Fleeing from the missionaries. An elder serving in central Indiana said he and his companion had a knack for "clearing the neighborhood" when they appeared. They would drive onto a street and see children playing in their yards, garage doors open, and people working in their yards or washing their cars. But as soon as the missionaries got out of their car, children would be hurried into houses, garage doors would close, and when they knocked on doors it appeared no one was home. In one instance, only one man in the entire neighborhood answered his door, and he talked with them for a very long time.

It was only as the elders were leaving that the man confessed he had detained them for a reason: so they wouldn't bother his neighbors.

Afraid to open doors. Some are afraid to open their doors to strange men, especially women living alone. Some don't open their doors because they think two men in dark suits, white shirts, and conservative ties are plain-clothes police officers or other government officials. Sisters are even misidentified. A sister who served in Washington, D.C., knocked at a door, and two young boys answered. When asked if their mother was home, the older boy said she wasn't, but the younger one turned to his brother and said, "Yes, she is. She is hiding in the closet." When the woman realized who the visitors were, she came out. She thought they were tax collectors.

Missionaries will sometimes take a different approach to avoid the perception of being government authorities. An elder working with a large immigrant population in southern California, many who were in the country illegally, found that when he and his companion went into a new area, they had a much better chance of meeting and talking with people if they initially wore jeans, T-shirts, and their nametags. Only later, once they were known and it was clear they weren't immigration officers, did they put on their missionary uniform of suits, white shirts, and ties. Such changes in practice have to be approved in advance by the mission president, and he did in this instance.

A sister described how the police stopped her on her first night tracting. She and two companions were going door to door after dark when a police car suddenly appeared and the officer asked them what they—three people in dark clothes, carrying a flashlight, and knocking on peoples' doors—were doing. When they explained they were missionaries, the officer said the police had received numerous calls about three strangers in the neighborhood who were bothering people. He asked them to stop, because they were scaring people.

Small kindnesses. Some will invite the missionaries in because they appear hot, cold, tired, or thirsty. In the face of constant rejection and boredom, missionaries appreciate small kindnesses like this.

When asked to describe the highlights of his mission, an elder who served in Northern Europe told of knocking on a woman's door, who, while not interested in their message, said since it was a hot day, invited he and his companion in for a glass of cold lemonade. They had a pleasant conversation, in which they talked about their respective families. The elders then thanked her for the lemonade and left.

What was striking about our interview was that the experience remained a vivid memory for him, even though it had occurred thirty years previously.

Hesitant to talk. Missionaries may also discover that some people don't want to talk about their faith because it is a very private matter for them. Inquisitive sisters serving in Northern New England found that some people weren't open to talking about such topics. The sisters wanted to talk about God, to ask people how they felt about religious matters, to ask probing questions, but some were not willing to respond. The sisters got the feeling they were thinking, "It's none of your business, thank you very much!" They said it was difficult to engage such people in conversation.

An American elder who served in Europe said he never got used to tracting, and he hated doing it. He did it because he had to, but he felt very hypocritical because he would never let someone like that into his home. It is not in his nature to invite strangers into his home, especially if they want to talk with him about religion. He had to do it on his mission to fill the time and to do the work, but every time someone would slam the door on him or tell him they didn't want to talk about religion, he would think, "I don't blame you."

Dog stories. Many missionaries tell stories about dogs they encountered. An elder who served in Peru told how he and his companion went up a dusty drive to an isolated house. As they knocked on the door, a number of dogs suddenly appeared and started chasing them. Running backwards, he tripped over a root and was quickly surrounded by the dogs. The owner eventually appeared and called off the dogs, but until then the elder held the dogs at bay by vigorously swinging a Book of Mormon at them.

An elder who served in South Africa told of using the "fake rock" technique in dealing with dogs. He would lean down and appear to pick up a rock, and dogs would generally back off. In one instance, when he and his companion approached a house, three huge, growling, German shepherds appeared. His companion was ready to move on, but the interviewee told the companion: "I have come thousands of miles to share an important message that I feel these people need to hear, and I am not going to let some dogs scare me away."

The fake rock technique worked for a while. The dogs backed off, until they figured out he didn't have any rocks. The missionaries got to the front door, where the dogs surrounded them, barking and foaming at the mouth. The elders pounded on the door, hoping someone would come.

A man opened the door, looked at the missionaries, and said, "How did you get here? I am surprised those dogs didn't rip you apart."

He then closed the door.

The elder pretended to pick up another rock and backed away.

"We barely made it," he reported.

In another instance, a dog suddenly appeared as an interviewee and his companion knocked at a door. The dog started running after them. A narrow path led away from the house, and the elder was the first down the path. His companion followed, and was bit from behind.

This illustrates a missionary truism: you don't have to outrun the dog; you just have to outrun your companion.

A sister was suffering at the time of our interview from a painful dog bite received while tracting, and she had become afraid of dogs because of it. But, she added positively, the experience did make her "an official missionary."

Latinos were never rude. Interviewees who went Spanish-speaking in the United States said they had a different experience at doors. Latinos were never rude to them, harsh words were never spoken, and doors were never slammed in their faces. Latinos were much too nice to do that, they said. Missionaries were shown great courtesy and were frequently invited into homes. And whether a Church member or not, Latinos wanted to feed them.

An elder who served in both a Spanish-speaking area and an English-speaking area in New England said it was like being in two different missions. It is part of Latino culture to be hospitable, he said, and when he spoke their language he was made to feel as though he was part of the family. They were surprised and appreciated that he spoke to them in Spanish, and they wanted to listen to what he had to say. There were people who were "down and out with no place to go," but they were still friendly.

"They didn't have much," he said, "but they gave us what they had. It taught me a lot about that money isn't everything; it is about giving, not receiving. So I think I learned more from them than they learned from me."

He contrasted this with those in the English-speaking areas where he served, who had comfortable lives and lifestyles, who didn't show much interest in their message, and who didn't feel a need for change in their lives.

Small miracles. Some non-Mormons show genuine interest in the missionaries. They will listen at the door or invite them in to see what they have to say. Some will become "investigators," participate in the lessons, find the message compelling, and join the Latter-day Saint Church. Missionaries do not believe these encounters are accidental; they feel they are led to these people by God's hand.

A very high percentage of Latter-day Saints believe in continuing revelation, and in miracles, and that they still occur today.[72] A committed sister reported: "We believe of course that God the Father and Jesus Christ communicate to us just as they did in Bible times, just as they did in the Old Testament, just as they did in the New Testament. They do it today, to me. That is very exciting; that is neat that we have continuing revelation."

This belief and expectation is evident in missionaries' day-to-day lives, and many talk of miraculous events and circumstances that led them to knock on a particular door or to approach a particular person—the belief being that such positive encounters are a direct result of prayer and of being "led by the Spirit."

Missionaries typically begin their day by praying and seeking Divine guidance regarding where they should tract. "We always prayed about where to go before doing any street contacting or knocking on doors," said an elder who served in Germany. "We prayed first, asking to be led to the right place." Missionaries continue to pray throughout the day, seeking guidance at specific streets and doors. Positive responses to their knocks are interpreted as being a result of being led, miraculously, to that location.

An elder who served in Massachusetts said on his first day in the mission field his trainer, whom he described as "a great missionary who followed the Spirit," prayed, "Heavenly Father, tell us where we need to tract." The trainer said they needed to go to a particular street, and when they arrived they started knocking on doors. At the first three doors, they found three families "ready for the gospel."

He added, "Ever since that point, I knew it was the work of miracles, that it wasn't just something I was doing, but it was something important to the Lord, it was the Lord's work. My trainer taught me to follow the Spirit."

An elder serving in Bristol, England, described a similar experience, how his companion and he felt led to knock on a particular door. As they passed it, his companion said, "We need to knock on that door." When they did, an elderly widow answered, and they felt led to say, "We are here to share a message about how families can be together; death isn't the end, we can be together after death."

She immediately invited them in and they began teaching her. Two meetings later, she shared an experience she had had in the hospital: while in and out of consciousness, her deceased husband appeared to her and gave her comfort.

She told them she let them in that first day because she knew death wasn't the end, and she felt their message could help her.

An elder who served in England in the mid-1960s described the process whereby he and his companion approached opening a new area. They reviewed maps, prayed for guidance, and fasted for twenty-four hours several times before setting out on their bikes for a specific area to which they felt led. But when they approached their first door in the new area, they looked at each other and decided something wasn't right. They returned to their bicycles, discussed it, and prayed. They returned to the same door, and before knocking, they again felt something was wrong; it was not where they were supposed to be. For a second time they retreated to their bikes. They felt led to ride farther down the road, where they discovered a new subdivision, which wasn't shown on their map. They felt it was the right place, and within a matter of minutes they found a family who invited them in and who soon converted to the LDS faith. He said it was a very special experience that showed how God led them in their day-to-day activities.

He also added, with a laugh, that the people in the first house, if they were watching, must have thought those two Mormon missionaries were acting very strangely, coming twice to their door but never knocking.

Apathy. The most common response to their knock, at least in the United States and much of Western Europe, is apathy. Most are indifferent and turn them away, saying, "No, thanks, I am not interested," or "Thanks, I am all set," or, "Thanks, but I have my own religion." The response of a woman in Kentucky to an elder's offer of a Book of Mormon is typical: "I attend where my mother and grandmother went to church. It is a family tradition. I am fine. I don't need anything else."

Missionary Reactions to Tracting

Some enjoy it. How do missionaries react to the struggles that go along with "knocking doors"? Some (a minority it seems) actually enjoy it. They like meeting and talking with new people, they are motivated by the possibility that a new convert is behind the door, or they like the challenge.

Two gregarious sisters said they loved tracting because they never knew what was on the other side of the door: it could be a big dog, someone who didn't like them, or someone who was excited about their coming. They didn't mind doors being slammed in their faces, because it meant they could move on to the next door much more quickly—to the next potential convert.

A sister who served in Northern New England humorously described how she loved tracting, but only on a seasonal basis. In the summer she could be outside in the pleasant weather and meet new people. She continued to enjoy it through the fall when she could admire the spectacular autumn leaves. But tracting lost its appeal when it got cold and started snowing, as she wore drafty skirts. She hated the cold and snow and she thought the Lord must have chuckled when He sent her to Northern New England, because it says in Proverbs 31:21 that one of the signs of a virtuous woman is that she isn't afraid of the snow. She thought that was why God sent her there.

Greenies and their first door. For many greenies, their first missionary experience comes at their first door. Some trainers may ease them into their new role by first demonstrating at multiple doors what to do and say, while some will push them up to the first door and tell them to go for it. Many reported they were nervous and scared and hoped the person wasn't home. They were afraid there was a big dog on the other side of the door, that the person would yell at them, or that the door would be slammed in their face.

When I asked an elder what it felt like during those first days of knocking on doors, he said: "I felt fear. The idea of knocking on someone's door and telling them what I believed scared me to death." An apprehensive sister described her first days of knocking on doors as "horrible." She didn't know how people were going to react, and she could only say, "Hi," and introduce her companion and herself before she would go silent and look to her trainer for help. She said things got better with time, because she learned how most people would respond to her knock.

An elder reported that people would say to the missionaries at the door, "Oh, you must have extensive training before you come out." He would smile, thinking, "No, we don't!"

An insecure sister from Idaho shared her experience at her first door. A man answered her knock, and she began: "Hi, uh, we are, uh, missionaries of The Church of Jesus Christ of Latter-day Saints and, uh." But the man interrupted her and said, "Not interested," and slammed the door in her face. At which point, the new sister turned to her trainer and said, "Okay, let's go home!"

A greenie's nervousness isn't necessarily assuaged once she or he is invited in. After knocking on many doors during his first day in the mission field, with no interest whatsoever being shown, an elder serving in Indianapolis said when a woman finally responded that she would like to hear what he had to say, his first thought was, "Okay, now what do I do!"

Entertaining moments. Tracting has its entertaining moments. Missionaries will stumble over their introductory greetings. A popular story in missionary lore is that instead of saying, "Good morning, ma'am, I am a Mormon missionary," it comes out, "Good ma'am, morning, I am a mission mormonary."

They also make mistakes while learning a new language. An elder serving Spanish-speaking in Delaware and New Jersey and still learning the language said at the door: "Muestreme su ombligo" ("Show me your navel") and, "Ponga su codo en mi oreja" ("Put your elbow in my ear").

A woman raised as a staunch Roman Catholic was tracted into one day by two elders. They had a pleasant conversation, but she told them she had no interest whatsoever in their message or in converting. They thanked her for her time, and as they were leaving the seventeen-year-old daughter of the woman came home and was struck by how handsome the young men were. When she heard that her mother had turned them away and that they would not be returning, she was very disappointed.

Two days later she happened to run into the elders, and she told them how much her mother had enjoyed talking with them and how her mother hoped they would return (which, of course, wasn't true). The elders returned, there was confusion, the daughter was in trouble, but the woman eventually joined the Latter-day Saint Church. She felt the missionaries were able to answer questions that her original faith was unable to answer.

Cultural differences. While missionaries serving in foreign countries frequently encounter cultural differences and behaviors that they have trouble identifying and interpreting, it isn't uncommon for the same thing to happen when they serve in different regions of the United States.

A sister from Utah serving in Georgia said she and her companion tracted into a home where a woman invited them in. They talked for a while, the woman showed mild interest in their religious message, and as the sisters were leaving the woman said, "Ya' all come back now, ya' hear."

Taking her words literally, the sisters returned two days later. Again, they had a pleasant conversation, but this time the woman showed less interest in their message. As they were leaving, she said, "Ya' all come back now, ya' hear."

Again, taking her words literally, the sisters returned two days later. The woman seemed surprised to see them, but invited them in. She showed no interest whatsoever in their message, and they stayed but a short time. As they left she said, "Ya' all come back now, ya' hear."

Learning their lesson, they never returned.

On a more serious note, missionaries from the Northern and Western United States spoke of racial tensions they experienced in the Southern United States. An interviewee whose father served in the Southern States Mission in the 1950s said his father was "out of his element" in the Deep South; as a polite, white farm boy from Utah, he didn't know his place in Southern culture, and it nearly got him into serious trouble a number of times—with whites, who didn't like that he was teaching blacks, and once with a mob of men who nearly threw him off a bus when he gave up his seat to a black woman.

Caucasian missionaries spoke of their unease in tracting into integrated or all-black neighborhoods, because up until the late 1970s black males couldn't enjoy the same status (of holding the priesthood) in the Latter-day Saint Church as white males. A sister who served in North Carolina in the 1970s said the practice made her very uncomfortable, and she was thrilled when, in 1978, President Kimball said he received a revelation that said that all worthy males, without regard to race or color, could hold the priesthood. The interviewee remembered where she was when she heard the announcement, and she wished she could go back and revisit her mission and the black neighborhoods.

Many Church members wanted the change in racial policy to happen, but it showed their faith and trust in the Church leadership, that change had to come through proper channels: it had to come through a revelation given to the president of the Latter-day Saint Church.

Jehovah's Witnesses: Tables are turned. Sometimes the tables are turned and missionaries become the subject of tracting. Two sisters answered a knock at their apartment door to find two Jehovah's Witnesses standing there. The Witnesses, not knowing who the sisters were, introduced themselves, showed the sisters a picture of heaven, and said they would like to tell them how to get there. The sisters said they would like to hear the Witnesses' message, if they could share their message with them. Confused, the Witnesses asked what they meant. The sisters introduced themselves as LDS missionaries.

"Mormons!" the Witnesses responded.

They thanked the sisters for their time and left.

"I guess they realized they would not change us, and we would not change them," observed the sister.

Latter-day Saint missionaries are frequently mistaken for Jehovah's Witnesses. Two elders told how when they knocked on a door the man told them they had been there two days earlier, he had told them he wasn't interested in talking with them then, and he certainly wasn't interested now, and he slammed the door in their faces. The previous visitors had been Jehovah's Witnesses. The LDS missionaries had seen Witnesses in the area, and the elders knew that they had not knocked on that particular door.

Relieving the boredom: In order to relieve the boredom of tracting, some missionaries will engage in unusual practices (some more acceptable than others). They will play what they call "the word game." As they approach a door, the missionary making the door approach is given a word by his companion, which has to be used during the conversation. One elder told of giving his companion the word "orange," while in return he was given "shark." Other words missionaries said they used included "broccoli," "cauliflower," and "front-end loader."

An elder said he actually learned something from the experience; he felt that, regardless of the word, it could be tied to the Latter-day Saint gospel in some way.

An elder who served in Sweden said he and his companion would get so bored with what they were doing, and being "the silly teenagers" they were, they started doing things they shouldn't. At one door the companion told the woman that they had come all the way from America to tell her about a book that had come down from God. The interviewee, standing behind the door, dropped the Book of Mormon over the door, and the companion caught it.

"And here it is!" said the companion.

"I think we will probably burn in Hell for that one," mused the interviewee.

An elder serving in the Northwest said they came upon a house with a sign in the front yard: "No Trespassing, Especially Mormans" (*sic*). Saying he couldn't resist the urge, the elder leaned against the sign while his companion took his picture. They then ran. After the picture was developed, they could see the owner through a window, heading toward the door to chase them away.

Missionaries have also posted videos of themselves on the Internet, sometimes in a less than positive light. Church officials find them embarrassing.

Laughing at adversity. Some try to find humor in their negative experiences, and they laugh about them afterwards. A man responded to the elders' knock by saying, "Sure, I'd like to talk with you. Let's go out and talk on the porch." The missionaries went out on the porch, at which point the man shut and locked the door behind him, leaving them standing alone. The elders looked at each other, laughed, and moved on.

At the end of a long day, two sisters laughed about experiences they had had that day, including a woman who told them, "See the end of my driveway? I want you over there, right now!" At another point, they were talking with a man, and his next door neighbor yelled over the fence, "Before you bother, don't bother!" They said initially such responses hurt, but eventually they would look back on such experiences and laugh.

Another sister agreed humor has to be found: "Missionary life is funny. Sometimes you just have to laugh. If you don't, you cry."

Aggressiveness and argumentation. Missionaries are told not to be aggressive when knocking on doors. Non-Mormons especially appreciate this aspect of missionary behavior. A student in a religion class described Mormon missionaries as "the nice ones, who will take 'no' for an answer."

A non-Mormon acquaintance said that while he finds it bothersome when they knock and that he doesn't agree with their beliefs, he does feel that missionaries have always been very pleasant. He and they have agreed to disagree, "and they haven't stuck their foot in the door."

But some missionaries can be aggressive, who stay longer at the door, pressing their point. Some interviewees said missionaries *did* stick their foot in the door as it was being shut. In at least one instance, it resulted in the missionaries being invited in and the family eventually joining the Latter-day Saint Church.

Missionaries are advised not to argue, but some can't resist the temptation. Non-Mormons will sometimes invite them in either to argue, or to convert them to *their* faith. An aggressive elder said early on in his mission he argued with people if he felt they were misinformed or said untruths about the Latter-day Saint Church. But by mid-mission, he agreed it was not the best approach, and he tempered his reactions. He said it didn't get him anywhere to argue. "I never once, in an argument, converted someone to the Church," he observed.

An elder who served in Germany said he didn't go on his mission to argue or to prove that some people were wrong and that he was right. He considered it his function to provide information to people and to talk about his personal experiences, about what his faith had done for him and why he thought the Latter-day Saint Church was true. He felt his duty was to provide the person with something to pray about. When faced with someone who started to "bash," he would leave, because he knew the discussion wasn't going anywhere.

But he knew missionaries who liked to argue. "Give them a good brawl with Bible bashing, and they would love it."

Most don't enjoy tracting. Based on my interviews, it appears that most missionaries, especially those who have to engage in knocking doors much of the time, don't enjoy tracting. They don't like doors slammed in their faces, rejection of their message, or apathetic responses to their appeals—in all kinds of weather. They find it frustrating, because they feel they have an important message to share, and they are devoting eighteen or twenty-four months of their lives to do it, but few seem interested in hearing what they have to say.

An elder serving in Switzerland, which is an area of limited baptisms, said he was amazed at how few people would take the time to even hear what he had to say. He was happy when they took a few minutes just to listen, even if they didn't agree. Another elder said he found it frustrating when people wouldn't accept a free copy of the Book of Mormon; all he asked of them was that they read it and find out for themselves if it was true. They wouldn't take it, saying, "You guys are wrong."

Missionaries who grew up in areas where Latter-day Saints were in the majority and where they had limited contact with non-Mormons, spoke of the religious culture shock they experienced when they served in areas where the Church had a limited presence. They were used to a culture that assumed Joseph Smith was a prophet and that the Book of Mormon was Divinely inspired, but once they were in a region where this was not generally believed, and where most didn't come to believe it, the experience of knocking on doors and being rejected proved to be very frustrating and very unsettling.

Doubts. Negative responses can cause missionaries to have doubts. An elder said his first antagonistic response caught him off guard, upset him, and put doubts in his mind. He was told he was lost and that Joseph Smith was not a prophet. To feel the person's disgust at what was precious to him disturbed him. He said he eventually came to realize that none of the detractors knew what they were talking about, that they had secondhand and thirdhand sources.

Rejection. A sister said that, next to living with a companion every hour of every day, the hardest part of being a missionary is the rejection. It is especially difficult because they want to share something that is so important to them, but people don't seem interested, or they think it has no value.

An elder said he started to "form a callus" against rejection when he realized that he shouldn't take it personally: people weren't rejecting him—they didn't even know him—they were rejecting his message. A sister added that rejection isn't so bad if people are at least cordial, if they say something like, "I am not really interested, but thanks so much for coming."

"I mean, we are human, too," continued the sister, "and it is nice when they treat us with respect."

"But rejection is still hard," added an elder, "it still hurts."

In the face of constant rejection, some try to remember the limits of their responsibility. They say that while tracting isn't very effective, there are some people who can't be found any other way. It is the missionaries' responsibility to share their message, and it is up to the person to receive it, or to reject it.

"I felt my message was important enough to give them an opportunity to listen to it, and if they didn't want to, then that was their choice," added an elder. "Of course, I am not accountable for their choice."

Some spoke of the importance of attitude when dealing with rejection. Said a sister, "You have to have a positive attitude, otherwise it will be a very long eighteen or twenty-four months."

When I asked him how he remains enthusiastic and happy in the face of constant rejection, an elder replied, "Sometimes you just have to fake it." He learned that as he was knocking on doors, if he wasn't happy, people with whom he was trying to communicate could sense that and they wouldn't respect his message or even want to hear it. He could imagine the person thinking, "If you aren't happy, what makes you think your message will make me happy?" He said eventually his happiness would become authentic during the day; belief followed behavior.

When I asked an elder who served in Portugal how he handled stress and rejection, he responded: "You had faith that what you were teaching was true and that in the end the person would receive something. That is why you are doing it. That is what motivates missionaries, and you need it to be successful as a missionary. You have to exercise faith to save people."

Some try to remain optimistic, flavored with a sense of humor. An elder serving in southwestern Pennsylvania said his goal was to baptize a thousand people. At the end of a day when he didn't have much success, he looked forward to the next day, when he would go out and look for a house with a thousand people in it.

Continual rejection can lead to discouragement. A disheartened sister said at first she had a really hard time with rejection: with doors being slammed in her face, with people telling her she was wrong, to go away, and to not come back. It was hard to keep a positive attitude, and sometimes it was hard to even open her mouth and talk with people.

Others also spoke of getting discouraged. An elder said he and his companion felt that way when faced with so much rejection, when they didn't have many teaching appointments, when they would come home wet, cold, and tired from tracting in the rain, and have no appointments on their calendar for the next day, which had a forecast of more rain.

To deal with weather-related discouragement, there is a missionary myth that the more you tract in the rain, the better looking your spouse will be. An elder who tracted during twenty straight days of rain said he was counting every raindrop and trying to picture what his future spouse would look like.

An elder who served in Paris said he experienced discouragement when he and his companion would work very hard, but they had no sense of accomplishment. Another elder said there were times when he struggled to get up the energy to go out and do the work, and while he knew he shouldn't, he would think about what he could be doing if he were at home. He said at times it was depressing to think he had a two-year obligation.

Discouragement was in the voice of an elder when he asked himself, "Why am I knocking on doors, in the snow, when nobody wants to listen to me?" This was echoed by a sister who served in Spain in the early 1990s when she observed, "You think you are doing right, but you keep getting 'No.'"

The rejections, the discouragement, and the thoughts of home cause many (some say *most*) missionaries to ask: "What am I doing here?" Gordon B. Hinckley asked that question when he served his mission in England in the 1930s. Elder Hinckley wrote to his father expressing his frustrations, and his father gave a response that is now famous throughout the Church: forget yourself, and go do the work.

Missionaries who form strong bonds with their companions seem to be in a better position to deal with the stress that arises from rejection and dejection, as they can be mutually supportive in times of need. Elders and sisters who had what they considered good companions talked of the mutual support they gave each other; they talked through their frustrations, they were sympathetic to one another's needs, and when one was down, the other was generally up.

Getting more proficient and comfortable. Most say that with time they become more comfortable talking with people. While they may marvel at how adept their trainer seemed to be in the early days, they find that, with practice, with learning new techniques, and with thinking of stories and analogies to illustrate their points, they become more proficient in engaging people in conversations.

But one's comfort level is relative. A hesitant elder serving in Pennsylvania said he started out his mission feeling "really uncomfortable." Six month later, he just felt "uncomfortable."

In spite of their comfort level, it seems that getting started each day is still a challenge. Said an elder who served in New Jersey: "The hardest thing each day was to knock on that first door. But then it was okay for the rest of the day."

The value of tracting. Some people do respond positively to the missionaries' knock and invite them into their homes to hear what they have to say. As a result, tracting is the most common way non-members are first exposed to detailed information about the Latter-day Saint Church. However, few approached in this way go on to be baptized. The Church estimates that only 2 to 3 percent of individuals found through such efforts join the Church.[73]

When missionaries have exhausted other, more successful approaches, they start knocking on doors. Granted, some experience success while tracting, and some enjoy the challenge, but there is a certain irony in the fact that the practice we most often associate with LDS missionaries—their signature activity of door-to-door evangelism—isn't very effective, or desirable.

Thus, if Latter-day Saint missionaries are knocking at your door, it probably means they have run out of other, more effective ways, of finding potential investigators.

They may be smiling, but they are struggling.

"Without Purse or Scrip"

One of the most unique interviews for this study was with a missionary who served in New England in the late 1940s. He must have been one of the last in this country to travel "without purse or scrip": the practice of proselytizing with little money, food, or clothes in hand, depending on the goodwill of people to house and feed the missionary. It is an approach to missions that missionaries from many different faiths have practiced over the centuries, including Latter-day Saint missionaries in the nineteenth and early twentieth centuries. The practice is inconceivable among Mormon missionaries today, and it was a special set of circumstances that led the interviewee to engage in it in eastern Massachusetts and in the Connecticut River Valley in the late 1940s.

Latter-day Saint missionaries weren't having much success in the larger cities in New England following WWII, because Yankee Calvinists had been replaced by Irish, Polish, and Italian immigrants, most of whom were devoutly Roman Catholic. They had been told by their priests not to talk with representatives of other faiths, because it was said to be harmful to their spiritual well-being. The interviewee said that when they knocked on the door and the person realized they weren't from the local parish, older women would appear frightened, while the men (as he recalled in one instance) would tell them they had ten seconds to get off of the porch, or they would be thrown off.

The mission president, realizing they weren't going to get anywhere in the cities and that the shrinking Yankee population was still out in the countryside, decided missionaries should concentrate on small towns instead of big cities. He sent them out two-by-two with the barest of necessities—a change of underwear and some literature—and that was about it.

The mission president referred to it as "country work." As soon as the snow melted, missionaries gave up the place where they stayed in the winter, and they started walking. The interviewee stressed that they walked (they didn't have bicycles), and he did it for thirteen of his twenty-four month mission. They slept outside maybe five times during the entire time. Every other night they found people to take them in, or they were in jail. They didn't have to twist arms; all they had to do was tell people their situation and they experienced considerable hospitability.

They walked from one town to another, and they corresponded through the mail every week with the mission president. They told him what town they expected to be in the next week, and he would forward their mail from home to them, care of general delivery at the post office in the next small town, a distance of perhaps twenty to thirty miles.

It was an experience "that separated the men from the boys," he said, and while some elders broke down during the process, very few went home early. Most who engaged in the practice were WWII veterans who had seen worse (which may help account for the fact that the mission president allowed it). The interviewee wasn't a veteran, but a nineteen year old from California who found it to be a scary experience; but he finally took to it, because it was a challenge to do something that was really "flaky," and he was just enough of a kid that the idea of doing something unconventional like that appealed to him.

"Not my better instincts," he added, "but it had its appeal."

In the summer of 1947, he and his companion walked up the Connecticut River on the New Hampshire side, and down the river on the Vermont side, stopping at all the towns along the way. They would go into a town, typically containing a few hundred people, and they lined up a meeting hall to which they invited people that night. It could be a grange hall, or a church if the minister wasn't anti-Mormon, or a school if they found someone on the school board who was friendly. On occasion they were turned away pretty abruptly from all of these possibilities and would have to depend on some friendly soul whose door they knocked on and who had a living room large enough to invite.

Almost without exception (and there were exceptions, to be sure), they succeeded early in finding some kind of meeting hall, and then they would canvas the whole town, knocking on every door, telling people who they were and why they were there, and inviting them to a meeting that evening.

He and his companion played the piano at the meeting, sang, prayed, and gave a sermon. They left behind pamphlets and copies of the Book of Mormon. They asked for fifty-cent donations for the books, which people usually paid.

They were thrown on their own resources and had to improvise in order to find teaching opportunities. He and his companion were in a drugstore in a small town in New Hampshire in July 1947 when they overheard a man from the Rotary Club bemoaning the fact that the guest speaker for the day's meeting was unable to attend at the last minute and that the Rotarians would be expecting a speaker, but that he as the program chairperson didn't have anyone else he could turn to. The interviewee said he noticed on the newsstand a picture of Brigham Young on the cover of a magazine, commemorating the centennial anniversary of the arrival of Young and the Mormon Pioneers to the Great Salt Lake Valley. He walked over to the man, introduced himself and his companion, pointed to the magazine and said, "Would you like to know about this? We will come and talk to you for free."

The man gave them lunch, and they spoke to the Rotarians for around thirty minutes. This opened up speaking opportunities at other Rotary Clubs.

The elders weren't always so well-received. There were nights when they had to sleep in jail. Sheriffs would pick them up under vagrancy laws, which required strangers in town to be able to cover a night's lodging, and, if they couldn't, they were operationally defined as a vagrant and would be locked up for the night. Thus they had to compromise and carry enough money to cover a night's lodging, but they hoped they wouldn't have to use it. In a lot of towns it was five dollars each for lodging, so that is how much they each carried.

Some local sheriffs weren't very friendly, and they looked for excuses to trick the missionaries. They would ask the missionaries if they had enough money for a night's lodging, and they would say, "Yes." The sheriff would respond, "How much have you got?" and the elders would say, "Five dollars, and here it is."

But the sheriff would say, "Sorry, boys, in this town it is ten dollars," and he would lock them up.

The elders quickly caught on to the system, and they would make the sheriff commit to the amount first. He would ask how much they had and they would say five dollars, and the sheriff would say, "Sorry, boys, but it is ten dollars," and the missionaries would respond, "And in this other pocket we have another five dollars!" They would go through this good-natured game if the sheriff's demeanor didn't threaten them.

Sometimes they would arrive in a town and people would start calling friends and relatives, warning them that Mormon missionaries were in town, so elders would not receive a good reception. Some local officials would tell the sheriff to pick them up on any excuse they could muster and get them out of town as quickly as possible. In one New Hampshire town, they were met at the town line by a delegation of eight men, one of whom carried a shotgun, while the others carried pitchforks. They were told in no uncertain terms that they weren't welcome in the town and that they should just keep on going, otherwise they would be sorry.

The interviewee reported, "We, of course, weren't predisposed to press the matter, or to ask what it would mean for us 'to be sorry,' so we went right on through town and that night we slept as much as we could in the rain. It was one of the most miserable nights I have spent in my life. And it kind of made us tough."

And they had to be tough, because he and his companion, after all that effort, only baptized about four people each summer—which, he said, was actually quite a few in those days.

The experience created a special bond between the missionaries involved. They met periodically for local, district-wide, or mission-wide missionary conferences. As he described it: "We, of course, had war stories to tell, which was a great part of the fun, but of course these war stories took on a life of their own, and, like all war stories, they got well-embroidered with each new telling, each trying to top the other."

Their relationship remained strong for many years thereafter, renewed by annual missionary reunions in Salt Lake City.

Street Contacting

In cities with locked apartment buildings and doormen and in areas with gated communities it is difficult for missionaries to gain access to peoples' homes, so they must try other techniques, including talking to people on the street, known as "street contacting." They may try to engage people by using approaches similar to their door approaches, or they may ask if they can give the person a brief questionnaire relating to their thoughts about religion. They may set up religious displays on the street, sing Church songs to gain attention, or preach short sermons.

A sister who served in California said she and her companion would stand on a busy sidewalk and when someone walked by one of the sisters would walk with the person, saying she was a representative of Jesus Christ and that she was there to share a message. She would say Heavenly Father has a plan for us and could she talk with the person for a moment? Some would let out a groan and run away. Many would be respectful, slow down, and let her offer the message, before politely declining. Some would actually stop. The sister then showed them a copy of the Book of Mormon, shared the First Vision, gave them some literature with the missionaries' names on it, and asked if they could come to their home and talk further.

They did get some appointments and were able to continue conversations in the person's home, although some people weren't always at home when they went for their appointment. She said they got to talk to many more people using this approach, versus knocking on doors.

She assured me that she and her companion were always in sight of each other, thus remaining true to the mission rules. And no, she added, they didn't chase after people who ran away.

An elder who served in Germany said he didn't like knocking doors, but he did enjoy street contacting, or "ATAPing": sharing the message "any time, any place." He and his companion would set up easels on the street decorated with pictures and a sign asking, "What is God's Plan?" Some people would stop and talk with them.

A sister who served in Japan in the early 1970s said they did mainly street contacting. Houses were walled off but there were a lot of people on the streets. Westerners were unusual at that time and people would stare at them. People were also "shocked" the missionaries could speak their language, and out of curiosity they were drawn to the missionaries when they appeared on the streets passing out leaflets. She said they just had to show up and people would gather around. While the missionaries were glad of the attention, she said the stares gave them a strong sense "of being different."

An elder who served in Portugal did what they called "the morning program." Missionaries would be on the streets by 7:30 A.M. so they could talk to men going to work. He said they found the approach to be very effective, and they gained converts that way.

The missionaries targeted men, because the Church has a special interest in converting men. Males hold positions of leadership in the Church, they hold "the priesthood," and there is a need to replenish their numbers in order to keep these positions filled. Husbands and fathers are considered the heads of households in the Latter-day Saint Church, and experience has shown that if they convert to the Church, there is a greater likelihood that their wives and children will, too.

A sister from Utah said street contacting forces missionaries to stretch and to do things they normally wouldn't consider. Before becoming a missionary, she would never have walked up to someone on the street and offered them a Book of Mormon. "That is not something I would ever have chosen to do," she said. "I have left my comfort zone miles and miles behind, millions of miles behind! I am way out there!"

Wearing the nametag can change their self-perception and help them overcome these inhibitions. A sister said she normally wouldn't walk up to people on the street and talk with them about her faith, but wearing her nametag made it easier for her to do so because it gave her a new identity. The nametag defined who she was. The collective had replaced her individuality.

Missionaries spoke of unusual experiences on the street. People came up to them and poured out their problems to them, believing they could solve them. Missionaries are told not to engage in any type of counseling, but to refer people to appropriate resources in the community. Missionaries are also exposed to colorful characters on the street, balanced and unbalanced, who corner them and talk at length about things missionaries may have only limited knowledge of or interest in.

Street Meetings

Putting on street meetings can be scary for missionaries, when they stand up in public places, bear their testimony, and give a sermon. New missionaries arriving in Boston from Salt Lake City in the mid-twentieth century were required to do this; it was considered a rite of passage, and they were confronted with it as soon as they got off the train. Their baptism by fire was a street meeting on the Boston Common, in which they would have to take a turn for five minutes, giving a sermon and bearing their testimonies "to whatever disrespectful and uncouth people" might gather around to make fun of them. An elder who was forced to do this said it was a big letdown spiritually; that things he had learned to consider as sacred were scoffed at by "the not-too-savory-types" gathered on the Common.

However, it did what a rite of passage is supposed to do: it humbled him. Many missions put new missionaries through similar experiences.

An interviewee who served in Boston in the early 1960s had to go through a similar roughing-up on Boston Common. It left such a bad taste in his mouth that, even though he has lived in New England for many decades since then, he is no fan of the Boston Red Sox, the Boston Celtics, or the Boston Bruins.

Street contacting and street meetings open missionaries up to various perils. They are harassed and sometimes assaulted. An elder serving in Lyon, France, said they were frequently accosted by men on the street and would sometimes be physically assaulted. It was difficult, because as missionaries they weren't supposed to retaliate or fight back. They stuck out, and because there had been missionaries there for so long, people knew they could push them around because they knew the missionaries wouldn't do anything back.

Missionaries are advised to ignore negative comments and to move on. In some cases it is easy, because people will swear at them in a language they don't understand, so they don't know what they are being called.

But missionaries are human. An elder serving in Mexico reported that people would make nasty comments behind their backs as they walked along, and some elders would want to go back and confront them.

A sister with backbone said on her first occasion of street contacting in California someone said something rude to her and she responded, "Excuse me, you can't talk to me like that!" She said there was a lot of learning that took place in those early days. "I learned I shouldn't be telling people off on the street," she observed.

"Golden Questions"

An elder who served in New England in the early 1990s said when they had no referrals and had tired of knocking on doors, he, his companion, and other missionaries would go to the town center, talk with people, and "G.Q."—that is, ask them "Golden Questions," such as: "What is the purpose of life?" "Why do you think you are on this earth?" "What are your feelings about God?" Such questions engaged the person and hopefully led to a conversation.

Initially it was hard for him to stop and talk with people like this. He would think they didn't want to be bothered, but then he realized he was there to help people but they didn't know it. Plus, he had nothing to lose, because he would never see them again. Missionaries would have contests to see how many people they could talk to in a day, which he said made the exercise interesting and fun. He said they had to enjoy what they were doing, because if they were miserable doing it, people would sense it.

I myself was "G.Q.ed" by missionaries in Harvard Square, Cambridge, Massachusetts, and it was an awkward, but humorous experience.

It was a warm afternoon in November 2000 and the sidewalks were filled with jugglers, street musicians, and people enjoying the late-autumn sunshine. I was on a break from a seminar, and I had settled onto a low wall to read a book. Then I noticed the missionaries, sisters and elders, ten in all, moving through the crowds, two-by-two, stopping and talking with as many people as they could engage. Most encounters were brief, but occasionally they engaged in longer conversations. A frequent topic was the Latter-day Saint temple that was being built in nearby Belmont. Its construction had been delayed by numerous lawsuits and by concerns from residents that it would decrease their property values.

I went out of my way to engage missionaries while I was writing this book, and I frequently accosted them before they accosted me. Thus I intentionally caught the eye of one of the elders; he immediately came over. He introduced himself, said he was a missionary, and asked if I had ever thought about life after death.

I assured him that I had.

He proceeded to talk about Joseph Smith, the First Vision, and the Book of Mormon.

Not wanting to hide my identity, I told him I was especially interested in what he was doing, because I was writing a book on Mormon missionaries. I explained that I wasn't a member of the Latter-day Saint Church, but that I wanted to tell *his* story.

His response was typical of missionaries who didn't know me: there was wariness, combined with inquisitiveness. He didn't know my motivation for writing such a book, but he was intrigued that an outsider was interested in the missionaries. When I told him I had interviewed hundreds of missionaries, including General Authorities, he warmed to the idea. He called five other elders to where we were sitting, and we talked briefly about their backgrounds, their mission experiences, and how people reacted to them that day.

When I said I had to return to my seminar, they asked if they could sing a song for me. Standing as I was with my back to a wall and with six elders standing in a semi-circle in front of me, I felt I had no choice, so I said, "Sure."

They proceeded to sing, with great gusto, the popular missionary song, "Called to Serve."

This caused heads—hundreds of heads—to turn.

Thinking this looked very strange—six missionaries singing to a middle-aged man—I took out my notebook, put my head down, and started writing notes about my conversation with them.

"Oh, I don't know who they are. Are they singing to me? I am just standing here, writing in my notebook."

After they finished, I asked if they sang often. "We sing when things slow down," replied one of the elders. "It draws attention to us." Since "us" in this instance was me, I took heart that no one in Harvard Square knew me. I thanked them for their time, shook their hands, and hurried back to my seminar.

When I walked into the seminar room, the program coordinator said, "Well, Rob, did they convert you?" He had seen the whole episode while strolling through Harvard Square and he had been quite amused by the scene. I told him they had not, and, as I always do in situations where missionaries are mentioned, I asked if he had ever had contact with them or with the Latter-day Saint Church.

He assured me he had, and he had fond memories of the experience. He had visited Salt Lake City, toured Temple Square, and had gone inside the Mormon Tabernacle. He had seen a number of young female missionaries from various countries on Temple Square, talking with visitors in their native languages, and he wondered who they were and how the Church was so successful in recruiting such a broad array of young international missionaries to serve as tour guides. I told him he wasn't alone in wondering about the missionaries—about who they are, why they serve, and what they and the Church gain from it. I told him I was wondering the same thing, and that was why I was writing a book about them. I said many non-Mormons entertain such questions, but they prefer not to seek the answers through conversations with the missionaries themselves. He said he could understand that, because he felt the same way.

"I look forward to reading your book," he said. He then smiled, turned, and walked away, humming "Called to Serve."

Finding potential investigators can be a challenge, but with just one "Yes," with just one person saying she wants to hear their message, missionaries forget the rejections and the discouragement.

We will now turn to what missionaries say when they are invited into a home, the baptismal and confirmation process, and the challenges and trials that go along the way.

CHAPTER 7

Teach, Baptize, and Confirm

"To teach someone who wants to learn and progress, that is what makes it all worth it. There is nothing better."

AN ELDER'S REFLECTIONS ON WHAT HE CONSIDERED TO HAVE BEEN A GOOD TEACHING SESSION.

"That was really hard for me. It wasn't supposed to go like that! They were supposed to react differently!"

A GREENIE SISTER'S LAMENT AFTER THE SIXTY-FIVE-YEAR-OLD COUPLE HER COMPANION AND SHE HAD BEEN TEACHING REFUSED TO ATTEND CHURCH OR PRAY TO ASK IF THEIR MESSAGE WAS TRUE. THEY DIDN'T WANT TO KNOW IF IT WAS TRUE, THEY SAID, BECAUSE IF IT WAS, THEY WOULD HAVE TO CHANGE, AND THEY DIDN'T WANT TO CHANGE. THEY FELT THEY WERE TOO OLD TO CHANGE, AND THEY REFUSED TO BE BAPTIZED.

The missionaries' goal is to locate potential converts, teach them the doctrines and practices of the Latter-day Saint Church, and baptize them into the faith. They teach from Church-provided materials to ensure doctrinal consistency, but they tailor their presentations to the needs of the individual. They look to publications from the Church's Missionary Department and obtain guidance from their mission presidents for advice on best practices.

They may have grown up seeing films that gave the impression that the missionary experience is a seamless, dynamic process centered on working with ideal investigators: who are easily found; who faithfully meet with missionaries; who thoughtfully study passages from the Book of Mormon; who keep various commitments such as stopping smoking and drinking coffee; who are baptized; who become faithful members of the Church; and who, along with other Church members, introduce missionaries to friends and relatives so that they too may learn about the faith. It is portrayed as a self-perpetuating process that carries on throughout the missionaries' time of service.

That, they quickly discover, is only the theory. The reality depends in large part on the initiative of missionaries, the helpfulness of local Church members, and where and when missionaries are serving. Hardworking missionaries in Latin America may baptize scores, even hundreds, of converts, whereas missionaries serving in areas with rocky religious soil, such as Western Europe and Northern New England, will baptize only a few. Some will have no baptisms at all. "Success" is thus a relative term. If missionaries work hard, keep the mission rules, and do what is asked of them, they are told their mission should be considered a success—regardless of the number of converts they bring into the Church. Still, they compare themselves to relatives and friends who enjoyed more baptisms during their time of service, and some find themselves wanting.

Some investigators are lackadaisical: they cancel meetings or fail to show up at scheduled times; they forget to read assigned passages in the Book of Mormon; they don't keep commitments; and they back out of baptisms. Many missionaries become frustrated as a result and struggle to find the inner resolve to continue on, day after day, in the face of such experiences. But, as is true of life in general, one positive experience, especially a baptism, wipes away the negatives and energizes them to continue on. Most emerge from the trials with a stronger testimony and a greater commitment to the Church. They have gone through a refiner's fire.

This chapter considers what they teach, the baptismal and confirmation process, and the roadblocks, detours, and successes along the way.

Teach

Missionaries are told their commission is to teach the gospel of Jesus Christ as restored through the prophet Joseph Smith. Theirs is a special calling in the Church. They are the "authorized representatives" of Jesus Christ, and through the power vested in their Melchizedek priesthood (which is held only by males), they have the power and authority to preach the gospel and baptize converts into the faith. They seek to help people identify and repent of their sins, commit to living a life according to the teachings of the Mormon Church, and to have faith in the Restored Gospel. They are to help converts to "put off the 'natural man' and become a Saint 'through the atonement of Christ the Lord.'"[74]

The task of missionaries is to teach lessons and baptize new members. They try to schedule as many evening teaching appointments as possible, to increase the likelihood that all family members can attend. Otherwise they teach when it is convenient for the investigator and the missionaries. Generally sisters are to teach females, and elders to teach males, but it doesn't always work out that way. If the missionaries are one sex and the investigator is the other, frequently the mission president will require that a Church member of the same sex of the investigator be present. Emphasis is placed on recruiting males, particularly males who are the heads of their households, because males "hold the priesthood" and thus provide leadership at all levels of the Church. This places the LDS Church at somewhat of a disadvantage, since statistically (and this is true in many religious traditions) more women than men engage in religious activities.[75]

Missed meetings are common. A time to meet will be agreed upon, but the investigator will not be there, frequently with no explanation given. A sister who served in France in the 1960s said many investigators didn't have telephones, so it was not possible to confirm previously agreed upon meeting times. The missionaries would make lengthy crosstown trips, only to find no one home. They would then have to contact the person again to set up a new meeting time. They had a fair number of evening teaching sessions, but they weren't allowed to tract after dark because it was considered too dangerous.

The lessons. Once people say they want to learn more about the Latter-day Saint Church, they become "investigators" and engage in a series of conversations around five lessons that focus on the beliefs and practices of the Church. The end result, it is hoped, is that the person will seek baptism. Lesson titles include: (1) "The Message of the Restoration of the Gospel of Jesus Christ"; (2) "The Plan of Salvation"; (3) "The Gospel of Jesus Christ"; (4) "The Commandments"; and (5) "Laws and Ordinances." All missionaries teach from the same lessons, thus providing consistency in the message given to investigators. The lessons are discussed in detail in *Preach My Gospel: A Guide to Missionary Service*, and they represent the core of missionary training at the MTC.

The manner in which missionaries present the material to investigators is still evolving. Prior to the introduction of *Preach My Gospel* in 2004, missionaries engaged in a series of six "discussions," which had evolved since the 1950s, with investigators. Earlier missionaries were expected to memorize the discussions and to present them in a preset way. Missionaries today, in contrast, are advised not to memorize lessons, but to focus on understanding the underlying doctrines and principles, to listen closely to an investigator's questions, and to tailor a curriculum specific to that individual's needs.

Missionaries still memorize particular passages of scripture, but the goal is to get away from what was perceived as wooden, uninspired presentations of the past. Flexibility and creativity are encouraged. It is referred to as "Teaching by the Spirit." They may depart from the order of the lessons, but they must cover the material in each lesson.

An elder noted: "We are taught the doctrine, then sent out to talk *with* people, not *at* them."

While there are great variations among the world's religions, many share a common starting point: they ask the same types of questions. Religions differ because they answer the questions differently. Questions include:

- What must one do to be "saved"? (However "salvation" is defined.)
- What is the nature of the Divine being(s)?
- How does one communicate with the Divine, and how does the Divine make known its will to humans?
- What is the nature of humans?
- How should one behave?
- What is the nature of the creation, and what is one's place in it?
- What will become of the creation?
- What outward manifestations should a religion take on? How should it be organized? What are the titles and roles of various religious personnel? What is the place of architecture, ritual, and vestments?

What is found in the five lessons that missionaries teach is how The Church of Jesus Christ of Latter-day Saints answers many of these basic questions of religion. What follows is a summary of the lessons, taken from *Preach My Gospel.* (The entire document is found at: https://www.lds.org/manual/preach-my-gospel-a-guide-to-missionary-service. See Chapter 3, "What Do I Study and Teach?" for a detailed discussion of the five lessons.)

Lesson One:
"The Message of the Restoration of the Gospel of Jesus Christ"

Central to understanding the Latter-day Saint Church and its theology is the concept of "The Restoration." This is the belief that: the authority and message of the original Christian Church was lost through a falling away, or "Great Apostasy," after the first generation of Christians died; this truth and authority was lost for 1,900 years; and "the fullness of the gospel" was restored through revelations given to the nineteenth century prophet Joseph Smith.

Lesson One teaches that there is a God who loves us and who sent His Son, Jesus Christ, to earth to establish His Church. Jesus called and ordained apostles, gave them priesthood authority to teach and to baptize, and continued to guide them through revelation after his death. But after the apostles were gone, people quickly fell away from the truth, and the priesthood authority to instruct and to baptize was taken away by God. As a result, doctrines were corrupted and unauthorized changes were made in church organization. This led to the creation of many different Christian churches.

This lesson explains that this falling away is part of a cyclical pattern that began in the Old Testament:

- God communicates to His people through prophets who hold the priesthood and who have the authority to lead and instruct His people
- People follow God's prophets for a while, but then reject them and ignore their teachings
- People fall into apostasy and lose knowledge of the gospel, so God takes away the priesthood authority
- God eventually sends another prophet who restores the priesthood and who teaches the people the true gospel.

The Latter-day Saint Church teaches that this cycle was repeated after Jesus's death:

- People fell away from the truth, into the Great Apostasy, after the apostles were gone
- God took away priesthood authority and the ability to receive revelation
- It was only when God revealed to the fourteen-year-old Joseph Smith the "Restored Gospel," and when God reinstituted priesthood authority, that truth and authority was once again

> on earth. "As God had done with Adam, Noah, Abraham, Moses, and other prophets, He called Joseph Smith to be a prophet through whom the fullness of the gospel was restored to earth."[76]

Lesson One explains that Joseph Smith was led through revelation to discover and translate a set of golden plates, which were published as the Book of Mormon. The Latter-day Saint Church describes the Book of Mormon as "Another Testament of Jesus Christ" and says it complements the Bible. It is an account of the earliest Indian inhabitants of the American continent, their Hebraic origin (it is said they are a remnant of the Lost Tribes of Israel), and it contains "the fullness of the everlasting Gospel," which Christ preached to these inhabitants in America, after his death but before his ascension into heaven. Joseph Smith described the Book of Mormon as the "keystone" of the faith, and *Preach My Gospel* states that its existence is proof that Smith was a prophet and that the gospel of Jesus Christ has been restored.[77]

It is said the head of the Latter-day Saint Church, the president, is a living prophet who is the successor to Joseph Smith. The president is described as a prophet, seer, and revelator. While Latter-day Saints revere Joseph Smith and succeeding prophets, they do not worship him. Their focus is on Christ.

It is also said we are living in the End Times, the "Latter Days" discussed in Revelation, and that is why the Church is named The Church of Jesus Christ of Latter-day Saints.

Lesson One talks of God being a loving God who "has a body of flesh and bones that is glorified and perfected." God wants to have a relationship with us, but since we are sinners, it is only through Christ's atonement, his suffering and death, that we "can be freed from the burden of our sins and develop faith and strength to face our trials."

The importance of families is emphasized: "Because families are ordained of God, they are the most important social unit in time and in eternity."

Lesson One ends with an appeal to investigators to keep certain "commitments," activities designed to help them make changes in their lives and to prepare them for baptism. They are asked to read suggested passages from the Book of Mormon, to pray to know that Joseph Smith was a prophet, and to believe that the Book of Mormon is the word of God. They are encouraged to attend services at a Mormon church, to think about a possible date for baptism, and to set a date when they will meet with missionaries to discuss Lesson Two. [78]

Lesson Two:
"The Plan of Salvation"

Lesson Two addresses the eternal questions of religion: Where did we come from? Why are we here? Where will we go? Latter-day Saint theology teaches we consist of a spirit body and a physical body. The spirit body (or soul) lived with God in heaven before we were born, but in order to enjoy fully God's blessings, we need to take on a physical body and come to earth. Our earthly life is a time of probation and testing, when we are given freedom or "agency" to make choices, and our duty is to make correct choices—to avoid sin, to believe in Jesus and His atonement, to repent, to be baptized, and to believe in the Restored Gospel of The Church of Jesus Christ of Latter-day Saints. It is said we don't remember our pre-earth life while we are alive on earth.

In order to progress and become like God, each has to obtain a body and be tested during a time of probation on earth. While on earth we are out of God's physical presence. After physical death, we enter the spirit world and stand before God, who will judge us on our actions and thoughts. We then live in a state of glory, of which there are three levels: the "Celestial Kingdom," where God and Jesus reside, and where those who embrace the Restored Gospel of the Latter-day Saint Church and who live righteous lives will dwell; the "Terrestrial Kingdom," where those who refuse the Restored Gospel but live honorable lives will dwell; and the "Telestial Kingdom," where those who continue to sin and do not repent will dwell.

Investigators are to continue reading the Book of Mormon, to pray, to attend church, and to *set a date* for their baptism.[79]

Lesson Three:
"The Gospel of Jesus Christ"

Lesson Three addresses the question of salvation. For Latter-day Saints, it involves faith in Jesus Christ and his atonement, repentance, baptism and receiving the Holy Ghost, and a lifelong commitment to the Latter-day Saint Church and its teachings. We must believe that Jesus is the Son of God and that he suffered and died for our sins. We also must change our lives: recognize our sins and stop doing what is wrong; confess our sins to God and ask forgiveness; make restitution for our actions; serve others; and attend church. We need to be baptized (even if we were previously baptized in another faith) and receive the Holy Ghost. With that, we are spiritually reborn. We then should attend church, participate in the weekly sacrament service, and remain faithful and "endure to the end."

Investigators are encouraged to continue reading the Book of Mormon and to attend church, to set a date for baptism, and to schedule the next meeting with the missionaries.[80]

Lesson Four:
"The Commandments"

The Latter-day Saint Church places heavy expectations on its members, and this becomes apparent in Lesson Four. They are to live the Law of Chastity, which precludes sex outside of legal marriage. They are to obey the Word of Wisdom by avoiding alcohol, tobacco, tea, coffee, and harmful drugs. They are to keep the Law of Tithing by contributing 10 percent of their gross yearly income to the Church. Also, they should not participate in abortions or homosexual relations. They are to observe the Law of the Fast, which is typically on the first Sunday of each month, when members go without food or drink for two consecutive meals. The money that would have been spent on the meals is donated to the Latter-day Saint Church for the care of the poor and needy.

Investigators are encouraged to continue reading the Book of Mormon, attend church, begin to live the various commandments, prepare for baptism, and set a date for the next meeting with the missionaries.[81]

Lesson Five:
"Laws and Ordinances after Baptism and Confirmation"

Lesson Five normally is taught to converts after baptism, although it is recommended that they be made aware of its contents before baptism. It includes: a discussion of the Melchizedek and Aaronic Priesthoods held by males; the responsibility to engage in missionary work; eternal marriage (that husbands and wives are married for eternity); and the roles of fathers and mothers in the family.

It is said that it is by design that fathers are the heads of their households and that they are to provide for their families and to protect them, while the care and nurturing of children is mothers' primary responsibility. Husband and wife are to help one another as equal partners. They are to engage in rituals in the temple, including participating in the ceremony for the baptism for the dead, in which a person stands as a proxy in the baptismal ceremony for a deceased relative who had not heard, or who had not accepted, the Restored Gospel. It is believed this grants access to salvation in the next life, should the deceased person choose to accept it. The names of the deceased are gleaned from genealogical research. This is the theological basis for, and motivation behind, the Mormon Church's well-known interest in genealogy.

Converts can also expect to be asked to accept a responsibility in the Church—to receive a "calling."[82]

The Teaching Experience

Missionaries study the lessons at the MTC and practice presenting them to one another and to volunteers from the community, although they probably are adept at presenting only the first and second lessons when they leave the MTC. Once in the field, they study and practice the remaining lessons with one another and at meetings with guidance from the mission president and the A.P.s. Interviewees told of presenting the lessons to Church members when the work was slow, just to keep in practice. Some also approached lapsed members and asked if they could "practice" on them.

Missionaries find that people react differently in different parts of the United States depending on the historical and cultural background of the region. They need to be aware of this and tailor their lessons accordingly. An elder who served both in the "Bible Belt" of the American South, and in California, found he had to be far more adept in citing the Bible in the South than in California and that challenges in the South were far more likely to be Biblically-based from people whose family roots went back generations in the area and whose religious roots were in conservative, Protestant faiths. This was in contrast to his teaching in California, where there was a much more heterogeneous population of people from all over the world. His quoting the Bible and the Book of Mormon wasn't challenged nearly as often in California as in the South.

Throughout their teaching of the lessons missionaries are concerned with more than just conveying information about beliefs and doctrines, for they also want to engage the investigator in the process. Thus they ask investigators to read aloud from the Book of Mormon, they ask if they have questions, and they ask them a variety of questions to judge their understanding of the concepts and their feelings about them. The elders and sisters are provided with a variety of teaching helps on how to do this. They ask questions such as, "How do you feel about?" or "What do you think about?" They also employ techniques such as offering their own testimony and saying that they know what they are saying is true.

Studies by the Latter-day Saint Church show missionaries serving in the United States and Canada spend on average nine hours a week teaching investigators. They are advised to limit their sessions to forty-five minutes, although they are provided guidelines in *Preach My Gospel* on what to teach if they have shorter periods of time available to them, including a short plan (three to five minutes), a medium plan (ten to fifteen minutes) and the full lesson plan (thirty to forty-five minutes). If the investigator is a referral from a Church member, it is desirable if the member either accompanies the missionaries to the investigator's home or hosts the session in her or his own home. Missionaries are to try to teach a lesson to the investigator every two or three days. The elders and sisters, or Church members, will stay in daily contact with investigators, which is a practice referred to as "friendshipping."

It is up to the missionaries to determine how many times they meet with investigators before they prepare them for baptism. Missionaries will check to see if commitments (such as reading the Book of Mormon, attending church, and following the Word of Wisdom) are being kept. Missionaries are advised not to proceed with the next lesson if the earlier commitments haven't been fulfilled. They should teach the first four lessons before baptism.

I participated in the earlier six-part discussions, and then in the current five-part lessons, with elders and with sisters on three different occasions. Each remained consistent with the outlines of the discussions or lessons, although each was personalized through individual testimonies, analogies, and visual aids. What was striking was the extent to which reference was made to the Book of Mormon. It is central to the lessons. It was referenced repeatedly during our sessions, and we read from it on many occasions. I was often asked to read aloud from it, alone. The importance of the Book of Mormon in the Latter-day Saint faith thus cannot be overstated. To Mormons, its existence is proof that Joseph Smith was a prophet, that the gospel of Jesus Christ has been restored, and that God loves us. It truly is the keystone of the faith, and while missionaries study and quote the Old and New Testaments, the Book of Mormon is the primary scripture they appeal to because, as *Preach My Gospel* states, the Book of Mormon is "the most powerful resource" for teaching their message.[83]

Investigators must therefore decide for themselves whether to accept the Book of Mormon as a Divinely inspired revelation from God. Missionaries are counseled to encourage people to read it, to pray about it, and to ask God if it is true. It is felt the witness of the Holy Spirit will attest to the truthfulness of the Book of Mormon and to the veracity of the missionaries' claims that Joseph Smith was a prophet of God. It is said these will serve as the cornerstones of their faith, that Christ has restored the true Church.[84]

Investigator Record

Missionaries maintain an Investigator Record for those they have taught. It includes basic information on investigators and their families, along with information on their jobs, hobbies, interests, religious backgrounds, if they have friends in the LDS Church, and if they were referred (and by whom). Information on the progress of each lesson is also kept in the Record: the date the lesson was given; the investigator's reaction to the session; what commitments they have kept; the reasons given if they stop the discussions; and the results of any follow-up. The Record remains in the missionary apartment for the next missionaries to consult.

Some go through the lessons more than once before committing to baptism. An Eastern European convert who joined the Church at the age of eighteen said she had the discussions, "Many, many times. At least three times, actually more like five times." They would have been chronicled in the Investigator Record.

Given the frequent number of transfers missionaries experience, it's not uncommon for multiple missionaries to play a role in assisting someone with the decision to be baptized, even if it only involves them teaching one or two of the lessons before moving on to a new location. The new missionary then joins the companion and takes up where the departing missionary left off. This is another reason missionaries are told to maintain good records and to keep the Investigator Record up to date.

The Theory and the Practice of Teaching

Just as they go through a range of experiences while seeking investigators, the same is true for missionaries while teaching them. Just as they find there is a difference between the theory and the practice of finding investigators (that they aren't as easy to find as they thought they would be), so is there a difference between the theory and practice of teaching investigators—that things don't always progress as smoothly as they hope. The lessons are designed to move the investigator along in a smooth and steady progression toward baptism, but, as missionaries soon discover, things don't always go according to plan. Some sessions go even better than planned, and some do not. Some provide humor, and some sadness. Some leave missionaries confused as to how to interpret the investigator's words and actions. Some provide high points, while some include low points that leave missionaries in tears.

Missionaries leave teaching sessions with a wide range of perceptions and feelings: from a sense of elation to a sense of failure. An elder who served in Portugal in the early 1990s said there were times when he was so happy with the way the discussion went that he was close to "passing out" and that they gave him spiritual highs that he will never forget. An elder who served in England recalled "the strong sense of the Spirit" that he felt during a teaching session with a man who considered himself an atheist: "I remember sharing with him the story of Joseph Smith, and I have never had the Spirit come over me so strongly. I don't think they were my words coming out of my mouth. Everything I said just fell right into place and the Spirit just bore witness so strongly." Reflecting on the teaching experience itself, an elder who served in Hungary said there was nothing as good as coming out of a good teaching experience, where the Spirit was present and where investigators understood and embraced what was said. "There is no drug in the world that is better than that spiritual feeling," he said. He came out of those situations "on cloud nine."

At the opposite end of the spectrum are those sessions that missionaries feel are a disaster. The investigator doesn't seem interested and may even be rude. There are dogs, cats, and small children disrupting the lesson, and the television is on so loud they have trouble hearing each other. They think nothing is accomplished, but their mission president and others remind them they don't know what people are thinking and feeling, and perhaps they have planted a seed that will someday grow into a baptism.

The Book of Mormon sometimes confuses investigators. Two missionaries received a media referral of an elderly woman who had requested a Book of Mormon. She had already received the book when the missionaries called on her, and they found she was puzzled by it. She was trying to figure out who the people were in the book, because she thought it was the Bible with different names. They reported that once she understood what it was, "she read it nonstop and was baptized."

"Golden" Investigators

All missionaries hope they encounter a "golden" investigator at least once during their mission. A "golden" is a person who, in a very short period of time, believes in the truthfulness of their message, embraces it, and is baptized. They are rare, memorable people, who in some cases seek out the missionaries—like the bus driver in New England who saw two sister missionaries walking along the street, pulled his bus over to the curb and asked: "Are you Mormon missionaries?" They replied, "Yes," and he said, "I want to know more about your religion." They met with him later that day, and he was baptized soon thereafter.

Or the time two elders were tracting, and a man answered the door and said, "I am glad you have come back. I am ready to be baptized." Other missionaries had left a copy of the Book of Mormon with him several years earlier, he had become convinced of what he heard and read, and he had waited for them to return.

A Guatemalan convert who went on to serve a mission in his own country said he had always been impressed by the quality of the lives of his Mormon friends. One day as he was walking along the street he saw two Latter-day Saint missionaries. He went up to them and said, "Would you like to teach me?" He was baptized two weeks later. "I had the feeling what they were telling me was true," he said. "It was from the Spirit. I believed the Book of Mormon was true."

"Goldens" are rare, and most missionaries never experience one, but some teaching situations do progress as hoped and planned. They may meet with the investigator in a member's home, or the member may accompany them to the inquiring friend or neighbor's home. The lessons progress relatively smoothly, the message is tailored to the needs of the person, the person is engaged, attends church, reads the Book of Mormon, keeps the commitments, and eventually seeks baptism.

Missionaries love such investigators.

We Aren't Counselors, But...

Since missionaries are in such close contact with investigators and members, they frequently are aware of their emotional or medical problems. They are counseled not to get involved in such issues but to refer them to Church leaders or appropriate community professionals. But people baring their souls to missionaries are fairly common. An elder serving in the early 1990s said people they hardly knew shared personal and family problems, and he and his companion felt "way over our heads."

They would pray with the person and try to connect them with someone who could help. "The trust they put in us is incredible," mused the elder, "the fact that they can talk to us like that. It would be hard for me to tell a stranger I have only met once or twice my problems. I guess they just trust us."

An elder who served in Mexico said when getting involved in people's lives, there is a "real element of reality" that enters into it, and it was a profound learning experience for him. He was called upon to bless dying Church members and to administer to Church members who were ill. He was asked to minister to a member's daughter who was "pretty much out of control." He, the daughter, the mother, and his companion fasted for twenty-four hours, and then he and his companion ministered to her. He recalled, "She got a lot better, she really relaxed, and the tension went away." He paused during our interview, then commented, reflecting on his young age at that time: "It surprised me."

An elder who served in California described how he and his companion received a call one day from a drug addict who said he needed help. They were hesitant to get involved, since they weren't counselors or drug rehabilitation specialists, but they met with him anyway. That first visit began a seven-month journey of meeting with him practically every day, reviewing his drug usage, praising him when he hadn't used drugs since their last conversation, and encouraging him when he had. They read the Book of Mormon with him, taught him the discussions, and took him to church. He started taking his family to Church activities. He stopped taking drugs after the sixth month, and after he had been clean for five weeks the interviewee baptized him. As they stepped out of the water, the elder gave the man a big hug, and the man started crying. The elder described the experience as one of the "greatest highs" of his mission; he had grown to love the man, he had seen him change, and it was something he would never forget.

Humorous and Unusual Experiences

Missionaries experience humorous and unusual experiences while teaching. An elder spoke of a companion who had a tendency to fall asleep during teaching sessions, especially in the winter when they were bundled up in warm clothing and went into warm houses. The interviewee would start the lesson, glance at his companion, and notice that he was falling asleep. His head would start to nod, it would drop to his chest, and he would start to snore. Investigators would watch the elder and try not to laugh, while the companion just ignored it and kept on teaching.

A sister who served in the mid-1990s went to the home of a less active member, whose little daughter sat on her lap. She looked down and saw lice in her hair. She asked the parents if she had been scratching her head. They asked why. The sister said she had lice. They said, "Again?"

The sister commented during our interview: "It says in our mission call that we will teach all nations and all creatures. I guess that includes lice."

Sometimes it is the investigator's personality that makes missionary work so difficult, but in the end it is what endears him to the missionaries. A sister observed: "I found that New England people are quite stubborn to convert, but once they are converted they make stubborn Mormons. They aren't wishy-washy ones!"

Low Points in Teaching

Things don't always progress smoothly. Investigators don't always keep appointments, read the Book of Mormon, attend church, keep commitments, or follow through on plans for baptism. This frustrates missionaries, and there are many reasons why investigators behave this way.

Declining interest with each lesson. There is declining interest among some investigators with each succeeding lesson. Lesson One is the lesson taught most often in the field, which is why it is given the most attention at the MTC.

Some investigators engage the missionaries because they want to know more about the Latter-day Saint Church and its beliefs. Once they have an understanding of the basics of the faith, they may decide it isn't for them and have no more interest in meeting with missionaries.

Some want to hear the first lesson because they are interested in Jesus. An elder serving in the Bible Belt said people responded to the title of the lesson "The Message of the Restoration of the Gospel of Jesus Christ" with comments like, "Oh, yes, I am interested to hear what you have to say about Jesus," or, "I'm always interested in knowing more about Jesus." But once it became clear that the missionaries were Mormons—that they were talking about the restoration of the gospel through the prophet Joseph Smith, and that they were reading from the Book of Mormon—investigators immediately said they were no longer interested and didn't go beyond the first lesson.

Just say, "No thanks." Some people have trouble saying "No" to missionaries. They may feel sorry for how hard the missionaries are trying and agree to meet with them, even though they have little interest in their message. Some people may say they are busy at the moment but will meet with the missionaries at a later date. A meeting time is set, but the person may not be there, or they may cancel at the last minute. Additional meetings may be set up, but with little enthusiasm. Their lack of interest is apparent to missionaries. Missionaries say they prefer that if people aren't interested in meeting with them, they should say so. They shouldn't worry about hurting the missionaries' feelings, because they feel to string them along is worse.

A sister and her companion went for a scheduled appointment and knocked on the door, but there was no answer. Peeking in the window, they saw the woman crouched down behind a chair in the living room. "I guess she didn't want to meet with us," quipped the sister. They didn't attempt to reschedule the meeting.

Another sister told of calling an investigator five minutes before their meeting to confirm the appointment. The person affirmed the time and place but wasn't there when the missionaries arrived. The sister observed during our interview: "I just can't figure people out sometimes. I thought people were a lot more responsible than they are. Why don't they just tell us they are not interested? It won't hurt our feelings. When I go back home, I will have more respect for others, for when I say I will do something, I will do it."

A frustrated sister said people should express their lack of interest if that is the case. She said it would be nice if they were polite about it and not slam the door in her face, although she would prefer a slammed door, rather than continuing to go back for scheduled appointments, time after time, when they have no interest whatsoever.

Missionaries ask that people be honest with them, because they feel they are being honest with investigators.

A sister serving on Temple Square summed up missionaries' feelings about investigators who don't want to meet with them when she said, "'No' is good."

Just want to be friends. A sister who served in Central America spoke of the difficulties of working with people who only wanted to be friends. When people invited the missionaries over it soon became obvious whether they wanted to learn more about the LDS Church or just to be friends. There were those who didn't want to discuss religion, and it was hard because she didn't want to be rude, but she felt it was a waste of time to continue to meet with the person. "You are not there for yourself, to make friends, but to preach the Gospel," she said. "You can't get too close to somebody; it just doesn't work. You have to keep that distance. If they are not willing to listen, then you need to move one and find someone who is."

An elder who served in Mexico said there were times when, after several visits and getting into the lessons, the investigators were more interested in the missionaries as people, rather than in their religion, and the elders had to make a decision—would they confront the investigator with this?

Missionaries say those who want to be friends—not potential converts—are some of the hardest people to work with. Missionaries are told they have to be very careful about relationships in the mission; they can't get too close to anybody.

The Latter-day Saint Church is aware of the potential for investigators becoming too close and too attached to missionaries (and vice versa), and it is one of the reasons why missionaries are told to always be formal in their language. These practices help create boundaries between them and their investigators, their companions, and Church members. It avoids too personal a relationship forming between them.

A missionary serving in a Spanish-speaking country said there is a formal and informal way of speaking in Spanish. They were told to always use the formal manner, regardless of how well they knew the person, for it kept respect and distance, even with children.

This is another way for missionaries to be set apart from the world.

Missionaries admit it is hard to maintain distance with investigators. "It's hard," observed a sister, "for you want people to know that you love them and care for them, you want them to trust you enough that they open their lives to you, but you have to be careful, for they may take it the wrong way. What is their motivation for listening to you and maybe wanting to join?"

She summed it up succinctly when she observed, "The mission is not a time to make friends."

Missionaries are transferred immediately when it becomes evident the investigator is more interested in the missionary for romantic reasons (and vice versa), than for spiritual ones.

Reservations. Investigators may have reservations about meeting with missionaries. A young woman confessed she hesitated to meet with missionaries because she had been exposed to anti-Mormon preaching as she grew up in an evangelical Protestant church. She was told to never talk with Mormon missionaries, because they would brainwash her and would do whatever it took to convert her. She was told that they were evil. "That is what I have grown up with my whole life," she told the elders, "and so it is hard for me to sit here and talk with you, but I honestly do want to learn more about your church."

"Nobody ever tells us that is what they think," remarked the missionary during the interview, "and that was an eye-opener to me. Now I see why it is hard for some people to talk with us."

Don't want to keep the commitments. Significant demands are placed on investigators by the fourth lesson, and this can lead to cancelled sessions and declining interest. They are taught the Word of Wisdom, which enjoins them to abstain from alcohol, tobacco, coffee, tea, and harmful drugs. They are taught sex outside of marriage is a sin and they must either marry or separate if they are living with someone. They are also told to begin planning to tithe 10 percent of their gross income after joining the Church. Some are not serious enough to take on these commitments, and they drift away.

An elder described the Word of Wisdom as "the breaking point" in the lessons—as the point at which many investigators lose interest.

Family/friend/personal resistance. Not all are pleased when a family member expresses interest in joining the Latter-day Saint Church. Two sisters told of meeting with a nineteen-year-old woman whose mother joined the Church, and then divorced the girl's father. The father blamed the Church for the breakup of his marriage and family, and when the sisters would call he would be very rude and sarcastic with them. The young woman still wanted to be baptized, but she first had to work on her relationship with her father.

When a middle-aged mother decided to join the Latter-day Saint Church after having raised her family in a very conservative faith, her adult daughter refused to speak to her for two years. The mother's decision to join the Mormon Church "devastated" the young woman. The mother tried to introduce the upset daughter to the missionaries, thinking she would convert once the missionaries taught her the lessons, but it didn't work.

The daughter told the parent: "If they ever come to my door, I will hit them with whatever is at hand. I don't want them near me. They took you away from me!"

Two sisters told of delivering a Book of Mormon to a man who had expressed interest in seeing a copy, but when they arrived his live-in girlfriend became upset and started screaming at them. Neighbors called the police, who had to take the missionaries back to their car for protection. "That looked good," recalled the mortified sister sarcastically, "being escorted to our car by the police." That was the last they saw of their potential investigator; the sisters said the girlfriend "put a damper" on his interest.

Family members (often husbands and fathers) may not approve of missionaries meeting with their spouses and children and may forbid them from doing so, even if the spouse and children want to continue meeting. It is Church policy that a spouse must give permission for their spouse to be baptized.

One young investigator stopped meeting with missionaries after a Church "friendshipper" told him he would have to go on a mission after he joined the Church. The thought "scared him to death." When the missionaries heard what had been said to their investigator, they reacted: "Wait a minute! He isn't even baptized and you are pushing a mission on him? Stop right there!"

He said he would call when he wanted to get back together with the missionaries, but he never did.

"And don't come back." And there are those who, quite inexplicably, refuse to meet any further with the missionaries. This was the case with two sisters who appeared in the doorway of my office one day, their eyes red, looking very dejected. As they slumped into chairs, I asked what was wrong. They said it was the lowest point of their mission. When I asked what had happened, they recounted an experience shared by many missionaries.

They had been meeting with an investigator, who was excited and showing interest in their message. She was reading the Book of Mormon and praying as they had asked her to, and there had even been talk of baptism. But suddenly she wanted nothing more to do with them. The sisters had returned for an appointment with her the previous day, but they found the Book of Mormon on the porch with a note saying, "I am no longer interested. Here is your book, and don't come back."

"We were shocked," said the sister, "and we just looked at each other in disbelief."

When I asked why they thought the woman changed her mind, they said they didn't know. They tried knocking on her door, but there was no answer. They went home and cried.

Their experience, and reaction to it, is not uncommon according to many of my interviewees. An elder who served in Kentucky remembered how a woman had gone through four of the discussions and had talked of baptism. When the elders arrived at her door for the fifth discussion, they found the Book of Mormon on the porch with a note telling them not to come back, plus she "cussed them out." It happened with other investigators, he recounted, and each time the elders cried.

Two other sisters told of teaching an investigator all the discussions, but then suddenly being told, "Sorry girls, but get out of my house and don't come back again." They were never told why.

The most common reason why investigators back out of lessons in such a manner is exposure to anti-Mormon sentiment and literature. Someone has given the person books or websites that "tell the truth about Mormonism" or "expose Mormonism for what it really is." Family members, clergy, or friends are frequently the source of the materials.

The elder in Kentucky who had been left the note on the porch saying not to come back later saw the investigator and asked her why she had changed her mind. She said a friend had told her Mormon missionaries were false prophets and antichrists. He said they heard that a lot, but it was especially hurtful in this case because the woman had made so much progress toward baptism. It was experiences like that that made him wonder why he was on a mission.

"This is the low point of my mission," confided another sister, who was recounting a similar experience with an investigator that had happened just the night before. "You work so hard, and pray so hard, you are excited for them, then you arrive at their home and you can immediately sense that they are different. Their attitude has changed, they are confrontational, and then they produce the book that has caused them to change. You try to address their doubts without being confrontational, but their mind is already made up. This man's mother had given it to him. I don't think he wanted to go against his mother's wishes."

Another sister who had a similar experience said: "Sometimes people are appalled that we don't tell them about the anti-Mormon literature that is out there, and they are surprised when they are exposed to it. They then think we are hiding something, when we are not. We would have talked about it, had the topic come up."

And there is plenty of anti-Mormon literature out there, although the LDS commentator Jerry Earl Johnston feels he sees a shift in Protestant books on Mormonism: moving away (although some still exist) from the strident anti-Mormon works of earlier years to an approach that advocates ministering to Mormons, who, while decent people, are thought to be misguided.[85]

Today the Internet plays a powerful role in shaping peoples' perceptions of the Latter-day Saint Church, and a growing number of potential investigators first turn to the Web, where they find both negative and positive information about the Church. There are numerous websites and blogs that are avidly anti-Mormon, and these now account for many of the instances in which investigators tell missionaries, "Don't come back."

The Latter-day Saint Church, realizing the importance and power of the Web, launched its own proselytizing/missionary web site (www.mormon.org) in 2001, which served as a platform for interested people to learn about the doctrines and beliefs of the LDS Church. It went through a significant makeover in 2010. Members are encouraged to write about themselves and their beliefs, to create personal profiles, to show that they are common, everyday people who have families, jobs, and interests just like everyone else—who are also Mormon. The Church has found that such personal connections are one of the most effective means of dispelling myths and misperceptions about the faith. There is also a message board where potential investigators can ask questions. A free copy of the Book of Mormon can be requested, as well as visits from missionaries.

The Church also encourages members to present a positive image of the Church, its values, and its teachings through their personal blogs and on social networking sites.[86] The unofficial More Good Foundation, which was created in 2005 by David Neeleman, founder of JetBlue Airlines, is an online source for people seeking information about the Latter-day Saint Church. According to their website: "It [the site] was created...as a solution to the overwhelming need for increased positive and accurate information about the LDS faith on the Internet." The foundation operates hundreds of websites in numerous languages.[87]

Visitors to all of the Church websites can request that missionaries visit them in their homes.

"Is it me?" Some elders and sisters, especially new ones, question if they are to blame for investigators canceling meetings or not showing interest in hearing future lessons. They speak of arriving in the mission field and, during their first week, appointments getting cancelled and people backing out of baptisms. A new sister asked, "Is it me?" Her trainer assured her it happened all the time. The greenie reflected: "I knew it would be hard, but not this hard. We work on every day, even P-Day."

Another greenie was becoming discouraged because no one seemed to show much interest. "I felt like I was an ineffective teacher and maybe I wasn't prepared enough. I should have started preparing earlier in my life."

A self-reproachful elder said the hardest thing for him "is seeing a weakness I have that gets in the way of someone progressing because I know it is something I did that affected them not for the good." An elder who said he felt guilty added: "You can get them to the point where they know it is true, you can feel it, but then they back away. It is frustrating, you think it is something you have done wrong that didn't help them progress, or there was something more you should have done and you question yourself about what is going on."

A reflective elder who was going home in two weeks said: "What has been hard? For me to be in a discussion and you are telling the truth to somebody and they don't get it, it doesn't seem to sink in and I wonder, 'Did I not say it right, or what?' Something that means very much to me doesn't mean much to them."

A sister who served in France said she found missionary work very challenging; she worked very hard and had a sense of urgency all of the time. She knew she had just a few minutes with people and that what she said to them was crucial, but people constantly told her, "No": they had no interest in her message.

"But if they understood, they wouldn't say no," she said. "Perhaps if I would have said it right, or they sensed something spirit-to-spirit with me, then they wouldn't say no. So I was constantly wishing that I could do that and feeling disappointed that it didn't happen very often."

But most work through the self-blame, and they provide counsel for later missionaries. A sister said: "That is one thing I have learned on my mission. I cannot convert. I cannot make someone believe what I believe, and I think the earlier a missionary knows that, the easier it is."

Said an elder, reflecting on an investigator who stopped meeting with the missionaries, "I know it is not my fault."

"Mormon Busters"/"Mormon Bashers"

Another way missionary efforts are undermined is through the efforts of "Mormon Busters" or "Mormon Bashers," people who follow along after missionaries to discredit what they say.

One of my interviewees served in this role. Raised a Roman Catholic, he converted to a conservative Protestant group after marriage. He became a Mormon Basher at the suggestion of his minister, a man he described as a "knocker" of Latter-day Saints and Jehovah's Witnesses. The minister recognized that he was a good public speaker and asked him to choose one of the two groups to study and to bash. He chose the Mormons, since his mother had told him as a child to hide under the bed when missionaries knocked at their door. The pastor gave him anti-Mormon materials, and he soon started speaking out against the Latter-day Saint Church.

He described himself as "an argumentative anti-Mormon with a gift for gab, not one who came in lightly." He found the more he attacked the LDS Church, the more popular he became. He was invited to people's homes when they arranged to meet with missionaries (unbeknownst to the missionaries), and he then gave them a difficult time. The technique he used when attacking their religion was to talk faster than they did—to talk faster than they could think. Common approaches he used included "scripture chasing," criticizing Church leaders, and getting missionaries angry.

He described scripture chasing as taking a passage of scripture and asking missionaries what they thought of it. When they responded, the conversation would proceed something like this:

> **Basher:** "Where did you get that interpretation?"
>
> **Missionaries:** "The Bible."
>
> **Basher:** "Which Bible?"
>
> **Missionaries:** "What do you mean, which Bible?"
>
> **Basher:** "There are very many different versions of the Bible."
>
> **Missionaries:** "King James."
>
> **Basher:** (Talking faster.) "There are many different translations of the Bible, and before we can agree on the meaning of the passage in question, we have to look it up in all the

translations. We don't want to jump to a conclusion based on only one Bible, so we need to look at all of them, to see what they all have to say."

Missionaries: *Somewhat confused, silent.*

Basher: "And then we need to see what related passages say."

Missionaries: "Well, okay."

He described the process as "throwing a scripture chase at them," and the faster he talked, the more confused the missionaries became. He said Mormon missionaries generally don't have much knowledge of the Bible beyond the average person of the same age, but when they come up against those from conservative Protestant groups, especially Fundamentalists and Pentecostals, they are at a real disadvantage, because members of these groups are trained from an early age to memorize passages from the Bible and to do scripture chasing to defend their faith.

He also focused on apparent mistakes in statements made by Church leaders, making the point that their prophet is fallible. He would find such statements and then "magnify them, twist them, and make them practically anything I want."

Another approach was to anger missionaries. He attacked them personally: "What makes you think you are so good? What makes you think you are so right?" In many cases the missionaries reacted to it; once they were riled up, he started to break them down, to get them to make an angry statement. Once he had done that, he had won, and the missionary and the Latter-day Saint Church had lost.

The impression he formed of Mormon missionaries was that they weren't slick, well-trained, forty year olds, but naïve late adolescents who wanted to go out and tell people about their beliefs, though few were interested in hearing it. Before they went out they didn't know the abuse they would get, and he felt it was worse in the South, in the Bible Belt. They took a tremendous amount of abuse, because they would walk into a home, not suspecting the family had set them up. Someone would think, "We will have some fun with the Mormons, let's invite them back," and they would get someone from their church who said he knew all about Mormons, and he would meet with them to give them a hard time.

"Thus these kids get submitted to a lot of abuse," he said. "A *lot* of abuse."

Ironically, the Mormon Basher eventually converted to the Latter-day Saint faith. He had been argumentative and caustic toward the Church, but through personal experience he said he had come to know it to be true. Because of his unique experiences, he was set apart in the Latter-day Saint Church to deal with anti-Mormon issues, materials, and questions. He described himself as a public relations man for the Church, an educator to the public, and he holds periodic "Meet the Mormons" sessions for non-members. He also counsels missionaries on how to handle situations like the ones he once subjected missionaries to. He tells them they are not unarmed, because they are ordained and set apart and God has a way of protecting His own. He also reaffirms what they are taught at the MTC and by their mission president: don't scripture bash or get contentious with people, and if people don't want to hear what they have to say, walk away.

An elder spoke of how his anger interfered with his missionary work. He reacted negatively to anti-Mormon literature, which he considered to be an insult to his faith, and he admitted yelling at people who produced such materials. He spoke of an investigator who showed him a book that claimed to "tell the truth about Mormonism." The man accused the missionaries of belonging to a cult and of worshipping Joseph Smith.

The elder started yelling at the man: "You think this is new to me, buddy? You think I haven't read it? I have read plenty of it!"

He knew he had "lost it" at that point and that his behavior wasn't missionary-like.

His embarrassed companion agreed: "I think that is why I don't like anti-Mormon material; just the fact that it gets you acting like you shouldn't be acting. It is not the standard you are supposed to be living up to. They get you edgy, and they get you contentious, and that is not how you are supposed to be as a missionary."

The Mormon Basher knew what he was doing.

An elder who served in Connecticut in the late 1950s said his experiences were very similar to what missionaries experience today. He didn't have a lot of success, very few people listened, a lot of doors were slammed in his face, and he had to learn to be gracious in spite of it.

He and his companion got very discouraged, but one day they walked past a car with the radio on and the Mormon Tabernacle Choir was singing the popular Latter-day Saint hymn, "Come, Come, Ye

Saints." The returned missionary said, "I thought, 'The world isn't so bad after all.'"

It is little instances like that that he remembers; he doesn't remember the frustrations, except the big ones, which he and his companion talked about and laughed about later. He observed: "There are a lot of challenges when you work with the public and your ideas aren't the same as everybody else's, when you have a body of belief you want others to consider."

But he found that some did respond positively, participated in the discussions, kept the commitments, and sought baptism. Those kinds of experiences were the highpoint of his mission.

Baptize

Qualifications for baptism. The qualifications for baptism are found in *Doctrine and Covenants* 20:37: "All those who humble themselves before God, and desire to be baptized, and come forth with broken hearts and contrite spirits, and witness before the church that they have truly repented of all of their sins and are willing to take upon them the name of Jesus Christ, having determined to serve him to the end, and truly manifest by their works that they have received of the Spirit of Christ unto the remission of their sins, shall be received by baptism into his church."

Investigators are encouraged to consider baptism and to set a date for the event very early on during the lessons, but before they can carry through with the ritual they must make changes in their lifestyle and must show commitment to the Latter-day Saint Church. Thus it isn't a simple process. It is the responsibility of missionaries to help investigators meet all requirements for baptism and meet the qualifications as spelled out in *D & C* 20:37: have developed faith in Christ; have repented of transgressions; lived moral lives; obeyed the Word of Wisdom; committed to pay tithing; received missionary Lessons One through Four; and met with the head of the local congregation—the bishop or branch president—and attended several church services (sacrament meetings).[88] In addition, those seeking baptism are interviewed by a district or zone leader, who asks if they have ever committed a serious crime, if they have ever participated in an abortion or a homosexual relationship, and if they will live by the law of chastity, which prohibits a sexual relationship between a man and a woman outside marriage. They are required to be interviewed by the mission president if they answer yes to any of these questions, and the baptismal ceremony is postponed if they don't live up to these standards.

The ritual. The missionaries, along with the investigator and local Church leaders, plan a "spiritually uplifting" baptismal service that includes music, songs, prayers, and short talks. The investigator is asked to identify friends, relatives, and neighbors who should be invited to the ceremony. They are also asked to identify which of these people might be interested in taking part in the lessons. Missionaries also meet regularly with the investigator to offer encouragement and support and to reconfirm their desire to be baptized.

Latter-day Saints believe in total immersion baptism. Thus no part of the body (including hair and clothing) may remain above the water during the actual ritual. LDS meetinghouses include an indoor, walk-in, baptismal pool where the ceremony takes place. It may also be held outdoors in lakes, streams, or swimming pools, if they are considered safe and if the weather is conducive. A person must be a worthy priest or a Melchizedek priesthood holder in order to conduct the ceremony; thus only males may baptize, for only they hold these offices. Sisters may teach all of the lessons and prepare the individual for baptism, but an elder will conduct the ceremony.

The elder goes into the water with the person to be baptized. Both are dressed in white. He holds the person's right wrist with his left hand, and the person holds the elder's left wrist with his or her left hand. The priesthood holder then raises his right arm about the person, states the person's name, and says, "Having been commissioned of Jesus Christ, I baptize you in the name of the Father, and of the Son, and of the Holy Ghost. Amen" (*D&C* 20:73). With the elder's right hand on the person's back, and the person holding her or his nose, the person is totally immersed in the water. The new convert is then helped out of the water, changes into dry clothes, and rejoins the service, where she or he may bear her or his testimony.

The ceremony must be performed *exactly* as described, and to insure compliance two priests or Melchizedek priesthood holders must serve as witnesses. If the words aren't spoken exactly as noted above, or if any part of the body or clothing is not completely immersed, then the ceremony must be performed again.

There can be complications. An elder who baptized a young woman in the ocean off the coast of France said that he, the convert, and two elders serving as witnesses went into the ocean to perform the ceremony. As he was about to immerse her, a huge wave knocked all of them over, and the witnesses couldn't tell if the convert had experienced total immersion or not. They had to appeal to two elders standing on the shore to confirm that she had.

Church members living along the coast in Ghana go into the ocean to perform baptisms, and the current and waves are so strong that other Church members encircle the baptismal party to lessen the force of the waves.

Baptize Quickly

Missionaries suggest baptism to investigators very early on. At the end of the first lesson they are challenged to *think* about a date for the ritual, and at the end of the second and succeeding lessons they are asked to *set* a date for their baptism. When I asked interviewees why they stress it so early, they pointed to the example in Acts 2:38-41, when Peter on the Day of Pentecost told his listeners that they must repent and be baptized for the forgiveness of their sins. It is said around three thousand were baptized that day. They didn't wait; they did it then.

This is in contrast to the approach taken by interviewees who served in earlier decades. Two elders who served in the 1940s said they didn't baptize right away, but would sometimes work with investigators up to six months before baptizing them. That approach changed after the mid-twentieth century, when greater speed of decision was advocated.

Pressure to Baptize

Interviewees spoke of feeling varying amounts of pressure to baptize investigators. *Preach My Gospel* states that baptizing and confirming investigators is "central" to the missionaries' purpose, because it leads to eternal life.[89] Many mission presidents set weekly and monthly expectations and goals for the number of Books of Mormon placed, of lessons taught, and of baptisms performed. Missionaries are required to submit weekly progress reports that record this information, and they are closely reviewed by the A.P.s and by the mission president.

Some missionaries say they appreciate quotas because they motivate them and provide clear guidance on how they should spend their time. Some admit to padding their numbers in their weekly reports because if they don't fulfill their quotas, they will be called on it. Some spoke of physical and psychological ailments that surfaced because of the pressure they felt to succeed. They felt stress and tension trying to find investigators and to baptize them, but they received conflicting messages from their leaders. When their numbers were down, they were told numbers weren't that important, that they should be concerned about caring for people. But then they were reminded their numbers were down.

It's not that missionaries aren't trying. Certain areas, such as Western Europe and Northern New England, have low rates of baptism and cannot be compared to regions of high baptisms such as Latin America. Sometimes missionaries, regardless of where they are, can't get out and proselytize because they or their companion is ill. Multiple interviewees spoke of being confined, and frustrated, because of a companion's physical or mental illness. Some spoke of being frustrated with their own illness.

There are other reasons why baptismal numbers are low. Investigators may not be willing to live up to all of the commitments. A French investigator said she was ready to be baptized, but she had a weekly rendezvous with a man at a hotel and did not want to give it up. She couldn't be baptized.

Sometimes missionaries just have to be patient. They sometimes work with investigators for *years* before they commit to baptism. A sister spoke of meeting with a family that had been talking with missionaries for six years. They had a problem with some of the commitments. Missionaries became frustrated with their inaction, but they kept coming back because the woman confided, "I wouldn't keep meeting with you if I didn't think it was true."

A senior couple in central Indiana spoke of working with an eighty-four-year-old woman who said she believed in the teachings of the Latter-day Saint Church, but who kept resisting the idea of baptism. Realizing they needed to get to the root of her hesitancy, they asked why she didn't want to go through with the ceremony. She confessed that she had a breathing problem and the idea of being totally submerged under water "scared her to death." They worked through her fears, she was baptized, and as she came out of the water she said to the elder: "I'm surprised you didn't hold me under. I have been such a bother for you!"

Missionaries refer to people like the former family who kept meeting with the missionaries as "eternal investigators," while they call people like the older woman, "dry Mormons." They are believers; they just haven't been baptized.

Sometimes missionaries just need to ask, to offer what is referred to as the "soft challenge." This is when missionaries tell investigators, "When you come to the point of knowing these things are true, we hope you will be baptized." A missionary told of giving a Book of Mormon to a young man and teaching him the first lesson. Baptism wasn't mentioned. When the missionaries returned for the second lesson, they talked about baptism and they invited the investigator to set a date for his. He responded: "I thought you were never going to ask. Can we do it right now? There is a pool outside."

Baptismal High Points

Baptisms are a highpoint of the missionaries' experience. They have met with the investigators, taught them, and in many cases struggled with them as they overcame doubts, fears, and addictions to coffee, alcohol, and tobacco. They have witnessed marital and family issues they have never seen before and for which they are not prepared to address. They have prayed with the family and possibly referred them to counselors and agencies for help. And in the end the family is baptized, becomes engaged in the life and work of the Latter-day Saint Church, and (the missionaries say) have their lives turned for the better.

Such was the experience of an elder who served in California. After helping a family sort through a myriad of family issues, he recalled: "We then finished the discussions and they joined the Church, and a son went on a mission. It was a happy ending to a dire circumstance. I always felt at the time, and later, that the Lord had really helped us, that He knew the family was in need and He knew that we, and others, could help them. That was the most dramatic experience we had."

An elder who served in Brazil in the early 2000s recalled his feeling at his first baptism: "One of the feelings I felt as I entered the water was that it was not me that was speaking, but the Lord was using me as an instrument to do this work and it really helped me to feel the spirit of that and the ordinance of baptism."

An elder who served in Hungary said: "There is nothing as exciting for a missionary as having a baptism, for all of your goals and desires are toward that during your mission. You have nothing else going on in your life. You are totally focused on bringing people to the gospel, to the Church, and when you have a baptism, it is a great feeling."

A sister who served in Italy said the high point for her came on the last day of her mission, when a man they had been working with was baptized. It was gratifying to see how much he had progressed, she said, how happy and strong he was in the faith, and to see him share in what she had.

Baptismal Low Points

Events surrounding the baptismal ceremony can also lead to missionary lows. Some investigators lapse back into drinking, smoking, and taking drugs just prior to the ceremony, and some back out of the ceremony at the last minute when family members threaten to disown them if they go through with it.

An elder recounted the experience of planning a baptismal service. The investigator invited friends and relatives to observe the ceremony, but then she didn't appear for the service. Spouses are required to give permission for their spouses to be baptized into the LDS faith, and at the last minute the husband told his wife she couldn't be baptized, and if she went through with it, he would "beat her up."

The elder who taught her spoke of his frustration: "You get attached to them. You are just about there, you are excited, you have grown to love the people and you are rooting for them. You would do anything you could for them, but they get to a point where they deny it, or someone denies them the opportunity." He described the moment when the woman didn't appear as a "harsh moment." "I felt very bad, and then when we found out why, it was even worse. It was the husband who was denying her the opportunity. She is not going to be held accountable for that as far as I am concerned. It was her husband who was holding her back."

A sad sister said, "It breaks your heart to see people move toward baptism, and then all of a sudden back away." She spoke of meeting with a woman she described as "glowing." She experienced a positive change in her life, she stopped smoking and drinking, and she was ready to be baptized. But then she called the sister and said she needed to cancel her baptism. Someone had given her some anti-Mormon material and it "scared" her. She started smoking again. The sisters cried.

Studies by the Church show that those investigators who participate in the first lesson are most often found by missionaries. Next in number are those found by media campaigns, and lastly are those found through member referrals (only 10 percent). In contrast, of the number of investigators who go on to be baptized, 59 percent have been invited to look at the Church by members or were referred to missionaries by members. Thus missionary efforts help identify the greatest number of investigators who participate in the first lesson, but member contact and referrals lead to the greatest number of converts to the Latter-day Saint Church.[90]

Confirmation

A confirmation ceremony follows baptism, typically the following Sunday at sacrament meeting. It is believed to be the time when the person receives the gift of the Holy Ghost. It is performed because in John 3:5 Jesus is quoted as saying that unless a person is born of water and of the Spirit, he cannot enter the kingdom of God. (*D & C* 33:10).

The newly baptized person appears in front of the congregation. The bishop, and frequently the missionaries who baptized him, stand over him and lay their hands on his head. The person's name is stated; it is said the ordinance is performed by the authority of the Melchizedek priesthood; the person is confirmed a member of the Latter-day Saint Church; the words, "Receive the Holy Ghost," are said; a priesthood blessing is given; and the ceremony is closed in the name of Jesus Christ.

Missionary contact with converts doesn't end with their baptism and confirmation. Missionaries are advised to continue "fellowshipping" new members for several weeks after their baptism, to read the Book of Mormon with them, and to sit in on the first two or three lessons of the new members' class, "Discussions for New Members." Members are also encouraged to continue fellowshipping new converts. The new member has periodic interviews with the bishop and is given a calling or responsibility in the congregation. For men this means ordination to the Aaronic, and then the Melchizedek priesthood, and for women this means involvement in the women's' parallel organization, the Relief Society. New members are also asked to provide names of referrals that missionaries might contact.

Retention

Retention is a major concern in the Latter-day Saint Church. Attention to and engagement of new converts is not taken lightly. Like other religious groups who rely on a conversion experience, or who demand major changes in a person's lifestyle and beliefs, there is a high attrition rate among converts. In the Latter-day Saint Church, the greatest number of new converts stops attending within the first two months after baptism. This fact motivated President Hinckley to stress the need for members to pay special attention to new converts: to help them with their questions and concerns; to help them become part of the Church community; and to serve as examples of what a faith-centered life can and should be. He also spoke of three things he felt aided in their retention: make a friend in the Church, take on a task, and read the scriptures.[91]

The Mormon Church also recognizes that the requirements of the Word of Wisdom create major stumbling blocks for new converts and that help must be provided. It was found that 75 percent of North American adult converts had to give up at least one of the following—tobacco, alcohol, coffee, or tea—and that 31 percent had to give up smoking. A third to a half further reported they had occasional, frequent, or even complete lapses in living up to the Word of Wisdom. Support from missionaries and members are cited as the single most helpful influence in helping converts address these issues.[92]

Recent converts are not immune to anti-Mormon material. A disheartened sister said a recently baptized member was the recipient of anti-Mormon material that she said "came out of nowhere." It undermined the person's faith and he drifted away from the Church.

It appears investigators' relationship with missionaries during the lessons can have an effect on whether they remain active in the Church. An insightful sister from Utah observed that she has seen three types of converts. First are those who have a change of heart and who want to follow Jesus Christ. They keep the commitments, are baptized ("no matter what"), and they become faithful members of the LDS Church. She has seen just a few of these.

Next are investigators who perceive missionaries as counselors and friends and who agree to baptism to please the missionaries. She hopes they have a necessary change of heart and are making the commitment to Jesus Christ, and not to the missionaries. They can tell if someone is really converted, or if, as missionaries describe it, they are "converted to the missionary." Such people are a concern to missionaries. Investigators fall in love with missionaries and get converted to the missionaries, and not to the Church. The sister said if it is apparent the investigator is getting attached to one or both of the missionaries, they step back and have other missionaries finish the lessons. Such a move usually solves the problem; it reveals whether the investigator is committed or not.

Two other sisters speaking of the dynamic added, "We don't want people to be baptized if they are just going to go inactive once we go home."

Finally there are those who feel pressured into baptism. They are active for a short while and then fall away from the Church.

An elder who served in the early 1960s said he found another type of person—those who are gullible and who agree to just about anything. He said they had to back off because they didn't want to exploit the person. They would say: "Wait, you need to *seriously* think about this. Are you *sure* you want to do this?"

Harder Than Expected

Many missionaries are surprised at the trials and tribulations they face, and some wonder if they are given too rosy a picture of what it is like in the mission field. They feel the image of missionary life as portrayed in film and otherwise is too idealistic, that it isn't always a smooth process of recruiting, teaching, and baptizing. Some are probably overly optimistic when they leave the MTC, and it takes a dose of reality to help them realize what they are facing.

Two sister missionaries described the frustration they felt once they got into the mission field and experienced how difficult it was. It wasn't like what they were led to believe, where sisters worked with an investigator who kept appointments, did the readings, kept the commitments, was baptized, became a faithful member of the Church, all along being helped by involved Church members.

What they found was that many people thought there was nothing to their message, investigators were hard to find, many cancelled or skipped appointments, they didn't do the reading or keep the commitments, and some backed out of baptisms. The sisters' frustration came from the fact that the image on the films—of both the investigators and the sisters—was the ideal, not necessarily the reality. They said it was a hard lesson to learn.

Chapters 6 and 7 have embodied the essence of what missionaries do: they find, teach, and baptize investigators. The *ideal* day would be a day of "balanced service," a combination of proselytizing, member contact (both current and lapsed), and service. They would have a specific destination in mind when they left their apartment in the morning. It could be to meet a referral for the first time, begin or continue the lessons with an investigator, meet with a Church member, or arrange or conduct a baptismal service. They may knock on doors, and they may help out at a soup kitchen or some other service activity. They would move from appointment to appointment throughout the day, stopping for lunch and dinner either at a member's home or going back to their apartment. If eating dinner at a member's home, they would stay for only an hour. They would continue their searching and teaching activities into the evening and return to their apartment by 9:00 P.M., where they would unwind, plan for the next day, write in their journals, and be in bed by 10:30 P.M.

Thus they could look back on a busy, productive, albeit exhausting, day. More than one missionary told of kneeling by the side of the bed to say their prayers, only to wake hours later in the same position, with the lights still on. I spoke with a German sister in Berlin, Germany, who had a cast on her foot. When I asked what happened, she said she had fallen asleep while kneeling and saying her prayers. She awoke hours later, and when she tried to stand, her leg was asleep, and she fell and fractured a bone in her foot.

But not all days go smoothly. Missionaries face significant challenges: living successfully with a companion around the clock is frequently cited as the biggest hurdle, while learning to live with rejection (and to not take it personally) is a close second. This is followed by the tedium that arises from doing the same thing over and over again, especially if it is knocking on doors with little success. They face rejection and apathetic responses to their message, and they need to find the inner resolve and strength to carry on. But with one baptism, all of the negatives are forgotten.

Many liken the missionary experience to a roller coaster ride. Said a sister who served in the mid-1990s: "If you are really committed and love what you are doing, and have people reject it, it can be awfully destructive. But to have them accept it, then you can't find better happiness, and this leads to extreme highs and lows. It is very challenging."

Another sister said she experienced a roller coaster of emotions, that a mission had every element of emotion in it—"happiness, joy, sadness, sorrows, anything you could possibly feel, I felt it." A sister who served in Argentina agreed. The highs on her mission were higher than at any time in her life, and her lows were lower. She said it was because she was working for something that was extremely important for her and that had the potential to have a life-changing effect on peoples' lives. She said when she puts her heart into something like that, she is setting herself up for a lot of emotional extremes.

There is a sense of urgency in the missionaries' message. As their name implies, The Church of Jesus Christ of *Latter-day* Saints (my emphasis) is awaiting Christ's Second Advent, and, while not date-setters, Mormons believe they are living in the End Times predicted in Revelation. Significantly, they feel *they* have a responsibility to help bring it about, because *Doctrine and Covenants* 90:11 states: "For it shall come to pass in that day, that every man shall hear the fulness (*sic*) of the gospel in his own tongue, and in his own language, through those who are ordained unto this power, by the administration of the Comforter, shed forth upon them for the revelation of Jesus Christ."

At the 181st Annual General Conference of the LDS Church held in Salt Lake City in April 2011, the Apostle Neil L. Anderson spoke on the topic "Preparing the World for the Second Coming." Speaking particularly to twelve-to-twenty-five-year-old young men, he asked, "Have you ever thought about why you were sent to earth at this specific time?" He said the Lord is preparing for His Second Coming and it is their responsibility as priesthood holders to help bring it about by serving as missionaries. Indeed, he said it is largely through the efforts of missionaries that the Second Coming will take place, and they therefore have an obligation to serve. They should be preparing to do so, being careful to live lives worthy of receiving a missionary call.[93]

Accordingly, the Latter-day Saint Church places great emphasis on missions, including international missions, and the young men Elder Anderson was talking to, along with young sisters and older senior missionaries, are the ones who are to take the message to the world.

We will now turn to their stories.

PART IV

International Missions

CHAPTER 8

International Missions: Training, Transitions, and Trials

"But purify your hearts before me;
and then go ye into all the world, and preach my gospel
unto every creature who has not received it."

DOCTRINE & COVENANTS 112:28

"We had two choices—beans and rice, or rice and beans."

AN AMERICAN SISTER MISSIONARY
WHO SERVED IN CENTRAL AMERICA

It is unusual to see eight Mormon missionaries in one day. Thus I was surprised in 1999 to see eight American elders in, of all places, Ulaanbaatar, the capital of Mongolia. Two were walking along a street in the city, two were walking along a dirt road on the outskirts of the city (on their way, they told me, to teach an English class), and four were gathered outside the largest department store in the city. All were easy to identify, since they were wearing their missionary "uniform" of dark suit, white shirt, conservative tie, and black nametag.

I approached the four and explained that I was interested in their work as missionaries. When I asked what they were doing, they said they were "trolling." Since that isn't a common missionary term, I asked what that meant. They explained that "trolling" in Ulaanbaatar is standing in public places and talking with as many people as possible, getting to know them but without "proclaiming the gospel." Laws prohibit active proselytizing by religious groups in Mongolia; thus missionaries can't go door to door or initiate conversations about religion with people on the street. Rather, they have to take a more passive approach. If asked who they are and what they are doing, missionaries can discuss their faith and their reasons for being there.

I mentioned that I had briefly spoken with the elders who were going to teach an English class. All four said they had taught similar classes.

Mongolia has been a popular recruiting ground for Western religions since the early 1990s. A huge, landlocked country, it is situated between China and Russia, which played significant roles in the country's recent history. China controlled the country until 1911, after which the Soviets dominated it until 1990. Mongolia was heavily dependent upon Soviet subsidies, since it was one of the most isolated and underdeveloped of any of the Soviet satellites. When the Soviets pulled out in the 1990s, Mongolians, fearing a renewal of Chinese domination, turned to the West and embraced Western practices and values, perhaps more so than any other Eastern country. The 1990s saw a democratic revolution that sought to introduce capitalism and democracy into the country. There was also an influx of new religions into the country, including Mormonism.

The Latter-day Saint Church is thus relatively new in Mongolia. Senior missionary couples arrived in Ulaanbaatar in the early 1990s, entering the country as English teachers, followed by elders not long thereafter. The Ulaanbaatar Branch was organized in 1993, the LDS Church was registered with the Mongolian government in 1994, and the Mongolian Ulaanbaatar Mission was established in 1995. The first native members, two young women, received mission calls in 1995. One served in Temple Square in Salt Lake City, while the other served in Provo. The first American sisters arrived in Mongolia in 1996. The Church bought and renovated an old theater in Ulaanbaatar and dedicated it as a church in 1999. As is its practice where it is found and wherever there is need, the LDS Church provided international aid in 2000 after Mongolia experienced a severe winter followed by a severe drought.

The work proceeded slowly, because of the prohibition on proselytizing, and the Church grew with around four hundred baptisms a year. One of the "trolling" elders I met said the Church's emphasis on the family strikes a chord with Mongolians and the English classes are an effective tool for raising awareness and questions about the Latter-day Saint Church. While the Church is not mentioned during the lessons, he said students do inquire about it after class.

Another elder explained that a goal of the Church is to train male converts to take over positions of leadership in the indigenous Church, so young Mongolian men are being encouraged to serve a mission, because it is felt the mission experience is excellent preparation for these future responsibilities.

A third elder said he liked the idea of being a pioneer, and he knew that some day when a temple is built there he will know he contributed to it. He is good at languages, but it still took him four to six months before he felt comfortable speaking Mongolian.

I returned to Mongolia eight years later, in 2007. As friends and I were driving about an hour outside of Ulaanbaatar, we came around a bend in a small, isolated village, and, much to my surprise, there stood a new Latter-day Saint church. Its fresh, yellow brickwork stood in stark contrast to the drab huts, houses, and dark apartment buildings around it, but it didn't appear inviting, as it was surrounded by a fence and locked gate.

My interviews with missionaries serving in 2007 confirmed that the LDS Church had been growing since my visit in 1999. The Book of Mormon had been translated into Mongolian and distributed to Church members in late 2001, and the Church reported 7,306 members at the end of 2006.[94] An American elder who served as a zone leader said the mission had received one thousand referrals that year. He repeated an earlier missionary's comment that Mongolians are family-centered and that the Church's emphasis on the family is attractive to them. He went on to say that while older Mongolians want to hang on to their Buddhist roots, younger people have different traditions, are less interested in the past, and are interested in trying new things.

The zone leader also commented on something I wondered about when I saw the new Church building in the drab village, in spite of the fence and locked gate: "LDS Church buildings look great," he said. "It brings them in."

He said it wasn't an easy mission. Gaining proficiency in the language was a challenge for him (it also took him almost six months before he felt comfortable speaking Mongolian), and teaching was awkward early on. People would look at him as if to say: "What are you saying?" During the long, dark, cold, Mongolian winters, he and his companion spent up to four hours a day teaching English, and they met with people either at the Church building or in peoples' homes. The depression and frustration that came with learning a difficult language, combined with the harsh Mongolian winter, contributed to occasional conflicts. Both he and his American companion had had Mongolian companions, whom they said were "good." Both of their mothers worried about them going to such an isolated country, and the mom of one of the elders "went crazy" buying him warm clothing.

The Latter-day Saint Church continues to grow in Mongolia. As of January 1, 2015, the Church reported there were 10,763 members in the country.[95]

The Latter-day Saint Church's experience in Mongolia is illustrative of what it is experiencing in the twenty-first century. There is a strong international outreach. There are laws unique to each country that must be obeyed. It can take a significant amount of time to gain proficiency in the new language. Younger, indigenous people may not feel as bound to tradition and may be more willing to try new things. The Church's goal is to develop the leadership skills of native members, and their serving missions contributes to it. And English classes, while not directly related to the Church's religious message, are frequently held in Church buildings or in member's homes, where conversations about the Mormon Church often follow the lessons.

There are mixed reactions worldwide to missionaries teaching English classes. An American elder who served in Japan described the classes as a "hook," as a way to draw people into discussions about the Latter-day Saint Church, whereas Russian Orthodox clergy I spoke with in Russia were not at all pleased with the practice. They considered the English classes a devious way to proselytize for the Latter-day Saint Church.

The International Impetus

The Latter-day Saint Church has an extensive international presence. Conference sessions for the 185th Annual General Conference, in April 2015, were translated into more than seventy-five languages and broadcast to more than 170 countries. In that same year, Church materials were published in 188 languages.[96]

Non-Mormons find the extensive international outreach of the Latter-day Saint Church surprising, for Mormonism is traditionally viewed as an "American" religion—and for apparent good reason: its prophet and founder Joseph Smith was born in Vermont; the Church's headquarters is in Salt Lake City, Utah; and the Book of Mormon has Jesus visiting the American Midwest after his resurrection, but before his ascension (3 Nephi 11-26).

Two significant events occurred at the dawn of the twenty-first century that changed the face of The Church of Jesus Christ of Latter-day Saints. In February 1996, for the first time in its history, there were more members outside of the United States than inside it, and in September 2000, again for the first time in its history, there were more non-English-speaking members than English-speaking in the Church.[97]

The impetus for this international outreach comes from the fact that Latter-day Saints take Jesus's missionary directive literally: "Go ye therefore and teach all nations" (Mt 28:19), a philosophy of evangelism that is echoed in *Doctrine and Covenants* 133:37: "And this gospel shall be preached unto every nation, and kindred, and tongue, and people."

International missions have been a part of Mormonism since its earliest days. Joseph Smith sent missionaries to Canada in 1833, just three years after the Church was established, and by mid-century missionaries had been dispatched to a number of European countries and as far afield as China, the Society Islands, the Cape of Good Hope, the West Indies, British Guiana, Australia, and the Sandwich Islands. The greatest success was experienced in Great Britain, where thousands joined the Church. By mid-century, the Latter-day Saint Church had become the most successful millenarian group proselytizing in Great Britain.[98]

Joseph Smith was martyred in Illinois in 1844, and leadership devolved upon the chief apostle in the Church, Brigham Young, who led the majority of the Saints on their famous trek across the Plains to the Great Salt Lake Valley. A new era began for Mormon missions when the Church's headquarters and the majority of its members were located in the Mountain West. The new situation and relative isolation brought about important changes in both mission policy and institutions. One of the most significant changes that occurred in 1846, which continued for decades, was that the Church placed great emphasis on foreign missions while practically ignoring the United States and Canada as fields for missionary activity.[99]

There were several reasons for this development. The Saints experienced a feeling of disaffection toward the United States because of the assassination of their leader and because of the persecution they suffered. Just before the Saints had to leave Nauvoo, Illinois, Brigham Young said, "We don't owe this nation another gospel sermon, they are left to feel the wrath of an angry God."[100] Anti-Mormon sentiment was strong in the United States, especially over Mormon non-cooperation and interference with federal appointees to civil offices in the Utah territory. The "Mountain Meadows Massacre" also contributed to anti-Mormon sentiment; this massacre occurred in southern Utah in 1857, when over 120 people in an emigrant party bound for California, who were outspokenly anti-Mormon, were killed by Mormons and Indians. The Saints also ran afoul of public sentiment and the federal government due to their practice of polygamy, or "plural marriages," and it delayed Utah's entry into statehood well into the 1890s, when the Church officially abandoned the practice. Church authorities were especially interested in foreign missions, particularly in the mission to Great Britain. Apostles Brigham Young, Heber C. Kimball, and Wilford Woodruff, individuals who had enjoyed considerable success in Britain during the late 1830s and early 1840s, were among the leaders of the Church in Utah, and their experiences influenced, and indeed determined, the nature of missionary outreach from Utah.

The most favorable response to their message—and for the call to come to the United States to build the kingdom of God on earth, or "Zion," in the intermountain West—occurred in Great Britain and northern Europe. At the height of the British Mission's success in 1851, the Mormon Church had over twenty-five thousand members in England and Wales, with an additional eight thousand having already immigrated to the Mormon Zion in America. It is estimated that approximately fifty-five thousand Mormons immigrated to America from Great Britain between 1840 and 1890, with an additional twenty-five thousand emigrating from Scandinavia, Germany, and Switzerland.[101] The Latter-day Saint Church was enjoying greater success in Great Britain and Europe than in the United States.

This success could have been even greater had it not been undermined in 1853 when Joseph Smith's revelation advocating plural marriages was published in the British Mission's periodical, *The Latter-day Saint Millennial Star*.[102] Thereafter, Mormon polygamy became a cause célèbre in England and Europe, and the practice generated massive amounts of anti-Mormon sentiment and literature.

The Birmingham anti-Mormon riots of 1857 saw unruly mobs numbering in the hundreds interrupting LDS church services with howling, whistling, and groaning, and members were pelted with rocks and mud as they walked home. After one serious rock-throwing and window-breaking episode, these words were chalked on the doorway of the chapel yard: "Brigham Young has got forty-two wives, damn him!"[103]

The plot in Arthur Conan Doyle's first Sherlock Holmes novel, *A Study in Scarlet* (1887), centers on the murder of a Mormon elder by the vengeful fiancé of a young woman whom the Mormon captured and forced into a polygamous marriage, a union that Doyle called "a shame and a disgrace." The young woman didn't last long in the "hateful marriage," we are told, but rather pined away and died within a month.

Membership in the Latter-day Saint Church in Great Britain went into serious decline as a result of the polygamy revelation, and it would not revive until the twentieth century.

Changes in practice, significant historical events, and an important policy change took place in the twentieth century, which had profound effects on the Church and its international missionary program. A major shift occurred in the first decade of the twentieth century when the Church stopped encouraging converts from around the world to "gather to Zion." It was having a weakening effect on local congregations, since members and leaders were disappearing to the Mountain West. Converts were counseled to remain in their communities, whether in the United States or abroad, and to build the Latter-day Saint Church there. As a result, the Church took on a pronounced international identity in the twentieth century.

A massive building and rebuilding campaign took place after World War II in Europe and elsewhere to erect new meetinghouses and to replace those that had been destroyed in the war, thus providing places of worship for members in their own countries. To help defray the cost, young men, or "building missionaries," were called, who served their two-year mission helping to build new schools and churches.

In 1974 President Spencer W. Kimball told Church members that "we must 'lengthen our stride'" in international outreach, with the result that an increased emphasis was placed on missionary service. There was a dramatic increase in the numbers of those who served through the end of the twentieth century and into the twenty-first century. The momentum continues today with sons and daughters, and grandsons and granddaughters, following in the footsteps of those who served in the latter part of the twentieth century.

One of the most profound changes in the twentieth century occurred in 1978, when President Kimball said he received a revelation that said that all worthy males, without regard to race or color, could receive the priesthood: a status that had up until that time been restricted to white males. This had worldwide implications, particularly for missionary work in Africa and for building the Church there.

Other building projects were undertaken to meet the needs of the expanding international Church, including the construction of temples, where faithful members participate in important rituals and ceremonies. Their numbers have increased exponentially since the latter part of the twentieth century, particularly outside of the United States. Seventeen temples had been built from 1830 to 1979, six of them outside of the United States; whereas it was reported in 2014 that when all of the current construction is completed, there will be 170 temples around the world, with the majority outside of the United States. It is thus easier for indigenous members to do their "temple work" closer to home.[104]

Membership statistics below show that the Latter-day Saint Church enjoys the greatest success in the United Sates, South America, and the Philippines. Surprisingly, the greatest concentration of Latter-day Saints after Utah (where they make up 68 percent of the state's population) is in Tonga, where the Church says its members constitute 45 percent of the total population.[105]

January 1, 2015, Membership by Regions, with the country with the highest membership number in parentheses:[106]

Africa	421,892 (Nigeria 118,139)
Asia	1,058,757 (Philippines 688,117)
North America	8,822,912 (United States of America 6,398,889)
Europe	498,668 (United Kingdom 186,768)
South America	3,750,440 (Brazil 1,250,073)
Pacific	507,972 (Australia 140,797)

The Latter-day Saint Church is adjusting to its worldwide presence. Historically a tightly and centrally controlled church (which it still is), it has had to adapt to the sheer distances of members from Salt Lake City, as well as the laws and customs of other countries. The Church has reorganized itself administratively, such that the world is divided into regions or areas, each overseen by three General Authorities living in the area (the "Area Presidency"), who provide oversight for the LDS Church and its missions. The number of missions overseen by mission presidents has also expanded over the years, so that by 2015 there were 406 missions worldwide.

A sense of eschatological urgency and purpose are motivating forces behind this dramatic expansion over the past four decades, because most good Latter-day Saints, as their name implies, see themselves as living in the End Times. Jesus told his followers to prepare for his Second Coming and that they must spread his word throughout the world for it to happen. "And the gospel must first be published among all nations," he told his disciples (Mark 13:10). Latter-day Saint missionaries see themselves as participants in this momentous effort. They believe they are helping to build the worldwide Kingdom of God on earth, which will greet Christ at his Second Advent.

Receiving the International Call

Many factors contribute to determining whether a missionary is called to his home country or if he is sent abroad: health; academic ability; previous language training; ability and interest in learning a new language; and regional needs. The large number of American interviewees who said they wanted to "go foreign" (who wanted to learn a new language, travel to new places, and experience different cultures) was quite striking. Many who weren't chosen for an international mission were initially disappointed with their call, but most came to accept it, believing they were being sent where they were most needed.

But there were those who were just as happy to stay in their home country. They could "hit the ground running" as they said, because they wouldn't have to struggle for several months learning a new language. Some also admitted that they were pleased to not have to adjust to new food, a new culture, and possibly uncomfortable living conditions.

It is true that international missions present special challenges for non-native missionaries. In addition to the need to become proficient in a new language, adjust to a new environment, and adapt to new and unusual foods, they may be exposed to special risks and dangers: primitive sanitation practices; minimal medical facilities; unstable political situations; and natural disasters.

American missionaries in foreign lands often experience paradoxical reactions to their nationality. Some people will embrace them because they are Americans, whereas others will reject them for that reason. For those who respond favorably to missionaries, they may wonder: "Why do they want to talk with me? Are they interested in my message, my country, or do they want to practice their English?" In some instances, especially among young local women, their interest may be marriage.

Missionaries aren't always welcomed in foreign lands, because some see them as yet another arm of American imperialism, bringing American values, behaviors, and an unusual American religion to a country where they aren't wanted. The occasional insensitive and immature missionary, who shows a lack of respect for local faiths and customs, or who exhibits a condescending attitude toward the host country and its people, doesn't help the image.

The Latter-day Saint Church faced two challenges when calls for more missionaries and for the worldwide expansion of the Church was made beginning in the 1970s—one internal to the Church in the United States, and one external. Some American members didn't like the idea of bringing "different" people into the LDS Church; they were uncomfortable with seeking converts among people of different cultures, languages, and races. Church leaders had to speak out against these biases and prejudices.[107]

Another challenge was to convince young men outside of the United States that missionary work was their responsibility, too—and not just a task for Americans. Speaking at a conference in the United Kingdom in 1976, President Spencer W. Kimball told the young men there that they had a responsibility to serve a mission: "There have been many young men who have felt they didn't need to go on a mission, that it's an American job. That's not so." This concern was expressed again in 2007, when Apostle M. Russell Ballard said the United States won't supply all of the world's missionaries: "We're at a time in the Church's history when young men and young women all over the world need to rise up and serve as missionaries. They can't assume there are enough young people in the United States to do all that the Lord needs. He needs the youth everywhere the Church is organized to prepare themselves to bring souls to Him."[108]

The Latter-day Saint Church has built fifteen MTCs around the world in order to facilitate this international buy-in. The goal is to train missionaries locally, have them serve in their own or other countries, return home, and assume leadership positions in the LDS Church.

Training: Missionary Training Centers Worldwide

International training. The international scope of the Latter-day Saint Church becomes evident when we look at the number of MTCs it maintains around the world, while their geographical distribution is an indication of the relative importance the Church places on various regions of the world. In 2015 there were fifteen MTCs. In addition to the largest MTC at Provo, Utah, there were seven in Latin America (Argentina, Brazil, Chile, Columbia, Guatemala, Mexico, and Peru), two in Europe (England and Spain), two in Africa (Ghana and South Africa), and one each in the Caribbean (the Dominican Republic), the Philippines, and New Zealand.

Provo still trains the largest number of missionaries. In 2010, a total of 31,755 missionaries were trained at the various MTCs, of which 65 percent (20,750) were trained in Provo. With the age change in 2012, the eighty-eight thousand missionaries serving in 2014 represented missionaries from 143 countries, being taught in fifteen MTCs, learning fifty-five languages (the greatest number being taught at the Provo MTC), who went on to serve in more than 150 countries. After the Provo MTC, the Mexico MTC is the next largest and can house more than one thousand.[109]

It is reported that 50 percent of all missionaries worldwide serve in their own homelands, but that percentage is lower for American missionaries serving in the United States.[110]

An American elder assigned to Brazil in the early 2000s went to the Brazil MTC to learn Portuguese and was met at the airport by someone who didn't speak English. (And he didn't speak a word of Portuguese.) The São Paulo MTC is a large facility, which includes classrooms, residence halls, computer rooms, a cafeteria, and a gym. The elder reported that language training was rigorous and intense: twelve hours a day, working at computers and with Portuguese speakers. The first thing they taught them was to pray in Portuguese. He said prayer is the basis of everything, so it made sense to start with prayer. He had a teacher of Portuguese who had recently returned from his mission and who was especially helpful and supportive. They were expected to speak Portuguese at lunch and with their companion, and while none from his district went home early, a couple of elders struggled with the language.

He said the training became monotonous after two months of classroom work, and they were very excited, but anxious, when they left the MTC for Fortaleza, where they would put into practice what they had been learning. It was "quite a shock" when they arrived, because people talked fast, and he couldn't understand what was being said. This was in contrast to the MTC, where teachers were taught to speak slowly. It took him four months before he could understand what people were saying and could respond.

The Latter-day Saint Church strives to keep its MTCs updated and focused on the regions they serve. A new, expanded, state-of-the-art

Philippines MTC was dedicated in 2012, replacing the original MTC that dated from 1983. The new facility can house up to 144 missionaries and serves missionaries from the region—the Philippines, Cambodia, Hong Kong, India, Indonesia, Mongolia, Pakistan, Sri Lanka, Taiwan, and Thailand. Instruction is in their native languages.[111]

While there are differences between the various MTCs in regard to their sizes and the languages of instruction, all use the same training materials: all work from *Preach My Gospel.*

All missionaries are given practical and legal advice, some of which particularly applies to those serving international missions. They are to respect the culture, customs, beliefs, practices, and sacred sites of other faiths, and they are not to evangelize at or near other houses of worship. They are reminded that it is illegal in many countries to place flyers or pamphlets in mailboxes or on cars. They must return home immediately at the end of their mission, because, if they don't, future missionaries may not be allowed into the country.

A returned missionary from Columbia who teaches the Columbia culture course at the Provo MTC for Columbian-bound missionaries said one of his most important goals is that missionaries come to understand that their role is to teach the Mormon gospel and to leave investigators as what they are, Columbians. MTC officials don't want international investigators to become Americans; they want them to become indigenous members of the LDS Church.

I spoke with the man who served as the president of the Chile MTC in the mid-1980s. He said that at that time in Latin America less than half of the missionaries had families in the Church. The exception was Mexico, where many were born into it. Many were very poor when they arrived at the MTC. He would write home and tell his children how the new missionaries didn't have enough clothes. An Eagle Scout took on the project of getting white shirts for the missionaries through individuals and stores and he collected over one hundred new shirts. The duty officer said he would have to pay a high duty, but the scout talked him into calling them rags and thus had to pay only a six dollar duty. The MTC president said the new clothes made the missionaries feel more confident and look like "real missionaries."

Stories of personal and family sacrifice were common, reported the MTC president. At the initial interview he would always ask if the missionary's parents were members of the LDS Church, and what he did prior to his mission. Some elders reported their parents weren't members and were very upset with their decision to serve a mission.

Some said they gave up promising jobs, bright careers, and significant educational opportunities to serve. One said he had just finished his internship as an M.D., but he gave up a very prestigious scholarship in medicine because, he said: "It was more important to me to serve a mission. I knew that is where Heavenly Father wanted me to be."

The Latter-day Saint Church's biggest problem in Latin America (then and now) is that mission work is growing so rapidly that they can't keep up with providing leadership.

It isn't uncommon for international missionaries to be older and to have made significant sacrifices to serve a mission. A Spanish instructor recalled a group from Spain who was trained at the Provo MTC, who then went back to their country to serve their missions. She found them "amazing." Many were older because they were converts to the Church, and many had given up good jobs in order to serve. In one sister's case, while all in her family were Church members, they still found it difficult to accept that she was going on a mission, because she was the main provider in the family. "It's hard to find work here," they said. "We can't believe you are going to leave your job and go on a mission. Who will work and earn money for the family?"

A visit to the Surrey, England, MTC. Prior to the 1998 construction of the MTC in Preston, England, the England MTC was located in a manor house on the grounds of the London Temple in Surrey, south of London. With its half-timbered walls, oak paneling, and heavy doors, it was a charming site for my three-day visit in 1994. It had been established in 1985 and was one of the smaller MTCs. Unlike the Provo MTC, with its constant turnover of overlapping groups of missionaries coming and going, the Surrey MTC served discreet groups; all arrived on the same day and left on the same day. Since it was small, it was a twelve-day program instead of the longer program typical of Provo at the time. Twenty-four groups of missionaries were served in 1993, with an average size of fourteen members.

The MTC staff referred to it as the "United Nations" MTC, because it served missionaries from the United Kingdom and Western, Central, and Eastern Europe. Twenty-seven countries were represented at the MTC in 1993, and most missionaries returned to serve in their home country. Most instruction was in English, although there were so many Spanish-speaking missionaries that instruction in Spanish was available. Theoretically, missionaries were fluent in either English or Spanish when they arrived, but that wasn't always the case. Thus the staff learned to speak slowly, or one of the missionaries served as a translator. There were a high percentage of sisters: they constituted 40 percent of missionaries in 1993. There were twenty missionaries from eleven countries when I visited.

The MTC president and his wife felt the MTC's small size was an asset because it was possible for them to develop close relationships with the missionaries. Their first goal was to be parents to them: to love and support them. They encouraged missionaries to be themselves and to accept that all have strengths and weaknesses.

The president said all MTCs hope to accomplish at least four things during the missionaries' stay: increase their desire to serve; improve their teaching skills; increase their spirituality; and increase their love for their Savior. Their biggest concern was that since there were so many countries and languages represented, they hoped the missionaries understood what was being said and done. The couple's greatest satisfaction came from seeing missionaries grow from being shy and quiet to gaining a testimony and developing a sense of community.

The president gave me the use of his office to talk with eight missionaries. There were two sisters and six elders: two British; one American living in Europe; two Scandinavians; one Croatian; one Belgian; and one Czech. The young woman from Croatia was the first sister to serve from her country. Some had been born into the LDS Church, but none had a father who had served a mission. One had two older brothers who had served, and he was the only one of the group who knew early on (at the age of twelve) that he was going on a mission. Most therefore didn't grow up in a culture where going on a mission was the expected norm. They waited until they had a testimony that the Latter-day Saint Church was true before putting in their papers. For some this decision came just months before applying. They seemed a more mature group as a result. Not all of their parents were supportive of their decision to serve.

I had lunch with all of the missionaries. Many from Eastern Bloc countries were recent converts and were very dedicated. Two sisters were going on a deaf mission. The missionaries' perception was that they belonged to a worldwide church, although their non-member friends referred to the LDS Church as "that American religion." Language was a problem for some. A friendly, talkative, Italian sister, when asked if she wanted seconds to eat, meant to say, "I am full," but said instead, "I am pregnant." That stopped the lunchroom conversation for a moment, and then everyone laughed.

Their days were filled with personal study, classes that focused on learning and teaching the discussions, and group meetings. They used the same learning materials used in Provo. The group was given a "final exam" on their last day, which consisted of two short quizzes: one on doctrine, and a fill-in-the-blank quiz on teaching the discussions.

They held a going-away ceremony on the final evening. It began at 6:30 P.M. and ended at 10:00 P.M. We sat in a circle, and all twenty spoke. They introduced themselves, said something about their lives, and described where they were going. It was obvious that the small size of the MTC, and the discreet groups, had contributed to a strong sense of community. The impact of their stay, their love for their fellow missionaries, and their love for the MTC president and his wife was striking. Some contributions were quite moving; there were many tears and a box of tissues was passed around the circle. One sister told how her parents had divorced when she was eight, and she said she had never seen love in a couple like she saw with the MTC president and his wife. "You are my role models," she said, "and I hope my marriage will be as good."

The session ended, as all farewell sessions ended at the Surrey MTC, with the singing of "God Be with You Till We Meet Again," the same song sung by sister missionaries in the stairwells of the Provo MTC on their last night. While there was little opportunity for traditions to be passed from group to group because of their arriving and leaving in discreet groups, singing that song is the one tradition they all shared.

I came away from the Surrey MTC visit (as I did with my interview with the Chilean MTC president) with a greater appreciation of the strength of conviction of international missionaries, since in many cases their serving involves a considerable amount of sacrifice. Joining the LDS Church isn't an easy thing for many, because it frequently involves changing their religion, which leads to conflicts in their family. Some are the only Church members in their families. Many consider serving a mission to be a privilege, not just something expected of them, and for some it creates even greater challenges, because in many cases serving leads to even more conflicts in their families. Some have to give up college places and scholarships, and some have to give up good jobs, which have an adverse effect on the family's finances. In spite of this, they choose to serve. They thus show a very high level of commitment to the LDS Church and generally are very good missionaries.

The Surrey MTC was bursting at the seams in the mid-1990s. It housed the younger missionaries, as well as older temple workers who served at the Surrey Temple on the same grounds. Typically retired couples, the Temple workers didn't always appreciate sharing living space with younger, enthusiastic, and not-so-quiet elders.

A new MTC was built in Preston in conjunction with the construction of a new temple there. It opened in 1998. While the new MTC is relatively small, serving cohorts of around forty, the fear was that it would lose some of the intimacy of the Surrey MTC.

Transitions: Initially Feeling Like Fish Out of Water

Arrival in the mission field. Missionaries arrive in the international mission field anxious and exhausted. They have endured a rigorous training regimen at a MTC and they don't quite know what to expect once they arrive. They wonder who their new trainer will be and whether they will get along. Those learning a new language fear they have not mastered their new language to the level expected of them.

An American elder who arrived in Geneva said all he wanted to do at first was sleep; he was "in a daze" the first few days. He was "really scared" as the plane landed, because he had no idea what to expect, and he thought that as soon as he got off the plane everyone would speak French to him and he would have no clue what was going on. He feared his mission president would meet his group and speak to them only in French and ask them questions about the investigator lessons. But, he was happy to discover, the mission president was "normal"; he spoke in English and made the new missionaries feel comfortable.

An A.P. who met new missionaries as they arrived in Portugal said they would be wide-eyed as they deplaned, and he would greet them in Portuguese. They would give a weak response in the language, and he would then start speaking in English. Relieved, they would say they thought he was only going to speak in Portuguese. He would respond: "Dude, no way. I came off of that plane, too."

Some missionaries spoke of their first impressions of their new country and how they were immediately taken out of their comfort zones. An American elder who arrived in Hungary, his first time out of the United States, said it felt different, it was gray, everything was dark, and people were unhappy. The airport was small and depressing. It was the grimmest and grayest place he had ever seen. No one was smiling, and there was a gloomy, depressing feeling about the place.

An American elder who served in Brazil said they were "wide-eyed" as they drove from the airport, seeing people living in shacks under bridges, next to dirty rivers.

Another new arrival expressed fear about native drivers when first riding along narrow, Japanese roads.

Missionaries meet with the mission president upon arrival for a personal interview, instruction, and training. Then their trainers come, and they are off to their fields of labor. In some instances, interviewees had to make it to their assigned area on their own. The elder who served in Brazil said he took a long bus ride to his area, and, when he arrived around 3:00 A.M. at the bus station, expecting to be met by the four elders serving in the town, they weren't there. The station was deserted. So he sat on a bench and nervously waited. Several thoughts went through his mind, including, "I am going to get robbed," and, "I have no idea where I am in the world." Someone eventually told him the elders were asleep in hammocks outside. He went out and woke them.

The elder who served in Hungary was put on a train and was told his companion would meet him at a particular stop. He found it "scary, really scary," because he didn't know the language, the country, or his soon-to-be companion. When he later worked in the mission president's office, he said it was common for new missionaries who were traveling by themselves to get lost and to get off at the wrong train stop. The greenies would be "traumatized" by the experience, but they would eventually be found.

Speaking a new language. For those going to a place where another language is spoken, their arrival is sometimes a shock. They believe they have been sent to the wrong country, because what they hear on the streets doesn't sound like what they learned at the MTC. An elder said on their first day in Paris he and his fellow missionaries were sure they were in the wrong place; they didn't understand a word that was said. They weren't prepared for the idioms and for how quickly people spoke. It took them a while to understand what was being said.

Two American elders I spoke with on the streets of St. Petersburg, Russia, echoed the same experience. They thought they had gotten off in the wrong country when they first arrived in Russia, because the Russian they heard spoken didn't sound like the Russian they had learned at the MTC.

A sister who served in France said she had four years of French in high school and a year in college, but when she arrived in the country she wondered, "What have I been studying all these years?"

Trainers are to help the new missionary become comfortable and proficient with the language, and it is common for greenies to look to the trainer when trying to talk with investigators. An elder serving in a Spanish-speaking mission in California said he could speak Spanish a little bit, could ask investigators questions, but he had to turn to his trainer for an explanation of their responses, because he didn't have a clue what they were saying.

Trainers and senior companions can also bail greenies out of awkward situations. An American elder serving in Italy said he thought he knew Italian pretty well after spending two months at the Language Training Mission in Provo, but his first month in Italy was a "language disaster." His first investigator became very responsive and animated during the discussion, and the new missionary thought he was getting excited about the message, but when he looked at his companion it was obvious he wanted to leave. After they left the greenie asked what the problem was, because he thought it was going great. The senior companion reported that the man said he was an atheist and if they ever came back, he would shoot them.

"I had no clue," said the greenie.

Maintaining a productive relationship with companions is hard enough in the best of circumstances, but the difficulty in doing so seems to be accentuated when serving in a foreign country and the missionary is struggling with the language. An American elder serving in Japan said he had been struggling during the early part of his mission. He was frustrated with the language, and he was afraid he was holding his senior companion back, who was one of the best in the mission. His companion was a very hard worker and much more comfortable with the language and with proselytizing than the junior companion. The senior comp liked to do street proselytizing, where the missionaries walk along with the person and talk at the same time. The interviewee felt a lot of pressure from his companion and was getting discouraged; he didn't want to slow him down. By six or seven in the evening he could hardly function anymore; he would be tired, feel sick (occasionally homesick), and occasionally get depressed. It was only after he felt comfortable with the language and could keep up with his hardworking companion that he got over his discouragement and felt he became effective in finding investigators. That took him three or four months.

Missionaries are typically assigned as senior companions some months after being in the mission field, but because of a large number of missionaries going home, a young elder in Paris was made a senior companion after just two months, when he was still struggling with the language. There were times when he didn't understand what the investigator was saying, but he couldn't look at his companion for help, because he would be there yawning, having just arrived in the country and still suffering from jet lag. Having this responsibility was "one of the most frightening experiences" of his mission. He said it required spiritual strength and close cooperation with his companion in order to succeed. It was a very challenging time, but also a time of real growth. "You had nothing but the guy next to you and help from our Father in Heaven to get us through it," he said. "And so we grew rapidly. We worked hard together, the time went by fast, and we were able to do some good work there."

Even those who go to a country where they think they speak the same language are challenged. An American elder who served in the south of England reported with a laugh that he thought he was going to an English-speaking country, but his first experience there was not being able to understand what people were saying. He got on a train in Bristol to go to Southampton, and he didn't understand a word the conductor was saying. He knew Southampton was the end of the line, so he waited until the train stopped and wasn't going any farther—then he got off.

Missionaries make honest mistakes with their new language. The elder who served in Hungary said there are particular words in Hungarian that are close in sound—one is a profanity, and one is not—and they would make mistakes. Sometimes people would laugh it off, but sometimes people would become offended and get angry with them.

An American elder who served in Mexico said missionaries rode buses as their major means of transportation. Not long after arriving in the country a new American missionary noted that the driver would make unscheduled stops if a passenger called out *"baja,"* which means "go down" or "get off." Wanting to get off at an unscheduled stop, the missionary yelled out *"vaca,"* which means "cow." (Although the two words look nothing alike, they sound very similar, in some regions more so than others. A non-native speaker could certainly confuse the two sounds.) Nothing happened when he called out. So the elder started saying it louder, people began turning around, staring, and laughing, and the driver didn't stop. The missionaries wondered why they were being discriminated against, and it was only later that they realized people thought they were two crazy "gringo" teenagers, sitting in the back of the bus, yelling something about a cow.

A new sister serving in a Spanish-speaking mission in California was called to the front of the church by the bishop to introduce herself to the congregation. What she meant to say was that she didn't speak Spanish very well, that she was embarrassed, and that it was the bishop's fault for asking her to come forward. But what she said was that she was pregnant and it was the bishop's fault. The congregation laughed, the bishop turned red, and one of the members explained to her what she had said. She too turned red, and then corrected herself.

A sister who served in France talked of the hazing of greenies by senior missionaries who would coach them to say things that were absolutely inappropriate, but the greenies had no idea what they were saying. An American elder serving in the early 1990s said it was quite common to play tricks on each other, especially if the companion was a greenie. They would be coached to say the wrong thing when ordering at a restaurant, sometimes saying something rude, and they wouldn't know what they said. Greenies are "a sitting duck" for those kinds of jokes, he reported.

When I asked missionaries how long it took them to learn the language, their answers generally ranged from three to six months. An American elder who served a Spanish-speaking mission in California and who had Spanish all through high school and a year in college said it still took him three or four months before he was comfortable with the language. An American sister in Italy said that by four months she was comfortable with the language. She couldn't express everything, but she could talk around the concepts. If she didn't know a particular word to explain what she meant, she would look it up in a dictionary. One of the American elders I spoke to on the street of St. Petersburg, Russia, said it took him eight months before he began to feel comfortable with the language and with his ability to communicate in it.

Missionaries speaking another language are advised to create a language study plan in the field. The plan has them setting aside thirty to sixty minutes each day to work on improving their language skills. They are also to work on their ability to read and write in their mission language and to learn about the culture of the country.

While today's missionaries are encouraged to memorize phrases and key scriptural passages in their mission language, their experience is unlike missionaries of previous generations who memorized entire lessons. Today's missionaries are told not to memorize lengthy passages or entire lessons. They are to retain the flexibility to react to the questions and situations at hand, not to present a canned speech.[112]

An elder who served in Japan said he got good at the language as soon as he stopped studying it in his room and took his dictionary out into the street. He became so proficient that he served as a translator for American visitors, which gave him status in the mission.

Some became so proficient in their new language that they set a goal of speaking without an accent, but it was difficult. An elder speaking Portuguese in Brazil said he finally gave up trying to get rid of his accent, while a sister who served in France, who became quite fluent in French, was told near the end of her mission that she still sounded like she had a hot potato in her mouth.

But the challenges remain when trying to communicate in another language, especially in the early days. Said a sister who served in Japan: "Teaching grand ideas is a problem when you sound like an idiot."

Mixing companions from different countries. Missionaries serving in countries other than their own are likely paired with companions from another country. Interviewees spoke of the many positive aspects of the experience, but also of the challenges it presented. They tended to learn their new language faster if they were paired with a native speaker, they gained a greater understanding of and appreciation for the people and the culture, and they tended not to make as many cultural faux pas when paired with a native. Their mutual need to sort through the language and cultural differences served as the basis for some to develop close, positive relationships with their companions.

But they also found the experience discomforting at times. It allowed them no break in speaking the new language, since they needed to communicate in their new language at all times. They may have been paired with a companion of a different race, who may have had a different sense of humor and a different way of looking at the world.

One interviewee said that sometimes "you just like to be with your own"—to be able to unwind, to comment on unusual experiences, to blow off steam, "to be with the guys." A sister serving in Italy said while she valued her time with her Italian companion and learned the language much faster because her companion didn't speak English, there still were times when she missed home and was lonely. It was good to be able to talk with other Americans, to hear American expressions, and to have American conversations.

Interviewees spoke of having both positive and negative reactions to having a native companion appear with them at a person's door. An American elder who served in Japan said he was surprised to discover that people were more likely to talk with two Americans, than if one of the companions was Japanese; they would think the Americans were "kind of cool and interesting," and while they may not have been interested in their message, they were interested in talking with them about America. When he had a Japanese companion, people weren't as interested in hearing their message and weren't as interested in talking with them.

Mixed companionships sometimes don't work. An American elder spoke of having a foreign companion who made anti-American remarks, who had hit one American companion and thrown a bowl of cereal at another. The interviewee described their six weeks together as "an awful experience" and as the low point of his mission. The companion would walk behind him and not go into peoples' houses. The interviewee said it was difficult to project a positive image and message under those conditions. He threatened to go to the mission president to ask for a transfer. The companion immediately apologized and was transferred not long thereafter.

An American elder who served in Japan in the early 1990s and had good experiences with two Japanese companions observed philosophically regarding mixed companionships: "People are people no matter what language, culture, or faith. They all have hearts and feelings."

Housing and bugs. Missionaries spoke of various housing arrangements, including having a room in a member's house, a room in a non-member's house, and having an apartment. Those who served in hotter climates faced special challenges. A sister who served in Central America said tarantulas flooded into their apartment through a hole in the wall when it rained hard, but she said they stung just "a little." They had trouble with cockroaches, ants, and "bugs with hundreds of legs." They were "everywhere," and they would find them on the kitchen counter each morning. They also had problems with fleas and lice. Fleas would get in their beds and bite, which hurt and itched. Her head began to itch, but she didn't want to consider she might have lice. But after washing her hair, she found lice on her comb, and her companion had them, too.

Transportation. Missionaries utilize various means of transportation: they walk, ride bicycles, use public transportation, and some drive cars.

Mopeds or motorized bicycles were popular in France in the 1960s and early 1970s. An elder who served in Paris in the mid-1960s said they would meet new missionaries at the train station and take them straight to the moped shop where they would buy their own. An elder who served in Paris in the early 1970s said they were a great means of transportation and that is how they got around. They had to wear helmets and could get up to thirty miles per hour going downhill. When they were transferred they would put their trunk and their bike on the train and move onto their next area. Occasionally they were stolen, and they were so beat up by the end of their mission that they would give them away to a member or to a neighbor.

Accidents are a constant worry for mission presidents, and accidents were common with mopeds, especially when it rained and the cobblestone streets were slippery from the rain and from oil from cars. The elder who served in Paris recounted the story of a companion who was unsteady on his moped, crashed on the cobblestones during a rainstorm, and when the interviewee returned to the scene, the elder's pants were ripped, he was bleeding, and a Roman Catholic priest was tending to him. The interviewee thought the priest was administering last rites to his companion. He often crashed his moped and ripped his pants. He would ask young women from the Church to sew them up for him, which they did.

Sisters had extra challenges on their mopeds. A sister who served in France in the mid-1960s said companions would share mopeds; one would drive while the other sat on the back carrying their gear, which included a flannel board for street displays, a large tape recorder for street music, and their scriptures. She imagined they looked quite a sight, especially the day they were crossing a bridge in Lyon and the wind caught the flannel board and everything blew away. She said they probably looked pretty ridiculous.

But mopeds could be dangerous. There was "Sister Lurch," who would forget to put her feet down when she came to a stop, and she would fly over the handlebars. There were so many accidents, and even some missionary deaths, that a General Authority came to France in the early 1970s, and he stopped the use of mopeds. Missionaries converted to ten-speed bicycles.

Bicycles present their own challenges, especially for sisters in their long dresses. An elder who served in Japan said the American sisters were not used to riding a bike, in a long dress, while holding an umbrella.

A sister who served in Italy said she preferred riding on the bus, because people were naturally inquisitive; they would recognize the missionaries as Americans, and people would strike up a conversation about their nametags and what they were doing. She said it was a perfect opening for her to talk about the Mormon gospel and why she was there. But, as she found out, standing out in the crowd can also be a distraction. This particular American sister, who is fair-haired and fair-skinned, stood out especially in southern Italy where she attracted even more attention, especially from men, which is not what she wanted.

Young men in dark suits. Missionaries tend to stand out regardless of where they are assigned, since young men in dark suits, white shirts, conservative ties, and black nametags are unusual. But their distinctive dress can be misinterpreted. In countries where it is unusual to see men attired in such outfits, it is frequently assumed the missionaries have sinister motives. An elder who served in Eastern Europe in the early 1990s said they quickly gave up going door to door. In his words: "After all those years of communism, two guys in dark suits knocking on your door just wouldn't work. People would freak out." He said people on the street knew immediately from their looks and accents that they were Americans, and they assumed they were CIA agents. An American elder in Brazil said people thought they were with the FBI. They were asked if they were going to kidnap children and take them to the United States. A young man from Utah who had just returned from his mission in Japan said people thought they were either with the CIA or they were there to take away their young women.

Even when people don't hear them speak, Americans find they are recognizable overseas. An American elder who served in southern England said they wore the standard missionary outfit, but no nametags (this was in the 1960s). One day he and his companion were riding through a town on British bikes, wearing British clothes, and two little boys yelled, "Hey! Look at the Americans!" He said sometimes people recognized them as Mormon missionaries, but, if not, they were seen as two odd-looking, twenty-year-old Americans, wearing suits. Other American missionaries said they tended to be recognizable regardless of what they were wearing. An elder serving in Japan said Americans stood out because they were taller, and an American elder over six feet tall serving in Brazil said the same thing: Americans tended to be taller, and kids even called him "a giant."

Cultural adjustments. Missionaries have to get used to cultural differences regarding dress and various stages of undress. An American elder I spoke to in Berlin said a woman answered her door in her underwear. It didn't seem to bother her, but it made him and his companion uncomfortable. Another said a man in Switzerland invited them in to talk, and when they got inside they discovered he was completely naked. Two elders in Mongolia talked of trying to teach the first lesson to a woman who was breast-feeding a baby. They looked at the floor, at the ceiling, and over her head while they spoke with her. An American elder who served in Japan said the local custom was to go to the public baths. They usually weren't coed, and people would be naked, although one time a Japanese man brought his girlfriend with him. The missionaries were embarrassed and put on towels.

Missionaries sometimes have to unlearn etiquette lessons they learned at home. An American missionary serving in France said sometimes at zone conference the mission president's wife would give missionaries tips and tell them what they were doing wrong. The missionary discovered it is very impolite in France to put a hand in his lap while eating: both hands are always to be on the table.

Food. Missionaries serving in foreign lands are frequently fed food they have never seen or eaten before. They may think it is wonderful, disgusting, or hard to digest. A sister who served in Central America said the food was incredible and tasted wonderful, but it was cooked in highly saturated fat coconut oil, and she gained weight.

Missionaries frequently work among poor people, and interviewees spoke of being served soup with scraps of meat in it, and sometimes finding a chicken foot or head. Or they would be offered fried pigskin with the hair still on it. Some sisters swore they were vegetarians and said they couldn't eat meat. A sister spoke of being served a "mystery meat," which she and her companion ended up putting in plastic bags, because there was no way they could eat it. They felt bad, but the family didn't know because they were outside.

The food sometimes doesn't agree with them. A sister said she ate a lot of chili, and it irritated her gastritis. Regarding the food at the Provo MTC, a Brazilian elder there in 2008 said, "It tastes good, but my body doesn't recognize these foods."

The sister who served in Central America said in some areas she and her companion would cook for themselves, whereas in other areas they would walk to members' homes for breakfast, lunch, or dinner. All members wanted to feed them well, and all of the sisters gained "enormous" amounts of weight. She gained "tons" of weight too, but she got sick near the end and lost it. She said that was fairly typical.

An elder who served in Germany said it was customary for people to give missionaries something to eat when they visited, and they would be invited to have dinner on Sunday with members, and sometimes during the week. He saw things he had never seen or eaten before (he spoke of a raw, smoked, ground beef spread). Elders are known for having large appetites, and it was customary that whatever elders were fed, they would eat. "I never refused anything," he said. "If they gave it to me, I ate it." One family was known for serving very large meals, and they proposed a contest: that the elders couldn't eat all the food put in front of them. Eight elders came to dinner that evening, but they still couldn't eat everything. The interviewee said he thought his stomach was going to "blow up."

An elder who served in Eastern Europe said the food was very good and they ate a lot, but the meat was fatty and greasy and not good for them. It was the tradition that if he and his companion had an appointment and were invited to the investigator's house, they would feed them. There were days when they had five appointments and would eat five times that day. He said it felt like all they did was study, walk, teach, baptize, eat, and sleep.

Missionaries may be humbled by the experience, because people will want to feed them but may have little to give. An elder serving in northwest Mongolia said his cleaning lady had been involved in slaughtering sheep over the summer, and she brought him and his companion a bowl of boiled entrails. He said it was humbling to see her giving practically everything she had.

According to the Word of Wisdom, Latter-day Saints are not to drink alcohol, and missionaries are well aware of the prohibition. But in some circles and in some cultures, alcohol is consumed at an early age. A sister serving in France told the story of attending a Church primary picnic not long after her arrival and being offered a drink from a little girl's thermos. She drank it and thought it tasted a little strange and then realized she had drunk wine, for the first time in her life, and it had happened while on her mission. She said many drank watered-down wine in France, including children, but not missionaries. The little girl didn't know missionaries shouldn't be drinking wine or that it shouldn't be drank at Church primary picnics.

Illness: a fact of life for some. Sickness is a fact of life for many missionaries, particularly those serving in areas with poor health standards. A sister who served in Guatemala said sanitation and contaminated food was an ongoing concern while working in poorer areas. She felt guilty when she was served food and wondered if she would get sick from it—and she did. All of the missionaries became sick from water and food, all had diarrhea, and they openly talked about it. It was a fact of life and of the mission. She also contracted a jungle virus that "knocked her socks off," and she was in bed for two weeks with a high fever. The disease made her think and feel as if all her bones were broken. She said missionaries would be sick and have no energy, but they would work anyway. One of her companions was really ill for the whole mission, having contracted a disease that was thought to be incurable. When I asked how that made her feel, she said it gave her pause when it happened and that she considered quitting and returning home. She was thinking about marriage and having children, and she wondered if she might contract something that would make that impossible; she worried that twenty years from then she would have a heart attack and die. Things like that happen, she said, and she wondered why she was putting herself at risk like that on her mission. She did continue on, but she did have amoebas in her body at the end of her mission.

Others reported being sick throughout their mission. An elder who served in Chile said he became frustrated because he was sick so often, and he frequently had to go to the doctor. He spent much of his time in his apartment while his companion went out with a local member. It was a trying time for him, not being able to do what he wanted to do. But he said he learned a lot from the experience. It wasn't his fault that he got sick, so he accepted it and moved on. He learned to have a positive attitude about everything he did. His health problems affected him so much that he was sent back to the United States after twenty-one months, where he completed his mission.

An interviewee who served in New England said he was just as happy to be called to the United States, because his brother lost thirty-five pounds on his mission in Columbia, where he was sick much of the time.

As we discussed earlier in Chapter 5, the Church has put in place resources that address the medical and emotional needs of missionaries and staff, and the number of missionaries sick on any particular day has decreased considerably from previous decades.

Unusual and dangerous situations. Missionaries face other issues and perils. Their high public profiles, brought about by frequent appearances on the streets and by knocking on peoples' doors, make them vulnerable, and interviewees recounted numerous uncomfortable situations. An elder who served in Paris said he and his companion had a gun pulled on them while tracting, and after they backed out of the situation they got on their mopeds and drove for around forty-five minutes before stopping. They also had a knife brandished at them at a door. He never told his mother of these experiences until he got home, because he felt she didn't need to hear them. He said mothers get "kind of excited about things like that. Dads are okay, but moms aren't."

Two sisters were kidnapped at gunpoint in Guatemala City, Guatemala, in July 1994, and were held for a $53,000 ransom. The kidnapper said two elders should deliver the money to a specified location. Two police officers put on white shirts and ties, dark trousers, and missionary nametags and delivered the money. The kidnapper was arrested when he came to collect the money.[113] A sister interviewee who served in Guatemala at the time of the kidnappings said they had to be very careful after that event. The mission president imposed a curfew, and they had to be in before dark.

The same sister said she and her companion went into another area of Guatemala where an American woman had been killed because people thought she was there to kidnap children. The sister said people would pass them on the street and yell, "Are you going to steal our children?" The sisters had "many problems," she reported. They had to be very careful and had to stop wearing their more casual preparation day clothes so that they didn't look like tourists. They had to wear their missionary attire with their nametags at all times, and they couldn't play in public with children like they had before. "We were just walking on eggshells all the time," she said.

American missionaries may be subjected to anti-American sentiment. An American elder serving in Chile said he experienced "a lot of it." People would yell anti-American slogans at him and swear. It was something he had to learn to ignore. Someone threw a rock at him, but it didn't hit him. A couple of LDS chapels were bombed while he was there, but he didn't know any missionaries who were physically harmed. He did hear of missionaries being beat up by drunks. His appearance drew attention to hm. He was probably the blondest and lightest-skinned missionary in the mission, and, together with his "missionary outfit," he always stood out. Buses would go by, and everyone would turn and look at him. He would just wave. It worked to his advantages at times, being so conspicuous and noticeable; people would come up to him and talk with him.

Missionaries face difficult situations when they serve in their home country, too, but such instances seem to be magnified when they take place in a foreign country. A sister who served in Northern New England reflected on how "easy" she had it compared to her brothers who served overseas. One was shot at in Germany, while another had stones thrown at him and his companion while they ran down a street in Madagascar. "I have been really blessed compared to what my brothers and sisters have gone through. I really think that I have had it really easy in the States. I go through hard times, but it is nothing compared to what other people go through."

Sometimes missionaries find themselves in bizarre situations. An interviewee who served in Mexico in the mid-1960s said he and his companion had a little cottage on a beach, and one day a busload of Americans parked their vehicle right next to the house. The bus was painted in psychedelic colors and designs, and the people who got out were equally colorful, with their long beards and psychedelic clothing. The missionaries went over to talk with them ("Since they were neighbors," reported the elder), and it turned out it was the American author Ken Kesey, one of the earliest proponents of psychedelic drugs, and his disciples, the "Merry Pranksters." (Tom Wolfe wrote about them in the 1960s in *The Electric Kool-Aid Acid Test*. There is a chapter in the book that talks about their flight to Mexico. Kesey is better known as the author of *One Flew Over the Cuckoo's Nest*.) Kesey and his band of disciples had been charged with drug violations in the United States and had fled to Mexico. The group wandered around town and attracted a lot of attention, and the American authorities soon became aware of their presence. The American authorities got in touch with the Mexican authorities, seeking to have them extradited to the United States. But the Pranksters heard they were being watched and left in the middle of the night, which embarrassed the authorities.

Meanwhile, my interviewee and his companion were the first Mormon missionaries in the town. The local Roman Catholic priest was irate at their presence, and he wanted something done about them. The interviewee was then transferred to another town—and just in time, because the police came and arrested the missionaries. It seemed the authorities had to do something, and since they couldn't get the Merry Pranksters, they arrested the missionaries instead. The mission president eventually orchestrated their release.

The missionaries had been invited onto Kesey's bus during their initial visit. There was a big vat of orange juice in the back, which the Pranksters offered the missionaries, but they declined. It was laced with LSD. "They were missionaries in a sense, too," observed the interviewee. "They just wanted to turn people on in a different way."[114]

Extremes of weather and temperature. Weather and temperature extremes can motivate missionaries to want to be invited into peoples' homes. A sister who served in Belize and Guatemala said the high humidity and scorching heat in the summer (over one hundred degrees Fahrenheit) provided a real incentive to get into houses and out of the heat. There were days when she and her companion felt like they couldn't take the heat anymore, and then the sky would open and they would get huge storms, which would cool them off. In areas where there were dirt roads, it would turn into mud with the rain. In the morning they would put on clean clothes, but with the hot sun and rain they would start to look shabby. That, together with the people who didn't want to hear their message, made it hard to keep a good attitude. They used bicycles in the beginning, but they were stolen. The mission president banned the use of bicycles, because if they were walking they could interact with the people.

At the other end of the temperature spectrum was the elder who served in eastern Canada in the early 1950s, who said he and his companion agreed they would tract as long as the temperature didn't go below minus twenty degrees Fahrenheit (minus twenty-nine degrees Celsius). It was rare for people to open their doors at that temperature, although some did.

Anti-Mormon sentiment and misinformation. As in the United States, missionaries sometimes suffer rude and offensive behavior. An elder who served in Portugal had doors slammed in his face, was chased away from homes, and had someone spit in his face. A sister serving in France had garbage dumped on her head from a third floor in Paris.

Anti-Mormon sentiment naturally has a negative impact on missionary effectiveness. An American elder who served in the Swiss mission had to contend with negative representations of the Latter-day Saint Church in the press. The 1993 siege at David Koresh's Branch Davidian Compound in Waco, Texas, took place during the interviewee's mission, and it was frequently featured on the news. Mormons were categorized as another American "cult" in some broadcasts, and it made missionary work difficult. The general impression of the Swiss people was the Mormon Church was there to take their money, and they were very distrustful of missionaries. It was fourteen months before he baptized his first convert.

A sister who served in Italy found a similar attitude, that people sometimes had the perception that missionaries were out to lure them into the Church to get their money; as a result, people would become defensive. That made it hard for her to get up in the morning and to carry on. She said her motivation was one of wanting to share something with them that was of value to her, that had brought her happiness, and that she was sure would improve their lives, though they showed little interest.

The anti-Mormon film *The God Makers: A Shocking Expose of What the Mormon Church Really Believes* (1982) was translated and shown in Germany. An elder who served in the country in the late 1990s said ministers would show it when their members began to express interest in the Latter-day Saint Church, and, in the elder's words, "And of course, it scared the dickens out of them and they ran away."

The same missionary had to contend with another misrepresentation of the Latter-day Saint Church rendered through a movie. In the Academy Award-winning movie *Witness* (1985), Harrison Ford goes undercover in an Amish community to serve as a bodyguard for a young Amish boy who witnessed a murder. The person who translated the script into German inserted "Mormon" for "Amish," and the elder said people would say to him, "Oh yeah, you are the guys without electricity." He would say it was the Amish who didn't have electricity, not Mormons, but they would tell him it was Mormons, because they had seen Harrison Ford in a movie about it.

The elder was in Germany when a rare tornado struck Salt Lake City on August 11, 1999, causing extensive damage, many injuries, and one fatality. There were pictures of the damage in German newspapers, and the accompanying article said Mormons were allowed to have four wives. The elder said such instances irritated him, and he wished people would have asked him about the Church, but they didn't because their sense was that they couldn't get the truth from a member.

Anti-Mormon sentiment can also be found in the most out-of-the-way places. An elder who served in the remote Tonga Islands in the South Pacific in the mid-1950s said that when he visited the tiny, isolated island of Tafahi (population eighty when he visited), where there was no telegraph and no scheduled boat service, he decided to see how aware the inhabitants were of the outside world. They had never heard of President Eisenhower, Nikita Khrushchev, or Charles de Gaulle, and they had never heard of the United States, Russia, or France, but when the missionary mentioned Joseph Smith, one of the islanders responded, "Don't talk to us about that false prophet! Not in our home! We know all about him. Our minister has told us!"

The missionary could hardly believe his ears; it showed the extent and pervasiveness of anti-Mormon sentiment around the world. But he put a positive interpretation on it—he felt it fulfilled a prophecy found in the *Pearl of Great Price* that said that Smith's name "should be had for good and evil among all nations."[115]

Clergy of other faiths will sometimes organize against the Latter-day Saint Church. When the Church was seeking government recognition in Slovakia in 2006, they had to present a petition signed by twenty thousand members of the public, saying they supported the group being made a recognized religion in the country. Without official recognition, the Mormon Church could not own property, build chapels, or apply for missionary visas. The number of actual Slovakian members was very small at the time (around 125), and collecting that many signatures seemed an impossible task. The Church initially hired a Slovakian public relations firm to collect the signatures, thinking countrymen approaching fellow countrymen would be the most successful approach. That didn't work (only two hundred signatures were obtained in two weeks), so the Church sent all sixty to seventy missionaries serving in the Czech Republic at the time (mainly Americans who spoke Czech, not Slovakian) to Slovakian cities, where they circulated petitions. Roman Catholic clergy told their parishioners not to sign it, saying Mormon beliefs were at odds with Roman Catholic doctrines. This had little effect, for within a week missionaries were able to collect over thirty-three thousand signatures, and the Latter-day Saint Church was recognized on October 18, 2006.

This seemingly impossible task and outcome is referred to as "The Slovakian Miracle."

This caught the attention of Slovakian officials, and the church registration law was further tightened in 2007. Now twenty thousand signers must be permanent residents in the country and must belong to the religion in question. The law is not retroactive; otherwise it would be impossible for the Church to be recognized at this time, because as of January 1, 2015, there were only 239 members in the country.[116]

The Latter-day Saint Church in Ghana experienced considerable anti-Mormon sentiment and persecution, some of it at the instigation of clergy from Christian churches. This resulted in what is referred to as "The Freeze," a seventeen-month period beginning in June 1989, when all missionary work was banned, missionaries were expelled from the country, and the government took over some Church buildings. Sunday meetings were banned, but members could meet in their homes. Anti-Mormon articles appeared in the press, and Church members were harassed. Some drifted away from the Church as a result of the persecution. The ban was lifted in November 1990, when the Church convinced authorities that it was not an anti-government movement. Church numbers have continued to grow since then, with membership standing at 57,748 as of January 1, 2015.[117]

Missionaries aren't always blameless in generating anti-Mormon feelings overseas, because they will sometimes do dumb things, such as showing a lack of respect for local peoples, cultures, or religious institutions.

All of the above—struggling with a new language, cultural adjustments, illness, anti-Mormon sentiment—can generate the "fish out of water" feeling, which can lead to unease and depression, which can lead to a "dark night of the soul."

Trials: The Dark Night of the Soul.

The term "dark night of the soul" comes from a poem of the same name written in the sixteenth century by the Spanish Carmelite priest, Saint John of the Cross. In the poem he speaks of the spiritual crises many go through as they seek a relationship with God. The term has come to represent a sense of separation from God. Prayer seems to have lost its relevance, the person feels abandoned by God, and doubt is prevalent. But all is not lost, for in retrospect such struggles are seen as a blessing in disguise; they are part of a journey one must endure in order to achieve a closer relationship with the Divine. It is necessary in order to gain a greater sense of purpose.

Many LDS missionaries talk of going through a similar painful experience, but also of how it leads to a more significant and fulfilling mission.

Anyone who has lived in another country and culture for any length of time has probably experienced the inevitable roller coaster of emotions that accompanies the dislocation, particularly in the early months. Commonly referred to as "culture shock," those affected tend to go through a predictable range of emotions and feelings, missionaries and non-missionaries alike.

> There is the honeymoon stage, when newcomers are curious, excited, and stimulated by their new environment, and while they may note differences from their own culture, they intrigue them. Their status and identity remain in tact.
>
> Next is the stage when things begin to fall apart, when they feel disoriented, depressed, and lonely. Cultural differences become apparent, and there is a loss of self-esteem; they know they are "different." This can lead to negative attitudes and behaviors: rejection of the new culture; anger and frustration; and holding negative opinions about the culture and the people. Mocking the natives, the country, and the culture is not uncommon at this point.
>
> With time they begin to feel more comfortable in their new environment. They become more adept at the language, they are able to interpret cultural clues, and they begin to appreciate cultural differences.
>
> Finally they reach the stage of understanding and embracing cultural differences. They successfully negotiate various situations and experiences, they become fluent in the language, and they regain their self-esteem.
>
> They go through a similar process, albeit not as pronounced, when they return home.[118]

Latter-day Saint missionaries who go foreign (and even those who serve in other regions of their own country) go through this range of emotions and experiences—this culture shock—but theirs is compounded by the fact that they have to adjust to living so closely with a companion, are expected to evangelize for their faith in the midst of this, and have to learn to live with rejection on a regular—oftentimes daily—basis.

Based on the predictable pattern of culture shock many go through, it can be expected that Latter-day Saint missionaries will reach a low point of their mission in their second to fourth month. They will have gone through the honeymoon stage and will be struggling with the new culture, the new language, their status of being different, the difficulty of missionary work, living with a companion, and the depression and negativity that accompany it.

Many interviewees confirmed this was their experience: by the fourth month they questioned their faith and wondered why they were on a mission, and it was at that point that they were most tempted to quit and return home. An American elder who served in Germany said he began to question his mission after serving two or three months.

The language was hard, he was trying to understand the culture, people were yelling at him, they were angry with him, and he faced considerable rejection. Outwardly he looked and acted as though he was confident, but inwardly it was a struggle: a struggle of faith, motivation, and dedication, of trying to understand what he was doing and what he was *supposed* to be doing.

A sister serving in Central America recounted: "It was hard, for there were times when I really wanted to quit; I just didn't want to do it anymore. I had been out three or four months and I felt like if I had a chance to go home, I would. I got to the point where I thought: 'I don't want to be here one more day. I will die if I have to be here one more day!'"

Two brothers who served in Mexico in the 1960s said they found the first few months "bewildering and disorienting." They had memorized the discussions, but beyond that they were pretty limited conversationally, and they were limited in terms of understanding. They found it very frustrating, given the high level of motivation they had. They wanted to succeed but felt very incompetent and wondered whether they would be able to function adequately.

The dark night of the soul can also occur when serving in a different region of one's own country. A sister from Northern New England who served in Washington, D.C., said after being there awhile she felt like she was "sinking into herself." She "fell down and down and things got blacker and blacker," and she "hit bottom and had never felt so terrible." It was her third or fourth month.

Another sister who was early in her mission said, "If I would have known it was going to be like this, I might not have come, or if I could stop now, I probably would."

An elder from the Northeastern United States who served in small towns in Kentucky said he had a hard time adjusting to Southern living and Southern people, and they teased him about being a Yankee. It was hard physically, and it bothered him emotionally. He didn't know why, but it took him three or four months to adjust.

But this dark night of the soul is also a turning point for many. They have reached rock bottom, but with time and perseverance they begin to feel more comfortable in their new environment, and their faith grows, as does their commitment to serve a mission. Thus their dark night becomes a very important period in their missionary experience.

The elder who served in Germany said in spite of his depression he felt a great responsibility to the people in his area. He knew that knocking on doors wasn't very effective, but it was the only way some people would hear about the LDS Church, and if he didn't do it, then probably no one would. So he continued on. He eventually came through the difficult period, and in hindsight he found that it was a very formative period in his mission.

The sister who struggled in Washington, D.C., said she came out of her depression, and she knew that she wouldn't go lower than that again in her mission. "It's not that we love God less, or that we don't appreciate our experiences," she said. "It's just that it is so hard, there is another trial around the corner. A mission is not an easy thing. The Lord is not going to give you an easy mission. You go through the refiner's fire, you suffer a lot."

Another sister said: "It was after the struggles that I had my best experiences. There were days when I thought, 'I don't ever want to go home, I don't ever want to stop doing this.'"

An American elder who served in Chile said the early months were probably the most trying of his mission, but if missionaries can make it through the first four months, they can make it through the whole thing. But he said those first months were also the most memorable—it's when he learned the most about who he was, why he was there, and why it really was the right thing for him to do. He said he was being blessed by being able to learn the language and to teach people. That was an answer to any doubts he might have had as to why he was there. He didn't have any doubts after that.

Others spoke of inner struggles and self-doubt in the early months of the mission, but of positive results in the end. An elder who served in England said his low points came early on when he felt he wasn't adequate to the task. He questioned if he was doing all that he could and should, and he wondered why he couldn't be more self-disciplined. He said they were "tough times," and they were times of prayer and meditation, when he sought very earnestly the Lord's assurance and guidance. One evening in prayer he had a "very special experience" that helped him come to a resolution of his doubts and concerns. Thus what began as the lowest point of his mission became the highest point as well.

Missionaries, particularly missionaries on international missions, struggle in many ways and a sister who served in Japan in an earlier decade described it well. She said it was physically and emotionally very demanding work, and she was taken "out of every source of comfort she had." Her language was taken away from her. Her food was taken away from her. Her housing was taken away from her. "Everything was different," she said, and it took a while to adjust. She said her youth got her by somewhat, but she lost many ways of coping.

Thus the trials of learning a new language, adjusting to a new culture, eating different foods, coping with extremes of temperature, dealing with ubiquitous anti-Mormon sentiment, and experiencing culture shock all contribute to making it a difficult, but formative, experience. Their challenges don't end there, for (as we will see in the next chapter) they may have to live and serve under numerous restrictions, they aren't always welcomed in foreign lands, and there are times when the missionary system itself goes in inappropriate and misguided directions.

But they also experience success, when their efforts help bring converts into the Church, and when they help grow the International Church.

These experiences are discussed in Chapter 9.

CHAPTER 9

International Missions: Containment, Conversions, and Controversy

"There are times and seasons for people in different areas, when their interest or ability to receive the Mormon gospel message is different, based both on their culture and the environment in which they are living. Economically and socially, it can have a profound influence on whether or not they have time to listen."

AN AMERICAN ELDER WHO SERVED IN HONG KONG AND VIETNAM IN THE MID-1970S

Containment: Restrictions on Proselytizing

It is inherent in the commission of Christians and Muslims that they are to proselytize throughout the world, and Article 18 of the 1948 United Nations Declaration of Human Rights would appear to support their right to do so: "Everyone has the right to freedom of thought, conscience and religion; this right includes freedom to change his religion or belief, and freedom, either alone or in community with others in public or private, to manifest his religion or belief in teaching, practice, worship and observance."

But not all embrace Article 18, because they consider proselytizing an unethical and dangerous practice.

Proselytizing raises the difficult question of the appropriateness of bringing a religion rooted in one country and culture into another, especially when it has the potential to interfere with, disrupt, or displace native religions, traditions, and cultures. As is evident in the histories of Christianity and Islam, their presence has generated tension in many different spheres and at many different levels, in the realms of private, religious, and public life. As a result, proselytizing is frequently viewed with suspicion, and many countries restrict religious proselytizing and religious activities. The fear is that the effects of the activity will go beyond the religious sphere and spill over into the social and cultural fabric of the society, frequently causing tension within families and communities and creating conflicts with religious and secular institutions.

Countries retain the right to control their borders, and many extend that right to regulating religious pluralism within.

Even in those countries where people enjoy freedom of religion and freedom of religious choice, does this mean external groups have the right to come in and proselytize? And in those countries were proselytizing is allowed, how much respect should be afforded the religion(s) of the host country or host community?

These questions and issues were most evident in my conversations in Russia with clergy and members of the Russian Orthodox Church. As we will see later in this chapter, they weren't pleased with Western religions (of *any* stripe) invading their country after the fall of communism. Not only were they concerned that members were being drawn away from the Russian Orthodox Church, but also that the outsiders' presence, values, and aggressive approach to evangelism was undermining Russian culture.[119]

The manner and means by which Latter-day Saint missionaries seek potential investigators vary with time and place. Some countries are very restrictive. As of 2010, LDS missionaries and missionary activity was not permitted in North Africa, India, the Middle East, certain countries in South and Southeast Asia, and Mainland China.[120] If there is an LDS presence in these countries, it is generally because Church members are expatriates working there for international companies or because they entered the country on tourist, teacher, student, or diplomatic visas.

China. While the Latter-day Saint Church may not proselytize in certain countries, it is allowed a presence in some, including Mainland China, but under very restricted conditions. Latter-day Saints may meet, but they may not engage in active or passive evangelism. Also, non-Chinese Latter-day Saints and Chinese national Latter-day Saints may not have any contact with one another. Each have their own meeting places, don't attend each other's services, and don't participate in Church-sponsored social events. There were eleven international branches of the Church in China in 2010, with two in Beijing. There was one Chinese national branch in Beijing, which included members from Hong Kong and Taiwan, but non-Chinese members were not to associate with them in any way.

An impenetrable wall has been built between them.

The Latter-day Saint Church has provided some resources for its Chinese members. The Book of Mormon, *Doctrine and Covenants*, and *Pearl of Great Price* ("the triple combination") were published in 2007 and 2008 in both traditional and simplified Chinese characters.[121]

At meetings of non-Chinese Church members in Beijing in spring 2010, the following statement appeared in the program and was read each Sunday at the beginning of the sacrament meeting. Latter-day Saint Church leaders, not Chinese officials, wrote it.

> *The branch presidency wishes to draw your attention to the following:*
>
> *1. It is important for foreign members of The Church of Jesus Christ of Latter-day Saints living in or visiting China to be aware of the unique restrictions on religious activities here. While China permits freedom of religious belief, it requires all religious activities in China to comply with relevant laws and regulations.*
>
> *We would like to remind you of the following:*
>
> *(1) no active or passive proselytizing is permitted among local nationals in China,*
> *(2) only individuals who hold foreign passports, and their spouses, may attend meetings or other activities of this branch,*
> *(3) no foreign nationals are permitted to participate in activities of any kind with Chinese nationals who are members of our church, and*
> *(4) religious materials may not be disseminated to Chinese nationals in China.*
>
> *2. Your strict observance of these rules enables us to build a foundation of trust with government authorities and enables us to continue to meet as the government permits us to do so.*

I don't know what is said at the beginning of the Chinese national LDS services.

A university colleague who is LDS regularly attended foreign national services in Beijing in spring 2010. They met on the fourth floor of an office building, above a Dairy Queen. (The number four is considered bad luck in China, because the word for "four" sounds like the word for "death." Just as thirteen is sometimes avoided in the West and thirteenth floors aren't included in some buildings, so fourth floors are sometimes omitted in China. My colleague thought the Church had sole use of the fourth floor.)

One hundred to 125 foreign nationals attended services each week in spring 2010, with roughly half of them being Americans—expatriates working there, many of whom were young couples with small children, and BYU college students and university professors on education exchanges. He said Canadians and Europeans passed through, and there were a number of non-Chinese Asians from Japan, Korea, Southeast Asia, Thailand, Malaysia, and Hong Kong. The congregation engaged in service projects including gathering money, supplies, and clothing for earthquake relief. They also had picnics and other social get-togethers, but never with Chinese national members.

The Church's profile in China was raised when Jon M. Huntsman Jr., the one-time Republican governor of Utah, was chosen in 2010 by President Obama to serve as the United States Ambassador to China. Huntsman is LDS and fluent in Mandarin, a skill he gained while serving his mission in Taiwan in the 1980s. His tenure as ambassador was short-lived, because he resigned his position and returned home in May 2011 to engage in a brief race for the Republican nomination for the 2012 presidential election.

While missionary activity is not permitted, ongoing conversations between Chinese officials and LDS Church officials took place in 2010 on how to "regularize" the relationship, on how Latter-day Saints may continue to exist in China in conformity to Chinese law. The topic of missionaries being permitted to come into the country wasn't even discussed.

The Latter-day Saint Church is hopeful that someday it will be. China (and other countries where the Church is currently not allowed to evangelize), is perceived as a huge, potential mission field. In his opening address to the 179th Semiannual General Conference held in Salt Lake City in October 2009, President Thomas S. Monson said members should pray for a miracle, that the LDS gospel will be allowed to be proclaimed where it is forbidden at the moment. It is recognized that it is unlikely to happen anytime soon, but he asked for their faith and their prayers that it happen eventually.

"Miracles can occur as we do so," he said.[122]

Except for the statement read at the beginning of each Latter-day Saint service in Beijing, my colleague was struck more by the similarities than the differences between the Church in the United States and the Church in Beijing. The language and services reflected the culture of Salt Lake City and Utah. He said it felt like being in the United States.

The Church adapts when necessary, but it maintains its unique sense of identity.

Find

Developing sensitivity to cultural clues. Missionaries have to develop sensitivity to cultural clues that tell them whether a person is interested in talking with them. In some cultures, being blunt is considered good, while those in other cultures communicate in more subtle and circumspect ways, where indirectness is considered polite. Interviewees said most Americans tended to be direct in responding to their knocks; they gave an answer, they meant what they said, and they said it in a straightforward manner. A sister who served in France found a similar reaction. People said "No" quite quickly when asked if the missionaries could talk with them. They typically said they were Roman Catholic, that nobody was going to change them, and that it would be a disgrace to the family if they did change. Germans were also said to be direct in communicating with missionaries.

In contrast, an interviewee who served in Switzerland said the Swiss he interacted with had a hard time saying they weren't interested. They would say to come back at a certain time, but then not be there, or they would say to come back in two weeks, but then say they were busy and ask for the missionaries to come back the next week. He felt they were trying to be polite, but that they weren't interested; they were hoping the missionaries would just give up—which they eventually did.

An elder who served in Spanish-speaking California said at times it was difficult to interpret the clues; usually Latinos wouldn't come right out and say, "I'm not interested." Rather, they would try to come up with some way of communicating that information in a way that wouldn't hurt his feelings. Sometimes it was a challenge to figure out what they were trying to tell him.

Missionaries who served in Japan found that instead of saying they weren't interested, meaning was communicated in other ways. An elder said people in Japan never slammed doors in his face and rarely said they weren't interested, but instead would almost always make excuses for why they couldn't let the missionaries in: they would say they were too busy, had already talked with missionaries, or were Buddhist. In one instance, a woman said she couldn't let him in because she was giving birth. They didn't want to give a straight answer, he said, to make them feel bad. Thus they tried to "soften the blow." After a while, it became easy for him to determine if the person wanted to talk.

Americans at the door, and speaking the native's language. Some are impressed by the fact that American LDS missionaries meet them in their homes, and they are doubly impressed by the fact that LDS missionaries (of any nationality) speak the language of the country. An American elder who served in Brazil said they were told it was an honor for Brazilians to have Americans in their home. An American elder who served in an Afrikaans area of South Africa worked with an Afrikaans companion and became proficient with the language, because they agreed to speak Afrikaans all the time. They taught and baptized an Afrikaans mother and daughter, and the interviewee said it was a highlight of his missionary experience. He was able to teach them in their native tongue, and they were thrilled that an American, "with an American twang in Afrikaans," would teach them and have the respect to learn their language.

An American elder who served in smaller, rural towns in Mexico said he and his companion would tract out the whole town, and in some places people were quite willing to talk with them. They may not have been interested in religion, but they were willing to invite them in and talk with them. In one town they were the first Mormon missionaries to visit there, and they were something of a curiosity. The local Roman Catholic priests viewed them as a tremendous threat, but they got into almost everyone's home. People were curious and charmed, for here were two young gringo missionaries at their door. People weren't always sure who the young men were, even when they were told, but they were impressed with these two young, clean-cut men who were speaking pretty good Spanish.

The interviewee surmised the combination of native hospitality for a foreigner, plus a charming foreigner, was the basis for letting them into their homes. A lot of them almost seemed flattered that young foreigners were talking with them; they often got the sense they were flattering the Mexicans by coming into their homes and giving them attention. If the missionaries continued to be charming, knew the language, were comfortable with the customs, and were interested in coming back, sometimes out of that, would develop a more serious commitment on the Mexican's part, and they would want to participate in the discussions.

Approaches. In those countries where active proselytizing is allowed, missionaries use many of the same techniques as in the United States: knocking on doors, public displays, and street contacting. Some, especially in earlier decades, knocked on doors almost exclusively. This was the experience of many interviewees who served in the 1960s and 1970s. An elder who served in Mexico in the mid-1960s said they didn't rely on referrals, phoning, or working with members. Rather, his days were filled with what he described as "old-fashioned knocking on doors." He spent most of his mission in two large cities (Mexico City and Guadalajara), and he and his companion went to huge apartment complexes and didn't spend much time at doors. They introduced themselves and asked if the person was interested in hearing their message. If the response was no, they moved on to the next door. They knocked on hundreds of doors a day in this manner, up to twelve hours a day.

The standard expectation (the "idealized norm") was they would work around seventy hours a week tracting and giving lessons, or an average of ten hours a day. What they actually did depended on the energy, dedication, and motivation of the senior companion, who set the expectations.

Another elder who served in Mexico in the mid-1960s said on his first day in the country he went tracting with his trainer, and after his first door he thought, "That wasn't so bad," but then he looked down the street and saw all of the doors, and then he thought of all of the doors on the next street, and it came to him what his mission was going to be about. But the approach proved fruitful, because membership in the country exploded at that time, and Mexican convert baptisms led the entire LDS Church system.

Success. Latin America in general has proven to be a fertile recruiting ground for the Church. An elder serving in Chile in the early 1990s said there were times when they didn't need to knock on doors at all. People sought them out. An American elder who served in São Paulo, Brazil, said he baptized hundreds of converts with his companions over a two-year period.

But missionaries still have to work hard. An elder who served in Brazil said a typical day included talking with people on the street, sometimes knocking on doors, asking members to give them names, visiting with inactive members and trying to address their issues, and teaching. People had a siesta after lunch, and it was hard to find people to teach then. They found it was much more effective to be teaching them in the evening.

An American sister who served in Guatemala talked of the success, but also the strenuous activity, involved in tracting. During her first week in the mission, she and her companion walked from five to eight miles a day, up and down very steep hills. But their efforts were rewarded. They found seven families to teach that first week.

Latter-day Saint missionaries have also been very successful in the Philippines and the South Pacific, particularly in Tonga. The Church's success in Tonga in the 1960s is illustrated by the fact that in 1961, the General Conference was translated into four languages—Spanish, French, German, and Tongan. It is also reported that today Latter-day Saints constitute an amazing 45 percent of the Tongan population.[123]

The work, however, got off to a rocky start in Tonga, and missionaries had to get creative when faced with an initial lack of interest, or unwillingness, to talk with them. An American elder serving on the Tongan island of Niuatoputapu in the 1950s found that people didn't want to be seen talking with him and his companion because of social pressure. Islanders were members of churches where their parents and grandparents had belonged, and it was expected that they would remain members, too. To change religions was socially unacceptable. The island was so small that word quickly spread if someone was seen talking with Mormon missionaries. Some told him that even if they wanted to join, they couldn't because of the social issues involved.

As a way to deal with this perception, the young elder volunteered to help weed or hoe alongside people working in their garden. He then tried to discuss gospel principles while working. If the person said he wasn't interested, the missionary would stop talking about the Church, but continue to help as promised, wanting to be known as someone who kept his word.

Some Tongan non-members were kind to the missionaries and invited them to dinner, although they made a point of saying they were not interested in hearing their message. They didn't want to give even the *appearance* of talking with missionaries about their church, because they knew their friends, relatives, and neighbors were watching.

Given these constraints, the elder devised another plan. He normally would say a blessing before the meal, and at his next invited meal he asked if he could include a blessing on the house as he gave a blessing for the food. The family said that would be fine. With heads bowed, he proceeded to give a thirty-minute blessing on the food, the family, and the home. He thanked God for Joseph Smith, the First Vision, the Book of Mormon, the restored gospel, the atoning sacrifice of Jesus, the restoration of the priesthood to missionaries, and the authority of missionaries to baptize.

The food got cold during the blessing, but his hosts didn't seem to mind. Their minister had a reputation for long prayers, too.

The elder was able to do this at two or three other homes, but word soon spread around the island, and dinner invitations from nonmembers dropped off considerably. When missionaries did receive such invitations, the host made a point of saying *he* would say the blessing.[124]

Rocky religious soil. Proselytizing isn't nearly as fruitful in other parts of the world. An American elder who served in Germany said people in German cities frequently live in apartment buildings and often there are call boxes at ground level. The typical response to their buzz was, "Not interested," "No time," or "No thank you." Rude responses were not typical, but a lack of interest was common. Those who did express interest were more interested in the fact that they were Americans—they wanted to practice their English, to talk about the country—but there wasn't much interest in religion. He said tracting was not an easy experience for him. He always found it a struggle to force himself to talk to strangers. Their lack of interest only compounded his unease.

Another American elder serving in Germany said he knocked on literally thousands of doors before he found the first family he baptized.

An American elder serving in France in the early 1970s said they did a lot of tracting, but it was slow going because cold contacting took a lot of time, effort, and people to find the few people who were interested. They didn't work with members for referrals as much back then, but in hindsight he thinks it would have been a more effective approach.

Interviewees serving in Japan did a lot of tracting, but with little success. An elder who served in Japan in the late 1980s said when he served in the southernmost part of the country, they knocked on many, many doors, but never got in. In many cases people wouldn't even open the door. He described it as "drudgery." Another elder serving at the same time went a year in Japan before he had his first baptism.

But an elder who served in Japan in the early 1990s spoke of the hospitality he experienced there. He and his companion would come home, and sometimes people they had just met or spoken to had left fruit baskets or other presents at their door, or even invited them to dinner. He said it was normal to be invited to dinner three or four times a week to non-member homes, to social functions, and to community events.

Lack of interest in the missionaries' message is not restricted to areas of the northern hemisphere. An American elder who served in South Africa said nine out of ten people didn't want to hear what he had to say, and two to four out of one hundred would react "vehemently" against him. It was hard to deal with people who responded in this manner, he said, and initially it caught him off guard. He had come from a comfortable lifestyle in Utah where no one questioned his beliefs, but when he would say to people, "Hello, we are from The Church of Jesus Christ of Latter-day Saints," and they would react with vehemence, he would think, "My goodness!" It hurt at first, and he found he hesitated to speak to people because he was very shy. He had to push himself, he had to "get out of himself" to do something he normally wouldn't do. He felt these people weren't antagonistic so much against the Mormon Church, but against religion in general. There was a sense of bitterness in their lives, and they made it known that it was none of the missionary's business what it was about.

As in other parts of the world, he said street contacting and knocking on doors were the least effective ways to reach people. The best was when members had friends who were interested. They would refer the missionaries, and they would go into peoples' homes and teach them. For the majority who were neutral, that is where the skills missionaries were taught about communicating with people, and with doing door approaches, came to bear. The goal was to convince people they had an important message, and sometimes it worked.

Some missionaries have trouble grasping why people aren't interested in their message. A zone leader who served in Japan said it was especially hard for missionaries who came from sheltered environments (he specifically mentioned Utah and Idaho). They couldn't understand why people weren't interested when they said they had a new scripture and a living prophet. They just couldn't understand why people wouldn't respond affirmatively.

Times and seasons: the effects of historical events. Missionaries serving in the latter half of the twentieth century saw the effects of dramatic world events on people's lives, and they saw how these events affected their success (or lack thereof) at proselytizing.

A sister who served in France in the mid-1960s said the work was pretty slow in Europe at that time. She taught two or three investigators, who were then baptized by elders, in a year's time. Many people she encountered "had a pretty grim view of life." They had been through some very hard times: World War II and the Algerian War, a decolonization war which took place between 1954 and 1962 in which Algeria gained its independence from France. Both wars were quite a part of many people's lives. At many of the doors on which she and her companion knocked people would say that anyone who believes in God is foolish, for He wouldn't allow all of the suffering to go on that they saw in the world. They didn't even want to hear about God.

A woman who lived in Italy as a teenager during World War II, and who lived through American air raids, confronted American missionaries when they appeared at her door in Brazil many years later. She asked how Americans could drop bombs on her head but then want to talk with her about the gospel. She had particular reservations about Joseph Smith, questioning how he could be a modern day prophet, especially since he was an American. She eventually had a change of heart and joined the Church.[125]

An American elder who served in Germany in the late 1990s said they tracted into a man in his eighties in Schwarzenberg, and they taught him the first discussion. At the end he told the elders he respected them for coming so far from their homes, but there was something they had to understand. First, he said, the country had Hitler, who promised that everything would be better if they followed Nazism—but it wasn't. Then the Communists came and said if they followed communism, life would be good—but it wasn't. Then the Berlin wall came down, and capitalism came in, and everyone promised life would be better—but it wasn't.

"So now," continued the elderly man, "you two young men from America come and tell me that if I join this religion, everything will be better. You will have to forgive me, but I don't believe you."

The elder said it put things into perspective, and he could see the man's point.

A missionary's experience can thus differ depending on the social, economic, and historical factors of the country in which he is serving. An American elder who served in Hong Kong and Vietnam in the mid-1970s reported contrasting experiences in the two locations. In Hong Kong, people would hardly give him the time of day if he stopped them on the street, but in Vietnam people would stop and talk with him and even invite his companion and him to come to their home. He found Hong Kong a much more materialistic society, where citizens were concerned about making a living and so they had no time for the missionaries. In Vietnam, he found they were a much more cheerful people and willing to talk with missionaries, even though they had been through amazing war experiences and their economy was worse than any place he could imagine. He found it an interesting contrast. He observed: "There are times and seasons for people in different areas, where their interest or ability to receive the gospel message is different, based both on their culture and the environment in which they are living. Economically and socially, it can have a profound influence on whether or not they have time to listen."

He eventually had to flee Vietnam, because of the war.

Atheistic communism has presented challenges to Mormon missionaries. An American elder who served in Paris in the early 1970s said he was in a Communist part of the city and it was difficult making progress, as Communists didn't want to have anything to do with Christians, Mormons, or religion in general. An elder who served in Germany in the late 1990s said those who had lived under communism found the notion of God strange, and missionaries had to begin at a pre-discussion stage, one that discussed the idea and characteristics of a supernatural being. A non-member interviewee who lived in the Russian city of Medvezhyegorsk, three hundred miles north of St. Petersburg, had never seen an American prior to 1993, let alone an American missionary. They had been forbidden to interact with them.

The dissolution of the Soviet Union in 1991 opened new possibilities for Western missionaries, and representatives of various religious groups flooded into the region, including Latter-day Saints.

An American elder who served in Hungary in the early 1990s said people were receptive after the fall of communism. Very few had a religious upbringing, and while some held fast to their atheism, some were inquisitive. They were curious, he said, and even if they didn't have an interest in the sense of joining or investigating, they wanted to know more about the LDS Church, since they didn't know anything about God or religion. Being American was a great advantage; people picked up quickly on their accents, it piqued their interest, and people wanted to talk with them. And so they had no problems setting up appointments.

He began his mission by serving in the smallest village in the mission, and in his first evening they were able to set up eleven appointments with full families. He couldn't believe it: he could teach all day if he wanted to. The attitude of those meeting with the missionaries was: "We want to believe in something, we want to raise our family with some kind of faith. That is why we invited you here to tell us. We feel impressed with you and we with open hearts are asking what we should believe in."

The elder said there is nothing better than the feeling of investigators being totally receptive to their message.

Opening new areas will sometimes lead to an initial burst of activity and baptisms. Seventy-five missionaries accounted for six hundred baptisms that first year in Hungary. They held baptisms in rivers and swimming pools, and in one town they rented a spa in the hospital and held the ritual there. He felt blessed having been sent to Hungary, and the high points of his mission were the relationships he formed. He would go back to cities where he had served and visit with his newfound friends. Seeing how much they had progressed since baptism was for him "a great reward."

But things weren't always so easy. When he was transferred to Budapest, everything, he said, "turned cold, stone cold." He told of getting up early each morning of his companion and he going to the subways to find people interested in hearing their message. There were none. It was the middle of winter, cold, dark, and frustrating.

But then they met a family who appeared to be "golden." They had good meetings around the first three discussions. A baptismal date was set. The elders were excited as they went back for their fourth visit. When they arrived at the apartment, the woman opened the door, gave back their Book of Mormon, said, "Don't ever come back. We need God, not this," and closed the door. The elder said he and his companion were like "deflated balloons." They sat down on a bench and cried. He never saw the family again. They tried to go back and talk to them, but they never let them in. It was frustrating, the lowest point of his mission. He started to think about home. He wondered what he was doing there, he was frustrated and unhappy, and he started to lose his focus. It was around the fourth month of his mission.

(Given the manner in which the woman cut off contact with the missionaries, I expect she was exposed to anti-Mormon material.)

The elder said things eventually got better, that he even was glad he had the difficult experience, because he learned a lot from it: he better appreciated the successes that came later on. Had everything been easy, he would not have gone through what was a crucial part of his mission, the tough times. He said he thought everyone has a period like that on their mission, and that it is an important part of the experience and that a person misses something if they don't have challenges and struggles.

While there was a high rate of baptisms in the former Communist countries, there was also a high rate of attrition among converts. They were religious seekers. A whole new world of religious opportunities was made available to them, and many shopped around. Mormonism requires such a high level of commitment that the less committed quickly fell away. Retention was thus a problem in former Soviet Bloc countries. There was a rush to learn more about the Church, to experiment with it, but then many stepped away from it. The elder who served in Hungary said it was frustrating to see people he had worked with get baptized, do well for a while, and then fall away. They would be smoking again, and he found it frustrating. "We would work with people and work with them and they would go inactive. It happened a lot. That was tough."

Service and teaching free English classes. Missionaries on international missions perform service, as do those on domestic missions. Interviewees spoke of helping in orphanages, visiting sick members, reading the scriptures to them, doing their washing and outdoor work, playing the piano at Church services, doing community service, and volunteering with social service agencies. As in the United States, missionaries are frequently enlisted to aid in disaster relief, including delivering supplies and cleaning up debris, where they wear distinctive yellow T-shirts and vests with a logo showing two hands and the words "Mormon Helping Hands." Latter-day Saints are a model of community help and assistance during times of need.

Teaching free English classes is considered service, and conversations about the Mormon Church can evolve from the classes. An American elder who served in Ukraine said they didn't talk about the LDS Church during English classes (they didn't teach "Church terms and Church language," he said), but classes were held in the Church building, and people often asked about it. He found it to be an effective proselytizing tool.

The elder who found tracting "drudgery" in Japan said teaching free English lessons was a more effective tool. It provided a "hook" to open up a dialogue, because the Japanese were interested in studying with native English speakers.

There is a long tradition of missionaries teaching English classes and of discussions about the Latter-day Saint Church evolving from them. The Norwegian Sara Elvira Eriksen wrote about attending English classes in Norway in the early twentieth century. Her first exposure to the Latter-day Saint Church came when she and her father attended a service at an LDS church and they spoke briefly with a missionary. She didn't return to the church until a year later, when she began attending English classes taught by the missionaries. She said when each class ended, "We drifted into religious discussions," and over succeeding weeks the missionaries taught her about prayer, the Restoration, Joseph Smith, and the Book of Mormon. She joined the Church soon thereafter.[126]

The Mormon Church and many non-members perceive teaching free English lessons in a positive light, but there are those who consider it a backhanded way to introduce people to the faith.

Who is the competition? Mormon missionaries encounter various forms of religious competition. Buddhist beliefs prevail in East Asia and Southeast Asia, while identification with the Roman Catholic Church is strong in Italy, France, and Latin America (although missionaries find that church attendance isn't always tied with identification). But their biggest competitor appears to be Jehovah's Witnesses, who have usually preceded Latter-day Saints in communities, and with whom they are frequently confused. A middle-aged piano teacher in a college of music in the remote city of Medvezhyegorsk, Russia, reported during our interview in 1998 that Latter-day Saint missionaries had not yet been to her city, but Jehovah's Witnesses had. Witnesses had arrived in Hungary five years before Latter-day Saints, and in the words of a Mormon missionary in Hungary, "had gotten a lot of good people." An elder serving in Switzerland in the early 1990s said the Witnesses were very strong, stronger than Latter-day Saints. In some cities there were three or four congregations of Jehovah's Witnesses, but just one of Latter-day Saints.

Because of the aggressive approach to evangelism shared by Jehovah's Witnesses and Latter-day Saints, it is common for people to confuse the two groups. Mormon interviewees spoke of this confusion in the United States, England, Switzerland, and Brazil.

An American elder in Brazil said Jehovah's Witnesses knocked on their door one day. The LDS missionaries invited them in, but the Witnesses wished them a good day and left once it was clear they were

Mormon missionaries. He said they were Brazilians, and that all of the missionaries he saw from other faiths were Brazilians, never Americans.

Conversions

Teach. LDS missionaries worldwide teach the same lessons. The Book of Mormon and the handouts they use are usually in the native tongue, and the material covered remains the same. Various teaching aids have been utilized over the years. An elder who served in France in the early 1970s said they had some somewhat crude audio-visual aids they brought to the investigator's home, some film strips, and some audio tapes, and they would play them during their teaching sessions. Today missionaries provide pamphlets that relate to the lessons being taught, may share Church DVDs, and point investigators to official Church web sites.

Missionaries have to continually assess investigators' real interest: are they interested in my message, my country, my language, my passport, friendship, or sex? Americans said many times investigators wanted to talk more about the United States than the LDS gospel, and, as one missionary described it, they would try to "ferret that out." If that were all investigators wanted to do, he would give them a Book of Mormon and say that if they were interested, they should come to church.

Many spoke of the challenge of assessing a person's real motivation. An elder who served in Hungary said a big problem in Eastern Europe was "Young girls interested in what we had, it was called a passport, and they tried to hit on the missionaries all the time. It was a big problem." (He assured me during our interview that none of his missionary colleagues succumbed to the flirtations of the young women.)

Interviewees spoke of awkward moments during teaching sessions. An elder serving in Mexico said he and his companion were giving lessons to an extended family, and they were in a back room with the door shut. The father came home drunk and heard that Mormon missionaries were in the back room with his family. He got out his machete and started pounding on the door. He threw them out.

Others spoke of angry scenes when the husband/father discovered missionaries were teaching his family. This caused inner tension for some missionaries. An elder who served in Japan said he felt awkward at times, because the wife would be receptive to the message, and she and her children would meet with the missionaries, but sometimes the husband was not aware of it, or he would find out about it and get angry. The elder said it made him very uncomfortable; he never felt right about it, and he feared he was dividing the family. He is no longer active in the Church. Spousal permission is now required before missionaries may start teaching in a home.

Missionaries meet resistance on other fronts. A sister who served in Italy said it was especially hard to work in a county with such a strong Roman Catholic culture and history. They would work with people who were accepting of their message, who would suddenly stop meeting with the missionaries. Families would put pressure on them and threaten to cut them off if they joined another faith. Part of being Italian is being Catholic, missionaries were told. They were very proud of it; it is their roots. "It is my heritage," they would say. "Why would I want to change? Why would I want to give up my culture and identity?"

Missionaries spoke of Roman Catholic resistance in other countries, particularly in Latin America, but some were able to find some common beliefs. A Latter-day Saint sister serving in Argentina said while the influence of the Roman Catholic Church was very strong and some would not even *consider* changing their religion, once they started talking she found their Roman Catholic background served as a basis for fruitful conversations between them, because they shared some common ground: a belief in God, in angels, in miracles, and in the scriptures.

Latter-day Saints make significant demands on the personal habits of its members, and these become clear during the lesson when the Word of Wisdom is introduced. An elder who served in Brazil said low points in his mission came when he would work with people and teach them the lessons, and they knew it was true, but they still rejected it. They weren't willing to make the sacrifices, and smoking was a particularly hard addiction for them to break. A missionary who served in Portugal echoed this. He worked with an investigator who he said started smoking at the age of three.

An elder who served in Mexico said the nature of the missionary program is to get investigators to make commitments right from the very beginning, and missionaries talk about a baptism date early-on if investigators believe the message is true. By the time of the fourth lesson, they are asking them to give up cigarettes, coffee, and alcohol, and pretty soon people find themselves being able to make these commitments—or not. The elder said if the investigator balked, they would discuss it. If the person lost interest, then the missionaries would move on.

Interviewees could be quite candid during our interviews. A convert from Venezuela said he had not read the Book of Mormon or had a testimony when he began his mission, and during his first week he was "practically lying" when he said he believed in the Book of Mormon. But he did what he asked of others—he read the Book of Mormon, he prayed about it, and he asked God's guidance—and he said he came away with a strong testimony as a result.

Baptize. Baptisms are the goal of every missionary. They speak of satisfaction when they perform them, and of discouragement when they don't. Baptisms are more common in some regions of the world than others, and there are a greater number of female converts than males.

Missionaries are encouraged to baptize whole families, and sometimes this is the case. An elder who served in Mexico found that when one or two family members were baptized, on occasion the whole family would follow. Emphasis is clearly on recruiting men, since only men hold the priesthood and are needed to assume positions of leadership in the local Church. An elder who served in Japan said they were told they had to find men, married ones were better, and the male head-of-household was best. When a whole household was converted, including the father, word quickly spread throughout the mission: "They baptized a family!"

But such instances were rare in Japan. The interviewee said there were a disproportionate number of female converts to male converts, and he described it as "unusual" when he baptized a young man in his twenties.

Another American elder who served in Japan in the 1980s said one of the disappointments of his mission was that he didn't get to baptize a whole family. Out of 150 baptisms in his mission, the majority were women, there was only one couple, and the rest were single baptisms. He said it is very difficult in Japan to baptize families, and it is difficult to keep the faith if you are the only convert in the family. The interviewee was personally involved in twenty baptisms, either through teaching or by conducting the ceremony: seventeen women and girls, and three young men in their late teens. It was very rare for men established in their careers even to be interested, let alone join. He hardly taught any.

Most joiners were college-aged. It was the people who had the least to lose who were most interested. They didn't have a lot of friends, they were going through a transition period in their lives—starting college, getting into a career—and they were the most interested, in contrast to people who were well-established, who would have to make a lot of changes, and perhaps would have much to lose.

The American elder who served in Tonga in the 1950s spoke of a similar experience. Early converts to the Mormon Church were those who were on the margins of society, who had the least to lose by joining the Church, which involved a certain social stigma for doing so.[127]

Missionaries in such disparate places as Japan and Brazil confirmed that women show more interest in the LDS Church than men. The phenomenon is also true in the United States. A mission president serving in Japan in the 1980s said all female investigators should be referred to sister missionaries, if there were sisters in the district. An elder serving at that time said he found this frustrating at times, since most of the investigators were women. He didn't feel sisters got as much training and support as elders, since A.P.s and zone leaders could go on "splits" with newer elders, where they would help train them in the field. They were not able to do that with sisters.

(This is not to suggest that sisters in Japan weren't dedicated and hardworking. The elder said that eighteen of the twenty sisters in his mission were Japanese and they "ran the American sisters ragged.")

Some sisters do serve in a training role. An interviewee who served in France in the 1960s said she served as a "traveling sister" and would meet with sisters in the communities where they were assigned. A more recent addition is the role of Sister Training Leader; a sister who serves in a comparable role to that of a zone leader, with responsibility for sisters in the mission.

Interviewees who served in secularized countries of Western Europe performed few baptisms. An American elder who served in Paris in the early 1970s said the baptism rate in France at that time was about one baptism per year per missionary. There were excellent missionaries who were district and zone leaders who didn't baptize anyone during their whole mission. An elder who served in Germany as an A.P. in the late 1990s said in one year there were around 130 elders and sisters in the mission and they performed sixty-four baptisms.

An elder who served in Germany in the 1960s said it was "slow going" at the beginning of his mission. His first mission president didn't allow missionaries to work with American military personnel stationed in the country, and two hundred missionaries baptized only ninety-seven in a year. The next mission president reversed that decision and encouraged working with Americans. The elder reported a significant increase in the number of baptisms that took place: 150 the first year; three hundred the following year; and four hundred the next year. Many were Americans, but the number of Germans increased too. The missionaries were energized with the American successes.

There is an inherent tension in evangelism. An A.P. said there is a dichotomy between those who say too much focus is placed on numbers at the expense of the individual and those who say too much focus on the individual clouds the primary goal of baptism. Are you more interested in the depth and validity of a person's religious experience, or in the number of baptisms performed? Mission presidents set the expectation, but they too feel the tension, since their perceived effectiveness may be based in part on the number of baptisms performed during their tenure.

An elder serving in Japan in the early 1990s said their baptismal rate was very low—maybe one or two people a month in an area. That didn't bother him, he added, because what was important was the quality of the relationship between the missionary and the person he was talking with, and how well the missionary fulfilled the role of ambassador for the LDS Church. He said they weren't interested in numbers and statistics, and then he opined: "I am sure God isn't interested either, when you get down to it. He doesn't care."

Not all interviewees were as sanguine as the elder. A frustrated sister who served in France spoke of her inner struggles over the lack of baptisms. When asked what challenges she faced, she said the greatest challenge for her was frustration that she didn't accomplish more as far as seeing more people come into the LDS Church. She constantly said to herself that it must be because she didn't have enough faith or that she wasn't working hard enough. She would drive herself "terribly," and she frustrated herself, because she thought it was her fault. When I asked how she feels about it today, decades later, she said she wished she had been more easygoing about it, because she did work hard, she kept the rules, and she wishes she hadn't taken it personally. She said missionaries have to do a certain amount of that, but she shouldn't have felt so frustrated. But in the end it didn't destroy her good feelings about her mission.

There are challenges sometimes between the time when the person says she or he wants to be baptized and when the ceremony takes place. An A.P. who served in Germany said at one point there were eight people committed to baptism, but "some were tracked down by their preacher and talked out of it," some had lingering problems that were discovered at the baptism interview and so couldn't be baptized, and some just disappeared. In the end, none of the group was baptized.

A common impediment, in addition to the Word of Wisdom, is unmarried couples living together. They can't be baptized in the Latter-day Saint Church. They either have to marry or split up.

A missionary "success" can lead to unintended consequences. An American elder who served in Chile said the high point of his mission was a "golden," a divorced woman in her fifties who said she had been searching for the truth for twenty years. She invited the missionaries in right away, accepted everything they had to say, "with emotion," and sought baptism soon thereafter.

Ironically, the only time the interviewee was bitten by a dog was while teaching her, his golden investigator.

Who are the converts, and why? A General Authority told me that the majority of international converts to the Latter-day Saint Church today are either Roman Catholics or the un-churched. Roman Catholics are coming especially from Latin America, and part of that success may be the Book of Mormon itself, since it claims to be the history of the peoples who inhabited the area, thus giving Divine importance to their ancestral heritage.

An American anthropologist colleague encountered Mormon missionaries while working in Peru in the 2000s, and she commented that evangelical movements and Latter-day Saints were making definite headway in the south-central Peruvian Andes. She observed that the nicest building in the entire town of Andahuaylas was the Mormon church, but what was unusual about it was that, unlike other churches in town, the Mormon church had a large iron fence around the compound, giving the impression that it was completely off limits to non-members. (I observed the same thing in Mongolia.) She didn't personally encounter Mormon missionaries in Andahuaylas, but she was told that groups of Latter-day Saints from the United States periodically came to build houses in the Andahuaylas area. People were always amazed at how fast a group of Americans could build a house, as compared to how long it typically took locals to build one.

While she wasn't researching the Latter-day Saint Church in Peru, Peruvians told the anthropologist that the primary reason why people were switching from Catholicism to the Mormon faith was the prohibition on drinking alcohol. The conversion process was typically led by women in an attempt to get their husbands to stop drinking, because heavy consumption of alcohol was strongly associated with domestic violence.

A Venezuelan convert who served his mission in his home country said his mother prayed for help because his father was a heavy drinker; the Latter-day Saint missionaries appeared at their door not long thereafter—the only door in the apartment building they knocked on. The family converted.

A Russian Orthodox priest I spoke to in Petrozavodsk, Russia, while no fan of Western missionaries pouring into his country and luring his flock away, did concede that Latter-day Saints were having some success in helping Russians who had drinking problems.

When I asked a returned missionary and current college professor why the Latter-day Saint Church is so successful in Latin America, he said the Church offers something very different for families: it offers "a real lifestyle change" that is very attractive to people. Spiritual principles are taught, help is available—whether in combating alcoholism or an addiction to tobacco—and practical assistance is offered, whether it is improved health care or building a new home. "These things change lives," he observed, "and it does something for them spiritually and physically. It makes quite a difference in their lives, they are excited by it, they share that with their friends, and pretty soon their friends want to know about it, and their friends end up joining the Church."

He went on to say that in Brazil (in contrast to countries like the United States and Western Europe, where the Church has had a presence since the nineteenth century), the Latter-day Saint Church hasn't been there that long and Brazilians are still meeting Mormon missionaries for the first time. "They have not seen them at the door ten times before," he observed. "I suppose that is part of it, too."

Conversion stories and missionary experiences. What follows are conversion and mission stories of Church members who are natives of other countries. Some held preconceived (and incorrect) images and ideas about the Church, some experienced tensions within their family because of their interest in the Church, and some had to make cultural adjustments, but in the end all said they valued their conversion and mission experience. Their names have been changed to protect their anonymity.

Slovakia: Daniela

The Church's strict guidelines requiring dark, conservative clothing makes missionaries seem out of place in some parts of the world. That was Daniela's feeling. Had it been left up to the teenager in the late 1980s, she wouldn't have talked with the Mormon elders. She found them "scary" in their dark suits and long, black trench coats. Men didn't dress like that in her Slovakian town of fifty thousand, and had they appeared at her door she wouldn't have let them in. They looked like gangsters.

Also, she had grown up in a socialist society where people didn't talk about religion very much. She had often heard that "bad things" happened to people who went to church, things like losing their jobs, or students not getting into good schools. She had been to the Lutheran Church for the occasional wedding and Christmas service, but other than that her family and she didn't attend. She described not attending as a "safety choice."

She first encountered Mormon missionaries in 1989, during her teenage years. Her mother had a Latter-day Saint friend who introduced Daniela and her mother to the Mormon gospel. He arranged for them to meet with elders. There were very few members and no missionaries in Slovakia at the time, and the elders had to come on a bus from the Czech Republic each week.

She, her mother, a friend, and the friend's brother met with the elders. Her lack of a religious background and the American elders' limited language skills made it difficult to understand what they were saying. None of her family spoke English. On their way home after the first discussion, the little group of investigators agreed they didn't understand, or remember, anything that was said. They were given passages to read in the Book of Mormon, but Daniela didn't understand them. "They went way over my head," she said. The copies of the Book of Mormon they were given had red covers on them so they would look like Communist literature.

Her conversion was a very slow process. She lost track of the number of times she had the discussions: at least three times, maybe as many as five. The elders, one Czech and the rest Americans, weren't too concerned; they were just as happy to have someone to talk to. She didn't have any major issues with the beliefs. The elders visited her home, had meals with her family, and always left with a spiritual message. Her father, who in general was distrustful of clergy, began to warm to the elders.

She visited Utah for a summer, where she joined the Church in 1994, at the age of eighteen. She called her mother and told her she was being baptized and she hoped she would tell her dad. She wasn't sure her mother ever told him. Six months after her baptism, her father had a dream where she appeared to him and told him she had joined the Latter-day Saint Church and that she was sorry she hadn't told him ahead of time. He was afraid it meant she had passed away, and he and his wife called Daniela at 3:00 A.M. to make sure she was okay. They didn't discuss the content of the dream. She found the dream very strange and rarely talks about it.

There wasn't anything in particular that struck her as unusual or hard to adjust to living in the United States, although she did find it odd that Americans would ask, "How are you?" when first meeting her, but then appear to have no interest in her answer to the question.

She lived in England to develop her English skills and then moved to Germany to work on her German. She started at Brigham Young University in 1997 and taught Czech at the Senior MTC. Her roommates, who had served missions, encouraged her to consider serving one herself. Her mother, who still hadn't joined the LDS Church, was surprised when she decided to serve, and she had reservations. Daniela would have to give up a scholarship, and that worried her mother.

"Have you prayed about it?" asked her mother.

"Not exactly," responded Daniela.

When she finally did pray about it, she was convinced it was the thing she should do. She made a quick decision in July to serve and left for her mission in October of 1998. She had completed one year at BYU and was twenty-two years old. She had very little money saved, and Church members from Utah, England, and Germany helped support her mission. Women weren't being called to Slovakia at that time, and she hoped she would be sent to Germany or Russia so she could work on her languages. She was called to California, which initially disappointed her, but in the end she said it was a great assignment.

She enjoyed her mission and only doubted her decision to serve on the very first day in the field, when she and her companion were stopped at a traffic light in San Francisco, and she thought, "What have I done? This isn't for me. I can't do this thing." Like her fellow missionaries, she struggled with knocking on doors, with the occasional rude person, and with finding interested investigators. It took her almost six months to memorize the discussions, and it was six months before she had her first baptism. She then felt like she actually knew what she was doing. When a less-active family started coming to church again, she and her companion would see them there and think, "Wow, we did something good!"

She taught at the Provo MTC after her mission, married a returned missionary, finished her degrees as a linguist, and has three children. The original small band of Slovakian investigators all joined the LDS Church. Her mother joined in 2006 and remains in the Slovakian town, where there is a small branch of the Mormon Church. Ten to twelve people attend weekly. With the age change in 2012, there have been up to four missionaries in her hometown at a time, including sisters. She also hopes the little branch will grow, but not many young people stay because of the economy. There were 239 members in the country as of early 2015.

There weren't any huge successes or huge struggles on her mission. It was difficult, but she knew she was expected to carry through the hard times. She feels she is a better person for it, because it was her own decision. She became more outgoing as a result of her mission, and she is not afraid to talk with people about the Church. It feels much easier now, and she is pleased to have served as an ambassador of the Latter-day Saint Church. Most importantly for her, she can explain things to her children about Heavenly Father and Jesus Christ, things that she wouldn't have known how to do before.

Bolivia: Diego

Diego was surprised to discover that Mormons are normal-looking people. He pictured them as having shaved heads and wearing tunics. He gained this impression from a priest who was his religion teacher at school. One day the priest started talking about the Mormon Church in a mocking tone, saying there is a church called The Church of Jesus Christ of Latter-day Saints, who call themselves Mormons, whose leader is Joseph Smith. Diego said he really felt sorry for them, those poor Mormons, because from the description, he pictured them as having no hair and wearing funny clothes.

Diego had been baptized a Roman Catholic in his native Bolivia, but he didn't attend church. He felt confused about religion as a teenager, and he had a lot of questions, one being why he had been baptized in the first place. He discovered the Latter-day Saint Church when he was fourteen years old. He was playing basketball with a boy his age, and after the game the boy asked Diego if he wanted to go to a meeting with him. Diego asked what kind of meeting, and the boy said he went to the Mormon Church. That caught Diego's attention, because he thought all Mormons were different, but the boy was just like him. He went to church and there were lots of boys his age, but they too were normal, so he thought it must be the leaders who were without hair and wore tunics. He looked in vain for leaders fitting that description, but he found they too were normal. He was surprised how wrong he had been. He was baptized two weeks later, without having read the Bible or the Book of Mormon. "I accepted everything," he said.

He left on his mission at the age of nineteen in the mid-1980s and immediately got into trouble. His companion did something that had the appearance of them stealing money, they were observed, and they were arrested and put in jail. The elders told the authorities they weren't thieves, they had no intention of stealing money, they knew they had done something wrong, and they were sorry. Diego was "really scared" during their time in jail, but his companion, the perpetrator, said he didn't need to worry, because they were meant to be there.

"God brought us to this jail for a reason," said his companion.

Diego wondered what kind of God he was talking about.

The offending companion turned to the policeman guarding them, told him they were missionaries for The Church of Jesus Christ of Latter-day Saints, and could they take a few minutes of his time to explain to him what they teach? The policeman was surprised, looked a little nervous, and didn't know what to say. The companion quickly bowed his head and began saying a prayer. The policeman automatically bowed his head. The elders then taught him the first discussion.

Diego knew nothing bad would happen after that. The mission president wasn't so sure. He interceded on the elders' behalf, and two days later they were released from jail. The offending companion was quickly transferred to a different area.

Diego became depressed because his mission had gotten off to such a bad start. He was given a new companion, an American. Diego was shy and very timid when he knocked on doors. He and his companion went up to their first door, and Diego knocked on it very lightly. The new companion told Diego to step aside and banged on it loudly. Diego asked why he was knocking on the door so loudly, and the new companion responded: "When it comes time for the Final Judgment, nobody will be able to say we didn't do good work, for even the Lord in heaven will be able to hear us knocking on these doors!" Diego found his companion's example helpful.

Diego's mission helped him both personally and spiritually. While he was shy (and still is, he says), his mission made his personality stronger. It helped him to be more sincere with himself and with others. His mission also helped make him stronger spiritually. It made him feel like a more worthy person and more worthy to teach. He is no longer afraid; he feels a kind of power that he can talk to whomever he wants.

Diego feels if he hadn't gone on a mission, he wouldn't be such a strong member of the Church today. He is now a leader in the Church in Bolivia, and while he got off to a rough start in his mission, he attributes his leadership skills and his current role in the Church to the knowledge, skills, and values he learned as a missionary.

"Those of us who are leaders in the Church owe it to the mission," he observed, "for the mission encouraged us to be different kind of men."

England: Stephen

In retrospect, Stephen is just as happy the elders did something they weren't supposed to do. Had they not, he probably wouldn't have joined the LDS Church.

They stuck their foot in the door.

They did it when Stephen's father answered their knock, said he wasn't interested, and started to close the door. One of the elders (one was American and one German) blocked the door with his foot and said they felt led to talk with him. He said "okay," and let them in. Stephen was baptized three weeks later at the age of nine.

The missionaries said they had prayed about whom to approach and had been led to knock on that specific door southwest of London in 1978.

When he was thirteen, Stephen's home teacher asked him when he wanted to go on a mission, and it was then that he began to think about it. He watched his older Mormon friends get ready and go and saw what good experiences they had, and he started saving money. At eighteen he told his bishop he wanted to serve. His parents weren't very strong in the Church and got a little worried that he, their eldest son, was going. But they supported him, and it strengthened their own faith.

He witnessed a tragedy just before leaving for the MTC, and it had a powerful impact on him. A cyclist was involved in an accident, and Stephen was with him when he died. Thereafter he felt, "I am living on and I must do my best."

He was assigned to a French-speaking mission in Montreal and spent nine weeks studying French at the Provo MTC. He felt privileged to be in Utah, the hub of Mormon culture. He said that Salt Lake City and Provo are "like Disneyland" to a Mormon. When they had large group meetings at the MTC with two thousand missionaries, it was the biggest group and largest Church function he had ever experienced. Going to the temple in Provo was one of the happiest times in his life.

He also brought an outsider's perspective. He felt Utah and Western Mormons took it all for granted and that some American missionaries were immature. He had to be very careful expressing humor, more so than had he been in England. The standards were very high at the MTC, and some humor was not acceptable. He wasn't so much homesick, as he missed "the Englishness of England." On Remembrance Day (comparable to Memorial Day in the United States; it is held the second Sunday in November and is marked by ceremonies and two minutes of silence), he and two other missionaries from the United Kingdom went behind the Provo temple and observed a moment of silence.

The Montreal Mission spanned three different cultures and two different languages, as it dipped into New York, Ontario, and Quebec. He experienced high points, low points, and unusual experiences.

He and his companion were invited late one evening into the Montreal home of a man. The man was old enough to be Stephen's father, and their initial impression was that he was going to be antagonistic toward them, but the man participated in the discussions, made significant changes in his life, and was baptized. Stephen said the changes were dramatic, and they helped the man's family life. It was a high point of his mission—to be instrumental in bringing something so important into the man's life. He felt the Lord brought them together.

He also faced challenges. He couldn't understand Canadian French in the early days, and he didn't always like his companions. His first antagonistic response at a door caught him off guard. He was told that he was lost and that Joseph Smith wasn't a prophet. To feel their disgust for what was precious to him disturbed him and upset him, and it put doubts in his own mind. He came to realize, however, with the help of his companion, that none of the detractors knew what they were talking about.

Stephen faced challenges on his return home. He was engaged to be married when he left for his mission, he and his fiancée wrote the entire time, but near the end he felt he was drifting away and said so. She was engaged to someone else when he returned home. He also felt very different from his old friends. They had carried on with their old lives, whereas he had experienced significant changes.

Looking back on his mission, Stephen said he learned to cope with anxiety and depression. He found that he could determine how he felt. If he didn't like something, then he should change it. He found companionships more difficult than marriage. While he couldn't always change difficult companions, it was the first time he had to learn to love someone, even if he didn't like them. It taught him tolerance, to look for the good in others. He also now knows how to act to feel closer to God. He came to appreciate solitude and to use it constructively—for prayer.

Columbia: Santiago

Santiago came from a large Columbian family of nine children. He described it as a traditional Roman Catholic family where you are born, raised, and die a Roman Catholic. He first became aware of the LDS Church when his sister-in-law met with missionaries and was baptized. The missionaries lived two doors down from his house, but he thought they were Jehovah's Witnesses. His mother invited them to the house to learn more about their teachings. The whole family attended, including Santiago, who was a university student at the time.

He said he went strictly for the cultural experience. He had read that Mormons practiced polygamy, and he wanted nothing to do with it, or them. But he did everything they asked of the family after the first meeting. He read selections from the Book of Mormon and was convinced he would never join. The elders asked him to be baptized at the second discussion, and he said to not even ask him. He would tell them if he wanted to. He continued with the discussions, which made his father nervous, because he was going to the university on a scholarship, and the family had great hopes for him. Joining the Mormon Church was not one of the hopes of his father. Plus, Santiago was nineteen at the time, like the missionaries, and his dad feared that if he joined, he too would want to go on a mission. His father pressured him not to join.

Santiago finished the discussions and went to church, but he wouldn't commit to baptism. He kept coming up with questions, but the missionaries were very patient. He read the Bible and the Book of Mormon, looking for "mistakes," but the elders always had answers that satisfied him.

He grew close to one of the elders, and one day the elder told him he was being transferred the next day and that he would like to baptize

Santiago before he left. Santiago said he would think about it. He had finished the discussions a month before, and he had been praying for what he called an "overwhelming answer" to his question of whether he should join the Church. The answer came that night through a powerful dream, where he experienced a sense of peace. He knocked on the missionaries' door the next morning and said he wanted to carry through with it. He was baptized one-half hour later. It was January 1988. He didn't tell his family for a few months. When he finally showed his dad a picture of his baptism, he reported his dad "wasn't real excited."

And his dad's fears were realized. Santiago got very involved with the missionaries. He had found answers to questions he had been struggling with about the meaning of life, and he wanted to share his excitement with others. He felt a lot of people were looking for the same answers. He knocked on doors with the missionaries, and they came to his house often. He told his parents he wanted to go on a month-long mini-mission, but they weren't supportive. He went anyway, and he loved it. They baptized people, and the Church was growing.

He decided he wanted to go on a mission about the same time that he applied to schools in Utah. His parents said he could go there, but only on one condition—that he not serve a mission. He told them he was okay with that, but deep in his heart he felt bad, because he knew he would do it anyway. His plans were different from theirs, and he felt he should do it.

"I knew I was doing the right thing," he said.

He went to school in Utah for a semester and then applied to serve a mission. He was assigned to serve in the Florida Miami Spanish-speaking mission. He informed his parents the day before he entered the Provo MTC, and they took his decision very hard. They thought he would be a missionary for the rest of his life and never go back to school.

He loved his mission, taught Spanish at the Provo MTC upon his return, finished his college degree at BYU, and returned to his home country, where he holds a leadership position in the Church. His parents are now more accepting of the choices he made. They saw what a powerful and positive influence his mission had on him both personally and spiritually, and they are relieved he isn't a missionary for life.

The Middle East: Mustafa

One of my most unusual interviews for this study was with a young man born and raised in a Middle Eastern Muslim country who converted to the Latter-day Saint Church while a college student in Western Europe.

Mustafa wasn't raised in a religious home, and he described his youth as growing up in a home without spiritual guidance. He always knew there was something lacking spiritually in his life, that there was something he needed to find that God was going to bring to him one day. He wanted to go to different countries and learn different languages. Thus when he was awarded a scholarship to Norway, he knew something was waiting for him there.

Mustafa watched a film on Jesus Christ one evening, and while he couldn't understand it very well (it was in English, with Norwegian subtitles), he was touched by Jesus's life, and it touched his heart. He went into his room and said, "Jesus Christ, I don't know who you are, I don't know if you can help me. I have lots of questions; I need help. If you can help me, please help me."

But nothing happened. As time went by, Mustafa felt more and more discouraged. He had many spiritual questions, he wondered how he could be closer to God and learn His ways, but his questions weren't being answered. He wondered if he should return home to be with his family. But at the same time he felt compelled to stay on in Norway.

One evening Mustafa had the urge to immediately leave his room, and when he opened the door two American Mormon missionaries were passing by. He had no idea who or what they were, but he knew young men in suits were uncommon in Norway. He said a power almost "pushed him" out the door; he felt it was one of the most important moments of his life. He stopped the elders and said he needed to talk with them. They looked at him, "rather worried and scared," and said they would speak with him, but they had come to visit his neighbor, and they would talk with him after they visited the neighbor. They returned at 9:30 P.M. and said they had to be in by 10:30 P.M., and they asked if they could come back tomorrow. No, he said, he wanted to talk with them right then. They spent a long time with him that evening, answering his questions, and they gave him a Norwegian translation of the Book of Mormon.

He said when he took the book in his hands he felt it was true without even reading it. The missionaries' testimonies had convinced him. They had left everything behind, they came on a mission, they were paying for it, they sacrificed their schooling, and they traveled to another country. He wondered how someone could do all of that if their message wasn't true.

He admired the missionaries as he was taking the discussions. He was twenty, and they were nineteen. He told them he was impressed with them and he wanted to be like them. He wanted to go on a mission some day.

Mustafa joined the Mormon Church in 1988, while a student in Norway. Not long thereafter, he had a dream where he saw himself as a missionary and heard people speaking in English in the dream. He believed God inspired the dream, and he took it as a sign that God wanted him to go on a mission. He awoke weeping. There were people waiting for him in a part of the world where he had never been before, and he would touch their lives. But he was living in Norway, burdened with school loans, and with no way to pay for a mission. He prayed for help. He found a good job, his bishop found some sponsors, and his ward gave him some money. He submitted his papers from Norway and was called to serve in Arizona. He entered the Provo MTC in November of 1989.

His parents were very upset and embarrassed when he told them that he had joined the Mormon Church, was dropping out of college, and was going on a mission. They told him he was brainwashed, ruining his life, and crazy to quit school. They told him to convert from Islam to another faith is "a big thing" in his country, that people would call him an infidel, and that there is no forgiveness for those who leave the faith. They said it is blasphemy and the greatest shame for the person and for the family. They told him to leave his things at school and to take the first plane home. He said it was a command on their part, but he didn't call or write until he was in the mission field.

Their reaction caused him to have many worries, and he felt insecure at times, "but God replaced them with peaceful feelings." He carried these worries and feelings throughout his mission.

He gained thirty pounds in three weeks at the MTC, and while people were nice to him as a foreigner, he felt like an outsider. He was uneasy with certain aspects of American society, particularly the practice of men taking communal showers. He felt it was disrespectful to God; he said it would be considered blasphemy at home and that Islamic Fundamentalists would "trash you" if it occurred in his country. He didn't mention his concerns to the MTC administrators, because he recognized the practice was part of American culture. He acknowledged that Latter-day Saints are modest in their dress and hold high moral standards, but the practice still bothered him throughout his stay. But he enjoyed his time at the MTC, saying the feeling of the Spirit was the high point for him there.

Mustafa had to adjust to other cultural differences. He had been working with an investigator who was trying to stop smoking, but one day it was obvious the investigator had a relapse. Mustafa became upset and started shaking his finger at the investigator, telling him he needed to stop. His companion took him aside and said that while he may shake his finger at someone at home, it isn't done in the United States. It became a joke between them, but was a good lesson learned.

Mustafa had a number of international companions—English, Samoan, Canadian, Kenyan (who was actually the first missionary from that country)—and he found it an international learning experience. He loved tracting, because he enjoyed meeting people. Arizonians didn't quite know what to think when he and his Kenyan companion appeared at their door, trying to tell them, in broken English, about their American prophet. Some were entertained by it, while some were irritated and offended. They were told to go back to their own countries. A woman screamed at them, saying she didn't like being bothered by Mormon missionaries. She threatened to get her gun and shoot them. They quickly left on their bicycles.

He gave a number of talks at LDS churches while on his mission. People were intrigued by his conversion story. He developed into a good public speaker.

He had a number of worries. Military service was mandatory in his country, and he would have to face that when he returned home. He also lived in fear of not having his passport and visa renewed, because he wasn't a student anymore and wasn't working. There were times when his mission president told him that he may be sent home the next week. Then he would have to face military service. He lived under that cloud for a year and a half. He said he learned to trust God, he read his scriptures daily, and he prayed that he would be able to finish his mission. In the end he was able to complete his mission, and even extended it by a month. But he had worries and concerns throughout his entire time in the field.

After his mission, he went to BYU on a scholarship as a graduate student in political science and international relations. He also worked in the telecenter at the MTC, training young missionaries to field calls from those requesting Church materials.

He felt that going on a mission was the greatest privilege a man or woman can have. He also felt that coming from an Islamic country, becoming a Latter-day Saint, going on a mission, and serving God was a privilege, and he said he thanks God for it. His life changed as a result of his mission. He now knows what God expects of him, he knows what his goals are, and he is stronger in Christ, which to him is the most important thing in his life.

Mustafa said the quality of his mission depended on his attitude and on the choices he made each day. He said a mission can be a heaven, or it can be a hell. He could obey the mission rules, do his part, and have a wonderful time. There were struggles, but it was good, because he loved the work and he loved teaching. He became a stronger person for it. He saw missionaries make wrong choices (sleeping in, not obeying mission rules), and they were miserable for it; their mission became a hell for them. "It's all up to your attitude," he concluded.

He said he felt that going on a mission and working at the MTC prepared him to be "a good man" for his country. He planned to go into politics at home and felt his mission experience helped him to become a better person. He was sad the Latter-day Saint Church wasn't established in his country, because it was so important to him. He said he would teach the Mormon Church's message in his home country, but not proselytize, because it isn't permitted there.

Controversy

"Baseball Baptisms." Pressure to produce baptisms reached an extreme point during what is referred to as the "Baseball Baptism" controversy. During a period in the late 1950s and 1960s in the British Mission and in continental Europe, a program was put in place to increase the number of young male converts into the Church to counterbalance the larger number of females who were joining the Church, and eventually to increase tithing, which would help support the Church's extensive building program. One ruse used was missionaries would get young boys involved in playing on baseball teams, and one of the requirements was that they would go through what the boys thought was an initiation ceremony—but what was actually a baptism ceremony. This was sometimes done without the parents' knowledge or consent. Sometimes there would be spiritual follow-up work and teaching, and sometimes not. Their names were then carried on the rolls to inflate membership figures. This went on for a number of years. Some mission presidents advocated it; baptismal quotas were set, contests were held between missionaries to see who could generate the greatest number of baptisms, and winning missionaries were granted special favors, such as being given a special pin to wear or having dinner with the mission president.

Not all General Authorities, mission presidents, and missionaries supported the program or engaged in the practice, seeing it for what it was. The president of the Church eventually realized that abuses were taking place, and he called a halt to the practice.

I interviewed Elder Marion D. Hanks, the General Authority taxed to bring the quotas and the practice to a halt. He went to England and did so. Worthy missionaries around the country were pressed into service to interview the young boys baptized under these conditions, to see if they knew what they had done and to ask if they wanted to remain on the Church rolls. Some did; most didn't. Technically, they had to be excommunicated in order for their names to be removed, and the missionaries did that. Immediately thereafter, there was a sharp decline in membership figures. The controversy generated such bad feelings among parents and friends of the young boys that missionaries had to avoid going into certain areas, otherwise they would have rocks thrown at them.

Similar interviews and a purging of the Church rolls also took place in France. A sister who served there in the 1960s saw the emphasis on increasing the number of baptisms in the mission. She said her mission president, an American who owned a car dealership, approached baptisms like selling cars: missionaries got their "commissions" based on the number of baptisms they performed. Elders were given pins to wear for above average numbers of baptisms, or were given a flag to fly at their apartment. Information was starting to leak out about the baseball controversy in England and that it had spread to France. There were two elders in her mission who spent most of their mission interviewing boys who had been involved in the episode, asking what they knew about the Latter-day Saint Church and if they wanted to stay in it. She said the ones she knew chose not to stay, thus they were excommunicated.

The sister referred to what she called "the huge maturation difference" between nineteen-year-old males and twenty-one-year-old females; while young elders got very excited about and were motivated by wearing a mission pin or flying the mission flag at their apartment, sisters, who found the practice immature and wrong, "just looked at each other and rolled our eyes." She said other than being shamed for *not* wearing the mission pin, there was no motivation to engage in the practice.

The view of Russian Orthodox clergy and academics: missionaries go home. The tension between external faiths and internal faiths—the issues surrounding the appropriateness of religious groups trying to convert others in different countries and of different cultures to their faith—was especially evident during my interviews and research on Latter-day Saint missionaries in Russia.

It is said that upon meeting Alexander the Great, a Buddhist monk asked him three questions: "Who are you?" "Do you not have a home?" and, "Why are you not at home?"[128] Clergy of the Russian Orthodox Church feel the same way about Western faiths and their missionaries, including Mormon missionaries, because it is felt they undermine Russian religion and culture.

I was made aware of the depth of this feeling in 1998, when I visited with the bishop of the Russian Orthodox Church in the city of Syktyvkar, the Komi Republic, eight hundred miles northeast of Moscow. The potential for negative attitudes toward Western faiths became evident to me in the hour before my translator friend and I were to meet with the bishop. We had visited the only two Russian Orthodox churches in Syktyvkar, a city of 230,000. Both were small, and one had been in such a state of disrepair that up until the mid-1990s it had a tree growing out of its roof.

As we drove to our meeting with the bishop, we passed a very large, newly constructed Baptist church that stood on the highest prominence in the city. Its size and location were striking, and my friend said that it had become very popular, especially for the periodic meals that were served there.

The bishop was not pleased with the size, location, and even the presence of the Baptist church, and when my friend first spoke with him to arrange our meeting, his first question to her was: "Is he Baptist? Because if he is, I don't want to speak with him."

She assured him I wasn't Baptist, and since she had heard that he liked Episcopalians, she took it upon herself to say that I was of that faith (which wasn't true). He then agreed to talk with me.

The question of my religious persuasion didn't come up during our conversation, but the bishop did express his concerns regarding religious outsiders. He felt they were drawing members away from the Russian Orthodox faith. "We did not die spiritually when they closed the church," he said, referring to the atheistic rule of the Communist Party. "The Russian Orthodox faith is in the genes of the Russian people. These outsiders hinder our work with the Russian people. They use deceptive practices like feeding them meals and teaching them English, then getting them to join their church. They are seducing the Russian people."

(The bishop's comment regarding teaching English as a proselytizing tool caused me to remember that a few days earlier I had stopped two American elders on a street in St. Petersburg, seeking to talk with them about their experiences. They apologized and said they couldn't stop; they were late for the weekly English class they were teaching to a group of Russians. I didn't mention my experience to the bishop.)

The bishop felt his concerns about Western faiths were justified, and he contrasted the size and newness of the Baptist church with the two, small, Russian Orthodox churches my friend and I had visited just hours before.

The bishop said there were some grounds for optimism. With the fall of communism in the early 1990s, the Russian Orthodox Church began to regain the place it had lost in Russian society. Numerous Orthodox churches were constructed or repaired (including the church with the tree growing out of it in Syktyvkar), and an Orthodox cathedral was being erected in Moscow to commemorate the year 2000. It also became fashionable to belong to the Russian Orthodox Church, and many politicians claimed membership and attended services. He said Russia was in a state of renewal, and the renewal of the Russian Orthodox Church was an important part of the process. Religious outsiders only hindered the process.

The bishop's concerns regarding Western faiths coming into Russia were echoed by a Russian Orthodox priest in Petrozavodsk, a city of 266,000 people, 280 miles north of St. Petersburg. Like Syktyvkar, Petrozavodsk could claim only two small Russian Orthodox churches. The priest I spoke with represented a new breed of Russian Orthodox priests. In his late thirties when I interviewed him in 1998, he was fluent in English, having lived in the United States for four years. Acknowledging that Russia was in the process of recovering after a long religious coma, he feared young people faced "a huge spiritual vacuum" because the country's spiritual roots were nearly destroyed. The Russian Orthodox Church was the root of the society, he said, the Communists knew it, and they tried to destroy it. He said that while communism held sway for ninety years, we must not forget that the Russian Orthodox Church has been in existence for one thousand years. The Russian Church fell apart when the country fell apart, and, in the early 1990s, when there was the threat of starvation, Western missionaries came with humanitarian goods. He felt the fact that the Russian people looked to outsiders was a natural and understandable attitude, given the conditions in the country at the time, but he wasn't impressed with the missionaries.

"They were well-fed and they had big egos," he observed.

He said Westerners recognized that Russia holds great potential, but Western missionaries "are taking advantage of the people, are sneaky, and aren't civilized."

American missionaries especially offended him. He said they think, "The Evil Empire has now collapsed and we will bring them the Truth. They come with their big egos and treat Russians like (American) Indians."

He went on to say that Western missionaries acted in primitive, un-Russian ways. An Orthodox priest would never knock on doors and invite people to come to his church. "Quantity is never what matters," he added. "It's sincerity toward God."

Latter-day Saints, members of the Unification Church, Jehovah's Witnesses, and Scientologists all had appeared in Petrozavodsk, all claiming to be Christian. He said Mormon missionaries felt like they were "little kings," sent there to save them: "I will teach you English, but through the avenue of my faith." He said being from America added to their mystique.

The Russian Orthodox priest found it "pretentious" that Americans came there to teach them what the Church is and what it stands for. He recognized that the Russian people weren't well-prepared to deal with outsiders. He said the answer to the threat rested on the shoulders of the Russian Orthodox priests, but their numbers were limited and an adequate ecclesiastical structure was lacking. He took heart in the fact that a new generation of bishops was rising who had international experience, as he had, and that they were in the process of recovering after a long coma. He felt people from foreign countries needed to be more modest. When he was in the United States, he saw this type of proselytizing coming. Now that he was seeing it come into Russia, he was tempted to say, "Leave us alone. Give us a break."

A university professor of religion and history in Petrozavodsk shared the concerns of the bishop and priest. He "felt bad" about the inroads Western faiths were having in Russia, because they were destroying the national consciousness. They isolated converts from their families and friends, although he did acknowledge that a positive byproduct of groups like the Latter-day Saints and Krishna Consciousness was that they had some influence over drug and alcohol addictions. He said Latter-day Saint missionaries had trouble converting Russians because of language limitations, but they had some success by teaching English. He questioned the motivation of Russians who agreed to talk with missionaries—were they interested in the religion, or did they want to hear native speakers and practice their English?

Some younger Russians felt differently about the Russian Orthodox Church. When I asked for their impressions, a group of college students at the Komi State Pedagogical Institute in Syktyvkar responded that they felt the Russian Orthodox Church was too formal. There was too much standing and bowing, the services were too long, and the priests seem too distant. By contrast, they found Western-style churches more informal and the clergy more approachable.

They did add that many older Russians distrusted what they called "the American smile," the tendency of Americans to smile a lot. They didn't think it was genuine, and they thought Americans were naïve. They themselves didn't smile often, they said: since they had been isolated from the world for so long, they didn't know there were things to smile about.

A middle-aged teacher in a college of music in Medvezhyegorsk, three hundred miles north of St. Petersburg, spoke of the attraction of Western faiths, but of the tension she felt because of her Russian roots. An American evangelical Protestant missionary and his wife (not Latter-day Saints) came to her city in 1993, bringing with them a bus and a computer. They opened a church and lived there for a year.

It was a hard period in the woman's life when the missionary first arrived. She was ill and felt very alone. The missionary and his wife visited her often, prayed with her, and supported her. This gave her strength and health. They taught her that she must have hope. She was baptized into the evangelical church. She is now healthy and believes the church helped her. "I feel like new blood has been poured into me," she said.

Around the same time, Russian Orthodox and Baptist churches were opened in Medvezhyegorsk, which caused people and families to divide and to go to separate churches. When I asked if she felt her life would have been any different had she remained in the Russian Orthodox Church, she replied that while she still visited Orthodox churches and lit candles, and while she respected the fact that the Russian Orthodox Church was a source of Russian culture, she didn't feel as strong a sense of community there as she did in her Western church. She didn't feel the inner freedom in the Orthodox Church that she found in her Western religion. "I keep the Russian culture inside me," she said, "but I also respect Western religion." She meets twice daily to pray with other evangelical church members. Some of them also attend the Orthodox Church.

She was impressed by the fact that when she asks an American, "How are you?" they always say, "Fine." Russians, she said, start to complain.

The Latter-day Saint Church is making modest progress in Russia. The Russian Book of Mormon was published in 1981, the first congregation was organized in Leningrad in 1990, official state recognition was granted in 1991, and the number of congregations and missionaries increased "dramatically" after that. The LDS Church was granted a new certificate of recognition in 1998, and, in 2011, the first stake was organized, the Moscow Russia Stake. As of January 1, 2015, the Church reported 22,039 members in Russia.[129]

The priest in Petrozavodsk remained unmoved in the face of the positive endorsements of Western faiths by the college students in Syktyvkar, by the music teacher in Medvezhyegorsk, and by the growth of the Latter-day Saint Church in Russia. "The Russian Church will not become the minority faith," he said. "It is the spirit that moves the country and its culture. It is the backbone of the country." But he did express concern: "If you throw away the Russian Orthodox Church, you will lose Russia. You will have nothing."

Effects of the International Missionary Experience and Efforts

International experiences have a significant impact on Latter-day Saint missionaries. Most missionaries from the United States have had minimal exposure to other religious faiths, and for many their mission represents the first time they have been outside of the United States. These combine to make their mission a challenging, but formative, experience. They gain unique language, cultural, and interpersonal skills, which make them highly desirable to employers when they return from their mission. Their experiences also contribute to the increased internationalization of the Latter-day Saint Church, which is a dominant trend in the twenty-first century. As was mentioned earlier, there are now more Latter-day Saints outside of the United States than in it.

Parents naturally worry about children serving overseas, but those who have done it themselves say it better prepares them for when their children serve. A sister who served in France and Switzerland said her experience helped her to relate to what her own children experienced when they went on their missions (all served internationally). Some of her children were assigned to areas where the work was slow and difficult, and she could relate to that became she had experienced the same thing. They would arrive energized, but when faced with language barriers and little interest in their message they were shocked and became discouraged. A son who served in Japan reported that it was the most difficult experience of his life. She said as a mother she worried, but had she not had a similar experience and knew that they would survive and grow as a result, then she would have worried "ten times more." "I am glad I know how they feel," she reported.

Indigenous missionaries and leaders. The twenty-first century is seeing the Latter-day Saint Church continue to strive toward its goal of calling more indigenous missionaries to their home country, growing local leadership, and having American missionaries step back. American interviewees who served in other countries spoke of training local men and working on improving their leadership skills. Some missionaries even served as branch presidents while on their mission. A General Authority told me that native missionaries are returning to their countries, becoming bishops and stake presidents, and then are in a position to lead and to encourage others to go on missions.

Many Latin American countries today have mainly indigenous missionaries. An elder who served in Mexico in the mid-1960s said there were only a handful of Mexican missionaries serving at the time, but at the turn of the twenty-first century, 80 percent of missionaries there were Mexicans. An American A.P. in Peru in the early 2000s said when he began his mission, 80 percent of the missionaries were from North America, but two years later the number had dropped to 20 percent.

The same is true in other parts of the world. An American sister who served in Italy in the late 1980s said an increasing number of Italian missionaries were called to their country while she served; while Tonga has few missionaries from the United States, since there is such a high percentage of Latter-day Saints in the Tongan population. An elder who served in Hungary said most branches now have Hungarian branch presidents.

A young couple who were instructors at the MTC in Provo, who served missions in the United States (she was from Uruguay and served in North Carolina, and he was from Columbia and served the Spanish-speaking population in Florida), told me that their goal was to return to Columbia after they graduated from BYU, so that they could help build the Church there and provide local leadership in the country. They felt they could do more in service to the Church there than in Utah. They said there are so many LDS people in Utah that "sometimes you go to a ward and you kind of get lost in the crowd." They added there is a need for people who know how things are done in the Mormon Church to train others, especially in a country like Columbia, where there are so many recent converts. "Sometimes, in South America," she observed, "there are little personal doctrines that are not really true, and beliefs that are sometimes a little weird. People will hold personal views, but may not know they are wrong. We look forward to helping them understand the correct way of believing and doing things. So there is a lot that can be done and local leaders will be welcomed."

Locals are expected to assume a heavy responsibility for the Latter-day Saint Church according to a General Authority I spoke with. He said the Church is a lay church and a missionary church, and locals have to become self-supporting and self-sustaining. They are to build or rent a church, and they receive little assistance from the United States. The big challenge, he said, is the development of local leadership—with the goal of getting away from American missionaries serving as bishops.

The locals share this goal. My interviews with Church members in England and Western Europe revealed that they have great affection for the American leadership in their countries, but they look forward to the day when more English and Europeans can serve in those roles.

The Perpetual Education Fund. At General Conference in 2001, President Hinckley announced the formation of the Perpetual Education Fund. Modeled on the Perpetual Emigration Fund popular in England in the nineteenth-century (a program that aided converts immigrating to the United States), the Perpetual Education Fund provides financial aid to returning non-American missionaries to help them further their education, to increase their knowledge and skills, and to aid them in finding gainful employment. Funded by donations, the aid is in the form of a loan, and the expectation is that recipients will repay the loan when they are in a position to do so. Participants have to take

"Planning for Success" courses and career workshops offered through LDS employment resource centers, prior to receiving the money. As of 2015, thousands of returned foreign missionaries had taken part in the program.

Living in the Latter Days. A senior couple serving at the London MTC said that most "good" Latter-day Saints believe they are living in the End Times spoken of in Revelation. The husband said they are aware the gospel must be preached to all people before Christ comes again, and as a result they have been praying that international missions can be expanded to all people. He said the reason they are so dedicated is because Jesus said to teach the gospel to the entire world; the Savior's command is why they are serving a mission. "Jesus gave the command to the apostles, he said it again to Joseph Smith, and it is the last time the command will be given," he said. "Our responsibility is to tell people that the restored gospel is back. What people do with it is up to them."

Missionaries as ambassadors. American missionaries in foreign lands have an important impact on locals, because it gives them contact with America. A returned missionary who is no longer active in the Church observed that nineteen-year olds don't make good theologians, but they make good ambassadors for the United States and for the Latter-day Saint Church. They are well-dressed, polite, and non-confrontational.

However, the presence of American missionaries overseas can at times make even their fellow countrymen uneasy—but they still can leave a positive impression. This tension is seen in an e-mail I received from a retired non-Mormon State Department official who served in a number of countries throughout his long government career. "I have encountered Mormon missionaries in several foreign countries," he said. "They are not always welcomed by the host government and thus are often considered an irritant to bilateral relations by U.S. officials. Nevertheless, I have never met one that was not a credit to his/her religion, as well as a positive example of American culture and values."

PART V

Sisters and Seniors

CHAPTER 10

Sister Missionaries

"I am proud of you, sister."

A WOMAN'S COMMENT AS SHE PASSED A SISTER MISSIONARY IN CHICAGO O'HARE INTERNATIONAL AIRPORT IN THE LATE 1990'S (SHE DIDN'T STOP OR IDENTIFY HERSELF)

"Sisters serving missions is the Mormon Church's closest expression of equal rights."

AN ELDER WHO SERVED HIS MISSION IN CANADA

"No, I didn't serve a mission. I decided to get married and have babies instead."

THE RESPONSE OF A UTAH WOMAN IN HER LATE TWENTIES, WHEN I ASKED IF SHE HAD SERVED A MISSION.

There is a story that circulates at the Provo MTC:

> Three elders found a magic lamp at the Provo MTC, and when they rubbed it a genie appeared.
>
> "Since there are three of you," said the genie, "I will grant you each one wish."
>
> "I want to perform two hundred baptisms during my mission," said the first elder.
>
> "Consider it done," said the genie.
>
> "I would like to be a mission president some day," said the second elder.
>
> "It will be granted," said the genie.
>
> "I would like to be the *best* missionary in the history of the Church!" exclaimed the third elder.
>
> "It too shall be," said the genie—and the young elder was immediately turned into a sister missionary.

There has been a decided shift in the Latter-day Saint Church over the past three or four decades regarding how Church members perceive young LDS women serving missions. What used to be seen as an unusual activity, or one even worthy of pity, has been replaced by attitudes of acceptance, and even of encouragement.

Young Latter-day Saint women aren't expected to serve—that is the responsibility of the young elders—rather, their role in the Church is that of spouse, mother, and homemaker. When a young woman did go on a mission in earlier decades of the twentieth century, some Church members would wonder: "Why is she serving a mission? Can't she find a husband? Is a mission her last resort?"

This questioning has given way in more recent decades to a more positive attitude about sisters serving, which is shaped by forces both within and without the Latter-day Saint Church. Interviewees spoke of watching brothers, relatives, and friends return from their missions and of being struck by what a positive experience it had been for them: they were more mature, had better communication skills, and exhibited a deeper spirituality. The sisters wanted the same for themselves. Attitudes by and about women were also changing in the wider American society; postponing marriage, personal independence, and considering options outside of marriage and motherhood were accepted, and even encouraged.

As a result, many young Latter-day Saint women now actively seek to serve their Church through missions. They want to help spread the Latter-day Saint gospel, and they want to share in the benefits that come from the experience.

While the Church leadership says that it values the sisters' contributions in the mission field and that the experience can have a positive effect on sisters' lives, they are ambivalent about young sisters serving. They advise that if a young woman has a viable marriage offer, she should choose that over serving a mission. "Marriage over mission," is the watchword.

A theological reason is advanced for the sisters to marry instead of serving a mission. Latter-day Saint theology teaches that all humans began as preexisting souls with God and that in order to work out their salvation the souls must first be given a body on earth. Consequently, Latter-day Saints tend to marry early and have large families.

Some young sisters report they don't want to marry early—they want to consider other options first, be it further education, employment, or a mission. But with options come choices, and some sisters report that having more choices makes their decision to serve that much more difficult. It comes down to following the counsel of Church leaders, or not.

"Do I date and marry, or do I postpone marriage until *after* my mission?" asked a sister.

Earlier generations of sisters said they didn't have to face this dilemma. Serving a mission "wasn't even on their radar screen," as one older woman described it. Since it was not expected of them, they didn't even think about it. Many of today's younger sisters *do* think about it, but since they don't have a mandate to serve, since it isn't a clear-cut decision as it is for young men, some sisters decide to serve only at the last minute. And when they do serve, some carry lingering doubts about whether they should have stayed home and married.

Until October 2012, young LDS women had to wait until they were twenty-one years old before they could serve, and while this may have increased the likelihood that they would marry before they could go, many sister interviewees said they consciously chose not to get married before their mission—and that they dated, or didn't date, accordingly. Serving a mission, not marriage, had become their immediate goal. "We are normal," a sister from California assured me while serving in the mid-1990s. "If you have a belief and a desire, you can serve. It is a lot more acceptable to go on a mission today. I want to help others, and I know that the Gospel can bring happiness. More and more sisters are realizing they don't need to get married as soon as they get out of high school. We have goals, we will get married, and we will have a family—eventually."

This changing attitude, along with the age change that allows sisters to begin serving at nineteen, have opened up new missionary possibilities for sisters and have led to a significant increase in their numbers. (They constituted between 10 and 15 percent of missionaries in the field in 2012, while their numbers jumped to around 28 percent by 2014.) The sisters' excitement over the age change is best illustrated by the fact that when the missionaries-in-training at the Provo MTC heard the announcement about the age changes, there was stunned silence when the age change for the young men was made (from nineteen to eighteen), but when the age change for young women was announced, it was greeted with loud cheering, particularly by the young women present.

What the long-term effects of this will be for Latter-day Saint women, and for the Church, remains to be seen. A marked decline in female enrollments was experienced at BYU after the age change, and some wonder if sisters will choose to continue their education after they return from their mission, or if they will marry and raise their children as stay-at-home-mothers instead.[130]

While sisters and elders share common experiences—they attend the same MTCs, teach the same lessons, and gain similar personal and spiritual benefits—the fact that sisters serve voluntarily, are generally older than elders, serve eighteen months instead of twenty-four months, and serve other types of missions besides proselytizing missions, all contribute to them having a different kind of missionary experience. Sisters, for example, serve as tour guides at Church visitors' centers, at historic sites, and at Temple Square in Salt Lake City. They may also engage in humanitarian and social service missions, where they assist in providing health care, education, and community development. Sister and senior missionaries typically perform these activities.

Their being older and female brings a note of seriousness and maturity to the mission that is sometimes lacking among eighteen and nineteen-year-old elders. This contributes to the image illustrated in our earlier story of the elders and the genie; that sisters are more effective as missionaries. The disparity in ages and maturity levels can lead to tension between sisters and elders, and patience and negotiation are sometimes necessary to keep the peace between them.

However, as in the Latter-day Saint Church in general, sister missionaries lack the spiritual authority of the priesthood that is enjoyed by elders. This is most clearly seen in the mission field by the fact that sisters cannot baptize converts, even if they have taught them all the lessons and brought them to the point where they are ready to join the Church. They must turn to the elders, for only elders are authorized to baptize; only they "hold the priesthood."

Non-Mormons generally perceive women as having a second-class status in the Latter-day Saint Church. Such attitudes are a carry-over from the nineteenth century when Mormon women were portrayed as innocent victims of a lecherous patriarchal construct—polygamy. This perception is reinforced by the fact that women do not hold the priesthood and cannot hold positions of leadership in the Latter-day Saint Church, with the result that all bishops, presidents, stake presidents, mission presidents, and General Authorities are men.

The Church responds that women have their own organization in the Church, the Relief Society (which is run entirely by women), and that women have made significant contributions to the faith throughout its history. They also repeat their position that a woman's role is first and foremost that of spouse, mother, and homemaker, and for that the Church leadership offers no apologies.

Latter-day Saint women have tended to lag behind in social trends found in wider society, but they are not immune to them. Like their non-Mormon female counterparts, an increasing number of today's LDS women are postponing marriage to pursue their education and other interests outside of the home, including employment and serving a mission. Thus the sister missionary interviews provide a window that allow non-Mormons to observe the changing experience of women in the Latter-day Saint Church. They also provide the Church with a mirror, for they reflect the greater participation of sisters in the missionary experience.

It remains to be seen how the Church will be affected by the new breed of sister missionaries. One might expect that by taking on increased responsibilities and hardships as missionaries, sisters will return home with the expectation that their voice should take on added weight in the male-dominated organization. Or the opposite may occur. Their missionary experience may reinforce the roles and relationships between males and females that already exist in the Mormon Church. Sisters expressed both expectations and predictions during our interviews. Time will tell. In either case, the missionary experience for women, as it is for men, is a life-changing event.

The Sister Interviews

The sisters were a delight to interview. They were bright, articulate, and engaging. They tended to be more verbal than the elders (especially the younger elders) and more expressive of their feelings. They were frank about the highs and lows of their missionary experiences. Since their interviews tended to include insightful, colorful, and extended discussions of topics, I had to guard against drawing on them too heavily throughout this book. As a wise colleague pointed out, sisters are in the minority in the missionary workforce, and I should be careful not to give the impression that their experience is the majority experience.

(It also should be noted that by the time the elders were getting near the end of their missions, and thus were older, their interviews tended to be as insightful and articulate as the sisters.)

Eighty-five Latter-day Saint sisters were interviewed for this project. Seventy-two were serving their mission at the time of the interviews. The interviews took place in New England; Salt Lake City, Utah; Berlin and Dresden, Germany; and London, England. Those serving in Western Europe faced the same lack of interest in their message as their counterparts in Northern New England. Most sisters were from Utah and the Mountain West. The majority came from families in which siblings, parents, grandparents, and close relatives had served missions before them. In some instances siblings, along with cousins, were serving concurrently.

Thirteen sisters who had served a mission in the past (they are referred to as "returned missionaries," or "RMs") were interviewed, and their dates of service ranged from the 1960s to the 2000s. They had served in various parts of the United States, as well as in Argentina, Belize, France, Guatemala, Italy, and Japan. They were able to put their mission experiences in the context of their longer life stories.

Of special significance is that many of those who were serving their mission at the time of the interviews were part of a transitional generation of sisters. They were born in a time when sisters weren't expected to serve a mission, but by the time they were of age attitudes had changed and they were encouraged to serve—even *expected* to serve by some—which put some of them in an awkward position.

Sisters Serving Missions: Earlier Perceptions

While the history of single Latter-day Saint sisters serving missions extends back at least as far as the end of the nineteenth century, their numbers were very small. It has only been since the latter part of the twentieth century that their representation has risen. The unease felt about sisters serving missions—that they weren't following the normal progression of education, marriage, and motherhood—extends well back in the twentieth century, and various interviewees, female and male, alluded to it: the perception was that if they were serving, it was because they couldn't find a mate.

A General Authority explained that until 1964 sisters had to be twenty-three years old to serve. (The age was lowered to twenty-one in 1964.) He felt there was a grain of truth to the earlier perception; the sisters he encountered when he served his mission in Colorado in the 1940s seemed to confirm it. A sister who served in Washington, D.C., after graduating from college in the early 1970s, confirmed that many of her companions were serving a mission because they couldn't get married. A sister who grew up in California in the 1970s said there was a "stigma" associated with sisters serving, the assumption being that it was their last option.

Various names were given to sister missionaries who served in earlier decades. An elder who served in California in the mid-1960s remembers them being called "lady missionaries." A sister born in Salt Lake City in the early 1940s remembers sister missionaries being referred to as "spinsters" when she was growing up in the Church, while an elder who served in Japan in the mid-1980s said there were just a few sisters in Japan and that they were "marginalized." They were referred to as "sweet spirits," and it was assumed they would never marry.

A sister who served her mission in Northern New England in the 1990s recalled that as she was growing up in Utah in the 1970s little boys, but not little girls, would be called to the front of the congregation to sing "I Hope They Call Me on a Mission." It made her angry, because she too wanted to serve. Another sister reported that while attending a female friend's missionary farewell in the 1980s, the friend told the story of when she was in primary school and they sang the same missionary song, a volunteer would be sought to stand and represent the missionary, but when she volunteered, the female primary teacher told her, "No, little girls do not go on missions." From that time on, she reported, she was determined she was going on a mission, in spite of what her teacher had said. A sister who served in the Mid-Atlantic States in the mid-1970s was discouraged from serving a mission by her female friends because they said she would die an "old maid" if she served, because no one would want to marry her when she returned. She thus came to believe that serving a mission and getting married were mutually exclusive choices.

"I truly believed in personal revelation and I felt God wanted me to go on a mission," she said. "I felt a compulsion to serve, but I also realized that if I did, I would never marry. I truly believed it."

All three women acknowledge that attitudes are different today in the Latter-day Saint Church. The first interviewee was happy to report that by the 1990s little boys and little girls were singing the missionary song together in church. The second interviewee said she couldn't imagine a primary teacher saying that women don't serve missions. The third (who did marry when she returned from her mission) noted that sisters now choose to serve a mission, not because they can't marry, but because they want the missionary experience before they marry.

Marriage or mission is thus no longer seen as a mutually exclusive choice.

As one sister commented, "Yes, I plan to marry, *after* my mission."

Certainly, not all sister interviewees who served in earlier decades fit the negative stereotype. A sister who served in France in the mid-1960s said she started thinking about a mission when her boyfriend, who had been on his mission in California for about a year, wrote and told her how phenomenal the sister missionaries in his mission were, and that she should consider serving, too. She discussed it with her parents and her bishop (who happened to be her father), and they too were very supportive. She turned twenty-one as a younger brother turned nineteen, and they had the unusual experience of sharing a missionary farewell service together, and they left on their missions at the same time. She had a successful mission and married her boyfriend upon their return. Thus not all sisters were discouraged from serving, and certainly not all fit the negative stereotype.

But sisters who served in earlier decades did face special challenges. A sister who served in Japan for twenty-four months in the early 1970s described her time of service as being "on the cusp of sisters going on missions." She spoke of how "isolating" the experience was for women—since there were so few sisters. She was the only sister missionary in her Japanese language class, and there were only twelve sisters among 170 elders in her mission.

The general feeling among women of earlier generations, however, was that it was not their responsibility to serve a mission. Their duty was to be a wife and a mother, and serving a mission wasn't even a consideration for most. Some older sisters who had not served a mission when younger confessed to being glad they didn't have to serve at that point in their life; they were just as happy to let the young men do it. But by the time they reached retirement age, they had changed their minds, and they went on to serve as senior missionaries.

Changing Attitudes and Perceptions

Changes in Church policy, along with societal changes, have contributed to changes in attitudes and perceptions about LDS women serving missions. When the minimum age for women to serve was dropped from twenty-three to twenty-one in 1964, a General Authority said he felt the change had a positive effect on women's decisions to serve. The option of serving at twenty-one came at a much more desirable time in their life. They could complete much of college, serve a mission, return and complete their education, and get married, and in some cases do it all by the age of twenty-three.

With their now being able to serve at nineteen, sisters can pursue their passion to serve a mission and still return home before their twenty-first birthday. This appears to be even more desirable for young women.

Social changes have also contributed to changes in attitudes. When asked why more sisters are serving missions, a sister who served in Argentina said she thinks it is partly generational and that society has opened up the possibility for sisters to "look outside of the box" for more options. Their sense of possibilities has expanded, and serving a mission is a natural consequence of that. She said that people are marrying later, including Mormon women, and so a larger percentage of them are still single when they reach the appropriate age, so it makes a mission a possibility. She also believes our society today generally encourages women to pursue independence and competence more than it did forty years ago, and going on a mission is a reflection of that.

As a result, she feels more LDS sisters are asking God if they should serve and the more they ask, the more "Yeses" they are going to get. While not required of young women, she sees serving a mission as a personal commitment to God and as a widening of possibilities for young women, whereas for previous generations serving a mission wasn't even a consideration for most LDS women. "It just wasn't what they thought about," she said.

Now a sister serving a mission is no longer seen as being odd.

A father of four children (two girls and two boys) who served his mission in the late 1960s talked of the "balancing act" he went through in discussing missions with them. He made it very clear with his sons how important it was that they serve a mission, but he didn't discuss the topic with his daughters. He found it a challenge. He would love for them to go on a mission, but he would also love for them to get married. He didn't want to preach a mission as strongly as he did with the boys, because the girls would feel like they should go on a mission, and they would feel conflicted if they wanted to get married. But at the same time he didn't want to downplay a mission as though it was a consolation prize, because he thought it was a wonderful experience. He struggled to find a balance. His sons went on missions, but his daughters did not.

Some LDS women who didn't go on a mission when they were younger now regret that they didn't and are unhappy that they weren't encouraged to go. A one-time mission president told how he had four children, also two boys and two girls. The boys went on missions, and the girls married, but now his daughters are "after him" for not encouraging them to go on missions, too. They ask: "Why didn't you suggest to us that we also consider a mission? We wish we would have done it!"

The perceptions, expectations, and role of sister missionaries are certainly changing. In a chapter in the book *The Missionary Kit* (published in 1979) entitled "About Lady Missionaries," the author, a sister who had served a mission earlier in the decade, suggests that sisters should bake cookies for elders, be "cheerleaders" for them on Preparation Day, expect and allow elders to open doors to buildings and cars for them, allow elders to help them put on their coats, and let elders start their motorbikes. (She doesn't identify where she served, but it may have been in France, since missionaries rode motorbikes there in the 1960s and early 1970s.) She said sisters should acknowledge the elders' efforts on their behalf, but not be "obnoxious" if elders forget. Particular attention in the article is paid to the importance of sisters' physical appearance, that they present a "proper picture." She wrote that elders complained most frequently about the sisters' hair. (Sisters' hair was never mentioned in my interviews with elders.) The author also added: "If you are one pound overweight, it is too much. Take it off!"[131]

Today's sisters find these suggestions humorous. "Bake for the elders? O, heavens! I have a problem with that!" reported a sister. Her companion added: "We bake for the elders if we *feel* like it. If they ask for cookies we say, 'Here is the recipe, go do it yourself!'" Added the first: "And be cheerleaders? It sounds like being a wife, without being married."

Sisters are also better off not acting so dependent upon the elders. An elder told of playing a joke on two sisters in France in the early 1970s. The elders, after apparent attempts to start the sisters' motorbikes proved unsuccessful, told the sisters their motorbikes wouldn't start, so the sisters pushed them home, a mile away. Of course, there was nothing wrong with the bikes.

The author of *The Missionary Kit* also advised sisters to "honor and support" the priesthood authority over them, even if it was wielded by a younger and less experienced elder, because it "is an important lesson to learn, for the line of authority is an eternal principle of the gospel and the home." She also said to "work so that you never have to be excused because you are a sister missionary." Acknowledging that depression can be an issue, the author counseled sister missionaries to take some extra time for themselves, whether working on their hair, or taking a longer shower, and praying for the Lord's help. Her last words of advice: "Lose yourself in the Spirit and work very, very hard."[132]

A sister who had just returned from serving her mission in the early 1990s also found parts of the article humorous, but said she felt much of the article was true, expressing as it did general principles that are taught and believed in the LDS Church.

There are practical considerations for having more sisters serve. The Church's goal is to spread the gospel worldwide, and in order to do that it needs more missionaries. Having more women serve seems a logical choice, especially since the cohort of eligible young males is shrinking nationwide. And as more women serve, they will return and encourage other women to do the same.

A young woman raised in the Mormon Church and preparing to go on her mission in the late 1990s summed up the perceptions and feelings regarding sisters serving missions. She said there were many reasons why she wanted to go: 1) she had seen the growth in the elders who had served, and she wanted the same for herself; 2) while she felt a strong need to get married, it wasn't the only thing in life for a woman, and she didn't feel a need to rush into it as her mother's generation had felt; 3) it wasn't because she couldn't get married or had nothing else to do (she had a goal to attend graduate school); and 4) at a more profound level, she wanted a deeper knowledge of the gospel, she wanted to serve others, and she wanted to share a message and a Church that she had been fortunate to be born into. She said it was a message that she didn't have to search for or struggle to find, and she wanted the opportunity to share it with others. She also felt the knowledge and skills she would gain on her mission would help her be a better spouse, mother, and Church member.

The Church's Position

While the Latter-day Saint Church is conservative on social issues and teaches that a woman's primary role is to raise a family, Church authorities do acknowledge a shift in attitudes among younger LDS women, particularly regarding postponing marriage. While such a tendency was seen in the wider American society decades ago, and while the LDS Church generally lags behind in social change (by choice), it recognizes that Church members are not immune to these forces. They just come later.

This has impacted women's decision to serve a mission. While the Church hierarchy supports women missionaries (a number of daughters and granddaughters of General Authorities have served missions), and while the Church recognizes the sisters' unique contributions (a number of mission presidents told me they *requested* sisters), the Church has not changed its position on what it considers a woman's priorities to be: marriage over mission, since marriage is considered "the higher calling." As a result, many sisters struggle with the question, "Should I go on a mission, or should I get married?" A sister missionary observed, "I think with sisters there is always that thought in the back of their head, 'What if I am supposed to stay home and get married, and if I don't, will I miss something?'" This tension was clearly expressed by another sister missionary: "Deciding between getting married and going on a mission was the hardest decision I have had to make in my life."

She chose the mission.

But in spite of the counsel of Church authorities of marriage over mission, and in spite of lingering doubts expressed by some, some sisters will do what they want to do. An interviewee said she has known women whose boyfriends have said, "I want to marry you," and the women responded, "Sorry, I am going on a mission instead."

Mission Before Marriage

The fact that perceptions of sisters serving missions have changed and that an increasing number of young women are doing so has forced sisters to at least consider it as an option—something their mothers and grandmothers didn't have to struggle with. Many of the interviewees were part of the transitional generation; when they were little, sisters weren't expected to go on missions, but by the time they were in their late teens and early twenties, the pendulum had swung in the opposite direction, such that they felt pressure *to* serve. Some spoke of how awkward and uncomfortable it made them feel. And many said that the fact that it was an option, and not an expectation, made their decision-making all the more difficult. The result was that while some decided early-on to serve, others waited until the very last minute.

Early deciders. Some sister interviewees decided at an early age to serve, and many of those who did spoke of the influence of a family culture of serving missions. One had a family tradition of serving missions, which extended back to her great, great-grandfather, with an unbroken continuity of successive generations serving thereafter. Another sister spoke of coming from a family in which both her parents and two older brothers had served. Her mother had frequently talked about her mission as if it were the normal thing for Latter-day Saint women to do, and just as she assumed she would go to college, the young sister also assumed she would serve a mission.

One gave a more unusual explanation for her early decision. She described herself as a "tomboy" as she was growing up, and since boys go on missions, she decided at the age of ten that she would do the same.

Another sister's mother was especially excited that her daughter had decided by the age of sixteen that she was going, because, the mother confessed, she had wanted to go when she was younger, but she lacked the courage to do so.

The example of young women serving prompted others to want to serve. A sister who served in the late 1990s said she started thinking about a mission when she was twelve, when she heard a sister missionary talk about her experiences. She decided she wanted to have the same and that if that sister could do it, so could she. She said to her mother, "Mom, I want to go on a mission." Her mother was very supportive and excited by her wish. The sister then watched her brother leave for his mission, and at his farewell she thought, "I want to go." At his homecoming she thought, "Okay, I want to go, *now*!" She and another brother entered the MTC together.

Interviewees also spoke of how impressed they were with their older (biological) sisters when they returned from their missions. One told the touching story of an older sister who came home a little early from her mission because her father was dying. The interviewee said it was her sister who held the family together after his passing. She had become very strong spiritually because of her mission, and she was the "glue" who held the family together and helped it carry on after her father's death. The interviewee said: "I remember thinking, 'I want to be like her. I want to have that spiritual backbone. I want to help people.'" She went on to serve a successful mission.

Hadn't given a mission much thought. In contrast, many said they never gave serving a mission much thought as they were growing up. Some reported that the normal progression of education, marriage, and family "was working for them." They had finished high school and were in a serious relationship, and marriage was their next logical step.

Some said they hadn't considered a mission because they had good jobs that they didn't want to give up.

Some said they actively resisted the idea. "I never wanted to go on a mission and I thought that way all along," reported a sister from Nevada. "I never thought about going on a mission," reported another sister, while a third said: "I didn't think much about going on a mission when I was growing up. I thought it was a 'boy thing.'"

Some said they had heard of sisters who became ill during their mission and had negative effects that had followed them home. The sisters said they didn't want to do something that might preclude them from having children someday.

Some didn't want to serve because they didn't want to go tracting and to knock on peoples' doors. They didn't want to walk the streets, and they didn't like talking with people. These things were outside of their comfort zone, they said, and it would be hard for them.

Part of the transitional generation. Sisters growing up in the Latter-day Saint Church in the last quarter of the twentieth century and later became exposed to a new phenomenon: instead of it just being a "boy thing," serving a mission became a possibility, even an expectation, for young women. They were part of the transitional generation, whose attitudes and expectations were shifting, and it made many of them uncomfortable. Ironically, the stigma attached to serving a mission took a 180-degree turn, such that the stigma became attached to those who did *not* serve a mission, as opposed to those who did.

This was especially evident on the Brigham Young University campus.

The pressure to serve at Brigham Young University. One of the largest concentrations of future and returned missionaries is found at Brigham Young University (BYU) in Provo, Utah, and missions are a common topic of conversation. An elder who served his mission in Eastern Europe said the missionary atmosphere was especially strong for women when he attended BYU in the mid-1990s. He had talked with many women who were quite clear in their desire to serve and who said that nothing was going to get in their way, including marriage. They were "adamant" about it, and the trend was spreading on campus; going on a mission was the thing for young BYU women to do. A General Authority confirmed this, saying that serving a mission had become "trendy" among young women at BYU at that time. A sister who started at BYU in 1996 said it was quite common for fellow students, both male and female to ask her, "and everybody else," if they were going on a mission. She recalled: "I remember that everyone kept asking everyone that. For the men, it was assumed they would go, but for the sisters, everyone would ask, 'Are you planning on going on a mission?'"

A sister who spent three years at BYU and then served her mission in Guatemala in the mid-1990s said there was pressure from peers to serve, especially when sisters turned twenty-one. People would say: "You are twenty-one. You are going on a mission, right?"

If the response was "No," people would wonder, "What's the matter with her?"

She had a roommate who said she didn't want to serve a mission because she felt completing her education was more important. When her roommate turned twenty-one, a friend asked, "So, are you going on a mission?"

"No, I am not," responded the young woman.

"Well, why not?" the friend asked, perplexed.

"BECAUSE I DON'T WANT TO!" yelled the young woman.

"Oh!" responded the friend, surprised.

Another interviewee told of a friend, a twenty-one-year-old BYU woman, who said she would be happy when she turned twenty-two, so that she won't be asked so often if she was going on a mission.

Some expressed reservations about this trend. A sister who served in Belize in the mid-1990s felt the need to raise a note of caution with sisters who thought that going on a mission would be a "fun thing" to do. They needed to give it serious thought, because, she counseled: "You go into the mission field and you get knocked over the head and you realize this isn't just an adventure. It's hard. You better be serious about this because it is more than just a cool thing to do."

A sister who had recently returned from her mission agreed. She said there were many days while on her mission in the Northeastern United Sates that she thought: "I don't have to be here. Why am I subjecting myself to such pain? This is torment!"

Other BYU women expressed concern, saying they felt undue pressure to serve from friends, boyfriends, and even professors. The First Presidency became aware of this pressure and released the following statement in 1994: "There is increasing evidence that some young women are being strongly encouraged to serve full-time missions. Though capable and effective, young women do not have the same responsibility to serve full-time missions, as do young men who hold the priesthood. We are grateful that some desire to serve but they should not feel obligated to do so. A young woman should not be recommended for a mission if it would interfere with a specific marriage proposal."[133]

This prompted discussions on the BYU campus regarding sisters serving missions. In the September 28, 1994, edition of the BYU campus newspaper, *Daily Universe,* the article "Marriage vs. Mission" discussed the Church's above position statement on sister missionaries. It alluded to what it called the "domino effect": as the number of sister missionaries increased, so would the number of women who wished to go on a mission, or who would be expected to do so. It also pointed out that half of the students in BYU's "Sharing the Gospel" class (a missionary preparation class) were women, and some professors actively encouraged women to consider a mission. Another article pointed out how the cliché "waiting for a missionary," common in LDS circles, no longer applied only to girlfriends waiting for elders to return home, but also to boyfriends waiting for sisters to return home.

The articles generated letters to the editor, which told of the tension that some women felt. Two said they had experienced pressure to serve a mission before marriage, and they were also aware of the First Presidency's counsel that missions shouldn't interfere with a specific marriage proposal. They felt the two came into direct conflict with each other, which they said turned it into a very sensitive issue for them. They had also talked with young men who said they wouldn't marry a woman unless she had served a mission. The women stated: "We would love to serve a mission and we both struggle with this decision. We also recognize that marriage is a higher priority. Yet the pressure we have felt to serve a mission has caused us to feel that if we were to marry without serving a mission, somehow we have failed."[134]

Sisters serving missions was still a point of discussion among General Authorities and sisters over a decade later. In 2007, Apostle M. Russell Ballard reminded young women that they don't have a responsibility to serve, that it is an obligation of the elders that comes with holding the priesthood, and that marriage should come before mission for sisters. But, he continued, a full-time mission is appropriate for a woman if she is worthy and if it fits her circumstances. It was also recognized that sisters bring particular assets to the mission field that mission presidents value: they are good teachers, they are empathetic, and they relate particularly well to other females.[135] When President Monson announced the lowering of the age requirements for elders and sisters in 2012, he reminded young men that serving a mission is a priesthood responsibility, and that while sisters aren't under the same mandate to serve, the Church does recognize that sisters make valuable contributions as missionaries and that their service is welcomed.

In talking with two nineteen-year-old sisters who had just completed their first year at BYU and who were in the mission field in 2015, they reported that the interest and pressure for sisters to serve at the younger age is still pervasive on the BYU campus.

Pressure away from BYU and Utah. The pressure to serve doesn't appear to be as intense for prospective sisters away from the BYU campus, the state of Utah, BYU-Idaho, and BYU-Hawaii, but the pressure is still evident. A sister from Maine preparing to leave for her mission said she has seen a growing tendency in the Latter-day Saint Church to think that sisters who are of age (twenty-one at the time of the interview), who aren't married, who may be in college or even graduated, "who aren't really doing anything with their lives," are (in the sister's words) considered a "horrible member" of the Church if they don't serve. Serving a mission is the best thing they can do; it is the only thing they should do. She sees this attitude particularly at the family level; parents are now realizing that it is a good thing for their daughters to go on a mission, not just their sons.

The pressure to decide. A sister who served in the early 2000s said her seminary (high school) teacher said girls should really pray about going on a mission, even though it isn't an expectation. She said some of the girls in the class were "taken aback," because it hadn't even been discussed in their homes. Some sisters said they only began to think about it when they were asked (or prodded) by friends, relatives, bishop, or stake president. When the topic of serving would come up the sisters were asked, "Well, won't you at least pray about it?" A sister said initially she became defensive when asked about her plans. She would think, "I don't have to go on a mission! Leave me alone!" One sister who originally was "dead set" against serving a mission said her older brothers and a sister kept asking her if she was going, and it got to the point of her saying, "If anyone else asks me, I am going to scream!" But she agreed to pray about it, and as she was sitting in church one Sunday she saw the image of a missionary nametag with her name on it, and she felt an "overwhelming peace." She knew she was to go. She was twenty-two at the time, and she left four months later.

Another sister told of a more dramatic experience. She had no desire to go, but after persistent enquiries from friends and relatives, she agreed to pray about it. She had been praying for a month, and she still didn't want to go. But during a friend's farewell service, she reported: "I was sitting there when I got my answer, 'You are supposed to go on a mission' and I said, 'No!' The answer came again, 'You are supposed to go on a mission,' and then I knew the answer was from God, that I was supposed to go on a mission, and that is why I am here today."

"Tell him the whole story," whispered her companion during our interview. It seems her "No" was not a mental "No," but rather a loud, audible "No!" heard by many people in the congregation. "Everyone turned and looked at me," she said, "thinking I was disagreeing with something the speaker had said. That never happens in a Mormon church. I was so shaken by the force of the answer to my prayer that I ran from the meeting, crying."

She went on to have a successful mission.

Not all responded in a defensive manner. Sometimes a comment or simple question sparked an interest in serving. For some it was a comment made by someone they respected. One sister said she had never thought about going on a mission until her brother encouraged her to think about it. Then an LDS college official from her school told her she would always have time for school, but she wouldn't always have time for a mission. She was in the mission field four months later.

A sister from southern California reported she hadn't considered a mission because she had other plans; she was waiting for her boyfriend to return from his mission, and then they would get married. As she was seeing her brother off on his mission at the airport, her grandfather asked, "When are you going to send in your mission papers?" She responded she wasn't going on a mission because she had other plans. But the seed had been planted. She eventually turned in her papers and left on her mission.

The boyfriend returned home and married someone else.

How to decide: to pray, or not to pray? Sisters have therefore been placed in the position of having to seriously consider whether to serve. When asked how they went about deciding, many said they turned to prayer and, in many cases, "fervent prayer," and to fasting, too. A sister said it involved "a lot of soul-searching, prayer, and fasting." When I asked a sister from the Northwest, who served in the Northeast and who waited until she was older than twenty-one to serve, how she decided it was right for her, she said, "When you pray about it and it feels good about going, then you do it."

Another who said she hadn't thought much about going on a mission while growing up said that people kept asking her if she was going, so she finally agreed to pray about it. She struggled and prayed for three months until one day, "My heart changed and it filled with love and peace. I realized I should go."

A sister who served in Italy shared, "I prayed about it and I wanted the Lord to tell me, 'Go on a mission,' or to do this or whatever. I wasn't getting an answer and then I finally realized I needed to make a decision and ask Him for confirmation. So I thought and decided there really was nothing better I could be doing with my life at this point in time than to go on a mission. So I decided to go and I prayed about it and I felt that would absolutely be the best thing I could be doing with my life at this point. So I left."

Some sisters chose *not* to pray, but for opposite reasons. A sister who said she never wanted to go on a mission said when she turned twenty a friend asked if she was going on a mission when she turned twenty-one. She said she wasn't because she wanted to finish her schooling. But then she kept getting "feelings" that she should go on a mission, and she kept thinking that she didn't want to do it. She said she didn't want to pray about it, because she knew that if she prayed about it, she would get an answer she didn't want. She finally decided to pray about it, she felt she should go on a mission, everything "fell into place," and she was soon on her mission. She said she didn't have to go, but she needed to.

Another sister took the same approach—of not wanting to pray about it because she was afraid of the answer—but for the opposite reason. She *wanted* to go. She chose not to pray if she should go, fearing she would get an answer that she didn't want to hear. She said: "I didn't want God to tell me, 'No,' so I didn't ask. I never asked, and still haven't." She decided that if she wasn't meant to serve, some disaster would befall her; but short of that, she was going. She went on to have a successful mission.

Delaying the decision. The majority of sister interviewees delayed deciding until much closer to the time when they would serve. A sister commented, "My basic frame of mind is that I would like to go, but I am not going to make the decision until I get to that point in time when I need to make the decision." Some hadn't even thought that far ahead.

Some described it as a "snap decision" made when they reached the required age, or had passed it.

The decision to serve a mission at the last minute came as a surprise or even as a shock to many families, creating (at least initially) concern, worry, and, in some cases, resistance. A sister shared that her mother had been planning on sending her sons on a mission ever since they were born, but she hadn't considered it a possibility for her daughter. Thus the mother was shocked when her twenty-one-year-old daughter announced that she too was going on a mission in just three months time. She struggled with saying goodbye.

Some who decided late faced parental opposition. Most sisters hadn't started a mission fund or didn't have much money saved, and parents were concerned with how to pay for the mission. This especially was the case for families who were already supporting a son and in some cases two sons in the mission field. Some parents didn't initially admit to this concern, saying instead things like, "I think it is fine for sisters to go on missions, but I would be concerned if it were my daughter," and, "I think it is a good idea, but I don't think you are quite ready for it." One sister told of having lengthy, frustrating discussions with her father about the topic until finally she said to him, "I think you are being a poop about it!" Her father laughed and said maybe he was. He then became supportive of her plans.

Last-minute decisions also surprised boyfriends. A sister told of getting to the point of looking at wedding rings with her boyfriend, but then deciding to serve a mission instead. She said she vacillated; she wanted to go, she didn't want to go. But she had an "overwhelming feeling" that it was God's will for her. Her boyfriend was disappointed and wavered back and forth in supporting her. "But," she said, "he knew, and I knew, that is what I needed to do." When she finally decided to serve, she said it was more exciting than all of the diamonds she had looked at. She left for the MTC within a matter of months.

Her boyfriend married someone else while she was gone.

Some had graduated from college but were undecided what they wanted to do. They didn't want to go to graduate school or get a job. They decided it was a good time to go on a mission.

Some had been waiting for their missionary boyfriends to return from their missions, but things didn't work out in their relationships. They decided to go on a mission.

Almost to a person, sisters said they eventually gained the support of their parents and families, but such support wasn't always forthcoming from their LDS friends or non-LDS acquaintances. Some said it was a painful process deciding to serve; when they expressed interest in going they got mixed responses from LDS friends. Some thought it was a wonderful idea and encouraged them to go, whereas others told them that since they were females they didn't have to, so why do it? One kept her going a secret from her friends, because she was afraid "opposition" would come. Everyone's mouth dropped open when she made her announcement.

A sister who was halfway through her college career and was turning twenty-one in a few months and seriously considering a mission said that a number of non-members ("influential adults" as she described them) told her, "it was a stupid idea and a waste of her time to go," that she should finish her education instead. It had a negative effect on her, and she wasn't sure what to do. Finally she opened *Doctrine and Covenants* and saw this highlighted passage: "But purify your hearts before me; and then go ye into all the world, and preach my gospel unto every creature who has not received it." (*D & C* 112:28). She decided to go, and she frequently returned to the passage, because non-members continued to tell her it was a bad idea. She didn't think they understood.

Motivation to serve. Interviewees gave a variety of reasons for what motivated them to serve a mission. I had expected many of them, but was surprised by some. Family members who had served missions were some of the most powerful influences on sisters: fathers; in a few cases, mothers; brothers; and older sisters who had served. Watching siblings and attending their homecomings had a powerful influence. A sister whose older brother served said she saw the blessings, benefits, and personal growth he experienced while on his mission, and that motivated her to want to go. She wanted the same for herself.

Many said they wanted to spread the Mormon gospel and to serve others out of thankfulness for what the Lord had done for them. One said she felt she had been given so much, and while she knew she wasn't expected to go on a mission, she almost felt obligated to share with others what had been given to her. This line from a Latter-day Saint hymn summed up her feelings: "Because I have been given much, I too must give."

Children of divorce said they wanted to repay what the Lord had done for them. They reported having a difficult time growing up and coming to terms with divorces that had "dissipated" their families. They felt as though they were "marked" in school, different from everyone else. It took them a long time to get over it, and they said they learned to depend on Jesus throughout the ordeal. Now they wanted to serve a mission to share the joy and strength they had received in their relationship with Jesus; to "pay back" Jesus, although they knew they couldn't do it completely.

Some spoke of the ideal, or the normal progression that a Latter-day Saint woman is supposed to experience—education, marriage, family—and how it didn't work out for them. Some lacked a sense of direction after high school, some didn't have a good, initial college experience, and some couldn't find employment. They said they prayed about it, and they received an answer that was undeniable; it was a "swift kick" to go into the mission field, as one described it, because they were wasting their time where they were and doing what they were doing. They came to realize that these negative experiences prepared them to understand that they needed to go on a mission.

Some expected they would follow the "normal progression," but when it didn't work out, it forced them to confront their assumptions and their identity. A sister from Utah talked of how her mother had married and started a family at the age of nineteen and how she assumed she would do the same. But when she turned nineteen and there were no marriage prospects ("It looked like I wouldn't get married for another ten years"), she spent the next two years feeling directionless. She worked, she went to night school, and she dated some. That's when she started thinking: "I am not my mom and my life is not turning out like hers. I am a completely different person and that's okay." She needed to decide what her own belief systems and values were and to get a direction for her life. That is when she decided to serve a mission. "This is a really important time in my life," she said during our interview, "and I know coming on my mission was the right decision."

A sister from Utah said she and her girlfriends agreed they would go on missions if they weren't married when they turned twenty-one. When they all eventually reached that age, she was the only one not married, and she fulfilled her promise.

Many spoke of believing they are living in the End Times, that the Mormon gospel must be proclaimed, and how that motivated them to want to serve. They spoke of "Heavenly Father sending his royal army to earth in the next generation." While Latter-day Saints aren't date setters, a sister said she believes Christ's second coming is "rapidly approaching." Another said she feels the Last Days are coming and that much work needs to be done; many still need to hear the gospel, and that is why she and other sisters she knows have chosen to serve.

Family dynamics of various sorts influenced why some sisters chose to serve. For some, they were fulfilling a role for their family. One said she was the only sibling in the family to serve, and it made her mother happy. Another considering a mission spoke of how all of her other siblings had served, and while she didn't feel pressure from her parents to serve, she knew they would be happy if she did, so she felt pressure from within not to disappoint them. "Maybe that is the kind of pressure I feel," she said. "Not negative pressure from my parents, but pressure from within to please."

Another reason to serve that related to family dynamics, that I was not expecting, were those instances where sisters stepped in to fill a void left when a brother either didn't go on a mission, or when he came home early. Girlfriends tripped up mission plans of young men in some instances, or serving a mission didn't work out for the young men and they returned home early. In both circumstances parents were very upset by the sons' actions. Some parents refused to go to farewells and homecomings thereafter, because it upset them and they worried about what fellow Church members would think of them and their family.

A sister who had a brother who returned home after a few weeks in the mission field said she hadn't considered a mission before then, but she struggled as she approached her twenty-first birthday, "when it came my turn," and whether to serve in his place. She said she wasn't ready to go on a mission at that point, and she feared that should she go then, she too might feel a need to come home early, and she didn't want to put her mother through that agony again. She decided to go a year later, and she served a successful mission, much to her mother's delight.

A sister whose brother's mission plans were derailed by a girlfriend said she decided she would take over his work, fill that void in the family, and make her mother proud of her children. It meant a lot to her parents to have at least one child go on a mission.

Regardless of their initial motivation to serve, or when they decided, all said they served because they wanted to share their faith with others. A sister who attended BYU summed up the general motivation of sisters: "I wanted to spread the gospel and tell others of its importance. It is an urgent message and people need to know the truth."

Doubts do linger for some, even after a decision has been made to serve. One sister said she struggled with the decision prior to her mission, and she continued to have doubts even halfway through the MTC where, she said, her doubts increased "one hundred fold." Finally, she felt it was God's will for her, and she continued on. Another confessed she still questioned whether she wanted to do it until the very end of her stay at the MTC. She was glad she continued on with her mission. One interviewee was halfway through her mission, and she was still unclear why she was serving.

Sister Safety

Safety is an issue for all missionaries, especially for sisters. They can be targets for harassment, perhaps because they appear vulnerable. Sisters told of being spit on, of garbage being dumped on them, and of being run off properties. An elder who served in Mexico said sisters were treated "roughly" in the streets, while a missionary who served in Eastern Europe said sisters faced special challenges in his mission. They were harassed "a lot" on the streets and on buses, particularly by drunk men. Certain rules applied to sisters in the Eastern European mission: they couldn't go tracting or street contacting like the elders, and they had strict curfews.

Others spoke of special conditions that applied only to sisters. A sister who served in Washington, D.C., said her mission president was very strict; sisters lived outside the city, they weren't allowed to go out at night, and they had to have a Church member present when teaching an investigator. A returned missionary who served in Paris in the early 1970s said there weren't many sisters in the city because of the potential danger.

Scary experiences. A sister serving in southern Italy said her fair complexion and blond hair made her stand out; she was "really noticed," and she got a lot of attention "to say the least." Not all of the attention was welcomed. Sisters also weren't supposed to be out after dark, and she remembered a couple of times when she and her companion got caught out late and had "scary" experiences. They were walking along a deserted side street in Naples when two young men going by on a motorcycle grabbed her bag. She held on to it, and they started dragging her along the street until she finally let go. For their efforts the thieves got her letters from home, a Book of Mormon, and Book of Mormon videos.

It happened a second time. This time she had her bag strapped across the inside of her coat, and two young men on a motorcycle must have thought she had something valuable in there, for they rode by and tried to rip it off her. They dragged her along until finally the strap broke, and they got away with it.

"Those were kind of scary experiences," she said in an understated way.

She felt vulnerable at times and was glad she was always with a companion. If they were going to be out late, they would have elders go with them. There were strict rules about teaching people of the opposite sex. They couldn't go into a house and teach a man without elders coming with them.

The three Nephites. As is true of folklore stories in general, stories about missionaries and their experiences provide insights into the mission experience, as well as deeper insights into missionary beliefs and attitudes. There is a rich folklore of how missionaries are given Divine protection while involved in what are potentially dangerous situations, and there are an increasing number that relate to sister missionaries.

A popular story has two sister missionaries knocking at the door of a deserted house. A man answers the door, but he quickly turns them away. Later that day they see his face on a wanted poster. He is an escaped prisoner who had been jailed for the murder of a number of young women in their early twenties. The sisters lead the police to the man, and as he is arrested they ask him why he didn't try to hurt them. He responded there were three large men with swords standing behind them and had he tried to hurt them, he would have been killed.

William A. Wilson, Emeritus professor of English at BYU and director of the BYU Folklore Archives, has done considerable research on Mormon folklore and says there are two important features to the story. The first is that it draws on the "Three Nephites" story found in the Book of Mormon (3 Nephi 28). The three Nephites are said to be disciples of Jesus who remain on earth until Christ's Second Advent, and until that time they are to help bring converts to the LDS Church. Wilson has collected over 1,400 Nephite stories, and they frequently play the role of protectors of missionaries. Their presence is typically not known to the missionaries, only to those who would do them harm.

Wilson also observes that while Nephites as bodyguards of missionaries has been a part of Mormon folklore for a long time, the fact that it is sister missionaries in this case is a relatively recent phenomenon. The first time such a story was recounted by a returned missionary was in 1985, and none refer to events before 1980. Wilson sees this as another instance where women and sister missionaries are assuming new roles in the Latter-day Saint Church, and that it is being reflected in the folklore of the Church.[136]

Types of Sister Missionary Service

There is a broad array of missionary activities available to sisters. In addition to proselytizing missions, they may serve as tour guides at Temple Square in Salt Lake City, as tour guides at historic Church sites, in Church visitors' centers, and in social service missions. I was able to interview sisters who had served in three of these settings.

Proselytizing sisters. The majority of sister interviewees were serving or had served proselytizing missions. Sisters and elders share similar proselytizing experiences: they keep the same schedule, they tract and street contact when it is safe, they visit with lapsed members, and they teach. They too have the occasional door slammed in their face. They provide service in the community, and they engage in social and cultural activities on Preparation Day.

People aren't as used to encountering sister missionaries as they are elders, and when they see the nametags with "Sister Jones" and "Sister White" on them, people frequently assume the young women are Roman Catholics nuns. A sister from Utah said that having "Sister" on the nametag, but not one's first name, is a bit "scary" for some people. Initially it can create a perceived barrier, but most sisters are able to engage people in conversation, and they soon become comfortable with the sisters.

A sister from California said her mission president told sisters not to be afraid of husbands and to engage them in conversation. She and her companion looked at each other and laughed, because they didn't have a problem with them. In fact, men were the only ones they were teaching. Men are sometimes more receptive than women, they said. The sisters wondered if it was because men want to talk with cute, young girls, but they said that didn't seem to be the case.

Sisters at Temple Square. The smallest mission in the Latter-day Saint Church is at Temple Square in the heart of Salt Lake City, Utah. Encompassing thirty-five acres, the Square is the spiritual and administrative center of the Latter-day Saint Church. It includes the Salt Lake City Temple, the Mormon Tabernacle, the Church Headquarters building, two visitors' centers, the Conference Center, and Brigham Young's house, the Beehive House. Temple Square is the most-visited tourist site in Utah, with up to five million members and non-members visiting annually.

Until 1995, tours of Temple Square were conducted by volunteers and returned missionaries who lived in the area. In that year President Hinckley said there should be a permanent presence of tour guides there, and a mission comprised of sisters and senior missionaries was established. President Hinckley further stated their goal was to answer questions about the Latter-day Saint Church, to show that it is a Christian church, and, to the extent possible, provide this information in the language of the visitors, further advancing the Church's goals of providing its message to all nations and tongues. An amazing number of languages are available for Temple Square tours in 2015—over forty—from Albanian to Urdu.

When I visited Temple Square in May 2008, two smiling sisters greeted me at the entrance. One had a Mongolian flag below her nametag, while the other wore an Italian flag. I asked the purpose of the flags. They said it represented their home countries. They were on call to lead the thirty-minute tours in their native tongues. Otherwise they led the tours in English. Both spoke excellent English. They said many of the sisters speak more than two languages. (I later observed the Mongolian sister leading a French-speaking tour.) The multilingual missionaries played a vital role during the 2002 Winter Olympics held in Salt Lake City, and they received worldwide attention from the media and from the many international visitors.

I asked the sisters if I could interview them about their missionary experiences on Temple Square. They informed me I would need to get permission from their mission president, since they receive frequent requests from the media and others to talk with them. After a brief conversation with the mission president, where I explained my project, he kindly granted me permission to interview some of the sisters. I interviewed four of them: they were from Australia, Germany, South Africa, and Zambia. I talked with them two at a time, and the mission president didn't sit in on the conversations. Two of the sisters were his assistants, the only two sister assistants to the president in the mission field.

I asked how they felt when they opened their white envelopes and discovered they were assigned to Temple Square. They reported great excitement; they had wanted to go foreign, and to be called to the spiritual center of the Church was the best calling they could imagine. But being called there also caused them to feel some sense of inadequacy; they said they focused on their perceived weaknesses and didn't feel confident they could do it.

I asked how their mission experience differed from that of proselytizing missionaries. It differed in two ways, they explained. People interested in the Latter-day Saint Church come to them instead of their having to seek them out, and since they spend only thirty minutes with visitors and never see them again, they have no idea what long-term effects their message might have. "It has taught me how vital those thirty minutes are," commented a sister, "for it gives me the opportunity to share my testimony many times each day and to answer questions they don't ask when missionaries appear at their door." She added that many visitors say their knowledge of the Church comes from secondhand sources, and thus she is acutely aware that people will leave with an impression and understanding of the LDS Church that is based largely on their impressions of her: her demeanor, her knowledge of the Church's history and beliefs, and the sincerity of her testimony that the Church is true.

I asked what challenges they face. They said while they find it enriching that their companions are typically from another country and thus provide them with great cross-cultural experiences, it can be a challenge to adjust to each other's cultural background, especially since their companions change periodically and they have to go through a new adjustment period with each new person. They also find it frustrating not knowing what impact the tours have on visitors. They find it physically and emotionally demanding since they are on their feet all day long, and they have to project their best image at all times.

They also have to deal with hecklers. Anti-Mormon detractors will join tour groups and want to argue with the sisters. They question that Joseph Smith was a prophet and that the Book of Mormon is sacred scripture, and they question the sisters' salvation, telling them they are misguided and going to Hell.

I asked how they handle such situations. They responded they are not to argue with people; their role is to explain the beliefs of the Latter-day Saint Church and to share their testimony. And, yes, it does bother them. They tell the hecklers they are welcome to stay with the tour, but they will not debate with them. A sister said it makes her sad to see someone who is so unhappy with something she finds so sacred. Plus, it takes away from the experience of others on the tour; she isn't able to devote as much attention to them as she would like.

The sisters said groups of detractors come and split up among various tour groups. They said General Conference time, which is held twice yearly in April and October, is especially challenging because busloads of anti-Mormons will appear in Temple Square. Some are even flown in, they added.

Some proselytizing missionaries in the field perceive Temple Square missionaries as having the "easy life," as being "pampered," as being able to passively wait for people to come to them, instead of having to go out and find investigators. Some proselytizing sisters I interviewed in the field said they wouldn't want to serve on Temple Square, because they say finding people, going into their homes, teaching them, and watching them change and progress is more fulfilling.

The Latter-day Saint Church understands the value of the traditional proselytizing experience, and Temple Square sisters are also assigned to traditional missions for four months during their mission, typically in the United States. Sisters say they enjoy the experience, as it gives them the opportunity to find and teach investigators, to see lives change over time, and to work with local members. They also have their share of doors slammed in their faces.

It is true that Temple Square missionaries have a different mission experience when compared to the more traditional proselytizing missionaries, but neither have it easy. I interviewed a sister tour guide while visiting Temple Square in 1994. She said Church members would come up to her and say, "You have a cushy mission." General Authorities countered by telling the guides they had the hardest mission, since they are always representing the LDS Church to non-members and their days are very long. The young woman showed me a slip that indicated where she was supposed to be and what she was supposed to be doing from 8:00 A.M. to 10:00 P.M. Her schedule had her rotating through various locations on the Square throughout the day. Four different people had her schedule and were potentially watching her.

This is in stark contrast to missionaries in the field where there is little or no direct daily supervision.

Sisters at the Joseph Smith Birthplace Memorial in Sharon, Vermont. Another popular destination for members and non-members alike is Joseph Smith's birthplace in Sharon, Vermont, which includes a visitors' center overseen by a senior missionary couple and staffed with senior and sister missionaries.

A sister who served at the Joseph Smith Memorial found it "an incredible opportunity." She grew up hearing prophets of the Church say that the Holy Land is the most holy ground because that is where Christ walked, and the second most holy ground is that associated with the prophet of the Restoration, Joseph Smith. She said that while serving there she gained a strong testimony of the Restoration and what kind of man Joseph was.

One sister confessed to being somewhat skeptical about Joseph Smith when she arrived there, wondering whether he was in fact a prophet or whether he had other, more human, motives when founding the Church. She said that after spending three months there reading about Smith, meditating on his life, writings, and teachings, and sharing his story time and again with visitors, she came away with a greater appreciation of his prophetic role. She attributed her change to the strong sense of "the Spirit" that she found there. She thought how appropriate it was the birthplace of the prophet is where she gained her knowledge that he was indeed a prophet of God.

Another sister said she loved non-members coming through the memorial. One of the first things she would ask non-member visitors would be what their idea of a prophet was, and what a prophet should be. They typically responded with the Old Testament description of a prophet having a beard, cane, and robes. She would agree with them that that was definitely a prophet, and then she would say how she believed God had sent a prophet in modern times, and just as Moses was commanded to deliver the Ten Commandments, so was Joseph Smith commanded to deliver the Book of Mormon. She said every prophet has a message that the Lord wants shared with humanity, and she would then share the First Vision with the visitors and Joseph's other miraculous experiences. She went on to say there is a living prophet on earth today, the President of The Church of Jesus Christ of Latter-day Saints, that he is in direct communication with the Divine, and that he is God's messenger on earth with a message for us all.

She said she could be quite bold and candid with visitors regarding Joseph, because that is what they expected at his memorial.

A Bimodal Distribution?

One of the more awkward topics that surfaced during research for this book had to do with what a returned sister missionary and current college professor labeled as the perceived "bimodal distribution" of the effectiveness of sisters. Put more bluntly, there is the perception among some that sisters make the best missionaries—and that they also make the worst missionaries; that committed and motivated sisters can do wonders, while sisters who came out for the wrong reasons may not contribute much to the mission. On the one end of the spectrum are the very committed, true believers who are very bright, very smart, and who come into the mission with the attitude, "I'm taking control," whereas at the other end are those sisters who say, "I am not married, what shall I do? If I go on a mission, maybe I will meet someone."

A sister who served in Japan in the early 1970s described this bimodal perception. She said sisters were either perceived as an "anchor," as more mature, and as contributing to more baptisms, or they were perceived as being emotionally and physically weak and a "bother."

There were female and male interviewees who said they felt there was some truth to the stereotype, but there were also those, sisters and elders, who said it wasn't a true representation, that there are effective and not-so-effective elders, just as there are effective and not-so-effective sisters. Some suggested that the sisters' smaller numbers contributed to the bimodal perception, that since they are fewer in number they are more noticeable. Others said that the sisters' greater propensity to talk about their feelings and concerns, as compared to the more reticent elders, contributed to the perception that sisters complain more and are less stable emotionally.

Enough spoke of it that I felt it necessary to include it in this book.

Positive impressions of sister missionaries. General Authorities, mission presidents, A.P.s, and elders sing the praises of sister missionaries, and especially of their spirituality. The Apostle Boyd K. Packer said while he didn't like to admit it, he thinks women are more spiritual than men. A General Authority told me that sisters are more likely to want to discuss deep spiritual things—the meaning of life, happiness, etcetera—whereas it has to be "pulled out" of elders. A one-time mission president said sisters have a broad spiritual base and that spiritual things come more quickly to them. He believes women are more spiritually orientated than men; they come on their mission because they want to, and thus sisters tend to be more dedicated. He pointed to the fact that more women than men convert to the Latter-day Saint Church.

Sisters were described as putting "a lot more feeling into the work," as more apt to share their true feelings, whereas elders were more likely to just go through the motions. Sisters were described as being more loving, more compassionate, more empathetic, more sensitive to other's feelings, more patient, more responsible, harder workers, better listeners, better at details and recordkeeping, better able to relate to women, able to strike up conversations more easily than elders, and as having a good influence on younger elders, because sisters were more stable, had a calming influence on them, and helped the elders become more sensitive.

It is felt that because of their maturity, empathy, and communication skills, they can reach people elders cannot.

Others spoke of sisters as being less intimidating than elders, of people not feeling as threatened by sisters, of feeling closer to them, of their having a friendliness and love about them, and thus their being more successful in being invited into peoples' homes. A sister who served in France said she observed that when two, tall, American young men in dark clothing showed up at the door of a sixty-five-year-old female, she found it scary, whereas this wasn't the case when two young women appeared. A mission president who served in Venezuela said that he *begged* for more sisters because they did such a good job. Macho fathers didn't want young elders teaching their daughters, but they welcomed sisters.

The sister who served in France also said that many sisters paid much more attention to integrating the new person into the Church after baptism. She did add, however, that she felt sisters didn't always know when to "let go" of the person.

A district leader in Canada said the joke among elders was that all sisters did was bake cookies for investigators. He said they had a knack for leaving baked goods and thoughtful notes for investigators, and consequently sisters had a better relationship with them.

It was also said that sister missionaries tend to "liven things up" at meetings. An A.P. said elders would get kind of boring; they would go to the same old meetings and do the same old thing, whereas sisters were more jovial and outgoing.

An elder who served as an A.P. in the Northwest echoed many of the above descriptions of sisters. He said sisters were typically smarter, more mature, and more spiritual than elders, and thus didn't require as much oversight. He said many of them were "phenomenal." "In general," he said, "I think they were our superiors. There is no doubt about that."

He went on to describe how effective sisters could be, compared to elders. There were situations when elders had been meeting with investigators for months, sometimes years, but the person wouldn't agree to baptism. Sisters would go into the situation, and they would bring the hesitating investigators to the baptismal pool in a short period of time.

Many interviewees, sisters and elders, echoed this experience. A sister who served in California in the late 1990s said there was an elderly gentleman with whom the elders had worked for years, but who had resisted baptism. She and her companion began meeting with him, and two visits later he said, "Sisters, I want to be baptized." For some reason, he wanted sisters to bring him to that point. The sister said they really didn't do anything different or extraordinary; she thought maybe he just related better to women. The sisters asked him why he chose to be baptized at that time, and he said, "It is you, sisters."

A sister shared an experience where she and her companion worked with an investigator with whom elders had become frustrated and who thought he had no potential for baptism. He was a "dry Mormon," someone who the missionaries said knows the message is true, but who hasn't entered the baptismal waters. (She said every area has at least one of these investigators.) It turned out the investigator had anxiety problems. He would go to church and feel overwhelmed by all the people and by all the expectations the Church placed on its members. He said it felt like his chest was caving in, and he couldn't breathe. The sister shared that she could identify with him, because while at the MTC she had gone through major anxiety attacks herself, where she too felt like her chest was caving in and she couldn't breathe. She and her companion were extra patient with him and taught him the discussions, but she admitted they too became frustrated because he wasn't keeping all of the commandments. But in the end he was baptized before the sisters left the area. He said the sisters had "a special effect" on him; he felt "a certain spiritual feeling when meeting with them," and said they had a "special spirit about them."

A returned sister missionary from New York said she feels one of the reasons sisters are more effective is because they don't hold the priesthood and are not eligible for leadership positions; thus there isn't the competitiveness for advancement among sisters that can be found among elders. Sisters don't aspire to move up the hierarchy, and she found that a much more liberating experience during her mission. She felt sisters aren't as focused on numbers as elders are; rather, they're focused on people. She added that sisters had their own support network when she served, and they wrote to companions after moving on, which is something elders typically don't do.

"Sisters are on a whole different wavelength," she said.

A young elder struggled to find the words when asked how sisters are different. He said he didn't think he could describe it. "Sisters just have a different way of doing things. It is a mystery we elders will never understand. Some things you don't question. Women are just different from men."

His companion agreed: "They just don't do things the same as elders. They are more sensitive and more caring. They are just sisters."

Negative impressions of sister missionaries. The perceived weaknesses of sisters as enumerated in the bimodal theory also surfaced in the interviews—mental health issues, emotionalism, and dependency.

An A.P. who served in the 1980s said he knew sisters would be upset with him for saying it, but he felt there was some truth to the theory of the bimodal distribution of sisters. He said there were some extremely hardworking, dedicated sister missionaries, but once in the mission office he found some had serious emotional issues, especially depression. Looking back on it today, given the stresses of the mission, he thought, "and no wonder." He said some had emotional baggage from the past, including abuse, which was brought to the surface during the rigors of the mission. He wondered if for some a mission was an attempt for a possible solution for that; to rise above it, to go out and serve others instead of focusing on their past.

An A.P. who served in Germany said when sisters were healthy and active, they were very effective, but they tended to take up more of the mission president's time than elders. He thought missions were harder, both physically and emotionally, for sisters; there was a lot of stress, and as a result the president had to deal with a number of issues. He said the president and his wife spent "a lot of time" dealing with issues relating to the sisters' physical and emotional well-being.

A sister said her mission president's wife discussed with sisters how a mission is such an emotionally trying time. They are constantly facing rejection, and it can't help but undermine their self-confidence and self-image, as well as dredge up old problems, fears, and doubts. It also intensifies un-confessed baggage they may still be carrying. "You are human before you are anything else," the mission president's wife would say.

A sister observed that she saw more weaknesses in herself since she went on her mission, much more than she ever did before. She was more aware of them because of being on her mission. She observed: "I have learned that I am so human, that it's not even funny!" Some sisters said they did share their feelings of inadequacy and anxiety during interviews with the mission president.

A sister who served in Washington, D.C., said sisters tend to be more mature, but they also tend to complain more. She then added (with tongue in cheek), "At least that is what I have heard!" A mission president who served in Mexico said sisters tended to be sick more, to whine more, and to play up their dependency.

A sister who served in France in the 1960s as a traveling sister (one who visited all the sisters and helped with their training, teaching, and personal problems) said she saw both types in her role as a travelling sister, that bimodality was evident, and one of the reasons for the traveling sister role was clearly counseling. She heard how difficult the work was, how isolated they felt, and their complaints about younger, less-educated elders who lorded their authority over the sisters. The personal costs were very high for some sisters, and she spent much of her time serving as a counselor. She said the "worst" missionaries probably had the greatest needs, wanting the elders to give them a blessing, wanting the elders to come and fix their faucets, to play up their dependencies, which she suggested would play out in their own marriages when they came home. She also noted there could be "hiding out": the sisters would avoid tracting and not do other things expected of them, because it was much safer to stay in the apartment and be with someone like themselves. She said she was very sympathetic with that, because she too experienced emotional issues, but she said she didn't allow herself to withdraw. Looking back on it now, she said she probably would have been a healthier person had she done it, rather than trying to rigidly follow the rules.

A no-nonsense sister and her companion said some of the stigmas that are placed on sisters come from those sisters who go on a mission for the wrong reasons. They are there to find a husband and will play up their dependency while doing so. Said she, mockingly: "Elder, can you come over and change my light bulb? After all, you are my zone leader." They said there are some who aspire to marry only a zone leader or an A.P. It takes a long time to overcome the negative effects of missionaries—sisters and elders—who are out for the wrong reasons.

Their advice for sisters who are looking for husbands—stay home and go to BYU.

Sisters can also be too independent, that being older they don't feel rules that are appropriate for younger elders apply to them. A mission president recounted that two sisters informed him that they weren't going to submit weekly reports anymore, which they felt they didn't need to do. The mission president responded, "Yes, you are, or I will send you home." They resumed sending their reports. Mission presidents and A.P.s commented that some sisters will have the attitude, "I don't have to do this, I volunteered for it, so I will determine how much effort I will put into it," with the result that they don't give one hundred percent.

Bowing to the spiritual authority of elders, especially younger, immature elders, is a point of contention for many sisters. An A.P. who served in Germany said many older sisters don't want to be bossed around by an eighteen or nineteen-year-old young man.

Some elders counter that they find sisters to be too bossy, to act too much like a mother, with the result that some elders don't get along well with sisters. Elders refer to such sisters as SWATs—"Sisters With Attitudes."

"'SWATs' are nasty," reported an elder. "Don't mess with them."

A sister reported that sometimes there is competition between missionaries, with sisters trying to outdo elders: "You may have the priesthood, but I will show you!"

A returned sister missionary wrote that her trainer taught her a valuable lesson: sisters had to work harder than elders to gain their respect, and sisters shouldn't cry in front of elders. To show such emotions was perceived as weakness, whereas she said it actually was a sign of frustration and exhaustion. She said not causing trouble was what was most valued by elders, and if a sister ever did need help or a blessing (since only elders could do it—since only they held the priesthood), sisters had to go to the elders, and then they were considered a problem, because they were sick or troubled. Thus they were in a bind.

Mormon folklore doesn't always cast sister missionaries in a positive light. An elder interviewee shared a story that was popular among elders. Two sisters were driving down an isolated road, and they ran out of gas. They had a bottle of water with them and said: "We have faith and know the Lord is looking out for us. If we pray, we know the Lord will turn this water into gas." They poured the liquid into the gas tank, it didn't turn to gas, and it fouled the engine.

"Shame on them," said the elder recounting the story. "They should have prayed first and made sure the water had turned into gasoline before putting it into the gas tank. They should have been more mindful. You would never see an elder do that."

In a similar vein, the Mormon folklorist William Wilson pointed out that there are varying interpretations given to the story of the Three Nephites who were protecting the sisters from the murderer. While sisters say it legitimates their serving as missionaries, that the Lord protects sisters as well as elders, Wilson said that a male student told him that in his mission elders interpreted it as a negative statement about sisters. The three Nephites are no longer present in similar stories involving elders—the message being that elders, through their inner strength and inspiration, can take care of themselves—whereas sisters need external help. Wilson said he hopes this is an isolated instance, but he says it is an example of how folklore is "a sensitive indicator of missionary attitudes and beliefs, helping to take the pulse of missionary life."

A candid sister who served in the mid-1990s said sisters probably have the capacity to be the worst, because women are catty in general, or can be, and they can get upset over the "dumbest things." She said if there is a contention between two sisters who are companions, they are not going to get any work done. She also said it would be very easy for two sisters to not get along, "for women are sort of competitive and jealous and stuff like that."

A sister suggested sisters' "whining tendency" is greater. If things aren't going right, sisters tend to whine and say, "I can't bear this," whereas elders usually don't say this, or keep it to themselves.

A sister serving in Northern New England said she had heard the talk before that sisters make the best and the worst missionaries. She said that a male friend who had served a mission advised her not to go on a mission, because all that sisters did was cry and make cookies.

"Two things I do really well," she observed.

A sister suggested that the statement that sisters make the worst missionaries is really just "sour grapes" on the part of elders. She said that while elders are expected to serve and do, sisters are not under the same obligation, but Church members like sisters better. She said members feed sisters more often than they do elders, and they always wish for more sisters in their ward. And she added, with a wink: "If I have one regret, it is that here are elders coming out to do their duty, and then we sisters come along and spoil it for them!"

No, there is no bimodal distribution. And there are those who feel there is no truth to the stereotype, but that there are explanations for the perceived weaknesses of some sisters. Multiple interviewees, women and men, suggested that the emotional instability attributed to some sisters may actually be a reflection of the fact that females tend to be more open to emotional issues than men and that they are more likely to talk about their problems with their companions, other sisters, and with the mission president's wife.

Elders on the other hand are perceived as more rigid and less emotional, and they are more likely to hide issues, keep them to themselves, or just ignore them. A sister who served in California said: "Hardly ever did I hear about an elder who was having an emotional problem, but we *always* knew about the sisters! But we talked more, too; we would share if there was something happening, whereas the elders might just not talk about it."

As a result, elders were perceived as being less problematic. It was conjectured that if elders were more forthcoming about their feelings, if they weren't as constrained by cultural norms and expectations regarding their feelings and issues they faced, then the percentage of troubled elders would be similar to the percentage of troubled sisters.

Today it is culturally more acceptable for missionaries, sisters and elders, to talk about their problems, to say if they are hurting. A Latter-day Saint physician said today he sees more and more elders, as well as sisters, struggling with mental health issues, a trend also seen on college campuses. Some interviewees suggested that the same numbers of troubled sisters and elders may have existed in earlier days, but today it is culturally more acceptable to talk about it.

An A.P. who served in the 1960s said in general he wouldn't say that sisters were either the best or the worst missionaries they had. He said that in certain kinds of situations, and in certain kinds of wards, they were very effective. The same applied to elders, he added. A sister agreed that sisters and elders each have their particular strengths and that they can complement each other. One should not be demeaned while the other is exalted.

A sister serving in Northern New England in the mid-1990s said she was encouraged to go because elders and sisters can complement each other in the mission field. She said there is the realization in the LDS Church that sisters can do some things elders can't, and vice versa; that women have a different "touch," different attitudes, are more nurturing, and have a greater understanding of women. She found that some people are more partial to women and some to men. She said that together sisters and elders make a good team when seeking to meet the needs of investigators.

It was also suggested that since there are fewer sisters serving, the really good ones stand out, and the ones who aren't so strong also stand out; whereas elders, being greater in number, show a more normal range of abilities.

"There are good and bad sisters and elders, but since we are in the minority, we tend to stick out," said a sister.

Advice for Sisters Considering a Mission

Sisters offered a number of suggestions for young women considering a mission: start praying about it early in life; start a mission fund early-on; attend seminary and pay attention; read and study the scriptures (especially the Book of Mormon, because they will be challenged on it); work on strengthening their testimony; go tracting with sister missionaries in the area; maintain their moral purity; and, once a decision has been made to serve a mission, don't look back, because it is very difficult if one foot remains at home and the other is in the mission field, wondering if marriage would have been a better choice.

And, most loudly and clearly, don't get into a serious relationship, especially with a returned missionary. BYU, BYU-Idaho, and BYU-Hawaii were variously described as "meat markets" and "marriage capitals," where returned missionaries are looking for a spouse. A sister offered this advice: "Don't date anyone right before you go out. That right there could alleviate a lot of problems; just don't date. If you know you are going to go on a mission, just don't get serious with anyone, because they never wait."

The Impact of Returned Sister Missionaries on the Role and Status of Women in the LDS Church

I had a theory when I began this project that as increasing numbers of women went into the mission field, it would have a long-term effect on the role and status of women in the LDS Church. Having committed eighteen months of their lives to the Church, experienced the rigors of a mission, and gained self-confidence, interpersonal skills, and organizational skills, they would want to command greater equality with men. They would want to assume more authority and responsibility in the Latter-day Saint Church.

That may or may not be the case. When I shared my theory with a twenty-three- year-old sister who had just returned from her mission in Spain, she said that in the early days of her mission she would have been offended if someone had said to her, "Once you are done with your mission, I expect you will go home and get married." She had a college degree in business and marketing and she had career plans for after her mission.

But having watched the elders' contributions and the sisters' contributions in the mission field, she felt now she would happily say, "Yes, that's right. That's the next step in my life," and she would feel good about it. She said she came to respect and value the priesthood, and she developed a greater appreciation for the roles women and men fill in the LDS Church. She was more willing to accept them, having gone on her mission. She said she spoke about this with two other sisters in her mission before she returned home, and they felt the same way.

Many other sisters I interviewed said the same thing. A common response was that they now understood and appreciated the responsibilities and hard work that went along with the priesthood and they were just as happy to let the men do it. When I asked if they felt women might someday hold the priesthood in the Church, they said, no: the priesthood is eternal, men have always filled positions in the priesthood, and it won't change just because someone wants it to. A sister added that she is okay with that because being a mother is a lot of work in and of itself. "We each have our own responsibility and it is a big load at times. So I am fine with it."

But there are also those who feel they have paid their dues, and they want to have a greater presence in the Latter-day Saint Church. Indeed, they feel that it would strengthen the Church if they did so and that there is more sisters can offer. A returned sister missionary wrote: "Culturally the Church is a male organization, and the assets that women could bring to the Church are usually ignored or limited to a narrow domestic field."[137] She went on to say her mission gave her courage and confidence she doubts she would have had had she not served. She now speaks in Sunday School and expresses an opinion—"sometimes any opinion"—just so there is at least one female voice among the male voices. She said women in her congregation offer intelligent and insightful comments within the context of the women's Relief Society meetings, but they rarely speak up in Sunday School. She feels they are intimidated by "the quick, sure answers of the men." But she says she isn't intimidated because she had known and worked with men like that when they were nineteen.[138]

Thus it is too early to tell what the long-term effects of more sisters serving missions might be. However, a sister who served in Japan said she didn't return home thinking she wanted to take on a leadership role in the Church, but given the increasing number of sisters serving, she felt the mission experience had created a leadership class that was beginning to show itself in the Church.

Sisters serve for many reasons. They believe that it is God's will for them, they want to serve others both spiritually and temporally, and they want the blessings and benefits that come from a mission. Granted, some said they lacked direction prior to their mission, others talked of plans that had not come to pass, while for some it was a last-minute decision. But regardless of their initial reasons for serving, it was seen as an important step prior to marriage and parenthood.

A sister who served in Northern New England in the mid-1990s echoed the feelings of many sisters interviewed for this book when she said: "Before becoming somebody's wife or mother, I want to become somebody. I want to know who I am first. Serving a mission will help me do that."

CHAPTER 11

Senior Missionaries and Other Types of Missionary Service

"They were a force, they were incredible,
and they could work magic."
AN AMERICAN ELDER'S
IMPRESSIONS OF SENIOR MISSIONARIES

"Rarely a week goes by that I do not receive a
desperate phone call from a mission president,
begging for more senior missionaries."
ELDER RICHARD G. HINCKLEY, EXECUTIVE DIRECTOR OF
THE CHURCH'S MISSIONARY DEPARTMENT,
2011 SEMINAR FOR NEW MISSION PRESIDENTS

"On the whole, people were pretty nice to us,
two old ladies knocking on doors."
A WIDOWED, SENIOR MISSIONARY WHO SERVED IN
BRITISH COLUMBIA IN THE MID-1980'S

The youthful sisters and elders aren't the only Latter-day Saints who volunteer for missionary service. Many retired Church members, like their retired counterparts in wider society, seek new challenges and experiences, and thousands serve in a variety of missionary roles around the world. They include senior couples and senior sisters, and they are in great demand because they typically are faithful, long-standing members who bring a wealth of knowledge and skills to the mission field.

Some engage in proselytizing missions characteristic of younger missionaries, but the majority prefer other types of activities that fall under a broader definition of "mission," activities that draw on their training, experience, and special abilities. These can include leadership support for members at the local level, genealogical research, temple work, medical assignments, social and educational services, and serving at visitors' centers and historic sites and in mission offices. While the senior's numbers pale in comparison to the younger missionaries' (there were around seven thousand serving in 2015), their maturity, commitment, and life experiences make them among the most effective of all missionaries.

Emphasis on seniors serving is a relatively recent phenomenon. It was President Spencer W. Kimball who said members must do more with regard to missionary work. "We must lengthen our stride and must do it now," he said. He was the first president to urge older couples to serve a mission if their health permitted.

Seniors are to conform to the dress and grooming standards that apply to younger missionaries, and, to the extent possible, given their primary assignment, they are to find, friendship, and teach the Latter-day Saint gospel. They do enjoy greater flexibility than younger missionaries: they have some say in what they do, where they serve, and for how long. Their day-to-day schedules are not so rigid. They may take the occasional nap when they feel tired.

They do face special challenges, which limit the numbers who serve. Some have lingering health problems; they worry about what to do with their homes and gardens while they are away; and they miss their grandchildren and great-grandchildren. They have also faced financial constraints, because most (until September 2011) paid all of their mission expenses, which could be significant. The recession in the latter part of the 2000s had a negative effect on recruiting seniors, and Church leaders, in an attempt to make senior missionary service more appealing and doable, relaxed some of their expectations regarding how long seniors can or must serve, how flexible their schedules can be, and how much they are expected to pay.

Like younger missionaries, seniors say the positives outweigh the negatives. They are pleased they can be of service to others and to the Church, they serve as parents or grandparents to the younger missionaries, and they enjoy both spiritual and personal growth. It can also be a time of self-discovery. They see that even in their advancing years they can learn new things, do new things, and change in ways they hadn't thought possible.

There are other categories of service that don't fit the traditional picture of a missionary. There are Church-Service Missionaries: people who may work from home or who serve in various capacities at Church sites close to home. Members of the Mormon Tabernacle Choir are considered missionaries, and they are formally set apart for that role. They too are dedicated to supporting the Church and furthering its message, or, as is said, "helping move the work along."

Senior Missionary Training Center, Provo, Utah

Training for senior missionaries, like training for younger missionaries, has evolved over time. Advances in transportation, communication, and the use of electronic media have made training more efficient, and stays at the Senior Missionary Training Center in Provo have been shortened as a result.

Some things don't change, however: the reasons for going, and the reservations about going, have remained pretty constant over time.

I had the pleasure and unusual opportunity of spending a day at the Senior Missionary Training Center in Provo in April 1994, with the Director of Administrative Services of the MTC. The Senior MTC at that time was located in a renovated motel that had been donated to Brigham Young University. It accommodated up to 150 older missionaries. It was separate from the larger MTC in Provo, and since seniors had more freedom than younger missionaries (the seniors could have cars and come and go as necessary), MTC administrators were just as happy to keep the two groups apart.

I was given a tour of the complex. My host began by pointing to a quote, displayed in the lobby, made by the General Authority Robert L. Backman at the October 1992 General Conference: "Senior missionaries perform a unique service in the mission simply by being there. Their experience, example and faith serve as tremendous resources in building inexperienced members of the Church. They are absolutely indispensable to the growth of the kingdom across the world."

Senior missionaries interviewed that day said they hoped they could live up to that confidence placed in them. While some expressed insecurity about their potential contributions, all were excited about serving.

During our tour I noticed there were older couples and single, senior sisters (a senior sister is defined as forty years of age or older), but there were no older, single men preparing for a senior mission. A General Authority told me they typically don't go on a senior mission; older, single men are needed for other Church callings, especially leadership positions in local churches. He said there also have been problems in the past because women sometimes perceived single men in the mission field as being eligible bachelors, and they pursued them. There had also been issues with older men serving as companions; they didn't always get along too well, living in such close quarters with one another. Single, senior sisters would confirm they faced similar companion issues.

I sat in on classes, interviewed seniors, and ate lunch with recently arrived couples. They had classes in the morning and afternoon, and in the evening they had classes or a devotional with a General Authority. They used the same study materials as the younger missionaries, and young returned missionaries studying at BYU taught them. In 1994, those going on an English-speaking mission stayed less than two weeks, while those learning a language stayed two months.

I interviewed a group of fifteen seniors. As we sat in a circle, I told them they reminded me of Elderhostelers (Elderhostel is an educational program for seniors) and of older continuing-education students with whom I had worked. They were enthusiastic, bright-eyed, and at a point of transition in their lives when they wanted to do something new and different. They smiled and nodded in agreement. I asked why they were choosing to serve a mission, and their responses included: as a way to show thanks to the Lord for what He had done for them; to serve others; and to help build the Latter-day Saint Church. They also expected to gain spiritual and personal benefits. Some said they felt it would contribute to their salvation, some had just retired and wanted something new and challenging to do, and some, for whom this was their third or fourth mission, said missionary work "was in their blood" and they were going to continue to serve until they could do so no longer. They also felt the mental stimulation was good for them, that it helped stave off dementia.

One sister offered a very personal reason. She said her husband had just died not too long ago, and going on a mission was the right thing to do at that point in her life. Otherwise, she said, she would sit at home and feel sorry for herself. I got a sense of the camaraderie and mutual support of the group when the sister seated next to her reached over and patted her hand.

A couple going to England had other reasons for serving. He was in college during the Korean War, and the Latter-day Saint Church had reached an agreement with the U.S. government that fewer missionaries would serve during that time. Thus he didn't go. (Restrictions on the number of young men who can serve missions during wartime are common.) He said he had always hoped and dreamed of going, and he was glad he could do it now. His wife added that she had always wanted to serve a mission, but young women weren't encouraged to do so as she was growing up in the 1930s and 1940s. She was now fulfilling her dream.

Another reason surfaced, which I hadn't expected, and which was echoed around the room. A member of the family (typically a son or daughter) had drifted away from the Church, and the parents hoped their example of dedication and sacrifice would impress their offspring, such that he or she would become active again in the Church. One couple told of a son who had served a good mission, and who was very bright, but who began to question the doctrines of the Church not long after returning home from his mission. He stopped attending, and he remained inactive to that day. They hoped their service would motivate him to start attending again.

"Words haven't worked," added a couple from South America, who were going to Italy and whose children had left the Church. "Perhaps our example will get them back into the fold."

A sister who had been quiet during the session said she faced other issues with her children; they hadn't supported her joining the Latter-day Saint Church or going on a mission. She had raised her large family as a single mother and as strong members of another religious faith, but when she converted to the Latter-day Saint Church in her early fifties, at least one of her children was "devastated" by her decision and wouldn't speak to her. She was made to feel guilty about going on a mission, because she would miss the wedding of one of her children and the birth of a grandchild. The sister said she was going anyway, because she had been looking forward to it for thirteen years, and if she didn't go then, she probably never would.

Another senior said her children thought that when she turned sixty she should just curl up on the sofa and watch TV. "I might do it at ninety," she quipped, "but for now, I'm going on a mission!"

When I asked what could keep seniors from going, the group quickly listed five things: health, finances, houses, grandchildren, and leaving their comfort zones. Applicants must undergo a physical exam and are asked about their finances and preferences. The results help determine if they can serve, where they can serve, and for how long. They are told no missionary calls will be given that jeopardize health, finances, or safety. The upper age limit at that time was seventy years of age. Anyone older than that required special permission and had to prove they were in good health. Ages in the room ranged up to seventy-two years old.

I later interviewed a senior missionary in Solihull, England, who was seventy-five and who was going to apply to serve yet another mission after the current one was over.

A couple in the group said they chose to serve a mission while their health was good so that Church leaders could send them where they were needed, be it anywhere in the world. They were going to the Caribbean.

The health of family members was also a consideration. A couple heading for a two-year temple mission said the timing was right for them, because their aging parents were still managing on their own. Had they waited any longer, they surmised they might not have been able to go because of caregiving responsibilities for the parents.

Paying for a senior mission can be a family affair. Some interviewees at the Senior MTC said their children were helping with their expenses, thus serving as another example of the family support system that is at the heart of the missionary enterprise. Only, in this instance, it was operating in reverse: just as parents had financially supported their children's missions, so now children were supporting the parents'. Contributors even included children who had drifted away from the Church. In one instance, a son who had left the LDS Church spearheaded the effort among his siblings to raise money for the parents. He said that even though he was no longer active, he was proud of his parents for what they were doing at this stage in their lives. Others added that siblings grew closer as a result of their joint efforts in supporting their parents' mission.

The economic downturn in the late 2000s impacted seniors' ability to afford serving a mission. A senior missionary who had worked as an electrical engineer before retiring, and who had served a mission with his wife in the Midwest in the late 2000s, said he observed that it became harder to recruit seniors at that time due to the economy. Prior to September 2011, when the financial burden of serving a mission was relaxed, serving a senior mission could be an expensive proposition, because participants who weren't on proselytizing missions were required to pay all their expenses. There was no equalization program for them, where all pay the same monthly amount, as is the case with younger missionaries (the Equalized Missionary Support Fund program). The Church provided estimates of monthly expenses for senior missions on the website http://lds.org. In September 2010, expenses ranged from $500 a month for certain locations in Brazil and for native couples serving in Tonga Nuku'alofa, to $5,000 a month for couples in Bermuda. The estimates included apartment rentals, utilities, food, and transportation. They didn't include prescriptions, tithing, fast offerings, cell phones, automobiles, personal care items, and apartment setup costs.

Single sisters could expect to pay about 65 percent of the amount paid by couples.

At the same time when it was becoming more and more difficult to recruit senior missionaries for full-time missions, the demand for their services was growing. Elder Richard G. Hinckley, the Executive Director of the Church's Missionary Department, said in 2011 that in recent years requests from mission presidents for senior couples had been as high as 3,200 couples, or 6,400 individuals, far more than the approximately 1,900 couples serving that year.[139] Church leaders took a serious look at the senior missionary program and decided there were a number of impediments to senior service that needed to be addressed: length of service; transportation costs; perceived inflexibility of the schedule; and the cost of serving.

Regarding the length of service and transportation costs, under the old policy senior couples given calls to serve a mission outside their country of residence were called for at least eighteen months. The Church paid for transportation to and from the field. Under the new policy, senior couples could serve a mission outside of their country of residence for a shorter term of six or twelve months, but had to pay for transportation costs to and from the field. Transportation costs for terms of eighteen or twenty-three months continued to be paid by the Church.

With regard to senior missionary housing costs, under the old policy housing costs (including rent, utilities, and furnishings) associated with a senior couple's assigned area of service were paid completely by the missionary couple. They paid the full amount of the expense. Under the new policy, local Church leaders responsible for senior missionaries would secure housing and pay all housing costs. Missionary couples then reimburse local leaders some or all of the costs up to a cap of $1,400 per month. Missionaries from the United States, Canada, Western Europe, Japan, and Australia are expected to reimburse local leaders the cost of housing up to the cap of $1,400, or, if less, the actual amount for expenses. Those from other countries are expected to reimburse the costs up to their individual ability to pay (but not to exceed $1,400 a month). All couples pay for food and other personal expenses.

Many prospective senior missionaries perceived the schedule as being too inflexible; like younger missionaries, they weren't allowed to return home until the end of their mission. Couples may now, at their own expense, take a short leave of absence from their mission (not normally more than ten days) to return home for important family events.

The new policies went into effect September 1, 2011, with the hope that they would contribute to increased numbers of seniors who would serve, to more positive missionary experiences, and to encouraging others to serve.[140] The changes appear to be having a positive effect, as senior numbers increased to around seven thousand in 2015.

What to do with their homes while they were gone was an important consideration for those in our circle at the Senior MTC. Some rented them, some had children staying in them, and some left them vacant. A couple and a sister in the group said they didn't have to worry about their houses because they were homeless; they had sold their homes, and they weren't sure what they were going to do when they returned from their missions. "The Lord will provide," they said.

Leaving grandchildren and great-grandchildren was especially difficult because they would miss interacting with them and watching them grow. There were also concerns about aging parents. One couple said their parents were likely to die while they were gone, and the wish of their parents was that they not return home for the funerals, that they not interrupt their mission. They felt especially conflicted by the possibility and by what they would do.

Given the advances in communication, seniors today say it is relatively easy to stay in touch with their families, even when they are half-a-world away. Some say they stay in closer touch than when they lived at home.

Some seniors said they initially balked at the idea of serving a mission. One man said he delayed the decision because he was shy and felt insecure, and because to go on a mission would mean he would have to leave his comfort zone. A widow shared she hadn't thought about going on a mission until her husband died, but she delayed volunteering because she didn't think she could do it. She felt "very inadequate." She said she didn't know enough about the scriptures, and she could think of any number of reasons why she wouldn't be a good missionary. "But," she said, gesturing toward the people in the circle, "they have assured me my fears are unfounded. We will see. I hope so."

A divorcée said she knew that spiritually she was ready to go, and she desperately wanted to go, but she was afraid she wasn't intelligent enough. She shared her fear with her stake president during her pre-mission interview, but he said not to worry about it: he said she would do just fine and that IQ tests were not part of the application process. The sister also confessed to being nervous when speaking in public; she would make a point of arriving at church one minute late so that she wouldn't be asked to do the opening or closing prayer. She also couldn't use notes while speaking because her hands trembled and she couldn't read the small print. She hoped a year as a missionary would help her get over some of her fears.

Others spoke of the excitement, and frustration, of going back to the classroom. They were glad to be learning new things, but they were frustrated with how long it was taking them, especially things that had come easily when they were younger, such as learning a new language. A senior who was losing his hearing and who was preparing to serve a deaf mission said he was especially frustrated: his hands were arthritic, he was the slowest student in his American Sign Language class, and he was embarrassed by it. But he wasn't going to give up; he was going to succeed. (The MTC administrator later told me that very few seniors drop out of the program by that point, so he wasn't surprised by the gentleman's tenacity.)

The Senior MTC was moved to the main MTC campus in November 2003. Space was available because the number of younger missionaries in residence in Provo had declined due to the increase of MTCs around the world. Forty-seven apartments were set aside for seniors. Thirty senior apartments were included in a new building constructed at the MTC in 2011.

The length of stay at the Senior MTC has been shortened over the past two decades. Those learning a new language now receive language tutoring from a returned missionary fluent in the language over the telephone in advance of their arrival at the MTC. Those living in the Provo area go to the MTC for individual tutoring sessions prior to entry into the MTC. A couple who lived about fifty miles from Provo and who were going on a Spanish-speaking mission said they went to the MTC two nights a week for two-hour sessions for around two months for tutoring in Spanish by a young returned missionary who had served in Argentina.

The current emphasis in language instruction for seniors, as it is for younger missionaries, is on conversational skills, on the "phrase approach" (versus the earlier emphasis on grammar).

Seniors enter the MTC on an assigned day and stays have been shorted to about a week. Those who live some distance from Provo spend their nights there, but those within commuting distance drive back and forth each day. The couple who lived fifty miles away thus commuted one hundred miles each day while they were receiving their language training and while they were at the MTC.

A couple who served in the mid-2000s said they were among fifty new senior missionaries who entered the MTC together. Their colleagues were going to a host of assignments in a variety of locations around the world. The seniors met in groups, listened to talks, and had training. Young, returned missionaries provided instruction, including work in *Preach My Gospel.* They were given training in proselytizing, but few were expecting to perform such work (and they didn't, the interviewees confirmed). They had a session with a pretend investigator, as do younger missionaries. They had virtually no contact with the younger missionaries at the MTC.

When compared to what was observed at the Senior MTC in 1994, today's seniors do have a different training experience. Some preparation begins before they arrive, language training has a more practical focus, and their stays are shorter. However, some things haven't changed: they still worry about finances, health, family, homes, and leaving their comfort zones.

Full-time Mission Opportunities

For seniors, "missionary" is used in a much broader sense than just the activities of tracting, or going door to door. The term used is "Missionaries with Additional Assignments" which retains the sense that the first assignment of a missionary is proselytizing, but suggests most of their attention will be focused on other types of service and work. Mission rules aren't as strict as they are for younger missionaries, although seniors need to conform to a lifestyle that is more limited than what they are used to at home.

There is a wide array of full-time senior missionary opportunities. There are domestic and foreign missions, and seniors who speak Spanish or Portuguese are in particular demand. They can provide shadow leadership for new or struggling congregations. There is a worldwide need for healthcare professionals to serve the health needs of missionaries, mission presidents, and locals. Seniors are needed in mission offices, visitors' centers, historic sites, temples, and in the Family and Church History Departments in Salt Lake City, where genealogical work is carried out. Their help is also needed in welfare services, humanitarian services, and in LDS Family Services, which provides mental health services to Church members. Employment counselors are needed to support the Church's Perpetual Education Fund, which seeks to improve the education level and employment skills of members overseas. Professionals in law, accounting, and education are needed, as are skilled agricultural, construction, maintenance, and grounds workers. The needs of this lay organization are great, requiring knowledge and expertise at many different levels and with varying amounts of sophistication.

Those who have significant personal or family responsibilities or financial limitations are still encouraged to become engaged because the need is so great and because they can serve as live-at-home missionaries while fulfilling many of the above needs.

Seniors have multiple choices, but they aren't always assigned their first choice. Some list no preferences, saying they will leave it to the Lord to send them where they are most needed. The Church prefers the latter approach.

Since my visit to the Senior MTC in 1994, I have been fortunate to interview senior couples and senior sisters who were serving or who had served a variety of missions around the world. These included leadership and proselytizing missions, overseeing a historic site and visitors' center, genealogical research, temple work, providing health services, and providing Church education services. While they are not exhaustive of the range of mission opportunities, they do provide insight into the individuals involved, their unique experiences, and the experiences common to them all.

Leadership and proselytizing mission. I spoke with three couples who had been involved in leadership and proselytizing missions. They had served in England, the Caribbean, and Singapore and Pakistan. They worked with local congregations who were new or were struggling. They assisted the local leadership, and they provided spiritual guidance and counseling for members. On occasion they referred members to social agencies for specialized help when it was available. They helped men develop their leadership skills. They contacted lapsed members and tried to reactivate them. Sometimes they were able to address the reasons why the person left the Church, such as a personality clash or a misunderstanding. They also worked with families which only partially consisted of members.

They may have done some proselytizing such as knocking on doors, but this was not very popular with seniors. Younger elders and sisters tended to do the proselytizing and teaching, while seniors did the follow-up work with recent converts.

They said they were "growing, learning, and becoming" during their missions—which they attributed to "the Spirit."

One of the couples, who were both converts, hadn't thought about going on a mission until a recently returned missionary (and eventual son-in-law) started dating their daughter. He was a convert whom they described as "gung-ho." Practically the first thing he asked them was when they were going on a mission. They told him they hadn't given it much thought. He never let up thereafter; he would ask them about it each time he saw them. At Christmas he gave them a piggy bank with the words "Missionary Fund" written on it, and each time he visited he would shake it to see how much they had saved. This was in the early 1980s, and the beginning of their seriously thinking about going.

The wife of this couple had reservations. She didn't like change or leaving her comfort zone. She would have been happy to serve six months in the next town over, had that been a possibility, but her husband wanted to go overseas, which meant serving eighteen months at that time. She prayed about it and eventually came around to the idea of going foreign.

They volunteered for an eighteen-month Leadership and Proselytizing mission in 1992 and assumed they would go overseas. When the large white envelope arrived from Salt Lake City announcing their assignment, she could see nervousness on his face as he read where they were going: to the Singapore Mission. He had worked in the Philippines forty years earlier and found it difficult because it was so hot. She began to have second thoughts. They looked at a map and realized the mission wasn't just in Singapore, but it included Pakistan, India, Malaysia, and East Malaysia. They wondered where they would end up. They said goodbye to their children and grandchildren and handed the keys to their home to a Church member, who watched over it during their absence.

Their experience at the MTC paralleled that of younger missionaries. They were kept very busy (all they did was go to meetings and eat), and they were exhausted after a few days. They were there over Christmas, and a number of General Authorities came to speak to bolster their spirits during the holiday away from home. They found it quite stirring when two thousand missionaries sang "Called to Serve."

They were assigned to a Singapore branch. The Latter-day Saint Church had experienced a checkered presence in Singapore. The first full-time missionaries arrived there in 1968, and there were forty converts by the end of the year. Forty-eight missionaries were in Singapore at the end of 1969. Anti-Mormon and anti-missionary sentiment erupted in 1970, which was led by the press and by Christian clergy. Twenty-nine Mormon missionaries had to leave Singapore because the government refused to renew their visas, which left only three foreign-born missionaries. The mission was temporarily dissolved in 1978. The Latter-day Saints Donny and Marie Osmond performed in Singapore in 1980 to (it is said) a crowd of thirty thousand fans. That stimulated interest in the Latter-day Saint Church—as did the appointment of Jon M. Huntsman Jr. (who was LDS and a future presidential candidate), to the position of U.S. Ambassador to Singapore in 1992. The Church's acceptance grew through the 1990s, and there were 1,650 members in Singapore in 1995. The number had grown to 3,608 as of January 1, 2015.[141]

The senior couple arrived in 1992 and worked with two elders in Singapore (one from Hawaii and one from Utah.) During the day they looked up referrals and reactivated people, and at night they taught with the elders. There were a number of elders and sisters in Singapore for whom they became father and mother figures. One thing that surprised them was that a few of the young elders didn't see seniors as being "real" missionaries. One once said when talking about an assignment, "Oh, I think they want the full-time missionaries to do that." It was tactfully pointed out to the young elder that seniors also are full-time missionaries.

They were reassigned to Pakistan, where they entered on a tourist visa. They were not given missionary visas, because the Church is not recognized in Pakistan. There was one other senior couple in the country at the time. They were assigned to the Lahore branch, which was only four months old, with twelve members. They weren't allowed to proselytize since it is a Muslim country, but members kept bringing people to them who wanted to be taught. They had to make sure investigators weren't Muslim, because they said that if they converted it could mean the death penalty for them. The branch president screened them. They found many Catholics and other Christians in Punjab. The rule of the mission was that they had to teach in English. They remained busy all day long.

The Church in Lahore grew from twelve when they arrived in 1992, to eighty in January 1994. Up to one hundred would attend services. As the membership grew, the area presidency told them to rearrange their priorities; they were to devote 80 percent of their time to leadership training and only 20 percent to teaching the discussions. The membership was growing faster than they could gain leadership skills.

They had to adjust to cultural differences. Latter-day Saint families sit together at their services, but out in the country the practice was resisted, with women sitting on one side and men on the other at meetings. The American sister wore native clothing. She didn't show her bare arms or legs. While they found Lahore a beautiful city, they had to contend with heat, dust, and flies, and they had to be very careful what they ate and drank.

As they reflected on their mission experience, which they described as "wonderful," the husband said he felt health was the only reason why a person should not consider a mission. He said the money will always be there, that someone will help. He recounted a story told by a fellow senior at the MTC, whose son had said to his parents, "Now it is your turn to go. We (the children) are all going to chip in and help pay for your mission. You helped us, now we will help you." Regarding the other reservations seniors have about going—leaving their homes, families, and grandchildren—the senior elder said, "I don't think there is anything you can miss that is as bad as what you miss by not going." The senior sister agreed, saying that so much is gained by going, that the eighteen months missed will be made up in other ways, and that the time goes by very fast.

Historic Sites and Visitors' Centers. The Latter-day Saint Church maintains numerous historic sites and visitors' centers. They commemorate significant people, places, and events in the Church's history, and the sites map the experiences, travels, and travails of the Saints as they moved, or were forced to move, westward. The majority of sites are found in New York, Illinois, and Utah. Many of the sites have a visitors' center associated with them. Millions of people, both Mormons and non-Mormons, visit these sites and centers each year, with Temple Square in Salt Lake City receiving the largest number of visitors, around five million a year. Many Mormon Church members set a goal of visiting as many of them as possible during their lifetimes. The sites and their maintenance require the service of thousands of volunteers, senior missionaries, younger sister missionaries, and Church-Service Missionaries, along with paid employees of the Church.

The Church constructs, restores, and maintains these sites at great expense (they are free and open to the public), and while the Church is pleased to see an interest in its history, the sites serve a deeper, more spiritual purpose. It is believed all have played a role in the restoration of the Latter-day Saint gospel, and it is this spiritual message that is conveyed during site tours and through literature available at the locations.

Joseph Smith Birthplace Memorial in Sharon, Vermont. While each site holds great significance for the Latter-day Saint Church and its members, none is considered more sacred than the Joseph Smith Birthplace Memorial in Sharon, Vermont. Situated at the top of a hill in a bucolic setting in central Vermont, it commemorates the location of the Smith family home and Joseph's birthplace. The home is no longer extant, but the granite front step and the hearthstone remain. The 360-acre site includes a director's home, a visitors' center, gardens, and a thirty-eight and one-half foot high polished, granite shaft commemorating the memory of Joseph, with each foot representing a year in his life. The grounds are impeccably maintained, as are the buildings.

Church members feel the site is special. A General Authority told a young sister beginning her mission there that next to Bethlehem and Jerusalem, Joseph Smith's birthplace is the most sacred place in the world. A General Authority told a director of the site that if he could choose to serve anyplace in the world, it would be at the Joseph Smith Memorial, while another General Authority told the same director that the place is so sacred that angels watch over it.

The site is located within the New Hampshire/Manchester Mission, and younger missionaries, particularly sisters, are sometimes assigned to serve there as tour guides, particularly during the busy summer season. I had occasion to interview some of them, and they too agreed the site is special. To a person they spoke of the strong sense of "the Spirit" they found there.

I visited the site in October 2010, when the Vermont leaves were ablaze with their autumn colors. The music of the Mormon Tabernacle Choir on outdoor speakers greeted me as I got out of my car. I had called ahead and was graciously met by the director and his wife. We met in their living room, which was bright and tastefully furnished. The walls included pictures of and paintings relating to the life of Joseph

Smith. The director's position was a two-year calling, and they had been at the site for twenty-one months.

The director and his wife were from Utah, and this was their first senior assignment. He had been raised in the Church and served a mission in Utah. She was a convert to the Church at age fourteen and had met her husband at BYU not long after he returned from his mission. She did not serve a mission, saying it wasn't a consideration for young women when she was growing up. He described himself as an entrepreneur, succeeding at some businesses, and not at others. Their company had been chosen for a Small Business of the Year award, and they received it at the White House. A son was currently running their family's international business.

They had not listed preferences on their senior mission application, saying they felt it would have defeated the purpose of the Lord sending them where they were needed. They were thrilled to be chosen to serve at the Joseph Smith Birthplace Memorial. (Like all assignments in the Latter-day Saint Church, one does not volunteer for a specific position, nor should someone advocate for someone to serve in a particular position. I have been told that such volunteering or advocacy practically guarantees that one will *not* get the position.) They attended a training workshop for new historic site and MTC directors at the Provo MTC. They were surprised that there was very little on the "nuts and bolts" of running such a site. They worked some from *Preach My Gospel*, and there was a lot of teaching on motivation and "seeking the Spirit."

They reported a similar experience when they arrived in Vermont. They spent a brief time with the outgoing director, who "showed us where the light switches were," and who emphasized the importance of fostering a sense of the Spirit. He then left them to develop their own approach to their new responsibilities.

They felt they would take a similar approach when they met with their successors in a few months' time.

One of their main responsibilities was to provide guided tours through the visitors' center and around the grounds. I noticed that a buzzer would periodically sound as we talked, and I was told it indicated a vehicle approaching the center. The number of visitors varied depending on the time of year. They received around 1,500 visitors a month in the winter, but the numbers jumped to four to five thousand a month in the summer. They had as many as five hundred in a single day. He estimated around 20 percent of the visitors were non-Church members.

In October they were assisted in giving tours by two senior couples, one of whom had been there a month. It wasn't a particularly busy day, although there were always cars in the parking lot. A Latter-day Saint couple from Utah came into the visitors' center, saying they had been visiting other sites, but this was the one they had been waiting to see.

Christmas is a popular time: they string 180,000 Christmas lights throughout the property and feature a live-animal nativity display. Facilities management missionaries and employees of the site were beginning to string the lights on the trees and bushes when I visited in October. Thousands of visitors drive through the grounds during the holiday period, many of them non-LDS. Many stop to see the live-animal display, and missionaries circulate among the visitors, encouraging them to go into the visitors' center.

I asked if visitors ever want to argue, as is sometimes the case on Temple Square. They said not often, although such an incident had occurred just the day before. The sister said a couple had asked for a tour, and as she was telling them about Joseph Smith's early life, she heard the man mutter something under his breath. He became more vocal as the tour progressed, citing various anti-Mormon opinions and books. She had learned not to argue or debate with visitors, "because no one wins" (at this her husband nodded in agreement), but she finally told the man that he was citing anti-Mormon sources and she asked him why he didn't just ask a Mormon if he had questions about the faith. The man's wife was becoming embarrassed, he held his remarks thereafter, and the couple left at the end of the tour.

The sister said she is always surprised when such exchanges occur, because she would never go to a place considered sacred by others and argue with them. I asked how often this occurs and if they perceived it as a problem. They said it didn't happen very often, perhaps twelve to fifteen times a year.

The sister said a more pressing problem for seniors is aching feet, from having to give so many walking tours.

The director took me on a tour of the visitors' center and the grounds. We went into a small theater in the center and watched a movie on the life of Joseph Smith, *Joseph Smith: Prophet of the Restoration*, which had been featured in the Legacy Theater in the Joseph Smith Memorial Building in Salt Lake City since 2005, and which is also shown at various visitors' centers. It shows Joseph's early personal and religious experiences, his various travails, and his final moments in

Carthage Jail. A parallel story running through the film tells of a young English woman who is emigrating from England to join the Saints in Nauvoo. She is a believer, but her father, who is accompanying her, is a skeptic. He couldn't let her travel four thousand miles alone.

As with any Latter-day Saint production, the quality of the film was first-rate. We were the only two in the little theater, and I imagined the director had seen the movie scores of times before.

We then toured the visitors' center, which included a statue of Joseph Smith, a timeline of his life and the restoration of the gospel, the hearthstone from the Smith fireplace, and a display of books by and about Smith. There were some academic books there, too, including volumes from the new series, the Joseph Smith Papers Project. Many paintings and pictures of key early LDS leaders were on the walls, along with the presidents/prophets of the Church. There was also a topographic display of the area, showing the location of the site in relation to the surrounding area.

We went up the hill to the site of the house where Smith was born. It is no longer extant, but a garden, a bench, and the granite front step of the original house mark its location. We then walked around the monument. The front of it reads: "Sacred to the memory of Joseph Smith the prophet born here 23 December 1805 martyred Carthage Illinois 27 June 1844." It includes a forty ton, thirty-eight and one-half foot shaft carved from one piece of granite, which was quarried in Barre, Vermont. Each foot represents a year in Joseph's life. It was erected in 1905 to commemorate the one-hundred-year anniversary of Smith's birth. The base of the shaft rests on a foundation on which is inscribed the scripture that Smith said motivated him to seek God's guidance when he was a teenager: "If any of you lack wisdom, let him ask of God, that giveth to all men liberally, and upbraideth not; and it shall be given him." (James 1:5). Smith's testimony appears on another side of the monument.

There are also trails on the 360-acre site where people may walk, meditate, and pray.

The director's wife said they entertain quite a bit, with invitations to younger and older missionaries serving in the area, as well as to members and non-members. I was served an excellent lunch of soup, salad, and dessert, and I noticed there was a very large pot of soup on the kitchen stove in preparation for other visitors expected later in the day.

While it is an historic site in a charming location, its real purpose is to advance the message of the Restoration and the gospel. The director's home is used to this end. They open the home to younger proselytizing missionaries so that they can bring investigators there to teach lessons in the rarified atmosphere of the director's living room. It is felt "the Spirit" is especially strong there. They also make themselves available to answer questions from members and non-members. On the day I was there, a Church member brought a non-member who had questions about the faith, which the director answered.

The director shared stories of his serving as a spiritual counselor to members and investigators. He told of talking with a young man who didn't think he would go on a mission. His mother was very disappointed and asked the director to talk with him. The director spoke with the young man over the course of a couple of hours. As they sat on the bench in the garden that marked the location of Smith's house, he impressed on the young man that he had lived with God for thousands of years prior to his birth, and now that he had been sent to earth, it was God's wish that he serve a mission. The young man disappeared for a few hours along the trails that surround the 360-acre site, and when he reappeared he said he was going on a mission.

The director and his wife said that it was these types of experiences that will provide them with their fondest memories of their time at the memorial site.

Genealogical research. Latter-day Saints are famous for their genealogical work, and the results of their labors are stored in a bunker cut deep into the Wasatch Mountains, southeast of Salt Lake City. There are names—billions of names—stored there. Gleaned from census, parish, and family records, some extending back to the Middle Ages, the names are recorded on 2.4 million rolls of microfilm housed in the Granite Mountain Records Vault. Commonly referred to as "The Vault," the facility was built in the early 1960s to house the microfilm and other important Church records and documents in a secure and controlled environment. The facility is designed to withstand earthquakes, fires, and other disasters. It is set seven hundred feet into the mountain with a covering of 675 feet of granite rock overhead. Entrances are protected by one fourteen-ton and two ten-ton bank vault doors. The temperature and humidity are controlled. It is not open to the public.[142]

There are two sources of names: genealogical research of one's ancestors; and, for those who don't have family names, names that come from records such as census, birth, marriage, death, residence, and cemetery, which are referred to as extraction and index projects. The names are gleaned by individuals, by part-time Church-Service Missionaries serving from their homes around the world, and by full-time senior missionaries who are dispatched throughout the globe. Part-time Church-Service Missionaries provide telephone and e-mail support for those seeking information about family history programs, products, and software, and they typically serve thirty months. Full-time missionaries typically serve up to twenty-three months.[143] All are aided by "film missionaries," who are full-time missionaries equipped with digital cameras who capture images of old records found in churches, town halls, and cemeteries. They are called from twelve to eighteen months. It is said this role is especially appropriate for single seniors.

Those participating in genealogical work are an avid bunch. I had occasion in 1994 to attend a biweekly meeting of the Family History Missionaries who meet at 7:00 A.M. in the ballroom of the Joseph Smith Memorial Building in Salt Lake City. There were three hundred present, all seniors. After announcements, several spoke about their lives, their families, and how much they enjoyed what they were doing. Their talks were then printed, bound, and shared with the group.

A widowed sister who had participated in an earlier group wrote that after her husband had died in an accident, she had had her ups and downs, and then she decided to go on a Family History Mission. "I felt this was the right time to come on my mission," she wrote. "I need a purpose. I didn't ask how long I would be able to stay. The most important thing is that I'm here, serving my Father and His Son Jesus Christ. A professor in my psychology class said: 'Everyone needs something or someone in their lives.' This is the only thing on which I ever agreed with him."[144]

At the end of their talks I was asked to say a few words about my book. I assured them I was including a chapter on senior missionaries. I told them as I looked out on their gray hair and bright faces, that they reminded me of Elderhostelers I had worked with in the past. They laughed. Many came up afterwards to talk about my research.

In that same year I spoke in England with four senior missionaries (two couples), all from the United States, serving in Solihull in the West Midlands, England. All were involved in the Church's genealogical program FamilySearch, analyzing the 1881 census data. One man was seventy-five, and they talked of a sister who was seventy-eight and who had just asked to go on another FamilySearch mission. The two men had been pretty heavily involved in genealogy prior to their mission, although none of their occupations related directly to it. One was a farmer, and one had sold insurance.

The Church is currently digitizing its collection, and making it available online to anyone at no cost. The information is accessed through thousands of Family History Centers which are located in Latter-day Saint Churches around the world. Non-members are particularly appreciative that the Church has made the records available, and they are taking advantage of the opportunity. The director of a Family History Center in Maine said that non-members constituted the majority of her patrons.

While non-Mormons hold the genealogical work of Latter-day Saints in high regard, many are not aware of the theological basis of the practice. The reason for collecting names is not just to serve an interest in ancestral history; the names are collected in order to fulfill one of the most important spiritual tasks of living Church members—to engage in proxy baptisms for the deceased through the ritual of "baptism for the dead."

Latter-day Saints, like any religious movement that includes a prophetic figure who claims a final, divine revelation, must address the question: "But what about all of those who lived prior to the prophet? Will they be lost since they have not heard 'the fullness of the gospel'? Will they have no chance of salvation?"

Latter-day Saints respond by saying that deceased individuals can receive the ordinance of baptism, and thus salvation, through someone standing in proxy for them in a baptismal ceremony. Volunteers go through the ceremony for deceased relatives or for people whose names have been gleaned through genealogical research. If it is the latter, the volunteer is given a card with the person's name on it.

As we will see below, the practice is not without its critics, who question involving deceased people in a ritual they might not have chosen to engage in had they been alive.

Latter-day Saint interest in genealogy is thus more than an interest in family history: it has a theological goal. And the place where the baptism for the dead ritual is performed is in a Latter-day Saint temple, often with the help and support of senior missionaries who are engaging in what is referred to as "temple work."

Latter-day Saint ritual. To outsiders, the Latter-day Saint Church may appear to have a split personality when it comes to the role and place of ritual. Their houses of worship ("meetinghouses," "chapels," or "units") and the services therein are plain. There are no crosses, statues, or stained glass windows on the outside or inside of their meetinghouses. (Stained glass windows are occasionally found on older chapels, but not on newer ones. The goal now is to build smaller, more numerous chapels, rather than fewer, more ornate meetinghouses.) No candles are lit, no incense is burned, and vestments are not worn. The leader of the local congregation, the bishop or branch president, wears a business suit when conducting services. There are few rituals. There is a weekly sacrament service where bread and water are shared communally, but beyond that the service consists of talks, singing, and prayers. In this regard, Latter-day Saints mirror a plainer, Protestant approach to ceremony.

Temples and temple rituals. But the Church also maintains another set of buildings—temples—that are more dramatic in size and in appearance, are considered sacred spaces, and are where elaborate rituals and ceremonies considered necessary for salvation are performed. A gold statue of the angel Moroni, the angel who appeared to Joseph Smith on several occasions, stands on the highest steeple, stained glass adorns the windows, and the grounds and interior are impeccably maintained.

Latter-day Saints explain the contrast between their worship and their rituals by pointing to ancient Israel and how synagogues were used for worship, while special rituals were performed in the Temple.

Members have been told throughout the history of the Church that performance of rituals ("ordinances") in a temple is vital to their salvation. There were relatively few temples around the world until the late 1970s, and members generally had to travel considerable distances to participate in these important ceremonies. The international growth of the Church has spurred it to build more temples worldwide, such that when those that are under construction in 2014 are completed, there will be one hundred and seventy temples around the world, the majority of which will be outside the United States.[145]

One of the changes brought about was that all temples didn't need to be built on a grand scale; rather, through the use of technology that allowed for instruction to be provided in a more efficient manner, in a smaller space, and in different languages simultaneously if necessary, their size could be tailored to meet the needs of the Saints in the area.[146]

New temples are open to the public for a brief period after their construction, but once the temple is dedicated, access to it (as was the case with the ancient Temple of Israel) is restricted to members in good standing. Members are required to produce a "temple recommend" to enter a temple; this is a document issued by their bishop or branch president, who has interviewed them and who attests to their belief in the Latter-day Saint Church and that they have kept the commandments, supported Church leaders, obeyed the Word of Wisdom, paid tithing, and are honest.

Attendees wear all-white clothing in the temple. It symbolizes purity, and it is also a social and economic leveling device; all are considered equal in the temple, since all are considered brothers and sisters in the Lord.

A sister said that when she steps into a temple she feels like she has left this world and worldly things. She has stepped out of her troubles and challenges. She has left the world behind. Her removing her worldly clothing and putting on the pure, white clothes of the temple symbolize this.

Non-Mormons who attend temple open houses are frequently surprised to discover the interior is not a large, open space designed for congregational worship, but rather a number of smaller rooms where ceremonies and rituals ("initiating ordinances") are performed, which focus on the individual, the family, and those who have passed on.

The endowment ceremony. At the individual level, a person goes through an "endowment ceremony," a ritual that typically takes place just prior to a young man or woman going on a mission, or just before a couple is married.

Temples are divided into women's and men's sections. The sexes are separated during the endowment ceremony, because participants begin with a symbolic washing and anointing, and they put on sacred clothing, a type of undergarment that is always worn thereafter. It is said the undergarment provides spiritual protection from evil and temptation, and it serves as a reminder of the covenants made during the endowment ceremony. A tunic-type garment is then donned over the endowment undergarment.

They attend lectures, receive instruction of God's purpose for mankind, consider their relationship with the Deity, and view representations of the Creation Story and the story of Adam and Eve. Life is seen as a journey from a primordial life with God, to an earthly life, to a life after death. This occurs in an "ordinance room," which includes scenic murals painted on the walls and sometimes on the ceilings. The ceremony is considered a very sacred event, characterized by the presence of God, with whom promises and covenants are made.

Others beside youthful missionaries and couples may participate in the ceremony, but they must be mature individuals, because they make adult covenants. Converts generally have to wait a year before they can participate in an endowment ceremony. The ceremony takes one and a half hours.

Celestial marriage. Latter-day Saints believe in marriage for "time and eternity," and that they and their children will be together forever, even after death. It is referred to as "eternal marriage" or "celestial marriage." The ceremony takes place at an altar in a "sealing room," where bonds and covenants are made during a "sealing ceremony." Children born later to the sealed couple are "born in the covenant" and do not go through an additional sealing ceremony with the parents. For converts who already have children before being sealed, the couple goes through the ceremony first, and then the children come into the sealing room, also dressed in white, where they join hands, all kneel at the altar, and the children are sealed to the parents. Subsequent children born to the couple are "born in the covenant."

Baptism for the dead. As we have seen, Latter-day Saint interest in genealogical research extends far beyond an interest in family history; the countless hours devoted to it is motivated by a theological reason. In answer to the question, "Are people lost who have died before hearing the Restored Gospel?" Latter-day Saints answer, "No." They believe the potential exists for the deceased person to accept the message if a living person can go through a baptism ceremony by proxy. This vicarious event takes place in a temple, in an ornate baptismal font that rests on the backs of twelve, life-size oxen (2 Chronicles 4: 2-4). As is the case with convert baptism, total immersion is required, and two witnesses must attest that the ceremony was carried out correctly.

To those who express concern about involving deceased people in the ritual, a ritual they may not have engaged in had they been alive, the Latter-day Saint Church explains that they are not actually baptizing the person, but are opening up the potential that should the person who now exists in the spirit world want to take advantage of it, he or she can do so from the other side. It is not baptism *of* the dead, they say, but baptism *for* the dead.

The Church has met with members of religious groups to discuss their concerns about the practice, and it reports that it has implemented safeguards to help guard against inappropriate submissions of names and baptisms. The practice has been a particular concern for Holocaust survivors, who don't want their relatives included in the ceremony. Present Church policies stipulate that Church members shouldn't submit the names of famous people for temple ordinances unless they demonstrate they are descended from them, and they shouldn't submit names of close friends or acquaintances to which they are not related unless they have permission from the person's most direct descendant. They also shouldn't submit the name of one of their own ancestors unless they are a direct-line descendent, they have evidence of his or her death, or they have obtained permission for the work from a direct-line descendent. Members are required to indicate their compliance with these policies when submitting names.

Volunteers also serve vicariously for deceased relatives and others in endowment, celestial marriage, and sealing rituals. Men and women participate equally in the rituals. Women do almost all in the temple that men do, albeit in a separate section. Men always do endowments, and sealers are always men.

Secret, or sacred? Non-Mormons question why Latter-day Saints are so secretive about what goes on in temples, because participants aren't allowed to discuss the details of the various rites and ceremonies. Church leaders respond that what goes on in a temple is sacred, not secret, and one doesn't discuss the details of sacred things. Some non-Mormons have drawn parallels between temple ordinances and the rituals of Freemasonry, saying the latter influenced Joseph Smith. The Church acknowledges similarities, but says they may stem from common roots, not direct influence.

Staff, volunteers, and senior missionaries. The number and complexity of the ceremonies that take place in temples require close administrative oversight, along with the help of numerous volunteers, including senior missionaries. A husband and wife, referred to as the president and matron, oversee each temple. Training for the president and matron takes place at the Provo MTC, and it is a three-year calling. Two counselors assist the president, and the matron has two assistants. They work in different parts of the temple: women with women; men with men. There is a paid recorder, who supervises the paid staff, including guards, custodians, and office staff.

Temples are very busy places, and the president and matron have to depend on many volunteers to help support the work and to carry out the involved ceremonies. According to a friend who has served there, the Provo, Utah, Temple (which is among the busiest in the Church), served over thirty thousand patrons a month in 2010. There are around four thousand volunteers at Provo, including retirees and BYU students. There are around twelve volunteers on a shift, and Provo did three million names in 2009. More and more retired General Authorities are overseeing temples.

When I asked volunteers at the Provo Temple why so many volunteer, they said their motivation is to serve others. They said volunteers do rituals for the deceased because they feel they are helping those who cannot help themselves. They said it also gives volunteers a new life and something to look forward to. Many retiree volunteers aren't in good health, have arthritic hands, and don't hear too well, but they do "find joy in serving others."

Temple workers. Temples require the assistance of thousands of volunteers worldwide, and among them are senior missionaries who are serving full-time missions as temple workers.

I had the pleasure of interviewing a senior couple who served a two-year mission in the mid-2000s as temple workers in Santo Domingo, the capital of the Dominican Republic. Both were born into the Church and were in their early sixties when they served. He was a retired college professor who served a mission in the 1960s, and subsequently served as a bishop and stake president. She too served a mission in the 1960s and had fulfilled various responsibilities in the Latter-day Saint Church. They had eight children, seven of whom served missions (they said the eighth, a daughter, fell in love and married before reaching her twenty-first birthday.)

When I asked why they chose to serve a senior mission, they responded that the need was there, they wanted to serve others, and the timing was right for them. They knew that senior missionaries are badly needed throughout the world and in a wide variety of capacities. Being committed to "helping move the work along," they felt the desire to contribute too. They had made covenants in the temple to serve the Lord, and this was a fulfillment of those promises. They said they had long known that happiness comes from serving others, and this too was part of their motivation. They added that in the broad scheme of things for their family, the timing was right for them to be absent for two years. Their aging parents were managing all right, and other family members were able to help out as needed. They feared that had they waited much longer, it might have been difficult to leave them. Further, their own health was good enough to enable them to pass the Church's physical exam, to serve anywhere in the world, and they felt enough vigor to make this venture. They also saw it as a challenge and an adventure; to live in a different place, to make new friends, to figure out how best to fit in, and to serve.

They left blank the type of assignment and location they desired on their missionary application, believing that Church leaders making those assignments ought not be constrained by the personal preferences of the applicants. They believed they were assigned to the temple because they had worked previously in the Washington, D.C., and Boston temples, and thus were already trained to do the work. It takes months to train someone to be a temple worker, as there are many ordinances that must be memorized, along with procedures to learn, and they felt older people often have a difficult time memorizing. They added it seems likely they were sent to the Caribbean because of the need for French-speaking workers to serve patrons from Haiti and Guadeloupe. The sister is fluent in French (having served her mission in France), and they felt that was probably a key factor in their assignment.

As they were assigned to a Spanish-speaking country, he observed the Church obviously took a chance on them in this regard. The expectation was that they would learn what Spanish they could to fulfill the assignment, and if that proved impossible the Church would use them as best it could. Working in the laundry takes no language skills, he pointed out. They were never told they had to become fluent, but it was obvious that the more conversant they became, the more valuable their service would be. So this was their incentive to learn the language.

They had their own tutor for about six weeks at the Provo MTC, meeting twice a week in the evening, but all this did for them was to get them "off the ground" on pronunciation and a few other matters. They felt there's really no substitute for intensive language immersion, such as young missionaries are given. In retrospect, they wished they had been taught more key phrases, which is the best approach for those not expecting to become highly fluent. After their arrival in the Dominican Republic, they studied the language every day for about six months and then tapered off at their own respective levels. Both memorized the temple ordinances in Spanish (she also memorized them in French), and they learned enough Spanish to communicate with patrons, workers, and outside the temple in normal situations, such as on the street, in stores, and on the telephone. He felt a missionary couple with no previous second-language experience and not "into books or study" would find learning a new language very difficult, particularly in their senior years.

The role of the senior temple workers was to help train the local members, to get them involved in the work, and to remain in the background. The seniors didn't expect to be the leaders, but rather worked alongside the Dominicans. They helped with things Dominicans couldn't do. They worked full-time, around six hours a day. He taught, supervised, and trained local members to do the ordinances. He performed marriages, served a shift (five hours) a week as a worker, and scheduled the activities of around two hundred volunteers, which he described as a huge job.

They did face a staffing problem in the Dominican Republic. There is not a retirement age there, and so people work until they die. In contrast, most of the temple workers in Provo are retired or are BYU students.

The temple president assigned them to organize and carry out a "dedication day celebration," which was held every year at the temple. The concept for the day was to keep the temple as busy as possible, and patrons were urged to attend in large numbers, which they did. The president wanted the islanders to experience what a very busy temple, like the Provo Temple, is like. An additional aspect was to keep the eight to ten senior missionaries in the background, giving the actual assignments to the Dominican workers, particularly the leadership assignments.

They spent about two months preparing for this day, making assignments, working out complicated schedules, and holding meetings (all in Spanish, which wasn't easy). The sister was in charge of the women workers, and her husband the men. They were up nearly all night several days before preparing and fine-tuning the schedules and assignments. In terms of technical details, and despite their previous temple experience, it was the most complicated and challenging assignment they had ever had.

And to the Dominicans' credit (and theirs, I would add), it went like "clockwork."

Over a twelve-hour period that day, around 2,200 patrons attended the temple and around 5,500 ordinances were completed. The temple was the busiest in the Mormon Church on that day. All were impressed that when called to the task, the Dominicans could run their own temple quite well, and on an extremely busy day at that.

It was quite a lot of fun, they said, and when it was all over they felt a wonderful satisfaction to have given the Dominicans a stage on which they could show their talents and dedication.

The senior couple performed some proselytizing here and there, befriending several shoeshine boys, for instance. They drove fifteen miles to their ghetto out in a suburb and took them to church nearby. One of them and his family took the lessons and probably were baptized after they left. When the couple returned to Utah, one of them begged them to take him with them. They had his friend and him to dinner twice in their apartment. These kinds of relationships meant a lot to them.

They also visited several orphanages and a children's hospital. The sister organized a gift-giving visit to the latter, and one of their granddaughters in Idaho raised nearly one thousand dollars and then visited the country with her family and presented the funds to one of the orphanages.

The seniors also performed more mundane tasks. They pulled weeds in the temple garden, folded temple clothes in the laundry, and repaired clothing.

They reported that working one-on-one with islanders who needed help proved to be one of the high points of their assignment. For instance, he did what he could to promote young temple workers, because older temple workers tended (because of their culture) to keep young people in menial tasks. So he would often step aside and invite a young man to take his place and learn by doing, rather than taking the important tasks for himself or allowing the older Dominican workers to take all the important tasks.

Another high point of their stay was continual association with the small (seventy-capacity) MTC in their apartment building within the temple compound. They saw many North American and island missionaries come and go, and they were sometimes asked to help teach them gospel lessons on Sunday (particularly the sister, who was asked to teach French-speaking Haitian sister missionaries). They developed strong friendships with quite a few island missionaries, most notably from Haiti and Jamaica, as well as the Dominican Republic. They enjoyed additional associations with them in the temple, as they came to the temple weekly. Four years later they were still corresponding with some of them. All were poor, humble, and spiritually-minded, and the senior missionaries said they learned much from them.

Each wrote in the others' mission journals before they departed, and the seniors said the islanders were astonished that a rich, white, North American couple would invite them to do such a thing.

Health service. Latter-day Saints are well known for their community service, for providing disaster relief, humanitarian service, and serving others in their time of need, whether Church members or not. These activities were given greater emphasis in the latter part of the twentieth century, such that by 1990 missionaries were expected to provide up to four hours a week of non-proselytizing community service. Beginning in 1983, those with a health background were sent out as "health missionaries," to bring their knowledge and skills of nutrition, sanitation, and disease prevention to developing countries around the world. Senior missionaries, older sisters, and senior sisters in particular serve in these roles.[147]

I had the pleasure of interviewing a senior couple who served a two-year health service mission in Mongolia in the mid-2000s. She was raised in the Church in Utah, while he was raised a Roman Catholic in Salt Lake City. He became a convert at age eighteen in the late 1950s when they were graduating from high school. He didn't go on a mission, nor did she, but she said she always wanted to go. She said young women weren't encouraged to serve missions back then, and those who did were labeled "spinsters." Seniors didn't go on missions back then either, she added. She earned a master's degree in Cross Cultural Training and he earned a master's and a Ph.D. in Public Health. His background was in the management of health care institutions, and he gained international experience while taking students abroad on health-related internships and field experiences.

They were sixty-two when they applied for a mission. They weren't interested in proselytizing, so they volunteered to provide international, humanitarian aid. They were assigned to Mongolia, which was considered a hardship mission.

He was made the branch president of the local congregation the week after they arrived in the capital city of Ulaanbaatar, taking over from a Mongolian. He found it a very difficult calling. His Mongolian initially wasn't very good. He said the people were great, but there was no consistency in attendance. He went on "splits" with younger missionaries, and they were limited in what they could do because of the law that prohibited active evangelism. They had to wait until someone inquired of them who they were and what they were doing. He said while people knew they were Mormons, not many engaged them in conversation.

The senior drew on his expertise in health care management. There is a high infant mortality rate in Mongolia, and he directed a neo-natal resuscitation program. He arranged to have the American Medical Association manual on neonatal resuscitation translated into Mongolian, and he distributed it around the country. The program was very successful.

He started a burn unit. Nomadic Mongolians live in "gers" (the Mongolian equivalent of a Russian yurt), which include a metal stove in the center of the structure. Burns are common. He was able to obtain hospital equipment, and he wrote twelve medical grants, which were funded after they left.

He taught an English language course for physicians, which included general and medical English. He also served as a consultant to a national drug abuse prevention program.

The senior sister created her own project, a non-residential school that fed and educated street children. For that, much to her surprise, she was awarded the highest honor Mongolia bestows on its non-citizens.

There are thousands of street children in Ulaanbaatar. They are orphans and runaways, and many have been abused. They don't attend school, and many are in poor health. Some spend their nights underground next to the steamy pipes in the city's hot water system, which keeps them alive during the long, brutal Mongolian winters. They emerge from "the hole" each day through uncovered manholes to scrounge for food at dumps, work at markets, steal, or engage in prostitution. Experience has shown that if intervention can occur within the first six months of their being on the street, there is a greater likelihood that their lives can be turned around; but after that, they seem impervious to positive intervention.

The senior couple became aware of the plight of homeless street children when they noticed that a dog was chewing on a bone that had been thrown in the garbage. Later that day they noticed that a street child was chewing on the same bone.

They were aghast.

She spoke with city officials and said she wanted to do something for the children; she wanted to start a soup kitchen and non-residential school for them. She was told she could use a facility near the American Embassy, but the city had no money to help fund it. The Latter-day Saint Church walks a fine line to avoid conflict with the Mongolian government, so the Church couldn't help fund her program either.

She contributed one thousand dollars of her own money, and, together with the Latter-day Saint wife of a U.S. Embassy employee, they opened the school. They fed street children and held classes for them throughout the day, getting them out of the harsh weather and teaching them how to read. Other Latter-day Saints carried on with the school after she and her husband returned to the United States.

For her outstanding efforts, the senior sister was awarded the Order of the Polar Star, the highest civilian award given to a non-Mongolian. Not one to seek attention for what she considered the right thing to do, she admitted that she wasn't aware of the significance of the award. A city official presented it to her, nice things were said about her and the school, she thanked him, and she went home and put the medal in a drawer. She said that it was only when leaving the country and a customs agent saw it and expressed amazement at it, that she realized its significance. She was told by the customs official (who first assumed it had been awarded to her husband) that any time she wants to return to the country all she needs to do is show it to border officials, and she will immediately be welcomed back into the country.

The framed medal now adorns a wall in their home.

The couple considered their mission a positive experience. It taught them how to survive at many different levels, both personally and professionally, and they learned to endure the Mongolian winter. They said if the right call came, they would do it again.

Church membership continues to grow in the country. It stood at 4,358 when the couple arrived in Mongolia in 2002, and there were 10,763 members as of January 1, 2015.[148] It is felt the Mormon Church's emphasis on the family strikes a chord with Mongolians.

Church Educational System. The LDS Church maintains an extensive continuing education program for young adults ages eighteen to thirty through its Institutes of Religion. There are over 2,500 Institutes worldwide, which served nearly 360,000 students as of January 1, 2015.[149] They offer educational, social, and spiritual opportunities for participants, providing a safe haven away from the temptations of the secular world. Classes offered include the Book of Mormon, *Doctrine and Covenants*, *Pearl of Great Price*, Old Testament, New Testament, LDS Church History, Presidents of the Church, Introduction to Family History, Mission Preparation, and Marriage Preparation. Institutes provide social activities including talent shows, performances, sports events, and choirs, as well as weekly devotional meetings. Institutes are popular places for returned missionaries who are seeking a spouse. Full-time senior missionaries and part-time service missionaries support the work of the Institutes as teachers and support staff. The ability for senior missionaries to interact with young adults is said to be an especially important trait.

A senior sister who served an eighteen-month mission at an Institute in Utah in the early 2000s was raised in a Scandinavian village in Northern New England. Her grandfather was an emigrant from Norway and was Lutheran. She attended his church, then a Congregational, then a Baptist, and then she married a Methodist. But she said she still felt like she "didn't have it all." She joined the Latter-day Saint Church in 1975 and has been a member ever since.

After her second husband passed away in the late 1990s, she decided to serve a mission, "to give it a try." She volunteered to go on a service mission, but she didn't indicate a preference. She said she wanted to leave that decision up to the Lord. When she received her call in 2002, informing her that she would be serving a Church Educational System (CES) mission in Utah, she didn't know what a CES mission was.

She found her time at the senior MTC in Provo "inspiring." She was one of thirty seniors who entered the MTC at the time, and she was impressed by the power of the Spirit she felt there. The young elders who would stream into the cafeteria over a two-hour period especially struck her. While "not quite dry behind the ears," she sensed they possessed a special power because of the Melchizedek priesthood they held. She described the cafeteria food as "stupendous." She had a ten-day training period and spent the last two days in Salt Lake City.

Her fellow senior missionaries at the MTC, most of whom were assigned to exotic places around the world, were quite amused when she reported that she would be serving just six miles up the road. Their laughter didn't bother her, because being two thousand miles from home was something new and different for her.

Her companion at the MTC went on to serve as her companion at the Institute. Once at their mission assignment, she and her companion shared an apartment; each had her own bedroom. They were allowed to go out by themselves, but were told to be careful. They could call home any time they liked.

She filled a number of roles at the Institute. She worked in the registration office, in the library, and did office jobs. She found the Institute director and staff very helpful. The director encouraged her and her companion to get immersed in the life and culture of Utah, and she reported they were "treated like royalty." They were taken to plays and performances and were included in Church activities. They traveled around the state and marveled at its geography. They went to a semi-annual General Conference meeting held in Salt Lake City, visited the Family History Library, and visited twelve Utah temples.

When asked why she served a mission, she responded that it was for the Church, for her grandchildren, and for herself. She was pleased to serve the young adults at the Institute, to see them grow spiritually and intellectually and to watch them interact with one another, particularly the returned missionaries who were looking for a spouse. She also wanted to be an example to her grandchildren, and while she missed two of their high school graduations, she felt it was worth it because she set an example of service and commitment to the Mormon Church. She also served herself. She traveled by air for the first time by herself, and she got to experience a part of the country where she had never been before.

It was also an opportunity to see what it is like to live inside the "Zion Curtain" (the invisible curtain said to surround Utah) and to live in a community where practically everyone on the block was LDS. This was in stark contrast to what she experienced living in Northern New England, where none of her neighbors were Latter-day Saints.

The senior sister attended a Family History class at the Institute that taught her how to seek out her ancestors and prepare their names for temple ordinances. She now serves as the Family History Librarian at her local church/unit.

I asked what she felt she gained from her mission, and she said she gained self-understanding and self-confidence, knowing who she is and being able to do things on her own. "It was a wonderful, wonderful, experience," she reported. "I am glad I went. It changed who I am."

"But," she added with a smile, "I am also happy to be back home."

Challenges and Blessings of Serving a Senior Mission

To a person, senior interviewees said they valued their mission experience. They helped strengthen the Latter-day Saint Church, they provided service to others, and they learned things about themselves. But they also faced challenges. Some found it harder than they had expected, some had to adjust to difficult living conditions and some found they didn't have the energy they once had. Some had to reassess their marriages, and some became frustrated with the Church bureaucracy. But all said they enjoyed the experience and many said they would do it again.

Challenges. Seniors face some of the same challenges as younger missionaries: they have to get used to people staring at them and their nametags; doors are slammed in the faces of proselytizing missionaries; and they don't always get along with their companion, even if it is their spouse. Depending on where they serve, they may have to disinfect food, cope with fleas and lice, have intermittent electrical service, and share a house with lizards or tarantulas. They may have to deal with extreme heat or extreme cold, medical care may be lacking, and they may have to adjust to cultural differences. Those who serve in third-world countries are often depressed at the poverty they witness, yet they are advised not give handouts to those in need. One couple spoke of observing many beggars on the streets in the city where they served, particularly at stoplights, most either severely disabled or using small children to procure a handout.

Some single, senior sisters face problems of compatibility with their companions (as did senior single males when they used to serve on senior missions). Many senior sisters are either widowed or divorced, have lived alone for years, and find it especially hard to adjust to living in such close proximity with someone they don't know.

A senior sister observed that she found it hard to adjust to living with another adult because each was "set in her own ways." She had to learn to love her companions, even if she didn't like them. Another senior said she got along fine with her first companion, but regarding her second, "We just didn't hitch horses." She tried to make their relationship work by working on her attitude, hoping her companion would do the same, but to no avail. In the end she decided she just had to endure it. It was a learning experience for her. She didn't feel she had the skills to make it work.

A sixty-three-year-old widow observed: "It's a challenge, a big challenge, to be able to get along with your companion for twenty-four hours a day. You can't even go shopping without them. When you do your laundry, they have to do their laundry. I used to think: 'Thank goodness for the bathroom!'"

When I met with the seniors at the MTC in Provo, senior sisters expressed concern about their future companions, fearing they would be paired with younger, more energetic partners. A senior sister is defined as a woman forty years of age or older, and a sixty-five-year-old sister said she was afraid that being paired with a companion twenty-five years her junior "would run her ragged." Another senior sister said the idea of being matched with an even younger companion bothered her "immensely." She wondered what twenty-one year old would want to be paired with a sixty-six year old and whether it would be fair to the younger companion. She didn't want her companion to feel she was being cheated by not being with someone her own age.

She did express a note of optimism. She had gone back to college at the age of fifty-three and found she could bridge the gap in age with younger students as long as she didn't act like she knew more than they did, and as long as they didn't think old people couldn't learn new things.

For some, their fears at the MTC about younger companions were justified once they got into the field. A sixty-two year old said one of her companions was fourteen years her junior and she found it physically difficult to keep up with her. A sixty-three-year-old senior was teamed with a twenty-six-year-old sister who, in the words of the older sister, "was very resentful that they had stuck her with an old lady and she let the whole world know it, including me."

Challenges in getting along with one's companion aren't restricted to single seniors, because one of the biggest issues many older couples face in the mission field (and something I didn't expect) is that of compatibility. "It is a revelation how little you know your spouse," exclaimed a senior husband serving in England. Some have to work through issues in their relationships that have been ignored for years. They are now "companions" in the LDS missionary sense; they are not only living together, but they are also working together. One is not the "boss" as he or she may have been when employed. They are coequals in a team. They are no longer two separate entities. "You are used to living together," observed a married senior, "but now you are living *and* working together." Thus compatibility is important.

Many couples said they got to know one another anew. A senior couple said they lived in one room in a foreign country for two years, and they had to work on their relationship. They knew of couples who had considered divorce as a result of the personal tensions that surfaced during their mission, but they weren't aware of any who had carried through with it. Some had a more positive outcome: they reported growing closer to their spouse as a result of working through their issues.

Cultural differences are another area that takes getting used to. A couple on a tropical foreign mission said members would arrive twenty minutes late to services if the weather was good, but they wouldn't show up at all if it was raining. Walking, riding a bicycle, or driving a car can be a challenge, depending on the culture, norms, and practices where they serve. A senior serving in Latin America said that people drove on the sidewalks in order to get around traffic jams, while a couple who served in Southeast Asia said a traffic stop sign "was merely a suggestion."

Like younger missionaries, seniors need to discern whether people are interested in their message, in financial support, or in knowing and talking with foreigners. One couple described how the Church had financially helped some people and some tried to see how much they could get. A large meal would be served when having meetings, and some came only for the food. In some countries status comes with associating with Americans and American institutions, but little interest would be shown in the Church's spiritual message.

Seniors also experience frustrations unique to their age. They aren't as proficient technologically as their children and grandchildren, and some need computer training. Learning a foreign language does not come as easily as it does for younger missionaries. Seniors are more likely to experience health issues. Some are surprised at what hard work a mission can be, and they get frustrated with the fact that they are not able to do as much as when they were younger. They tire more easily. Good mission presidents tell them to take a nap when they feel that way. A hardworking couple reported they were "quite tired" when they returned from their two year mission.

Some seniors who held positions of some authority while employed find it difficult to do routine work and to accept directions from someone who would have worked for *them* just a few months earlier. A retired college professor serving in a mission president's office in England was given the task of tracking down lost and lapsed members. It involved looking through numerous records and making many telephone calls. She described it as a desk job, a secretarial job, which she found routine and boring. As a professor, she was used to telling others what to do; now everyone was telling her what to do.

Some senior men report it is a challenge to function effectively as "shadow leaders" and advisors; their tendency is to assert themselves continually in doing tasks they are well-trained to do. But the goal is for the local leadership to learn how to run their own unit, not for the missionaries to run it for them. An interviewee said he wasn't always sure when to help out and when to step back. He worked at letting local leaders manage on their own unless a crisis was impending, and then he and his wife kindly offered to help. But it wasn't always easy to determine when to step in.

A sister interviewed near the end of her two-year mission said that missing her fifty-two children and grandchildren was a "burden" and was the hardest part of the mission. She struggled with the separation but eventually got past it. She tells senior sisters they have to learn to let go; they should not stay in touch with their family every day, but restrict communication to once a week. Other seniors spoke of the difficulty of being separated from their family.

Seniors enjoy greater freedom than younger missionaries. Depending on their mission president, some don't have to be together at all times, are free to travel in their district, and can read what they want. Still, some seniors feel it is too restrictive. They feel they lack the freedom to do what they want to do. They aren't allowed to go beyond the boundaries of their mission, and some, because it is felt they don't need them, are not allowed cars.

Some, including those located great distances from the United States, expressed frustration with working with headquarters in Salt Lake City. They found the "Wasatch Mentality" to be at odds at times with the realities of the field. (Salt Lake City sits in the shadow of the Wasatch Mountain Range.) They found communication very cumbersome, and they felt the bureaucracy was slow and unresponsive to workers in the field, that they didn't value the opinion of those on the front lines, and that people in Salt Lake City were afraid to make decisions. They felt the Church needed to do a better job researching the needs of the country in which they would be serving.

One couple was told they would be involved in a particular project when they arrived at their assigned location, but once there they discovered the project had been completed a few years earlier by another agency. They were told to find something else to do. They were disappointed and considered returning home, but they stayed. They identified other projects that needed to be done, but they knew approval from Salt Lake City would be a long-time coming. Using their professional judgment and keeping their mission president informed, they proceeded on their own and set up their own projects, not waiting to hear back from Salt Lake City.

They followed the philosophy, "It is better to ask forgiveness, than permission."

They shared their frustrations with Church authorities and surmised they became known as "the outspoken couple," but they wanted to provide constructive feedback to the Missionary Department. They were especially appreciative of their mission president, who supported them throughout their mission. They also found the lack of continuity a problem. They felt they had just gotten their bearings and then their mission was over.

In spite of these challenges, they still found the experience "wonderful."

When asked if they experienced challenges, the couple that served in Pakistan responded that "every day" was a challenge. The language was a challenge. They had to soak vegetables in bleach for twenty minutes because human fertilizer was used to grow them. They were served drinks in bottles or cans when visiting members or investigators, because it was understood they couldn't drink the water. The sister said that if someone would have told her what it was like before they went—sweltering heat, meat hanging in markets and covered with flies, the dirt, the dust, the open sewers—she probably wouldn't have wanted to do it. But once she was there and working, she never once thought about going home early, even though each day brought new and unexpected challenges. And in spite of the dirt and dust, they found the city where they were serving a beautiful place; they called it the city of flowers. They found that while houses were full of flies, they were clean. And they noted that the women always looked clean and neat wearing their long dresses.

The couple who served a two-year temple mission in the Caribbean said the whole experience humbled them in many ways, reminding them continually that although they were well-educated, "rich" (in contrast to most Dominicans), committed to the Latter-day Saint Church, resourceful, and capable, they were lacking on many fronts: language, health and vigor, being "shadows" in leadership roles, working effectively with the temple presidents (they had two), and working with patrons in five languages (Spanish, French, Dutch, and English, plus Haitian Creole). They reported that at their most challenging and frustrating times, they pleaded for support and guidance, and the Lord blessed them greatly, far beyond what they deserved, enabling them to survive trials and afflictions and to come through the better for them. They reported this was a great blessing because it reminded them the Lord doesn't abandon His children in their times of need, particularly if they are trying to keep His commandments and follow Him.

Blessings. A senior couple who served in a mission office in a large Midwestern city in 2009 said their greatest joy was working with others—providing service to others and seeing their lives change. He was in charge of eighty missionary apartments and fifty-nine vehicles, and she was in charge of finances. She said she was learning new things, including how to use a computer, and it gave her hope and understanding. He was happy the experience kept him mentally active.

A senior couple who served in England said the most gratifying aspect of their service was seeing lives change. They enjoyed seeing local members grow as they worked with them on developing their leadership skills and taught them how to fulfill their Church responsibilities.

Another senior couple felt their family was blessed for their service, both during their absence and following it. Specifically, they earnestly prayed that a son and a daughter would find the right companions and marry, and they did: the daughter while they were gone (they returned briefly for the wedding), and their son soon after their return. Two grandchildren were also born during their time away.

I asked them what the experience meant to them. They listed a variety of things. It provided them the satisfaction of serving others full-time for two years. It expanded their capacities to adjust to a new culture and to make a comfortable life among people quite different from them. It enabled them to work through small and large challenges, including disinfecting all their food and coping with small health issues (such as fleas and lice). They worked effectively and compatibly with other senior missionaries. It helped them to stay in the background rather than assert themselves because of their previous Church experiences. It also gave their extended family a legacy of service to Jesus Christ—it sent a message to them that their parents considered it important enough to leave the comforts of home and family to serve in this way.

When asked what she learned about herself, the sister who served in Singapore and Pakistan said she learned she could do things she didn't think she could do. She drew closer to her spouse and to the

Savior. "When you are set apart by Church authorities, and with the Lord's help, you can do anything," she observed.

She said she had been hesitant about going because she found it difficult to accept change. She then stopped and corrected herself: "I *had* found it difficult to accept change in my life, but not anymore."

Part-time Church-service Missionary and Volunteer Opportunities

There are thousands of service opportunities for those who cannot commit to a full-time mission. They can be seniors or younger Church members. Part-time Church-Service Missionaries serve in their own country from eight to thirty-two hours a week, for six to twenty-four months. They can serve from home. These missions can include: computer-based work assisting patrons around the world who are doing genealogical work; hosting and leading tours at historic sites; teaching English as a second language; assisting in employment centers; building and maintenance work; administrative work in mission offices; working with prison inmates; computer hardware and software support; making telephone calls to obtain updated addresses of those who have moved or who are not attending church; and assisting at Church camps, to name just a few.

There are also volunteer opportunities requiring a wide range of skills. Foreign language volunteers are needed to assist foreign language tutors at the MTC in Provo. Volunteers are sought to serve as missionary housing inspectors, as facilitators for LDS twelve-step addiction-recovery support groups, in healthcare, and to serve as investigator role-players at the Provo MTC.

Member engagement is vital in a lay organization and the importance of their contributions is clearly evident in the work that is performed by the full-time, part-time, and volunteers workers. The Latter-day Saint Church could not survive without them.[150]

The Mormon Tabernacle Choir

There are other types of missionary service that reflect the very broad definition of "mission" the Church employs. Members of the Mormon Tabernacle Choir, for example, are considered music missionaries. They are called and set apart, as are younger and senior missionaries. They all advance the work of the Mormon Church, each in their own way.

Referred to as "America's Choir" by President Ronald Reagan, the 360-member Mormon Tabernacle Choir has been in existence for over a century. It has produced scores of recordings, earned two platinum records, and was awarded a Grammy. The program that showcases the choir, "Music and the Spoken Word," had its first radio broadcast from the Tabernacle on Temple Square, Salt Lake City, on July 15, 1929. Since that date the program has enjoyed an uninterrupted series of weekly performances, making it the longest-running continuous network broadcast in the world. In recognition of its many achievements, "Music and the Spoken Word" has been named to the National Radio Hall of Fame. In 2015, the choir was inducted into the American Classical Music Hall of Fame. The choir travels worldwide, has performed in many of the world's greatest concert venues, and has performed before millions. It is the very public face of the Latter-day Saint Church.

The standards and expectations for participation in the choir are very high. Members must be Church members in good standing, they must undergo a series of rigorous auditions, and those selected must participate in music training classes. They must live within a one-hundred-mile radius of Temple Square, Salt Lake City, attend at least 80 percent of the rehearsals and performances, make an initial commitment of five years, and step down when they reach the age of sixty or have served twenty years—whichever come first. It is estimated that members devote between fifteen and twenty hours a week to the choir. Spouses of members are referred to as "choir widows," because of the heavy time commitment of members.

While singing is their passion, choir members say their real role and assignment is that of music missionaries. They wear missionary-like nametags when they travel, coordinate missionary activities with mission presidents in the areas where they perform, and carry pass-along cards and CDs to share with non-members, with whom they mingle after performances. Full-time missionaries make a point of bringing investigators to hear the choir perform and to meet the choir members.[151]

Bearing one's testimony is a common practice in the Latter-day Saint Church. For members of the Mormon Tabernacle Choir, they bear theirs through their music. As I mentioned in the Prologue, a student in one of my religion classes observed that it was because of the Mormon Tabernacle Choir that she had not rejected the missionaries' appeal to consider the LDS Church; she said that something that can produce something *that* good, warrants her serious consideration.

The choir, too, "helps move the work along."

Conclusion

There is a huge, worldwide demand for senior Latter-day Saint missionaries. Virtually every mission president would like to have more serving with him. Their age and maturity have a stabilizing effect. They give strength to the mission, provide shadow leadership in a branch, and provide support for younger missionaries.

Interviewees young and old commented on how the seniors' age can be a positive influence when talking with investigators. A young sister who served in California said senior missionary couples are dignified, experienced, and could do things she and her companion could never do. Older investigators would look at her and her companion and communicate the attitude, "And what are *you* going to tell me?" When senior couples joined them, the seniors did a much better job of communicating than the young sisters could, given the tools they had with their limited twenty-two years of age.

An older sister agreed, having observed that people frequently relate better to older missionaries. "A lot of people will listen to an older person quicker than they will to a nineteen-year-old boy," she observed. "They are good boys and very sincere, but sometimes people will associate better with older people."

A younger sister serving in the early 2000s was so impressed by how well senior missionaries related to investigators that she wrote to her parents and told them they too needed to go on a senior mission. She was so inspired by the senior's example that she plans to serve a senior mission herself some day. An interviewee who served in Mexico in the mid-1960s said he and his wife planned to go on at least two senior missions after he retired. He had watched his mother go on two missions after his father passed away, and he said it was good for her. He interviewed couples who had served multiple missions in Africa, and he spoke of their excitement. "It can get in their blood," he said. "They go on a mission, come back for a bit, and then go out again."

Another interviewee said he too planned to serve multiple missions with his wife after he retired. He would love to work until he is sixty-five or seventy, retire, go on a mission for two years, come back for a while, go back out for two more years, return for a while, and repeat the process until he died. When asked what kind of mission he would like to serve, he responded: "I am easy. Just send me. The Restored message is what I would like to share. That is what motivates me. I just need to come home periodically to see my grandkids."

I contacted a senior missionary in the late 2000s who served as an administrative assistant in the mission president's office in a large city in the American Midwest. I explained my project and asked if I could interview her; I said I wanted to tell her story. She seemed surprised by the request and said that she felt "ordinary," that she felt her story was not unusual when compared to the stories of other senior missionaries she knew. I assured her that it was not ordinary in the eyes of the wider society and that non-Mormons perceived what she was doing as being quite unusual.

She was in her late fifties and from the American Southwest. She converted to the LDS faith at age eight. Her mother joined, but her father did not. She became active in the Church as a teenager. She didn't serve a mission in her twenties because young women didn't serve missions back then, but she watched young men go and thought she would like to do the same someday. After raising a large family as a single parent, she felt it was time to pursue her dream of serving a mission. Her children were very supportive, including a son who had served a mission and a son who had left the Church, but who was proud she was serving. She wanted to go foreign, but said she was happy to serve where she was needed. She felt her previous work experience as an office assistant in a Church office in the American Southwest prepared her for her current administrative position as the referral secretary, where she handled referrals, requests for DVDs and Books of Mormon, and recorded baptisms.

Her experiences paralleled those of the younger missionaries in some ways. She felt uncomfortable wearing the nametag. "I feel like a bug," she said, because people stared at her and didn't know what to think of her. She had a great companion, but it was hard to live with someone after having lived alone for so many years. She found it hard to give up her freedom, to not be able to come and go as she pleased.

She also had experiences that were more unique to seniors. She described herself as homeless, because she had sold her house before leaving on her mission. She had lingering health issues, and she regretted not being able to visit her family. She had twenty-five grandchildren and nine great-grandchildren, and she missed the births of five great-grandchildren while on her two-year mission. But she said it was worth it. A high point was working with the young sisters and elders whom she described as the "cream of the crop." They worked hard and were dedicated. It was a real treat and an honor to watch them grow. She said inner growth, both spiritual and personal, was what was important—both theirs and hers.

As with most missionaries, regardless of their ages, her mission was a time of self-discovery. She successfully faced new challenges, and skills surfaced she didn't know she had. She said she was learning who she really was. Her mission was a time to see "if what she was on the outside was what she was on the inside."

She said they didn't always agree, but she was working on it.

PART VI

After the Mission

CHAPTER 12

Going Home: An Uncomfortable Return, a "Successful" Mission, and the Benefits of Serving

"I am going home a different person than when I came out."
AN AUSTRALIAN SISTER WHO SERVED ON TEMPLE SQUARE, SALT LAKE CITY, ON THE EVE OF GOING HOME IN 2008

"I came out to serve others, but I have been blessed more than I can ever say."
A SISTER WHO SERVED IN NORTHERN NEW ENGLAND IN THE MID-1990'S

"Going home is highly overrated."
AN AMERICAN ELDER, NOT LONG AFTER RETURNING HOME FROM HIS MISSION

As Elder Livingston's plane taxied to the gate, bringing him home from his mission in Guatemala, he thought back to what his returned-missionary brother had said to him two years earlier: "You think it's hard leaving home? You will find it's even harder when you leave your mission."

Elder Livingston said that at the time he thought: "That's ridiculous. I am ready to turn around and go home right now. What a dumb thing to say."

But now he realized his brother was right; it *was* harder to return home. He was a different person than when he left for his mission. He had grown to love Guatemala and the Guatemalans he had worked with, he had become fluent in Spanish, and he felt comfortable in the culture.

If anything, it was returning home that made him uncomfortable.

He worried because things probably hadn't changed much at home, and he feared he might slide back into old habits. He felt insecure about his future; his life had been planned from birth through his mission, but now there were many unknowns ahead—schooling, marriage, occupation.

"Will I make the right choices and decisions?" he wondered.

Other returning missionaries on the flight expressed similar feelings and concerns. As if to hang on to their mission experience as long as they could, they were the last to exit the airplane.

As his mother ran to greet him, Elder Livingston realized how difficult his mission had been: to be away from home for two years, the rejection, the discouragement, the poverty he had seen.

As he hugged her tight, he said, "I did it! I did it! I did it!" In that instant came the realization that he had accomplished something, and it wasn't an easy task. It was a difficult task, but it was good, and it was worthwhile.

Thinking back on that moment years later, Elder Livingston said it was a good thing he realized that, because it helped him as he has faced other challenges. There have been many times since then when he thought, "We will get through this, we will ride this out, because I have done things that are as hard, or even harder."

Most missionaries return home exhausted, but with ambivalent feelings. They have led intense, focused lives for eighteen or twenty-four months, and they are ready to move on with their lives, but part of them wants to remain in the mission field. They have changed in significant ways, but they return to home environments that may not have changed much, and they have to work at not falling into old habits and attitudes. They find it difficult to suddenly be alone and to be responsible for structuring their days. They may try to impose structure on their families, such as having regular scripture study and weekly planning meetings, but these don't last long. They may share missionary stories, but they fear their family and friends will soon tire of hearing them. They discover that going home is not as great as it is made out to be, and some wish they had never left the mission field.

They are experiencing reverse culture shock, and many find that returning home is even more difficult than leaving for their mission.

Missionaries reap significant benefits from their mission experiences. They return home with knowledge, skills and dispositions that can enrich their lives, lead to more satisfying employment, and contribute to stronger marriages and families. The Church also benefits, because research shows that returned missionaries are more active than the Latter-day Saint population as a whole; they are more religious, more likely to marry in the temple, and more likely to remain active in the Mormon Church.

Chapter 12 looks at this readjustment period and the benefits gained from the mission experience. Chapter 13 then follows the returned missionaries as they move on to the next phases of their lives. For many it is a time of increased commitment to the LDS faith; but for some, it sets the stage for them to leave the Church.

The Countdown

"Dump." As we saw in Chapter 5, missionaries divide their mission into six-month segments and assign terms that denote their experience: "bump," "hump," "slump," and finally, "dump," when they are sent home.

We will consider the "dump" phase in this section.

"Getting trunkie." There is an expression that describes how some missionaries feel as they approach the final few months of their mission: it's called "getting trunkie." Being trunkie is a state of mind. It manifests itself in their becoming increasingly preoccupied with going home; they think and talk about family, girlfriends, boyfriends, friends, jobs, and going back to school. Some pack their bags weeks in advance. Some coast; they relax in their missionary efforts, and they may sleep in. They are worn out, and they are holding on until the end.

An elder observed with classic understatement, "Being gone from home for two years starts to wear on you a bit near the end."

A conscientious elder who served in Switzerland said while he never stopped working, it was hard to remain focused on the work near the end of his mission. Mentally he had shifted to thinking about home during his last three months. He said the last month was especially hard, because he knew that any investigators he found would not be baptized before he left.

An elder who served as an A.P. in Eastern Europe said many good missionaries experience trunkiness; they don't have the energy they had as new missionaries, and it affects some more than others. In more serious cases, it is an issue mission presidents try to counter through increased oversight by district and zone leaders or by assigning new responsibilities that keep the missionary engaged.

There are also those who do the opposite when faced with their impending return home. They feel there is more for them to do, and they recommit to their work during the final months. An elder who served in England said when he had one month left in the mission field he decided he wanted to do all that he could with that month, since he would never again have the opportunity to devote twenty-four hours a day, seven days a week, to the Lord's work.

Some interviewees admitted that while they were exhausted, they felt a sense of possessiveness with regard to the investigators they had been working with, and they didn't want to leave them. They thought about other missionaries coming in and teaching "their people," and they wanted to be very much involved in making sure the next missionaries did a good job.

Some even chose to extend their mission by a few months when permitted to do so.

And there are those who are ready to return home. An A.P who served in Japan said he didn't consider extending because he had given his "best shot" for two years, and he needed to go back to college. A returning elder said he was ready to continue his education; he missed reading, learning, and school. He said it would feel good to go back and "get a life." A sister who served in Argentina said she remembered being physically and emotionally exhausted at the end of her mission. "I had given so much," she said, "up to the very end. I had experienced incredible love and incredible struggles, incredible highs and incredible lows, and I was ready to go home."

A sister who served as a trainer in the mid-Atlantic region—she trained missionaries who then went on to train other missionaries—said she worked hard to the very end of her mission. She said she was conscientious as a trainer, but by the end she was "weary." Each day was so busy she felt like she had lived a whole life over the course of her mission. She said she started out as a baby, and by the end of her mission she felt old like a grandmother. She explained that's what they call a sister missionary who has trained someone, who then goes on to train another: a "grandmother."

"So I was a 'grandmother,'" she said, "and I felt like it."

An elder who was returning home in six weeks spoke of conflicted feelings, of wanting to stay and work and of wanting to return home and see his family. He said it was a cycle he went through each day. He also found the future scary; his life had been planned for the first twenty-one years of his life, but in six week's time, nothing was planned.

Missionaries use vivid language to describe the end of their mission and going home. An elder who served in Japan said they didn't use the expression "to go home," but rather "to die." "When is your death date?" they would ask each other. "Have you gotten your death papers yet?" Missionaries also use the expression, "I killed my companion," when they are the departing missionary's last companion.

The departure of a missionary can affect the companion, especially if the companion is new to the field. A new sister said she had just left home, was homesick, and felt it was "kind of mean" to pair her with a companion who was going home, especially since the companion was trunkie and spoke at length about going home. Some missionaries try to avoid this dynamic by trying not to appear trunkie and by not telling the new missionary that they are going home soon; they wait until the greenie is settled in before revealing their impending exodus.

Returning missionaries say they find value in being paired with a greenie, because not only does it give them a chance to share their experiences and serve as a mentor, it also gives them a perspective on how much they have changed over the course of their mission. An elder who served in California said it was only at the end of his mission, when he served as a trainer for an elder fresh from the MTC, that he recognized how much he had changed over the previous two years. He realized he had grown in an "amazing" number of ways during that time. He said without that experience he would not have appreciated just how much he had matured.

A returned missionary who served in Germany said on his first day in the mission field he went street contacting in Leipzig with his Polish A.P. He said he found it an intense, but good, experience. He went on to say that on his last day in the mission field, when he was an A.P., he took a new elder out on foot. He said it was a "profound" experience. Not only was he able to see how much he had grown, but it also brought a sense of closure for him, that the cycle was complete.

Traditions. There are various traditions associated with going home, many of them involving destroying old, worn-out clothing. An elder serving in Paris in the early 1970s said the night before they went home, elders would take the trousers from their worn-out suits and rip them apart at the crotch. A sister who served in Spain said sisters would cut up a skirt, write messages on the pieces, and give them to their fellow sister missionaries. A mission president's wife cut up old ties and made them into a quilt.

Practices vary among missions regarding holding going-home parties for departing missionaries. Some mission presidents allow parties, and some don't. Some counsel their missionaries not to tell Church members when they are leaving, or only at the very end of their time in the community. They feel going-away parties detract from the work of the missionaries, plus it places undue emphasis on the missionaries themselves. Mission presidents want to avoid the tendency for investigators to be converted to the missionaries, not to the Mormon gospel.

Some missions allow small events. A retuned missionary who served in California said departing missionaries in his mission were allowed to invite all the people with whom they had worked to the mission headquarters on the night before returning home. He said it was hard to leave seeing them there, but it was a time when he could say goodbye to the people to whom he had become attached.

Final Meetings with the Mission President

Final interview. The departing missionaries meet at the mission home for final, personal interviews with the mission president and for a group discussion about what it will be like to return home. During the personal interview the mission president typically encourages returning missionaries to create structure in their lives as soon as they can, including faithful church attendance, marriage, school, and employment. They are encouraged to continue their daily practice of prayer, scripture reading, clean living, and to continue visiting the temple on a regular basis. They are counseled to willingly accept Church callings.

Individual plans for the future are discussed. A returning sister reported her mission president told her it was important for her to establish structure in her life as soon as she returned home, and since she was just one year away from receiving her college degree, he encouraged her to return to school. This is common advice given to returning missionaries—to begin, or to complete, higher education.

An elder who had just returned from his mission in Peru said that during his exit interview his mission president told him his mission is a lifelong event; that success in a mission isn't merely the number of baptisms during the mission, but that it serves as the foundation for a successful life. He had had a successful mission, and his mission president hoped he would continue on in the same way in his life: a life of dedication and service to his family, Church, and community. The missionary reported he found it to be a profound thought, and he was going to strive to live up to the expectation.

Others find the final interview to be a time when both they and the mission president share personal reflections on the missionary experience; when the more formal aura of previous one-on-one meetings is replaced with an informality, and where tears may even flow on both sides.

A young American missionary I met at Gatwick Airport in London, on his way home from his mission in Scotland, reflected on the close relationship he felt with his mission president and his wife. "The mission president and his wife became like parents. The hardest thing to do was to say goodbye to my missionary mom and dad."

Group session. Some of the same topics may be revisited in the group session, when the mission president and the returning missionaries consider what they can expect and what they should do when they return home.

I attended such a session along with six elders and three sisters. We were seated in the mission president's living room in New Hampshire, and a lively discussion ensued around a consideration of the adjustments they would need to make when they returned home, their plans for maintaining their spirituality, their plans for their education and employment, and their plans for dating and marriage.

The mission president warned that while they had changed during their mission, things at home probably had not, and their parents and friends would likely want to treat them as they were before their mission. He said they needed to be aware of this tendency and to watch they didn't get pulled back to being "their old selves." They needed to be true to what they had become. He advised them to continue reading the scriptures, to pray daily, and to honor the Sabbath by attending church regularly and by keeping the entire day as a day of rest, as a holy day. They were encouraged to return to school or to find employment as soon as possible and to apply the lessons they had learned on their mission to these endeavors: personal discipline, good study habits, and the ability to work with others.

They were reminded to dress modestly and to attend wholesome activities. Regarding dating and marriage, the president warned against getting into situations that could lead to serious moral transgressions. These included make-out sessions, French-kissing, and parking. They were encouraged to date in groups, because, they were told, not only is it more interesting, but it is also safer.

Regarding marriage, the mission president advised: "Go with someone long enough to get to know them. Marry when you know you know them."

Going Home, but with Mixed Feelings

Various interviewees spoke of how difficult it was to return home. An elder who served in the Midwestern United States in the late 1970s agreed it was much harder for him to return home than it was for him to go on his mission. He had a difficult time coming home; he didn't want to, and when he came home he found it to be "a scary world" for him because he so enjoyed the "protectiveness" of the missionary milieu. An elder who served in Southeast Asia in the 1970s reported that, yes, he was tired at the end of his mission, but he didn't want to leave. Serving as a missionary was his life, he loved it, and he couldn't even remember what he had done prior to his mission. A missionary who served in Bolivia in the mid-1970s recalled that he didn't want to return home, but since he had no choice, he chose to be the last person off the plane.

Other returned missionaries reported doing the same thing.

An elder who served in Japan said he began to feel homesick for Japan two months before returning home to the United States. He had developed such a love for the country and for the people; he had developed so many friendships, such that he didn't want to leave. And once he was home, he wanted to return. He doubted he could have developed such closeness had he not served in the role of a missionary, a role that brought him into close contact with people to deal with their issues, problems, and questions about the meaning of life.

A sister preparing to serve her mission spoke of how her brother experienced "major culture shock" when he returned to the United States from Hong Kong. He said he preferred to be there, instead of at home.

The return. The countdown also takes place at home. A countdown calendar is available in the shape of a temple with eighteen months on one side and twenty-four on the other. It is divided into small boxes representing the days, and the box is checked as each day passes until the missionary comes home.

It is common for family and friends to gather at the airport to greet the missionaries as they arrive home. Signs, balloons, and streamers are common. An elder who had just returned home from Geneva said he had thought about his family greeting him at the airport throughout his entire two years in the mission field.

An American who served in Western Europe recalled that he had never been so afraid in all his life as when he got off the plane. He wondered how much he had changed and what his parents would think of him. He also wondered if he would be able to cope in the "real world," as he called it. He and the other returning missionaries traveling with him were the last to get off the plane. He said they "held onto the seats" until the very end.

He gave this description of his arrival in the terminal: "My mom hurdled the barrier and she came running up to me and I tried not to cry, but to be in mom's arms again was special," (his voice broke at this point in the interview), "and as soon as she hugged me, I felt relief and no more nervousness."

Many, however, admitted that their nervousness remained after the initial hugs and kisses, because while their lives (particularly for elders) had been clearly planned up until that point—practically everything they had done had led toward serving a mission—life beyond it could be very vague.

But as those who have lived abroad for any length of time can understand and appreciate, there is something psychologically and emotionally liberating about returning home. An elder who served in Japan said it felt "safe" coming back to his own place; it felt good coming home.

He was no longer a foreigner.

Meeting with the Stake President

Missionaries are officially released from their calling during a meeting with their stake president, which takes place a few days after returning home. It is a private time with the missionary, and at some point the stake president says something to the effect, "I hereby release you from serving full-time as a missionary." The missionary will likely be wearing his nametag, and the fact he should no longer wear the nametag may come up. A returned-missionary told how his stake president asked for the nametag (which he gave up very reluctantly), only to have the stake president return it to him.

Another stake president felt such a transition at such a sensitive time was too abrupt, that the nametag was such a part of their identity, it would be too painful for them to give it up. That the nametag shouldn't be worn any longer seemed obvious, and he left it to the missionary to decide to stop wearing it.

When I asked the stake president what else is discussed during this time, he responded that he asked how the mission went and what the missionary planned to do, but he didn't offer a lot of advice. He generally left it up to the parents and bishop to cover the variety of topics for which advice might be offered. He considered it a release meeting, rather than a serious counseling meeting. The stake president generally doesn't know the missionary well, if at all, so there isn't a close bond that might prompt the missionary to take the advice to heart. "Besides," he continued, "the missionary is recovering from jet lag, is in a fog, his mind is still on the beloved friends left behind, and (at a more practical level) he is wondering why his car is all scratched up." (By this he meant that a missionary's family members had been driving his car—but not taking very good care of it—for the last two years.) He believed it was more effective to give the missionary a special blessing, and in the blessing he pronounced specific protections and offered counsel. He felt this seemed to help missionaries more than a lecture on what they should avoid doing. He said, why dwell on the negatives; here's the missionary before him, "full of the spirit, full of love for those that had to be left behind, full of love for home, and usually in tears."

There were instances when the returning elder virtually begged him not to release him; he would say that missionary service was his life, and he really didn't want to leave it, the people, or the country where he had served. The stake president would be sympathetic but would tell the returning missionary that it was time to move on with his life.

An elder who served in California said he felt a distinct change when his stake president released him from his mission. It felt like when he takes off a tie; it felt as though a part of him had been taken away, and he felt "empty" as a result.

The power and symbolism of the nametag can be long-lasting. A returned-missionary said that during his daily devotions he closes his door, puts on his nametag, reads his scriptures, and prays.

An Uncomfortable Return

Missionaries who successfully complete their mission are referred to thereafter as "returned missionaries," or "RMs," and they talk of how difficult it is to go from an action-packed missionary life to a life of no schedules, no boundaries, and no responsibilities. They recall how busy they were during their mission—talking with people, teaching lessons, getting involved in the lives of investigators—and they contrast that with their lives once they return home: lives that lack focus, are boring, and leave them with a sense that they are wasting time.

They wonder what is happening in their old mission and if missionaries are still meeting with "their" investigators, investigators that they miss.

"It's so mundane, so old, so slow," observed a recently returned missionary. Others described the return home as "anticlimactic" and as "not as great as it is cracked up to be." A missionary who served in the Washington, D.C., district described returning home as being "wonderful and horrible" at the same time. A sister who served in Central America said returning home was good for the first five minutes—then you are home, the excitement is over, and it's back to normal living.

They talked of how disoriented they felt. An elder who served in Germany felt "spacey" when he returned home, while others said they felt "weird."

A returned missionary who served in South Africa in the mid-1980s spoke of the "emotionally scary" adjustment period many missionaries go through upon their return home. They have developed new values and patterns of behavior while on their mission, but family and friends may not help during this adjustment period. The returned missionary has changed, but she is treated like she was when she left on her mission. A sister who was going home in three months said her parents wrote to her as if she were the person who left fifteen months ago, but that she had changed, her thinking had changed, and when she received their letters she had to guard against being like she used to be. She didn't want that to happen when she returned home.

Some missionaries talked of having trouble relating to family and friends when they returned home; they hesitated to talk about their missions for fear they would be considered "fanatics," that all they seemed to want to talk about was their mission. Finding herself in that situation, a recently returned sister missionary asked: "But what else can I talk about? It is the only life I have known for the past eighteen months!"

Returned missionaries confirm that they tend not to share missionary stories with their fellow returned missionaries. Unless it is something really unusual or dramatic, other RMs aren't that interested in hearing about it, because many missionary stories are similar.

Returned missionaries feeling adrift will sometimes try to impose structure on their family. A missionary who served in Spain tried to get his family to do a weekly planner like in his mission field, but they didn't think they could plan that far ahead. A missionary told of a returned-missionary friend who kept getting up at 6:30 A.M. to read the scriptures and who tried to get his family to do the same. He also had them gather around the piano to sing Church songs. The family put up with it, thinking it would pass in a couple of weeks.

The RM now sleeps in like everybody else.

Missionaries contrasted their changed lives with the lives of friends and neighbors who had remained in the same town, in the same home, and with the same way of life while the missionaries were away. An elder who served in Canada said he felt like he took a "time leap" on his return home, because he felt very different from his old friends. A returned sister missionary said she had matured far more in the mission field than she ever could have back home. She had gained valuable knowledge and skills while on her mission, whereas it appeared her old friends at home had done nothing with their lives. Her mission had set her apart from those who had stayed home. Some interviewees spoke of needing to find new friends after their return.

Some found that things had changed at home. Parents had moved to a new home or divorced, friends and relatives had died, and boyfriends and girlfriends, who had faithfully promised they would wait until the missionary returned home, had married someone else and had babies.

Being without a companion was also unnerving to newly returned missionaries. An elder who served in Peru said it felt especially strange when he was with groups of people without a companion; he would find himself looking around for someone to "grab on to."

RMs also talked of being glad they had more time for themselves and not living under so many restrictions. They could watch television, engage in social networking, read books, magazines, and newspapers, and build relationships.

But this could make them uncomfortable, since it was now up to them to set new boundaries. As missionaries, they knew what they were allowed to do, what was right and wrong, but once home they didn't have the same restrictions. They had to establish their own rules; they had to determine their new boundaries. And while they were glad to have more time for themselves, they spoke of feeling they had almost *too much* free time; as missionaries their time was devoted completely to others, but at home they had to fill their days with other activities, frequently focused on themselves and on their needs and wants. As an elder who served in Mongolia observed, "All of a sudden, you come back into your life."

It is a time when they have moved from an environment where their individuality was replaced with a collective identity, back to one where they are to be an individual again.

Many spoke of the difficultly of shifting their attention from others to themselves. An elder said the role of a missionary is to help others, but as soon as he wasn't a missionary, he was suddenly "left with himself," doing things for himself. He said it was a painful adjustment. A RM who served in England said that when he got home everything was focused on him—what his career would be, what school to attend, who would be his spouse. He said one of the most difficult things he had to do was to go shopping, trying to find fashionable clothes.

An elder said he didn't remember much about the ten days he spent at home after his return, but he did remember feeling a sense of loss when he got to Brigham Young University. He no longer felt so important in the lives of others. He had served as an A.P., and he had felt a strong sense of responsibility for the happiness and welfare of others. He had cultivated relationships with investigators, and he felt they depended on him. But once he was back in college, he was supposed to concentrate on himself, and it wasn't quite as enjoyable as getting close to someone and becoming his friend. He said it was a difficult adjustment.

It is not unusual for returned missionaries to write missionaries still in the field and tell them to value what they have—to treasure their mission experience and to not wish it away by dwelling on thoughts of returning home. They are told they don't realize what they have, until it is over.

A RM who had been home a few weeks said that going home is a popular topic among missionaries. They say they can't wait until they go home and that as soon as they get home everything will be great. He said initially being home is very exciting, but after a few days it set in how much fun his mission was and how much he missed it. This was especially the case when he was sitting there with nothing to do.

It is in this context of missing their mission that missionaries frequently remark at their homecoming, "My mission was the best two years of my life."

The Homecoming Talk

In order for a rite of passage to have meaning and to serve its purpose, it must include reincorporation into the community, typically with increased status. Ceremonies and rituals generally characterize this at the end of a period that has been marked by isolation and hardship. In the Latter-day Saint Church, this reincorporation takes place when missionaries speak at their local congregation upon their return from their mission, when they give their homecoming talk.

During the pre-departure session I attended at the mission home in New Hampshire, the mission president advised returning missionaries to gear their homecoming talks to the younger members of the congregation. He said they represented the next generation of potential missionaries and returned missionaries are the only speakers younger members listen to. The missionaries were told not to criticize companions or areas where they served, but to tell personal stories and conversion stories. They should thank those who helped them, especially their parents, and they should end by bearing their testimony of Christ and the influence of the Book of Mormon in their lives.

Interviewees confirmed the wisdom and accuracy of the mission president's counsel regarding gearing their message to the younger members of the congregation. A missionary serving in the mid-1990s said that as he was growing up he was struck at homecomings by how much people had changed on their missions. When they shared their experiences and success stories, he would think he too wanted these experiences. He said homecomings had a much more powerful impact on him than missionary farewells, because he was able to see the changes that had occurred in the missionary's life. There were instances during farewells when he would think, "There is no way this guy is going to make it for two years," but he would return a totally changed person.

I have attended numerous missionary farewells and homecomings and the contrast between missionaries-to-be and returned missionaries is indeed striking. The former may be tentative and nervous in front of large groups, with a testimony that sounds rote, whereas returned missionaries are more mature, better communicators, and exhibit a deeper spirituality.

An elder who returned from Brazil gave a moving homecoming talk, which included a consideration of the role of the Holy Ghost in one's life, the price of discipleship as one attempts to follow the promptings of the Spirit, and three conversion stories from his mission, which illustrated his points. He ended his talk by bearing his testimony in Portuguese, and while probably no one in the congregation understood what he said, the depth of his conviction was apparent to all; in his voice, in his demeanor, and in his body language.

It is common for returned missionaries to refer to their mission as the best eighteen or twenty-four months of their lives. When I asked a soon-to-return sister if she was going to say that at her homecoming, she said she was not, but instead she was going to say that it was the most productive eighteen months of her life, and also the hardest, because it was the hardest thing she had ever done.

An elder who served as an A.P. in Germany said he found his mission to be very hard, and when he heard of missionaries going home and saying it was the best time in their lives and that they would return in a heartbeat, he would think, "They are so full of it," because he was finding it so painfully difficult and hard. He wondered how anyone could call it the best two years of his life.

Looking back on it a decade later, he still wasn't prepared to call his mission the best two years of his life, because how could it compare to his marriage, family, and other important aspects of his life? Rather, it was two years of his life that he "wouldn't change for the world." He knew he was a different person as a result of the experiences, and, he thought, a much better person for it. He considered it a "great" two years.

The structure and content of missionary homecoming talks have changed in recent years, with the result being that they are more routinized today. As with missionary farewells, returned missionaries are now asked to speak on a specific theological topic for a specific length of time (fifteen minutes), the goal being to save time in the sacrament service.

I suggest to returning missionaries that as a non-Mormon what I am most interested in are their personal stories, the human dimension of their experience: how they struggled, how they overcame, how they changed. This may be somewhat at variance with the counsel of the Brethren, but as an outsider I find it far more interesting and meaningful (and I would think far more interesting for young listeners, too).

Folklore and jokes abound in most areas of the missionary experience, and homecomings are no exception. It is reported that a returned missionary, speaking at his homecoming, said that at his farewell his bishop told him that while on his mission he would either lose his hair or his girlfriend.

The balding missionary quipped: "I wish I would have had a girlfriend."

A "Successful" Mission?

At the 181st semiannual conference held in Salt Lake City on October 1, 2011, the General Authority Elder Christopher Waddell, addressing prospective missionaries in his priesthood session, said: "Arrive on your mission ready to work. Your success as a missionary will be measured primarily by your commitment to find, teach, baptize, and confirm. You will be expected to work effectively every day, doing your best to bring souls to Christ."[152]

While such a definition of "success" seems pretty straightforward, some missionaries find it problematic, because once in the field they find that "success" can be a relative term. Normally one thinks of the number of Books of Mormon placed, lessons taught, and baptisms performed as markers of a successful mission, but even these numbers are relative, depending on where one serves in the world. There are high baptism rates in Latin America, the Philippines, and parts of the United States (including missions in Utah, which have fairly high conversion rates). Conversely, there are low baptism rates in New England and Western Europe.

Thus missionaries' experience varies considerably. An elder who baptized over two hundred Brazilians felt he had a successful mission, whereas an elder who baptized eight in Germany felt *he* had a successful mission. An elder who served in Germany in the 1960s said two baptisms a year was the norm for missionaries. There were those in Northern New England and Western Europe who baptized none.

This can lead to frustration and discouragement. An elder who served in England, which is also an area of limited baptisms, spoke of this frustration. He had been out fifteen months, was a senior companion, and had never been involved in baptizing anyone. The responsibility was on his shoulders to baptize, and he found his lack of success to be "very, very difficult" to understand.

He finally let go of that definition of success and decided that success to him was the personal growth he was achieving and the difference he was making in people's lives. He was surprised to discover that the more he was able to see things in terms of that definition, the more success he had in baptizing people. He felt he had selfish motives when he tried to define success in terms of the baptisms he performed, because he feared what people would think of him when he went home and reported he had performed so few baptisms.

A sister who served in the rocky religious soil of Northern New England took a philosophical approach. She said that regardless of whether the person accepted a copy of the Book of Mormon or sought baptism, she felt she was doing a good job if she was able to get the person to understand a little bit more about what she and the Church were all about.

Another RM defined his success in terms of doing what was asked of him. He felt he had been an effective A.P. He had done the best he could, given his knowledge, skills, and preparation, and while it was far from perfect, he felt he did what he was supposed to do. Another RM agreed, saying that any success he experienced was because he worked at having the right attitude. He obeyed the mission rules, he did what was asked of him, and he "left the rest up to Heavenly Father."

An elder who served in Paris in the early 1970s said he considered his mission a success because he grew and developed personally, spiritually, and emotionally during that time, which set the tone for the rest of his life. It set the stage for achievement, family, education, and interpersonal contact with people. When he returned from his mission he was much more relaxed and could "talk with anyone," and he felt he could achieve educationally because of his ability to pick up a new language. He also felt he had a better understanding of people and their spirituality.

"It was clearly the best thing I had done in my life to that point," he reported.

A fellow RM agreed. He considered his mission a success because it was a period of personal growth and maturation. He felt there was nothing he could have done over the two years that could have better prepared him for the rest of his life. A RM who served in the 1960s said his mission made him a better person. It set him on a track of keeping his life clear and clean so that he wouldn't do things he felt guilty about. He would still make mistakes, and, if need be, he would confess them to his bishop, but it didn't happen very often. He worked hard during his mission, he saw a lot of people join the Latter-day Saint Church and live a better life, and it was a source of continuing satisfaction for him.

Interviewees spoke of the importance of obedience and its relationship to success and of how their mission helped them come to that understanding. A RM who served in the 1960s said he learned to listen to the counsel of Church leaders—that is, to be obedient. He learned to follow directions from leaders, "instead of trying to reason them out and to see if they made sense to him." He was willing to make that commitment when he entered his mission and that commitment followed him throughout his life. He considered his mission and his later Church life a success.

A sister who served in Washington, D.C., echoed this feeling. She learned on her mission to be obedient, and that, she said, is the first step to having a relationship with Heavenly Father. "Listen to what He says and do it. Listen to what the Brethren say and do it. Simply put, it really works." She said there is safety, comfort, and peace in doing what is right, even if she didn't see the results. She could put faith in knowing that what she did was right because she was obedient, whether it "pans out" immediately or not.

Another RM gave a more serious assessment of the relationship between obedience and success: he found it "detrimental" to not be obedient to those in authority in the LDS Church. He didn't elaborate.

Based on an analysis of two hundred missionaries, a General Authority told me he considered the following as characteristics of successful missionaries:

1. They are willing to abide by the schedule.
2. They become scripturally adept.
3. They are willing to get along with companions at any cost.
4. The better missionaries are able to shed other titles and statuses (such as athlete) and define themselves as a missionary.
5. They feel closeness at home (parental support), and they seek to please their mothers and fathers—even those who don't have family support.
6. "Personality" doesn't play as strong a role as thought. Some were dry and conservative personalities, but they succeeded.
7. Those not having a lot of money, those coming from a background of less money, do better.
8. Curiosity is important.
9. The Spirit has much to do with it. The good missionary would rather die than disappoint the Savior.
10. Effective missionaries hold something sacred, such as: their own priesthood; the Church; the scriptures; their mission.
11. Strict obedience is important. While serving as a mission president the General Authority told his missionaries he wanted not only their bodies, but their hearts, minds, and souls.

12. Those who did well separated from home successfully and adapted well to a new life.
13. The good missionary doesn't rationalize or make excuses.

While obedience is stressed, it is interesting to note that he never mentioned baptisms.

Some missionaries who served in difficult areas confessed they returned home with mixed feelings, or even with a sense of failure about their missions. An elder who served in Western Europe said to a certain extent he was aware that it was going to be a very difficult area in which to serve. He had been told there were some missionaries who didn't baptize anyone, but he still came home feeling he had not been very successful in accomplishing what he had been called to do. This feeling colored his missionary experience. This was especially the case when he compared his experience with those of his friends who served in Latin America, who reported having considerable success in finding, teaching, and baptizing investigators.

As he looks back on his mission now, years later, he isn't so hard on himself. He said in many ways it was a positive experience. There were a number of people, both members and nonmembers, who he felt he helped. He provided support and strength to small, struggling branches, and, in spite of a sense of failure, he felt to a certain extent that it was a positive, growing experience for him.

A Romanian sister who served on Temple Square observed: "Oftentimes we measure our success as a missionary by the number of people we taught and baptized, but that is not what it's all about. Success is measured in something greater, something deeper. It is measured in the hearts that we touched, in the people who are able to feel the Spirit and recognize it. Our purpose as missionaries is not to see how many people we can baptize, but to see how many hearts we can help the Spirit touch."[153]

Still, if missionaries are to serve as the "lifeblood of the Church," they must bring in new members.

Who Benefits, the Individual or the Church?

Church members sometime ask: is the missionary program for the benefit of the missionaries, or is it for the benefit of the Latter-day Saint Church? Is it designed to help younger generations of Latter-day Saints gain valuable knowledge and skills that will benefit them for a lifetime? Or is the goal of the missionary program to strengthen the missionaries' testimonies, train future Church leaders, and increase membership in the Church—to serve as the "lifeblood" of the Latter-day Saint Church?

The general consensus is that it serves both purposes; it helps the individual *and* the Church. Missionaries discover that as they move on to the next phases of their lives—marriage, school, employment—the knowledge, skills, and dispositions they developed during their mission serve them well in their new pursuits. The Mormon Church also gains, because most missionaries return with a stronger testimony, a greater commitment to the Church, and a greater likelihood that they will accept future Church callings.

Thus both gain in the end.

Personal and social growth. Returned missionaries cite a litany of benefits gained from the mission experience, and for many it set the tone for the rest of their lives. They spoke of how it helped them grow personally and how it helped them develop socially.

They developed a certain mental and physical toughness because they had successfully weathered eighteen or twenty-four months of hardship and rejection. They learned the importance of developing a positive mental attitude. Some spoke of gaining mental discipline, of becoming more introspective, of controlling their thoughts, of being aware of their self-talk. They learned to watch their language. Perfectionists who came into the mission field said they found it was okay to not succeed at everything they did.

They gained self-discipline through time management, money management, and setting goals and priorities. They learned the importance of perseverance, of not giving up when things got difficult. They became self-motivated. They developed a strong work ethic. An RM said he took his responsibilities more seriously, everything from paying bills on time and being punctual for meetings, to following through on his word and fulfilling his responsibilities.

RMs said they became more humble. Many learned to cook, wash, iron, and sew. Many learned they could do things they didn't think they could.

They gained social skills. They spoke of improved relations with others. They learned how to interact and communicate with a variety of people. They learned how to get along with people they didn't necessarily like. They spoke of the need to love someone, even if they didn't like the person. They became more patient with themselves and with others, and they became more forgiving. Some reported their missions made them better listeners, and they appreciated when people would stop to listen to what they had to say, even if they didn't agree with them. They learned they needed to do the same in return.

Many said they overcame shyness. One interviewee observed, "I came out of myself during my mission."

Missionaries gain skills in the areas of leadership, teaching, and public speaking. Americans consider public speaking as one of their greatest fears. An RM who said he was very shy before his mission shared how he developed an ability to speak on his mission. He decided that if he wanted to be a good missionary, he had to learn to speak in public. Initially it was hard, but eventually he came to enjoy it.

One said his mission helped him learn how to serve as a motivator; he learned how to appeal to people's better side. Missionaries spoke of gaining a love for people and of developing a desire to serve others.

They became more aware of the world. Those coming from "Mormon Country" in the Mountain West said they found it an eye-opening experience. An elder from Utah serving in Northern New England said: "It was a shock to come from my sheltered environment into the real world, into 'Babylon.' It was a real change."

Many gained competency in a foreign language, traveled to a different country, and were exposed to a different culture. An American elder who served in Bolivia observed that because of his mission he had been in the homes of people representing practically every social stratum in the country. He had been in the homes of wealthy Bolivians (although not the super-rich), the middle class, the lower class, and the "desperately poor." He had also spent time with street people. He doubted that he could have had the experience in any other context.

The maturation level of thinking of RMs also evolves over time. A RM who served in Japan returned to teach Japanese at the Provo MTC. He didn't see any changes between missionaries when he was there as a new missionary and when he returned to teach, but the biggest change he saw was in himself. He had become more open-minded about things and more prone to question things, instead of accepting them at face value as most missionaries do and as he did when he was a missionary. He felt it was a function of being older and of being more mature.

RMs spoke of gaining a greater understanding of other faiths. An RM said he felt he came back a better person: more patient and understanding, and more appreciative of other religions. A sister said it was only after she came to understand other faiths that she was able to more effectively communicate with people. She learned that the goal is not to tear down others' faith, but to build on a common religious foundation.

Finally, an RM said the attitudes and behaviors he developed during his mission served as a "blueprint" for the rest of his life.

Thus missionaries gain knowledge in a variety of areas and a number of significant life skills.

The experience of an American missionary who served in Latin America is a good example of how a mission can shape a person. He talked of his self-confidence and how it grew because he had rewarding and reinforcing (albeit stressful) experiences during his mission.

Initially he found being a missionary to be very challenging, because he was thrust into a role where people assumed he had the ability to do things he himself would have thought impossible prior to his mission. He was frequently called upon to give extemporaneous talks (in Spanish), and he was placed in situations in which he had real responsibilities and it was assumed that he would be able to exercise proper judgment in these situations. People the age of his parents came to him for help regarding serious marital, economic, and personal problems, issues he had never dealt with before.

"What should I do, elder?" they asked.

It was a role reversal that was initially intimidating, but he had no choice. In the eyes of the members, he had the wisdom and authority to deal with the issues, and they came to him trusting he would help them. Those who were living together, but not married, he would have get married (frequently with resistance). Members would die, and he would be called upon to make the funeral arrangements and preach the funeral sermon.

"The contrast couldn't be greater between this and what I had been doing nine months earlier in my life," he said during our interview.

But with time and experience, he grew comfortable in his new role, with conducting all of his conversations in Spanish, and he found it rewarding, even "exhilarating." He faced real tests during his mission, but he learned how to address them, and he returned home a stronger and more confident person because of it.

Others see changes in the RM. The youngest sister of a brother who returned from Hong Kong said she found him to be more mature, stronger spiritually, culturally more aware, more loving of people, more patient, more willing to compromise, and he didn't let things bother him.

A Columbian who served in his native country said his father initially was against him joining the Latter-day Saint Church, and he was especially against him serving a mission, because he was under the impression it was a lifelong commitment for his son. But after two years of successful missionary service, and having gained valuable leadership skills, he returned home, went back to school, and got married. His family saw what a positive influence the mission had had on him, and his father was pleased. "Now you can have a normal life and that is great," said his father, relieved.

In 2009, a mother living in Maine shared that she had sent three sons on missions: one to Peru, one to California, and one to Germany. She said, "They have all left boys and come back strong, confidant men. I love that."

Spiritual growth. Missionaries pointed to a variety of spiritual benefits gained on their missions, saying it provided a spiritual grounding that stayed with them for a lifetime. They included a closer relationship with God and Jesus Christ, a greater knowledge and appreciation of the scriptures, and a greater understanding of the importance of prayer and of relying on the Spirit. These led to a strengthening of their testimony, or the inward assurance of the truth of Mormonism. But it was not without struggles, because benefits came only after dealing with challenges from others, exposure to anti-Mormon attitudes and literature, and confronting their own doubts and lack of faith.

They spoke of a greater love and understanding of Heavenly Father. "I now know what God expects me to do," reported a returned elder. Another said his mission taught him to learn to rely on the Lord. His mission was characterized by extreme highs and extreme lows, and throughout it all he learned to give thanks when things were going well and to put the whole burden on the Lord when things weren't going well. An RM said he learned that if he did his part, then God would do the rest.

As one RM so clearly stated: "My mission forced me to be on intimate terms with God."

An RM who served in Mexico said part of the religious quest is to know what God will do in your life and what He *won't* do in your life. For him, his mission put religion in the context of reality. He saw that good, religious people still had to struggle with life and with their spirituality, and it was an important lesson for him as a nineteen-year-old boy and young missionary.

They spoke of a greater love for Jesus Christ and a strengthening of their relationship with him. "I am stronger in Christ now," reported an RM who served in the Southwestern United States. Another RM shared that during his pre-mission interview with his stake president, the president asked him about his testimony of Jesus Christ. He said as he served he came to realize the importance of a strong testimony of Jesus Christ—not just a simple "He exists," but to really believe in Him. He thought back on the question of his relationship with Jesus Christ during his mission, and he came to understand the importance of that in what he was doing.

An RM sister said she had faith now, not just belief. She had learned to love, trust, and respect the Savior; He was someone close to her, a friend. "That's who He is to me now," she reported.

RMs spoke of their motivation to serve in terms of their relationship with Heavenly Father and with Jesus. As he looked back on his mission, an elder said he wasn't sure who he had helped, but serving a mission was something he needed to do out of gratitude for what Christ had done for him. An RM sister said she wanted to do what the Lord would have her do, to serve a mission. She was happy to give up a year and a half of her life to show God her appreciation for all that He had done for her. This was her opportunity to "give back" something to God.

An RM said the highlight of his mission was learning who the Spirit is, how he communicates with Him, how he can benefit from it, and how he can help others to benefit from it. He said the Spirit testifies to the truth of Mormonism and that it is one of the most important feelings they need as missionaries. He said it is also one of the most important things investigators need—"to feel the Spirit"—so they know the message is true.

I asked two sisters what it means "to feel the Spirit." I wanted to know how they described and recognized the Spirit. They responded in terms of actual feelings. One spoke of getting an "overwhelming warmth" over her whole body, "a calm, peaceful feeling," when she is doing what is right. As a result, she has no doubts and no worries.

Her companion talked in terms of extremes. She said "feeling the Spirit" for her is a burning in her heart, which hurts because she is feeling it so overwhelmingly. It can also be a sudden chill in her body when she is saying a prayer or singing a hymn. It gives her peace.

They said they get the Spirit by working hard, and they know they have the Spirit because they experience the fruits of the Spirit that are found in Galatians 5:22-23: love, joy, peace, longsuffering, gentleness, goodness, faith, meekness, and temperance.

Some said their faith grew when they saw what a powerful impact their message had on the lives of others. A sister said before she served her mission she believed the Latter-day Saint Church was true, but she didn't have the firm conviction that she *knew* it was true, that the Book of Mormon was true, and that Joseph Smith was a prophet of God. But seeing peoples' lives change under the influence of the Spirit was such that she couldn't deny it. As a result, her own testimony grew and was strengthened.

The RM who traveled without purse or scrip up and down the Connecticut River Valley in the late 1940s said he found the experience of walking in the country to be an ongoing spiritual experience. He was without resources of his own, and he was thrown totally on Divine guidance, direction, and protection. "I had nothing else," he said.

He observed that a skeptic would say he didn't have that either. Maybe not, he noted, but he *thought* he did, and that is what mattered.

Non-Mormons ask about Joseph Smith and if Latter-day Saints worship him. No, they don't. RMs emphasized that their commitment is to Jesus Christ, not to Joseph Smith. They recognize Smith as a prophet, but their attention is on Christ.

On the eve of his return home, an elder spoke of the relative place of Christ, the LDS Church, the Book of Mormon, and Joseph Smith in his spiritual life. He said he knew that Jesus Christ is the savior of the world, that the Mormon Church is true, and that the Book of Mormon came from a prophet. Beyond recognizing Joseph Smith as a prophet, Smith didn't play a role in his spiritual life. His motivation to serve as a missionary came from his faith in Jesus Christ as savior, not Joseph Smith as prophet. He said he knew the LDS Church and the Book of Mormon to be true because the same Spirit that confirmed to him that Christ was the savior was the same Spirit he felt when he read the Book of Mormon, "the Spirit that confirms truth."

Missionaries said challenges to their beliefs generally caused them to grow stronger in their faith. Some had never been exposed to so much anti-Mormon sentiment before, but they said that (eventually) it had a positive effect on them; their personal testimony grew, along with their testimony of the LDS Church.

An RM said he felt that missionaries become strong when they are challenged, when they are forced to think about what they were taught when they were young. At a certain point in their lives they have to determine if they feel the Mormon Church is true, the Book of Mormon is scripture, and that Joseph Smith was a prophet. For him, these assurances came after being exposed to anti-Mormon sentiment during his mission and after much study and prayer.

Another RM said it was his spiritual growth that was the most important dimension of his missionary experience. It was after being forced time and again to stand up for the Church, to deal with people who asked him if he believed what he was saying (which people still ask him today), that reasoning didn't work, and that he was forced to ask himself, "Okay, do I believe this, or do I not?"

He believed it because of the feelings he had had and because of the testimony he received. He said serving a mission is like boot camp, because it was during his mission that his testimony went through a building process. He said it continues to grow today. He was very thankful he went on a mission, and while he found it very hard, and while he might not say it was the best two years of his life, it was two years of his life that he wouldn't change for the world. He felt he came back a different person, a better person, as a result of his mission experiences and because of the challenges he faced.

An RM who served in Japan said the most important spiritual lesson he learned is that he is literally a child of God and that his life has purpose. He said with that testimony within him he could withstand any assaults on his faith—which, he added, were many.

"The mission converts the missionary." There is an expression in the Latter-day Saint Church, "The mission converts the missionary," which means that while missionaries may start out with a belief in the Church and the Book of Mormon, many return home with new faith that they are true. They have undergone their own spiritual rebirth, and they return with an increased level of commitment to the Church, which, it is hoped, will last a lifetime.

An RM who served in New England in the late 1950s spoke of this experience when he said that as he attempted to answer peoples' questions, he was really investigating himself. He was deciding how he felt about the doctrines of the Church and their meaning. Why does the Mormon Church have them, and are they true?

It is a conversion process for the missionary, as well as for the investigator.

This emphasis on the missionary conversion experience is seen in the missionary guide *Preach My Gospel.* While speaking at a seminar for newly-called MTC presidents and visitors' centers directors at the Provo MTC in January 2008, the Apostle Jeffrey R. Holland, a member of the Missionary Executive Council and a person who played a role in the development of *Preach My Gospel*, said the guide seeks to strengthen the missionary as well as to convert the investigator. He said it is always regretful when a missionary returns home without a strong testimony. Regardless of how successful or how difficult a mission was, he hopes the missionary comes home with a testimony "burning in his or her soul." Once missionaries have a conversion experience of their own, when they experience what they are asking their investigators to experience, he said that is when they can become truly effective, when they can have a permanent testimony of their own. This theme is echoed throughout *Preach My Gospel.*

Elder Holland is thus giving expression to a hope and desire heard over and over again in LDS circles: that missionaries will experience at least one conversion during the course of their mission—their own.

This was echoed by an elder who served in England: "If you went on your mission and the only person you converted, or the only person who became converted to the true gospel of Jesus Christ, was you, then it would be a successful mission."

An elder reported that he observed this conversion process as it occurred. He would watch missionaries as they came into the field. The best missionaries were those who had the strongest testimony, while those who struggled throughout their mission had the weakest testimony. But there were also those who gained a testimony during their time on their mission. He said when they realized what their Savior had done for them, "it put fire in their eyes," and they became very effective. He could see the changing point when things "started to fall into place" for them, and he could see in their attitude and in their eyes the changes that had come about. He said the mission brings souls to Christ and into the Church, but it is also there to help the missionary. He said a favorite verse of his in this context is *Doctrine and Covenants* 18:15: "...and bring, save it one soul unto me, how great will be your joy with him in the kingdom of my Father!"

An RM sister who served in California recalled that during an interview with her mission president she lamented that she wasn't teaching many lessons or seeing many baptisms. He responded that baptisms were just a byproduct of her mission and that she was there for her: for her testimony, to convert her to the gospel, and to set her on a path for the rest of her life. She was surprised when he said it, because she thought she was there "saving everybody else." But as she thought about it, it made sense. Studying scriptures, praying, struggling with companions—those things were for her.

Now that she looks back on it, she knows she was doing something that would be beneficial for the rest of her life. She just didn't know that was what she was doing at the time.

On-going struggles. There are RMs who struggle today with various Church beliefs and practices, but because of their mission and the spiritual experiences they witnessed and experienced there, they remain in the Mormon Church.

An RM who became a college professor said his mission was a time for him to mature in many different ways and to enjoy spiritual experiences, but his adult experience since the mission has been on the whole a very secularizing one. As an academic social scientist, he has found the process of trying to negotiate between his faith and his worldly learning difficult to do, and he is sure many of his LDS academic colleagues would say the same thing. He said they have dealt with it in different ways. Some have drifted away from the Church and don't have much to do with it anymore, whereas others have somehow found a way to retain their activity as he has, and to bring their children up in the tradition, as he did.

He finds it hard to do, and he thinks the few special spiritual experiences he enjoyed on his mission (which were "of a very heavy and intense formative kind"—where he felt the immediate presence of Deity, where he saw coincidences occur of the most improbable kind in the direction of promoting the work, or contributing to someone's conversion) gave him the spiritual foundation that has made it possible for him to hold on to his attachment to the Latter-day Saint Church and to his commitment to the religion. This despite what he called a great many spiritual setbacks in the interim and despite a great many disheartening experiences in Church life. These spiritual experiences have kept him in the Church, even when he didn't always agree with its practices.

"My mission had that impact on my life," he observed, "and my experiences were intensely personal and subjective."

"I am an old man," he continued during our interview, "but I can't forget them." (His voice broke at that point, and there was a long pause.)

Benefits for the Church

A lay church. As has been previously mentioned, The Church of Jesus Christ of Latter-day Saints is a lay organization, which means it does not have a paid, professional clergy. Rather, it depends on its members, the laity, to conduct its business.

All positions at the local level are staffed by members who serve in a particular position for a particular period of time—everyone from the head of the local unit, the bishop, to Sunday School teachers, to those who handle the Church's financial records. But they are not "volunteers" in the traditional sense of the word; it is not something they *choose* to do. Rather, it as a responsibility they are "called" to fulfill; it becomes their "calling."

The process is explained in this way: "Those with the authority to issue callings need to prayerfully seek the inspiration from the Lord. When an inspired decision is made, the call needs to be extended properly in a dignified and reverent manner, with all involved realizing that the call comes from the Lord. We serve willingly. We do not volunteer. We are called."[154]

A lay church requires that there are enough members to fill the various positions, that the members are committed enough to devote hours of their time in service to the Church, and that they possess the necessary knowledge, skills, and dispositions to do their jobs well. Depending on the position, it may require leadership skills, communication skills, and a strong spiritual grounding. It may require administrative skills, teaching skills, or money-management skills. One need not be a returned missionary to possess these attributes, but it certainly helps, because the mission serves as an important training ground for future LDS Church leaders.

RMs who went on to serve callings in their local congregations pointed to the knowledge and skills gained on their missions and how that aided them in their Church work, including leadership, teaching, and public speaking skills. Those who served as A.P.s in the mission office said they gained considerable knowledge about Church administration and the workings of the Church bureaucracy and they honed their people skills. Another pointed to the organizational and administrative skills that he gained in the mission office; he learned how to be effective in carrying out Church assignments and responsibilities.

In conversations with staff members at Latter-day Saint Church Headquarters in Salt Lake City, they indicated that their research shows that returned missionaries are more active than the general LDS population. They are more religious, more likely to marry in the temple, and more likely to accept Church callings and to remain faithful members of the Church.

Thus serving a mission does have a lasting effect on people, on their religiosity and on their commitment to the Latter-day Saint Church.

An elder who served in England said the spiritual experiences he had during his mission have stayed with him throughout his life, and they have served as the basis for his continued commitment to, and service in, the Church. He has held various callings. He has worked with young men to prepare them for missions and he has shared with his own sons his mission experiences. He and his wife have opened their home for missionaries to teach there, and they have fellowshipped with those being taught. They have invited friends to hear about the Church. They have fed the missionaries once or twice a month. He has gone on "splits" with them occasionally when they need to be teaching multiple families. He has accepted such callings and said he is happy to do it. He said he doubted if he would be so willing to serve had he not served a mission. He felt returned missionaries are "a great boon to the LDS Church," because it depends on their lay leadership.

A Bolivian who served in his home country in the mid-1980s said his experience was that if someone were a good missionary, he would likely be a good member of the Church, but that those who weren't committed as missionaries would probably drift away from the Church. He said his mission helped him to be a better person and to be a stronger member of the Mormon Church, and that would not have been true had he not served a mission. He said others in positions of leadership in Bolivia felt the same way.

What is surprising to non-Mormons is that these are people who typically have full-time responsibilities at home or at work but who still devote large amounts of their time to the LDS Church.

A case in point is the RM and retired college professor who estimated that by the time he dies, he will have given ten full years of his life in service to the LDS Church. In addition to his two-year mission, he has served as a bishop (three times), a stake president, a patriarch, and a senior missionary. He devoted around seventy hours a month when he served as a bishop and the same amount of time again when he served as a stake president. (The length of term for the former calling is around five years, while the latter is around ten.) And he said he was pleased to serve. "I am grateful for the opportunity to repay what God has done for me," he said.

As was true for that individual, it is not unusual for a person to be released from one calling and then quickly be assigned another. An RM physician who served his mission in the late-1980s said that since then he has been in some form of calling almost constantly since then, including serving as a bishop and serving in the stake presidency. And this is on top of his heavy responsibilities as a physician.

He said one of the values of his mission was that many of the issues he now faced were ones he had already learned to face while on his mission: being involved in people's lives; helping them when they are at important crossroads; helping marriages that are in trouble; having a positive influence on the lives of young people; and to generally helping those who are facing challenges.

Returned missionaries as motivators and mentors. Serving a mission isn't just an individual experience: it is a family and a Church community experience.

The roots of missionary service run deep in many LDS families. As each generation of potential missionaries grows up, they are exposed to the expectations and hopes that they too will serve, and returned missionaries are key voices and influences in this endeavor. There is intergenerational support that is family-based. The family system is thus the foundation to the Church's missionary program.

An RM father said that he is already talking to his three-year-old son about missions. He tells him mission stories pretty much every night, telling him where he was and what he did. He tells his son that he hopes he too will want to go on a mission someday.

Other RMs spoke of talking with their children about the Church and missions and of how teaching skills gained in the mission field helped them explain Church beliefs and practices to their children, as well as to their non-Mormon friends and neighbors.

Missionaries for life. The "mission" doesn't stop at the end of eighteen or twenty-four months, because all members, regardless of whether they went on a mission or not, are expected to be "member missionaries," a concept enunciated by a head of the Latter-day Saint Church,

President David O. McKay, in the 1950s. "Every member a missionary" was the watchword of President McKay. It is not surprising, therefore, that members in general, and many returned missionaries in particular, continue throughout their lives to invite their friends, neighbors, and colleagues to investigate their faith.

The Church stresses the use of *Preach My Gospel* by all members for their own personal use, along with using its guidelines and recommendations as they pursue their responsibilities as "member missionaries." It is reported that those who are familiar with *Preach My Gospel* form a more effective working relationship with the missionaries serving in their area. Returned missionaries also report that prayerful reading and following of *Preach My Gospel* has rekindled the missionary zeal they felt while serving as full-time missionaries. It can also be used to prepare younger members to become full-time missionaries.[155] Indeed, given the shortened time missionaries now spend at the MTC and given the increased numbers being trained there, General Authorities counsel prospective missionaries-to-be to start studying and following *Preach My Gospel* at an earlier age.

Some interviewees said their mission inspired them to continue with their missionary work once they returned home. They spoke of being more comfortable talking with their friends and neighbors about the Church, of planning on going on splits with missionaries serving in the area, and of hoping to serve as senior missionaries with their spouses when they were older.

Few had any interest in knocking on doors once they returned home. A sister who never did develop a taste for "knocking doors" said a companion and her brother knocked on doors once they returned from their missions, but it wasn't something she would consider. "You won't find me doing that," she said. "No, sorry."

Another sister said she didn't know many non-Mormons as she was growing up and thus didn't talk with non-members about the LDS Church, but it was more likely that she would do so after her mission. She talked in terms of stepping outside of her comfort zone. She said missionaries aren't really normal people; serving a mission is like a strange, little time warp, when they do things they wouldn't normally do, but it is those things that will make a big influence on her later in life. She said hopefully she won't have to knock on doors, but she can talk with her non-Mormon friends about the Book of Mormon and the LDS Church. "It is not always good to be in your comfort zone," she said. "You should step outside and see what it is like out there."

The Apostle L. Tom Perry, while acknowledging that RMs sometimes have a difficult readjustment period, called on them to rededicate themselves, to rekindle the spirit of missionary work, and to proclaim the gospel.[156]

Advice for Prospective Missionaries

When asked what advice they would give prospective missionaries, interviewees gave consistent responses. They said it is important to set a goal of serving a mission early on, to keep their sights on that goal as they are growing up, and to make decisions that will pave the way to being a successful missionary and to having a good mission.

The motivation to serve is also important, added an elder. People must go for the right reason and make sure it is the right thing for them. Prospective missionaries should not let people pressure them into going on a mission, for oftentimes those missionaries serve without their heart, since they are only doing it to please their family or significant other.

"Having the right attitude, having the desire to do it, and being willing to work, will lead to a good experience," reported a returned missionary. "If they don't have the right attitude and they don't want to be there, then they could have a very bad experience."

An elder advised to come prepared to work hard. He didn't like it when missionaries came out and their whole focus was on going back home. His advice: "Remember, it is the Lord's time, and if you don't have a good work ethic, get one. Go work at a menial job for a while."

An elder recommended working with the full-time missionaries in the area. When he was in his teens, missionaries in his area called him a couple of times, inviting him to go, but he was either working or he made up an excuse saying he was busy. He didn't know what they wanted or what he would be doing. He didn't know what to expect. He said missionaries should spell out what they want young helpers to do, such as asking a question or sharing a scripture.

Missionaries can serve as examples to younger, prospective missionaries and not be aware of it. A sister said she received a letter from a young friend in college who told her she was getting ready to go on her mission, and she thanked her for being a good example of a sister serving a mission and of being a good missionary. The sister said the same was true for her; other sisters had served before her and had inspired her to serve.

Not all receive encouragement to serve. For some Latter-day Saint youth, their parents, even those who served a mission, don't discuss their experiences or encourage their children to go. The same is true of siblings. A sister said her brother returned from serving his mission in Boston, and he discouraged her from going on a mission. While he spoke highly of his mission, she thought he had a hard time there and didn't want her to have a similar experience. He didn't go into details, but she went anyway.

Another sister interviewee had a younger sister who was turning of age to serve and who wanted to go on a mission. While the interviewee was excited by it, she had reservations. She had had some negative experiences, and she didn't want her sister to go through the same thing. But it was not her role to say that, she decided, and her sister went on to serve.

Service to Others

A mission is also a time when missionaries develop a capacity for service to others. An RM said he worked from the premise that one of the major purposes of life is to be tried and tested and to develop capacities for service—to get away from our self-centeredness. He felt the mission provided an excellent opportunity not only to work, but also to learn how to serve and to learn the joys of serving. He "tasted" the joy of seeing what it's like for someone to become happy because of his missionary labors. "It is more delicious than chocolate, jogging, or sex," he said. "It's just better." He said missionaries are teaching people how to govern their lives and how to keep their lives clean and free from evil, how to serve others, and how to worship God. There is joy in that, he felt. He said people come back from their mission thinking, for the most part, that their time, money, and talents should not be directed only toward themselves. Thus RMs generally tend to be more service-orientated both in and out of the Church, although mainly in the Church, because of its heavy time demands.

"A mission introduces you to that world," he said. "Young missionaries have to get out of themselves. The Latter-day Saint Church takes them at eighteen or nineteen when they are least able to be responsible and puts them in a situation, while training them, to get outside of themselves and serve others. A mission opens the windows revealing that it is a good and happy thing to do something for others."

But it isn't easy, he added. He said missionary work, if it is done right and if a missionary is teaching a lot, is hard. "So many need you, and want you, and take from you, and demand from you, and it wears you down and is hard." As a result, he learned to work, and he learned to relate to people with problems "pretty well." It also paved the way for him to be called to other administrative duties in the Church, and, he felt, to be a better father.

The Social Value of a Mission

Interviewees spoke of the friendships and social relationships that developed as a result of their missions: with their companions, fellow missionaries in the field, converts, and Church members. Some spoke of ongoing communication with some of their companions. One continued to write and visit a Church member who fed him breakfast many mornings during his mission in California in the 1960s, while an elder who served in England in the 1960s reconnected with his landlady in England, who then visited him and his family at their home in the United States.

A returned missionary who has since left the Church said one of the high points of his mission was the social dimension. He valued the relationships and friendships developed during his mission and he said he still values them today.

Certainly not all stay in touch with their companions. A sister who served in Europe in the 1960s said she stayed in touch with some of her companions for a while, but then the letters stopped.

Missionary reunions are a common occurrence at General Conference time in April and October in Salt Lake City. It is an occasion when mission presidents, their wives, and missionaries who served with them meet to reconnect, provide updates on their lives, and relive old mission experiences. There are hundreds of such reunions every spring and fall. The missionary who served in New England in the late 1940s, at times serving "without purse or scrip," said their reunions lasted forty years, finally ending after the mission president, his wife, and some of the missionaries began to pass away. Not many RM reunions last that long, and he attributed the longevity to the unique bonding that took place because of their unusual mission. He said they always told stories at their reunions about their unique experiences, with the stories frequently becoming more grandiose with each retelling.

Some RMs will revisit their mission areas years later, often taking their spouses and children with them, so that they can see where they served. They often meet those with whom they worked and baptized into the Church.

An American elder who served in Mexico went to Costa Rica with his wife to pick up their daughter, who was finishing her mission. They then went to Mexico to the town where he was first assigned, and they visited some of the people he had known thirty years before. They visited one of the first families who had joined the Church. As they were talking, he noticed that everything was as he remembered: the family was living in the same house, with the same furniture, with the same pictures on the wall. But his daughter noticed something else. There was a large frame picture holding around twenty pictures of early LDS missionaries who had served in the town, including her father's picture.

During our interview, the RM observed that while Roman Catholic families have pictures of saints on their walls, at least one Mormon family in Mexico has pictures of Mormon missionaries prominently displayed on their wall.

The social value of a mission can also extend to a greater understanding of social class. An interviewee who served in France came to an unexpected realization regarding social class during our interview. She observed that she had been raised in a working class family in Utah; she did not eat in a restaurant and her family didn't have indoor plumbing until she was in high school. She said as a result, "Paris was about as exotic as anything could be."

She said she gained more than just a veneer of culture from her mission, and she gained more than she had gotten from her working class background. Latter-day Saint values are essentially middle-class values, she said, and a mission is a way to broaden them, to communicate them. It was her pairing—the matching with her companions who came from middle-class backgrounds—when she first came into contact with middle-class values. It was a way of communicating values that she would not have gotten from her family and that she didn't get through her education. She described it as a "leavening of class factors," and it was a part of her socialization.

"It was during my mission when I moved into the middle class," she observed, "at least mentally."

Conclusion

Serving an honorable mission is extremely important in Latter-day Saint culture. The pride of a father whose son was returning honorably was seen when he said: "Few things are as satisfying as seeing your sons return honorably from missions. When they were infants, I didn't bless them to be college grads, although they're all destined to be, nor did I bless them to become CEOs or NFL players. I blessed them to live that they may serve honorable missions and marry in the temple." Later the father said, "One of the most gratifying moments in LDS parents' lives (is) the reunion with faithful sons who have served their missions honorably and with distinction."[157]

Reflecting on his return home from his mission in France in the late 1960s, a BYU professor said it feels good to come back having served an honorable mission. There is a sense of having done a good thing reasonably well and of having done what was expected of you. It gives "a peace of conscience." He said it was a great feeling to have done it and to come home and feel good about it.

"Then you have to get on with your life," he said, "college, marriage, family. But then you become a proponent of the missionary program. You talk it up. You become a perpetuator of the system. And so the cycle repeats itself, over and over again."

CHAPTER 13

Transitions, Leaving the Church, and the Future of Missionary Work

"It's a good start."

A RETURNED MISSIONARY'S MOTHER,
COMMENTING ON THE FACT THAT HE HAD THREE CHILDREN

"We all have different stories."

A RETURNED MISSIONARY WHO SERVED IN PARIS, REFLECTING ON HIS MISSION EXPERIENCES AND THOSE OF MISSIONARIES HE HAS KNOWN; HE HAS SINCE LEFT THE LDS CHURCH

"The leadership of the Church has issued a clarion call to the rising generation to lead the way in the use of technology."

APOSTLE QUINTON L. COOK,
184TH SEMIANNUAL GENERAL CONFERENCE

"While social media will be an important missionary tool as we move forward, they (prospective missionaries) have got that down, but some have paid a price of not really learning how to communicate with others. Making sure they know how to listen to people and talk with them is a good idea."

STEPHEN B. ALLEN, MANAGING DIRECTOR,
LDS MISSIONARY DEPARTMENT, 2015

Transitions

As missionaries move on to the next phases of their lives—dating, marriage, and family; school; employment—many discover that the knowledge, skills, and dispositions they developed during their mission serve them well in their new pursuits. They have a better sense of what they want in a spouse, a marriage, and a family. They have gained valuable skills that will aid them in the classroom, such as time management and study skills. They have also gained knowledge and skills that will aid them in the workplace, including communication skills, interpersonal skills, and, for some, knowledge of a second language.

But for some, their mission opens a world to them that they had not known before, and they do not feel they can go back to what they perceive as the narrow confines of the Latter-day Saint Church. Some drift away, while others make a conscious break from the Church. Some are excommunicated. But while they may leave the Church, many still look back on their mission as a positive, life-changing event.

Few developments hold the potential for fundamentally impacting missionary work as have the advances in the Internet. The speed and range of communication and the Internet's capacity for storing information about the Church have profound implications for spreading the teachings of the Latter-day Saint Church. The Church has started to take advantage of this new tool: Church websites have been developed; members are encouraged to use the Internet to tell their faith stories; and pilot programs have missionaries working from computer screens in place of knocking on doors.

In spite of its advantages, the Latter-day Saint Church is wary of the Internet, because Church authorities cannot filter what members see and read—from pornography to anti-Mormon sites—so the potential exists for it to undermine the faith and morals of Church members. The Church struggles to find the right balance when it comes to accessing the Internet and these efforts continue into the first decades of the twenty-first century.

Dating, marriage, and family. It is said the expected sequence of events in an LDS man's life is mission, dating, marriage, children, education, and full-time employment. Consequently, considerable pressure is placed on young Latter-day Saint men to marry and have families. For Latter-day Saints, marriage and having children is central to God's plan on earth. They are told they have an obligation to future generations to provide physical bodies for souls that are waiting to come to earth so they can be tried and tested and so that they can work out their salvation. They also believe families are eternal and that after one dies he or she joins other deceased family members in heaven and that the larger one's family, the greater one's glory. Marriage in the Church is necessary in order to reach the highest levels of glory.

The pressure to marry is clear: "Church leaders have affirmed the command to marry and have assured young adults that eternal marriage is not only possible but also desirable."[158]

Studies show that Latter-day Saints do marry younger than the general population, although modern Latter-day Saints, like their non-Mormon counterparts, are delaying marriage. In 2008, non-Mormon young men on average were waiting until the historic high of twenty-eight to marry, while young women were waiting until almost twenty-seven. Latter-day Saints marry on average four and one-half years earlier, but they still are waiting later than earlier generations of Latter-day Saints.[159]

A survey of Latter-day Saints in 2009 found that one-third of LDS young adults ages twenty-one to twenty-five had concerns about their readiness for marriage. They cited economic concerns, and they worried about divorce.[160]

Church leaders have expressed concern that LDS young men are postponing marriage. They assure them they can have a successful marriage, and they even chide them for waiting. At the 181st Semiannual General Conference held in April 2011, President Monson questioned why so many young men of marriageable age are delaying marriage. He saw young women wanting to marry and raise a family, but young men weren't asking them for their hand. He said these young men were not doing their priesthood duty by not marrying. He appreciated that some may delay because of a concern about finances or of making the wrong choice, but he assured them that frugality and faith would help them through the trials they would face.

He then scolded them: "Perhaps you are having a little too much fun being single, taking extravagant vacations, buying expensive cars and toys, and just generally enjoying the carefree life with your friends. I've encountered groups of you running around together, and I admit that I've wondered why you aren't out with the young ladies."[161]

Young LDS women are also being encouraged to date. Elaine S. Dalton, Young Women General President, told women at a BYU-Idaho devotional in October 2011, to stop "hanging out" with their friends and to start dating.[162] Julie B. Beck, Relief Society General President, speaking to young women adults in California, gave the same message: get married and have families, because they have a great responsibility to the generation that is yet unborn.

The Church tries to do its part by playing matchmaker. It arranges social events for singles in various Church venues, including their Institutes of Religion that serve young adults, where dating is encouraged. Singles in the Mormon Tabernacle Choir are also encouraged to date one another.[163]

But dating can be a challenge for the newly returned missionary, because relations with the opposite sex can initially be awkward. A returned sister missionary reported how strange it felt to go on a date with a newly returned missionary. He seemed very nervous, and she told him to relax. He said he "was afraid his mission president would jump out of nowhere and yell at him for being with a girl."

"They are strange," reported the sister. "They are *very* strange when they return home."

Given the emphasis on marriage and raising a family, it isn't surprising that many interviewees said they would marry not long after they returned home. "Marriage will be the next logical step in my life," observed a sister as she prepared to return home. On the eve of his return home, an elder said he wanted to get married as soon as possible and that his mission president encouraged him to do so. When I asked why marry so quickly, he said it was to remain true to the gospel, to not get into trouble, and to remain chaste.

Large populations of returned missionaries are found at Brigham Young University, BYU-Idaho, and BYU-Hawaii. The BYU professor in Chapter 2 who observed that going on a mission is an integral part of BYU culture (one is considered "normal" and gains capital if he has gone on a mission) said it also applies when looking for a spouse. If one is a "normal" male on the marriage market at these schools, he has gone on a mission.

A sister referred to the schools as "meat markets," where dating is "a serious matter" and where the push to date and marry is "intense." Various sisters confessed to counseling younger women that if they want to serve a mission or are not ready to marry, they shouldn't date a returned missionary, because he probably has only one thing in mind.

Many interviewees, both sisters and elders, said that an unexpected benefit of their mission was that they came away with a greater sense of what they wanted in a spouse, what it would be like to live with another person, and what they wanted for their family. They observed how missionaries of the opposite sex handled themselves: how they interacted with their companions, with other missionaries of both sexes, with Church members, and with investigators. They saw characteristics they valued, including sensitivity, caring for others, and a strong testimony, but they also saw things they didn't like, such as self-centeredness, and a lack of respect for others. They would avoid those in their spouse.

Many reported that living under the extreme circumstances of a companionship prepared them for marriage. They felt living with a companion all the time gave them the opportunity to work on those skills that would help them in a marriage relationship, including communication, patience, and maintaining a positive attitude about the relationship. They learned not to let issues fester until there is a blowup, but rather they learned how to peacefully express their concerns and needs as they arose. Many said they learned this lesson the hard way with their companions, but while it may have been painful at the time, it had the positive effect of making them more aware of the need for loving communication with their spouse and children. They learned to address their weaknesses and irritating habits. They also learned to compromise; in a shared relationship they could not always have their own way. They became used to making joint decisions and to doing things with someone.

An elder who served in the 1960s said in retrospect, learning to live with a companion helped him in his marriage, but at the time of his mission he wasn't so sure. He remembered thinking: "How am I ever going to get married, for at four months, my companion and I are already getting on each other's nerves. How could I ever make it for a lifetime?" But then he (and other returned missionaries with him) reported that living with a spouse is easier than living with a companion. They have a choice in who their spouse will be; they are free to marry someone they like and love. And they don't have to be with the person literally twenty-four hours a day, seven days a week.

A sister observed, "If you can get along with a comp, someone you don't choose to be with, you probably can get along with someone you do choose to be with, and make it work."

Their approach to missions—going into people's homes—exposed them to family life and living situations they wouldn't have had the opportunity to see in practically any other context. Some situations were happy, and some were not. A returned missionary who served in the late 1950s observed, "Every door is a different person with different problems." Many said they came to realize what they wanted, and didn't want, in their own families and homes; they reassessed what was important to them. Their perceptions were heightened because they were outsiders. What may not have seemed obvious to those living in the midst of the family, was obvious to them.

An elder said his mission helped him rearrange his priorities—from being focused on himself, to what he would look for in a wife, how he would act as a husband and a father, and how he would help raise his children. He came away with a better understanding of the kind of family he wanted, of the amount of love, communication, and caring for one another he wanted, and of what he didn't want.

A sister said that an unexpected thing she learned was what to look for in a husband and how to raise her family. Every day she was able to view people and their family relationships, and she was able to evaluate the choices they made and how they had affected them. She said the benefit from doing that was that she could choose what she wanted her family to be, and she could see what it took to get there.

An elder said, "I remember many times thinking," (as he left a home), "'I don't want to be that way. I don't want to have a family like that. I don't want to live like that.'"

Given what missionaries experienced and learned on their missions, it is not surprising that many—sisters and elders—said they would only marry a returned missionary. They share a "common ground," as one sister described it. They have grown and matured personally and spiritually. They have successfully weathered a strong test. Serving a mission is a sign of a person's commitment and obedience to the Lord, to the Church, and to family. Their testimony has grown, they have gained knowledge of the gospel, and they share common commitments and values.

As a sister clearly stated, "You have to get with someone who is your equal."

Many young Latter-day Saint women who didn't serve a mission said they look for the same thing in their prospective spouse; they too want to marry a returned missionary.

Such a goal has historically been much easier for sisters to attain than for elders, since so many more elders serve. But with the increased number of sisters serving, more elders will now be able to marry a returned sister missionary.

A stake president said his mission prepared him for marriage, and as he started dating he consciously decided he wanted to marry a returned missionary. Being a returned missionary was a "significant attribute" he wanted in a spouse. And he did marry a returned missionary. Their joint missionary experience helped them prepare for marriage, he felt, and it brought strength to their relationship; it taught them to get along with others, to work hard, and to live righteous lives. He also saw this in the lives of people he respected; many had married returned missionaries. As a result, he now makes a conscious effort to encourage young women to serve a mission.

An elder who described himself as "a very practical person" said when he got back from his mission and returned to college, he decided he only wanted to marry an RM, because he saw so much growth in the sisters with whom he had worked on his mission. He decided to date thirty different women one semester as he looked for the right one. He saw a very big difference between the ones who had been on missions and the ones who hadn't. He felt they showed a greater level of maturity and spirituality.

He got as far as his seventeenth date, who was a returned missionary, and they are now happily married.

Some elders decide early on that they want to marry a returned sister missionary. I was eating lunch in the Provo MTC cafeteria with the MTC president and his wife when a young elder walked up to the table and announced, to no one in particular, and to everyone in general, "When I get married, I want to marry a returned missionary!" He then sat down and quietly started eating.

A sister who was about to go on her mission found it "disappointing" that a special male friend chose not to go on a mission. She said he had many wonderful qualities, but he didn't make the Church as much of a priority in his life as she felt was necessary, and he didn't feel serving a mission was that important. But it was important to her, and the person she married needed to feel the same way, she said.

Some said the probability of marrying an RM is very great, but they wouldn't rule out marrying someone who hadn't served a mission, as long as the person loved God, had a strong testimony, and knew that the LDS Church was true. Some said that serving a mission in and of itself was not sufficient for them; they knew elders serving a mission they would never marry.

A very small percentage of missionaries return to the significant other they left at the beginning of their mission, and an even smaller percentage go on to marry their pre-mission sweetheart. (Only three did so in my sample of eighty-five returned missionaries, and two of the returned missionaries were dating each other prior to their missions.) One couple had faithfully written to each other every week and were married five months after his return. They kept each other's letters, and she paired them up and put them in a scrapbook.

Some decided that waiting through the mission for the missionary to return wasn't such a good idea. A returned missionary described how he and his girlfriend wrote faithfully his entire mission, and she didn't date anyone while he was gone, but when he came home and they had one date, they agreed they shouldn't get married. Each had changed in significant ways, and it was best that they each went their separate ways.

The vast majority of missionaries return to no one, either because they didn't leave someone at home, or because they sent or received "Dear John" or "Dear Jane" letters, some as late as a few weeks before returning home.

In many cases they return home to find the earlier significant other engaged or married. President David O. McKay is quoted as promising a group of new elders ready to embark on their missions that their girlfriends would be waiting for them when they returned—with their husbands and their first children.[164]

The idea of marrying outside the faith is a foreign concept to highly religious Latter-day Saints. In analyzing data collected by the Relate Institute, a non-profit organization at BYU whose goal it is to collect data on relationships, a BYU professor found in 2011 that 98 percent of highly-religious Latter-day Saints date and marry within the faith, while the percentage drops to 65 percent for Mormons described as having low religiosity.[165] This has ritualistic implications, because mixed-faith couples would not be able to be married in a temple, which the highly religious consider a vitally important dimension of LDS belief and practice.

A candid sister missionary said she would not even consider marrying a non-member. She said she could fall in love with any number of people, but she wouldn't want to marry them, because spirituality is such a key part of her life. She could not have the marriage she is looking for unless her spouse shares her beliefs. Marrying outside the faith is not even an issue for her.

"It just won't happen," she said.

Some missionaries who serve in the same mission end up marrying each other when they return home. An elder who served in Canada said "a fair number" of sisters and elders from the mission eventually married each other. A mission president who served in Japan said there were one hundred elders and eighteen sisters serving with him, and after they returned home eight marriages came out of the group. An elder who served in Germany said he heard of similar marriages. Some even returned to the mission, married people in the area, and lived there.

Latter-day Saints are encouraged to have large families, since it is believed we all began as preexisting souls with God and that the duty of Church members is to give these souls a body so they can work out their salvation. Thus it isn't uncommon for LDS families to have six, seven, or eight children; some have even more.

A sociologist of religion who is a returned missionary and no longer active in the Church said there is an idealized type in the Latter-day Saint Church: the person is married, successful, and never divorced. He said it is very hard if one is outside these parameters, because it places him in an awkward position. He said single men over thirty are "disdained." They are perceived as a "menace" to LDS society. (Brigham Young is credited as saying, "Any unmarried man over the age of 27 is a menace to society," but researchers have been unsuccessful in substantiating the attribution.)

Given the current demographics of young people postponing marriage, an increasing number of young Latter-day Saint women fear they will never marry, even if they want to, which raises the uncomfortable question, "What does the Latter-day Saint faith have to offer me if I am single?" They feel out of place in the Church because they don't fit the expected mold of wife and mother. Articles regarding singles have appeared in Church publications, assuring them they do have a place in the Church, and bishops are instructed to find meaningful callings for all young single adults.

Education and schooling. The majority of interviewees had interrupted college careers to serve their missions, and when they returned home one of their first goals was to return to school. And most did. Many spoke of the positive influence of their mission on obtaining their degree. They took their schooling more seriously, they had developed a strong work ethic and good study skills, they knew how to set goals, they knew how to manage their time, and their mission had given them insight into their strengths, weaknesses, and interests. As a result, they had a better sense of what they wanted to study and the direction they wanted to take in their working lives. Almost to a person, they were more focused and earned better grades after their mission. For many, their mission made them confident about their future; if they could survive a mission and do it successfully, they could also achieve in other areas of their lives.

As all who teach at the college level know, this type of student is a welcome addition to the classroom.

Some parents and some missionaries expressed concern about interrupting their college career to serve a mission, for fear they would "lose time" and "be behind" when they returned to school. An interviewee who served in France said he was able to test out of sixteen credits of French after his mission. He took a language placement exam at BYU, and in one afternoon he was able to gain a whole semester's worth of credit. That, along with taking extra courses in the summer, allowed him to catch up with his original classmates.

Missionary training and experience is reflected in the BYU student body and in its curriculum. It is reported that 77 percent of BYU students speak a second language, with only 6 percent of them being international students. More than 90 percent of the returned missionaries at BYU who speak a second language possess advanced speaking skills. This number compares to 47 percent of five hundred language majors tested at five liberal arts colleges. BYU also has one of the largest language programs in the nation, with more than sixty languages offered regularly. Almost 31 percent of the student body is enrolled in a language course each semester. The national average is around 9 percent. It is also said that BYU offers more advanced language classes than any university in the country.[166]

Employment. The knowledge and skills missionaries gain in the mission field can have a positive effect on their potential for finding employment, including: communication, leadership, public speaking, and motivational skills; the ability to interact effectively with others and to work in groups; goal setting; time management; working with a budget; persistence; working under adversity; and a strong work ethic. All are traits that employers value.

For those who served overseas and learned a new language, their unique language and cultural skills have the potential to open up an even wider range of possibilities for them, although they may not want to take advantage of all of the opportunities available to them.

For some, their mission set the course for future employment. Some interviewees discovered they enjoyed teaching and were good at it, and they went on to teach at the elementary, high school, and college levels. For some, their close work with individuals and families and their exposure to the many issues people face motivated them to go into the helping professions, including counseling, social work, and rehabilitation services. Language skills gained while serving aided some in future employment and endeavors. The opera soprano Rachel Willis-Sørensen, winner of the 2010 Metropolitan Opera National Council Auditions, is a returned missionary who served in Germany. The judges were especially impressed with her ability to sing Wagner and with her command of the German language, which she learned during her mission. She went on to perform with the Metropolitan Opera.[167] A senior missionary who worked with Spanish-speaking missionaries at the London MTC said he became fluent in Spanish while serving his mission in Argentina, and his mission became the most influential thing in his life, because he went on to serve as a Spanish-speaking military attaché.

A college administrator who served a mission in Germany in the late 1960s said the knowledge and skills he gained during his mission have served him well in higher education because he gained important administrative, people, and organizational skills, which have been brought to good use in his various positions. He said there was little in his faculty training that prepared him as well for his administrative roles as did the things he learned on his mission and in the LDS Church. He said a mission is like a crucible, where there is intensity around the experience that gets imprinted on the individual. He was fortunate to work in the mission office for eight months, and he got to know his mission president very well, a man he described as "an extraordinary man and an outstanding mission president." The elder served as the mission financial secretary, and he audited the Church and mission financial reports. He went on to become the dean of a prestigious business school before becoming a college president.

Some employers seek out returned missionaries. This is particularly true in Utah, where the greatest concentration of returned missionaries are found and where employers, Mormons and non-Mormons alike, appreciate what returned missionaries can bring to their businesses and organizations.

Not all who seek work find it upon returning from a mission, and it can create personal and spiritual dissonance. A returned missionary who served in Canada was out of work for seven months after he returned from his mission. During the interim he asked with frustration, "I served a mission. Aren't I supposed to get blessed?"

In a follow-up interview with a missionary I had interviewed when she was serving years earlier, I asked if what she had learned during her mission helped her in her current position of teaching computer classes. She responded that *every* (her emphasis) part of her life has been affected by her mission, and that with regard to employment, the mission helped her self-confidence and her public speaking skills. She also learned good teaching skills, including the importance of taking time to prepare for each class, even over-prepare, so that she didn't find herself "teaching to the edge of her knowledge."

While some of the beliefs and practices of the LDS Church may put members at odds with mainstream religions and society, the skills and knowledge they gain on their missions that translate into the business world have caught the attention of business journalists, and they are enjoying a growing reputation in business circles. Returned missionaries are praised for their work ethic, their honesty, and, for those who served overseas, for their cultural awareness and language skills. As one commentator observed, "Mormons may be better understood in U.S. boardrooms and on Wall Street than they are in other segments of society."[168]

While returned missionaries may have gained the knowledge and skills needed for a particular profession, it doesn't necessarily mean they are interested in pursuing it. In an interview with a non-Mormon who is a retired Foreign Services Officer (who has "lived, worked, and traveled on every continent"), he spoke of how the knowledge and skills missionaries gain make them highly employable. Their language skills and experiences living overseas, along with their reputation for hard work and clean living, make them "highly desirable," and they are "eagerly sought" by U.S. firms with interests overseas. He added that various U.S. intelligence agencies try to recruit former Mormon missionaries with hard-to-find language skills, but that the CIA probably recruits fewer Mormons than other intelligence agencies, the reason being that neither the CIA nor returned missionaries are comfortable with one another. Latter-day Saints aren't comfortable going into environments where intelligence is commonly gathered—bars and brothels—so they show limited interest in the agency.

He described LDS colleagues who had worked with him in the Foreign Service as "top-flight diplomats, all of them, as well as pillars of the local American community." But he also pointed out that not many former LDS missionaries appear to be interested in the Foreign Service. He surmised that because of the Mormon emphasis on family and community, not many are attracted to a career that requires constant uprooting, unpredictable moves, possible separation from the basic nuclear family, and lengthy separation from the extended family.

Serving a mission impacts many important areas of a returned missionary's life, be it marriage, schooling, or employment. But there are those cases where the mission, or association with the Church, impacts the individual negatively, and he or she leaves the Church.

Not All Have a Good Mission Experience or Remain in the LDS Church

Not all have a good mission experience. Some don't get along with their mission president, some have negative mission experiences, and some should not have served in the first place.

A returned missionary said he found his mission experience discouraging. He didn't get along with his mission president, and his mission was "soured" because of it. He and his family continue to be active in the Church, but he's less active than his brothers who had more satisfying mission experiences.

An RM who served in the mid-1980s said his mission experience shaped his feelings regarding the Church, and it had an impact on his decision to leave it. He worked in the mission office, and he wasn't always impressed with some of the "bureaucrats" who came through the office. He wouldn't have had that close an exposure to the organization of the Church and the bureaucracy had he not had the mission experience. But he doesn't regret going on his mission, because it was an important two years in his life.

A self-confessed "slacker" who served in the Southern United States said he shouldn't have served at all. A native of Utah, he had doubts about serving a mission, but he went anyway because he found the family pressure and social pressure "overwhelming." He felt he had no choice. He constantly broke mission rules, he hated tracting, and he padded his numerical reports to the mission president. He was a good teacher, but he got to the point of not wanting to convert people to the LDS faith.

He is no longer a member of the Church.

For others, their beliefs and values were challenged (sometimes during their mission, and sometimes after), and they were unable to incorporate new views into their existing LDS frames of reference. Consequently, some drifted away from the Church, some made a conscious break, and some were excommunicated.

Theological doubts. Many interviewees who left the Church had theological concerns and doubts. There is the belief in the Church that Mormonism is the one, true faith and that it represents original Christianity. The Latter-day Saint science fiction author Orson Scott Card described the Church as the "chief organ" of God's work in the world. A sister observed that other religions might have part of the truth, but not all of it; only Mormonism has "the fullness of the gospel."[169]

Some interviewees began to question this assumption while on their mission. An RM who served in Switzerland said the more educated about the world he became, the more difficult it became for him to accept the literal statement that the Church has the only truth and that the Church's prophet is the only mouthpiece of God. He said in the end the LDS Church sent him on a mission that gave him a vision of the world that was much larger and more complex than the Church could nurture. His curiosity overflowed the bounds of what the Church could offer him. "From the age of eighteen to twenty-five the LDS Church nurtured me wonderfully and sent me on my way," he said, "but in the end it was not a way the Church could be a part of."

A returned missionary who served in Japan said that as he and his senior companion walked away from a door, after having been told by the person that he wasn't interested in their message, the senior companion said, "That is unfortunate, elder. He has missed his chance for salvation." The interviewee thought, "That can't be right." Exposure to other peoples, cultures, and religions started him thinking in relative terms. Is the Latter-day Saint Church just one of many options? How can so few be so right? He is no longer active in the Church.

An RM who served in Costa Rica had similar theological doubts. He thought he could hide them, but they became "overwhelming" during his mission. He stopped attending church after his return, and two years later he took his name off the Church rolls. He considers himself an atheist.

Racial issues. Interviewees who served in earlier decades raised issues of race. Prior to 1978, only white males could hold the priesthood. A returned missionary from Utah who served in California in the mid-1960s said the low point of his mission came as he struggled to justify the policy, a policy with which he did not agree. He recounted the experience of a black woman answering his knock, and while she graciously declined his invitation to attend church, he felt awkward extending it, given the Church's teaching at that time on who could and who could not hold the priesthood. He gradually eased himself out of the Church after returning home from his mission.

Others who served prior to the late 1970s, including those who remained active in the Church after their mission, said the same thing: they found it awkward when they tracted into a black home.

The policy was reversed in 1978 when Church President Spencer W. Kimball said he received a revelation to that effect, much to the relief of many Latter-day Saints. A sister who served in North Carolina in the mid-1970s said she can remember where she was when she heard the announcement regarding the prophet's revelation. She said she wished she could go back and reconnect with blacks she had encountered on her mission.

Gender issues. A missionary who served in the Midwest said issues of gender became apparent to him during his mission and contributed to his leaving the Church. He observed that sisters were more effective than elders in recruiting and teaching investigators, but since they didn't hold the priesthood, they couldn't participate in baptisms. This is when he first started seeing gender inequities that he felt existed in the Church. Now he considers himself somewhat of a feminist because of seeing that on his mission. He said it wasn't because of anything his mission president did, but that it was institutional.

Reacting against authoritarianism. Some interviewees who are no longer active reacted against the authoritarianism of the LDS Church. The mission president has considerable authority. He tells missionaries what they can and cannot wear, where they can and cannot go, and what they can and cannot do. While the local bishop doesn't wield that kind of power over the lives of regular Church members, the top-down organizational structure of the Church does impose greater expectations and restrictions on its members than is typical of most religious organizations. It is a question of obedience—what is the proper balance between the individual self and what the Church expects?

A missionary who served in Japan said the low point of his mission came when his grandfather passed away, but he wasn't allowed to return for the funeral. He found the experience "devastating," and he still regrets to this day that he didn't go home for the funeral. His mission president told him: "What can you do? He is in the afterlife. He would want you to stay in your mission."

He has since left the Church.

A square peg in a round hole. An interviewee who served his mission in the 1960s said he felt like a square peg in a round hole. His parents were Democrats in a Republican state, were working-class, and belonged to labor unions. They were liberal Mormons in Utah—liberal in the sense that the family would come home from church and discuss and question what was said, including the Church's stands on authoritarianism, race, and gender. This prepared him and his brothers to think of the LDS Church as something that could legitimately be criticized, since the Church generally took conservative positions that the family did not share. While it seemed inevitable that he would serve a mission, there was a certain ambiguity about it. He would have preferred a social mission, something like the Peace Corps, versus one of teaching doctrine, which he didn't view as the central part of religion, but which Mormon missionary activity seemed to be all about.

Going on a mission as a liberal young man involved doing something he thought was necessary in order to gain the respect he wanted to have later in his life: the respect of being able to engage in religious discussions with Latter-day Saints. He thus saw going on a mission as a necessary step, as a rite of passage, to become a religious adult. He wanted to be regarded with respect, because his goal as a liberal Mormon was to engage the Church in conversation and to change it.

He found his mission to be a frustrating experience. He felt having to memorize and repeat lessons did not allow his spiritual self to be expressed, because his language had to be what others had written, and he resented it. He would have preferred to be a "real missionary," one who went off without purse or scrip and who engaged people in terms of his own individual self instead of presenting standardized, memorized lessons, which for him was very alienating. It assumed his experiences could be put into the same form as everyone else's, and he could never quite adjust to that.

Another low point was the quantification forms he had to fill out each week. He resented the routinization and regimentation, the emphasis on numbers. Both the memorization and standardization alienated him; they were "thorns in his side." He wished the mission would be over.

In the end the mission experience taught him that he really didn't want to engage in the practice of changing the Church. Instead, he decided to leave it, although leaving took place gradually over a period of years. He had no concept of living outside Utah as he was growing up, but he chose to get away from it by going to graduate school on the East Coast, and he didn't return. His family and others he has known share his marginality. His brothers aren't practicing LDS and are liberal.

He sees leaving the Latter-day Saint Church as a natural evolution on his part, but it took a number of years to do it. It showed him how slowly his life changes. He could see from a younger age where he was headed, but it took a long time to get there.

Gay marriage and homosexuality. Some returned missionaries chose to leave the Church because of its stance on gay marriage and homosexuality. Gay marriage and homosexuality don't have a place in Mormon theology, because the Latter-day Saint Church, more than practically any other religious organization, ties its earthly and eternal life to heterosexual marriage. To achieve the highest level of glory in the next life, a person must be married ("sealed") to someone of the opposite sex, ideally in a temple. Thus gay marriage and homosexuality are seen as being at odds with Mormon theology and social values. The 1995 statement "The Family: A Proclamation to the World" stated that the LDS Church believes the family is central to God's plan, that marriage between a man and a woman is ordained by God, and that the formation of families is central to God's plan for his children. The family is thus of central importance to the Church, and at its core believes marriage is between one man and one woman. Anything else is seen as being contrary to God's laws, including homosexuality and gay marriage, which are seen as contributing to the disintegration of the family in modern society.[170]

While the Church is an advocate for conservative values, Utah is a Republican state, and the majority of Mormons vote Republican, it is rare for the Church to take a public stand on an issue that is to be decided at the ballot box. They have a standard neutrality statement: "The church's mission is to preach the gospel of Jesus Christ, not to elect politicians."[171]

The issue of gay marriage is an exception. The LDS Church became heavily involved in advocating for the passage of Proposition 8 in California in 2008, a proposition that sought to ban gay marriage in California. It is said Latter-day Saints donated nearly one-half of the nineteen million dollars raised in the campaign. The Church circulated flyers in support of "Prop 8" among its members, encouraging them to share them with their neighbors and on the street. While many churches and the majority of California citizens supported Prop 8, it was the LDS Church's backing of the cause, both financially and in volunteer support, which caught the public's attention, led to its passage, and generated outrage from the proposition's opponents. Anti-Mormon demonstrations took place across the country, including a thousand-strong demonstration by gay-rights activists in front of the LDS temple in Westwood, CA.

It is reported that anti-Mormon attitudes generated by the controversy hindered missionaries in their work of finding and teaching investigators. It also led to some returned missionary interviewees leaving the Church.

More recently, the Church has taken steps that are applauded by gay-rights activists. In 2015, the Church was actively seeking to help pass laws in Utah that would ban discrimination in housing and employment based on sexual orientation.

There are some Latter-day Saints who know they are gay, and they hope their missions will make them straight. In a study of gay, male Mormons, there were those who were attracted to members of the same sex while adolescents and who prayed that the attraction would be taken away. When that failed, they went on a mission to prove their dedication to God and to the LDS Church, with the hope and expectation that the attraction would cease. When that didn't happen, some became suicidal. [172]

An interviewee had a neighbor who was sent home early because he was gay, much to his and his family's embarrassment. The young man soon drifted away from the Church. The interviewee said in the eyes of Church members a person is better off being sent home early because he slept with a girl, than being sent home early because he engaged in a homosexual relationship.

Just didn't like it. And there are those who just didn't like their mission experience. A missionary who served in Canada reported that as his father was driving him home from his mission, his father asked him if he had enjoyed it.

"No, I didn't," replied the missionary.

"I didn't enjoy mine either," responded the father, and they never spoke of it again.

Leaving the Church

There are a variety of ways to "leave" the LDS Church. Members can stop attending, they can formally request that their names be removed from the Church rolls, and they can be excommunicated. The individual initiates the first two approaches, while the Church initiates the latter. A staff member who works at Church Headquarters in Salt Lake City told me not many choose to remove their names from Church rolls and not many are excommunicated.

Most interviewees who left the Church just stopped attending and became what is called "inactive." Their names continue on the membership rolls, and they may be periodically approached about becoming "active" again. Reactivating "inactives" is a goal of the current Church President, Thomas S. Monson.

Interviewees who formally removed their names said it wasn't easy. Almost all who went through the process of having their names purged from the Church records described the experience as long, hard, and painful. It caused hurt and confusion in their families, they were told their eternal salvation was in peril, and it ate away at their self-perception and identity. Some were bitter; some were not. None seemed to be crusading ex-Mormons.

A returned missionary said his departure from the Latter-day Saint Church sent "shock waves" through his family and that they felt disappointment. Rumors circulated in the family that he had been unfaithful to his wife and that was why he left the Church. He said it wasn't true. They couldn't accept the fact that he had lost his faith. He wanted to get on with his life, but he still hadn't lived it down in his extended family. He didn't talk with them about his leaving the Church, but he wouldn't back down if the topic came up.

Another RM said there was "a high cost" for him to disaffiliate from the Church and to leave the Latter-day Saint community. He recalled receiving a letter from Salt Lake City that said the effects of baptism and the temple were cancelled, and did he want to lose his eternal family?

"It hurt," he said.

He also felt anger. He said there are hard feelings still associated with it, but his anger has moderated with time. He still considers himself a Mormon in identity. It is part of his heritage and his past. "I accept my past," he said. "I did all the right things, channeled in the right direction, but then switched as an adult."

A returned missionary who served in the mid-1980s said his parents were so upset over his apostasy that his mother took his missionary journals away from him for fear of what he might do with them. He said his leaving the Latter-day Saint Church would create awkward family dynamics, because he expects his son will be the only grandchild in his extended Utah family who won't go on a mission. When asked if he will regret that, he said a study-abroad experience would be just fine for his son.

He is now past his anti-Mormon phase, and he has made peace with his family. They are feeling better about his decision, although his mother still won't return his journals.

One interviewee was excommunicated because he was a practicing homosexual. A sixth-generation Latter-day Saint from a family in which all the eligible male members in his family had served missions, who had served a successful mission himself where he enjoyed a number of baptisms, and who had prayed that by going on a mission that he might become straight, was excommunicated. He was excommunicated, in the words of his excommunication letter from Church authorities, "for the practice of homosexuality."

He was angry; he felt excommunication was a type of spiritual abuse and that he was being punished for what he *was*, not for what he had done. With time he mellowed. He now considered himself a humanist "with residual Christian tendencies." He still valued his mission experience, and he attended Church services with his children. He often took them to performances of the Mormon Tabernacle Choir in Salt Lake City. He reported, "Church was my life" as he was growing up. He continued: "I don't believe in 'church' anymore, but I will never give up on my people. Though I am no longer a Latter-day Saint, something about me will always be Mormon."[173]

They were not slackers. While it would be easy to assume that those who left the Latter-day Saint Church were not good missionaries, it is far from the truth. Many said that during their missions they were hardworking and were considered good missionaries by the objective criteria of the Church.

A returned missionary who was no longer a member cautioned that Church members shouldn't assume he was a slacker and a marginal missionary. On the contrary, he said, he was a faithful, obedient missionary during his mission, moving up the leadership ranks from district leader to zone leader and finally serving as an A.P. for his final seven months. He would call his mission successful by Church standards.

An RM who served in the Caribbean and was no longer a member of the Church described himself as a "straight arrow" while serving his mission. He was strict and hardworking, and he too was considered successful by the objective standards of the LDS Church.

Avid readers. Interviewees who left the Latter-day Saint Church tended to be avid readers who read far beyond the approved, standard LDS works and for whom their intellectual development was important.

An RM no longer affiliated with the Church served as the financial secretary in the mission office. He read all of the books in the mission president's library. He had a book by Karl Marx on his desk in the mission office, and a General Authority told him not to read it. He began to have doubts, which "ate away at his faith." When he would ask awkward questions, he would be told, "Elder, we don't ask those kinds of questions."

Another returned missionary who was no longer in the Church said he was a voracious reader throughout his mission. He "gobbled up" the scriptures as well as various Mormon and related texts. What he didn't realize at the time was that the intellectual quest he began on his mission would ultimately lead him out of the Church.

He began to "devour" various texts when he returned home from his mission—anything from Emerson, to the Koran, to postmodern philosophy. It was an intellectual journey that eventually resulted in the realization that, for him, Mormonism simply was not, and *could* not, be what it claimed to be—the only true and living Church upon the face of the earth. It was an epiphany that would not have seemed possible just a few years earlier. He realized he didn't have to believe in Mormonism because his parents had, or because his friends did, or because it was pretty much the whole of his experience up to that point. He realized that he could believe what he wanted to believe, how he wanted to believe it.

Today he considers himself an agnostic.

The academic study of religion. For some interviewees, while their missionary experiences contributed to their leaving the Church, it also provided new directions for their interests and careers. An RM who served in Latin America in the 1960s said he quickly fell outside the flock once he returned home from his mission. He felt it was a reflection of the times (the 1960s), plus he began studying the sociology of religion in college, which exposed him to critical analysis and the academic study of religion. It provided a different framework from which to analyze his experiences, and it became increasingly difficult to reconcile things he had always taken for granted.

He acknowledged that at the beginning of his mission he didn't have a testimony. He assumed it would come, he did what he thought was right, and he was committed to doing the best job he could. But he never had the experience that others talked about—a mystical confirmation of his testimony of the sort that people talked about in LDS meetings. It made him feel uncomfortable; he rarely bore his testimony in traditional LDS style, either before or after his mission, although during his mission it was easy because he did it in Spanish, and that didn't seem quite the same. He had it memorized and he could say the words, but it didn't have the same meaning. He had a very successful mission by all the objective standards used, but he didn't come away with a testimony or faith based on some spiritual experience.

His experiences made more sense to him after studying the social sciences, which led to some skepticism regarding the religious interpretation of his experiences. Thus he lacked a spiritual basis of faith for his experiences. He didn't denigrate it, because it was a valuable experience. It was just a loss of belief. It wasn't a loss of faith, since he didn't have it in the sense that Mormons talk about it. It was a rapid erosion of belief.

Thus the long-term consequence of the missionary experience for him was that "it was a wonderful, stimulating experience that brought from slumber many potential abilities and directions." But in terms of a religious orientation for the rest of his life, he was not able to overcome the secular exposure.

He retained an academic interest in religion. He had always been fairly tolerant of others' faiths and never went through a period where he became embittered or intolerant. Now, partly because of his mission, he had a sympathetic understanding for people who were religiously committed, and he had incorporated that into his professional life.

Still a good experience for most. While those who left the LDS Church had various issues with it, few regretted serving a mission. A social scientist who served in the 1970s reported that years later, when he was more distant from the Church, he still looked back on his mission as a "wonderful" experience. He had a number of disaffected Mormons as close friends, and many of them wanted their children to have the mission experience because they still looked back on theirs with real fondness.

An RM who served in Mexico in the mid-1960s took a retrospective look at his mission and those of others he had known. He said it was very hard for people to regret their missionary experiences, whether they stayed active in the Church or not, because it was such a formative period in their lives. As he looked back on it now, he had a great mission. At the time, he wasn't so sure.

An RM reported that the two years spent on his mission were two of the best years of his life. He said it must sound odd coming from someone who had since left the Church, but he wouldn't trade the lessons he learned on his mission for anything. He believed they are, in no small part, to thank for any achievement he had accomplished since his mission. He was a big believer that young people need to be involved in something bigger than them. For him, it was his mission.

The Move Toward Centralization and Routinization

The Church of Jesus Christ of Latter-day Saints is a highly centralized church with a rigid hierarchical organizational structure. Ongoing efforts to centralize and routinize various aspects of the organization are characteristic of the Church, including, since the mid-twentieth century, missionary training and the missionary experience.

The Latter-day Saint missionary system, like all organizations, experiences both continuity and change. The goal of the missionary program has remained consistent throughout the history of the Church—to bring investigators into the faith—and missionaries share common experiences regardless of when they serve. The system has also changed over time in ways it is felt have improved it. But depending on whom you talk to, not all agree that all of the changes are for the better.

Some things don't change. An interviewee said he had just come from a homecoming talk by a returned missionary and the young man said the exact same things he had said twenty-five years earlier at his homecoming. They shared the same kinds of experiences and the same sorts of feelings about Christ, their lives, their families, and the importance of service.

Some things are seen to change for the better. The infrastructure of the Mormon Church has been expanded in ways that strengthen the missionary program. A returned missionary said the Church is in a better position today to prepare young men and women to go on their missions because the seminary program is more widespread. When he was growing up in a small town in the Northern Plains in the 1940s and 1950s, there was no seminary to help prepare him for his mission. It was only after he arrived at BYU that he received the help he felt he needed.

Missionary training has changed over the decades, and it is much more structured today. What was a week's training in the mid-twentieth century, had evolved, prior to the age change in 2012, to a three to twelve week stay at the Provo MTC. There their days are tightly scheduled, their actions are closely monitored, and they receive training on what to say and how to say it. Missionary materials have also evolved over time, incorporating increased sophistication.

A General Authority told me that he sees these changes as a positive evolution. He said the Church now has a better understanding of what a missionary is supposed to do. The training is better, the message is "packaged" better, the lessons are shorter, and the Church has a better understanding of how people are going to react.

While older generations of missionaries agree today's missionaries are more thoroughly trained in the nuts and bolts of missionary work—some compared the regimentation and formalized training of the MTC to a military boot camp, without the military component—they aren't convinced it is necessarily for the better. The fear is that missionaries are programmed ("This is what you do and this is the way you do it"). As a result some come into the mission field lacking creativity and initiative, such that when they are confronted with situations different from those presented in the MTC, they don't know what to do.

A one-time bishop and stake president who served his mission in the 1960s and who lives in a community where there has been a steady presence of missionaries for decades observed that on occasion he has found fault with missionaries: with some he almost felt like he needed to wind them up, they would go until they stopped, and then they would sit and wait for the next assignment from the ward mission leader. While acknowledging there probably were lazy missionaries when he served, he felt his generation showed more self-motivation and were more likely to try a variety of approaches if the first didn't work. In this regard, he felt more training is not necessarily better. He said missionaries are a little *too* programed today. They get the notion at the MTC that, "This is how it is done" (he said with emphasis) and thus if it doesn't work just like that, they are lost.

A returned missionary who served in New England in the late 1940s agreed. He saw a number of differences between his experience as a missionary and what missionaries experience today. Today's missionary program is run much more by formula, and he didn't see how it could be nearly as "charismatic" an experience. He felt there was very little leeway left to missionaries to do anything really on their own. His mission president allowed his companion and him to wander from town to town over a large area, they were thrown on their own resources, and they had to improvise as they went along. They had no teaching materials or prescribed lessons to present to investigators. Rather, investigators had to be convinced through a series of persuasive conversations. He had to form a relationship with them so that they came to admire missionaries as people, as well as their message. They worked on the premise that people would be converted in their heads *and* in their hearts, and as a result they would want to join the local Mormon congregation.

But such opened-ended wanderings, with such unstructured teaching, are inconceivable now. Neither parents nor Church Fathers would tolerate such an approach today.

He felt today's lesson plans leave very little room for maneuvering for missionaries. While he acknowledged that structure, discipline, and regimentation are necessary when dealing with late adolescents, both at the MTC and in the mission field, he lamented that today's missionary experience is far from being the kind of morale-building, charismatic experience that he experienced during his training and on his mission.

And as we have seen above, increased routinization and centralization is also seen at the ritual level of the missionary experience, particularly the farewell talk, the arrival at the Provo MTC, and the homecoming talk.

Missionary training is still evolving. The Church acknowledges the benefits of relying more on the inspiration and creativity of missionaries, and it has moved away from requiring them to present memorized lessons in a set and (it was feared) wooden, uninspired, mechanical manner. It is felt the approach taken in *Preach My Gospel,* which teaches the principles of the faith and encourages missionaries to be creative and flexible as they tailor their conversations and lessons to the needs of the individual investigator, is a step in the right direction.

But the contrast with the training of earlier generations is still striking, and it is reflected in the comment of an elder who served in the mid-1960s. He recalled the basic message he took away from his six days of training at the Mission Home in Salt Lake City as being, "Here is what you need to do, here are the rules, and off you go."

The Changing Face of Missionary Work: Technology

Practically nothing has affected churches more than the growth of the Internet. It has moved religious discussion outside the traditional bounds of churches, where Internet technologies are creating new spaces where the religious can gather. It is a form of participatory media. Today's children are growing up in a digital world, a world that is not always understood or appreciated by their parents and grandparents. Youths find it extremely important that they remain connected electronically, around the clock for some, and they see their identity, both online and offline, as one. It is their social identity. For some, it is an addiction.

Older generations don't understand this, saying that while young people today want to stay connected, it is not a face-to-face connectedness, but rather connectedness at a distance. Older generations want the personal experience, and the fear is that younger generations are losing vital communication skills that come with the face-to-face experience.

A faculty colleague gave an example of this. He said historically when he would walk into the classroom students would be talking and socializing and the noise level could be pretty high. Today when he walks into the classroom there is total silence, with students hunched over their smartphones—often texting someone, who is somewhere else.

Technology favors the young because they understand it, whereas older generations may not, and they see it as a divider. Words on a page aren't how young people communicate today.

It is also feared that authority and control are lost when people communicate this way, because of the radical non-authoritarianism of the Internet. It is hard to maintain authority online, since all are authorities there. Conflicting points of view are found on the Internet, which can lead youths away from their faith.

The Latter-day Saint Church is aware that door-to-door proselytizing and street contacting are very inefficient approaches to spreading the gospel. Granted, they provide visibility for the missionaries and an awareness of the presence of the Church in communities, but, as we have seen, the appearance of missionaries can also be the reason why people disappear into their homes and don't answer knocks at their door. Such approaches to evangelism require considerable time, effort, and money, with few long-term results.

As a result, the Church is investigating the use of the Internet as a vehicle for reaching out to potential converts. Its advantages are many: it provides access to a world-wide audience; it allows for communication to take place twenty-four hours a day; and it allows investigators to pursue their questions at their own pace and in a private manner. The Church missionary program recognizes these advantages, plus it sees value in the current generation's addiction to technology, so it is taking steps to test such an approach.

A pilot program was implemented in upstate New York in May 2010, called "Missionaries on the Internet," where a dozen missionaries communicated with potential investigators via blogs and social networks. Companions had to work together at the same computer monitor, and they had to use computers at an LDS Church meetinghouse or at a Church visitors' center. They returned to tracting only after exhausting their Internet possibilities. Contacts made outside the mission area were referred to missionaries in the investigator's area, which could be anywhere in the world.[174]

Such an approach is proving to be effective. In 2013, a pilot program in the Arizona Phoenix Mission saw missionaries teaching online lessons to investigators in forty-two states and fifty countries. And in 2014 certain missions were being equipped with iPads and other digital devices.[175]

The Church even puts a theological interpretation on its use of technology: "The divine purpose of technology is to hasten the work of salvation."[176]

But in spite of its advantages, there is a push and a pull in the Latter-day Saint Church with regard to the use of technology. On a positive note, its award-winning weekly program *Music and the Spoken Word* has been broadcast since 1929 and reaches millions, and the Church's twice-yearly General Conferences are beamed to millions around the world in nearly one hundred languages. However, the Church was slow to adopt Internet technology because it poses a threat in terms of authority and control. Church authorities can't filter what members see and read—they are particularly concerned about pornography and anti-Mormon sites—which can undermine the faith and morals of Church members and can destroy marriages. There are also documented cases where young men, committed to online gaming groups, have chosen not to serve a mission, saying a two-year absence would have a negative impact on their group.[177]

But at the turn of the twenty-first century, the Church expanded its Internet presence with the websites www.lds.org and www.mormon.org. The sites explain the beliefs and practices of the Latter-day Saint Church and provide ways for non-members to learn more about the LDS faith, including requesting a visit from missionaries. A popular feature of www.mormon.org is that it tells the personal and spiritual stories of individual

Church members, the goal of which is to show that Mormons are common, everyday people and to aid in the Church's missionary efforts.

On a practical level, there are declining demographics of eligible teenage boys in the United States, and young men in other countries are being encouraged to assume greater responsibility for missionary labors, along with sisters and seniors in the U.S. and elsewhere. The increased use of the Internet may help offset the declining population by getting more people involved from their homes and by making missionary work, formal and informal, more efficient.

Time will tell how the missionary program will be affected by the Internet revolution. There are concerns that younger generations won't have the personal communication skills of their parents and grandparents, that they will be exposed to extensive anti-Mormonism on the Web, and that weaning them from video games, social networking, and staying connected twenty-four hours a day, seven days a week is a challenge that bishops, stake presidents, MTC officials, and mission presidents will have to address.

How to balance the positive aspects of technology with its dangers is an ongoing challenge for Latter-day Saint Church authorities.

My Plan

The Church implemented a new program for missionaries in July 2015: *My Plan*.[178] It is an online course, completed by missionaries at the beginning and at the end of their mission, where they set a path for their lives after their missions. The stated goal of the program is for returning missionaries to "consider how a mission can become a spiritual foundation for a righteous, successful life." They are to share their personal, professional, and spiritual goals with parents, bishops, stake presidents, and mission presidents, who can serve as mentors. By publically sharing these goals the hope and assumption is that the returned missionary will build upon the mission experience and become a lifelong, faithful member of the Church. It can also be a way to address those who may have a tendency to become inactive after their mission.

Tearing Up

In the devotional classic *The Imitation of Christ*, Thomas A'Kempis observes that our strengths are most often seen during times of trial and tribulation. Such times do not make us weak; rather, they show us what we are.[179]

Such is the experience of the men and women who serve as missionaries for The Church of Jesus Christ of Latter-day Saints. They face numerous trials and struggles—rejection, exhaustion, getting along with difficult companions, doubt, boredom, extreme highs and extreme lows, and, for a few, even assaults—but most say they are thankful they did it, that it was the greatest experience they had had up to that point in their lives.

The comment of a sister about her returned missionary father is illustrative. She said he talked about how difficult his mission had been and how much he had struggled, but he would say it with a big grin on his face. She said prior to her mission she couldn't understand his behavior, but afterwards, she could.

The mission is a pressure cooker, where missionaries face their weaknesses but also find they have strengths and skills they never knew they possessed. They also develop new ones. They forget the low points and remember the high points. They say the good things outweigh the bad.

"A high point erases twenty low points," reported an RM.

Returned missionaries who had served many decades earlier said it was hard for them to believe that such a short period of their lives could have had such lasting consequences, and they said it with tears in their eyes.

I asked an RM who served in the 1960s why it is that even after thirty or forty years, some returned missionaries will tear up when talking about their mission. He said that it is because the mission is such a powerful experience, that while serving they are instruments of God in other people's spiritual growth. He said they get to see things that are extraordinary; they get to see the Lord working in peoples' lives, and they get to see peoples' lives change. He said that in many ways the Lord works at the frontiers of peoples' lives, at the edges, and that missionaries work at those edges, where they see changes take place in investigators' lives. He said they have amazing experiences because of this, they remember them vividly, and even after thirty years, they tear up.

"I DID DO IT!"

A sister from the Northwest, who returned home from her mission in Northern New England, shared her homecoming story. She recalled that as her plane taxied to the gate, the airport windows were filled with signs saying, "Welcome Home, Kate!" There were so many signs that the pilot came on the intercom and said, "It looks like we have a passenger named Kate with us today."

Still wearing her missionary nametag, Kate was quickly identified by her fellow passengers, who encouraged her to be first off the plane.

As she exited, Kate recalled that as she was leaving for her mission eighteen months earlier from this very same airport, she had confided to her mother, "I hope I can do this."

As she entered the terminal and was greeted by her parents, sisters, brothers, aunts, uncles, and friends, her mother rushed to her—and as they embraced, Kate said through her tears: "I did do it, I *did* do it, and to the best of my ability. It was hard, very hard, but I was a good missionary."

To which her mother responded, "I knew you would be, Kate. I knew you would be. Welcome home."

ENDNOTES

PROLOGUE

1. Vermont, New Hampshire, and Maine are identified as the least religious states in the United States. Frank Newport, "Mississippi Most Religious State, Vermont Least Religious," *Gallup*, February 3, 2014, http://www.gallup.com/poll/167267/mississippi-religious-vermont-least-religious-state.aspx.

2. John Bytheway, *How to Be an Extraordinary Missionary* (Salt Lake City: Deseret Book, 2005); Brad Wilcox and Russell Wilcox, *Raising Ourselves to the Bar: Practical Advice and Encouragement for the Next Generation of Missionaries and Their Parents* (Salt Lake City: Deseret Book, 2007); Gary Shepherd and Gordon Shepherd, *Mormon Passage: A Missionary Chronicle* (Urbana: University of Illinois Press, 1998); also see DeseretBook.com. Craig Harline, *Way Below the Angels: The Pretty Clearly Troubled But Not Even Close to Tragic Confessions of a Real Live Mormon Missionary* (Grand Rapids: Wm. B. Eerdmans Publishing Co., 2014). Armand L. Mauss, *Shifting Borders and a Tattered Passport: Intellectual Journeys of a Mormon Academic* (Salt Lake City: University of Utah Press, 2012.)

3. Walter Kirn, "The Mormon Moment," *Newsweek,* June 5, 2011, http://www.newsweek.com/mormon-moment-67951.

4. Michael De Groote, "Hugh Nibley's secret coded language," *Deseret News,* November 19, 2009, http://www.deseretnews.com/article/705345502/Hugh-Nibleys-secret-coded-language.html.

5. *Deseret News 2013 Church Almanac* (Salt Lake City: Deseret News, 2013), 5; Tad Walch, "LDS missionary numbers to peak at 88,000; more to use and pay for digital devices," *Deseret News*, July 3, 2014.

INTRODUCTION

6. All biblical quotations are from the King James Version, since that is the translation used by Latter-day Saints.

7. Examples include the New York Missionary Society, the Connecticut Missionary Society, and the American Home Missionary Society. The American Bible Society was formed to support the missionary societies.

8. Smith himself subsequently wrote an account of his experiences, and the story has attracted a number of historians, both official Church historians, and others. Joseph Smith, *History of the Church of Jesus Christ of Latter-day Saints: Period I History of Joseph Smith, the Prophet, by Himself. Vol I. Joseph Smith History* (Salt Lake City: Deseret Book Co.,1927) 1:1-80. See also: *Doctrine and Covenants* (D&C) 13:1; 27:12; 128:20; Brigham H. Roberts, *Comprehensive History of the Church of Jesus Christ of Latter-day Saints, Century I* (Provo: BYU Press, 1975); Richard L. Bushman, *Joseph Smith: Rough Stone Rolling* (New York: Knopf, 2005); Fawn Brodie, *No Man Knows My History: The Life of Joseph Smith*. (New York: Knopf, 1945; second edition, 1971).

9. Smith, *History*, 1:85.

10. www.lds.org

11. *Ensign* 40, No. 3 (March 2010): 65. *Deseret News Church News* (November 20, 2010): 3.

12. Pew Research Center, "Public Expresses Mixed Views of Islam, Mormonism," Religion and Public Life Project, (September 25, 2007).

13. Gary C. Lawrence, *How Americans View Mormonism: Seven Steps to Improve Our Image* (The Parameter Foundation, 2008).

14. *Deseret News Church News* (May 9, 2009): 6.

15. Laurie Goodstein, "Mormons' ad campaign may play out on the '12 campaign trail." *New York Times* (November 18, 2011).

16. Cathy Lynn Grossman, "Pastor: I'll 'hold my nose,' vote for Mormon Romney," *USA Today* (February 22, 2012).

17. Jonathan D. Salant, "Some Voters Have Qualms About Mormon President, Poll Says," *Bloomberg Business* (June 8, 2011). http://www.bloomberg.com/news/articles/2011-06-08/a-third-of-voters-have-qualms-about-mormon-president-poll-says.

18. www.lds.org

CHAPTER 1

19. Spencer W. Kimball, "President Kimball Speaks Out on Being a Missionary," *The New Era* 11, No. 5 (May, 1981).

20. See: https://www.lds.org/prophets-and-apostles/unto-all-the-world/prepare-to-be-a-missionary.

21. *For the Strength of Youth: Fulfilling Our Duty to God* (Salt Lake City: Intellectual Reserve, Inc., 2001).

22. *Preach My Gospel. A Guide to Missionary Service* (Salt Lake City: Intellectual Reserve, Inc., 2004); *For the Strength of Youth: Fulfilling Our Duty to God* (Salt Lake City: Intellectual Reserve, Inc., 2001); M. Russell Ballard, "How to Prepare to be a Good Missionary," *The New Era* 37, No. 3 (March 2007): 8.

23. M. Russell Ballard, "The Greatest Generation of Missionaries," *Ensign* 32, No. 11 (November 2002): 47-48.

24. *Deseret News Church News* (January 18, 2003): 3.

25. *Mormon Times* (May 1, 2010): 1; Charles D. Knutson and Kyle K. Oswald, "Just a Game?" *Ensign* 39, No. 8 (August 2009): 48.

26. *Deseret News 2012 Church Almanac* (2012): 5, 202.

27. *Deseret News Church News* (July 31, 2010): 6.

CHAPTER 2

28. "Our Son's Choice," *Ensign* 38, No. 2 (February 2008): 11-13.

29. Quentin L. Cook, "LDS Women Are Incredible!" *Ensign* 41, No. 5 (May 2011): 20.

30. Mary Paulson Harrington, "Not Every Family Rejoices To Have A Child Go On A Mormon Mission," *Sunstone* 14, Issue 80 (December 1990): 51-53.

31. Gary Smith, "A Season for Spreading the Faith," *Sports Illustrated* (September 4, 1985).

32. *Deseret News Church News*, (August 3, 2002).

33. Sheri L. Dew, *Go Forward With Faith: The Biography of Gordon B. Hinckley* (Salt Lake City: Deseret, 1996), 259.

34. M. Russell Ballard, "How to Prepare to be a Good Missionary," *New Era* (March 2009).

35. Ronald A. Rasband, "The Divine Call of a Missionary," *Ensign* 40, No. 5(May 2010): 52-53.

36. Donald B. Doty, "Missionary Health Preparation," *Ensign* 37, No. 3 (March 2007).

37. "Church changes dress code for sister missionaries." *Daily Universe,* October 20, 2011. http://universe.byu.edu/2011/10/20/sister-missionary-fashion-changes/.

38. Gordon B. Hinckley, "My Testimony," *Ensign* 23, No. 11 (November 1993): 52.

CHAPTER 3

39. *Deseret News Church News* (January 15, 2011): 3.

40. *Deseret News Church News* (November 9, 2014): 2.

41. Neil L. Anderson, "Preparing the World for the Second Coming," *Ensign* 41, No. 5 (May 2011): 51.

42. "Missionary Leader's Responsibilities," MTC handout, 2008.

43. The document can be found at: https://www.lds.org/manual/preach-my-gospel-a-guide-to-missionary-service.

44. "Missionary Training Centers Help Hasten the Work of Salvation," *Ensign* 44, No. 5 (May 2014): 138.

45. See https://www.lds.org/music/library/hymns/called-to-serve?lang=eng

46. James B. Allen and John B. Harris, "What Are You Doing Looking Up Here? Graffiti Mormon Style," *Sunstone* 6, No. 2 (March-April 1981): 27-40.

47. "Children," *Missionary Handbook* (the "little white book") (Salt Lake City: The Church of Jesus Christ of Latter-day Saints, 2006), 35.

CHAPTER 4

48. "Elder Ronald A. Rasband: Prepared for a Lifetime of Service." http://www.mormonnewsroom.org/article/elder-ronald-a-rasband-prepared-for-a-lifetime-of-service.

49. See *Mission President Handbook (2006)* (Salt Lake City: The Church of Jesus Christ of Latter-day Saints, 2006).

50. Gary Avant, "Leaders Instruct New Mission Presidents, Wives," *Church News* (June 22, 2014).

51. *Deseret News Church News* (July 3, 2010).

CHAPTER 5

52. *Missionary Handbook*, Chapter 5.

53. *Preach My Gospel*, 150.

54. *Deseret News Church News* (July 16, 2011).

55. James Talmadge, *Jesus the Christ* (Salt Lake City: Deseret Book Co., 1915); *Our Heritage: A Brief History of The Church of Jesus Christ of Latter-day Saints* (Salt Lake City: The Church of Jesus Christ of Latter-day Saints, Intellectual Reserve, Inc., 1996); M. Russell Ballard, *Our Search for Happiness: An Invitation to Understand the Church of Jesus Christ of Latter-day Saints* (Salt Lake City: Deseret Book Co., 1993); *True to the Faith: A Gospel Reference* (Salt Lake City: The Church of Jesus Christ of Latter-day Saints, Intellectual Reserve, Inc., 2004).

56. *Collegium Aesculapium...an Organization for LDS Health Professionals*, April 2010.

57. Doty, "Missionary Health Preparation."

58. *Preach My Gospel*, 4.

59. Michael Paulson, "Survivors recall tragic car crash in France with Romney," *New York Times* (June 24, 2007).

60. Michael S. Nielsen, "Without Saying Goodbye," *Ensign* 20, No. 6 (June 1990): 30-31; *Deseret News Church News* (February 13, 2010); *Deseret News Church News* (March 15, 2003).

61. See Susan E. Woods, *The Transfer: Stories of Missionaries Who Gave the Last Full Measure of Devotion,* Volumes 1 and 2 (Digital Legend Press, 2010).

CHAPTER 6

62. Dallin H. Oaks, "The Role of Members in Conversion," *Ensign* 33, No. 3 (March 2003): 54.

63. Oaks, "The Role of Members in Conversion," 54.

64. *Deseret News Church News,* (July 6, 2002).

65. *Deseret News Church News,* (January 18, 2003).

66. *Deseret News Mormon Times* (September 5, 2009).

67. *Deseret News Church News* (June 25, 2011).

68. Oaks, "The Role of Members in Conversion," 54.

69. http://www.mormontabernaclechoir.org/events/visitor-information?lang=eng

70. Oakes, "The Role of Members in Conversion," 56.

71. Watchtower Bible & Tract Society of New York, Inc., v. Village of Stratton 536 U.S. 150 (2002).

72. In the Pew Forum on Religion & Public Life, "A Portrait of Mormons in the U.S." (July 24, 2009), 96 percent of LDS respondents said they believe that miracles still occur today; 80 percent said they believe "completely" in miracles; while 16 percent said they believe "mostly" in miracles.

73. Oaks, "The Role of Members in Conversion," 54.

CHAPTER 7

74. *Preach My Gospel* 1-2; Mosiah 3:19.

75. http://www.pewforum.org/religious-landscape-study/gender-composition/

76. *Preach My Gospel*, 37.

77. Book of Mormon, Introduction; *Preach My Gospel*, 7, 103.

78. *Preach My Gospel*, 31-46.

79. *Preach My Gospel*, 47-59.

80. *Preach My Gospel*, 60-70.

81. *Preach My Gospel*, 71-81.

82. *Preach My Gospel*, 82-88.

83. *Preach My Gospel*, 7.

84. *Preach My Gospel*, 7.

85. Jerry Earl Johnston, "Protestant books on Mormons show welcome change in attitude," *Mormon Times* (March 6, 2010): 9. Examples include: Mark J. Cares, *Speaking the Truth, in Love, to Mormons* (Northwestern Publishing House, 1998); Ron Rhodes and Marian Bodine, *Reasoning from the Scriptures with the Mormons* (Harvest House, 1995); Bill McKeever and Eric Johnson, *Mormonism 101:*

Examining the Religion of the Latter-day Saints (Grand Rapids: Baker Books, 2000); David L. Rowe, *I Love Mormons: A New Way to Share Christ with Latter-day Saints* (Grand Rapids: Baker Books 2005).

86. Breanna Olaveson, "Role of Members Important in Sharing the Gospel Online," *Ensign* 40, No. 9 (September 2010): 74-76; M. Russell Ballard, "Sharing the Gospel Using the Internet," *Ensign* 38, No. 7 (July 2008): 58-63.

87. More Good Foundation, http://www.moregoodfoundation.org

88. *Preach My Gospel*, 204.

89. *Preach My Gospel*, 9.

90. Oaks, "The Role of Members in Conversion," 54.

91. Gordon B. Hinckley, "Some Thoughts on Temples, Retention of Converts, and Missionary Service," General Conference, October 1997; Gordon B. Hinckley, "Every Convert is Precious," *Liahona* 23, No. 2 (February 1999).

92. Oaks, "The Role of Members in Conversion," 57-58.

93. Neil L. Anderson, "Preparing the World for the Second Coming," 49-52.

CHAPTER 8

94. *Deseret News 2008 Church Almanac* (2008): 422.

95. See http://www.mormonnewsroom.org/facts-and-statistics/country/mongolia

96. *Deseret News Church News* (April 12, 2015): 3. http://www.mormonnewsroom.org/facts-and-statistics

97. *Deseret News 2001-2002 Church Almanac* (2001-2002): 573.

98. Robert L. Lively, Jr., "The Catholic Apostolic Church and the Church of Jesus Christ of Latter-day Saints: A Comparative Study of Two Millenarian Groups in Nineteenth-century England" (doctor of philosophy dissertation, University of Oxford, 1977), 163-181, 206-212.

99. S. George Ellsworth, "A History of Mormon Missions in the United States and Canada, 1830-1860" (doctor of philosophy dissertation, University of California, 1951), 295, 305-306.

100. Brigham Young, *History of the Church of Jesus Christ of Latter-day Saints*, Period II, Vol. VII (Salt Lake City, 1952), 466. See also: *The Latter-day Saints' Millennial Star* VII: 38-39. The *Star* was the official publication of the LDS Church in Great Britain, 1840-1970.

101. P. A. M. Taylor, *Expectations Westward. The Mormons and the Emigration of Their British Converts in the Nineteenth Century* (Ithaca, N.Y.: Cornell University Press, 1966), 144.

102. *Millennial Star* XV (January 1, 1853): 5-8. The revelation is found in *Doctrine and Covenants,* Section 132.

103. *Millennial Star* XIX (August 22, 1857): 531-532.

104. Thomas S. Monson, "Welcome to Conference," *Ensign* 44, No. 11 (November 2014): 4.

105. *Deseret News 2012 Church Almanac* (2012): 394, 577.

106. See http://www.mormonnewsroom.org/facts-and-statistics

107. James B. Allen and Richard O. Cowan, "History of the Church: c. 1945-1990, Post-World War II International Era Period," *The Encyclopedia of Mormonism* (New York: Macmillan, 1992).

108. *Deseret News Church News* (June 23, 2001); M. Russell Ballard, "How to Prepare to be a Good Missionary," *New Era* (March 2007).

109. "Missionary Training Centers Help Hasten the Work of Salvation," *Ensign* 44, No. 5 (May 2014): 138. https://www.lds.org/locations/missionary-training-centers.

110. Anderson, "Preparing the World for the Second Coming": 51.

111. See: https://www.lds.org/locations/missionary-training-centers/philippines.

112. *Preach My Gospel*, 127-135.

113. *Lewiston Maine Sun Journal* (August 6, 1994).

114. Based on a personal interview. Also see Shepherd and Shepherd, *Mormon Passage*, 372-373, 383, 396.

115. John H. Groberg, *The Other Side of Heaven* (Salt Lake City: Deseret Book, 1993): 104-106.

116. *Deseret News 2013 Church Almanac* (2013): 561; Stefan M. Hogan, "Young Men in White Shirts," *The Slovak Spectator* (October 8,

2007); Jonathan Green, "Slovakia!" *Times and Seasons* (November 14, 2006); *LDS Church News*, "Daunting Task Known as Slovakian Miracle" (November 11, 2006); Jonathan T. Tichy, "The Registration of the Church of Jesus Christ of Latter-day Saints in Slovakia. An Insider's Report" *Osterreichisches archive fur recht & religion* (2009): 17-26.

117. *Deseret News 2013 Church Almanac* (2013): 487; Emmanuel Abu Kissi, *Walking in the Sand. A History of the Church of Jesus Christ of Latter-day Saints in Ghana* (Provo: BYU Press, 2004).

118. See Paul Pedersen, *The Five Stages of Culture Shock: Critical Incidents Around the World.* (Westport, CT: Greenwood Press, 1995).

CHAPTER 9

119. See "Georgetown Symposium on Proselytism & Religious Freedom in the 21st Century," March 3, 2010.

120. *Deseret News 2011 Church Almanac* (2011): 157, 168, 169; *Mormon Times* (August 28, 2010): 5.

121. *Deseret News Church News* (January 30, 2010).

122. Thomas S. Monson, "Welcome to Conference," *Ensign* 39, No. 11 (November 2009): 6. http://www.mormonnewsroom.org/article/church-in-talks-to-regularize-activities-in-china

123. *Deseret News 2012 Church Almanac* (2012): 577.

124. Groberg, *The Other Side of Heaven*, 70-74.

125. *Deseret News Church News* (September 12, 2009.)

126. Sara Elvira Eriksen, "One Stalwart Pioneer, Many Generations Blessed," *Ensign* 41, No. 8 (August 2011): 13.

127. Groberg, *The Other Side of Heaven*, 76.

128. Recounted by the religious historian Charles H. Long, in Jennifer I. M. Reid, *Religion and Global Culture* (Lanham, MD: Lexington Books, 2004): 1.

129. *Deseret News 2013 Church Almanac* (2013): 553-555.

CHAPTER 10

130. "Gospel v gown," *The Economist*, April 18, 2015. http://www.economist.com/news/united-states/21648694-more-mormon-women-are-going-missions-fewer-may-go-university-gospel-v-gown

131. Douglas Beardall and Jewel N. Beardall, *The Missionary Kit* (Provo: LDS Publications, 1979): 54-56.

132. *Missionary Kit*, 56.

133. "Official Policies and Announcements," *Deseret News Church News* (January 22, 1994): 2.

134. *Daily Universe* (October 4, 1994).

135. Ballard, "How to Prepare to be a Good Missionary."

136. William A. Wilson, "Mormon Folklore: Faith or Folly?" *Brigham Young Magazine*, 49, No. 2 (May 1995): 51. William A. Wilson, "Mormon Folklore: Cut from the Marrow of Everyday Experience," *BYU Studies* 33, No. 3 (1993): 532-535.

137. Tracie Lamb-Kwon, "Because I Was a Sister Missionary," *Dialogue: A Journal of Mormon Thought* 25, No. 2 (Summer 1992): 149.

138. Lamb-Kwon, "Because I Was a Sister Missionary," 137-8.

CHAPTER 11

139. *Deseret News Church News* (July 9, 2011).

140. *Deseret News Church News* (June 11, 2011; July 9, 2011).

141. *Deseret News 2012 Church Almanac* (2012): 560-561. http://www.mormonnewsroom.sg/facts-and-statistics

142. Scott Taylor, "Mormon church's storied Granite Mountain vault opens for virtual tour," *Deseret News Church News* (April 29, 2010).

143. "Missionaries Support Family History," *Ensign* 40, No. 4 (April 2010): 76.

144. Audry Sparks, *Mission Memories, Family History Missionaries, Devotional Talks. Life Sketches of the Family History Missionaries*, April 1, 1993 – October 1, 1993 (Salt Lake City, Family History Missionaries, 1993): 15: 104.

145. Thomas S. Monson, "Welcome to Conference," *Ensign* 44, No. 11 (November 2014): 4.

146. "Temples of the Church of Jesus Christ of Latter-day Saints," *Ensign Special Issue* 40, No. 10 (October 2010).

147. "Health Missionaries: Called to Serve Him," *Church News* (March 22, 2011).

148. See http://www.mormonnewsroom.sg/facts-and-statistics/country/mongolia

149. See http://www.mormonnewsroom.org/facts-and-statistics

150. Kent D. Watson, "Our Senior Missionaries," *Ensign* 40, No. 9 (September 2010): 26-29.

151. *Mormon Times* (June 5, 2010): 1, 6; *Mormon Times* (September 11, 2010): 1, 9; *Deseret News Church News* (July 17, 2010): 10.

CHAPTER 12

152. *Deseret News Church News* (October 8, 2011): 14.

153. Laura Vasilescu, "Hearts Changed on Temple Square," in *Eighteen Months: Sister Missionaries in the Latter Days*, ed. Melissa Baird Carpenter (Orem UT: Millennial Press, 2007), 128-129.

154. Robert D. Hales, "When is the Time to Serve?" *Ensign* 40, No. 2 (February 2010): 25.

155. Don L. Searle, "The Member Missionary Effect," *Ensign* 39, no. 10 (October 2009): 21.

156. L. Tom Perry, "To Returned Missionaries," *Ensign* 40, No. 9 (September 2010): 22-24.

157. *Deseret News Mormon Times* (July 2, 2011).

CHAPTER 13

158. "Making the Marriage Decision," *Ensign*, 40, No. 4 (April 2010): 21.

159. *Deseret News Church News* (March 29, 2008).

160. "Making the Marriage Decision," 20-21.

161. Thomas S. Monson, "Priesthood Power," *Ensign* 41, No. 5 (May 2011): 67.

162. *Deseret News Church News* (October 15, 2011).

163. *Deseret News Mormon Times* (June 5, 2010).

164. *Deseret News Mormon Times* (May 29, 2010).

165. *Deseret News Church News* (October 29, 2011).

166. *Deseret News Church News* (February 26, 2011).

167. *Deseret News Church News* (March 27, 2010; January 4, 2015).

168. Joel Campbell, "Mormon Media Observer: Business Journalists Giving Mormons a Fair Shake," *Deseret News Mormon Times* (July 14, 2010).

169. *Deseret News Mormon Times* (July 17, 2010).

170. "The Family: A Proclamation to the World." https://www.lds.org/topics/family-proclamation

171. "Mormons in America." The Pew Forum on Religion & Public Life (January 12, 2012): 56-57. *Deseret News Mormon Times* (January 1, 2012).

172. Richley H. Crapo, "Latter-day Saint Lesbian, Gay, Bisexual, and Transgendered Spirituality," in *Gay Religion*, eds. Scott Thumma and Edward R. Gray, (Lanham, MD: AltaMira Press, 2005), 107.

173. Steven Fales, *Confessions of a Mormon Boy. Behind the Scenes of the off-Broadway Hit*, 36, 41, 65, 72.

174. *Deseret News Mormon Times* (July 24, 2010).

175. See https://www.lds.org/church/news/more-missionaries-will-use-ipads-digital-devices-to-preach-gospel?lang=eng

176. Randall L. Ridd, "The Choice Generation," *Ensign* 44, No. 5 (May 2014): 56.

177. Charles D. Knutson, and Kyle K. Oswald, "Just a Game?" *Ensign* 39, No. 8 (August 2009): 46-51.

178. *My Plan: New Resource for Returning Missionaries*. https://www.lds.org/callings/missionary/my-plan.

179. Thomas à Kempis, *The Imitation of Christ*, transl. William Creasy (Notre Dame: Ave Maria Press, 1989), 45.

BIBLIOGRAPHY

à Kempis, Thomas. *The Imitation of Christ: A Timeless Classic for Contemporary Readers*. Translated by William C. Creasy. Notre Dame: Ave Maria Press, 1989.

Allen, James B., and Richard O. Cowen. "History of the Church: c. 1945-1990, Post-World War II International Era Period." In *The Encyclopedia of Mormonism*. Provo: Brigham Young University, 2007. http://eom.byu.edu/index.php/History_of_the_Church#History_of_the_Church:_c._1945-1990.2C_Post-World_War_II_International_Era_Period.

Allen, James B., and John B. Harris. "What Are You Doing Looking Up Here? Graffiti Mormon Style." *Sunstone* 6, no. 2 (1981): 27-40.

Anderson, Neil L. "Preparing the World for the Second Coming." *Ensign* 41, no. 5 (2011): 51.

Avant, Gerry. "Leaders Instruct New Mission Presidents, Wives." *Church News*, June 22, 2014. https://www.lds.org/church/news/leaders-instruct-new-mission-presidents-wives.

Ballard, M. Russell. "How to Prepare to be a Good Missionary." *The New Era* 37, no. 3 (2007). https://www.lds.org/new-era/2007/03/how-to-prepare-to-be-a-good-missionary.

Ballard, M. Russell. *Our Search for Happiness: An Invitation to Understand The Church of Jesus Christ of Latter-day Saints*. Salt Lake City: Deseret Book Co., 1993.

Ballard, M. Russell. "Sharing the Gospel Using the Internet." *Ensign* 38, no. 7 (2008): 58-63. https://www.lds.org/ensign/2008/07/sharing-the-gospel-using-the-internet.

Ballard, M. Russell. "The Greatest Generation of Missionaries." *Ensign* 32, no. 11 (2002): 47-48. https://www.lds.org/ensign/2002/11/the-greatest-generation-of-missionaries.

Beardall, Douglas, and Jewel N. Beardall. *The Missionary Kit: Hints, Tips and Smart Advice for Missionaries*. Provo: LDS Book Publications, 1979.

Brigham, Janet. "Tobacco: Quitting for Good." *Ensign* 32, no. 2 (2002): 50-57. https://www.lds.org/ensign/2002/02/tobacco-quitting-for-good.

Brodie, Fawn. *No Man Knows My History: The Life of Joseph Smith*. 2nd ed. New York: Knopf, 1971.

Burdett, Julie. "My Service as a Single Member." *Ensign* 41, no. 12 (2011): 34-35. https://www.lds.org/ensign/2011/12/my-service-as-a-single-member.

Bushman, Richard L. *Joseph Smith: Rough Stone Rolling*. New York: Knopf, 2005.

Bytheway, John. *What I Wish I'd Known Before My Mission*. Salt Lake City: Deseret Book, 1996.

Bytheway, John. *How to Be an Extraordinary Missionary*. Salt Lake City: Deseret Book, 2005.

Campbell, Joel. "Mormon Media Observer: Business Journalists Giving Mormons a Fair Shake." *Deseret News Mormon Times*, July 14, 2010. http://www.deseretnews.com/article/705385077/Mormon-Media-Observer-Business-journalists-giving-Mormons-a-fair-shake.html.

Cares, Mark J. *Speaking the Truth, in Love, to Mormons*. Milwaukee: Northwestern Publishing House, 1998.

Carpenter, Melissa Baird, ed. *Eighteen Months: Sister Missionaries in the Latter Days*. Orem: Millennial Press, 2007.

"Children." *Missionary Handbook*. Salt Lake City: The Church of Jesus Christ of Latter-day Saints, 2006: 35. https://www.lds.org/bc/content/ldsorg/topics/missionary/MissionaryHandbook2006Navigate.pdf.

Children's Songbook of The Church of Jesus Christ of Latter-day Saints. Salt Lake City: Intellectual Reserve, Inc., 2010.

"Church changes dress code for sister missionaries." *Daily Universe,* October 20, 2011. http://universe.byu.edu/2011/10/20/sister-missionary-fashion-changes/.

"Church Encourages Members Worldwide to Serve Local Communities." *Ensign* 43, no. 1 (2013): 74-75.

"Church in Talks to 'Regularize' Activities in China." *Mormon Newsroom*, August 30, 2010. http://www.mormonnewsroom.org/article/church-in-talks-to-regularize-activities-in-china.

Collegium Aesculapium.... An Organization for LDS Health Professionals (April 2010). http://www.collegiumaesculapium.org/newsletters/newsApr2010.htm.

Cook, Quentin L. "LDS Women Are Incredible!" *Ensign* 4, no. 5 (2011): 20. https://www.lds.org/ensign/2011/05/lds-women-are-incredible.

Crapo, Richley H. "Latter-day Saint Lesbian, Gay, Bisexual, and Transgendered Spirituality." In *Gay Religion*, edited by Scott Thumma and Edward R. Gray. Lanham: AltaMira Press, 2005.

Daily Universe, Letter to the Editor, October 4, 1994.

Daughters in My Kingdom: The History and Work of Relief Society. Salt Lake City: The Church of Jesus Christ of Latter-day Saints, 2011. https://www.lds.org/relief-society/daughters-in-my-kingdom.

Dew, Sheri L. *Go Forward With Faith: The Biography of Gordon B. Hinckley.* Salt Lake City: Deseret Book Co, 1996.

Doty, Donald B. "Missionary Health Preparation." *Ensign* 37, no. 3 (2007). https://www.lds.org/ensign/2007/03/missionary-health-preparation.

Eckholm, Erik. "Perry Ally Calls Mormonism a Cult." *New York Times,* October 7, 2011. http://thecaucus.blogs.nytimes.com/2011/10/07/blunt-talk-about-mormonism-at-the-values-voter-summit/.

Ellsworth, S. George. "A History of Mormon Missions in the United States and Canada, 1830-1860." PhD diss., University of California, Berkley, 1951.

Eriksen, Sara Elvira. "One Stalwart Pioneer, Many Generations Blessed." *Ensign* 41, no. 8 (2011): 12-13. https://www.lds.org/ensign/2011/08/one-stalwart-pioneer-many-generations-blessed.

Fales, Steven. *Confessions of a Mormon Boy. Behind the Scenes of the off-Broadway Hit*. New York: Alyson Books, 2006.

Faust, James E. "Welcoming Every Single One." *Ensign* 37, no. 8 (2007): 6. https://www.lds.org/ensign/2007/08/welcoming-every-single-one.

For the Strength of Youth: Fulfilling Our Duty to God. Salt Lake City: Intellectual Reserve, Inc. 2001, 2011. https://www.lds.org/youth/for-the-strength-of-youth.

Foster, Charles R., Lisa E. Dahill, Lawrence A. Golemon, and Barbara Wang Tolentino. *Educating Clergy: Teaching Practices and Pastoral Imagination.* San Francisco: Jossey-Bass, 2006.

"Georgetown Symposium on Proselytism & Religious Freedom in the 21st Century." March 3, 2010. http://berkleycenter.georgetown.edu/events/proselytism-and-religious-freedom-in-the-21st-century.

Godfrey, Kenneth W. "Freemasonry and the Temple." *The Encyclopedia of Mormonism.* Provo: Brigham Young University, 2007. http://eom.byu.edu/index.php/Freemasonry_and_the_Temple.

Goodstein, Laurie. "Mormons' ad campaign may play out on the '12 campaign trail." *New York Times,* November 18, 2011. http://www.nytimes.com/2011/11/18/us/mormon-ad-campaign-seeks-to-improve-perceptions.html.

"Gospel v gown." *The Economist,* April 18, 2015. http://www.economist.com/news/united-states/21648694-more-mormon-women-are-going-missions-fewer-may-go-university-gospel-v-gown.

"Granite Mountain Records Vault." http://www.mormonnewsroom.org/article/granite-mountain-records-vault.

Green, Jonathan. "Slovakia!" *Times and Seasons,* November 14, 2006. http://timesandseasons.org/index.php/2006/11/slovakia/.

Groberg, John H. *The Other Side of Heaven.* Salt Lake City: Deseret Book, 1993.

Grossman, Cathy Lynn. "Pastor: I'll 'hold my nose,' vote for Mormon Romney," *USA Today,* February 22, 2012. http://content.usatoday.com/communities/Religion/post/2012/02/baptist—jeffress-mitt-romney-mormon-cult/.

Hales, Robert D. "When is the Time to Serve?" *Ensign* 40, no. 2. (2010): 25. https://www.lds.org/ensign/2010/02/when-is-the-time-to-serve.

Harline, Craig. *Way Below the Angels: The Pretty Clearly Troubled But Not Even Close to Tragic Confessions of a Real Live Mormon Missionary.* Grand Rapids: Wm. B. Eerdmans Publishing Co., 2014.

Harrington, Mary Paulson. "Not Every Family Rejoices To Have A Child Go On A Mormon Mission." *Sunstone* 14, issue 80 (1990): 51-53.

"Health Missionaries Called to Serve Him." *Church News,* March 22, 2011. https://www.lds.org/church/news/health-missionaries-called-to-serve-him.

Hinckley, Gordon B. "Every Convert is Precious." *Liahona* 23, no. 2 (1999). https://www.lds.org/liahona/1999/02/every-convert-is-precious.

Hinckley, Gordon B. "My Testimony," *Ensign* 23, no. 11 (1993): 52. https://www.lds.org/ensign/1993/11/my-testimony.

Hinckley, Gordon B. "Some Thoughts on Temples, Retention of Converts, and Missionary Service." General Conference, October 1997. https://www.lds.org/general-conference/1997/10/some-thoughts-on-temples-retention-of-converts-and-missionary-service.

Hogan, Stephan M. "Young Men in White Shirts." *The Slovak Spectator*, October 8, 2007.

Institute of Religion. http://institute.lds.org.

Johnston, Jerry Earl. "Protestant books on Mormons show welcome change in attitude." *Deseret News Mormon Times*, March 6, 2010.

Kirn, Walter. "The Mormon Moment." *Newsweek*, June 5, 2011.

Kimball, Spencer W. "Advice to a Young Man: Now is the Time to Prepare." *The New Era* 3, no. 6 (1973): 8. https://www.lds.org/new-era/1973/06/advice-to-a-young-man-now-is-the-time-to-prepare.

Kimball, Spencer W. "President Kimball Speaks Out on Being a Missionary." *The New Era* 11, no. 5 (1981). https://www.lds.org/new-era/1981/05/president-kimball-speaks-out-on-being-a-missionary.

Kissi, Emmanuel Abu. *Walking in the Sand: A History of The Church of Jesus Christ of Latter-day Saints in Ghana.* Provo: BYU Press, 2004.

"Knocking at the College Door-2003. Projections of High School Graduates by State, Income, and Race/Ethnicity, 1998-2018."Western Interstate Commission for Higher Education.

Knutson, Charles D. and Kyle K. Oswald. "Just a Game?" *Ensign* 39 no. 8 (2009): 48. https://www.lds.org/ensign/2009/08/just-a-game.

Kunz, Ryan. "180 Years Later, Book of Mormon Nears 150 Million Copies." *Ensign* 40, no. 3 (2010): 74-76.

Lamb-Kwon, Tracie. "Because I Was a Sister Missionary." *Dialogue: A Journal of Mormon Thought* 25, no. 2 (1992).

Lewiston Maine Sun Journal (1994).

Lawrence, Gary C. *How Americans View Mormonism: Seven Steps to Improve Our Image*. The Parameter Foundation, 2008.

Linker, Damon. *The Religious Test: Why We Must Question the Beliefs of Our Leaders*. New York: W.W. Norton & Co., 2010.

Lively, Robert L. Jr. "The Catholic Apostolic Church and the Church of Jesus Christ of Latter-day Saints: A Comparative Study of Two Minority Millenarian Groups in Nineteenth-Century England." DPhil diss., University of Oxford, 1977.

"Making the Marriage Decision." *Ensign* 40, no. 4 (2010): 21. https://www.lds.org/ensign/2010/04/making-the-marriage-decision.

Mauss, Armand L. *Shifting Borders and Tattered Passport: Intellectual Journeys of a Mormon Academic*. Salt Lake City: University of Utah Press, 2012.

McKeever, Bill and Eric Johnson. *Mormonism 101: Examining the Religion of the Latter-day Saints*. Grand Rapids: Baker Books, 2000.

Mission Presidents Handbook (2006). Salt Lake City: The Church of Jesus Christ of Latter-day Saints, 2006. https://archive.org/details/MissionPresidentsHandbook2006.

"Missionaries Support Family History." *Ensign* 40, no. 4 (2010): 76. https://www.lds.org/ensign/2010/04/missionaries-support-family-history.

Missionary Handbook. Salt Lake City: Intellectual Reserve, Inc., 2006.

"Missionary Leader's Responsibilities." Provo MTC, 2008.

"Missionary Training Centers Help Hasten the Work of Salvation." *Ensign* 44, no. 5 (2014): 138. https://www.lds.org/ensign/2014/05/news-of-the-church/missionary-training-centers-help-hasten-the-work-of-salvation.

Monson, Thomas S. "Welcome to Conference." Ensign 42, no. 11 (2012): 4-5. https://www.lds.org/general-conference/2012/10/welcome-to-conference.

Monson, Thomas S. "Priesthood Power." *Ensign* 41, no. 5 (2011): 67. https://www.lds.org/ensign/2011/05/priesthood-power.

Monson, Thomas S. "Welcome to Conference." *Ensign* 39, no. 11 (2009): 6. https://www.lds.org/ensign/2009/11/welcome-to-conference.

Monson, Thomas S. "Welcome to Conference." *Ensign* 44, no. 11 (2014): 4. https://www.lds.org/ensign/2014/11/saturday-morning-session/welcome-to-conference.

More Good Foundation. http://www.moregoodfoundation.org.

"More Missionaries Will Use Ipads, Digital Devices to Preach Gospel." *Church News*, July 9, 2014. https://www.lds.org/church/news/more-missionaries-will-use-ipads-digital-devices-to-preach-gospel.

"Mormons and Proposition 8." *PBS Religion and Ethics Newsweekly*, May 22, 2009. http://www.pbs.org/wnet/religionandethics/2009/05/22/may-22-2009-mormons-and-proposition-8/3019/.

My Plan: New Resource for Returning Missionaries. https://www.lds.org/callings/missionary/my-plan.

Pew Forum on Religion & Public Life. "Mormons in America: Certain in Their Beliefs, Uncertain in Their Place in Society." January 12, 2012: 56-57.

Nielsen, Michael S. "Without Saying Goodbye." *Ensign* 20, no. 6 (1990): 30-31. https://www.lds.org/ensign/1990/06/without-saying-good-bye.

Nielson, Brent H. "A Call to the Rising Generation." *Ensign* 39, no. 11 (2009): 95. https://www.lds.org/ensign/2009/11/a-call-to-the-rising-generation.

Oaks, Dallin H. "The Role of Members in Conversion." *Ensign* 33, no. 3 (2003). https://www.lds.org/ensign/2003/03/the-role-of-members-in-conversion.

Official Declaration 2. https://www.lds.org/scriptures/dc-testament/od/2.

"Official Policies and Announcements." *Deseret News Church News*, January 22, 1994: 2.

Olaveson, Breanna. "International MTCs Play Important Role." *Ensign* 40, no. 12 (2010): 74-76. https://www.lds.org/ensign/2010/12/international-mtcs-play-important-role.

Olaveson, Breanna. "Role of Members Important in Sharing the Gospel Online." *Ensign* 40, no. 9 (2010): 74-76. https://www.lds.org/ensign/2010/09/role-of-members-important-in-sharing-the-gospel-online.

Our Heritage: A Brief History of The Church of Jesus Christ of Latter-day Saints. Salt Lake City: Church of Jesus Christ of Latter-day Saints, Intellectual Reserve, Inc. 1996. https://www.lds.org/bc/content/shared/content/english/pdf/language-materials/35448_eng.pdf.

"Our Son's Choice," *Ensign* 38, no. 2 (2008): 11-13.

Paulson, Michael. "Survivors recall tragic car crash in France with Romney." *New York Times,* June 24, 2007. http://www.nytimes.com/2007/06/24/world/europe/24iht-24Romney.6300715.html.

Pedersen, Paul. *The Five Stages of Culture Shock: Critical Incidents Around the World.* Westport, CT: Greenwood Press, 1995.

Perry, L. Tom. "To Returned Missionaries." *Ensign* 40, no. 9 (2010): 22-24. https://www.lds.org/ensign/2010/09/to-returned-missionaries.

Pew Forum on Religion & Public Life. "A Portrait of Mormons in the U.S." July 24, 2009.

Pew Forum on Religion & Public Life. "Mormons in America." January 12, 2012.

Pew Forum on Religion & Public Life. "Rising Restrictions on Religion." August 2011.

Phillips, Rick. *Conservative Christian Identity and Same-Sex Orientation: The Case for Gay Mormons*. Bern, Switzerland: Peter Lang, 2004.

"Plural Marriage in The Church of Jesus Christ of Latter-day Saints." https://www.lds.org/topics/plural-marriage-in-the-church-of-jesus-christ-of-latter-day-saints.

"Practical Preparation for a Mission." *Aaronic Priesthood Manual 2*. Salt Lake City: The Church of Jesus Christ of Latter-day Saints, 1993: 83-86.

Preach My Gospel: A Guide to Missionary Service. Salt Lake City: Intellectual Reserve, Inc., 2004.

Princeton Review. http://www.princetonreview.com.

Rasband, Ronald A. "The Divine Call of a Missionary." *Ensign* 40, no. 5 (2010): 52-53. https://www.lds.org/ensign/2010/05/the-divine-call-of-a-missionary.

Reid, Jennifer I. M. *Religion and Global Culture*. Lanham, MD: Lexington Books, 2004.

Rhodes, Ron and Marian Bodine. *Reasoning from the Scriptures with the Mormons*. Eugene, OR: Harvest House, 1995.

Ridd, Randall L. "The Choice Generation." *Ensign* 44, no. 5 (2014): 56.

Roberts, Brigham H. *Comprehensive History of The Church of Jesus Christ of Latter-day Saints, Century I*. Provo: BYU Press, 1975.

Rowe, David L. *I Love Mormons: A New Way to Share Christ with Latter-day Saints*. Grand Rapids: Baker Books, 2005.

"Safe in His Hand." *Ensign* 40, no.3 (2010): 62. https://www.lds.org/ensign/2010/03/safe-in-his-hand.

Salant, Jonathan D. "Some Voters Have Qualms About Mormon President, Poll Says." *Bloomberg Business,* June 8, 2011. http://www.bloomberg.com/news/articles/2011-06-08/a-third-of-voters-have-qualms-about-mormon-president-poll-says.

Searle, Don L. "The Member Missionary Effect." *Ensign* 39, no. 10 (2009): 21. https://www.lds.org/ensign/2009/10/the-member-missionary-effect.

Shepherd, Gary and Gordon Shepherd. *Mormon Passage: A Missionary Chronicle*. Urbana: University of Illinois Press, 1998.

"Single Members." *Handbook 2: Administering the Church* (2010): 16.3.3. https://www.lds.org/handbook/handbook-2-administering-the-church/single-members.

"Slovakia!" *Times and Seasons*, November 14, 2006.

Smith, Gary. "A Season for Spreading the Faith." *Sports Illustrated*, September 4, 1985.

Smith, Joseph. *History of The Church of Jesus Christ of Latter-day Saints. Period I History of Joseph Smith, the Prophet, by Himself.* Salt Lake City: Deseret Book, 1927.

Sparks, Audrey. *Mission Memories. Family History Missionaries. Devotional Talks. Life Sketches of the Family History Missionaries.* Vol.15, Salt Lake City: Family History Missionaries, April 1, 1993-October 1, 1993.

Sun Journal, Lewiston, Maine, August 6, 1994.

Talmadge, James. *Jesus the Christ*. Salt Lake City: Deseret Book Co., 1915.

Taylor, P.A.M. *Expectations Westward: The Mormons and the Emigration of Their British Converts in the Nineteenth Century*. Ithaca: Cornell University Press, 1966.

Taylor, Scott. "Mormon church's storied Granite Mountain vault opens for virtual tour." *Deseret News Church News*, April 29, 2010.

"Temples of the Church of Jesus Christ of Latter-day Saints." *Ensign Special Issue* 40, no. 10 (2010). https://www.lds.org/ensign/2010/10/temples-of-the-church-of-jesus-christ-of-latter-day-saints.

"Ten Basic Commandments of Good Health." Provo MTC Handout, 2008.

Tichy, Jonathan T. "The Registration of The Church of Jesus Christ of Latter-day Saints in Slovakia. An Insider's Report." *Osterreichisches archive fur recht & religion* (2009): 17-26.

"The Family. A Proclamation to the World." https://www.lds.org/topics/family-proclamation.

"Tips for Buying the Best Missionary Attire." *Deseret News Mormon Times*, May 1, 2010.

True to the Faith: A Gospel Reference. Salt Lake City: The Church of Jesus Christ of Latter-day Saints, Intellectual Reserve, Inc. 2004. https://www.lds.org/manual/true-to-the-faith.

Turkle, Sherry. *Alone Together: Why We Expect More From Technology and Less From Each Other.* New York: Basic Books, 2011.

Turner, Victor W. *The Ritual Process*. New York: Penguin, 1969.

Van Gennep, Arnold. *The Rites of Passage*. Chicago: The University of Chicago Press, 1961.

Vasilescu, Laura. "Hearts Changed on Temple Square." In *Eighteen Months. Sister Missionaries in the Latter Days*, edited by Melissa Baird Carpenter. Orem: Millennial Press, 2007.

Walch, Tad. "LDS Missionary Numbers to Peak at 88,000; More to Use and Pay for Digital Devices." *Deseret News*, July 3, 2014.

Watchtower Bible & Tract Society of New York, Inc., v. Village of Stratton 536 U.S. 150 (2002). https://supreme.justia.com/cases/federal/us/536/150/case.html.

Watson, Kent D. "Our Senior Missionaries." *Ensign* 40, no. 9 September 2010: 26-29. https://www.lds.org/ensign/2010/09/our-senior-missionaries.

White, Benjamin Hyrum. "The History of 'Preach My Gospel.'" *Religious Educator* 14, no. 1 (2013): 129-158. http://rsc.byu.edu/archived/volume-14-number-1-2013/history-preach-my-gospel.

Wilcox, Brad and Russell Wilcox. *Raising Ourselves to the Bar: Practical Advice and Encouragement for the Next Generation of Missionaries and Their Parents*. Salt Lake City: Deseret Book, 2007.

Wilson, William A. "Mormon Folklore: Cut from the Marrow of Everyday Experience." *BYU Studies* 33, no. 3 (1993).

Wilson, William A. "Mormon Folklore: Faith or Folly?" *Brigham Young Magazine* 49, no. 2 (1995).

Wilson, William A. *On Being Human: The Folklore of Mormon Missionaries*. Logan: Utah State University Press, 1981.

Woods, Susan E. *The Transfer: Stories of Missionaries Who Gave the Last Full Measure of Devotion*. Vols. 1 and 2. Honeoye Falls: Digital Legend Press. 2010.

Wrigley, Heather Whittle. "Church Encourages Members Worldwide to Serve Local Communities." *Ensign* 43, no. 1 (2013): 74-75. https://www.lds.org/ensign/2013/01/church-encourages-members-worldwide-to-serve-local-communities.

Wrigley, Heather Whittle. "Church Leaders Share More Information on Missionary Age Requirement Change." https://www.lds.org/church/news/church-leaders-share-more-information-on-missionary-age-requirement-change.

Young, Brigham. *History of The Church of Jesus Christ of Latter-day Saints, Period II, Vol. VII.* Salt Lake City: The Church of Jesus Christ of Latter-day Saints, 1952.

INDEX

C

M

N

P

R

32475890R00353

Made in the USA
San Bernardino, CA
06 April 2016